Natural Language Processing: Python and NLTK

Learn to build expert NLP and machine learning projects using NLTK and other Python libraries

A course in three modules

Packt

BIRMINGHAM - MUMBAI

Natural Language Processing: Python and NLTK

Published on: November 2016

Production reference: 1150617

Published by Packt Publishing Ltd.
Livery Place
35 Livery Street
Birmingham B3 2PB, UK.

ISBN 978-1-78728-510-1

www.packtpub.com

Credits

Authors
Nitin Hardeniya
Jacob Perkins
Deepti Chopra
Nisheeth Joshi
Iti Mathur

Reviewers
Afroz Hussain
Sujit Pal
Kumar Raj
Patrick Chan
Mohit Goenka
Lihang Li
Maurice HT Ling
Jing (Dave) Tian
Arturo Argueta

Content Development Editor
Aishwarya Pandere

Production Coordinator
Arvindkumar Gupta

Preface

NLTK is one of the most popular and widely used library in the natural language processing (NLP) community. The beauty of NLTK lies in its simplicity, where most of the complex NLP tasks can be implemented using a few lines of code. Start off by learning how to tokenize text into component words. Explore and make use of the WordNet language dictionary. Learn how and when to stem or lemmatize words. Discover various ways to replace words and perform spelling correction. Create your own custom text corpora and corpus readers, including a MongoDB backed corpus. Use part-of-speech taggers to annotate words with their parts of speech. Create and transform chunked phrase trees using partial parsing. Dig into feature extraction for text classification and sentiment analysis. Learn how to do parallel and distributed text processing, and to store word distributions in Redis.

This learning path will teach you all that and more, in a hands-on learn-by-doing manner. Become an expert in using NLTK for Natural Language Processing with this useful companion.

What this learning path covers

Module 1, NLTK Essentials, talks about all the preprocessing steps required in any text mining/NLP task. In this module, we discuss tokenization, stemming, stop word removal, and other text cleansing processes in detail and how easy it is to implement these in NLTK.

Module 2, Python 3 Text Processing with NLTK 3 Cookbook, explains how to use corpus readers and create custom corpora. It also covers how to use some of the corpora that come with NLTK. It covers the chunking process, also known as partial parsing, which can identify phrases and named entities in a sentence. It also explains how to train your own custom chunker and create specific named entity recognizers.

Module 3, Mastering Natural Language Processing with Python, covers how to calculate word frequencies and perform various language modeling techniques. It also talks about the concept and application of Shallow Semantic Analysis (that is, NER) and WSD using Wordnet.

It will help you understand and apply the concepts of Information Retrieval and text summarization.

What you need for this learning path

Module 1:

We need the following software for this module:

Chapter number	Software required (with version)	Free/ Proprietary	Download links to the software	Hardware specifications	OS required

1-5	Python/ Anaconda
	NLTK
		Free	`https://www.python.org/`
			`http://continuum.io/downloads`
			`http://www.nltk.org/`
				Common Unix Printing System	any

6	scikit-learn and gensim	Free	`http://scikit-learn.org/stable/` `https://radimrehurek.com/gensim/`	Common Unix Printing System	any
7	Scrapy	Free	`http://scrapy.org/`	Common Unix Printing System	any

Chapter number	Software required (with version)	Free/ Proprietary	Download links to the software	Hardware specifications	OS required

8	NumPy, SciPy, pandas, and matplotlib	Free	`http://www.numpy.org/`
			`http://www.scipy.org/`
			`http://pandas.pydata.org/`
			`http://matplotlib.org/`
				Common Unix Printing System	any

9	Twitter Python APIs and Facebook python APIs	Free	`https://dev.twitter.com/overview/api/twitter-libraries` `https://developers.facebook.com`	Common Unix Printing System	any

Module 2:

You will need Python 3 and the listed Python packages. For this learning path, the author used Python 3.3.5. To install the packages, you can use pip (`https://pypi.python.org/pypi/pip/`). The following is the list of the packages in requirements format with the version number used while writing this learning path:

- NLTK>=3.0a4
- pyenchant>=1.6.5
- lockfile>=0.9.1
- numpy>=1.8.0
- scipy>=0.13.0
- scikit-learn>=0.14.1
- execnet>=1.1
- pymongo>=2.6.3

- redis>=2.8.0
- lxml>=3.2.3
- beautifulsoup4>=4.3.2
- python-dateutil>=2.0
- charade>=1.0.3

You will also need NLTK-Trainer, which is available at `https://github.com/japerk/nltk-trainer`.

Beyond Python, there are a couple recipes that use MongoDB and Redis, both NoSQL databases. These can be downloaded at `http://www.mongodb.org/` and `http://redis.io/`, respectively.

Module 3:

For all the chapters, Python 2.7 or 3.2+ is used. NLTK 3.0 must be installed either on 32-bit machine or 64-bit machine. Operating System required is Windows/Mac/Unix.

Who this learning path is for

If you are an NLP or machine learning enthusiast and an intermediate Python programmer who wants to quickly master NLTK for natural language processing, then this Learning Path will do you a lot of good. Students of linguistics and semantic/sentiment analysis professionals will find it invaluable.

Reader feedback

Feedback from our readers is always welcome. Let us know what you think about this course—what you liked or disliked. Reader feedback is important for us as it helps us develop titles that you will really get the most out of.

To send us general feedback, simply e-mail `feedback@packtpub.com`, and mention the course's title in the subject of your message.

If there is a topic that you have expertise in and you are interested in either writing or contributing to a course, see our author guide at `www.packtpub.com/authors`.

Customer support

Now that you are the proud owner of a Packt course, we have a number of things to help you to get the most from your purchase.

Downloading the example code

You can download the example code files for this course from your account at `http://www.packtpub.com`. If you purchased this course elsewhere, you can visit `http://www.packtpub.com/support` and register to have the files e-mailed directly to you.

You can download the code files by following these steps:

1. Log in or register to our website using your e-mail address and password.
2. Hover the mouse pointer on the **SUPPORT** tab at the top.
3. Click on **Code Downloads & Errata**.
4. Enter the name of the course in the **Search** box.
5. Select the course for which you're looking to download the code files.
6. Choose from the drop-down menu where you purchased this course from.
7. Click on **Code Download**.

You can also download the code files by clicking on the **Code Files** button on the course's webpage at the Packt Publishing website. This page can be accessed by entering the course's name in the **Search** box. Please note that you need to be logged in to your Packt account.

Once the file is downloaded, please make sure that you unzip or extract the folder using the latest version of:

- WinRAR / 7-Zip for Windows
- Zipeg / iZip / UnRarX for Mac
- 7-Zip / PeaZip for Linux

The code bundle for the course is also hosted on GitHub at `https://github.com/PacktPublishing/Natural-Language-Processing-Python-and-NLTK`. We also have other code bundles from our rich catalog of books, videos and courses available at `https://github.com/PacktPublishing/`. Check them out!

Errata

Although we have taken every care to ensure the accuracy of our content, mistakes do happen. If you find a mistake in one of our books—maybe a mistake in the text or the code—we would be grateful if you could report this to us. By doing so, you can save other readers from frustration and help us improve subsequent versions of this course. If you find any errata, please report them by visiting `http://www.packtpub.com/submit-errata`, selecting your course, clicking on the **Errata Submission Form** link, and entering the details of your errata. Once your errata are verified, your submission will be accepted and the errata will be uploaded to our website or added to any list of existing errata under the Errata section of that title.

To view the previously submitted errata, go to `https://www.packtpub.com/books/content/support` and enter the name of the book in the search field. The required information will appear under the **Errata** section.

Piracy

Piracy of copyrighted material on the Internet is an ongoing problem across all media. At Packt, we take the protection of our copyright and licenses very seriously. If you come across any illegal copies of our works in any form on the Internet, please provide us with the location address or website name immediately so that we can pursue a remedy.

Please contact us at `copyright@packtpub.com` with a link to the suspected pirated material.

We appreciate your help in protecting our authors and our ability to bring you valuable content.

Questions

If you have a problem with any aspect of this course, you can contact us at `questions@packtpub.com`, and we will do our best to address the problem.

Module 1: NLTK Essentials

Module 2: Python 3 Text Processing with NLTK 3 Cookbook

Module 3: Mastering Natural Language Processing with Python

Module 1

NLTK Essentials

Build cool NLP and machine learning applications using NLTK and other Python libraries

1

Introduction to Natural Language Processing

I will start with the introduction to **Natural Language Processing** (**NLP**). Language is a central part of our day to day life, and it's so interesting to work on any problem related to languages. I hope this book will give you a flavor of NLP, will motivate you to learn some amazing concepts of NLP, and will inspire you to work on some of the challenging NLP applications.

In my own language, the study of language processing is called NLP. People who are deeply involved in the study of language are linguists, while the term 'computational linguist' applies to the study of processing languages with the application of computation. Essentially, a computational linguist will be a computer scientist who has enough understanding of languages, and can apply his computational skills to model different aspects of the language. While computational linguists address the theoretical aspect of language, NLP is nothing but the application of computational linguistics.

NLP is more about the application of computers on different language nuances, and building real-world applications using NLP techniques. In a practical context, NLP is analogous to teaching a language to a child. Some of the most common tasks like understanding words, sentences, and forming grammatically and structurally correct sentences, are very natural to humans. In NLP, some of these tasks translate to tokenization, chunking, part of speech tagging, parsing, machine translation, speech recognition, and most of them are still the toughest challenges for computers. I will be talking more on the practical side of NLP, assuming that we all have some background in NLP. The expectation for the reader is to have minimal understanding of any programming language and an interest in NLP and Language.

By end of the chapter we want readers

- A brief introduction to NLP and related concepts.

- Install Python, NLTK and other libraries.
- Write some very basic Python and NLTK code snippets.

If you have never heard the term NLP, then please take some time to read any of the books mentioned here—just for an initial few chapters. A quick reading of at least the Wikipedia page relating to NLP is a must:

- *Speech and Language Processing* by Daniel Jurafsky and James H. Martin
- *Statistical Natural Language Processing* by Christopher D. Manning and Hinrich Schütze

Why learn NLP?

I start my discussion with the Gartner's new hype cycle and you can clearly see NLP on top of the cycle. Currently, NLP is one of the rarest skill sets that is required in the industry. After the advent of big data, the major challenge is that we need more people who are good with not just structured, but also with semi or unstructured data. We are generating **petabytes** of Weblogs, tweets, Facebook feeds, chats, e-mails, and reviews. Companies are collecting all these different kind of data for better customer targeting and meaningful insights. To process all these unstructured data source we need people who understand NLP.

We are in the age of information; we can't even imagine our life without Google. We use Siri for the most of basic stuff. We use spam filters for filtering spam emails. We need spell checker on our Word document. There are many examples of real world NLP applications around us.

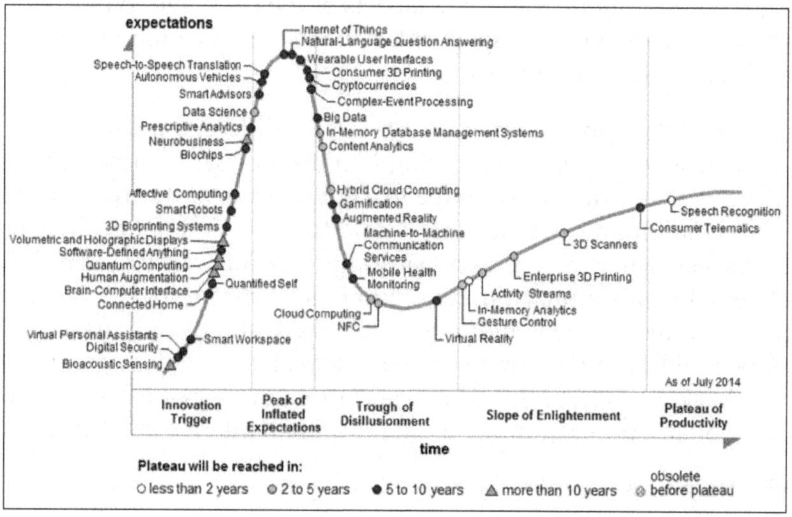

Image is taken from `http://www.gartner.com/newsroom/id/2819918`

Let me also give you some examples of the amazing NLP applications that you can use, but are not aware that they are built on NLP:

- Spell correction (MS Word/ any other editor)
- Search engines (Google, Bing, Yahoo, wolframalpha)
- Speech engines (Siri, Google Voice)
- Spam classifiers (All e-mail services)
- News feeds (Google, Yahoo!, and so on)
- Machine translation (Google Translate, and so on)
- IBM Watson

Building these applications requires a very specific skill set with a great understanding of language and tools to process the language efficiently. So it's not just hype that makes NLP one of the most niche areas, but it's the kind of application that can be created using NLP that makes it one of the most unique skills to have.

To achieve some of the above applications and other basic NLP preprocessing, there are many open source tools available. Some of them are developed by organizations to build their own NLP applications, while some of them are open-sourced. Here is a small list of available NLP tools:

- GATE
- Mallet
- Open NLP
- UIMA
- Stanford toolkit
- Genism
- **Natural Language Tool Kit (NLTK)**

Most of the tools are written in Java and have similar functionalities. Some of them are robust and have a different variety of NLP tools available. However, when it comes to the ease of use and explanation of the concepts, NLTK scores really high. NLTK is also a very good learning kit because the learning curve of Python (on which NLTK is written) is very fast. NLTK has incorporated most of the NLP tasks, it's very elegant and easy to work with. For all these reasons, NLTK has become one of the most popular libraries in the NLP community:

I am assuming all you guys know Python. If not, I urge you to learn Python. There are many basic tutorials on Python available online. There are lots of books also available that give you a quick overview of the language. We will also look into some of the features of Python, while going through the different topics. But for now, even if you only know the basics of Python, such as lists, strings, regular expressions, and basic I/O, you should be good to go.

> Python can be installed from the following website:
> `https://www.python.org/downloads/`
> `http://continuum.io/downloads`
> `https://store.enthought.com/downloads/`

I would recommend using Anaconda or Canopy Python distributions. The reason being that these distributions come with bundled libraries, such as `scipy`, `numpy`, `scikit`, and so on, which are used for data analysis and other applications related to NLP and related fields. Even NLTK is part of this distribution.

> Please follow the instructions and install NLTK and NLTK data:
> `http://www.nltk.org/install.html`

Let's test everything.

Open the terminal on your respective operating systems. Then run:

```
$ python
```

This should open the Python interpreter:

```
Python 2.6.6 (r266:84292, Oct 15 2013, 07:32:41)
[GCC 4.4.7 20120313 (Red Hat 4.4.7-4)] on linux2
Type "help", "copyright", "credits" or "license" for more information.
>>>
```

I hope you got a similar looking output here. There is a chance that you will have received a different looking output, but ideally you will get the latest version of Python (I recommend that to be 2.7), the compiler GCC, and the operating system details. I know the latest version of Python will be in 3.0+ range, but as with any other open source systems, we should tries to hold back to a more stable version as opposed to jumping on to the latest version. If you have moved to Python 3.0+, please have a look at the link below to gain an understanding about what new features have been added:

`https://docs.python.org/3/whatsnew/3.4.html`.

UNIX based systems will have Python as a default program. Windows users can set the path to get Python working. Let's check whether we have installed NLTK correctly:

```
>>>import nltk
>>>print "Python and NLTK installed successfully"
Python and NLTK installed successfully
```

Hey, we are good to go!

Let's start playing with Python!

We'll not be diving too deep into Python; however, we'll give you a quick tour of Python essentials. Still, I think for the benefit of the audience, we should have a quick five minute tour. We'll talk about the basics of data structures, some frequently used functions, and the general construct of Python in the next few sections.

> I highly recommend the two hour Google Python class. `https://developers.google.com/edu/python` should be good enough to start. Please go through the Python website `https://www.python.org/` for more tutorials and other resources.

Lists

Lists are one of the most commonly used data structures in Python. They are pretty much comparable to arrays in other programming languages. Let's start with some of the most important functions that a Python list provide.

Try the following in the Python console:

```
>>> lst=[1,2,3,4]
>>> # mostly like arrays in typical languages
>>>print lst
[1, 2, 3, 4]
```

Python lists can be accessed using much more flexible indexing. Here are some examples:

```
>>>print 'First element' +lst[0]
```

You will get an error message like this:

```
TypeError: cannot concatenate 'str' and 'int' objects
```

The reason being that Python is an interpreted language, and checks for the type of the variables at the time it evaluates the expression. We need not initialize and declare the type of variable at the time of declaration. Our list has integer object and cannot be concatenated as a print function. It will only accept a string object. For this reason, we need to convert list elements to string. The process is also known as type casting.

```
>>>print 'First element :' +str(lst[0])
>>>print 'last element :' +str(lst[-1])
>>>print 'first three elements :' +str(lst[0:2])
>>>print 'last three elements :'+str(lst[-3:])
First element :1
last element :4
first three elements :[1, 2,3]
last three elements :[2, 3, 4]
```

Helping yourself

The best way to learn more about different data types and functions is to use help functions like `help()` and `dir(lst)`.

The `dir(python object)` command is used to list all the given attributes of the given Python object. Like if you pass a list object, it will list all the cool things you can do with lists:

```
>>>dir(lst)
>>>' , '.join(dir(lst))
'__add__ , __class__ , __contains__ , __delattr__ , __delitem__ , __
delslice__ , __doc__ , __eq__ , __format__ , __ge__ , __getattribute__
, __getitem__ , __getslice__ , __gt__ , __hash__ , __iadd__ , __imul__
, __init__ , __iter__ , __le__ , __len__ , __lt__ , __mul__ , __ne__ ,
__new__ , __reduce__ , __reduce_ex__ , __repr__ , __reversed__ , __rmul__
, __setattr__ , __setitem__ , __setslice__ , __sizeof__ , __str__ , __
subclasshook__ , append , count , extend , index , insert , pop , remove
, reverse , sort'
```

With the `help(python object)` command, we can get detailed documentation for the given Python object, and also give a few examples of how to use the Python object:

```
>>>help(lst.index)
Help on built-in function index:
```

```
index(...)
    L.index(value, [start, [stop]]) -> integer -- return first index of
value.
This function raises a ValueError if the value is not present.
```

So `help` and `dir` can be used on any Python data type, and are a very nice way to learn about the function and other details of that object. It also provides you with some basic examples to work with, which I found useful in most cases.

Strings in Python are very similar to other languages, but the manipulation of strings is one of the main features of Python. It's immensely easy to work with strings in Python. Even something very simple, like splitting a string, takes effort in Java / C, while you will see how easy it is in Python.

Using the help function that we used previously, you can get help for any Python object and any function. Let's have some more examples with the other most commonly used data type strings:

- **Split**: This is a method to split the string based on some delimiters. If no argument is provided it assumes whitespace as delimiter.

  ```
  >>> mystring="Monty Python !  And the holy Grail ! \n"
  >>> print mystring.split()
  ['Monty', 'Python', '!', 'and', 'the', 'holy', 'Grail', '!']
  ```

- **Strip**: This is a method that can remove trailing whitespace, like '\n', '\n\r' from the string:

  ```
  >>> print mystring.strip()
  >>>Monty Python !  and the holy Grail !
  ```

  If you notice the '\n' character is stripped off. There are also methods like `rstrip()` and `lstrip()` to strip trailing whitespaces to the right and left of the string.

- **Upper/Lower**: We can change the case of the string using these methods:

  ```
  >>> print (mystring.upper()
  >>>MONTY PYTHON !AND THE HOLY GRAIL !
  ```

- **Replace**: This will help you substitute a substring from the string:

```
>>> print mystring.replace('!','''''')
>>> Monty Python  and the holy Grail
```

There are tons of string functions. I have just talked about some of the most frequently used.

> Please look the following link for more functions and examples: `https://docs.python.org/2/library/string.html`.

Regular expressions

One other important skill for an NLP enthusiast is working with regular expression. Regular expression is effectively pattern matching on strings. We heavily use pattern extrication to get meaningful information from large amounts of messy text data. The following are all the regular expressions you need. I haven't used any regular expressions beyond these in my entire life:

- `(a period)`: This expression matches any single character except newline `\n`.
- `\w`: This expression will match a character or a digit equivalent to [a-z A-Z 0-9]
- \W (*upper case W*) matches any non-word character.
- `\s`: This expression (*lowercase s*) matches a single whitespace character - space, newline, return, tab, form [`\n\r\t\f`].
- `\S`: This expression matches any non-whitespace character.
- `\t`: This expression performs a tab operation.
- `\n`: This expression is used for a newline character.
- `\r`: This expression is used for a return character.
- `\d`: Decimal digit [0-9].
- `^`: This expression is used at the start of the string.
- `$`: This expression is used at the end of the string.
- \: This expression is used to nullify the specialness of the special character. For example, you want to match the `$` symbol, then add \ in front of it.

Let's search for something in the running example, where `mystring` is the same string object, and we will try to look for some patterns in that. A substring search is one of the common use-cases of the `re` module. Let's implement this:

```
>>># We have to import re module to use regular expression
>>>import re
>>>if re.search('Python',mystring):
>>>     print "We found python "
>>>else:
>>>     print "NO "
```

Once this is executed, we get the message as follows:

```
We found python
```

We can do more pattern finding using regular expressions. One of the common functions that is used in finding all the patterns in a string is `findall`. It will look for the given patterns in the string, and will give you a list of all the matched objects:

```
>>>import re
>>>print re.findall('!',mystring)
['!', '!']
```

As we can see there were two instances of the "`!`" in the `mystring` and `findall` return both object as a list.

Dictionaries

The other most commonly used data structure is dictionaries, also known as **associative arrays/memories** in other programming languages. Dictionaries are data structures that are indexed by keys, which can be any immutable type; such as strings and numbers can always be keys.

Dictionaries are handy data structure that used widely across programming languages to implement many algorithms. Python dictionaries are one of the most elegant implementations of hash tables in any programming language. It's so easy to work around dictionary, and the great thing is that with few nuggets of code you can build a very complex data structure, while the same task can take so much time and coding effort in other languages. This gives the programmer more time to focus on algorithms rather than the data structure itself.

I am using one of the very common use cases of dictionaries to get the frequency distribution of words in a given text. With just few lines of the following code, you can get the frequency of words. Just try the same task in any other language and you will understand how amazing Python is:

```
>>># declare a dictionary
>>>word_freq={}
>>>for tok in string.split():
>>>     if tok in word_freq:
>>>         word_freq [tok]+=1
>>>     else:
>>>         word_freq [tok]=1
>>>print word_freq
{'!': 2, 'and': 1, 'holy': 1, 'Python': 1, 'Grail': 1, 'the': 1, 'Monty':
1}
```

Writing functions

As any other programming langauge Python also has its way of writing functions. Function in Python start with keyword `def` followed by the function name and parentheses `()`. Similar to any other programming language any arguments and the type of the argument should be placed within these parentheses. The actual code starts with `(:) colon symbol`. The initial lines of the code are typically doc string (comments), then we have code body and function ends with a return statement. For example in the given example the function `wordfreq` start with `def` keyword, there is no argument to this function and the function ends with a return statement.

```
>>>import sys
>>>def wordfreq (mystring):
>>>    '''
>>>    Function to generated the frequency distribution of the given text
>>>    '''
>>>    print mystring
>>>    word_freq={}
>>>    for tok in mystring.split():
>>>        if tok in word_freq:
>>>            word_freq [tok]+=1
>>>        else:
>>>            word_freq [tok]=1
```

```
>>>     print word_freq
>>>def main():
>>>     str="This is my fist python program"
>>>     wordfreq(str)
>>>if __name__ == '__main__':
>>>     main()
```

This was the same code that we wrote in the previous section the idea of writing in a form of function is to make the code re-usable and readable. The interpreter style of writing Python is also very common but for writing big programes it will be a good practice to use function/classes and one of the programming paradigm. We also wanted the user to write and run first Python program. You need to follow these steps to achive this.

1. Open an empty python file `mywordfreq.py` in your prefered text editor.
2. Write/Copy the code above in the code snippet to the file.
3. Open the command prompt in your Operating system.
4. Run following command prompt:

   ```
   $ python mywordfreq,py "This is my fist python program !!"
   ```

5. Output should be:

   ```
   {'This': 1, 'is': 1, 'python': 1, 'fist': 1, 'program': 1, 'my':
   1}
   ```

Now you have a very basic understanding about some common data-structures that python provides. You can write a full Python program and able to run that. I think this is good enough I think with this much of an introduction to Python you can manage for the initial chapters.

> Please have a look at some Python tutorials on the following website to learn more commands on Python:
> `https://wiki.python.org/moin/BeginnersGuide`

Diving into NLTK

Instead of going further into the theoretical aspects of natural language processing, let's start with a quick dive into NLTK. I am going to start with some basic example use cases of NLTK. There is a good chance that you have already done something similar. First, I will give a typical Python programmer approach, and then move on to NLTK for a much more efficient, robust, and clean solution.

We will start analyzing with some example text content. For the current example, I have taken the content from Python's home page.

```
>>>import urllib2
>>># urllib2 is use to download the html content of the web link
>>>response = urllib2.urlopen('http://python.org/')
>>># You can read the entire content of a file using read() method
>>>html = response.read()
>>>print len(html)
47020
```

We don't have any clue about the kind of topics that are discussed in this URL, so let's start with an **exploratory data analysis** (**EDA**). Typically in a text domain, EDA can have many meanings, but will go with a simple case of what kinds of terms dominate the document. What are the topics? How frequent they are? The process will involve some level of preprocessing steps. We will try to do this first in a pure Python way, and then we will do it using NLTK.

Let's start with cleaning the html tags. One ways to do this is to select just the `tokens`, including numbers and character. Anybody who has worked with regular expression should be able to convert html string into list of `tokens`:

```
>>># Regular expression based split the string
>>>tokens = [tok for tok in html.split()]
>>>print "Total no of tokens :"+ str(len(tokens))
>>># First 100 tokens
>>>print tokens[0:100]
Total no of tokens :2860
['<!doctype', 'html>', '<!--[if', 'lt', 'IE', '7]>', '<html', 'class="no-js', 'ie6', 'lt-ie7', 'lt-ie8', 'lt-ie9">', '<![endif]-->', '<!--[if',
'IE', '7]>', '<html', 'class="no-js', 'ie7', 'lt-ie8', 'lt-ie9">',
'<![endif]-->', ''type="text/css"', 'media="not', 'print,', 'braille,'
...]
```

As you can see, there is an excess of html tags and other unwanted characters when we use the preceding method. A cleaner version of the same task will look something like this:

```
>>>import re
>>># using the split function
>>>#https://docs.python.org/2/library/re.html
>>>tokens = re.split('\W+',html)
```

```
>>>print len(tokens)
>>>print tokens[0:100]
5787
['', 'doctype', 'html', 'if', 'lt', 'IE', '7', 'html', 'class', 'no',
'js', 'ie6', 'lt', 'ie7', 'lt', 'ie8', 'lt', 'ie9', 'endif', 'if',
'IE', '7', 'html', 'class', 'no', 'js', 'ie7', 'lt', 'ie8', 'lt', 'ie9',
'endif', 'if', 'IE', '8', 'msapplication', 'tooltip', 'content', 'The',
'official', 'home', 'of', 'the', 'Python', 'Programming', 'Language',
'meta', 'name', 'apple' ...]
```

This looks much cleaner now. But still you can do more; I leave it to you to try to remove as much noise as you can. You can clean some HTML tags that are still popping up, You probably also want to look for word length as a criteria and remove words that have a length one—it will remove elements like `7`, `8`, and so on, which are just noise in this case. Now instead writing some of these preprocessing steps from scratch let's move to NLTK for the same task. There is a function called `clean_html()` that can do all the cleaning that we were looking for:

```
>>>import nltk
>>># http://www.nltk.org/api/nltk.html#nltk.util.clean_html
>>>clean = nltk.clean_html(html)
>>># clean will have entire string removing all the html noise
>>>tokens = [tok for tok in clean.split()]
>>>print tokens[:100]
['Welcome', 'to', 'Python.org', 'Skip', 'to', 'content', '&#9660;',
'Close', 'Python', 'PSF', 'Docs', 'PyPI', 'Jobs', 'Community', '&#9650;',
'The', 'Python', 'Network', '&equiv;', 'Menu', 'Arts', 'Business' ...]
```

Cool, right? This definitely is much cleaner and easier to do.

Let's try to get the frequency distribution of these terms. First, let's do it the Pure Python way, then I will tell you the NLTK recipe.

```
>>>import operator
>>>freq_dis={}
>>>for tok in tokens:
>>>    if tok in freq_dis:
>>>        freq_dis[tok]+=1
>>>    else:
>>>        freq_dis[tok]=1
>>># We want to sort this dictionary on values ( freq in this case )
```

```
>>>sorted_freq_dist= sorted(freq_dis.items(), key=operator.itemgetter(1), reverse=True)
>>> print sorted_freq_dist[:25]
[('Python', 55), ('>>>', 23), ('and', 21), ('to', 18), (',', 18), ('the', 14), ('of', 13), ('for', 12), ('a', 11), ('Events', 11), ('News', 11), ('is', 10), ('2014-', 10), ('More', 9), ('#', 9), ('3', 9), ('=', 8), ('in', 8), ('with', 8), ('Community', 7), ('The', 7), ('Docs', 6), ('Software', 6), (':', 6), ('3:', 5), ('that', 5), ('sum', 5)]
```

Naturally, as this is Python's home page, Python and the `(>>>)` interpreter symbol are the most common terms, also giving a sense of the website.

A better and more efficient approach is to use NLTK's `FreqDist()` function. For this, we will take a look at the same code we developed before:

```
>>>import nltk
>>>Freq_dist_nltk=nltk.FreqDist(tokens)
>>>print Freq_dist_nltk
>>>for k,v in Freq_dist_nltk.items():
>>>     print str(k)+':'+str(v)
<FreqDist: 'Python': 55, '>>>': 23, 'and': 21, ',': 18, 'to': 18, 'the': 14, 'of': 13, 'for': 12, 'Events': 11, 'News': 11, ...>
Python:55
>>>:23
and:21
,:18
to:18
the:14
of:13
for:12
Events:11
News:11
```

Downloading the example code

You can download the example code files from your account at `http://www.packtpub.com` for all the Packt Publishing books you have purchased. If you purchased this book elsewhere, you can visit `http://www.packtpub.com/support` and register to have the files e-mailed directly to you.

Let's now do some more funky things. Let's plot this:

```
>>>Freq_dist_nltk.plot(50, cumulative=False)
>>># below is the plot for the frequency distributions
```

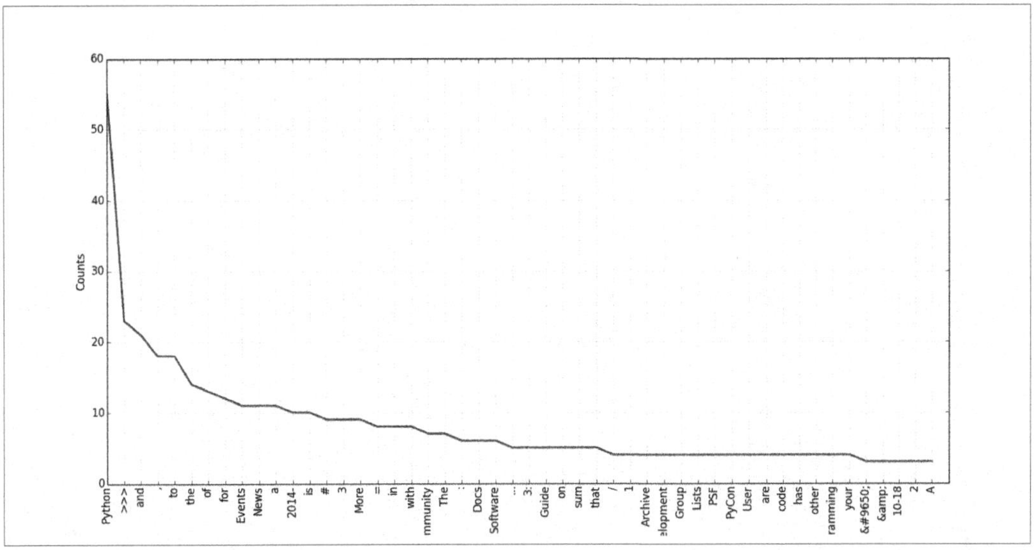

We can see that the cumulative frequency is growing, and at some point the curve is going into long tail. Still, there is some noise, there are words like `the`, `of`, `for`, and `=`. These are useless words, and there is a terminology for them. These words are stop words; words like `the`, `a`, `an`, and so on. Article pronouns are generally present in most of the documents, hence they are not discriminative enough to be informative. In most of the NLP and information retrieval tasks, people generally remove stop words. Let's go back again to our running example:

```
>>>stopwords=[word.strip().lower() for word in open("PATH/english.stop.
txt")]
>>>clean_tokens=[tok for tok in tokens if len(tok.lower())>1 and (tok.
lower() not in stopwords)]
```

```
>>>Freq_dist_nltk=nltk.FreqDist(clean_tokens)
>>>Freq_dist_nltk.plot(50, cumulative=False)
```

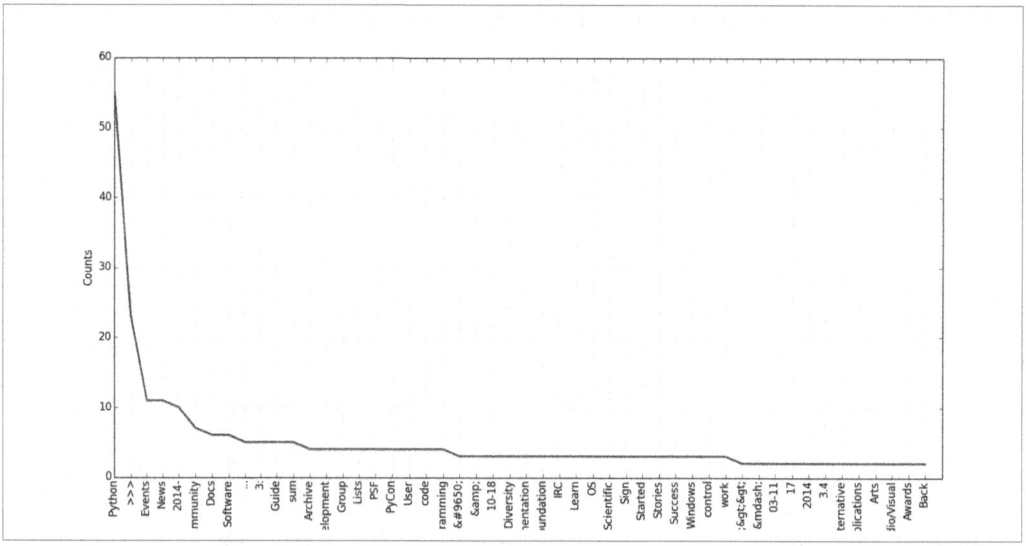

> Please go to `http://www.wordle.net/advanced` for more word clouds.

Looks much cleaner now! After finishing this much, you can go to **wordle** and put the distribution in a form of a CSV and you should be able to get something like this word cloud:

Your turn

- Please try the same exercise for different URLs.
- Try to reach the word cloud.

Summary

To summarize, this chapter was intended to give you a brief introduction to Natural Language Processing. The book does assume some background in NLP and programming in Python, but we have tried to give a very quick head start to Python and NLP. We have installed all the related packages that are require for us to work with NLTK. We wanted to give you, with a few simple lines of code, an idea of how to use NLTK. We were able to deliver an amazing word cloud, which is a great way of visualizing the topics in a large amount of unstructured text, and is quite popular in the industry for text analytics. I think the goal was to set up everything around NLTK, and to get Python working smoothly on your system. You should also be able to write and run basic Python programs. I wanted the reader to feel the power of the NLTK library, and build a small running example that will involve a basic application around word cloud. If the reader is able to generate the word cloud, I think we were successful.

In the next few chapters, we will learn more about Python as a language, and its features related to process natural language. We will explore some of the basic NLP preprocessing steps and learn about some of basic concepts related to NLP.

2

Text Wrangling and Cleansing

The previous chapter was all about you getting a head start on Python as well as **NLTK**. We learned about how we can start some meaningful **EDA** with any corpus of text. We did all the pre-processing part in a very crude and simple manner. In this chapter, will go over preprocessing steps like **tokenization**, **stemming**, **lemmatization**, and **stop word** removal in more detail. We will explore all the tools in NLTK for text wrangling. We will talk about all the pre-processing steps used in modern NLP applications, the different ways to achieve some of these tasks, as well as the general do's and don'ts. The idea is to give you enough information about these tools so that you can decide what kind of pre-processing tool you need for your application. By the end of this chapter, readers should know :

- About all the data wrangling, and to perform it using NLTK
- What is the importance of text cleansing and what are the common tasks that can be achieved using NLTK

What is text wrangling?

It's really hard to define the term text/data wrangling. I will define it as all the pre-processing and all the heavy lifting you do before you have a machine readable and formatted text from raw data. The process involves **data munging, text cleansing, specific preprocessing, tokenization, stemming** or **lemmatization** and **stop word removal**. Let's start with a basic example of parsing a `csv` file:

```
>>>import csv
>>>with open('example.csv','rb')  as f:
>>>     reader = csv.reader(f,delimiter=',',quotechar='"')
>>>     for line in reader :
>>>         print line[1]    # assuming the second field is the raw sting
```

Here we are trying to parse a `csv`, in above code line will be a list of all the column elements of the `csv`. We can customize this to work on any delimiter and quoting character. Now once we have the raw string, we can apply different kinds of text wrangling that we learned in the last chapter. The point here is to equip you with enough detail to deal with any day to day `csv` files.

A clear process flow for some of the most commonly accepted document types is shown in the following block diagram:

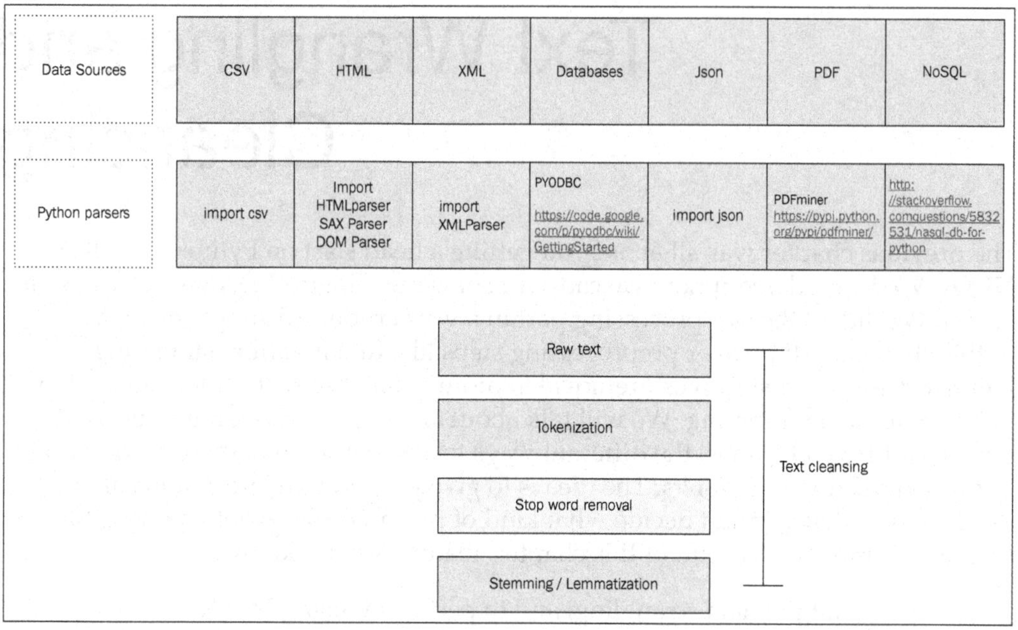

I have listed most common data sources in the first stack of the diagram. In most cases, the data will be residing in one of these data formats. In the next step, I have listed the most commonly used Python wrappers around those data formats. For example, in the case of a `csv` file, Python's `csv` module is the most robust way of handling the `csv` file. It allows you to play with different splitters, different quote characters, and so on.

The other most commonly used files are `json`.

For example, `json` looks like:

```
{
  "array": [1,2,3,4],
 "boolean": True,
  "object": {
    "a": "b"
  },
  "string": "Hello World"
}
```

Let's say we want to process the string. The parsing code will be:

```
>>>import json
>>>jsonfile = open('example.json')
>>>data = json.load(jsonfile)
>>>print data['string']
"Hello World"
```

We are just loading a `json` file using the `json` module. Python allows you to choose and process it to a raw string form. Please have a look at the diagram to get more details about all the data sources, and their parsing packages in Python. I have only given pointers here; please feel free to search the web for more details about these packages.

So before you write your own parser to parse these different document formats, please have a look at the second row for available parsers in Python. Once you reach a raw string, all the pre-processing steps can be applied as a pipeline, or you might choose to ignore some of them. We will talk about tokenization, stemmers, and lemmatizers in the next section in detail. We will also talk about the variants, and when to use one case over the other.

> Now that you have an idea of what text wrangling is, try to connect to any one of the databases using one of the Python modules described in the preceding image.

Text cleansing

Once we have parsed the text from a variety of data sources, the challenge is to make sense of this raw data. Text cleansing is loosely used for most of the cleaning to be done on text, depending on the data source, parsing performance, external noise and so on. In that sense, what we did in *Chapter 1, Introduction to Natural Language Processing* for cleaning the html using `html_clean`, can be labeled as text cleansing. In another case, where we are parsing a PDF, there could be unwanted noisy characters, non `ASCII` characters to be removed, and so on. Before going on to next steps we want to remove these to get a clean text to process further. With a data source like `xml`, we might only be interested in some specific elements of the tree, with databases we may have to manipulate splitters, and sometimes we are only interested in specific columns. In summary, any process that is done with the aim to make the text cleaner and to remove all the noise surrounding the text can be termed as text cleansing. There are no clear boundaries between the terms data munging, text cleansing, and data wrangling they can be used interchangeably in a similar context. In the next few sections, we will talk about some of the most common pre-processing steps while doing any NLP task.

Sentence splitter

Some of the NLP applications require splitting a large raw text into sentences to get more meaningful information out. Intuitively, a sentence is an acceptable unit of conversation. When it comes to computers, it is a harder task than it looks. A typical sentence splitter can be something as simple as splitting the string on (`.`), to something as complex as a predictive classifier to identify sentence boundaries:

```
>>>inputstring = ' This is an example sent. The sentence splitter will
split on sent markers. Ohh really !!'
>>>from nltk.tokenize import sent_tokenize
>>>all_sent = sent_tokenize(inputstring)
>>>print all_sent
[' This is an example sent', 'The sentence splitter will split on
markers.','Ohh really !!']
```

We are trying to split the raw text string into a list of sentences. The preceding function, `sent_tokenize`, internally uses a sentence boundary detection algorithm that comes pre-built into NLTK. If your application requires a custom sentence splitter, there are ways that we can train a sentence splitter of our own:

```
>>>import nltk.tokenize.punkt
>>>tokenizer = nltk.tokenize.punkt.PunktSentenceTokenizer()
```

The preceding sentence splitter is available in all the 17 languages. You just need to specify the respective pickle object. In my experience, this is good enough to deal with a variety of the text corpus, and there is a lesser chance that you will have to build your own.

Tokenization

A word (*Token*) is the minimal unit that a machine can understand and process. So any text string cannot be further processed without going through tokenization. Tokenization is the process of splitting the raw string into meaningful tokens. The complexity of tokenization varies according to the need of the NLP application, and the complexity of the language itself. For example, in English it can be as simple as choosing only words and numbers through a regular expression. But for Chinese and Japanese, it will be a very complex task.

```
>>>s = "Hi Everyone !    hola gr8" # simplest tokenizer
>>>print s.split()
['Hi', 'Everyone', '!', 'hola', 'gr8']
>>>from nltk.tokenize import word_tokenize
>>>word_tokenize(s)
['Hi', 'Everyone', '!', 'hola', 'gr8']
>>>from nltk.tokenize import regexp_tokenize, wordpunct_tokenize,
blankline_tokenize
>>>regexp_tokenize(s, pattern='\w+')
['Hi', 'Everyone', 'hola', 'gr8']
>>>regexp_tokenize(s, pattern='\d+')
['8']
>>>wordpunct_tokenize(s)
['Hi', ',', 'Everyone', '!!', 'hola', 'gr8']
>>>blankline_tokenize(s)
['Hi, Everyone !!  hola gr8']
```

In the preceding code we have used various tokenizers. To start with we used the simplest: the `split()` method of Python strings. This is the most basic tokenizer, that uses white space as delimiter. But the `split()` method itself can be configured for some more complex tokenization. In the preceding example, you will find hardly a difference between the `s.split()` and `word_tokenize` methods.

The `word_tokenize` method is a generic and more robust method of tokenization for any kind of text corpus. The `word_tokenize` method comes pre-built with NLTK. If you are not able to access it, you made some mistakes in installing NLTK data. Please refer to *Chapter 1, Introduction to Natural Language Processing* for installation.

There are two most commonly used tokenizers. The first is `word_tokenize`, which is the default one, and will work in most cases. The other is `regex_tokenize`, which is more of a customized tokenizer for the specific needs of the user. Most of the other tokenizers can be derived from regex tokenizers. You can also build a very specific tokenizer using a different pattern. In line 8 of the preceding code, we split the same string with the regex tokenizer. We use `\w+` as a regular expression, which means we need all the words and digits from the string, and other symbols can be used as a splitter, same as what we do in line 10 where we specify `\d+` as regex. The result will produce only digits from the string.

Can you build a regex tokenizer that will only select words that are either small, capitals, numbers, or money symbols?

Hint: Just look for the regular expression for the preceding query and use a `regex_tokenize`.

> You can also have a look at some of the demos available online: `http://text-processing.com/demo`.

Stemming

Stemming, in literal terms, is the process of cutting down the branches of a tree to its stem. So effectively, with the use of some basic rules, any token can be cut down to its stem. Stemming is more of a crude rule-based process by which we want to club together different variations of the token. For example, the word *eat* will have variations like eating, eaten, eats, and so on. In some applications, as it does not make sense to differentiate between eat and eaten, we typically use stemming to club both grammatical variances to the root of the word. While stemming is used most of the time for its simplicity, there are cases of complex language or complex NLP tasks where it's necessary to use lemmatization instead. Lemmatization is a more robust and methodical way of combining grammatical variations to the root of a word.

In the following snippet, we show a few stemmers:

```
>>>from nltk.stem import PorterStemmer # import Porter stemmer
>>>from nltk.stem.lancaster import LancasterStemmer
>>>from nltk.stem.Snowball import SnowballStemmer
>>>pst = PorterStemmer()   # create obj of the PorterStemmer
>>>lst = LancasterStemmer() # create obj of LancasterStemmer
>>>lst.stem("eating")
eat
>>>pst.stem("shopping")
shop
```

A basic rule-based stemmer, like removing *-s/es* or *-ing* or *-ed* can give you a precision of more than 70 percent, while **Porter stemmer** also uses more rules and can achieve very good accuracies.

We are creating different stemmer objects, and applying a `stem()` method on the string. As you can see, there is not much of a difference when you look at a simple example, however there are many stemming algorithms around, and the precision and performance of them differ. You may want to have a look at `http://www.nltk.org/api/nltk.stem.html` for more details. I have used Porter Stemmer most often, and if you are working with English, it's good enough. There is a family of **Snowball stemmers** that can be used for Dutch, English, French, German, Italian, Portuguese, Romanian, Russian, and so on. I also came across a light weight stemmer for Hindi on `http://research.variancia.com/hindi_stemmer`.

> I would suggest a study of all the stemmers for those who want to explore more about stemmers on `http://en.wikipedia.org/wiki/Stemming`.
>
> But most users can live with Porter and Snowball stemmer for a large number of use cases. In modern NLP applications, sometimes people even ignore stemming as a pre-processing step, so it typically depends on your domain and application. I would also like to tell you the fact that if you want to use some NLP taggers, like Part of Speech tagger (POS), NER or dependency parser, you should avoid stemming, because stemming will modify the token and this can result in a different result. We will go into this further when we talk about taggers in general.

Lemmatization

Lemmatization is a more methodical way of converting all the grammatical/inflected forms of the root of the word. Lemmatization uses context and part of speech to determine the inflected form of the word and applies different normalization rules for each part of speech to get the root word (*lemma*):

```
>>>from nltk.stem import WordNetLemmatizer
>>>wlem = WordNetLemmatizer()
>>>wlem.lemmatize("ate")
eat
```

Here, `WordNetLemmatizer` is using `wordnet`, which takes a word and searches `wordnet`, a semantic dictionary. It also uses a morph analysis to cut to the root and search for the specific lemma (variation of the word). Hence, in our example it is possible to get *eat* for the given variation *ate*, which was never possible with stemming.

- Can you explain what the difference is between Stemming and lemmatization?
- Can you come up with a Porter stemmer (Rule-based) for your native language?
- Why would it be harder to implement a stemmer for languages like Chinese?

Stop word removal

Stop word removal is one of the most commonly used preprocessing steps across different NLP applications. The idea is simply removing the words that occur commonly across all the documents in the corpus. Typically, articles and pronouns are generally classified as stop words. These words have no significance in some of the NLP tasks like information retrieval and classification, which means these words are not very discriminative. On the contrary, in some NLP applications stop word removal will have very little impact. Most of the time, the stop word list for the given language is a well hand-curated list of words that occur most commonly across corpuses. While the stop word lists for most languages are available online, these are also ways to automatically generate the stop word list for the given corpus. A very simple way to build a stop word list is based on word's document frequency (Number of documents the word presents), where the words present across the corpus can be treated as stop words. Enough research has been done to get the optimum list of stop words for some specific corpus. NLTK comes with a pre-built list of stop words for around 22 languages.

To implement the process of stop word removal, below is code that uses NLTK stop word. You can also create a dictionary on a lookup based approach like we did in *Chapter 1, Introduction to Natural Language Processing.*

```
>>>from nltk.corpus import stopwords
>>>stoplist = stopwords.words('english') # config the language name
# NLTK supports 22 languages for removing the stop words
>>>text = "This is just a test"
>>>cleanwordlist = [word for word in text.split() if word not in
stoplist]
# apart from just and test others are stopwords
['test']
```

In the preceding code snippet, we have deployed a cleaner version of the same stop word removal we did in *Chapter 1, Introduction to Natural Language Processing.* Previously, we were using a lookup based approach. Even in this case, NLTK internally did a very similar approach. I would recommend using the NLTK list of stop words, because this is more of a standardized list, and this is robust when compared to any other implementation. We also have a way to use similar methods for other languages by just passing the language name as a parameter to the stop words constructor.

- What's the math behind removing stop words?
- Can we perform other NLP operations after stop word removal?

Rare word removal

This is very intuitive, as some of the words that are very unique in nature like names, brands, product names, and some of the noise characters, such as html leftouts, also need to be removed for different NLP tasks. For example, it would be really bad to use names as a predictor for a text classification problem, even if they come out as a significant predictor. We will talk about this further in subsequent chapters. We definitely don't want all these noisy tokens to be present. We also use length of the words as a criteria for removing words with very a short length or a very long length:

```
>>># tokens is a list of all tokens in corpus
>>>freq_dist = nltk.FreqDist(token)
>>>rarewords = freq_dist.keys()[-50:]
>>>after_rare_words = [ word for word in token not in rarewords]
```

We are using the `FreqDist()` function to get the distribution of the terms in the corpus, selecting the rarest one into a list, and then filtering our original corpus. We can also do it for individual documents, as well.

Spell correction

It is not a necessary to use a spellchecker for all NLP applications, but some use cases require you to use a basic spellcheck. We can create a very basic spellchecker by just using a dictionary lookup. There are some enhanced string algorithms that have been developed for fuzzy string matching. One of the most commonly used is `edit-distance`. NLTK also provides you with a variety of metrics module that has `edit_distance`.

```
>>>from nltk.metrics import edit_distance
>>>edit_distance("rain","shine")
3
```

We will cover this module in more detail in advanced chapters. We also have one of the most elegant codes for spellchecker from Peter Norvig, which is quite easy to understand and written in pure Python.

> I would recommend that anyone who works with natural language processing visit the following link for spellcheck: `http://norvig.com/spell-correct.html`

Your turn

Here are the answers to the open-ended questions:

- Try to connect any of the data base using pyodbc.

  `https://code.google.com/p/pyodbc/wiki/GettingStarted`

- Can you build a regex tokenizer that will only select words that are either small, capitals, numbers or money symbols?

  [`\w+`] selects all the words and numbers [a-z A-Z 0-9] and [`\$`] will match money symbol.

- What's the difference between Stemming and lemmatization?

  Stemming is more of a rule-based approach to get the root of the word's grammatical forms, while lemmatization also considers context and the POS of the given word, then applies rules specific to grammatical variants. Stemmers are easier to implement and the processing time is faster than lemmatizer.

- Can you come up with a Porter stemmer (Rule-based) for your native language?

  Hint: `http://tartarus.org/martin/PorterStemmer/Python.txt`

  `http://Snowball.tartarus.org/algorithms/english/stemmer.html`

- Can we perform other NLP operations after stop word removal?

  No; never. All the typical NLP applications like POS tagging, chunking, and so on will need context to generate the tags for the given text. Once we remove the stop word, we lose the context.

- Why would it be harder to implement a stemmer for languages like Hindi or Chinese?

  Indian languages are morphologically rich and it's hard to token the Chinese; there are challenges with the normalization of the symbols, so it's even harder to implement steamer. We will talk about these challenges in advanced chapters.

Summary

In this chapter we talked about all the data wrangling/munging in the context of text. We went through some of the most common data sources, and how to parse them with Python packages. We talked about tokenization in depth, from a very basic string method to a custom regular expression based tokenizer.

We talked about stemming and lemmatization, and the various types of stemmers that can be used, as well as the pros and cons of each of them. We also discussed the stop word removal process, why it's important, when to remove stop words, and when it's not needed. We also briefly touched upon removing rare words and why it's important in text cleansing—both stop word and rare word removal are essentially removing outliers from the frequency distribution. We also referred to spell correction. There is no limit to what you can do with text wrangling and text cleansing. Every text corpus has new challenges, and a new kind of noise that needs to be removed. You will get to learn over time what kind of pre-processing works best for your corpus, and what can be ignored.

In the next chapter will see some of the NLP related pre-processing, like POS tagging, chunking, and NER. I am leaving answers or hints for some of the open questions that we asked in the chapter.

3

Part of Speech Tagging

In previous chapters, we talked about all the preprocessing steps we need, in order to work with any text corpus. You should now be comfortable about parsing any kind of text and should be able to clean it. You should be able to perform all text preprocessing, such as Tokenization, Stemming, and Stop Word removal on any text. You can perform and customize all the preprocessing tools to fit your needs. So far, we have mainly discussed generic preprocessing to be done with text documents. Now let's move on to more intense NLP preprocessing steps.

In this chapter, we will discuss what part of speech tagging is, and what the significance of POS is in the context of NLP applications. We will also learn how to use NLTK to extract meaningful information using tagging and various taggers used for NLP intense applications. Lastly, we will learn how NLTK can be used to tag a named entity. We will discuss in detail the various NLP taggers and also give a small snippet to help you get going. We will also see the best practices, and where to use what kind of tagger. By the end of this chapter, readers will learn:

- What is Part of speech tagging and how important it is in context of NLP
- What are the different ways of doing POS tagging using NLTK
- How to build a custom POS tagger using NLTK

What is Part of speech tagging

In your childhood, you may have heard the term **Part of Speech** (**POS**). It can really take good amount of time to get the hang of what adjectives and adverbs actually are. What exactly is the difference? Think about building a system where we can encode all this knowledge. It may look very easy, but for many decades, coding this knowledge into a machine learning model was a very hard NLP problem. I think current state of the art POS tagging algorithms can predict the POS of the given word with a higher degree of precision (that is approximately 97 percent). But still lots of research going on in the area of POS tagging.

Languages like English have many tagged corpuses available in the news and other domains. This has resulted in many state of the art algorithms. Some of these taggers are generic enough to be used across different domains and varieties of text. But in specific use cases, the POS might not perform as expected. For these use cases, we might need to build a POS tagger from scratch. To understand the internals of a POS, we need to have a basic understanding of some of the machine learning techniques. We will talk about some of these in *Chapter 6, Text Classification*, but we have to discuss the basics in order to build a custom POS tagger to fit our needs.

First, we will learn some of the pertained POS taggers available, along with a set of tokens. You can get the POS of individual words as a **tuple**. We will then move on to the internal workings of some of these taggers, and we will also talk about building a custom tagger from scratch.

When we talk about POS, the most frequent POS notification used is Penn Treebank:

Tag	**Description**
`NNP`	Proper noun, singular
`NNPS`	Proper noun, plural
`PDT`	Pre determiner
`POS`	Possessive ending
`PRP`	Personal pronoun
`PRP$`	Possessive pronoun
`RB`	Adverb
`RBR`	Adverb, comparative
`RBS`	Adverb, superlative
`RP`	Particle
`SYM`	Symbol (mathematical or scientific)
`TO`	to
`UH`	Interjection
`VB`	Verb, base form
`VBD`	Verb, past tense

Tag	Description
VBG	Verb, gerund/present participle
VBN	Verb, past
WP	Wh-pronoun
WP$	Possessive wh-pronoun
WRB	Wh-adverb
#	Pound sign
$	Dollar sign
.	Sentence-final punctuation
,	Comma
:	Colon, semi-colon
(	Left bracket character
)	Right bracket character
"	Straight double quote
'	Left open single quote
"	Left open double quote
'	Right close single quote
"	Right open double quote

Looks pretty much like what we learned in primary school English class, right? Now once we have an understanding about what these tags mean, we can run an experiment:

```
>>>import nltk
>>>from nltk import word_tokenize
>>>s = "I was watching TV"
>>>print nltk.pos_tag(word_tokenize(s))
[('I', 'PRP'), ('was', 'VBD'), ('watching', 'VBG'), ('TV', 'NN')]
```

If you just want to use POS for a corpus like news or something similar, you just need to know the preceding three lines of code. In this code, we are tokenizing a piece of text and using NLTK's `pos_tag` method to get a tuple of (word, `pos-tag`). This is one of the pre-trained POS taggers that comes with NLTK.

> It's internally using the `maxent` classifier (will discuss these classifiers in advanced chapters) trained model to predict to which class of tag a particular word belongs.
>
> To get more details you can use the following link:
>
> `https://github.com/nltk/nltk/blob/develop/nltk/tag/__init__.py`

NLTK has used python's powerful data structures efficiently, so we have a lot more flexibility in terms of use of the results of NLTK outputs.

You must be wondering what could be a typical use of POS in a real application. In a typical preprocessing, we might want to look for all the nouns. Now this code snippet will give us all the nouns in the given sentence:

```
>>>tagged = nltk.pos_tag(word_tokenize(s))
>>>allnoun = [word for word,pos in tagged if pos in ['NN','NNP'] ]
```

Try to answer the following questions:

- Can we remove stop words before POS tagging?
- How can we get all the verbs in the sentence?

Stanford tagger

Another awesome feature of NLTK is that it also has many wrappers around other pre-trained taggers, such as **Stanford tools**. A common example of a POS tagger is shown here:

```
>>>from nltk.tag.stanford import POSTagger
>>>import nltk
>>>stan_tagger = POSTagger('models/english-bidirectional-distdim.
tagger','standford-postagger.jar')
>>>tokens = nltk.word_tokenize(s)
>>>stan_tagger.tag(tokens)
```

> To use the above code, you need to download the Stanford tagger from `http://nlp.stanford.edu/software/stanford-postagger-full-2014-08-27.zip`. Extract both the jar and model into a folder, and give an absolute path in argument for the `POSTagger`.

Summarizing this, there are mainly two ways to achieve any tagging task in NLTK:

1. Using NLTK's or another lib's pre-trained tagger, and applying it on the test data. Both preceding taggers should be sufficient to deal with any POS tagging task that deals with plain English text, and the corpus is not very domain specific.
2. Building or Training a tagger to be used on test data. This is to deal with a very specific use case and to develop a customized tagger.

Let's dig deeper into what goes on inside a typical POS tagger.

Diving deep into a tagger

A typical tagger uses a lot of trained data, with sentences tagged for each word that will be the POS tag attached to it. Tagging is purely manual and looks like this:

```
Well/UH what/WP do/VBP you/PRP think/VB about/IN the/DT idea/NN of/IN ,/,
uh/UH ,/, kids/NNS having/VBG to/TO do/VB public/JJ service/NN work/NN
for/IN a/DT year/NN ?/.Do/VBP you/PRP think/VBP it/PRP 's/BES a/DT ,/,
```

The preceding sample is taken from the Penn Treebank switchboard corpus. People have done lot of manual work tagging large corpuses. There is a **Linguistic Data Consortium (LDC)** where people have dedicated so much time to tagging for different languages, different kinds of text and different kinds of tagging like POS, dependency parsing, and discourse (will talk about these later).

> You can get all these resources and more information about them at `https://www.ldc.upenn.edu/`. (**LDC** provides a fraction of data for free but you can also purchase the entire tagged corpus. NLTK has approximately 10 percent of the PTB.)

If we also want to train our own POS tagger, we have to do the tagging exercise for our specific domain. This kind of tagging will require domain experts.

Typically, tagging problems like POS tagging are seen as sequence labeling problems or a classification problem where people have tried generative and discriminative models to predict the right tag for the given token.

Instead of jumping directly in to more sophisticated examples, let's start with some simple approaches for tagging.

The following snippet gives us the frequency distribution of POS tags in the Brown corpus:

```
>>>from nltk.corpus import brown
>>>import nltk
>>>tags = [tag for (word, tag) in brown.tagged_words(categories='news')]
>>>print nltk.FreqDist(tags)
<FreqDist: 'NN': 13162, 'IN': 10616, 'AT': 8893, 'NP': 6866, ',': 5133,
'NNS': 5066, '.': 4452, 'JJ': 4392 >
```

We can see `NN` comes as the most frequent tag, so let's start building a very naïve POS tagger, by assigning `NN` as a tag to all the test words. NLTK has a `DefaultTagger` function that can be used for this. `DefaultTagger` function is part of the Sequence tagger, which will be discussed next. There is a function called `evaluate()` that gives the accuracy of the correctly predicted POS of the words. This is used to benchmark the tagger against the brown corpus. In the `default_tagger` case, we are getting approximately 13 percent of the predictions correct. We will use the same benchmark for all the taggers moving forward.

```
>>>brown_tagged_sents = brown.tagged_sents(categories='news')
>>>default_tagger = nltk.DefaultTagger('NN')
>>>print default_tagger.evaluate(brown_tagged_sents)
0.130894842572
```

Sequential tagger

Not surprisingly, the above tagger performed poorly. The `DefaultTagger` is part of a base class `SequentialBackoffTagger` that serves tags based on the Sequence. Tagger tries to model the tags based on the context, and if it is not able to predict the tag correctly, it consults a `BackoffTagger`. Typically, the `DefaultTagger` parameter could be used as a `BackoffTagger`.

Let's move on to more sophisticated sequential taggers.

N-gram tagger

N-gram tagger is a subclass of `SequentialTagger`, where the tagger takes previous *n* words in the context, to predict the POS tag for the given token. There are variations of these taggers where people have tried it with `UnigramsTagger`, `BigramsTagger`, and `TrigramTagger`:

```
>>>from nltk.tag import UnigramTagger
>>>from nltk.tag import DefaultTagger
>>>from nltk.tag import BigramTagger
>>>from nltk.tag import TrigramTagger
# we are dividing the data into a test and train to evaluate our taggers.
>>>train_data = brown_tagged_sents[:int(len(brown_tagged_sents) * 0.9)]
>>>test_data = brown_tagged_sents[int(len(brown_tagged_sents) * 0.9):]
>>>unigram_tagger = UnigramTagger(train_data,backoff=default_tagger)
>>>print unigram_tagger.evaluate(test_data)
0.826195866853
>>>bigram_tagger = BigramTagger(train_data, backoff=unigram_tagger)
>>>print bigram_tagger.evaluate(test_data)
0.835300351655
>>>trigram_tagger = TrigramTagger(train_data,backoff=bigram_tagger)
>>>print trigram_tagger.evaluate(test_data)
0.83327713281
```

Unigram just considers the conditional frequency of tags and predicts the most frequent tag for the every given token. The `bigram_tagger` parameter will consider the tags of the given word and the previous word, and tag as tuple to get the given tag for the test word. The `TrigramTagger` parameter looks for the previous two words with a similar process.

It's very evident that coverage of the `TrigramTagger` parameter will be less and the accuracy of that instance will be high. On the other hand, `UnigramTagger` will have better coverage. To deal with this tradeoff between precision/recall, we combine the three taggers in the preceding snippet. First it will look for the trigram of the given word sequence for predicting the tag; if not found it `Backoff` to `BigramTagger` parameter and to a `UnigramTagger` parameter and in end to a `NN` tag.

Regex tagger

There is one more class of sequential tagger that is a regular expression based taggers. Here, instead of looking for the exact word, we can define a regular expression, and at the same time we can define the corresponding tag for the given expressions. For example, in the following code we have provided some of the most common regex patterns to get the different parts of speech. We know some of the patterns related to each POS category, for example we know the articles in English and we know that anything that ends with *ness* will be an adjective. Instead, we will write a bunch of regex and a pure python code, and the NLTK `RegexpTagger` parameter will provide an elegant way of building a pattern based POS. This can also be used to induce domain related POS patterns.

```
>>>from nltk.tag.sequential import RegexpTagger
>>>regexp_tagger = RegexpTagger(
        [( r'^-?[0-9]+(.[0-9]+)?$', 'CD'),     # cardinal numbers
         ( r'(The|the|A|a|An|an)$', 'AT'),     # articles
         ( r'.*able$', 'JJ'),                  # adjectives
         ( r'.*ness$', 'NN'),              # nouns formed from adj
         ( r'.*ly$', 'RB'),                # adverbs
         ( r'.*s$', 'NNS'),                # plural nouns
         ( r'.*ing$', 'VBG'),              # gerunds
         (r'.*ed$', 'VBD'),                # past tense verbs
         (r'.*', 'NN')                     # nouns (default)
         ])
>>>print regexp_tagger.evaluate(test_data)
0.303627342358
```

We can see that by just using some of the obvious patterns for POS we are able to reach approximately 30 percent in terms of accuracy. If we combine regex taggers, such as the `BackoffTagger`, we might improve the performance. The other use case for regex tagger is in the preprocessing step, where instead of using a raw Python function `string.sub()`, we can use this tagger to tag date patterns, money patterns, location patterns and so on.

- Can you modify the code of a hybrid tagger in the N-gram tagger section to work with Regex tagger? Does that improve performance?
- Can you write a tagger that tags Date and Money expressions?

Brill tagger

Brill tagger is a transformation based tagger, where the idea is to start with a guess for the given tag and, in next iteration, go back and fix the errors based on the next set of rules the tagger learned. It's also a supervised way of tagging, but unlike N-gram tagging where we count the N-gram patterns in training data, we look for transformation rules.

If the tagger starts with a `Unigram` / `Bigram` tagger with an acceptable accuracy, then brill tagger, instead looking for a trigram tuple, will be looking for rules based on tags, position and the word itself.

An example rule could be:

Replace `NN` with `VB` when the previous word is `TO`.

After we already have some tags based on `UnigramTagger`, we can refine if with just one simple rule. This is an interactive process. With a few iterations and some more optimized rules, the brill tagger can outperform some of the N-gram taggers. The only piece of advice is to look out for over-fitting of the tagger for the training set.

> You can also look at the work here for more example rules.
> `http://stp.lingfil.uu.se/~bea/publ/megyesi-BrillsPoSTagger.pdf`

- Can you try to write more rules based on your observation?
- Try to combine brill tagger with `UnigramTagger`.

Machine learning based tagger

Until now we have just used some of the pre-trained taggers from NLTK or Stanford. While we have used them in the examples in previous section, the internals of the taggers are still a black box to us. For example, `pos_tag` internally uses a **Maximum Entropy Classifier** (**MEC**). While `StanfordTagger` also uses a modified version of Maximum Entropy. These are discriminatory models. While there are many **Hidden Markov Model** (**HMM**) and **Conditional Random Field** (**CRF**) based taggers, these are generative models.

Covering all of these topics is beyond the scope of the book. I would highly recommend the NLP class for a great understanding of these concepts. We will cover some of the classification techniques in *Chapter 6, Text Classification*, but some of these are very advanced topics in NLP, and will need more attention.

If I have to explain in short, the way to categorize POS tagging problem is either as a classification problem where given a word and the features like previous word, context, morphological variation, and so on. We classify the given word into a POS category, while the others try to model it as a generative model using the similar features. It's for the reader's reference to go over some of these topics using links in the tips.

> NLP CLASS: `https://www.coursera.org/course/nlp`
>
> HMM: `http://mlg.eng.cam.ac.uk/zoubin/papers/ijprai.pdf`
>
> MEC: `https://web.stanford.edu/class/cs124/lec/Maximum_Entropy_Classifiers.pdf`
>
> `http://nlp.stanford.edu/software/tagger.shtml`

Named Entity Recognition (NER)

Aside from POS, one of the most common labeling problems is finding entities in the text. Typically NER constitutes name, location, and organizations. There are NER systems that tag more entities than just three of these. The problem can be seen as a sequence, labeling the Named entities using the context and other features. There is a lot more research going on in this area of NLP where people are trying to tag Biomedical entities, product entities in retail, and so on. Again, there are two ways of tagging the NER using NLTK. One is by using the pre-trained NER model that just scores the test data, the other is to build a Machine learning based model. NLTK provides the `ne_chunk()` method and a wrapper around Stanford NER tagger for Named Entity Recognition.

NER tagger

NLTK provides a method for Named Entity Extraction: `ne_chunk`. We have shown a small snippet to demonstrate how to use it for tagging any sentence. This method will require you to preprocess the text to tokenize for sentences, tokens, and POS tags in the same order to be able to tag for Named entities. NLTK used `ne_chunking`, where chunking is nothing but tagging multiple tokens to a call it a meaningful entity.

NE chunking is loosely used in the same way as Named entity:

```
>>>import nltk
>>>from nltk import ne_chunk
>>>Sent = "Mark is studying at Stanford University in California"
>>>print(ne_chunk(nltk.pos_tag(word_tokenize(sent)), binary=False))
(S
  (PERSON Mark/NNP)
  is/VBZ
  studying/VBG
  at/IN
  (ORGANIZATION Stanford/NNP University/NNP)
  in/IN
  NY(GPE California/NNP)))
```

The `ne_chunking` method recognizes people (names), places (location), and organizations. If binary is set to `True` then it provides the output for the entire sentence tree and tags everything. Setting it to `False` will give us detailed person, location and organizations information, as with the preceding example using the Stanford NER Tagger.

Similar to the POS tagger, NLTK also has a wrapper around Stanford NER. This NER tagger has better accuracy. The code following snippet will let you use the tagger. You can see in the given example that we are able to tag all the entities with just three lines of code:

```
>>>from nltk.tag.stanford import NERTagger
>>>st = NERTagger('<PATH>/stanford-ner/classifiers/all.3class.distsim.
crf.ser.gz',...                    '<PATH>/stanford-ner/stanford-ner.jar')
>>>st.tag('Rami Eid is studying at Stony Brook University in NY'.split())
[('Rami', 'PERSON'), ('Eid', 'PERSON'), ('is', 'O'), ('studying', 'O'),
('at', 'O'), ('Stony', 'ORGANIZATION'), ('Brook', 'ORGANIZATION'),
('University', 'ORGANIZATION'), ('in', 'O'), ('NY', 'LOCATION')]
```

If you observe closely, even with a very small test sentence, we can say Stanford Tagger outperformed the NLTK `ne_chunk` tagger.

Now, these kinds of NER taggers are a nice solution for a generic kind of entity tagging, but we have to train our own tagger, when it comes, to tag domain specific entities like biomedical and product names, so we have to build our own NER system. I would also recommend an NER Calais. It has ways of tagging not just typical NER, but also some more entities. The performance of this tagger is also very good:

`https://code.google.com/p/python-calais/`

Your Turn

Here are the answers to the questions posed in the above sections:

- Can we remove stop words before POS tagging?

  No; If we remove the stop words, we will lose the context, and some of the POS taggers (Pre-Trained model) use word context as features to give the POS of the given word.

- How can we get all the verbs in the sentence?

  We can get all the verbs in the sentence by using `pos_tag`

  ```
  >>>tagged = nltk.pos_tag(word_tokenize(s))
  >>>allverbs = [word for word,pos in tagged if pos in
  ['VB','VBD','VBG'] ]
  ```

- Can you modify the code of the hybrid tagger in the N-gram tagger section to work with Regex tagger? Does that improve performance?

  Yes. We can modify the code of the hybrid tagger in the N-gram tagger section to work with the Regex tagger:

  ```
  >>>print unigram_tagger.evaluate(test_data,backoff= regexp_tagger)
  >>>bigram_tagger = BigramTagger(train_data, backoff=unigram_
  tagger)
  >>>print bigram_tagger.evaluate(test_data)
  >>>trigram_tagger=TrigramTagger(train_data,backoff=bigram_tagger)
  >>>print trigram_tagger.evaluate(test_data)
  0.857122212053
  0.866708415627
  0.863914446746
  ```

  The performance improves as we add some basic pattern-based rules, instead of predicting the most frequent tag.

- Can you write a tagger that tags Date and Money expressions?

  Yes, we can write a tagger that tags Date and Money expressions. Following is the code:

  ```
  >>>date_regex = RegexpTagger([(r'(\d{2})[/.-](\d{2})[/.-](\d{4})$'
  ,'DATE'),(r'\$','MONEY')])
  >>>test_tokens = "I will be flying on sat 10-02-2014 with around
  10M $ ".split()
  >>>print date_regex.tag(test_tokens)
  ```

> The last two questions haven't been answered.
>
> There can be many rules according to the reader's observation, so there is no Right / Wrong answer here.

Can you try a similar word cloud to what we did in *Chapter 1, Introduction to Natural Language Processing* with only nouns and verbs now?

References:

`https://github.com/japerk/nltk-trainer`

`http://en.wikipedia.org/wiki/Part-of-speech_tagging`

`http://en.wikipedia.org/wiki/Named-entity_recognition`

`http://www.inf.ed.ac.uk/teaching/courses/icl/nltk/tagging.pdf`

`http://www.nltk.org/api/nltk.tag.html`

Summary

This chapter was intended to expose the reader to some of the most useful NLP pre-processing steps of tagging. We have talked about the Part of Speech problem in general, including the significance of POS in the context of NLP. We also discussed the different ways we can use a pre-trained POS tagger in NLTK, how simple it is to use, and how to create wonderful applications. We then talked about all the available POS tagging options, like N-gram tagging, Regex based tagging, etc. We have developed a mix of these taggers that can be built for domain specific corpuses. We briefly talked about how a typical pre-trained tagger is built. We discussed the possible approaches to address tagging problems. We also talked about NER taggers, and how it works with NLTK. I think if, by the end of this chapter, the user understands the importance of POS and NER in general in the context of NLP, as well as how to run the snippet of codes using NLTK, I will consider this chapter successful. But the journey does not end here. We know some of the shallow NLP preprocessing steps now, and in most of the practical application POS, the NER predominantly used. In more complex NLP applications such as the Q/A system, Summarization, and Speech we need deeper NLP techniques like Chunking, Parsing, Semantics. We will talk about these in the next chapter.

4
Parsing Structure in Text

This chapter involves a better understanding of deep structure in text and also how to deep parse text and use it in various NLP applications. Now, we are equipped with various NLP preprocessing steps. Let's move to some deeper aspect of the text. The structure of language is so complex that we can describe it by various layers of structural processing. In this chapter we will touch upon all these structures in text, differentiate between them, and provide you with enough details about the usage of one of these. We will talk about **context-free grammar** (CFG) and how it can be implemented with NLTK. We will also look at the various parsers and how we can use some of the existing parsing methods in NLTK. We will write a shallow parser in NLTK and will again talk about NER in the context of chunking. We will also provide details about some options that exist in NLTK to do deep structural analysis. We will also try to give you some real-world use cases of information extraction and how it can be achieved by using some of the topics that you will learn in this chapter. We want you to have an understanding of these topics by the end of this chapter.

In this chapter:

- We will also see what parsing is and what is the relevance of parsing in NLP.
- We will then explore different parsers and see how we can use NLTK for parsing.
- Finally, we will see how parsing can be used for information extraction.

Shallow versus deep parsing

In deep or full parsing, typically, grammar concepts such as CFG, and **probabilistic context-free grammar** (**PCFG**), and a search strategy is used to give a complete syntactic structure to a sentence. Shallow parsing is the task of parsing a limited part of the syntactic information from the given text. While deep parsing is required for more complex NLP applications, such as dialogue systems and summarization, shallow parsing is more suited for information extraction and text mining varieties of applications. I will talk about these in the next few sections with more details about their pros and cons and how we can use them for our NLP application.

The two approaches in parsing

There are mainly two views/approaches used to deal with parsing, which are as follows:

The rule-based approach	**The probabilistic approach**
This approach is based on rules/grammar	In this approach, you learn rules/grammar by using probabilistic models
Manual grammatical rules are coded down in CFG, and so on, in this approach	This uses observed probabilities of linguistic features
This has a top-down approach	This has a bottom-up approach
This approach includes CFG and Regex-based parser	This approach includes PCFG and the Stanford parser

Why we need parsing

I again want to take you guys back to school, where we learned grammar. Now tell me why you learnt grammar Do you really need to learn grammar? The answer is definitely yes! When we grow, we learn our native languages. Now, when we typically learn languages, we learn a small set of vocabulary. We learn to combine small chunks of phrases and then small sentences. By learning each example sentence, we learn the structure of the language. Your mom might have corrected you many times when you uttered an incorrect sentence. We apply a similar process when we try to understand the sentence, but the process is so common that we never actually pay attention to it or think about it in detail. Maybe the next time you correct someone's grammar, you will understand.

When it comes to writing a parser, we try to replicate the same process here. If we come up with a set of rules that can be used as a template to write the sentences in a proper order. We also need the words that can fit into these categories. We already talked about this process. Remember POS tagging, where we knew the category of the given word?

Now, if you've understood this, you have learned the rules of the game and what moves are valid and can be taken for a specific step. We essentially follow a very natural phenomenon of the human brain and try to emulate it. One of the simplest grammar concepts to start with is CFG, where we just need a set of rules and a set of terminal tokens.

Let's write our first grammar with very limited vocabulary and very generic rules:

```
# toy CFG
>>>from nltk import CFG
>>>toy_grammar =
nltk.CFG.fromstring(
"""
  S -> NP VP                 # S indicate the entire sentence
  VP -> V NP                 # VP is verb phrase the
  V -> "eats" | "drinks"     # V is verb
  NP -> Det N    # NP is noun phrase (chunk that has noun in it)
  Det -> "a" | "an" | "the" # Det is determiner used in the sentences
  N -> "president" |"Obama" |"apple"| "coke"  # N some example nouns
   """)
>>>toy_grammar.productions()
```

Now, this grammar concept can generate a finite amount of sentences. Think of a situation where you just know how to combine a noun with a verb and the only verbs and nouns you knew were the ones we used in the preceding code. Some of the example sentences we can form from these are:

- President eats apple
- Obama drinks coke

Now, understand what's happening here. Our mind has created a grammar concept to parse based on the preceding rules and substitutes whatever vocabulary we have. If we are able to parse correctly, we understand the meaning.

So, effectively, the grammar we learnt at school constituted the useful rules of English. We still use those and also keep enhancing them and these are the same rules we use to understand all English sentences. However, today's rules do not apply to William Shakespeare's body of work.

On the other hand, the same grammar can construct meaningless sentences such as:

- Apple eats coke
- President drinks Obama

When it comes to a **syntactic parser**, there is a chance that a syntactically formed sentence could be meaningless. To get to the semantics, we need a deeper understanding of semantics structure of the sentence. I encourage you to look for a semantic parser in case you are interested in these aspects of language.

Different types of parsers

A parser processes an input string by using a set of grammatical rules and builds one or more rules that construct a grammar concept. Grammar is a declarative specification of a well-formed sentence. A parser is a procedural interpretation of grammar. It searches through the space of a variety of trees and finds an optimal tree for the given sentence. We will go through some of the parsers available and briefly touch upon their workings in detail for awareness, as well as for practical purposes.

A recursive descent parser

One of the most straightforward forms of parsing is recursive descent parsing. This is a top-down process in which the parser attempts to verify that the syntax of the input stream is correct, as it is read from left to right. A basic operation necessary for this involves reading characters from the input stream and matching them with the terminals from the grammar that describes the syntax of the input. Our recursive descent parser will look ahead one character and advance the input stream reading pointer when it gets a proper match.

A shift-reduce parser

The shift-reduce parser is a simple kind of bottom-up parser. As is common with all bottom-up parsers, a shift-reduce parser tries to find a sequence of words and phrases that correspond to the right-hand side of a grammar production and replaces them with the left-hand side of the production, until the whole sentence is reduced.

A chart parser

We will apply the algorithm design technique of dynamic programming to the parsing problem. Dynamic programming stores intermediate results and reuses them when appropriate, achieving significant efficiency gains. This technique can be applied to syntactic parsing. This allows us to store partial solutions to the parsing task and then allows us to look them up when necessary in order to efficiently arrive at a complete solution. This approach to parsing is known as chart parsing.

> For a better understanding of the parsers, you can go through an example at
> `http://www.nltk.org/howto/parse.html.`

A regex parser

A regex parser uses a regular expression defined in the form of grammar on top of a POS-tagged string. The parser will use these regular expressions to parse the given sentences and generate a parse tree out of this. A working example of the regex parser is given here:

```
# Regex parser
>>>chunk_rules=ChunkRule("<.*>+","chunk everything")
>>>import nltk
>>>from nltk.chunk.regexp import *
>>>reg_parser = RegexpParser('''
        NP: {<DT>? <JJ>* <NN>*}          # NP
         P: {<IN>}                       # Preposition
         V: {<V.*>}                      # Verb
        PP: {<P> <NP>}                   # PP -> P NP
        VP: {<V> <NP|PP>*}               # VP -> V (NP|PP)*
  ''')
>>>test_sent="Mr. Obama played a big role in the Health insurance bill"
>>>test_sent_pos=nltk.pos_tag(nltk.word_tokenize(test_sent))
>>>paresed_out=reg_parser.parse(test_sent_pos)
>>> print paresed_out
Tree('S', [('Mr.', 'NNP'), ('Obama', 'NNP'), Tree('VP', [Tree('V',
[('played', 'VBD')]), Tree('NP', [('a', 'DT'), ('big', 'JJ'), ('role',
'NN')])]), Tree('P', [('in', 'IN')]), ('Health', 'NNP'), Tree('NP',
[('insurance', 'NN'), ('bill', 'NN')])])
```

The following is a graphical representation of the tree for the preceding code:

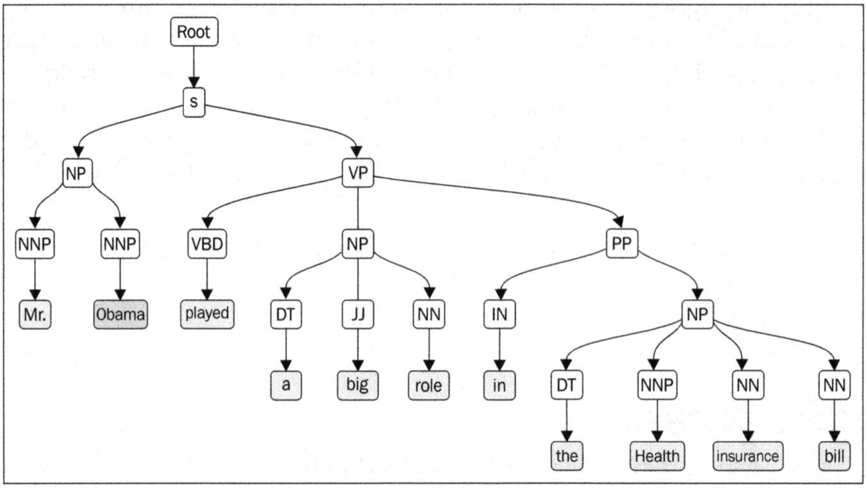

In the current example, we define the kind of patterns (a regular expression of the POS) we think will make a phrase, for example, anything that `{<DT>? <JJ>* <NN>*}` has a starting determiner followed by an adjective and then a noun is mostly a noun phrase. Now, this is more of a linguistic rule that we have defined to get the rule-based parse tree.

Dependency parsing

Dependency parsing (**DP**) is a modern parsing mechanism. The main concept of DP is that each linguistic unit (*words*) is connected with each other by a directed link. These links are called **dependencies** in linguistics. There is a lot of work going on in the current parsing community. While **phrase structure parsing** is still widely used for free word order languages (Czech and Turkish), dependency parsing has turned out to be more efficient.

A very clear distinction can be made by looking at the parse tree generated by phrase structure grammar and dependency grammar for a given example, as the sentence "The big dog chased the cat". The parse tree for the preceding sentence is:

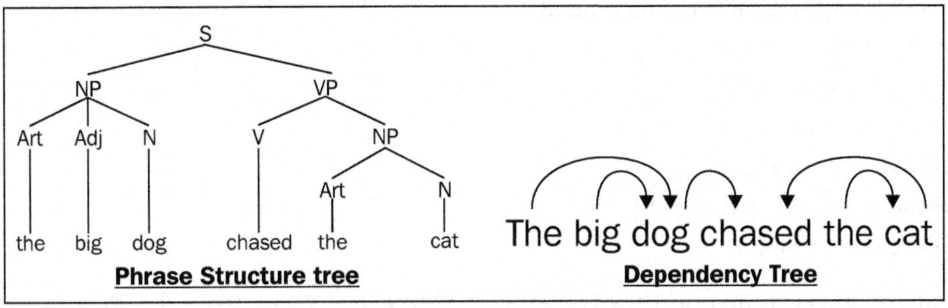

If we look at both parse trees, the phrase structures try to capture the relationship between words and phrases and then eventually between phrases. While a dependency tree just looks for a dependency between words, for example, *big* is totally dependent on *dog*.

NLTK provides a couple of ways to do dependency parsing. One of them is to use a **probabilistic, projective dependency parser**, but it has the restriction of training with a limited set of training data. One of the state of the art dependency parsers is a Stanford parser. Fortunately, NLTK has a wrapper around it and in the following example, I will talk about how to use a Stanford parser with NLTK:

```
# Stanford Parser [Very useful]
>>>from nltk.parse.stanford import StanfordParser
>>>english_parser = StanfordParser('stanford-parser.jar', 'stanford-parser-3.4-models.jar')
>>>english_parser.raw_parse_sents(("this is the english parser test")
Parse
(ROOT
  (S
    (NP (DT this))
    (VP (VBZ is)
      (NP (DT the) (JJ english) (NN parser) (NN test)))))
Universal dependencies
nsubj(test-6, this-1)
cop(test-6, is-2)
det(test-6, the-3)
amod(test-6, english-4)
compound(test-6, parser-5)
root(ROOT-0, test-6)
```

```
Universal dependencies, enhanced
nsubj(test-6, this-1)
cop(test-6, is-2)
det(test-6, the-3)
amod(test-6, english-4)
compound(test-6, parser-5)
root(ROOT-0, test-6)
```

The output looks quite complex but, in reality, it's not. The output is a list of three major outcomes, where the first is just the POS tags and the parsed tree of the given sentences. The same is plotted in a more elegant way in the following figure. The second is the dependency and positions of the given words. The third is the enhanced version of dependency:

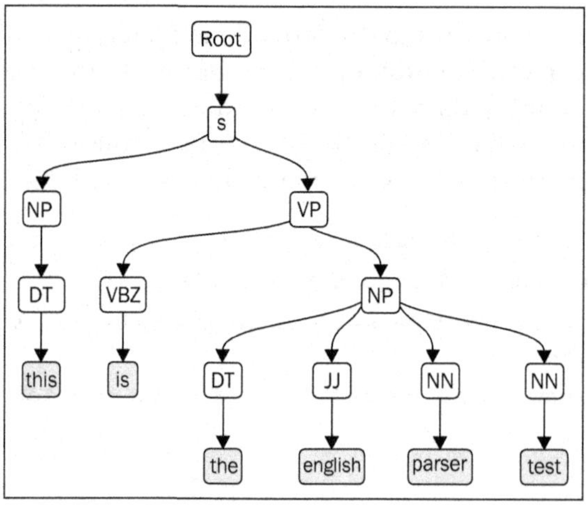

For a better understanding of how to use a Stanford parser, refer to http://nlpviz.bpodgursky.com/home and http://nlp.stanford.edu:8080/parser/index.jsp.

Chunking

Chunking is shallow parsing where instead of reaching out to the deep structure of the sentence, we try to club some chunks of the sentences that constitute some meaning.

A chunk can be defined as the minimal unit that can be processed. So, for example, the sentence "the President speaks about the health care reforms" can be broken into two chunks, one is "the President", which is noun dominated, and hence is called a **noun phrase (NP)**. The remaining part of the sentence is dominated by a verb, hence it is called a **verb phrase (VP)**. If you see, there is one more sub-chunk in the part "speaks about the health care reforms". Here, one more NP exists that can be broken down again in "speaks about" and "health care reforms", as shown in the following figure:

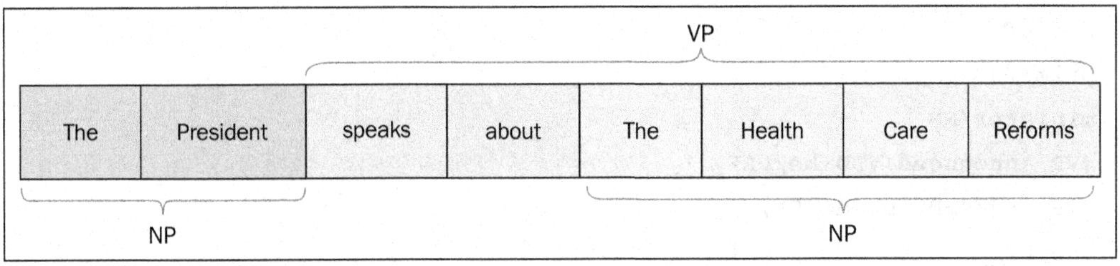

This is how we broke the sentence into parts and that's what we call chunking. Formally, chunking can also be described as a processing interface to identify non-overlapping groups in unrestricted text.

Now, we understand the difference between shallow and deep parsing. When we reach the syntactic structure of the sentences with the help of CFG and understand the syntactic structure of the sentence. Some cases we need to go for semantic parsing to understand the meaning of the sentence. On the other hand, there are cases where, we don't need analysis this deep. Let's say, from a large portion of unstructured text, we just want to extract the key phrases, named entities, or specific patterns of the entities. For this, we will go for shallow parsing instead of deep parsing because deep parsing involves processing the sentence against all the grammar rules and also the generation of a variety of syntactic tree till the parser generates the best tree by using the process of backtracking and reiterating. This entire process is time consuming and cumbersome and, even after all the processing, you might not get the right parse tree. Shallow parsing guarantees the shallow parse structure in terms of chunks which is relatively faster.

So, let's write some code snippets to do some basic chunking:

```
# Chunking
>>>from nltk.chunk.regexp import *
>>>test_sent="The prime minister announced he had asked the chief
government whip, Philip Ruddock, to call a special party room meeting for
9am on Monday to consider the spill motion."
>>>test_sent_pos=nltk.pos_tag(nltk.word_tokenize(test_sent))
>>>rule_vp = ChunkRule(r'(<VB.*>)?(<VB.*>)+(<PRP>)?', 'Chunk VPs')
```

```
>>>parser_vp = RegexpChunkParser([rule_vp],chunk_label='VP')
>>>print parser_vp.parse(test_sent_pos)
>>>rule_np = ChunkRule(r'(<DT>?<RB>?)?<JJ|CD>*(<JJ|CD><,>)*(<NN.*>)+',
'Chunk NPs')
>>>parser_np = RegexpChunkParser([rule_np],chunk_label="NP")
>>>print parser_np.parse(test_sent_pos)
(S
  The/DT
  prime/JJ
  minister/NN
  (VP announced/VBD he/PRP)
  (VP had/VBD asked/VBN)
  the/DT
  chief/NN
  government/NN
  whip/NN
….
….
….
(VP consider/VB)
  the/DT
  spill/NN
  motion/NN
  ./.)

(S
  (NP The/DT prime/JJ minister/NN)                    # 1st noun phrase
  announced/VBD
  he/PRP
  had/VBD
  asked/VBN
  (NP the/DT chief/NN government/NN whip/NN)           # 2nd noun
phrase
  ,/,
  (NP Philip/NNP Ruddock/NNP)
  ,/,
```

```
  to/TO
  call/VB
  (NP a/DT special/JJ party/NN room/NN meeting/NN)        # 3rd noun
phrase
  for/IN
  9am/CD
  on/IN
  (NP Monday/NNP)                                  # 4th noun phrase
  to/TO
  consider/VB
  (NP the/DT spill/NN motion/NN)                          # 5th noun phrase
  ./.)
```

The preceding code is good enough to do some basic chunking of verb and noun phrases. A conventional pipeline in chunking is to tokenize the POS tag and the input string before they are ed to any chunker. Here, we use a regular chunker, as rule NP / VP defines different POS patterns that can be called a verb/noun phrase. For example, the NP rule defines anything that starts with the determiner and then there is a combination of an adverb, adjective, or cardinals that can be chunked in to a noun phrase. Regular expression-based chunkers rely on chunk rules defined manually to chunk the string. So, if we are able to write a universal rule that can incorporate most of the noun phrase patterns, we can use regex chunkers. Unfortunately, it's hard to come up with those kind of generic rules; the other approach is to use a machine learning way of doing chunking. We briefly touched upon `ne_chunk()` and the Stanford NER tagger that both use a pre-trained model to tag noun phrases.

Information extraction

We learnt about taggers and parsers that we can use to build a basic information extraction engine. Let's jump directly to a very basic IE engine and how a typical IE engine can be developed using NLTK.

Any sort of meaningful information can be drawn only if the given input stream goes to each of the following NLP steps. We already have enough understanding of sentence tokenization, word tokenization, and POS tagging. Let's discuss NER and relation extraction as well.

A typical information extraction pipeline looks very similar to that shown in the following figure:

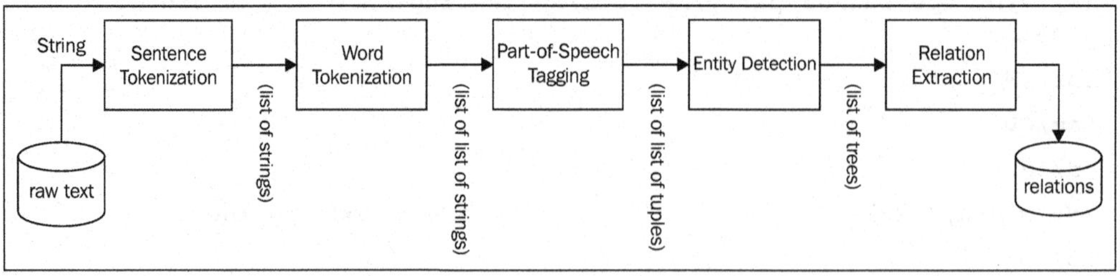

> Some of the other preprocessing steps, such as stop word removal and stemming, are generally ignored and do not add any value to an IE engine.

Named-entity recognition (NER)

We already briefly discussed NER generally in the last chapter. Essentially, NER is a way of extracting some of the most common entities, such as names, organizations, and locations. However, some of the modified NER can be used to extract entities such as product names, biomedical entities, author names, brand names, and so on.

Let's start with a very generic example where we are given a text file of the content and we need to extract some of the most insightful named entities from it:

```
# NP chunking (NER)
>>>f=open(# absolute path for the file of text for which we want NER)
>>>text=f.read()
>>>sentences = nltk.sent_tokenize(text)
>>>tokenized_sentences = [nltk.word_tokenize(sentence) for sentence in sentences]
>>>tagged_sentences = [nltk.pos_tag(sentence) for sentence in tokenized_sentences]
>>>for sent in tagged_sentences:
>>>print nltk.ne_chunk(sent)
```

In the preceding code, we just followed the same pipeline provided in the preceding figure. We took all the preprocessing steps, such as sentence tokenization, tokenization, POS tagging, and NLTK. NER (pre-trained models) can be used to extract all NERs.

Relation extraction

Relation extraction is another commonly used information extraction operation. Relation extraction as it sound is the process of extracting the different relationships between different entities. There are variety of the relationship that exist between the entities. We have seen relationship like inheritance/synonymous/analogous. The definition of the relation can be dependent on the Information need. For example in the case where we want to look from unstructured text data who is the writer of which book then authorship could be a relation between the author name and book name. With NLTK the idea is to use the same IE pipeline that we used till NER and extend it with a relation pattern based on the NER tags.

So, in the following code, we used an inbuilt corpus of `ieer`, where the sentences are tagged till NER and the only thing we need to specify is the relation pattern we want and the kind of NER we want the relation to define. In the following code, a relationship between an organization and a location has been defined and we want to extract all the combinations of these patterns. This can be applied in various ways, for example, in a large corpus of unstructured text, we will be able to identify some of the organizations of our interest with their corresponding location:

```
>>>import re
>>>IN = re.compile(r'.*\bin\b(?!\b.+ing)')
>>>for doc in nltk.corpus.ieer.parsed_docs('NYT_19980315'):
>>> for rel in nltk.sem.extract_rels('ORG', 'LOC', doc, corpus='ieer',
pattern = IN):
>>>print(nltk.sem.rtuple(rel))
[ORG: u'WHYY'] u'in' [LOC: u'Philadelphia']
[ORG: u'McGlashan &AMP; Sarrail'] u'firm in' [LOC: u'San Mateo']
[ORG: u'Freedom Forum'] u'in' [LOC: u'Arlington']
[ORG: u'Brookings Institution'] u', the research group in' [LOC:
u'Washington']
[ORG: u'Idealab'] u', a self-described business incubator based in' [LOC:
u'Los Angeles']
..
```

Summary

We moved beyond the basic preprocessing steps in this chapter. We looked deeper at NLP techniques, such as parsing and information extraction. We discussed parsing in detail, which parsers are available, and how to use NLTK to do any NLP parsing. You understood the concept of CFG and PCFG and how to learn from a tree bank and build a parser. We talked about shallow and deep parsing and what the difference is between them.

We also talked about some of the information extraction essentials, such as entity extraction and relation extraction. We talked about a typical information extraction engine pipeline. We saw a very small and simple IE engine that can be built in less than 100 lines of code. Think about this kind of system running on an entire Wikipedia dump or an entire web content related to an organization. Cool, isn't it?

We will use some of the topics we've learnt in this chapter in further chapters to build some useful NLP applications.

5
NLP Applications

This chapter discusses NLP applications. Here, we will put all the learning from the previous chapters into action and will see what kind of application can be developed using the concepts we have learned. This will be a complete hands-on chapter. In the last few chapters we have learned most of the preprocessing steps that are required for any NLP application. We know how to use tokenizer, POS tag, and NER and how to perform parsing. This chapter will give you an idea how we can developed some of the complex NLP application using the concepts we have learned.

There are so many applications of NLP in the real world. Some of the most exciting and common examples you can observe are Google Search, Siri, machine translation, Google News, Jeopardy, and spell check. Some of these took many years for researchers to reach this level and bring these applications to their current state. NLP is complicated too; we have seen in the previous chapters that most of the processing steps, such as POS and NER, are still research problems. But with the use of NLTK, we have solved many of these problems with reasonable accuracy. We will not cover the more sophisticated applications such as machine translation or speech recognition in this book. But at this point in time, you should have enough background knowledge to understand some of the basic blocks of these applications. As a NLP enthusiast we should have a basic understanding of these NLP applications. I urge you to try and look for some of these NLP applications on the web and try to understand them.

By the end of this chapter :

- We will introduce reader to few common NLP applications.
- We will develop a NLP application (News summarizer) using what we have learnt so far.
- The importance of different NLP applications and essential details about each of them.

Building your first NLP application

Let's start with one of the very complex NLP applications, which is **summarization**. The concept of summarization is quite simple. We are given an article/passage/story and you will have to generate a summary of the content automatically. Summarization actually requires deep knowledge of NLP because we need to understand not just the structure of the sentence but also the structure of the entire text. We also need to know about genre of the text and the theme of the content.

Since it all looks very complex to us, let's try a very intuitive approach. We will assume that summarization is nothing but ranking of the sentences based on their importance and significance to you. We will create a few rules based on the understanding and the preprocessing tools we have learned so far and will try to come up with an acceptable summary of the news article.

I have scraped an article from the *New York Times* in a text file `nyt.txt`, in the following example. The idea here is to summarize this news article for us. Let's build a version of Google News for our personal use.

To start off, we need to keep in mind that, typically, a sentence that has more entities and nouns has greater importance than other sentences. We will try to normalize the same logic while calculating an **importance score**, using the following code. To get the top-n sentence, we can choose a threshold for the importance score.

Let's read the content of the news article. You can choose any news article with only contents of the news dumped into a text file. The content will look like this:

```
>>>import sys
>>>f=open('nyt.txt','r')
>>>news_content=f.read()
""" President Obama on Monday will ban the federal provision of some
types of military-style equipment to local police departments and sharply
restrict the availability of others, administration officials said.


The ban is part of Mr. Obama's push to ease tensions between law
enforcement and minority communities in reaction to the crises in
Baltimore; Ferguson, Mo.; and other cities.
- - -
blic." It contains dozens of recommendations for agencies throughout the
country."""
```

Once we parse the contents of the news we will need to split the entire news article into a list of sentences. We will go back to our old sentence tokenizer to break the entire news snippet into sentences. Let's also provide some form of sentence number so that we can identify and rank a sentence. Once we have the sentence, we will pass it through a word tokenizer and eventually through the `NER` tagger and `POS` tagger.

```
>>>import nltk
>>>results=[]
>>>for sent_no,sentence in enumerate(nltk.sent_tokenize(news_content)):
>>>     no_of_tokens=len(nltk.word_tokenize(sentence))
>>>     #print no_of_toekns
>>>     # Let's do POS tagging
>>>     tagged=nltk.pos_tag(nltk.word_tokenize(sentence))
>>>     # Count the no of Nouns in the sentence
>>>     no_of_nouns=len([word for word,pos in tagged if pos in
["NN","NNP"] ])
>>>     #Use NER to tag the named entities.
>>>     ners=nltk.ne_chunk(nltk.pos_tag(nltk.word_tokenize(sentence)),
binary=False)
>>>     no_of_ners= len([chunk for chunk in ners if hasattr(chunk,
'node')])
>>>     score=(no_of_ners+no_of_nouns)/float(no_of_toekns)
>>>
>>>     results.append((sent_no,no_of_tokens,no_of_ners,\
no_of_nouns,score,sentence))
```

In the preceding code, we are iterating over a list of sentences calculating a score based on a formula that is nothing but the fraction of tokens being entities as compared to a normal token. We are creating a tuple of all these as the results.

Now, the result is a tuple with all the scores, such as the number of nouns, entities, and so on. We can sort it based on the score in descending order, as shown in the following example:

```
>>>for sent in sorted(results,key=lambda x: x[4],reverse=True):
>>>     print sent[5]
```

Now, the result of this will be sorted by the rank of the sentence. You will be amazed by the kind of results we get for the news article.

Once we have a list of `no_of_nouns` and `no_of_ners` scores, we can actually create some more complex rules around this. For example, a typical news article will start with very important details about the topic, and the last sentence will be a conclusion to the story.

Can we modify the same snippet to incorporate this logic?

The other theory of this kind of summarization is that the important sentences generally contain important words and that most of the the discriminatory words across the corpus will be important. The sentences that has very discriminatory words are important. A very simple measure of that is to calculate the **TF-IDF (term frequency–inverse document frequency)** score of each and every word and then look for an average score normalized by the words that are important; this can then be used as the criteria to choose sentences for our summary.

For explaining the concepts instead of the entire article, just take the first three sentences of the article. Let's see how you can implement something this complex using very few lines of code:

> This code require installing scikit. If you have installed anaconda or canopy you should be fine otherwise install scikit using this link.
> `scikit-learn.org/0.9/install.html`

```
>>>import nltk
>>>from sklearn.feature_extraction.text import TfidfVectorizer
>>>results=[]
>>>news_content="Mr. Obama planned to promote the effort on Monday during a visit to Camden, N.J. The ban is part of Mr. Obama's push to ease tensions between law enforcement and minority \communities in reaction to the crises in Baltimore; Ferguson, Mo. We are, without a doubt, sitting at a defining moment in American policing, Ronald L. Davis, the director of the Office of Community Oriented Policing Services at the Department of Justice, told reporters in a conference call organized by the White House"

>>>sentences=nltk.sent_tokenize(news_content)

>>>vectorizer = TfidfVectorizer(norm='l2',min_df=0, use_idf=True, smooth_idf=False, sublinear_tf=True)

>>>sklearn_binary=vectorizer.fit_transform(sentences)
>>>print countvectorizer.get_feature_names()
>>>print sklearn_binary.toarray()
>>>for i in sklearn_binary.toarray():
>>>    results.append(i.sum()/float(len(i.nonzero()[0]))
```

In the preceding code, I am using some unknown methods, such as `TfidfVectorizer`, which is a scoring method that will calculate a vector of TF-IDF scores for each sentence in a given list of sentences. Don't worry, we will talk about this in more detail. For this chapter, consider it as a black-box function that, for a given list of sentences/documents, will give you the score corresponding to each sentence and will also provide the ability to build a term-doc matrix that will look just like our output.

We got a dictionary of all the words present across all the sentences and then we have a list of lists where each element assigns each word its individual TF-IDF score. If you got that right, then you can see some of the stop words will get a near-zero score while some discriminatory words like `ban` and `Obama` will get a very high score. Now once we have this in the code, I will look for the average TF-IDF score by using only non-zero TF-IDF words. This will give us a similar kind of score as we got in our first approach.

You will be amazed by the kind of results a simple algorithm can give. I think now you are all set to write your own news summarizer that summarizes any given news article with the two preceding algorithms and the summary will look quite decent. While this kind of approach will give you a decent summarization, it's actually very poor when you compare it with the current state of summarization research. I would recommend looking for some literature relating to summarization. I would also like you to try and combine both the approaches for summarization.

Other NLP applications

Some of the other NLP applications are text classification, machine translation, speech recognition, information retrieval, information extraction, topic segmentation, and discourse analysis. Some of these problems are actually very difficult NLP tasks and a lot of research is still going on in these areas. We will discuss some of these in depth in the next chapter, but as NLP students, we should have a basic understanding of these applications.

Machine translation

The easiest way to understand machine translation is to know how we translate from one language to other. Our mind parses the sentence structure and tries to understand the sentence. Once we understand the sentence, we will try to substitute the words from the original language with those from the target language. While substituting, we use the grammar rules of the target sentence and finally achieve the correct translation.

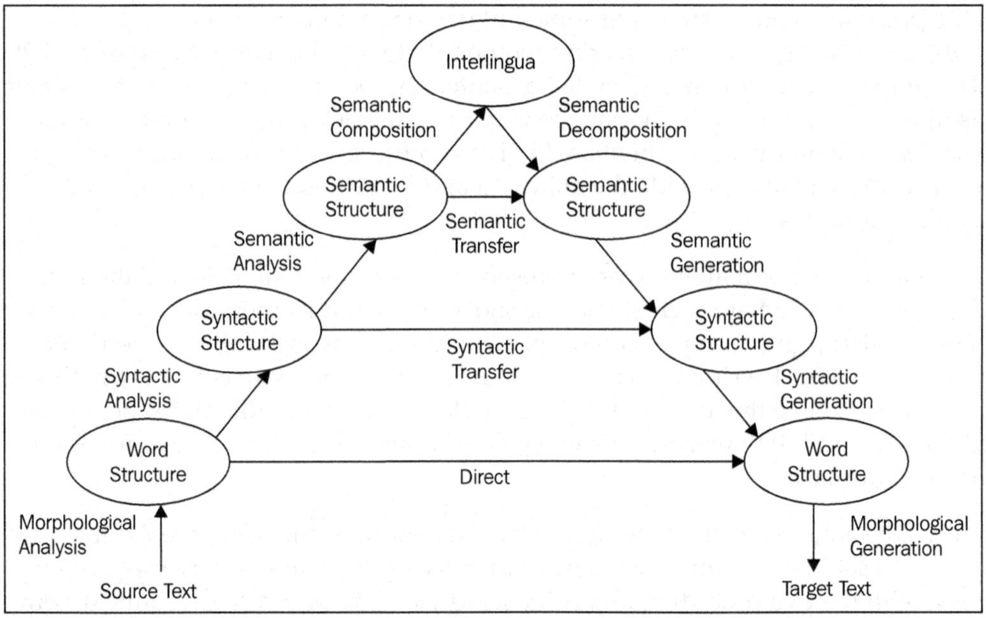

Loosely, the process can be translated to something like the pyramid in the preceding figure. If we start from the source language text, we have to tokenize the sentences that we will parse the tree (for syntactic structure in easy words) to make sure the sentences are correctly formulated. Semantic structure holds the meaning of the sentences, and at the next level, we reach the state of Interlingua, which is an abstract state that is independent from any language. There are multiple ways in which people have developed methods of translation. The more you go on towards the root of the pyramid, the more intense is the NLP processing required. So, based on these levels of transfer, there are a variety of methods that are available. I have listed two of them here:

- **Direct translation**: This will be more of a dictionary-based machine translation while you have huge corpora of source and target language words. This kind of transfer is possible for applications where we have a large corpus of languages available. It's popular because of its simplicity.
- **Syntactic transfer**: Here you will try to build a parser of the source language. There are varieties of ways in which people have approached the problem of parsing. There are deep parsers that actually take care of some parts of semantics too. Once you have a parser, target word substitution happens and the target parser can generate the final sentence in the target language.

Statistical machine translation

Statistical machine translation (**SMT**) is one of the latest approach of machine translation, where people have come up with a variety of ways to apply statistical methods to almost all the aspects of machine translation. The idea behind this kind of algorithm is that we have a huge volume of corpora, parallel text, and language models that can help us predict the language translation in the target language. Google Translate is a great example of SMT, where it learns from the corpora of different language pairs and builds an SMT around it.

Information retrieval

Information retrieval (**IR**) is also one of the most popular and widely used applications. The best exmple of IR is Google Search, where—given an input query from the user—the information retrieval algorithm will try to retrieve the information which is relevant to the user's query.

In simple words, IR is the process of obtaining the most relevant information that is needed by the user. There are a variety of ways in which the information needs can be addressed to the system, but the system eventually retrieves the most relevant infromation.

The way a typical IR system works is that it generates an indexing mechanism, also known as **inverted index**. This is very similar to the indexing schemes used in books, where you will have an index of the words present throughout the book on the last pages of the book. Similarly, an IR system will create an inverted index poslist. A typical posting list will look like this:

```
< Term , DocFreq, [DocId1,DocId2] >
{"the",2 --->[1,2] }
{"US",1 --->[2] }
{"president",2 --->[1,2] }
```

So if any word occurs in both document 1 and document 2, the posting list will be a list of documents pointing to terms. Once you have this kind of data structure, there are different retrieval models that can been introduced. There are different retrieval models that work on different types of data. A few are listed in the following sections.

Boolean retrieval

In the Boolean model, we just need to run a Boolean operation on the poslist. For example, if we are looking for a search query like "US president", the system should look for an intersection of the postlist of "US" and "president".

```
{US}{president}=> [2]
```

Here, the second document turns out to be the relevant document.

Vector space model

The concept of **vector space model** (**VSM**) derives from geometry. The way to visualize the documents in the high dimension space of vocabulary is to represent it as a vector. So each and every document is represented as a vector in that space. We can represent the vector in various ways, but one of the most useful and efficient ways is using TF-IDF.

Given a term and a corpus, we can calculate the **term frequency** (**TF**) and **inverse document frequency** (**IDF**) using the following formula:

$$\mathrm{tf}(t,d) = 0.5 + \frac{0.5 \times \mathrm{f}(t,d)}{\max\{\mathrm{f}(w,d) : w \in d\}}$$

The TF is nothing but the frequency in the document. While the IDF is the inverse of document frequency, which is the count of documents in the corpus where the term occurs:

$$\mathrm{idf}(t,D) = \log \frac{N}{\left|\{d \in D : t \in d\}\right|}$$

There are various normalization variants of these, but we can incorporate both of these to create a more robust scoring mechanism to get the scoring of each term in the document. To get to a TF-IDF score, we need to multiply these two scores as follows:

$$\mathrm{tfidf}(t,d,D) = \mathrm{tf}(t,d) \times \mathrm{idf}(t,D)$$

In TF-IDF, we are scoring a term for how much it is present in the current document and how much it is spread across the corpus. This gives us an idea of the terms that are not common across corpora and where ever they are present have a high frequency. It becomes discriminatory to retrieve these documents. We have also used TF-IDF in the previous section, where we describe our summarizer.The same scoring can be used to represent the document as a vector. Once we have all the documents represented in a vectorized form, the vector space model can be formulated.

In VSM, the search query of the user is also considered as a document and represented as a vector. Intuitively, a dot product between these two vectors can be used to get the cosine similarity between the document and the user query.

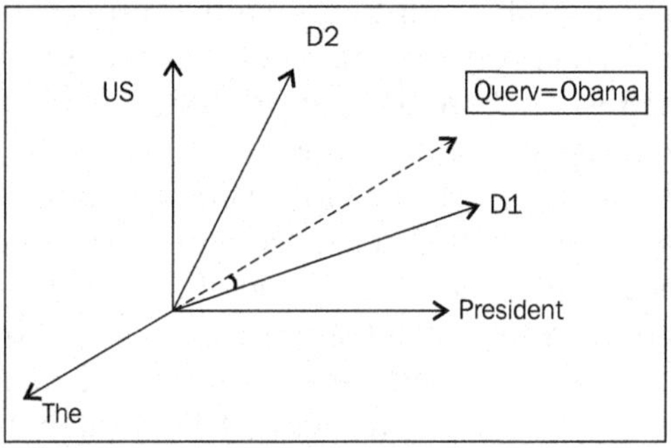

In the preceding diagram, we see that these same documents can be represented using each term as an axis and the query `Obama` will have as much relevance to *D1* as compared to *D2*. The scoring of the query for relevant documents can be formulated as follows:

$$\text{sim}\left(d_j, q\right) = \frac{\mathrm{d_j} \cdot \mathrm{q}}{\left\|\mathrm{d_j}\right\| \left\|\mathrm{q}\right\|} = \frac{\sum_{i=1}^{N} w_{i,j}, w_{i,q}}{\sqrt{\sum_{i=1}^{N} w_{i,j}^2} \sqrt{\sum_{i=1}^{N} w_{i,q}^2}}$$

The probabilistic model

The probabilistic model tries to estimate the probability of the user's need for the document. This model assumes that the probability of the relevance depends on the user query and document representation.The main idea is that a document that is in the relevant set will not be present in the non-relevant set. We denote `dj` as the document and `q` as user query; `R` represents the relevant set of documents, while `P` represents the non-relevant set. The scoring can be done like this:

$$\text{sim}\left(d_j, q\right) = \frac{P\left(R \mid \vec{d}_j\right)}{P\left(\bar{R} \mid \vec{d}_j\right)}$$

For more topics on IR, I would recommend that you read from the following link:

`http://nlp.stanford.edu/IR-book/html/htmledition/irbook.html`

Speech recognition

Speech recognition is a very old NLP problem. People have been trying to address this since the era of World War I, and it still is one of the hottest topics in the area of computing. The idea here is really intuitive. Given the speech uttered by a human can we convert it to text? The problem with speech is that we produce a sequence of sounds, called **phonemes**, that are hard to process, so speech segmentation itself is a big problem. Once the speech is processable, the next step is to go through some of the constraints (models) that are built using training data available. This involves heavy machine learning. If you see the figure representing the modeling as one box of applying constraints, it's actually one of the most complex components of the entire system. While acoustic modeling involves building modes based on phonemes, lexical models will try to address the modeling on smaller segments of sentences, associating a meaning to each segment. Separately language models are built on unigrams and bigrams of words.

Once we build these models, an utterence of the sentences is passed through the process. Once processed for initial preprocessing, the sentence is passed through these acoustic, lexical, and language models for generating the token as output.

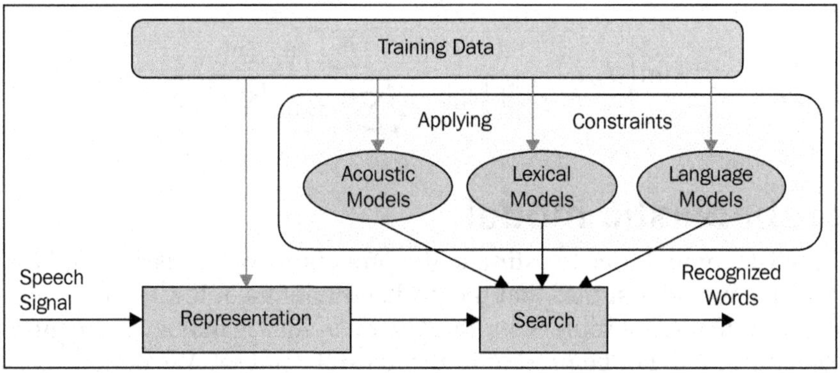

Text classification

Text classification is a very interesting and common application of NLP. In your daily work, you interact with many text classifiers. We use a spam filter, a priority inbox, news aggregators, and so on. All of these are in fact applications built using text classification.

Text classification is a well-defined and somewhat solved problem, and it has been applied across many domains. Typically, any text classification is the process of classifying text documents using words and the combination of words. While it's a typical machine learning problem, many of the preprocessing steps used in text classification are from NLP.

An abstract diagram of text classification is shown here:

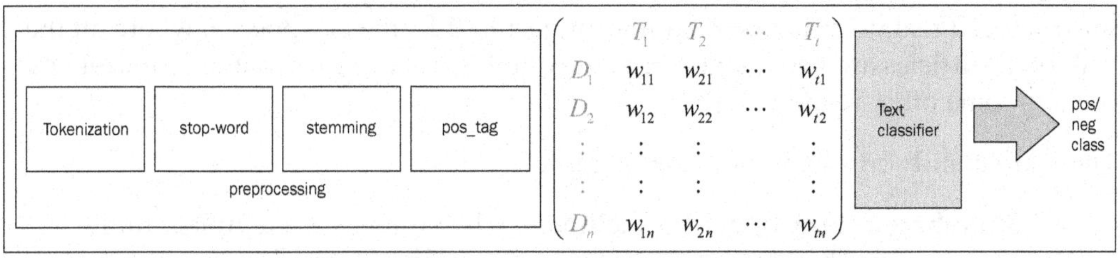

Here we have a bunch of documents for a set of classes. For simplicity, we will use just binary `1/0` as the class. Now let's assume it's a spam detection problem where 1 represents spam and 0 represents normal text which is not to be considered as spam.

The process involves some of the preprocessing steps we learned in previous chapters. While some of these are essential, it depends on the kind of text classification problem we are trying to solve. So in few cases, it's more a case of feature engineering while we drop some of the preprocessing steps. The final goal of feature engineering is to generate a **Term doc matrix (TDM)**, which holds the vocabulary of the entire corpus: columns and rows are the documents, while the matrix represents a scoring mechanism to show the **Bag of word (BOW)** representation. The weighting scheme can be varied to TF, TF-IDF, Bernoulli, and other variations of term frequency.

There are also ways to induce features such as the POS of a given feature, contextual POS, and others, to make our feature space more NLP intense. Once the TDM is generated, the text classification problem becomes a typical supervised/unsupervised classification problem, where given a set of samples, we need to predict what sample belongs to what class. The next chapter is dedicated entirely to this topic. This is definitely a splendid application of NLP/ML and is used quite often for commercial purposes.

Some of the most common use cases in day-to-day scenarios are sentiment analysis, spam classification, e-mail categorization, news categorization, patent classification, and so on. We will talk about text classification in more detail in the next chapter.

Information extraction

Information extraction (**IE**) is a process of extracting meaningful information from unstructured text. IE is yet another widely popular and highly important application. In general, an information extraction engine harnesses huge numbers of unstructured documents and generates some sort of structured/semi-structured **knowledge base** (**KB**) that can be deployed to build an application around it. A simple example is that of generating a very good ontology using a huge set of unstructured text documents. A similar project in this line is DBpedia, where all the Wikipedia articles are used to generate the ontology of artifacts that are interrelated or have some other relationship.

There are mainly two ways of extracting information:

- **Rule-based extraction**: This method is where one uses a template filling mechanism. The idea is to look for some kind predefined use cases for expected outcomes and try to mine the unstructured text for that specific template. For example, building a knowledge base of football will involve getting information on all the players and their profiles, the statistics, some personal information, and so on. All that can be well defined and extracted using either pattern-based rules or POS tags, NERs and relation extraction.
- **Machine learning based**: The other approach involves deeper NLP-based methods such as building a parser specific to the need of our knowledge base. Some of the KBs will require mining the entities that can't be extracted using a pre-trained NER, so we have to build a custom NER. We might want to develop a relation extraction algorithm specific to the KB we are trying to build. This is a more NLP-intensive approach, where we are developing a NLP-based parser or tagger to use for heavy machine learning.

Question answering systems

Question answering (**QA**) systems are intelligent systems that can address any question based on their knowledge base. One of the major examples of this is IBM Watson, which took part in the TV show *Jeopardy* and won over human opponents. A QA system can be broken down to building components from speech recognition for querying the knowledge base while the knowledge base is generated using information retrieval and extraction.

Once you have a question for the system, one big problem is to classify/categorize the question in different ways. The other aspect is to search the knowledge base effectively and retrieve the most precise document. Even after that, we have to generate the answer in a natural way using some of the other applications, such as summarization and parsing.

Dialog systems

Dialog systems are considered the dream application, where given a speech in source language, the system will perform speech recognition and transcribe it to text. This text will then go to a machine translation system that can translate the speech into the target language and then a text-to-speech system will convert it into speech in the target language. This is one of the most desirable applications of NLP, where we can talk to a computer in any language and the computer will reply in the same language. This kind of application can actually destroy the language barrier that exists in the world.

Apple Siri and Google Voice are examples of some of the commercial applications in the line of dialog systems intelligent enough to understand our information needs, try to address them in a set of actions or information, and respond in a human-like manner.

Word sense disambiguation

Word sense disambiguation (**WSD**) is also one of the difficult challenges not solved even after years of research and one of the major causes of application problems, such as question answering, summarization, search, and so on. A simple way to understand the concept is that many words have different meanings when used in different contexts. For example, "cold" in the following example:

- The ice-cream is really cold
- That was cold blooded!

Here the word "cold "has two different senses, and it's really hard for computers to understand this concept. Some of the other NLP processing options, such as `POS` tagging and `NER`, are used to resolve some of these problems.

Topic modeling

Topic modeling, in the context of a large amount of unstructured text content, is really an amazing application, where the primary task is to identify the emerging topics in the corpus and then categorize the documents in the corpus as per these topics. We will discuss this briefly in the next chapter.

Topic modeling uses the same NLP preprocessing, for example, sentence split, tokenization, stemming, and so on. The beauty of the algorithms is that we have an unsupervised way of categorizing the document; also, topics are generated without explicitly mentioning anything prior to the process. I encourage you to look at topic modeling in more detail. Try reading about **latent dirichlet allocation** (**LDA**) and **latent semantics indexing** (**LSI**) for more detail.

Language detection

Given a snippet of text, the detection of language is also a problem. The application of language detection is very important for some of the other NLP applications, such as search, machine translation, speech, and so on. The main concept is learning from the text as features what the language is. A variety of machine learning and NLP techniques are used for feature engineering in the process.

Optical character recognition

Optical character recognition (OCR) is an application of NLP and computer vision, where given a handwritten document/ non-digital document, the system can recognize the text and extract it into digital format. This has also been widely researched in the area of machine learning for many years. Some of the big OCR projects are Google Books, where they use OCR to convert non-digital books into a centralized library.

Summary

In conclusion, there are many NLP applications around us that we interact with in our day-to-day routines. NLP is difficult and complex, and some of these problems are still unsolved or do not yet have perfect solutions. So anybody who is looking for problems in NLP, try exploring the literature around that. It's a great time to be an NLP researcher. In the era of Big Data, NLP applications are very popular. Many research labs and organizations are currently working on NLP applications such as speech recognition, search, and text classification.

I believe we have learned a lot up until this chapter. For the next couple of chapters, we will delve deeply into some of the applications described here. We have reached a point where we know enough NLP related preprocessing tools and also have a basic understanding about some of the most popular NLP applications. I hope you leverage some of this learning to build a version of an NLP application.

In the next chapter, we will start with some of the important NLP applications, such as text classification, text clustering, and topic modeling. We will move slightly away from the pure NLTK applications on to how NLTK can be used in conjunction with other libraries.

6
Text Classification

We were talking about some of the most common NLP tools and preprocessing steps in the last chapter. This is the chapter where we will get to use most of the stuff we learnt in the previous chapters, and build one of the most sophisticated NLP applications. We will give you a generic approach about text classification and how you can build a text classifier from scratch with very few lines of code. We will give you a cheat sheet of all the classification algorithms in the context of text classification.

While we will talk about some of the most common text classification algorithms, this is just a brief introduction and to get to a detailed understanding and mathematical background, there are many online resources and books available that you can refer to. We will try to give you all you need to know to get you started with some working code snippets. Text classification is a great use case of NLP, but in this chapter, instead of using NLTK, we will use **scikit-learn** that has a wider range of classification algorithms and its library is much more memory efficient for text mining.

By the end of this chapter:

- You will learn and understand all text classification algorithms
- You will learn end-to-end pipeline to build a text classifier and how to implement it with scikit-learn and NLTK

The following is the scikit-learn cheat sheet for machine learning:

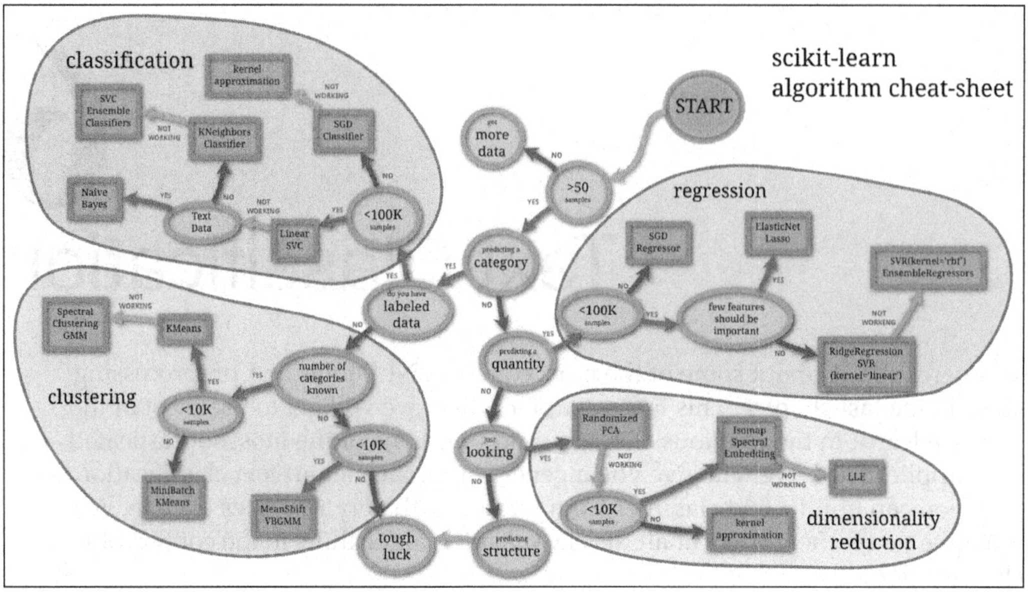

credit : scikit-learn

Now, as you travel along the process shown in the cheat sheet. We have a clear guideline about what kind of algorithm is required for which problem? When we should move from one classifier to another depending on the size of the tagged sample? It's a good place to start following this for building practical application, and in most cases this will work. We will focus mostly on text data while the scikit-learn can work with other types of data as well. We will explore text classification, text clustering, and topic detection in text (**dimensionality reduction**) with examples in this chapter and build some cool NLP applications. I will not go in to more detail about the concepts of machine learning, classification, and clustering in this chapter, as there are enough resources available on the Web for you. We will provide you with more details of all these concepts in the context of a text corpus. Still, let me give you a refresher.

Machine learning

There are two types of machine learning techniques—supervised learning and Unsupervised learning:

- **Supervised learning**: Based on some historic prelabeled samples, machines learn how to predict the future test sample, based on the following categories:

- **Classification**: This is used when we need to predict whether a test sample belongs to one of the classes. If there are only two classes, it's a binary classification problem; otherwise, it's a multiclass classification.
- **Regression**: This is used when we need to predict a continuous variable, such as a house price and stock index.

- **Unsupervised learning**: When we don't have any labeled data and we still need to predict the class label, this kind of learning is called unsupervised learning. When we need to group items based on similarity between items, this is called a clustering problem. While if we need to represent high-dimensional data in lower dimensions, this is more of a dimensionality reduction problem.
- **Semi-supervised learning**: This is a class of supervised learning tasks and techniques that also make use of unlabeled data for training. As the name suggests, it's more of a middle ground for supervised and unsupervised learning, where we use small amount of labeled data and large amount of unlabeled data to build a predictive machine learning model.
- **Reinforcement learning**: This is a form of machine learning where an agent can be programmed by a reward and punishment, without specifying how the task is to be achieved.

If you understood the different machine learning algorithms, I want you to guess what kind of machine learning problems the following are:

- You need to predict the values of weather for the next month
- Detection of a fraud in millions of transactions
- Google's priority inbox
- Amazon's recommendations
- Google news
- Self-driving cars

Text classification

The simplest definition of text classification is that it is a classification of text based on the content of that text. Now, in general, all the machine learning methods and algorithms are written for numeric features/variables. One of the most important problems with text corpus is how to represent text as numeric features. There are different transformations prescribed in the literature. Let's start with one of the simplest and most widely used transformations.

Now, to understand the processes of text classification, let's take a real word problem of spams. In the world of WhatsApp and SMS, you get many spam messages. Let's start by solving this real problem of spam detection with the help of text classification. We will be using this running example across the chapter.

Here are a few real examples of SMS's that we asked people to manually tag for us:

```
SMS001 ['spam', 'Had your mobile 11 months or more? U R entitled to Update to the latest colour mobiles with camera for Free! Call The Mobile Update Co FREE on 08002986030']

SMS002 ['ham', "I'm gonna be home soon and i don't want to talk about this stuff anymore tonight, k? I've cried enough today."]
```

> A similar tagged dataset can be downloaded from link here. Make sure you create a CSV like the one show in the example. 'SMSSpamCollection' in the following code which will correspond to this file.
> `https://archive.ics.uci.edu/ml/datasets/SMS+Spam+Collection`

The first thing you want to do here is what we learnt in the last few chapters about data cleaning, tokenization, and stemming to get much cleaner content out of the SMS. I wrote a basic function to clean the text. Let's go over the following code:

```
>>>import nltk
>>>from nltk.corpus import stopwords
>>>from nltk.stem import WordNetLemmatizer
>>>import csv
>>>def preprocessing(text):
>>>    text = text.decode("utf8")
>>>    # tokenize into words
>>>    tokens = [word for sent in nltk.sent_tokenize(text) for word in nltk.word_tokenize(sent)]

>>>    # remove stopwords
>>>    stop = stopwords.words('english')
>>>    tokens = [token for token in tokens if token not in stop]

>>>    # remove words less than three letters
>>>    tokens = [word for word in tokens if len(word) >= 3]
```

```
>>>     # lower capitalization
>>>     tokens = [word.lower() for word in tokens]
>>>     # lemmatize
>>>     lmtzr = WordNetLemmatizer()
>>>     tokens = [lmtzr.lemmatize(word) for word in tokens]
>>>     preprocessed_text= ' '.join(tokens)
>>>     return preprocessed_text
```

We have talked about tokenization, lemmatization, and stop words in *Chapter 3, Part of Speech Tagging*. In the following code, I am just parsing the SMS file and cleaning the content to get cleaner text of the SMS. In the next few lines, I created two lists to get all the cleaned content of the SMS and class label. In **ML** (**Machine learning**) terms all the X and Y:

```
>>>smsdata = open('SMSSpamCollection') # check the structure of this
file!
>>>smsdata_data = []
>>>sms_labels = []
>>>csv_reader = csv.reader(sms,delimiter='\t')
>>>for line in csv_reader:
>>>      # adding the sms_id
>>>     sms_labels.append( line[0])
>>>     # adding the cleaned text We are calling preprocessing method
>>>     sms_data.append(preprocessing(line[1]))
>>>sms.close()
```

Before moving any further we need to make sure we have scikit-learn installed on the system.

```
>>>import sklearn
```

> If there is an error you made some error installing scikit. Please go to below link and install scikit:
>
> `http://scikit-learn.org/stable/install.html`

Sampling

Once we have the entire corpus in the form of lists, we need to perform some form of sampling. Typically, the way to sample the entire corpus in development train sets, dev-test sets, and test sets is similar to the sampling shown in the following figure.

The idea behind the whole exercise is to avoid overfitting. If we feed all the data points to the model, then the algorithm will learn from the entire corpus, but the real test of these algorithms is to perform on unseen data. In very simplistic terms, if we are using the entire data in the model learning process the classifier will perform very good on this data, but it will not be robust. The reason being, we have to tune it to perform the best on the given data, but it doesn't learn how to deal with unknown data.

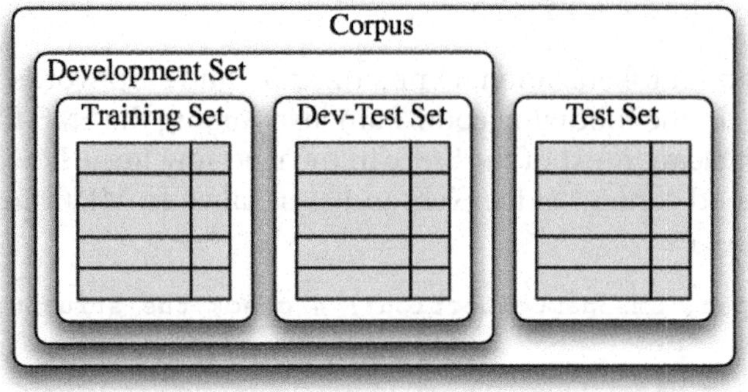

To solve this kind of a problem, the best way is to divide the entire corpus into two major sets. The development set and test set are kept away for the modeling exercise. We just use the dev set to build and tune the model. Once we are done with the entire modeling exercise, the results are projected based on the test set that we put aside. Now, if the model performs well on this set, we are sure that it's accurate and robust for any new data sample.

Sampling itself is a very complicated and well-researched stream in the machine learning community, and it's a remedy for many data **skewness** and overfitting issues. For simplicity, will use the basic sampling, where we just divide the corpus into a split of 70:30:

```
>>>trainset_size = int(round(len(sms_data)*0.70))
>>># i chose this threshold for 70:30 train and test split.
>>>print 'The training set size for this classifier is ' + str(trainset_
size) + '\n'
>>>x_train = np.array([''.join(el) for el in sms_data[0:trainset_size]])
>>>y_train = np.array([el for el in sms_labels[0:trainset_size]])
>>>x_test = np.array([''.join(el) for el in sms_data[trainset_
size+1:len(sms_data)]])
>>>y_test = np.array([el for el in sms_labels[trainset_size+1:len(sms_
labels)]])or el in sms_labels[trainset_size+1:len(sms_labels)]])
>>>print x_train
>>>print y_train
```

- So what do you think will happen if we use the entire data as training data?
- What will happen when we have a very unbalanced sample?

> To understand more about the available sampling techniques, go through `http://scikit-learn.org/stable/modules/classes.html#module-sklearn.cross_validation`.

Let's jump to one of the most important things, where we transform the entire text into a vector form. The form is referred to as the **term-document matrix**. If we have to create a term-document matrix for the given example, it will look somewhat like this:

TDM	anymore	call	camera	color	cried	enough	entitled	free	gon	had	latest	mobile
SMS1	0	1	1	1	0	0	1	2	0	1	0	3
SMS2	1	0	0	0	1	1	0	0	1	0	0	0

The representation here of the text document is also known as the **BOW (Bag of Word)** representation. This is one of the most commonly used representation in text mining and other applications. Essentially, we are not considering any context between the words to generate this kind of representation.

To generate a similar term-document matrix in Python, we use scikit vectorizers:

```
>>>from sklearn.feature_extraction.text import CountVectorizer
>>>sms_exp=[ ]
>>>for line in sms_list:
>>>     sms_exp.append(preprocessing(line[1]))
>>>vectorizer = CountVectorizer(min_df=1)
>>>X_exp = vectorizer.fit_transform(sms_exp)
>>>print "||".join(vectorizer.get_feature_names())
>>>print X_exp.toarray()
array([[    1,    0,    1,    1,    1,    0,    0,    1,    2,    0,
1,    0,    1,    3,    1,    0,    0,    0,    1,    0,    0,    2,
0,    0], [    0,    1,    0,    0,    0,    1,    1,    0,    0,    1,
0,    1,    0,    0,    0,    1,    1,    1,    0,    1,    1,    0,
1,    1,    ]])
```

The count vectorizer is a good start, but there is an issue that you will face while using it: longer documents will have higher average count values than shorter documents, even though they might talk about the same topics.

> To avoid these potential discrepancies, it suffices to divide the number of occurrences of each word in a document by the total number of words in the document. This new feature is called **tf (Term frequencies)**.

Another refinement on top of tf is to downscale weights for words that occur in many documents in the corpus, and are therefore less informative than those that occur only in a smaller portion of the corpus.

This downscaling is called **tf-idf (term frequency-inverse document frequency)**. Fortunately, scikit also provides a way to achieve the following:

```
>>>from sklearn.feature_extraction.text import TfidfVectorizer
>>>vectorizer = TfidfVectorizer(min_df=2, ngram_range=(1, 2),  stop_
words='english',  strip_accents='unicode',  norm='l2')
>>>X_train = vectorizer.fit_transform(x_train)
>>>X_test = vectorizer.transform(x_test)
```

We now have the text in a matrix format the same as we have in any machine learning exercise. Now, `X_train` and `X_test` can be used for classification using any machine learning algorithm. Let's talk about some of the most commonly used machine learning algorithms in context of text classification.

Naive Bayes

Let's build your first text classifier. Let's start with a Naive Bayes classifier. Naive Bayes relies on the Bayes algorithm and essentially, is a model of assigning a class label to the sample based on the conditional probability class given by features/attributes. Here we deal with frequencies/bernoulli to estimate prior and posterior probabilities.

$$\text{posterior} = \frac{\text{prior} \times \text{likelihood}}{\text{evidence}}.$$

The naive assumption here is that all features are independent of each other, which looks counter intuitive in the case of text. However, surprisingly, Naive Bayes performs quite well in most of the real-world use cases.

Another great thing about NB is that it's too simple and very easy to implement and score. We need to store the frequencies and calculate the probabilities. It's really fast in case of training as well as test (scoring). For all these reasons, in most of the cases of text classification, it serves as a benchmark.

Let's write some code to achieve this classifier:

```
>>>from sklearn.naive_bayes import MultinomialNB
>>>clf = MultinomialNB().fit(X_train, y_train)
>>>y_nb_predicted = clf.predict(X_test)
>>>print y_nb_predicted
```

```
>>>print ' \n confusion_matrix \n '
>>>cm = confusion_matrix(y_test, y_pred)
>>>print cm
>>>print '\n Here is the classification report:'
>>>print classification_report(y_test, y_nb_predicted)
confusion_matrix [[1205 5]
                  [26 156]]
```

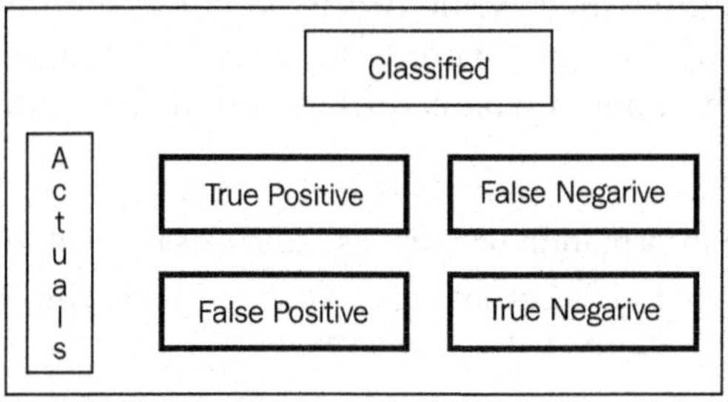

The way to read the confusion matrix is that from all the 1,392 samples in the test set, there were 1205 true positives and 156 true negative cases. However, we also predicted 5 false negatives and 26 false positives. There are different ways of measuring a typical binary classification.

We have given definitions of some of the most common measures used in classification measures:

$$\text{Accuracy} = \frac{tp + tn}{tp + tn + fp + fn}$$

$$\text{Precision} = \frac{tp}{tp + fp}$$

$$\text{Recall} = \frac{tp}{tp + fn}$$

$$F = 2 \cdot \frac{\text{precision} \cdot \text{recall}}{\text{precision} + \text{recall}}$$

Here is the classification report:

```
              Precision      recall      f1-score      support
ham           0.97           1.00        0.98          1210
spam          1.00           0.77        0.87          182
avg / total   0.97           0.97        0.97          1392
```

With the preceding definition, we can now understand the results clearly. So, effectively, all the preceding metrics look good, which means that our classifier is performing accurately, and is robust. I would highly recommend that you look into the module metrics for more options to analyze the results of the classifier. The most important and balanced metric is the `f1` measure (which is nothing but the harmonic mean of precision and recall), which is used widely because it gives a better picture of the coverage and the quality of the classification algorithms. Accuracy intuitively tells us how many true samples have been covered from all the samples. Precision and recall both have significance, while precision talks about how many true positives it got and what else got covered, hand recall gives us details about how accurate we are from the pool of true positives and false negatives.

> For more information on various scikit classes visit the following link:
> `http://scikit-learn.org/stable/modules/classes.html#module-sklearn.metrics`

The other more important process we follow to understand our model is to really look deep into the model by looking at the actual features that contribute to the positive and negative classes. I just wrote a very small snippet to generate the top *n* features and print them. Let's have a look at them:

```
>>>feature_names = vectorizer.get_feature_names()
>>>coefs = clf.coef_
>>>intercept = clf.intercept_
>>>coefs_with_fns = sorted(zip(clf.coef_[0], feature_names))
>>>n = 10
>>>top = zip(coefs_with_fns[:n], coefs_with_fns[:-(n + 1):-1])
>>>for (coef_1, fn_1), (coef_2, fn_2) in top:
>>>    print('\t%.4f\t%-15s\t\t%.4f\t%-15s' % (coef_1, fn_1, coef_2, fn_2))
-9.1602    10 den                    -6.0396    free
-9.1602    15                        -6.3487    txt
-9.1602    1hr                       -6.5067    text
-9.1602    1st ur                    -6.5393    claim
-9.1602    2go                       -6.5681    reply
-9.1602    2marrow                   -6.5808    mobile
-9.1602    2morrow                   -6.5858    stop
-9.1602    2mrw                      -6.6124    ur
-9.1602    2nd innings               -6.6245    prize
-9.1602    2nd ur                    -6.7856    www
```

In the preceding code, I just read all the feature names from the vectorizer, got the coefficients related to the given feature, and then printed the first-10 features. If you want more features, just modify the value of *n*. If we look closely just at the features, we get a lot of information about the model as well as more suggestions about our feature selection and other parameters, such as preprocessing, unigrams/bigrams, stemming, tokenizations, and so on. For example, if you look at the top features of ham you can see that `2morrow`, `2nd innings`, and some of the digits are coming very significantly. We can see on the positive class (spam) term "free" comes out a very significant term which is intuitive while many spam messages will be about some free offers and deal. Some of the other terms to note are prize, www, claim.

> For more details, refer to `http://scikitlearn.org/stable/modules/naive_bayes.html`.

Decision trees

Decision trees are one of the oldest predictive modeling techniques, where for the given features and target, the algorithm tries to build a logic tree. There are multiple algorithms that exist for decision trees. One of the most famous and widely used algorithm is **CART**.

CART constructs binary trees using this feature, and constructs a threshold that yields the large amount of information from each node. Let's write the code to get a CART classifier:

```
>>>from sklearn import tree
>>>clf = tree.DecisionTreeClassifier().fit(X_train.toarray(), y_train)
>>>y_tree_predicted = clf.predict(X_test.toarray())
>>>print y_tree_predicted
>>>print ' \n Here is the classification report:'
>>>print classification_report(y_test, y_tree_predicted)
```

The only difference is in the input format of the training set. We need to modify the sparse matrix format to a **NumPy** array because the scikit tree module takes only a NumPy array.

Generally, trees are good when the number of features are very less. So, although our results look good here, people hardly use trees in text classification. On the other hand, trees have some really positive sides to them. It is still one the most intuitive algorithms and is very easy to explain and implement. There are many implementations of tree-based algorithms, such as ID3, C4.5, and C5. scikit-learn uses an optimized version of the CART algorithm.

Stochastic gradient descent

Stochastic gradient descent (**SGD**) is a simple, yet very efficient approach that fits linear models. It is particularly useful when the number of samples (and the number of features) is very large. If you follow the cheat sheet, you will find SGD to be the one-stop solution for many text classification problems. Since it also takes care of regularization and provides different losses, it turns out to be a great choice when experimenting with linear models.

SGD, also known as **Maximum entropy** (**MaxEnt**), provides functionality to fit linear models for classification and regression using different (convex) loss functions and penalties. For example, with loss = log, fits a logistic regression model, while with loss = hinge, it fits a linear support vector machine (SVM).

An example of SGD is as follows:

```
>>>from sklearn.linear_model import SGDClassifier
>>>from sklearn.metrics import confusion_matrix
>>>clf = SGDClassifier(alpha=.0001, n_iter=50).fit(X_train, y_train)
>>>y_pred = clf.predict(X_test)
>>>print '\n Here is the classification report:'
>>>print classification_report(y_test, y_pred)
>>>print ' \n confusion_matrix \n '
>>>cm = confusion_matrix(y_test, y_pred)
>>>print cm
```

Here is the classification report:

	precision	recall	f1-score	support
ham	0.99	1.00	0.99	1210
spam	0.96	0.91	0.93	182
avg / total	0.98	0.98	0.98	1392

Most informative features:

-1.0002	sir	2.3815	ringtoneking
-0.5239	bed	2.0481	filthy
-0.4763	said	1.8576	service
-0.4763	happy	1.7623	story
-0.4763	might	1.6671	txt
-0.4287	added	1.5242	new
-0.4287	list	1.4765	ringtone
-0.4287	morning	1.3813	reply

-0.4287	always	1.3337	message
-0.4287	and	1.2860	call
-0.4287	plz	1.2384	chat
-0.3810	people	1.1908	text
-0.3810	actually	1.1908	real
-0.3810	urgnt	1.1431	video

Logistic regression

Logistic regression is a linear model for classification. It's also known in the literature as logit regression, maximum-entropy classification (MaxEnt), or the log-linear classifier. In this model, the probabilities describing the possible outcomes of a single trial are modeled using a logit function.

As an optimization problem, the `L2` binary class' penalized logistic regression minimizes the following cost function:

$$\min_{w,c} \frac{1}{2} w^T w + C \sum_{i=1}^{n} \log\left(\exp\left(-y_i \left(X_i^T w + c\right)\right) + 1\right)$$

Similarly, `L1` the binary class' regularized logistic regression solves the following optimization problem:

$$\min_{w,c} \frac{1}{2} \|w\|_1 + C \sum_{i=1}^{n} \log\left(\exp\left(-y_i \left(X_i^T w + c\right)\right) + 1\right)$$

Support vector machines

Support vector machines (**SVM**) is currently the-state-of-art algorithm in the field of machine learning.

SVM is a non-probabilistic classifier. SVM constructs a set of hyperplanes in an infinite-dimensional space, which can be used for classification, regression, or other tasks. Intuitively, a good separation is achieved by a hyperplane that has the largest distance to the nearest training data point of any class (the so-called functional margin), since in general, the larger the margin, the lower the size of classifier.

Let's build one of the most sophisticated supervised learning algorithms with scikit:

```
>>>from sklearn.svm import LinearSVC
>>>svm_classifier = LinearSVC().fit(X_train, y_train)
>>>y_svm_predicted = svm_classifier.predict(X_test)
>>>print '\n Here is the classification report:'
>>>print classification_report(y_test, y_svm_predicted)
>>>cm = confusion_matrix(y_test, y_pred)
>>>print cm
```

Here is the classification report for the same:

```
             precision    recall  f1-score   support
        ham       0.99      1.00      0.99      1210
       spam       0.97      0.90      0.93       182
avg / total       0.98      0.98      0.98      1392

confusion_matrix  [[1204    6] [  17  165]]
```

The most informative features:

```
    -0.9657     road                       2.3724     txt
    -0.7493     mail                       2.0720     claim
    -0.6701     morning                    2.0451     service
    -0.6691     home                       2.0008     uk
    -0.6191     executive                  1.7909     150p
    -0.5984     said                       1.7374     www
    -0.5978     lol                        1.6997     mobile
    -0.5876     kate                       1.6736     50
    -0.5754     got                        1.5882     ringtone
    -0.5642     darlin                     1.5629     video
    -0.5613     fullonsms                  1.4816     tone
    -0.5613     fullonsms com              1.4237     prize
```

These are definitely the best results so far from all the supervised algorithms we have tried. Now with this, I will stop with supervised classifiers. There are millions of books available related to the different machine learning algorithms; even for individual algorithms, there are many books that are available for you. I would highly recommend you to have a deep understanding of any of the preceding algorithms before you use them for any of the real-world applications.

The Random forest algorithm

A random forest is an ensemble classifier that estimates based on the combination of different decision trees. Effectively, it fits a number of decision tree classifiers on various subsamples of the dataset. Also, each tree in the forest built on a random best subset of features. Finally, the act of enabling these trees gives us the best subset of features among all the random subsets of features. Random forest is currently one of best performing algorithms for many classification problems.

An example of Random forest is as follows:

```
>>>from sklearn.ensemble import RandomForestClassifier
>>>RF_clf = RandomForestClassifier(n_estimators=10)
>>>predicted = RF_clf.predict(X_test)
>>>print '\n Here is the classification report:'
>>>print classification_report(y_test, predicted)
>>>cm = confusion_matrix(y_test, y_pred)
>>>print cm
```

> People who still want to work with NLTK for text classification. Please go through the following link:
> `http://www.nltk.org/howto/classify.html`

Text clustering

The other family of problems that can come with text is unsupervised classification. One of the most common problem statements you can get is "I have these millions of documents (unstructured data). Is there a way I can group them into some meaningful categories?". Now, once you have some samples of tagged data, we could build a supervised algorithm that we talked about, but here, we need to use an unsupervised way of grouping text documents.

Text clustering is one of the most common ways of unsupervised grouping, also known as, clustering. There are a variety of algorithms available using clustering. I mostly used **k-means** or **hierarchical** clustering. I will talk about both of them and how to use them with a text corpus.

K-means

Very intuitively, as the name suggest, we are trying to find k groups around the mean of the data points. So, the algorithm starts with picking up some random data points as the centroid of all the data points. Then, the algorithm assigns all the data points to it's nearest centroid. Once this iteration is done, recalculation of the centroid happens and these iterations continue until we reach a state where the centroids don't change (algorithm saturate).

There is a variant of the algorithm that uses mini batches to reduce the computation time, while still attempting to optimize the same objective function.

> Mini batches are subsets of the input data randomly sampled in each training iteration. These options should always be tried once your dataset is really huge and you want less training time.

An example of K-means is as follows:

```
>>>from sklearn.cluster import KMeans, MiniBatchKMeans
>>>true_k=5
>>>km = KMeans(n_clusters=true_k, init='k-means++', max_iter=100, n_
init=1)
>>>kmini = MiniBatchKMeans(n_clusters=true_k, init='k-means++', n_init=1,
init_size=1000, batch_size=1000, verbose=opts.verbose)
>>># we are using the same test,train data in TFIDF form as we did in
text classification
>>>km_model=km.fit(X_train)
>>>kmini_model=kmini.fit(X_train)
>>>print "For K-mean clustering "
>>>clustering = collections.defaultdict(list)
>>>for idx, label in enumerate(km_model.labels_):
>>>        clustering[label].append(idx)
>>>print "For K-mean Mini batch clustering "
>>>clustering = collections.defaultdict(list)
>>>for idx, label in enumerate(kmini_model.labels_):
>>>        clustering[label].append(idx)
```

In the preceding code, we just imported scikit-learn's `kmeans` / `minibatchkmeans` and fitted the same training data that we were using in the running examples. We can also print a cluster for each sample using the last three lines of the code.

Topic modeling in text

The other famous problem in the context of the text corpus is finding the topics of the given document. The concept of topic modeling can be addressed in many different ways. We typically use **LDA** (**Latent Dirichlet allocation**) and LSI (Latent semantic indexing) to apply topic modeling text documents.

Typically, in most of the industries, we have huge volumes of unlabeled text documents. In case of an unlabeled corpus to get the initial insights of the corpus, a topic model is a great option, as it not only gives us topics of relevance, but also categorizes the entire corpus into number of topics given to the algorithm.

We will use a new Python library "gensim" that implements these algorithms for us. So, let's jump to the implementation of LDA and LSI for the same running SMS dataset. Now, the only change to the problem is that we want to model different topics in the SMS data and also want to know which document belongs to which topic. A better and more realistic use case could be to run topic modeling on the entire Wikipedia dump to find different kinds of topics that have been discussed there, or to run topic modeling on billions of reviews/complaints from customers to get an insight of the topics that people discuss.

Installing gensim

One of the easiest ways to install gensim is using a package manager:

```
>>>easy_install -U gensim
```

Otherwise, you can install it using:

```
>>>pip install gensim
```

Once you're done with the installation, run the following command:

```
>>>import gensim
```

> If there is any error, go to
> `https://radimrehurek.com/gensim/install.html`.

Now, let's look at the following code:

```
>>>from gensim import corpora, models, similarities
>>>from itertools import chain
>>>import nltk
```

```
>>>from nltk.corpus import stopwords
>>>from operator import itemgetter
>>>import re
>>>documents = [document for document in sms_data]
>>>stoplist = stopwords.words('english')
>>>texts = [[word for word in document.lower().split() if word not in
stoplist] \ for document in documents]
```

We are just reading the document in our SMS data and removing the stop words. We could use the same method that we did in the previous chapters to do this. Here, we are using a library-specific way of doing things.

> Gensim has all the typical NLP features as well provides some great way to create different corpus formats, such as TFIDF, libsvm, market matrix. It also provides conversion of one to another.

In the following code, we are converting the list of documents to a BOW model and then, to a typical **TF-IDF** corpus:

```
>>>dictionary = corpora.Dictionary(texts)
>>>corpus = [dictionary.doc2bow(text) for text in texts]
>>>tfidf = models.TfidfModel(corpus)
>>>corpus_tfidf = tfidf[corpus]
```

Once you have a corpus in the required format, we have the following two methods, where given the number of topics, the model tries to take all the documents from the corpus to build a LDA/LSI model:

```
>>>si = models.LsiModel(corpus_tfidf, id2word=dictionary, num_topics=100)
>>>#lsi.print_topics(20)
>>>n_topics = 5
>>>lda = models.LdaModel(corpus_tfidf, id2word=dictionary, num_topics=n_
topics)
```

Once the model is built, we need to understand the different topics, what kind of terms represent that topic, and we need to print some top terms related to that topic:

```
>>>for i in range(0, n_topics):
>>>        temp = lda.show_topic(i, 10)
>>>        terms = []
>>>        for term in temp:
>>>            terms.append(term[1])
>>>            print "Top 10 terms for topic #" + str(i) + ": "+ ",
".join(terms)
Top 10 terms for topic #0: week, coming, get, great, call, good, day,
txt, like, wish
Top 10 terms for topic #1: call, ..., later, sorry, 'll, lor, home, min,
free, meeting
Top 10 terms for topic #2: ..., n't, time, got, come, want, get, wat,
need, anything
Top 10 terms for topic #3: get, tomorrow, way, call, pls, 're, send,
pick, ..., text
Top 10 terms for topic #4: ..., good, going, day, know, love, call, yup,
get, make
```

Now, if you look at the output, we have five different topics with clearly different intent. Think about the same exercise for Wikipedia or a huge corpus of web pages, and you will get some meaningful topics that represent the corpus.

References

- http://scikit-learn.org/
- https://radimrehurek.com/gensim/
- https://en.wikipedia.org/wiki/Document_classification

Summary

The idea behind this chapter was to introduce you to the world of text mining. We want to give you a basic introduction to some of the most common algorithms available with text classification and clustering .We know how some of these concept will help you to build really great NLP applications, such as spam filters, domain centric news feeds, web page taxonomy, and so on. Though we have not used NLTK to classify the module in our code snippets, we used NLTK for all the preprocessing steps. We highly recommend you to use scikit-learn over NLTK for any classification problem. In this chapter, we started with machine learning and the types of problems that it can address. We discussed some of the specifics of ML problems in the context of text. We talked about some of the most common classification algorithms that are used for text classification, clustering, and topic modeling. We also give you enough implementation details to get the job done. I still think you need to read a lot about each and every algorithm separately to understand the theory and to gain in-depth understanding of them.

We also provided you an entire pipeline of the process that you need to follow in case of any text mining problem. We covered most of the practical aspects of machine learning, such as sampling, preprocessing, model building, and model evaluation.

The next chapter will also not be directly related to NLTK/NLP, but it will be a great tool for a data scientist/NLP enthusiast. In most of NLP problems, we deal with unstructured text data, and the Web is one of the richest and biggest data sources available for this. Let's learn how to gather data from the Web and how to efficiently use it to build some amazing NLP applications.

7
Web Crawling

The largest repository of unstructured text is the Web, and if you know how to crawl it, then you have all the data you need readily available for your experiments. Hence, web crawling is something worth learning for people who are interested in NLTK. This chapter is all about gathering data from the Web.

In this chapter we will use an amazing Python library called **Scrapy** to write our web crawlers. We will provide you all the details to configure different settings that are required. We will write some of the most common spider strategies and many use cases. Scrapy also requires some understanding about **XPath**, crawling, scraping, and some concepts related to the Web in general. We will touch upon these topics and make sure you understand their practical aspects, before really getting in to their implementation. By the end of this chapter, you will have a better understand of web crawler.

- How we can write our own crawler using Scrapy
- Understanding about all the major Scrapy functionality

Web crawlers

One of the biggest web crawler is Google that crawls the entire **World Wide Web (WWW)**. Google has to traverse every page that exists on the Web and scrape/crawl the entire content.

A web crawler is a computer program that systematically browses the web page by page and also scrapes/crawls the content of the pages. A web crawler can also parse the next set of URLs to be visited from the crawled content. So, if these processes run indefinitely over the entire Web, we can crawl through all the web pages. Web crawlers are interchangeably also called spiders, bots, and scrapers. They all mean the same.

There are a few main points we need to think about before writing our first crawler. Now, every time a web crawler traverses a page, we must decide what kind of content we want to select and what content we want to ignore. For applications such as a search engine, we should ignore all the images, js files, css files, and other files and should concentrate only on HTML content that can be indexed and exposed to the search. In some information extraction engines, we select specific tags or parts of a web page. We also need to extract the URLs if we want to do the crawling recursively. This brings us to the topic of crawling strategy. Here, we need to decide whether we want to go recursively in depth first manner or breadth first manner. We want to follow all the URLs on the next page and then go in depth first manner till we get the URLs, or we should go to all the URLs in the next page and do this recursively.

We also need to make sure that we are not going in the self loop stage because essentially, we traverse a graph in most of the cases. We need to make sure we have a clear revisit strategy for a page. One of the most talked about crawled policies is focused crawling, where we know what kind of domains/topics we are looking for, and the ones that need to be crawled. Some of these issues will be discussed in more detail in the spider section.

> Take a look at the video on Udacity at `https://www.youtube.com/watch?v=CDXOcvUNBaA`.

Writing your first crawler

Let's start with a very basic crawler that will crawl the entire content of a web page. To write the crawlers, we will use Scrapy. Scrapy is a one of the best crawling solutions using Python. We will explore all the different features of Scrapy in this chapter. First, we need to install Scrapy for this exercise.

To do this, type in the following command:

```
$ pip install scrapy
```

This is the easiest way of installing Scrapy using a package manager. Let's now test whether we got everything right or not. (Ideally, Scrapy should now be part of `sys.path`):

```
>>>import scrapy
```

If there is any error, then take a look at http://doc.scrapy.org/en/latest/intro/install.html.

At this point, we have Scrapy working for you. Let's start with an example spider app with Scrapy:

```
$ scrapy startproject tutorial
```

Once you write the preceding command, the directory structure should look like the following:

```
tutorial/
    scrapy.cfg   #the project configuration file
    tutorial/      #the project's python module, you'll later import
your code from here.
        __init__.py
        items.py        #the project's items file.
        pipelines.py    #the project's pipelines file.
        settings.py      # the project's settings file.
        spiders/   #a directory where you'll later put your spiders.
              __init__.py
```

The top folder will be given the name of the example tutorial in this case. Then, there is the project configuration file (scrapy.cfg) that will define the kind of setting file that should be used for the project. It also provides the deploy URLs for the project.

Another important part of tutorial setting.py is where we can decide what kind of item pipeline and spider will be used. The item.py and pipline.py are the files that define the data and kind of preprocessing we need to do on the parsed item. The spider folder will contain the different spiders you wrote for the specific URLs.

For our first test spider, we will dump the contents of a news in a local file. We need to create a file named NewsSpider.py, and put it in the path /tutorial/spiders. Let's write the first spider:

```
>>>from scrapy.spider import BaseSpider
>>>class NewsSpider(BaseSpider):
>>>     name = "news"
>>>     allowed_domains = ["nytimes.com"]
>>>     start_URLss = [
```

```
>>>         'http://www.nytimes.com/'
>>>     ]
>>>def parse(self, response):
>>>         filename = response.URLs.split("/")[-2]
>>>         open(filename, 'wb').write(response.body)
```

Once we have this spider ready, we can start crawling using the following command:

```
$ scrapy crawl news
```

After you enter the preceding command, you should see some logs like this:

```
[scrapy] INFO: Scrapy 0.24.5 started (bot: tutorial)
[scrapy] INFO: Optional features available: ssl, http11, boto
[scrapy] INFO: Overridden settings: {'NEWSPIDER_MODULE': 'tutorial.
spiders', 'SPIDER_MODULES': ['tutorial.spiders'], 'BOT_NAME': 'tutorial'}
[scrapy] INFO: Enabled extensions: LogStats, TelnetConsole, CloseSpider,
WebService, CoreStats, SpiderState
```

If you don't see logs like the ones shown in the preceding snippet, you have missed something. Check the location of the spider and other Scrapy-related settings, such as the name of the spider matching to the crawl command, and whether `setting.py` is configured for the same spider and item pipeline or not.

Now, if you are successful, there should be a file in your local folder with the name `www.nytimes.com` that has the entire web content of the `www.nytimes.com` page.

Let's see some of the terms that we used in the spider code in more detail:

- `name`: This is the name of the spider that works as an identifier for Scrapy to look for the `spider` class. So, the crawl command argument and this name should always match. Also make sure that it's unique and case sensitive.
- `start_urls`: This is a list of URLs where the spider will begin to crawl. The crawler with start from a seed URL and using the `parse()` method, it will parse and look for the next URL to crawl. Instead of just a single seed URL, we can provide a list of URLs that can start the crawl.
- `parse()`: This method is called to parse the data from start URLs. The logic of what kind of element is to be selected for specific attributes of item. This could be as simple as dumping the entire content of HTML to as complex as many parse methods callable from parse, and different selectors for individual item attributes.

So, the code does nothing but starts with the given URLs (in this case, `www.nytimes.com`) and crawls the entire content of the page. Typically, a crawler is more complex and will do much more than this; now, let's take a step back and understand what happened behind the scenes. For this, take a look at the following figure:

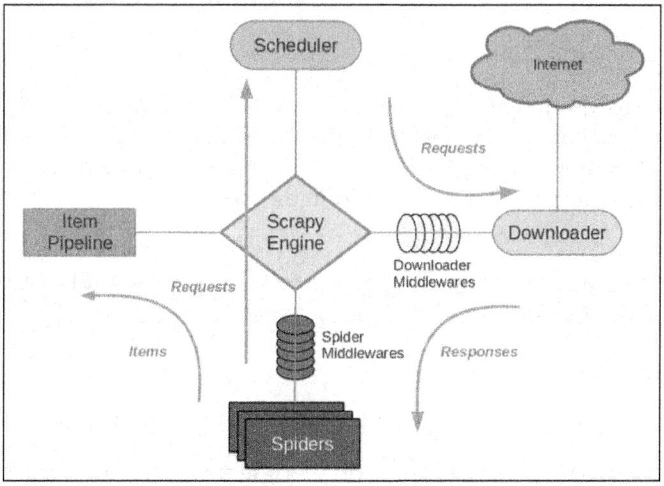

credit :Scrapy

Data flow in Scrapy

The data flow in Scrapy is controlled by the execution engine and goes like this:

1. The process starts with locating the chosen spider and opening the first URL from the list of `start_urls`.
2. The first URL is then scheduled as a request in a scheduler. This is more of an internal to Scrapy.
3. The Scrapy engine then looks for the next set of URLs to crawl.
4. The scheduler then sends the next URLs to the engine and the engine then forwards it to the downloader using the downloaded middleware. These middlewares are where we place different proxies and user-agent settings.
5. The downloader downloads the response from the page and passes it to the spider, where the parse method selects specific elements from the response.
6. Then, the spider sends the processed item to the engine.
7. The engine sends the processed response to the item pipeline, where we can add some post processing.
8. The same process continues for each URL until there are no remaining requests.

The Scrapy shell

The best way to understand Scrapy is to use it through a shell and to get your hands dirty with some of the initial commands and tools provided by Scrapy. It allows you to experiment and develop your XPath expressions that you can put into your spider code.

> To experiment with the Scrapy shell, I would recommend you to install one of the developer tools (**Chrome**) and Firebug (**Mozilla Firefox**) as a plugin. This tool will help us dig down to the very specific part that we want from the web page.

Now, let's start with a very interesting use case where we want to capture the trending topics from Google news (`https://news.google.com/`).

The steps to follow here are:

1. Open `https://news.google.com/` in your favorite browser.
2. Go to the trending topic section on Google news. Then, right-click on and select **Inspect Element** for the first topic, as shown in the following screenshot:

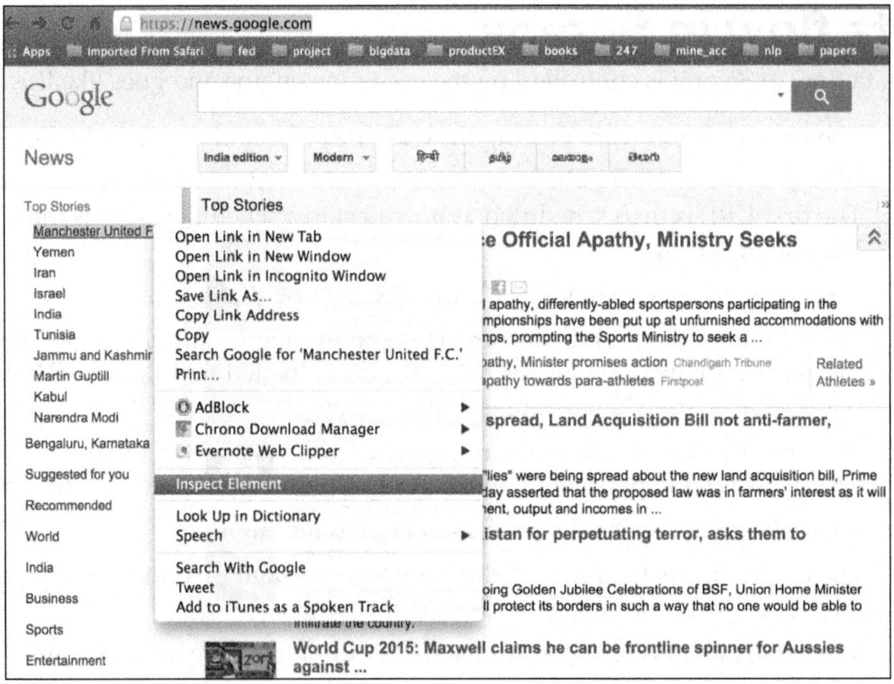

3. The moment you open this, there will be a side window that will pop up and you will get a view.
4. Search and select the `div` tag. For this example, we are interested in `<div class="topic">`.
5. Once this is done, you will come to know that we have actually parsed the specific part of the web page, as shown in the following screenshot:

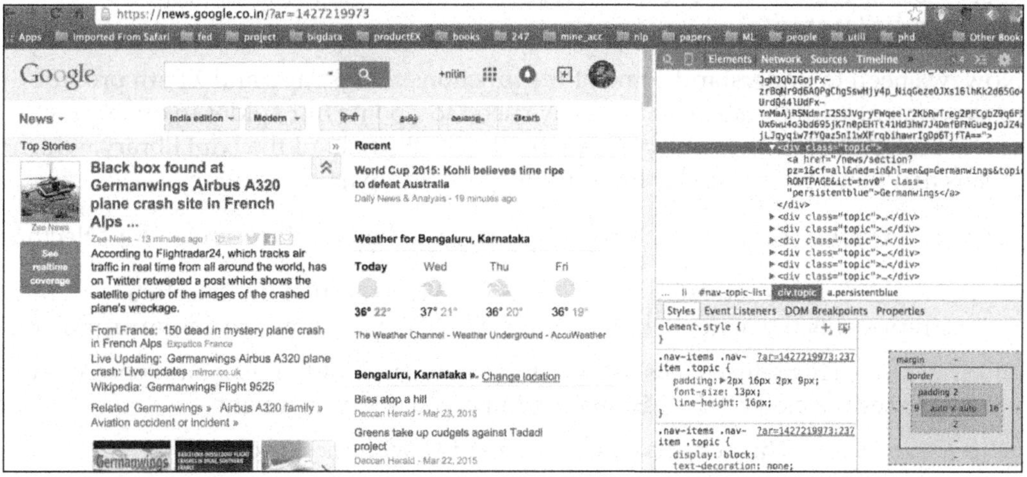

Now, what we actually did manually in the preceding steps can be done in an automated way. Scrapy uses an XML path language called XPath. XPath can be used to achieve this kind of functionality. So, let's see how we can implement the same example using Scrapy.

To use Scrapy, put the following command in you cmd:

```
$scrapy shell https://news.google.com/
```

The moment you hit enter, the response of the Google news page is loaded in the Scrapy shell. Now, let's move to the most important aspect of Scrapy where we want to understand how to look for a specific HTML element of the page. Let's start and run the example of getting topics from Google news that are shown in the preceding image:

```
In [1]: sel.xpath('//div[@class="topic"]').extract()
```

The output to this will be as follows:

```
Out[1]:
[<Selector xpath='//div[@class="topic"]' data=u'<div class="topic"><a
href="/news/sectio'>,
<Selector xpath='//div[@class="topic"]' data=u'<div class="topic"><a
href="/news/sectio'>,
<Selector xpath='//div[@class="topic"]' data=u'<div class="topic"><a
href="/news/sectio'>]
```

Now, we need to understand some of the functions that Scrapy and XPath provide to experiment with the shell and then, we need to update our spider to do more sophisticated stuff. Scrapy selectors are built with the help of the lxml library, which means that they're very similar in terms of speed and parsing accuracy.

Let's have a look at some of the most frequently used methods provided for selectors:

- `xpath()`: This returns a list of selectors, where each of the selectors represents the nodes selected by the XPath expression given as an argument.
- `css()`: This returns a list of selectors. Here, each of the selectors represent the nodes selected by the CSS expression given as an argument.
- `extract()`:This returns content as a string with the selected data.
- `re()`: This returns a list of unicode strings extracted by applying the regular expression given as an argument.

I am giving you a cheat sheet of these top 10 selector patterns that can cover most of your work for you. For a more complex selector, if you search the Web, there should be an easy solution that you can use. Let's start with extracting the title of the web page that is very generic for all web pages:

```
In [2] :sel.xpath('//title/text()')
Out[2]: [<Selector xpath='//title/text()' data=u' Google News'>]
```

Now, once you have selected any element, you also want to extract for more processing. Let's extract the selected content. This is a generic method that works with any selector:

```
In [3]: sel.xpath('//title/text()').extract()
Out[3]: [u' Google News']
```

The other very generic requirement is to look for all the elements in the given page. Let's achieve this with this selector:

```
In [4]: sel.xpath('//ul/li')
Out [4] : list of elements (divs and all)
```

We can extract all the titles in the page with this selector:

```
In [5]: sel.xpath('//ul/li/a/text()').extract()
Out [5]: [ u'India',
u'World',
u'Business',
u'Technology',
u'Entertainment',
u'More Top Stories']
```

With this selector, you can extract all the hyperlinks in the web page:

```
In [6]:sel.xpath('//ul/li/a/@href').extract()
Out [6] : List of urls
```

Let's select all the `<td>` and `div` elements:

```
In [7]:sel.xpath('td'')
In [8]:divs=sel.xpath("//div")
```

This will select all the `divs` elements and then, you can loop it:

```
In [9]: for d in divs:
    printd.extract()
```

This will print the entire content of each div in the entire page. So, in case you are not able to get the exact div name, you can also look at the regex-based search.

Now, let's select all `div` elements that contain the attribute `class="topic"`:

```
In [10]:sel.xpath('/div[@class="topic"]').extract()
In [11]:  sel.xpath("//h1").extract()          # this includes the h1 tag
```

This will select all the `<p>` elements in the page and get the class of those elements:

```
In [12 ] for node in sel.xpath("//p"):
print node.xpath("@class").extract()
Out[12] print all the <p>
```

```
In [13]: sel.xpath("//li[contains(@class, 'topic')]")

Out[13]:

[<Selector xpath="//li[contains(@class, 'topic')]" data=u'<li class="nav-
item nv-FRONTPAGE selecte'>,

<Selector xpath="//li[contains(@class, 'topic')]" data=u'<li class="nav-
item nv-FRONTPAGE selecte'>]
```

Let's write some selector nuggets to get the data from a css file. If we just want to extract the title from the css file, typically, everything works the same, except you need to modify the syntax:

```
In [14] :sel.css('title::text').extract()

Out[14]: [u'Google News']
```

Use the following command to list the names of all the images used in the page:

```
In[15]: sel.xpath('//a[contains(@href, "image")]/img/@src').extract()

Out [15] : Will list all the images if the web developer has put the
images in /img/src
```

Let's see a regex-based selector:

```
In [16 ]sel.xpath('//title').re('(\w+)')

Out[16]: [u'title', u'Google', u'News', u'title']
```

In some cases, removing the namespaces can help us get the right pattern. A selector has an inbuilt `remove_namespaces()` function to make sure that the entire document is scanned and all the namespaces are removed. Make sure before using it whether we want some of these namespaces to be part of the pattern or not. The following is example of `remove_namespaces()` function:

```
In [17] sel.remove_namespaces()

sel.xpath("//link")
```

Now that we have more understanding about the selectors, let's modify the same old news spider that we built previously:

```
>>>from scrapy.spider import BaseSpider

>>>class NewsSpider(BaseSpider):

>>>    name = "news"

>>>    allowed_domains = ["nytimes.com"]

>>>    start_URLss = [

>>>        'http://www.nytimes.com/'

>>>    ]
```

```
>>>def parse(self, response):
>>>     sel = Selector(response)
>>>         sites = sel.xpath('//ul/li')
>>>         for site in sites:
>>>             title = site.xpath('a/text()').extract()
>>>             link = site.xpath('a/@href').extract()
>>>             desc = site.xpath('text()').extract()
>>>             print title, link, desc
```

Here, we mainly modified the parse method, which is one of the core of our spider. This spider can now crawl through the entire page, but we do a more structured parsing of the title, description, and URLs.

Now, let's write a more robust crawler using all the capabilities of Scrapy.

Items

Until now, we were just printing the crawled content on `stdout` or dumping it in a file. A better way to do this is to define `items.py` every time we write a crawler. The advantage of doing this is that we can consume these items in our parse method, and this can also give us output in any data format, such as XML, JSON, or CSV. So, if you go back to your old crawler, the items class will have a function like this:

```
>>>fromscrapy.item import Item, Field
>>>class NewsItem(scrapy.Item):
>>>     # define the fields for your item here like:
>>>     # name = scrapy.Field()
>>>     pass
```

Now, let's make it like the following by adding different fields:

```
>>>from scrapy.item import Item, Field
>>>class NewsItem(Item):
>>>     title = Field()
>>>     link = Field()
>>>     desc = Field()
```

Here, we added `field()` to `title`, `link`, and `desc`. Once we have a field in place, our spider parse method can be modified to `parse_news_item`, where instead dumping the parsed fields to a file now it can be consumed by an item object.

A Rule method is a way of specifying what kind of URL needs to be crawled after the current one. A Rule method provides `SgmlLinkExtractor`, which is a way of defining the URL pattern that needs to be extracted from the crawled page. A Rule method also provides a `callback` method, which is typically a pointer for a spider to look for the parsing method, which in this case is `parse_news_item`. In case we have a different way to parse, then we can have multiple rules and parse methods. A Rule method also has a Boolean parameter to follow, which specifies whether links should be followed by each response extracted with this rule. If the callback is None, follow defaults to *True*: otherwise, it default to *False*.

One important point to note is that the Rule method does not use parse. This is because the name of the default callback method is `parse()` and if we use it, we are actually overriding it, and that can stop the functionality of the crawl spider. Now, let's jump on to the following code to understand the preceding methods and parameters:

```
>>>from scrapy.contrib.spiders import CrawlSpider, Rule
>>>from scrapy.contrib.linkextractors.sgml import SgmlLinkExtractor
>>>from scrapy.selector import Selector
>>>from scrapy.item import NewsItem
>>>class NewsSpider(CrawlSpider):
>>>    name = 'news'
>>>    allowed_domains = ['news.google.com']
>>>    start_urls = ['https://news.google.com']
>>>    rules = (
>>>        # Extract links matching cnn.com
>>>        Rule(SgmlLinkExtractor(allow=('cnn.com', ), deny=(http://
edition.cnn.com/', ))),
>>>       # Extract links matching 'news.google.com'
>>>       Rule(SgmlLinkExtractor(allow=('news.google.com', )),
callback='parse_news_item'),
>>>    )
>>>    def parse_news_item(self, response):
>>>        sel = Selector(response)
>>>        item = NewsItem()
>>>        item['title'] = sel.xpath('//title/text()').extract()
>>>        item[topic] = sel.xpath('/div[@class="topic"]').extract()
>>>        item['desc'] = sel.xpath('//td//text()').extract()
>>>        return item
```

The Sitemap spider

If the site provides `sitemap.xml`, then a better way to crawl the site is to use `SiteMapSpider` instead.

Here, given `sitemap.xml`, the spider parses the URLs provided by the site itself. This is a more polite way of crawling and good practice:

```
>>>from scrapy.contrib.spiders import SitemapSpider
>>>class MySpider(SitemapSpider):
>>>     sitemap_URLss = ['http://www.example.com/sitemap.xml']
>>>     sitemap_rules = [('/electronics/', 'parse_electronics'), ('/
apparel/', 'parse_apparel'),]
>>>     def 'parse_electronics'(self, response):
>>>         # you need to create an item for electronics,
>>>         return
>>>     def 'parse_apparel'(self, response):
>>>         #you need to create an item for apparel
>>>         return
```

In the preceding code, we wrote one parse method for each product category. It's a great use case if you want to build a price aggregator/comparator. You might want to parse different attributes for different products, for example, for electronics, you might want to scrape the tech specification, accessory, and price; while for apparels, you are more concerned about the size and color of the item. Try your hand at using one of the retailer sites and use shell to get the patterns to scrape the size, color, and price of different items. If you do this, you should be in a good shape to write your first industry standard spider.

In some cases, you want to crawl a website that needs you to log in before you can enter some parts of the website. Now, Scrapy has a workaround that too. They implemented `FormRequest`, which is more of a **POST** call to the HTTP server and gets the response. Let's have a deeper look into the following spider code:

```
>>>class LoginSpider(BaseSpider):
>>>     name = 'example.com'
>>>     start_URLss = ['http://www.example.com/users/login.php']
>>>     def parse(self, response):
>>>         return [FormRequest.from_response(response,
formdata={'username': 'john', 'password': 'secret'}, callback=self.after_
login)]
>>>     def after_login(self, response):
>>>         # check login succeed before going on
```

```
>>>        if "authentication failed" in response.body:
>>>            self.log("Login failed", level=log.ERROR)
>>>          return
```

For a website that requires just the username and password without any captcha, the preceding code should work just by adding the specific login details. This is the part of the parse method since you need to log in the first page in the most of the cases. Once you log in, you can write your own `after_login` callback method with items and other details.

The item pipeline

Let's talk about some more item postprocessing. Scrapy provides a way to define a pipeline for items as well, where you can define the kind of post processing an item has to go through. This is a very methodical and good program design.

We need to build our own item pipeline if we want to post process scraped items, such as removing noise and case conversion, and in other cases, where we want to derive some values from the object, for example, to calculate the age from DOB or to calculate the discount price from the original price. In the end, we might want to dump the item separately into a file.

The way to achieve this will be as follows:

1. We need to define an item pipeline in `setting.py`:

   ```
   ITEM_PIPELINES = {
       'myproject.pipeline.CleanPipeline': 300,
       'myproject.pipeline.AgePipeline': 500,
       'myproject.pipeline.DuplicatesPipeline: 700,
       'myproject.pipeline.JsonWriterPipeline': 800,
   }
   ```

2. Let's write a class to clean the items:

   ```
   >>>from scrapy.exceptions import Item
   >>>import datetime
   >>>import datetime
   >>>class AgePipeline(object):
   >>>    def process_item(self, item, spider):
   >>>        if item['DOB']:
   >>>            item['Age'] = (datetime.datetime.
   strptime(item['DOB'], '%d-%m-%y').date()-datetime.datetime.
   strptime('currentdate, '%d-%m-%y').date()).days/365
   >>>            return item
   ```

3. We need to derive the age from `DOB`. We used Python's date functions to achieve this:

```
>>>from scrapy import signals
>>>from scrapy.exceptions import Item
>>>class DuplicatesPipeline(object):
>>>    def __init__(self):
>>>        self.ids_seen = set()
>>>    def process_item(self, item, spider):
>>>        if item['id'] in self.ids_seen:
>>>            raise DropItem("Duplicate item found: %s" % item)
>>>        else:
>>>            self.ids_seen.add(item['id'])
>>>            return item
```

4. We also need to remove the duplicates. Python has the `set()` data structure that only contains unique values, we can create a pipline `DuplicatesPipeline.py` like below using Scrapy :

```
>>>from scrapy import signals
>>>from scrapy.exceptions import Item
>>>class DuplicatesPipeline(object):
>>>    def __init__(self):
>>>        self.ids_seen = set()
>>>    def process_item(self, item, spider):
>>>        if item['id'] in self.ids_seen:
>>>            raise DropItem("Duplicate item found: %s" % item)
>>>        else:
>>>            self.ids_seen.add(item['id'])
>>>            return item
```

5. Let's finally write the item in the JSON file using `JsonWriterPipeline.py` pipeline:

```
>>>import json
>>>class JsonWriterPipeline(object):
>>>    def __init__(self):
>>>        self.file = open('items.txt', 'wb')
>>>    def process_item(self, item, spider):
>>>        line = json.dumps(dict(item)) + "\n"
>>>        self.file.write(line)
>>>        return item
```

External references

I encourage you to follow some simple spiders and try building some cool applications using these spiders. I would also like you to look at the following links for reference:

- `http://doc.scrapy.org/en/latest/intro/tutorial.html`
- `http://doc.scrapy.org/en/latest/intro/overview.html`

Summary

In this chapter, you learned about another great Python library and now, you don't need help from anybody for your data needs. You learned how you can write a very sophisticated crawling system, and now you know how to write a focused spider. In this chapter, we saw how to abstract the item logic from the main system and how to write some specific spider for the most common use cases. We know some of the most common settings that need to be taken care of in order to implement our own spider and we wrote some complex parse methods that can be reused. We understand selectors very well and know a hands-on way of figuring out what kind of elements we want for specific item attributes, and we also went through Firebug to get more of a practical understanding of selectors. Last but not least, very importantly, make sure that you follow the security guidelines of the websites you crawl.

In the next chapter, we will explore some essential Python libraries that can be used for natural language processing and machine learning.

8
Using NLTK with Other Python Libraries

In this chapter, we will explore some of the backbone libraries of Python for machine learning and natural language processing. Until now, we have used NLTK, Scikit, and genism, which had very abstract functions, and were very specific to the task in hand. Most of statistical NLP is heavily based on the vector space model, which in turn depends on basic linear algebra covered by NumPy. Also many NLP tasks, such as POS or NER tagging, are really classifiers in disguise. Some of the libraries we will discuss are heavily used in all these tasks.

The idea behind this chapter is to give you a quick overview of some the most fundamental Python libraries. This will help us understand more than just the data structure, design, and math behind some of the coolest libraries, such as NLTK and Scikit, which we have discussed in the previous chapters.

We will look at the following four libraries. I have tried to keep it short, but I highly encourage you to read in more detail about these libraries if you want Python to be a one-stop solution to most of your data science needs.

- NumPy (Numeric Python)
- SciPy (Scientific Python)
- Pandas (Data manipulation)
- Matplotlib (Visualization)

NumPy

NumPy is a Python library for dealing with numerical operations, and it's really fast. NumPy provides some of the highly optimized data structures, such as ndarrays. NumPy has many functions specially designed and optimized to perform some of the most common numeric operations. This is one of the reasons NLTK, scikit-learn, pandas, and other libraries use NumPy as a base to implement some of the algorithms. This section will give you a brief summary with running examples of NumPy. This will not just help us understand the fundamental data structures beneath NLTK and other libraries, but also give us the ability to customize some of these functionalities to our needs.

Let's start with discussion on ndarrays, how they can be used as matrices, and how easy and efficient it is to deal with matrices in NumPy.

ndarray

An ndarray is an array object that represents a multidimensional, homogeneous array of fixed-size items.

We will start with building an ndarray using an ordinary Python list:

```
>>>x=[1,2,5,7,3,11,14,25]
>>>import numpy as np
>>>np_arr=np.array(x)
>>>np_arr
```

As you can see, this is a linear 1D array. The real power of Numpy comes with 2D arrays. Let's move to 2D arrays. We will create one using a Python list of lists.

```
>>>arr=[[1,2],[13,4],[33,78]]
>>>np_2darr= np.array(arr)
>>>type(np_2darr)
numpy.ndarray
```

Indexing

The ndarray is indexed more like Python containers. NumPy provides a slicing method to get different views of the ndarray.

```
>>>np_2darr.tolist()
[[1, 2], [13, 4], [33, 78]]
>>>np_2darr[:]
array([[1, 2], [13,  4], [33, 78]])
>>>np_2darr[:2]
array([[1, 2], [13, 4]])
>>>np_2darr[:1]
array([[1, 2]])
>>>np_2darr[2]
array([33, 78])
>>>    np_2darr[2][0]
>>>33
>>>    np_2darr[:-1]
array([[1, 2], [13, 4]])
```

Basic operations

NumPy also has some other operations that can be used in various numeric processing. In this example, we want to get an array with values ranging from 0 to 10 with a step size of `0.1`. This is typically required for any optimization routine. Some of the most common libraries, such as Scikit and NLTK, actually use these NumPy functions.

```
>>>>import numpy as np
>>>>np.arange(0.0, 1.0, 0.1)
array([ 0. ,  0.1,  0.2,  0.3,  0.4,  0.5,  0.6,  0.7,  0.8,  0.9,  1]
```

We can do something like this, and generate a array with all ones and all zeros:

```
>>>np.ones([2, 4])
array([[1., 1., 1., 1.], [1., 1., 1., 1.]])
>>>np.zeros([3,4])
array([[0., 0., 0., 0.], [0., 0., 0., 0.], [0., 0., 0., 0.]])
```

Wow!

If you have done higher school math, you know that we need all these matrixes to perform many algebraic operations. And guess what, most of the Python machine learning libraries also do that!

```
>>>np.linspace(0, 2, 10)
array([    0.,      0.22222222,     0.44444444,     0.66666667,
0.88888889,     1.11111111,     1.33333333,     1.55555556,     1.77777778,
2,     ])
```

The `linespace` function returns number samples which are evenly spaced, calculated over the interval from the start and end values. In the given example we were trying to get 10 sample in the range of 0 to 2.

Similarly, we can do this at the log scale. The function here is:

```
>>>np.logspace(0,1)
array([    1.,      1.04811313,     1.09854114,     1.1513954,     7.90604321,
8.28642773,     8.68511374,     9.10298178,     9.54095476,     10.,     ])
```

You can still execute Python's help function to get more details about the parameter and the return values.

```
>>>help(np.logspace)
Help on function logspace in module NumPy.core.function_base:


logspace(start, stop, num=50, endpoint=True, base=10.0)
    Return numbers spaced evenly on a log scale.


    In linear space, the sequence starts at ``base ** start``
    (`base` to the power of `start`) and ends with ``base ** stop``
```

```
(see `endpoint` below).

Parameters
----------
start : float
```

So we have to provide the start and end and the number of samples we want on the scale; in this case, we also have to provide a base.

Extracting data from an array

We can do all sorts of manipulation and filtering on the ndarrays. Let's start with a new Ndarray, `A`:

```
>>>A = array([[0, 0, 0], [0, 1, 2], [0, 2, 4], [0, 3, 6]])

>>>B = np.array([n for n in range n for n in range(4)])
>>>B
array([0, 1, 2, 3])
```

We can do this kind of conditional operation, and it's very elegant. We can observe this in the following example:

```
>>>less_than_3 = B<3 # we are filtering the items that are less than 3.
>>>less_than_3
array([ True,  True,  True, False], dtype=bool)
>>>B[less_than_3]
array([0, 1, 2])
```

We can also assign a value to all these values, as follows:

```
>>>B[less_than_3] = 0
>>>: B
array([0, 0, 0, 3])
```

There is a way to get the diagonal of the given matrix. Let's get the diagonal for our matrix `A`:

```
>>>np.diag(A)
array([0, 1, 4])
```

Complex matrix operations

One of the common matrix operations is element-wise multiplication, where we will multiply one element of a matrix by an element of another matrix. The shape of the resultant matrix will be same as the input matrix, for example:

```
>>>A = np.array([[1,2],[3,4]])
>>>A * A
array([[ 1,  4], [ 9, 16]])
```

> However, we can't perform the following operation, which will throw an error when executed:
>
> ```
> >>>A * B
> ---------------------------------------------------------------
> ----------------
> ValueError Traceback (most recent call last)
> <ipython-input-53-e2f71f566704> in <module>()
> ----> 1 A*B
> ```
>
> **ValueError**: Operands could not be broadcast together with shapes (2,2) (4,).
>
> Simply, the numbers of columns of the first operand have to match the number of rows in the second operand for matrix multiplication to work.

Let's do the dot product, which is the backbone of many optimization and algebraic operations. I still feel doing this in a traditional environment was not very efficient. Let's see how easy it is in NumPy, and how super-efficient it is in terms of memory.

```
>>>np.dot(A, A)
array([[ 7, 10], [15, 22]])
```

We can do operations like add, subtract, and transpose, as shown in the following example:

```
>>>A - A
array([[0, 0], [0, 0]])
>>>A + A
array([[2, 4], [6, 8]])
>>>np.transpose(A)
array([[1, 3], [2, 4]])
>>>>A
array([[1, 2], [2, 3]])
```

The same transpose operations can be performed using an alternative operation, such as this:

```
>>>A.T
array([[1, 3], [2, 4]])
```

We can also cast these ndarrays into a matrix and perform matrix operations, as shown in the following example:

```
>>>M = np.matrix(A)
>>>M
matrix([[1, 2], [3, 4]])
>>> np.conjugate(M)
matrix([[1, 2], [3, 4]])
>>> np.invert(M)
matrix([[-2, -3], [-4, -5]])
```

We can perform all sorts of complex matrix operations with NumPy, and they are pretty simple to use too! Please have a look at documentation for more information on NumPy.

Let's switch back to some of the common mathematics operations, such as min, max, mean, and standard deviation, for the given array elements. We have generated the normal distributed random numbers. Let's see how these things can be applied there:

```
>>>N = np.random.randn(1,10)
>>>N
array([[    0.59238571,     -0.22224549,     0.6753678,     0.48092087,
-0.37402105,     -0.54067842,     0.11445297,     -0.02483442,
-0.83847935,     0.03480181,     ]])
>>>N.mean()
-0.010232957191371551
>>>N.std()
0.47295594072935421
```

This was an example demonstrating how NumPy can be used to perform simple mathematic and algebraic operations of finding out the mean and standard deviation of a set of numbers.

Reshaping and stacking

In case of some of the numeric, algebraic operations we do need to change the shape of resultant matrix based on the input matrices. NumPy has some of the easiest ways of reshaping and stacking the matrix in whichever way you want.

```
>>>A
array([[1, 2], [3, 4]])
```

If we want a flat matrix, we just need to reshape it using NumPy's `reshape()` function:

```
>>>>(r, c)  = A.shape  # r is rows and c is columns
>>>>r,c
(2L, 2L)
>>>>A.reshape((1, r * c))
array([[1, 2, 3, 4]])
```

This kind of reshaping is required in many algebraic operations. To flatten the ndarray, we can use the `flatten()` function:

```
>>>A.flatten()
array([1, 2, 3, 4])
```

There is a function to repeat the same elements of the given array. We need to just specify the number of times we want the element to repeat. To repeat the ndarray, we can use the `repeat()` function:

```
>>>np.repeat(A, 2)
array([1, 1, 2, 2, 3, 3, 4, 4])
>>>>A
array([[1, 2],[3, 4]])
```

In the preceding example, each element is repeated twice in sequence. A similar function known as `tile()` is used for for repeating the matrix, and is shown here:

```
>>>np.tile(A, 4)
array([[1, 2, 1, 2, 1, 2, 1, 2], [3, 4, 3, 4, 3, 4, 3, 4]])
```

There are also ways to add a row or a column to the matrix. If we want to add a row, we use the `concatenate()` function shown here:

```
>>>B = np.array([[5, 6]])
>>>np.concatenate((A, B), axis=0)
array([[1, 2], [3, 4], [5, 6]])
```

This can also be achieved using the `Vstack()` function shown here:

```
>>>np.vstack((A, B))
array([[1, 2], [3, 4], [5, 6]])
```

Also, if you want to add a column, you can use the `concatenate()` function in the following manner:

```
>>>np.concatenate((A, B.T), axis=1)
array([[1, 2, 5], [3, 4, 6]])
```

> Alternatively, the `hstack()` function can be used to add columns. This is used very similarly to the `vstack()` function in the example shown above.

Random numbers

Random number generation is also used across many tasks involving NLP and machine learning tasks. Let's see how easy it is to get a random sample:

```
>>>from numpy import random
>>>#uniform random number from [0,1]
>>>random.rand(2, 5)
array([[ 0.82787406, 0.21619509, 0.24551583, 0.91357419, 0.39644969], [
0.91684427, 0.34859763, 0.87096617, 0.31916835, 0.09999382]])
```

There is one more function called `random.randn()`, which generates normally distributed random numbers in the given range. So, in the following example, we want random numbers between `2` and `5`.

```
>>>>random.randn(2, 5)
array([[-0.59998393, -0.98022613, -0.52050449, 0.73075943, -0.62518516],
[ 1.00288355, -0.89613323,  0.59240039, -0.89803825, 0.11106479]])
```

This is achieved by using the function `random.randn(2,5)`.

SciPy

Scientific Python or SciPy is a framework built on top of NumPy and ndarray and was essentially developed for advanced scientific operations such as optimization, integration, algebraic operations, and Fourier transforms.

The concept was to efficiently use ndarrays to provide some of these common scientific algorithms in a memory-efficient manner. Because of NumPy and SciPy, we are in a state where we can focus on writing libraries such as scikit-learn and NLTK, which focus on domain-specific problems, while NumPy / SciPy do the heavy lifting for us. We will give you a brief overview of the data structures and common operations provided in SciPy. We get the details of some of the black-box libraries, such as scikit-learn and understand what goes on behind the scenes.

```
>>>import scipy as sp
```

This is how you import SciPy. I am using `sp` as an alias but you can import everything.

Let's start with something we are more familiar with. Let's see how integration can be achieved here, using the `quad()` function.

```
>>>from scipy.integrate import quad, dblquad, tplquad
>>>def f(x):
>>>     return x
>>>x_lower == 0 # the lower limit of x
>>>x_upper == 1 # the upper limit of x
>>>val, abserr = = quad(f, x_lower, x_upper)
>>>print val,abserr
>>> 0.5 , 5.55111512313e-15
```

If we integrate the `x`, it will be x2/2, which is `0.5`. There are other scientific functions, such as these:

- Interpolation (`scipy.interpolate`)
- Fourier transforms (`scipy.fftpack`)
- Signal processing (`scipy.signal`)

But we will focus on only linear algebra and optimization because these are more relevant in the context of machine learning and NLP.

Linear algebra

The linear algebra module contains a lot of matrix-related functions. Probably the best contribution of SciPy is sparse matrix (CSR matrix), which is used heavily in other packages for manipulation of matrices.

SciPy provides one of the best ways of storing sparse matrices and doing data manipulation on them. It also provides some of the common operations, such as linear equation solving. It has a great way of solving eigenvalues and eigenvectors, matrix functions (for example, matrix exponentiation), and more complex operations such as decompositions (SVD). Some of these are the behind-the-scenes optimization in our ML routines. For example, SVD is the simplest form of LDA (topic modeling) that we used in *Chapter 6, Text Classification*.

The following is an example showing how the linear algebra module can be used:

```
>>>A = = sp.rand(2, 2)
>>>B = = sp.rand(2, 2)
>>>import Scipy
>>>X = = solve(A, B)
>>>from Scipy import linalg as LA
>>>X = = LA.solve(A, B)
>>>LA.dot(A, B)
```

[Detailed documentation is available at `http://docs.scipy.org/doc/Scipy/reference/linalg.html`.]

eigenvalues and eigenvectors

In some of the NLP and machine learning applications, we represent the documents as term document matrices. Eigenvalues and eigenvectors are typically calculated for many different mathematical formulations. Say A is our matrix, and there exists a vector v such that $Av=\lambda v$.

In this case, λ will be our eigenvalue and v will be our eigenvector. One of the most commonly used operation, the **singular value decomposition** (**SVD**)will require some calculus functionality. It's quite simple to achieve this in SciPy.

```
>>>evals = LA.eigvals(A)
>>>evals
array([-0.32153198+0.j, 1.40510412+0.j])
```

And eigen vectors are as follows:

```
>>>evals, evect = LA.eig(A)
```

We can perform other matrix operations, such as inverse, transpose, and determinant:

```
>>>LA.inv(A)
array([[-1.24454719, 1.97474827], [ 1.84807676, -1.15387236]])
>>>LA.det(A)
-0.4517859060209965
```

The sparse matrix

In a real-world scenario, when we use a typical matrix, most of the elements of this matrix are zeroes. It is highly inefficient to go over all these non-zero elements for any matrix operation. As a solution to this kind of problem, a sparse matrix format has been introduced, with the simple idea of storing only non-zero items.

A matrix in which most of the elements are non-zeroes is called a dense matrix, and the matrix in which most of the elements are zeroes is called a sparse matrix.

A matrix is typically a 2D array with an index of row and column will provide the value of the element. Now there are different ways in which we can store sparse matrices:

- **DOK** (**Dictionary of keys**): Here, we store the dictionary with keys in the format (*row*, *col*) and the values are stored as dictionary values.
- **LOL** (**list of list**): Here, we provide one list per row, with only an index of the non-zero elements.
- **COL** (**Coordinate list**): Here, a list (*row*, *col*, *value*) is stored as a list.
- **CRS/CSR** (**Compressed row Storage**): A CSR matrix reads values first by column; a row index is stored for each value, and column pointers are stored (*val*, *row_ind*, *col_ptr*). Here, *val* is an array of the non-zero values of the matrix, *row_ind* represents the row indices corresponding to the values, and *col_ptr* is the list of *val* indexes where each column starts. The name is based on the fact that column index information is compressed relative to the COO format. This format is efficient for arithmetic operations, column slicing, and matrix-vector products.

> See `http://docs.scipy.org/doc/Scipy-0.15.1/reference/generated/Scipy.sparse.csr_matrix.html` for more information.

- **CSC** (**sparse column**): This is similar to CSR, except that the values are read first by column; a row index is stored for each value, and column pointers are stored. In otherwords, CSC is (*val*, *row_ind*, *col_ptr*).

> Have a look at the documentation at:
> `http://docs.scipy.org/doc/Scipy-0.15.1/reference/generated/Scipy.sparse.csc_matrix.html`

Let's have some hands-on experience with CSR matrix manipulation. We have a sparse matrix A:

```
>>>from scipy import sparse as s
>>>A = array([[1,0,0],[0,2,0],[0,0,3]])
>>>A
array([[1, 0, 0], [0, 2, 0], [0, 0, 3]])
>>>from scipy import sparse as sp
>>>C = = sp.csr_matrix(A);
>>>C
<3x3 sparse matrix of type '<type 'NumPy.int32'>'
    with 3 stored elements in Compressed Sparse Row format>
```

If you read very carefully, the CSR matrix stored just three elements. Let's see what it stored:

```
>>>C.toarray()
array([[1, 0, 0], [0, 2, 0], [0, 0, 3]])
>>>C * C.todense()
matrix([[1, 0, 0], [0, 4, 0], [0, 0, 9]])
```

This is exactly what we are looking for. Without going over all the zeroes, we still got the same results with the CSR matrix.

```
>>>dot(C, C).todense()
```

Optimization

I hope you understand that every time we have built a classifier or a tagger in the background, all these are some sort of optimization routine. Let's have some basic understanding about the function provided in SciPy. We will start with getting a minima of the given polynomial. Let's jump to one of the example snippets of the optimization routine provided by SciPy.

```
>>>def f(x):
>>>    returnx          return x**2-4
>>>optimize.fmin_bfgs(f,0)
Optimization terminated successfully.
         Current function value: -4.000000
         Iterations: 0
```

```
        Function evaluations: 3
        Gradient evaluations: 1
array([0])
```

Here, the first argument is the function you want the minima of, and the second is the initial guess for the minima. In this example, we already knew that zero will be the minima. To get more details, use the function `help()`, as shown here:

```
>>>help(optimize.fmin_bfgs)
Help on function fmin_bfgs in module Scipy.optimize.optimize:


fmin_bfgs(f, x0, fprime=None, args=(), gtol=1e-05, norm=inf,
epsilon=1.4901161193847656e-08, maxiter=None, full_output=0, disp=1,
retall=0, callback=None)
    Minimize a function using the BFGS algorithm.


    Parameters
    ----------
    f : callable f(x,*args)
        Objective function to be minimized.
    x0 : ndarray
        Initial guess.
>>>from scipy import optimize
          optimize.fsolve(f, 0.2)
array([ 0.46943096])


>>>def f1 def f1(x,y):
>>>    return x ** 2+  y ** 2 - 4
>>>optimize.fsolve(f1, 0, 0)
array([ 0.])
```

To summarize, we now have enough knowledge about SciPy's most basic data structures, and some of the most common optimization techniques. The intention was to motivate you to not just run black-box machine learning or natural language processing, but to go beyond that and get the mathematical context about the ML algorithms you are using and also have a look at the source code and try to understand it.

Implementing this will not just help your understanding about the algorithm, but also allow you to optimize/customize the implementation to your need.

pandas

Let's talk about pandas, which is one of the most exciting Python libraries, especially for people who love **R** and want to play around with the data in a more vectorized manner. We will devote this part of the chapter only to pandas; we will discuss some basic data manipulation and handling in pandas frames.

Reading data

Let's start with one of the most important tasks in any data analysis to parse the data from a CSV/other file.

> I am using `https://archive.ics.uci.edu/ml/machine-learning-databases/adult/adult.data and attributes`
>
> `https://archive.ics.uci.edu/ml/machine-learning-databases/iris/iris.names`
>
> Feel free to use any other CSV file.

To begin, please download the data to your local storage from the preceding links, and load it into a pandas data-frame, as shown here:

```
>>>import pandas as pd
>>># Please provide the absolute path of the input file
>>>data = pd.read_csv("PATH\\iris.data.txt",header=0")
>>>data.head()
```

	4.9	**3.0**	**1.4**	**0.2**	**Iris-setosa**
0	4.7	3.2	1.3	0.2	Iris-setosa
1	4.6	3.1	1.5	0.2	Iris-setosa
2	5.0	3.6	1.4	0.2	Iris-setosa

This will read a CSV file and store it in a DataFrame. Now, there are many options you have while reading a CSV file. One of the problems is that we read the first line of the data in this DataFrame as a header; to use the actual header, we need to set the option header to None, and pass a list of names as column names. If we already have the header in perfect form in the CSV, we don't need to worry about the header as pandas, by default, assumes the first line to be the header. The header 0 in the preceding code is actually the row number that will be treated as the header.

So let's use the same data, and add the header into the frame:

```
>>>data = pd.read_csv("PATH\\iris.data.txt", names=["sepal length",
"sepal width", "petal length", "petal width", "Cat"], header=None)
>>>data.head()
```

	sepal length	sepal width	petal length	petal width	Cat
0	4.9	3.0	1.4	0.2	Iris-setosa
1	4.7	3.2	1.3	0.2	Iris-setosa
2	4.6	3.1	1.5	0.2	Iris-setosa

This has created temporary column names for the frame so that, in case you have headers in the file as a first row, you can drop the header option, and pandas will detect the first row of the file as the header. The other common options are Sep/ Delimiter, where you want to specify the delimiter used to separate the columns. There are at least 20 different options available, which can be used to optimize the way we read and cleanse our data, for example removing Na's, removing blank lines, and indexing based on the specific column. Please have a look at the different type of files:

- `read_csv`: reading a CSV file.
- `read_excel`: reading a XLS file.
- `read_hdf`: reading a HDFS file.
- `read_sql`: reading a SQL file.
- `read_json`: reading a JSON file.

These can be the substitutes for all the different parsing methods we discussed in *Chapter 2, Text Wrangling and Cleansing*. The same numbers of options are available to write files too.

Now let's see the power of pandas frames. If you are an R programmer, you would love to see the summary and header option we have in R.

```
>>>data.describe()
```

The `describe()` function will give you a brief summary of each column and the unique values.

```
>>>sepal_len_cnt=data['sepal length'].value_counts()
>>>sepal_len_cnt

5.0    10
6.3     9
6.7     8
5.7     8
5.1     8
dtype: int64
>>>data['Iris-setosa'].value_counts()
Iris-versicolor    50
Iris-virginica     50
Iris-setosa        48
dtype: int64
```

Again for R lovers, we are now dealing with vectors, so that we can look for each value of the column by using something like this:

```
>>>data['Iris-setosa'] == 'Iris-setosa'
0      True
1      True

147     False
148     False
Name: Iris-setosa, Length: 149, dtype: bool
```

Now we can filter the DataFrame in place. Here the setosa will have only entries related to `Iris-setosa`.

```
>>>sntsosa=data[data['Cat'] == 'Iris-setosa']
>>>sntsosa[:5]
```

This is our typical SQL `Group By` function. We have all kinds of aggregate functions as well.

> You can browse through the following link to look at Dow Jones data:
> `https://archive.ics.uci.edu/ml/machine-learning-databases/00312/`

Series data

Pandas also have a neat way of indexing by date, and then using the frame for all sorts of time series kind of analysis. The best part is that once we have indexed the data by date some of the most painful operations on the dates will be a command away from us. Let's take a look at series data, such as stock price data for a few stocks, and how the values of the opening and closing stock change weekly.

```
>>>import pandas as pd
>>>stockdata = pd.read_csv("dow_jones_index.data",parse_dates=['date'],
index_col=['date'], nrows=100)
>>>>stockdata.head()
```

date	quarter	stock	open	high	low	close	volume	percent_change_price
01/07/2011	1	AA	$15.82	$16.72	$15.78	$16.42	239655616	3.79267
01/14/2011	1	AA	$16.71	$16.71	$15.64	$15.97	242963398	-4.42849
01/21/2011	1	AA	$16.19	$16.38	$15.60	$15.79	138428495	-2.47066

```
>>>max(stockdata['volume'])
   1453438639
>>>max(stockdata['percent_change_price'])
   7.62173999999999991
>>>stockdata.index
<class 'pandas.tseries.index.DatetimeIndex'>
[2011-01-07, ..., 2011-01-28]
Length: 100, Freq: None, Timezone: None
>>>stockdata.index.day
array([ 7, 14, 21, 28, 4, 11, 18, 25, 4, 11, 18, 25, 7, 14, 21, 28, 4,11,
18, 25, 4, 11, 18, 25, 7, 14, 21, 28, 4])
```

The preceding command gives the day of the week for each date.

```
>>>stockdata.index.month
```

The preceding command lists different values by month.

```
>>>stockdata.index.year
```

The preceding command lists different values by year.

You can aggregate the data using a resample with whatever aggregation you want. It could be sum, mean, median, min, or max.

```
>>>import numpy as np
>>>stockdata.resample('M', how=np.sum)
```

Column transformation

Say we want to filter out columns or to add a column. We can achieve this by just by providing a list of columns as an argument to `axis 1`. We can drop the columns from a data frame like this:

```
>>>stockdata.drop(["percent_change_volume_over_last_wk"],axis=1)
```

Let's filter out some of the unwanted columns, and work with a limited set of columns. We can create a new `DataFrame` like this:

```
>>>stockdata_new = pd.DataFrame(stockdata, columns=["stock","open","high"
,"low","close","volume"])
>>>stockdata_new.head()
```

We can also run R-like operations on the columns. Say I want to rename the columns. I can do something like this:

```
>>>stockdata["previous_weeks_volume"] = 0
```

This will change all the values in the column to 0. We can do it conditionally and create derived variables in place.

Noisy data

A typical day in the life of a data scientist starts with data cleaning. Removing noise, cleaning unwanted files, making sure that date formats are correct, ignoring noisy records, and dealing with missing values. Typically, the biggest chunk of time is spent on data cleansing rather than on any other activity.

In a real-world scenario, the data is messy in most cases, and we have to deal with missing values, null values, Na's, and other formatting issues. So one of the major features of any data library is to deal with all these problems and address them in an efficient way. pandas provide some amazing features to deal with some of these problems.

```
>>>stockdata.head()
```

```
>>>stockdata.dropna().head(2)
```

Using the preceding command we get rid of all the Na's from our data.

date	quarter	Stock	open	high	low	close	volume	percent_ change_ price
01/14/2011	1	AA	$16.71	$16.71	$15.64	$15.97	242963398	-4.42849
01/21/2011	1	AA	$16.19	$16.38	$15.60	$15.79	138428495	-2.47066
01/28/2011	1	AA	$15.87	$16.63	$15.82	$16.13	151379173	1.63831

You also noticed that we have a $ symbol in front of the value, which makes the numeric operation hard. Let's get rid of that, as it will give us noisy results otherwise (for example. $43.86 is not among the top values here).

```
>>>import numpy
```

```
>>>stockdata_new.open.describe()
count          100
unique          99
top        $43.86
freq          2
Name: open, dtype: object
```

We can perform some operations on two columns, and derive a new variable out of this:

```
>>>stockdata_new.open = stockdata_new.open.str.replace('$', '').convert_
objects(convert_numeric=True)
```

```
>>>stockdata_new.close = stockdata_new.close.str.replace('$', '').
convert_objects(convert_numeric=True)
```

```
>>>(stockdata_new.close - stockdata_new.open).convert_objects(convert_
numeric=True)
```

```
>>>stockdata_new.open.describe()
count     100.000000
mean       51.286800
std        32.154889
min        13.710000
25%        17.705000
50%        46.040000
75%        72.527500
max       106.900000
Name: open, dtype: float64
```

We can also perform some arithmetic operations, and create new variables out of it.

```
>>>stockdata_new['newopen'] = stockdata_new.open.apply(lambda x: 0.8 * x)
>>>stockdata_new.newopen.head(5)
```

We can filter the data on the value of a column in this way too. For example, let's filter out a dataset for one of the companies among all those that we have the stock values for.

```
>>>stockAA = stockdata_new.query('stock=="AA"')
>>>stockAA.head()
```

To summarize, we have seen some useful functions related to data reading, cleaning, manipulation, and aggregation in this section of pandas. In the next section, will try to use some of these data frames to generate visualization out of this data.

matplotlib

matplotlib is a very popular visualization library written in Python. We will cover some of the most commonly used visualizations. Let's start by importing the library:

```
>>>import matplotlib
>>>import matplotlib.pyplot as plt
>>>import numpy
```

We will use the same running data set from the Dow Jones index for some of the visualizations now. We already have stock data for company "AA". Let's make one more frame for a new company CSCO, and plot some of these:

```
>>>stockCSCO = stockdata_new.query('stock=="CSCO"')
>>>stockCSCO.head()
>>>from matplotlib import figure
>>>plt.figure()
>>>plt.scatter(stockdata_new.index.date,stockdata_new.volume)
>>>plt.xlabel('day') # added the name of the x axis
>>>plt.ylabel('stock close value') # add label to y-axis
>>>plt.title('title') # add the title to your graph
>>>plt.savefig("matplot1.jpg")  # savefig in local
```

You can also save the figure as a JPEG/PNG file. This can be done using the `savefig()` function shown here:

```
>>>plt.savefig("matplot1.jpg")
```

Subplot

Subplot is the best way to layout your plots. This works as a canvas, where we can add not just one plot but multiple plots. In this example, we have tried to put four plots with the parameters numrow, numcol which will define the canvas and the next argument in the plot number.

```
>>>plt.subplot(2, 2, 1)
>>>plt.plot(stockAA.index.weekofyear, stockAA.open, 'r--')
>>>plt.subplot(2, 2, 2)
>>>plt.plot(stockCSCO.index.weekofyear, stockCSCO.open, 'g-*')
>>>plt.subplot(2, 2, 3)
>>>plt.plot(stockAA.index.weekofyear, stockAA.open, 'g--')
>>>plt.subplot(2, 2, 4)
>>>plt.plot(stockCSCO.index.weekofyear, stockCSCO.open, 'r-*')
>>>plt.subplot(2, 2, 3)
```

```
>>>plt.plot(x, y, 'g--')
>>>plt.subplot(2, 2, 4)
>>>plt.plot(x, y, 'r-*')
>>>fig.savefig("matplot2.png")
```

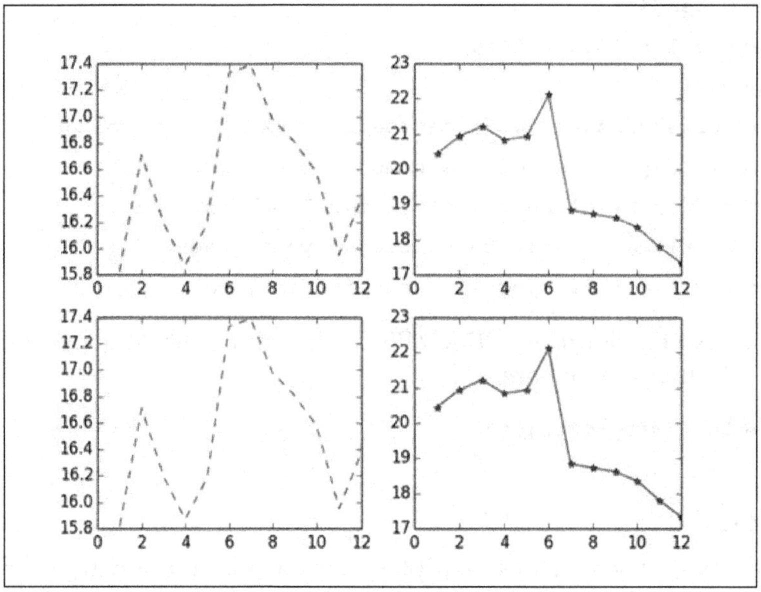

We can do something more elegant for plotting many plots at one go!

```
>>>fig, axes = plt.subplots(nrows=1, ncols=2)
>>>for ax in axes:
>>>      ax.plot(x, y, 'r')
>>>      ax.set_xlabel('x')
>>>      ax.set_ylabel('y')
>>>      ax.set_title('title');
```

As you case see, there are ways to code a lot more like in typical Python to handle different aspects of the plots you want to achieve.

Adding an axis

We can add an axis to the figure by using `addaxis()`. By adding an axis to the figure, we can define our own drawing area. `addaxis()` takes the following arguments:

```
*rect* [*left*, *bottom*, *width*, *height*]
>>>fig = plt.figure()
>>>axes = fig.add_axes([0.1, 0.1, 0.8, 0.8]) # left, bottom, width,
height (range 0 to 1)
>>>axes.plot(x, y, 'r')
```

Let' plot some of the most commonly used type of plots. The great thing is that most of the parameters, such as title and label, still work in the same way. Only the kind of plot will change.

If you want to add an x label, a y label, and a title with the axis; the commands are as follows:

```
>>>fig = plt.figure()
>>>ax = fig.add_axes([0.1, 0.1, 0.8, 0.8])
>>>ax.plot(stockAA.index.weekofyear,stockAA.open,label="AA")
>>>ax.plot(stockAA.index.weekofyear,stockCSCO.open,label="CSCO")
>>>ax.set_xlabel('weekofyear')
>>>ax.set_ylabel('stock value')
>>>ax.set_title('Weekly change in stock price')
>>>ax.legend(loc=2); # upper left corner
>>>plt.savefig("matplot3.jpg")
```

Try writing the preceding code and observe the output!

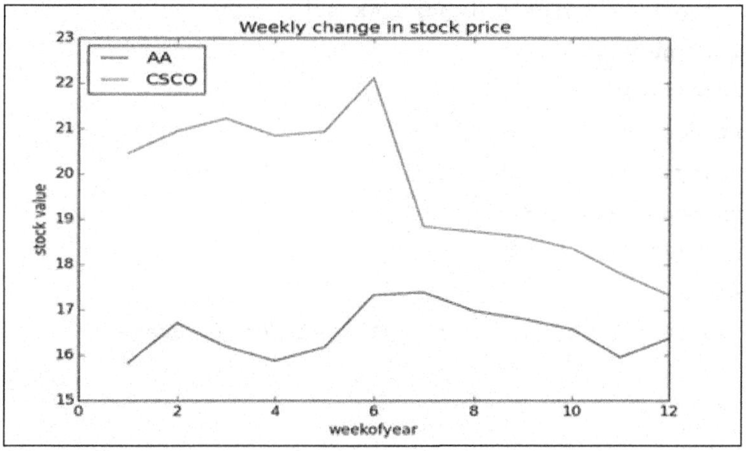

A scatter plot

One of the simplest forms of plotting is to plot the y-axis point for different x-axis values. In the following example, we have tried to capture the variation of the stock price weekly in a scatter plot:

```
>>>import matplotlib.pyplot as plt
>>>plt.scatter(stockAA.index.weekofyear,stockAA.open)
>>>plt.savefig("matplot4.jpg")
>>>plt.close()
```

A bar plot

Intuitively, the distribution of the y axis is shown against the x axis in the following bar chart. In the following example, we have used a bar plot to display data on a graph.

```
>>>n = 12
>>>X = np.arange(n)
>>>Y1 = np.random.uniform(0.5, 1.0, n)
>>>Y2 = np.random.uniform(0.5, 1.0, n)
>>>plt.bar(X, +Y1, facecolor='#9999ff', edgecolor='white')
>>>plt.bar(X, -Y2, facecolor='#ff9999', edgecolor='white')
```

3D plots

We can also build some spectacular 3D visualizations in matplotlib. The following example shows how one can create a 3D plot using matplotlib:

```
>>>from mpl_toolkits.mplot3d import Axes3D
>>>fig = plt.figure()
>>>ax = Axes3D(fig)
>>>X = np.arange(-4, 4, 0.25)
>>>Y = np.arange(-4, 4, 0.25)
>>>X, Y = np.meshgrid(X, Y)
>>>R = np.sqrt(X**2+ + Y**2)
>>>Z = np.sin(R)
>>>ax.plot_surface(X, Y, Z, rstride=1, cstride=1, cmap='hot')
```

External references

I like to encourage readers to go over some of the following links for more details about the individual libraries, and for more resources:

- `http://www.NumPy.org/`
- `http://www.Scipy.org/`
- `http://pandas.pydata.org/`
- `http://matplotlib.org/`

Summary

This chapter was a brief summary of some of the most fundamental libraries of Python that do a lot of heavy lifting for us when we deal with text and other data. NumPy helps us in dealing with numeric operations and the kind of data structure required for some of these. SciPy has many scientific operations that are used in various Python libraries. We learned how to use these functions and data structures.

We have also touched upon pandas, which is a very efficient library for data manipulation, and has been getting a lot of mileage in recent times. Finally, we gave you a quick view of one of Python's most commonly used visualization libraries, matplotlib.

In the next chapter, we will focus on social media. We will see how to capture data from some of the common social networks and produce meaningful insights around social media.

9
Social Media Mining in Python

This chapter is all about social media. Though it's not directly related to NLTK / NLP, social data is also a very rich source of unstructured text data. So, as NLP enthusiasts, we should have the skill to play with social data. We will try to explore how to gather relevant data from some of the most popular social media platforms. We will cover how to gather data from Twitter, Facebook, and so on using Python APIs. We will explore some of the most common use cases in the context of social media mining, such as trending topics, sentiment analysis, and so on.

You already learned a lot of topics under the concepts of natural language processing and machine learning in the last few chapters. We will try to build some of the applications around social data in this chapter. We will also provide you with some of the best practices to deal with social data, and look at social data from the context of graph visualization.

There is a graph that underlies social media and most of the graph-based problems can be formulated as information flow problems and finding out the busiest node in the graph. Some of the problems such as trending topics, influencer detection, and sentiment analysis are examples of these. Let's take some of these use cases, and build some cool applications around these social networks.

By the end of this chapter,:

- You should be able to collect data from any social media using APIs.
- You will also learn to formulate the data in a structured format and how to build some amazing applications.
- Lastly, we will be able to visualize and gain meaningful insight out of social media.

Data collection

The most important objective of this chapter is to gather data across some of the most common social networks. We will look mainly at Twitter and Facebook and try to give you enough details about the API and how to effectively use them to get relevant data. We will also talk about the data dictionary for scrapped data, and how we can build some cool apps using some of the stuff we learned so far.

Twitter

We will start with one of the most popular and open social media that is completely public. This means that practically, you can gather entire Twitter stream, which is payable, while you can capture one percent of the stream for free. In the context of business, Twitter is a very rich resource of information such as public sentiments and emerging topics.

Let's get directly to face the main challenge of getting the tweets relevant to your use case.

> The following is the repository of many Twitter libraries. These libraries are not verified by Twitter, but run on the Twitter API.
>
> `https://dev.twitter.com/overview/api/twitter-libraries`

There are more than 10 Python libraries there. So pick and choose the one you like. I generally use Tweepy and we will use it to run the examples in this book. Most of the libraries are wrappers around the Twitter API, and the parameters and signatures of all these are roughly the same.

The simplest way to install Tweepy is to install it using `pip`:

```
$ pip install tweepy
```

> The hard way is to build it from source. The GitHub link to Tweepy is: `https://github.com/tweepy/tweepy`.

To get Tweepy to work, you have to create a developer account with Twitter and get the access tokens for your application. Once you complete this, you will get your credentials and below these, the keys. Go through `https://apps.twitter.com/app/new` for registration and access tokens. The following snapshot shows the access tokens:

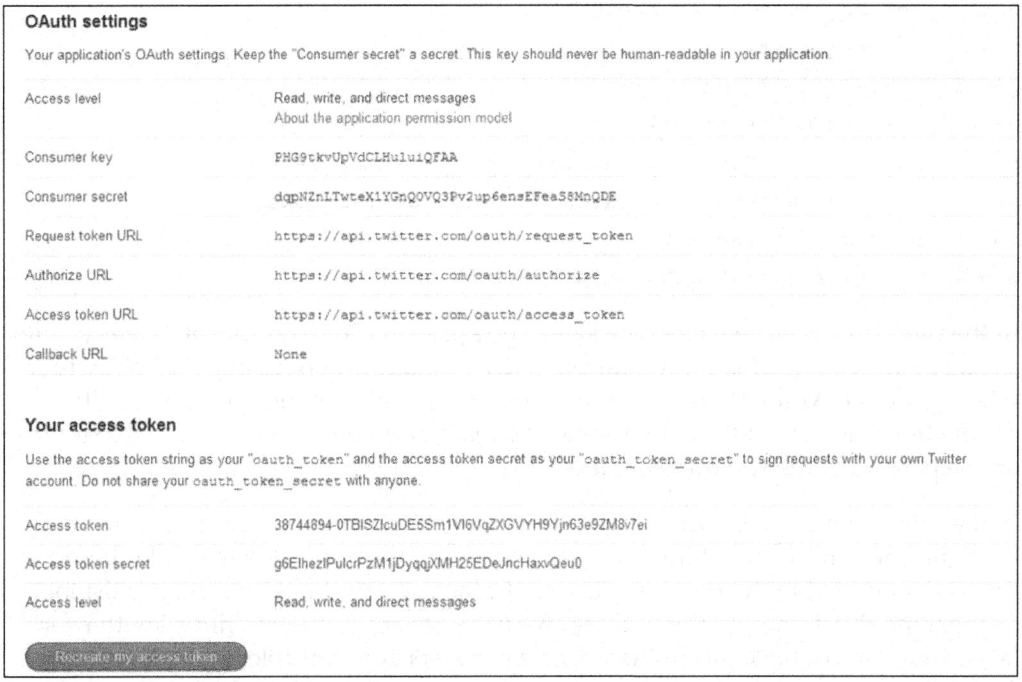

We will start with a very simple example to gather data using Twitter's streaming API. We are using Tweepy to capture the Twitter stream to gather all the tweets related to the given keywords:

```
tweetdump.py
>>>from tweepy.streaming import StreamListener
>>>from tweepy import OAuthHandler
>>>from tweepy import Stream
>>>import sys
>>>consumer_key = 'ABCD012XXXXXXXXx'
>>>consumer_secret = 'xyz123xxxxxxxxxxxxx'
>>>access_token = '000000-ABCDXXXXXXXXXXX'
>>>access_token_secret ='XXXXXXXXXgaw2KYz0VcqCO0F3U4'
>>>class StdOutListener(StreamListener):
>>>    def on_data(self, data):
>>>        with open(sys.argv[1],'a') as tf:
>>>            tf.write(data)
>>>        return
```

```
>>>     def on_error(self, status):
>>>         print(status)
>>>if __name__ == '__main__':
>>>     l = StdOutListener()
>>>     auth = OAuthHandler(consumer_key, consumer_secret)
>>>     auth.set_access_token(access_token, access_token_secret)
>>>     stream = Stream(auth, l)
>>>     stream.filter(track=['Apple watch'])
```

In the preceding code, we used the same code given in the example of Tweepy, with a little modification. This is an example where we use the streaming API of Twitter, where we track **Apple Watch**. Twitter's streaming API provides you the facility of conducting a search on the actual Twitter stream and you can consume a maximum of one percent of the stream using this API.

In the preceding code, the main parts that you need to understand are the first and last four lines. In the initial lines, we are specifying the access tokens and other keys that we generated in the previous section. In the last four lines, we create a listener to consume the stream. In the last line, we use `stream.filter` to filter Twitter for keywords that we have put in the track. We can specify multiple keywords here. This will result in all the tweets that contain the term Apple Watch for our running example.

In the following example, we will load the tweets we have collected, and have a look at the tweet structure and how to extract meaningful information from it. A typical tweet JSON structure looks similar to:


```
{
"created_at":"Wed May 13 04:51:24 +0000 2015",
"id":598349803924369408,
"id_str":"598349803924369408",
"text":"Google launches its first Apple Watch app with News & Weather
http:\/\/t.co\/o1XMBmhnH2",
"source":"\u003ca href=\"http:\/\/ifttt.com\" rel=\"nofollow\"\
u003eIFTTT\u003c\/a\u003e",
"truncated":false,
"in_reply_to_status_id":null,
"user":{
"id":1461337266,
"id_str":"1461337266",
```

```
"name":"vestihitech \u0430\u0432\u0442\u043e\u043c\u0430\u0442",
"screen_name":"vestihitecha",
"location":"",
"followers_count":20,
"friends_count":1,
"listed_count":4,
""statuses_count":7442,
"created_at":"Mon May 27 05:51:27 +0000 2013",
"utc_offset":14400,
},
,
"geo":{ "latitude" : 51.4514285, "longitude"=-0.99
}
"place":"Reading, UK",
"contributors":null,
"retweet_count":0,
"favorite_count":0,
"entities":{
"hashtags":["apple watch", "google"
],
"trends":[
],
"urls":[
{
"url":"http:\/\/t.co\/o1XMBmhnH2",
"expanded_url":"http:\/\/ift.tt\/1HfqhCe",
"display_url":"ift.tt\/1HfqhCe",
"indices":[
66,
88
]
}
],
"user_mentions":[
],
"symbols":[
```

```
]
},
"favorited":false,
"retweeted":false,
"possibly_sensitive":false,
"filter_level":"low",
"lang":"en",
"timestamp_ms":"1431492684714"
}
]
```


Data extraction

Some of the most commonly used fields of interest in data extraction are:

- `text`: This is the content of the tweet provided by the user
- `user`: These are some of the main attributes about the user, such as username, location, and photos
- `Place`: This is where the tweets are posted, and also the geo coordinates
- `Entities`: Effectively, these are the hashtags and topics that a user attaches to his / her tweets

Every attribute in the previous figure can be a good use case for some of the social mining exercises done in practice. Let's jump onto the topic of how we can get to these attributes and convert them to a more readable form, or how we can process some of these:

Source: `tweetinfo.py`

```
>>>import json
>>>import sys
>>>tweets = json.loads(open(sys.argv[1]).read())

>>>tweet_texts = [ tweet['text']\
                                  for tweet in tweets ]
>>>tweet_source = [tweet ['source'] for tweet in tweets]
>>>tweet_geo = [tweet['geo'] for tweet in tweets]
```

```
>>>tweet_locations = [tweet['place'] for tweet in tweets]
>>>hashtags = [ hashtag['text'] for tweet in tweets for hashtag in
tweet['entities']['hashtags'] ]
>>>print tweet_texts
>>>print tweet_locations
>>>print tweet_geo
>>>print hashtags
```

The output of the preceding code will give you, as expected, four lists in which all the tweet content is in `tweet_texts` and the location of the tweets and hashtags.

> In the code, we are just loading a JSON output generated using `json.loads()`. I would recommend you to use an online tool such as Json Parser (`http://json.parser.online.fr/`) to get an idea of what your JSON looks like and what are its attributes (key and value).

Next, if you look, there are different levels in the JSON, where some of the attributes such as text have a direct value, while some of them have more nested information. This is the reason you see, where when we are looking at hashtags, we have to iterate one more level, while in case of text, we just fetch the values. Since our file actually has a list of tweets, we have to iterate that list to get all the tweets, while each tweet object will look like the example tweet structure.

Trending topics

Now, if we look for trending topics in this kind of a setup. One of the simplest ways to find them could be to look for frequency distribution of words across tweets. We already have a list of `tweet_text` that contains the tweets:

```
>>>import nltk
>>>from nltk import word_tokenize,sent_tokenize
>>>from nltk import FreqDist
>>>tweets_tokens = []

>>>for tweet in tweet_text:
>>>     tweets_tokens.append(word_tokenize(tweet))
```

```
>>>Topic_distribution = nltk.FreqDist(tweets_tokens)
>>>Freq_dist_nltk.plot(50, cumulative=False)
```

One other more complex way of doing this could be the use of the part of speech tagger that you learned in *Chapter 3, Part of Speech Tagging*. The theory is that most of the time, topics will be nouns or entities. So, the same exercise can be done like this. In the preceding code, we read every tweet and tokenize it, and then use POS as a filter to only select nouns as topics:

```
>>>import nltk
>>>Topics = []
>>>for tweet in tweet_text:
>>>     tagged = nltk.pos_tag(word_tokenize(tweet))
>>>     Topics_token = [word for word,pos in ] in tagged if pos in
['NN','NNP']
>>>     print Topics_token
```

If we want to see a much cooler example, we can gather tweets across time and then generate plots. This will give us a very clear idea of the trending topics. For example, the data we are looking for is "Apple Watch". This word should peak on the day when Apple launched Apple Watch and the day they started selling it. However, it will be interesting to see what kind of topics emerged apart from those, and how they trended over time.

Geovisualization

One of the other common application of social media is geo-based visualization. In the tweet structure, we saw attributes named geo, longitude, and latitude. Once you have access to these values, it is very easy to use some of the common visualization libraries, such as **D3**, to come up with something like this:

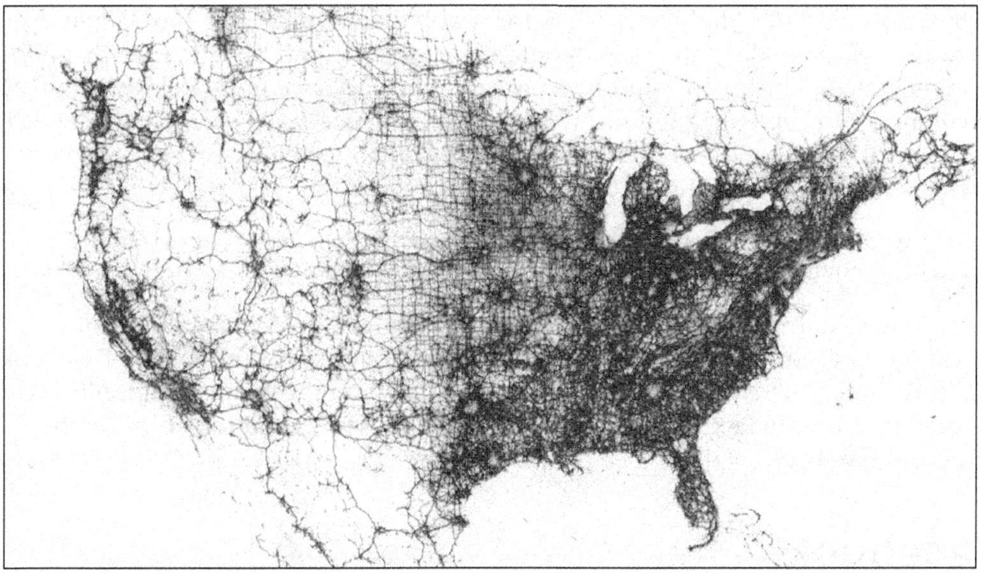

This is just an example of what we can achieve with these kind of visualizations; this was the visualization of a tweet in the U.S. We can clearly see the areas of increased intensity in eastern places such as New York. Now, a similar analysis done by a company on the customers can give a clear insight about which are some of the most popular places liked by our customer base. We can text mine these tweets for sentiment, and then we can infer insights about customers as to in which states they are not happy with the company and so on.

Influencers detection

Detection of important nodes in the social graph that has a lot of importance is another great problem in the context of social graphs. So, if we have millions of tweets streaming about our company, then one important use case would be to gather the most influential customers in the social media, and then target them for branding, marketing, or improving customer engagement.

In the case of Twitter, this goes back to the graph theory and concept of PageRank, where in a given node, if the ratio of outdegree and indegree is high, then that node is an influencer. This is very intuitive since people who have more followers than the number of people they follow are typically, influencers. One company, **KLOUT,** (`https://klout.com/`) has been focusing on a similar problem. Let's write a very basic and intuitive algorithm to calculate Klout's score:

```
>>>klout_scores = [ (tweet['user']['followers_count]/ tweet['user']
['friends_count'],tweet['user']) for tweet in tweets ]
```

Some of the examples where we worked on Twitter will hold exactly the same modification of content field. We can build a trending topic example with Facebook posts. We can also visualize Facebook users and post on the **geomap** and influencer kind of use cases. In fact, in the next section, we will see a variation of this in the context of Facebook.

Facebook

Facebook is a bit more personal, and somewhat private social network. Facebook does not allow you to gather the feeds/posts of the user simply for security and privacy reasons. So, Facebook's graph API has a limited way of accessing the feeds of the given page. I would recommend you to go to `https://developers.facebook.com/docs/graph-api/using-graph-api/v2.3` for better understanding.

The next question is how to access the Graph API using Python and how to get started with it. There are many wrappers written over Facebook's API, and we will use one the most common Facebook SDK:

```
$ pip install facebook-sdk
```

> You can also install it through:
> `https://github.com/Pythonforfacebook/facebook-sdk`.

The next step is to get the access token for the application while Facebook treats every API call as an application. Even for this data collection step, we will pretend to be an application.

> To get your token, go to:
> `https://developers.facebook.com/tools/explorer`.

We are all set now! Let's start with one of the most widely used Facebook graph APIs. In this API, Facebook provides a graph-based search for pages, users, events, places, and so on. So, the process of getting to the post becomes a two-stage process, where we have to look for a specific pageid / userid related to our topic of interest, and then we will be able to access the feeds of that page. One simple use case for this kind of an exercise could be to use the official page of a company and look for customer complaints. The way to go about this is:

```
>>>import facebook
>>>import json


>>>fo = open("fdump.txt",'w')
>>>ACCESS_TOKEN = 'XXXXXXXXXXX' # https://developers.facebook.com/tools/
explorer
>>>fb = facebook.GraphAPI(ACCESS_TOKEN)
>>>company_page = "326249424068240"
>>>content = fb.get_object(company_page)
>>>fo.write(json.dumps(content))
```

The code will attach the token to the Facebook Graph API and then we will make a REST call to Facebook. The problem with this is that we have to have the ID of the given page with us beforehand. The code which will attach the token is as follows:


```
"website":"www.dimennachildrenshistorymuseum.org",
"can_post":true,
"category_list":[
{
"id":"244600818962350",
"name":"History Museum"
},
{
"id":"187751327923426",
"name":"Educational Organization"
}
],
"likes":1793,
},
```

```
"id":"326249424068240",
"category":"Museum/art gallery",
"has_added_app":false,
"talking_about_count":8,
"location":{
"city":"New York",
"zip":"10024",
"country":"United States",
"longitude":-73.974413,
"state":"NY",
"street":"170 Central Park W",
"latitude":40.779236
},
"is_community_page":false,
"username":"nyhistorykids",
"description":"The first-ever museum bringing American history to life
through the eyes of children, where kids plus history equals serious
fun! Kids of all ages can practice their History Detective skills at
the DiMenna Children's History Museum and:\n\n\u2022 discover the past
through six historic figure pavilions\n\n\u2022!",
"hours":{
""thu_1_close":"18:00"
},
"phone":"(212) 873-3400",
"link":"https://www.facebook.com/nyhistorykids",
"price_range":"$ (0-10)",
"checkins":1011,
"about":"The DiMenna Children' History Museum is the first-ever museum
bringing American history to life through the eyes of children. Visit it
inside the New-York Historical Society!",
"name":"New-York Historical Society DiMenna Children's History Museum",
"cover":{
"source":"https://scontent.xx.fbcdn.net/hphotos-xpf1/t31.0-8/s720x720/104
9166_672951706064675_339973295_o.jpg",
"cover_id":"672951706064675",
```

```
"offset_x":0,
"offset_y":54,
"id":"672951706064675"
},
"were_here_count":1011,
"is_published":true
},
```

Here, we showed a similar schema for the Facebook data as we did for Twitter, and now we can see what kind of information is required for our use case. In most of the cases, the user post, category, name, about, and likes are some of the important fields. In this example, we are showing a page of a museum, but in a more business-driven use case, a company page has a long list of posts and other useful information that can give some great insights about it.

Let's say I have a Facebook page for my organization xyz.org and I want to know about the users who complained about me on the page; this is good for a use case such as complaint classification. The way to achieve the application now is simple enough. You need to look for a set of keywords in `fdump.txt`, and it can be as complex as scoring using a text classification algorithm we learned in *Chapter 6, Text Classification*.

The other use case could be to look for a topic of interest, and then to look for the resulting pages for open posts and comments. This is exactly analogous to searching using the graph search bar on your Facebook home page. However, the power of doing this programmatically is that we can conduct these searches and then each page can be recursively parsed for use comments. The code for searching user data is as follows:

User search

```
>>>fb.request("search", {'q' : 'nitin', 'type' : 'user'})
Place based on the nearest location.
>>>fb.request("search", {'q' : 'starbucks', 'type' : 'place'})
Look for open pages.
>>>fb.request("search", {'q' : 'Stanford university', 'type' : page})
Look for event matching to the key word.
>>>fb.request("search", {'q' : 'beach party', 'type' : 'event'})
```

Once we have dumped all the relevant data into a structured format, we can apply some of the concepts we learned when we went through the topics of NLP and machine learning. Let's pick the same use case of finding posts, that will mostly be complaints on a Facebook page.

I assume that we now have the data in the following format:

Userid	**FB Post**
XXXX0001	The product was pathetic and I tried reaching out to your customer care, but nobody responded
XXXX002	Great work guys
XXXX003	Where can I call to get my account activated ??? Really bad service

We will go back to the same example we had in *Chapter 6, Text Classification*, where we built a text classifier to detect whether the **SMS** (text message) was spam. Similarly, we can create training data using this kind of data, where from the given set of posts, we will ask manual taggers to tag the comments that are complaints and the ones that are not. Once we have significant training data, we can build the same text classifier:

```
fb_classification.py
>>>from sklearn.feature_extraction.text import TfidfVectorizer
>>>vectorizer = TfidfVectorizer(min_df=2, ngram_range=(1, 2),  stop_
words='english',  strip_accents='unicode',  norm='l2')
>>>X_train = vectorizer.fit_transform(x_train)
>>>X_test = vectorizer.transform(x_test)

>>>from sklearn.linear_model import SGDClassifier
>>>clf = SGDClassifier(alpha=.0001, n_iter=50).fit(X_train, y_train)
>>>y_pred = clf.predict(X_test)
```

Let's assume that these three are the only samples. We can tag 1st and 3rd to be classified as complaints, while 2nd will not be a complaint. Although we will build a vectorizer of unigram and bigram in the same way, we can actually build a classifier using the same process. I ignored some of the preprocessing steps here. You can use the same process as discussed in *Chapter 6, Text Classification*. In some of the cases, it will be hard/expensive to get training data like this. In some of these cases, we can apply either an unsupervised algorithm, such as text clustering or topic modeling. The other way is to use some different dataset that is openly available and build model on that and apply it here. For example, in the same use case, we can crawl some of the customer complaints available on the Web and use that as training data for our model. This can work as a good proxy for labeled data.

Influencer friends

One other use case of social media could be finding out the most influencer in your social graph. In our case, it could be finding out a clear node that has a vast amount of inlinks and outlinks will be the influencer in the graph.

The same problem in the context of business can be finding out the most influential customers, and targeting them to market our products.

The code for the Influencer friends is as follows:

```
>>>friends = fb.get_connections("me", "friends")["data"]
>>>print friends
>>>for frd in friends:
>>>     print fb.get_connections(frd["id"],"friends")
```

Once you have a list of all your friends and mutual friends, you can create a data structure like this:

source node	destination node	link_exist
Frind 1	Frind 2	1
Frind 1	Frind 3	1
Frind 2	Frind 3	0
Frind 1	Frind 4	1

This a kind of data structure that can be used to generate a network, and is a very good way of visualizing the social graph. I used D3 here, but python also has a library called **NetworkX** (`https://networkx.github.io/`) that can be used to generate graph visualization, as shown in the following graph. To generate a visualization, you need to arrive at a adjacency matrix that can be created based on the bases of the preceding information about who is the friend of whom.

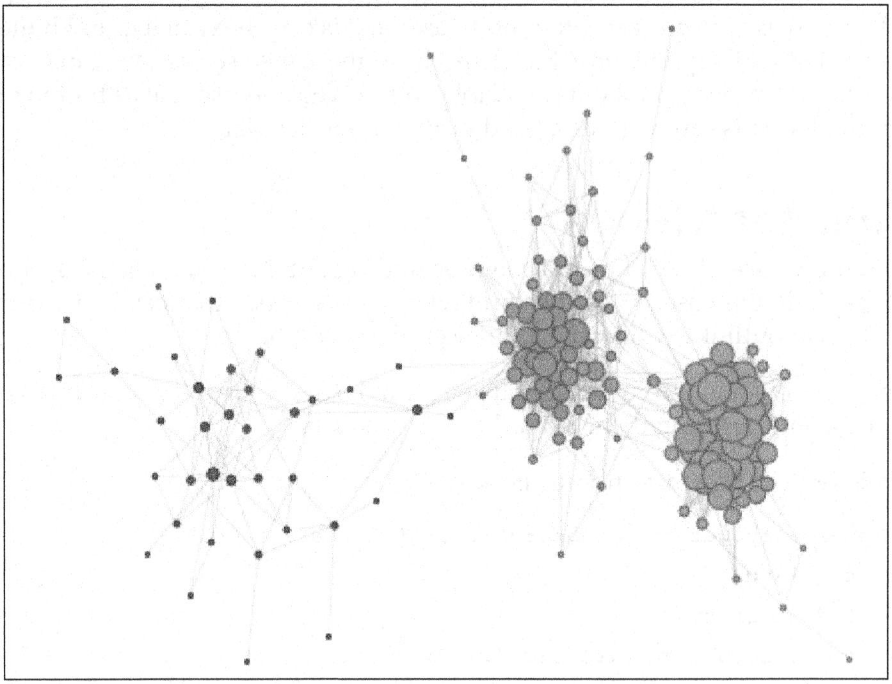

Visualization of a sample network in D3

Summary

In this chapter, we touched upon some of the most popular social networks. You learned how to get data using Python. You understood the structure and kind of attributes data has. We explored different options provided by the API.

We explored some of the most common use cases in the context of social media mining. We touched upon the use cases about trending topics, influencer detection, information flow, and so on. We visualized some of these use cases. We also applied some of the learnings from the previous chapter, where we used NLTK to get some of the topic and entity extraction, while in scikit-learn we classified some of the complaints.

In conclusion, I would suggest that you look for some of the same use cases in context of some other social networks and try to explore them. The great part of these social networks is that all of them have a data API, and most of them are open enough to do some interesting analysis. If you apply the same learning you did in this chapter, you need to understand the API, how to get the data, and then how to apply some of the concepts we learned in the previous chapters. I hope that after learning all this, you will come up with more use cases, and some interesting analysis of social media.

10
Text Mining at Scale

In this chapter, we will go back to some of the libraries we learned about in the previous chapters, but this time, we want to learn to learn how these libraries will scale up with bigdata. We assume that you have a fair bit of an idea about big data, **Hadoop** and **Hive**. We will explore how some of the Python libraries, such as NLTK, scikit-learn, and pandas can be used on a Hadoop cluster with a large amount of unstructured data.

We will cover some of the most common use cases in the context of NLP and text mining, and we will also provide a code snippet that will be helpful for you to get your job done. We will look at three major examples that can capture the vast majority of your text mining problems. We will tell you how to run NLTK at scale to perform some of the NLP tasks that we completed in the initial chapters. We will give you a few examples of some of the text classification tasks that can be done on Big Data.

One other aspect of doing machine learning and NLP at a very high scale is to understand whether the problem is parallelizable or not. We will talk in brief about some of the problems discussed in the previous chapter, and whether these problems are big data problems or not. Or in some case is it even possible to solve this using Big Data.

Since most of the libraries we learned so far are written in Python, let's deal with one of the main questions of how to get Python on Big Data (Hadoop).

By end of the chapter we like reader to have :

- Good understanding about big data related technologies such as Hadoop, Hive and how it can be done using python.
- Step by step tutorial to work with NLTK, Scikit & PySpark on Big Data.

Different ways of using Python on Hadoop

There are many ways to run a Python process on Hadoop. We will talk about some of the most popular ways through which we can run Python on Hadoop as a streaming MapReduce job, Python UDF in Hive, and Python hadoop wrappers.

Python streaming

Typically a Hadoop job has to be written in form of a map and reduce function. User has to write an implementation of map and reduce function for the given task. Commonly these mappers and reducers are implemented in JAVA. At the same time Hadoop provide streaming, you where a user can write a Python mapper and reducer function similar to Java in any other language. I am assuming that you have run a word count example using Python. We will also use the same example using NLTK later in this chapter.

> In case you have not, have a look at `http://www.michael-noll.com/tutorials/writing-an-hadoop-mapreduce-program-in-python/` to know more about MapReduce in Python.

Hive/Pig UDF

Other way to use Python is by writing a **UDF (User Defined Function)** in Hive/Pig. The idea here is that most of the operations we are performing in NLTK are highly parallelizable. For example, POS tagging, Tokenization, Lemmatization, Stop Word removal, and NER can be highly distributable. The reason being the content of each row is independent from the other row, and we don't need any context while doing some of these operations.

So, if we have NLTK and other Python libraries on each node of the cluster, we can write a **user defined function (UDF)** in Python, using libraries such as NLTK and scikit. This is one of the easiest way of doing NLTK, especially for scikit on a large scale. We will give you a glimpse of both of these in this chapter.

Streaming wrappers

There is a long list of wrappers that different organizations have implemented to get Python running on the cluster. Some of them are actually quite easy to use, but all of them suffer from performance bias. I have listed some of them as follows, but you can go through the project page in case you want to know more about them:

- Hadoopy
- Pydoop
- Dumbo
- mrjob

> For the exhaustive list of options available for the usage of Python on Hadoop, go through the article at `http://blog.cloudera.com/blog/2013/01/a-guide-to-python-frameworks-for-hadoop/`.

NLTK on Hadoop

We talked enough about NLTK as a library, and what are some of the most-used functions it gives us. Now, NLTK can solve many NLP problems from which many are highly parallelizable. This is the reason why we will try to use NLTK on Hadoop.

The best way of running NLTK on Hadoop is to get it installed on all the nodes of the cluster. This is probably not that difficult to achieve. There are ways in which you can do this, such as sending the resource files as a streaming argument. However, we will rather prefer the first option.

A UDF

There are a variety of ways in which we can make NLTK run on Hadoop. Let's talk about one example of using NLTK by doing tokenization in parallel using a Hive UDF.

For this use case, we have to follow these steps:

1. We have chosen a small dataset where only two columns exist. We have to create the same schema in Hive:

ID	Content
UA0001	"I tried calling you. The service was not up to the mark"
UA0002	"Can you please update my phone no"
UA0003	"Really bad experience"
UA0004	"I am looking for an iPhone"

2. Create the same schema in Hive. The following Hive script will do this for you:

   Hive script

```
CREATE TABLE $InputTableName (
ID String,
Content String
)
ROW FORMAT DELIMITED
FIELDS TERMINATED BY '\t';
```

3. Once we have the schema, essentially, we want to get something like tokens of the content in a separate column. So, we just want another column in the `$outTable` with the same schema, and the added column of tokens:

   Hive script

```
CREATE TABLE $OutTableName (
ID String,
Content String,
Tokens String
)
```

4. Now, we have the schemas ready. We have to write the UDF in Python to read the table line by line and then apply a `tokenize` method. This is very similar to what we did in *Chapter 3, Part of Speech Tagging*. This is the piece of function that is analogous to all the examples in *Chapter 3, Part of Speech Tagging*. Now, if you want to get POS tags, Lemmatization, and HTML, you just need to modify this UDF. Let's see how the UDF will look for our tokenizer:

```
>>>import sys
>>>import datetime
>>>import pickle
```

```
>>>import nltk
>>>nltk.download('punkt')
>>>for line in sys.stdin:
>>>     line = line.strip()
>>>     print>>sys.stderr, line
>>>     id, content= line.split('\t')
>>>     print>>sys.stderr,tok.tokenize(content)
>>>     tokens =nltk.word_tokenize(concat_all_text)
>>>     print '\t'.join([id,content,tokens])
```

5. Just name this UDF something like: `nltk_scoring.py`.
6. Now, we have to run the insert hive query with the `TRANSFORM` function to apply the UDF on the given content and to do tokenization and dump the tokens in the new column:

   Hive script

```
add FILE nltk_scoring.py;
add FILE english.pickle; #Adding file to DistributedCache
INSERT OVERWRITE TABLE $OutTableName
SELECT
        TRANSFORM (id, content)
    USING 'PYTHONPATH nltk_scoring.py'
    AS (id string, content string, tokens string )
FROM $InputTablename;
```

7. If you are getting an error like this, you have not installed the NLTK and NLTK data correctly:

```
raiseLookupError(resource_not_found)
LookupError:
*******************************************************************
****
  Resource u'tokenizers/punkt/english.pickle' not found.  Please
  use the NLTK Downloader to obtain the resource:  >>>
  nltk.download()
  Searched in:
    - '/home/nltk_data'
    - '/usr/share/nltk_data'
    - '/usr/local/share/nltk_data'
    - '/usr/lib/nltk_data'
    - '/usr/local/lib/nltk_data'
```

8. If you are able to run this Hive job successfully, you will get a table named `OutTableName`, that will look something like this:

ID	Content	
UA0001	"I tried calling you, The service was not up to the mark"	[" I", " tried", "calling", "you", "The", "service" "was", "not", "up", "to", "the", "mark"]
UA0002	"Can you please update my phone no"	["Can", "you", "please" "update", " my", "phone" "no"]
UA0003	"Really bad experience"	["Really"," bad" "experience"]
UA0004	"I am looking for an iphone"	["I", "am", "looking", "for", "an", "iPhone"]

Python streaming

Let's try the second option of Python streaming. We have Hadoop streaming, where we can write our own mapper and reducer functions, and then use Python streaming with `mapper.py`, as it looks quite similar to our Hive UDF. Here we are using the same example with map-reduce python streaming this will give us a option of choosing a Hive table or using a HDFS file directly. We will just go over the content of the file and tokenize it. We will not perform any reduce operation here, but for learning, I included a dummy reducer, which just dumps it. So now, we can ignore the reducer from the execution command completely.

Here is the code for the Mapper.py:

Mapper.py

```
>>>import sys
>>>import pickle
>>>import nltk
>>>for line in sys.stdin:
>>>     line = line.strip()
>>>     id, content = line.split('\t')
>>>     tokens =nltk.word_tokenize(concat_all_text)
>>>     print '\t'.join([id,content,topics])
```

Here is the code for the `Reducer.py`:

Reducer.py

```
>>>import sys
>>>import pickle
>>>import nltk
>>>for line in sys.stdin:
>>>     line = line.strip()
>>>     id, content,tokens = line.split('\t')
>>>     print '\t'.join([id,content,tokens])
```

The following is the Hadoop command to execute a Python stream:Hive script

```
hadoop jar <path>/hadoop-streaming.jar \
-D mapred.reduce.tasks=1 -file <path>/mapper.py \
-mapper <path>/mapper.py \
-file <path>/reducer.py \
-reducer <path>/reducer.py \
-input /hdfspath/infile \
-output outfile
```

Scikit-learn on Hadoop

The other important use case for big data is machine learning. Specially with Hadoop, scikit-learn is more important, as this is one of the best options we have to score a machine learning model on big data. Large-scale machine learning is currently one of the hottest topics, and doing this in a big data environment such as Hadoop is all the more important. Now, the two aspects of machine learning models are building a model on big data and to build model on a significantly large amount of data and scoring a significantly large amount of data.

To understand more, let's take the same example data we used in the previous table, where we have some customer comments. Now, we can build, let's say, a text classification mode using a significant training sample, and use some of the learnings from *Chapter 6, Text Classification* to build a Naive Bayes, SVM, or a logistic regression model on the data. While scoring, we might need to score a huge amount of data, such as customer comments. On the other hand building the model itself on big data is not possible with scikit-learn, we will require tool like spark/Mahot for that. We will take the same step-by-step approach of scoring using a pre-trained model as we did with NLTK. While building the mode on big data will be covered in the next section. For scoring using a pre-trained model specifically when we are working on a text mining kind of problem. We need two main objects (a vectorizer and modelclassifier) to be stored as a serialized pickle object.

> Here, pickle is a Python module to achieve serialization by which the object will be saved in a binary state on the disk and can be consumed by loading again.
>
> `https://docs.python.org/2/library/pickle.html`

Build an offline model using scikit on your local machine and make sure you pickle objects. For example, if I use the Naive Bayes example from *Chapter 6, Text Classification*, we need to store `vectorizer` and `clf` as pickle objects:

```
>>>vectorizer = TfidfVectorizer(sublinear_tf=True, min_df=in_min_df,
stop_words='english', ngram_range=(1,2), max_df=in_max_df)
>>>joblib.dump(vectorizer, "vectorizer.pkl", compress=3)
>>>clf = GaussianNB().fit(X_train,y_train)
>>>joblib.dump(clf, "classifier.pkl")
```

The following are the steps for creating a output table which will have all the customer comments for the entire history:

1. Create the same schema in Hive as we did in the previous example. The following Hive script will do this for you. This table can be huge; in our case, let's assume that it contains all the customer comments about the company in the past:

   Hive script

   ```
   CREATE TABLE $InputTableName (
   ID String,
   Content String
   )
   ROW FORMAT DELIMITED
   FIELDS TERMINATED BY '\t';
   ```

2. Build an output table with the output column like the predict and probability score:

   Hive script

```
CREATE TABLE $OutTableName (
ID String,
Content String,
predict String,
predict_score double
)
```

3. Now, we have to load these pickle objects to the distributed cache using the `addFILE` command in Hive:

```
add FILE vectorizer.pkl;
add FILE classifier.pkl;
```

4. The next step is to write the Hive UDF, where we are loading these pickle objects. Now, they start behaving the same as they were on the local. Once we have the classifier and vectorizer object, we can use our test sample, which is nothing but a string, and generate the TFIDF vector out of this. The vectorizer object can be used now to predict the class as well as the probability of the class:

   Classification.py

```
>>>import sys
>>>import pickle
>>>import sklearn
>>>from sklearn.externals import joblib

>>>clf = joblib.load('classifier.pkl')
>>>vectorizer = joblib.load('vectorizer.pkl')

>>>for line in sys.stdin:
>>>     line = line.strip()
>>>     id, content= line.split('\t')
>>>     X_test = vectorizer.transform([str(content)])

>>>     prob = clf.predict_proba(X_test)
>>>     pred = clf.predict(X_test)
>>>     prob_score =prob[:,1]
>>>     print '\t'.join([id, content,pred,prob_score])
```

5. Once we have written the `classification.py` UDF, we have to also add this UDF to the distributed cache and then effectively, run this UDF as a `TRANSFORM` function on each and every row of the table. The Hive script for this will look like this:

   Hive script

```
add FILE classification.py;

INSERT OVERWRITE TABLE $OutTableName
SELECT
    TRANSFORM (id, content)
    USING 'python2.7 classification.py'
    AS (id string, scorestringscore string )
FROM $Tablename;
```

6. If everything goes well, then we will have the output table with the output schema as:

ID	Content	Predict	Prob_score
UA0001	"I tried calling you, The service was not up to the mark"	Complaint	0.98
UA0002	"Can you please update my phone no "	No	0.23
UA0003	"Really bad experience"	Complaint	0..97
UA0004	"I am looking for an iPhone "	No	0.01

So, our output table will have all the customer comments for the entire history, scores for whether they were complaints or not, and also a confidence score. We have choosen a Hive UDF for our example, but the similar process can be done through the Pig and Python steaming in a similar way as we did in NLTK.

This example was to give you a hands-on experience of how to score a machine learning model on Hive. In the next example, we will talk about how to build a machine learning/NLP model on big data.

PySpark

Let's go back to the same discussion we had of building a machine learning/NLP model on Hadoop and the other where we score a ML model on Hadoop. We discussed second option of scoring in depth in the last section. Instead sampling a smaller data-set and scoring let's use a larger data-set and build a large-scale machine learning model step-by-step using PySpark. I am again using the same running data with the same schema:

ID	Comment	Class
UA0001	I tried calling you, The service was not up to the mark	1
UA0002	Can you please update my phone no	0
UA0003	Really bad experience	1
UA0004	I am looking for an iPhone	0
UA0005	Can somebody help me with my password	1
UA0006	Thanks for considering my request for	0

Consider the schema for last 10 years worth of comments of the organization. Now, instead of using a small sample to build a classification model, and then using a pretrained model to score all the comments, let me give you a step-by-step example of how to build a text classification model using PySpark.

The first thing that we need to do is we need to import some of the modules. Starting with `SparkContext`, which is more of a configuration, you can provide more parameters, such as app names and others for this.

```
>>>from pyspark import SparkContext
>>>sc = SparkContext(appName="comment_classifcation")
```

> For more information, go through the article at `http://spark.apache.org/docs/0.7.3/api/pyspark/pyspark.context.SparkContext-class.html`.

The next thing is reading a tab delimited text file. Reading the file should be on HDFS. This file could be huge (~Tb/Pb):

```
>>>lines = sc.textFile("testcomments.txt")
```

The lines are now a list of all the rows in the corpus:

```
>>>parts = lines.map(lambda l: l.split("\t"))
>>>corpus = parts.map(lambda row: Row(id=row[0], comment=row[1],
class=row[2]))
```

The part is a list of fields as we have each field in the line delimited on "\t".

Let's break the corpus that has [ID, comment, class (0,1)] in the different RDD objects:

```
>>>comment = corpus.map(lambda row: " " + row.comment)
>>>class_var = corpus.map(lambda row:row.class)
```

Once we have the comments, we need to do a process very similar to what we did in *Chapter 6, Text Classification*, where we used scikit to do tokenization, hash vectorizer and calculate TF, IDF, and tf-idf using a vectorizer.

The following is the snippet of how to create tokenization, term frequency, and inverse document frequency:

```
>>>from pyspark.mllib.feature import HashingTF
>>>from pyspark.mllib.feature import IDF
# https://spark.apache.org/docs/1.2.0/mllib-feature-extraction.html

>>>comment_tokenized = comment.map(lambda line: line.strip().split(" "))
>>>hashingTF = HashingTF(1000) # to select only 1000 features
>>>comment_tf = hashingTF.transform(comment_tokenized)
>>>comment_idf = IDF().fit(comment_tf)
>>>comment_tfidf = comment_idf.transform(comment_tf)
```

We will merge the class with the `tfidf` RDD like this:

```
>>>finaldata = class_var.zip(comment_tfidf)
```

We will do a typical test, and train sampling:

```
>>>train, test = finaldata.randomSplit([0.8, 0.2], seed=0)
```

Let's perform the main classification commands, which are quite similar to scikit. We are using a logistic regression, which is widely used classifier. The `pyspark.mllib` provides you with a variety of algorithms.

For more information on pyspark.mllib visit https://spark.apache.org/docs/latest/api/python/pyspark.mllib.html

The following is an example of Naive bayes classifier:

```
>>>from pyspark.mllib.regression import LabeledPoint
>>>from pyspark.mllib.classification import NaiveBayes
>>>train_rdd = train.map(lambda t: LabeledPoint(t[0], t[1]))
>>>test_rdd = test.map(lambda t: LabeledPoint(t[0], t[1]))
>>>nb = NaiveBayes.train(train_rdd,lambda = 1.0)
>>>nb_output = test_rdd.map(lambda point: (NB.predict(point.features),
point.label))
>>>print nb_output
```

The nb_output command contains the final predictions for the test sample. The great thing to understand is that with just less than 50 lines, we built a snippet code for an industry-standard text classification with even petabytes of the training sample.

Summary

To summarize this chapter, our objective was to apply the concepts that we learned so far in the context of big data. In this chapter, you learned how to use some Python libraries, such as NLTK and scikit with Hadoop. We talked about scoring a machine learning model, or an NLP-based operation.

We also saw three major examples of the most-common use cases. On understanding these examples, you can apply most of the NLTK, scikit and PySpark functions.

This chapter was a quick and brief introduction to NLP and text mining on big data. This is one of the hottest topics, and each term and tool which I talked about in the example snippet could be a book in itself. I tried to give you a hacker's approach, to give you an introduction to big data and text mining on a large scale. I encourage you to read more about some of these big data technologies such as Hadoop, Hive, Pig, and Spark and try to explore some of the examples we gave in this chapter.

Module 2

Python 3 Text Processing with NLTK 3 Cookbook

Over 80 practical recipes on natural language processing techniques
using Python's NTLK 3.0

1

Tokenizing Text and WordNet Basics

In this chapter, we will cover the following recipes:

- Tokenizing text into sentences
- Tokenizing sentences into words
- Tokenizing sentences using regular expressions
- Training a sentence tokenizer
- Filtering stopwords in a tokenized sentence
- Looking up Synsets for a word in WordNet
- Looking up lemmas and synonyms in WordNet
- Calculating WordNet Synset similarity
- Discovering word collocations

Introduction

Natural Language ToolKit (**NLTK**) is a comprehensive Python library for natural language processing and text analytics. Originally designed for teaching, it has been adopted in the industry for research and development due to its usefulness and breadth of coverage. NLTK is often used for rapid prototyping of text processing programs and can even be used in production applications. Demos of select NLTK functionality and production-ready APIs are available at `http://text-processing.com`.

This chapter will cover the basics of tokenizing text and using WordNet. **Tokenization** is a method of breaking up a piece of text into many pieces, such as sentences and words, and is an essential first step for recipes in the later chapters. **WordNet** is a dictionary designed for programmatic access by natural language processing systems. It has many different use cases, including:

- Looking up the definition of a word
- Finding synonyms and antonyms
- Exploring word relations and similarity
- Word sense disambiguation for words that have multiple uses and definitions

NLTK includes a WordNet corpus reader, which we will use to access and explore WordNet. A corpus is just a body of text, and corpus readers are designed to make accessing a corpus much easier than direct file access. We'll be using WordNet again in the later chapters, so it's important to familiarize yourself with the basics first.

Tokenizing text into sentences

Tokenization is the process of splitting a string into a list of pieces or tokens. A token is a piece of a whole, so a word is a token in a sentence, and a sentence is a token in a paragraph. We'll start with sentence tokenization, or splitting a paragraph into a list of sentences.

Getting ready

Installation instructions for NLTK are available at `http://nltk.org/install.html` and the latest version at the time of writing this is Version 3.0b1. This version of NLTK is built for Python 3.0 or higher, but it is backwards compatible with Python 2.6 and higher. In this book, we will be using Python 3.3.2. If you've used earlier versions of NLTK (such as version 2.0), note that some of the APIs have changed in Version 3 and are not backwards compatible.

Once you've installed NLTK, you'll also need to install the data following the instructions at `http://nltk.org/data.html`. I recommend installing everything, as we'll be using a number of corpora and pickled objects. The data is installed in a data directory, which on Mac and Linux/Unix is usually `/usr/share/nltk_data`, or on Windows is `C:\nltk_data`. Make sure that `tokenizers/punkt.zip` is in the data directory and has been unpacked so that there's a file at `tokenizers/punkt/PY3/english.pickle`.

Finally, to run the code examples, you'll need to start a Python console. Instructions on how to do so are available at `http://nltk.org/install.html`. For Mac and Linux/Unix users, you can open a terminal and type `python`.

How to do it...

Once NLTK is installed and you have a Python console running, we can start by creating a paragraph of text:

```
>>> para = "Hello World. It's good to see you. Thanks for buying this
book."
```

> **Downloading the example code**
>
> You can download the example code files for all Packt books you have purchased from your account at `http://www.packtpub.com`. If you purchased this book elsewhere, you can visit `http://www.packtpub.com/support` and register to have the files e-mailed directly to you.

Now we want to split the paragraph into sentences. First we need to import the sentence tokenization function, and then we can call it with the paragraph as an argument:

```
>>> from nltk.tokenize import sent_tokenize
>>> sent_tokenize(para)
['Hello World.', "It's good to see you.", 'Thanks for buying this
book.']
```

So now we have a list of sentences that we can use for further processing.

How it works...

The `sent_tokenize` function uses an instance of `PunktSentenceTokenizer` from the `nltk.tokenize.punkt` module. This instance has already been trained and works well for many European languages. So it knows what punctuation and characters mark the end of a sentence and the beginning of a new sentence.

There's more...

The instance used in `sent_tokenize()` is actually loaded on demand from a pickle file. So if you're going to be tokenizing a lot of sentences, it's more efficient to load the `PunktSentenceTokenizer` class once, and call its `tokenize()` method instead:

```
>>> import nltk.data
>>> tokenizer = nltk.data.load('tokenizers/punkt/PY3/english.pickle')
>>> tokenizer.tokenize(para)
['Hello World.', "It's good to see you.", 'Thanks for buying this
book.']
```

Tokenizing sentences in other languages

If you want to tokenize sentences in languages other than English, you can load one of the other pickle files in `tokenizers/punkt/PY3` and use it just like the English sentence tokenizer. Here's an example for Spanish:

```
>>> spanish_tokenizer = nltk.data.load('tokenizers/punkt/PY3/spanish.
pickle')
>>> spanish_tokenizer.tokenize('Hola amigo. Estoy bien.')
['Hola amigo.', 'Estoy bien.']
```

You can see a list of all the available language tokenizers in `/usr/share/nltk_data/tokenizers/punkt/PY3` (or `C:\nltk_data\tokenizers\punkt\PY3`).

See also

In the next recipe, we'll learn how to split sentences into individual words. After that, we'll cover how to use regular expressions to tokenize text. We'll cover how to train your own sentence tokenizer in an upcoming recipe, *Training a sentence tokenizer*.

Tokenizing sentences into words

In this recipe, we'll split a sentence into individual words. The simple task of creating a list of words from a string is an essential part of all text processing.

How to do it...

Basic word tokenization is very simple; use the `word_tokenize()` function:

```
>>> from nltk.tokenize import word_tokenize
>>> word_tokenize('Hello World.')
['Hello', 'World', '.']
```

How it works...

The `word_tokenize()` function is a wrapper function that calls `tokenize()` on an instance of the `TreebankWordTokenizer` class. It's equivalent to the following code:

```
>>> from nltk.tokenize import TreebankWordTokenizer
>>> tokenizer = TreebankWordTokenizer()
>>> tokenizer.tokenize('Hello World.')
['Hello', 'World', '.']
```

It works by separating words using spaces and punctuation. And as you can see, it does not discard the punctuation, allowing you to decide what to do with it.

There's more...

Ignoring the obviously named `WhitespaceTokenizer` and `SpaceTokenizer`, there are two other word tokenizers worth looking at: `PunktWordTokenizer` and `WordPunctTokenizer`. These differ from `TreebankWordTokenizer` by how they handle punctuation and contractions, but they all inherit from `TokenizerI`. The inheritance tree looks like what's shown in the following diagram:

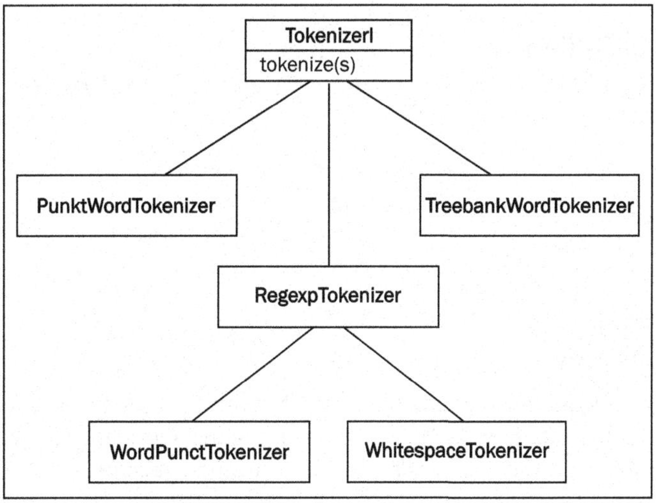

Separating contractions

The `TreebankWordTokenizer` class uses conventions found in the Penn Treebank corpus. This corpus is one of the most used corpora for natural language processing, and was created in the 1980s by annotating articles from the *Wall Street Journal*. We'll be using this later in *Chapter 4, Part-of-speech Tagging*, and *Chapter 5, Extracting Chunks*.

One of the tokenizer's most significant conventions is to separate contractions. For example, consider the following code:

```
>>> word_tokenize("can't")
['ca', "n't"]
```

If you find this convention unacceptable, then read on for alternatives, and see the next recipe for tokenizing with regular expressions.

PunktWordTokenizer

An alternative word tokenizer is `PunktWordTokenizer`. It splits on punctuation, but keeps it with the word instead of creating separate tokens, as shown in the following code:

```
>>> from nltk.tokenize import PunktWordTokenizer
>>> tokenizer = PunktWordTokenizer()
>>> tokenizer.tokenize("Can't is a contraction.")
['Can', "'t", 'is', 'a', 'contraction.']
```

WordPunctTokenizer

Another alternative word tokenizer is `WordPunctTokenizer`. It splits all punctuation into separate tokens:

```
>>> from nltk.tokenize import WordPunctTokenizer
>>> tokenizer = WordPunctTokenizer()
>>> tokenizer.tokenize("Can't is a contraction.")
['Can', "'", 't', 'is', 'a', 'contraction', '.']
```

See also

For more control over word tokenization, you'll want to read the next recipe to learn how to use regular expressions and the `RegexpTokenizer` for tokenization. And for more on the Penn Treebank corpus, visit `http://www.cis.upenn.edu/~treebank/`.

Tokenizing sentences using regular expressions

Regular expressions can be used if you want complete control over how to tokenize text. As regular expressions can get complicated very quickly, I only recommend using them if the word tokenizers covered in the previous recipe are unacceptable.

Getting ready

First you need to decide how you want to tokenize a piece of text as this will determine how you construct your regular expression. The choices are:

- Match on the tokens
- Match on the separators or gaps

We'll start with an example of the first, matching alphanumeric tokens plus single quotes so that we don't split up contractions.

How to do it...

We'll create an instance of `RegexpTokenizer`, giving it a regular expression string to use for matching tokens:

```
>>> from nltk.tokenize import RegexpTokenizer
>>> tokenizer = RegexpTokenizer("[\w']+")
>>> tokenizer.tokenize("Can't is a contraction.")
["Can't", 'is', 'a', 'contraction']
```

There's also a simple helper function you can use if you don't want to instantiate the class, as shown in the following code:

```
>>> from nltk.tokenize import regexp_tokenize
>>> regexp_tokenize("Can't is a contraction.", "[\w']+")
["Can't", 'is', 'a', 'contraction']
```

Now we finally have something that can treat contractions as whole words, instead of splitting them into tokens.

How it works...

The `RegexpTokenizer` class works by compiling your pattern, then calling `re.findall()` on your text. You could do all this yourself using the `re` module, but `RegexpTokenizer` implements the `TokenizerI` interface, just like all the word tokenizers from the previous recipe. This means it can be used by other parts of the NLTK package, such as corpus readers, which we'll cover in detail in *Chapter 3, Creating Custom Corpora*. Many corpus readers need a way to tokenize the text they're reading, and can take optional keyword arguments specifying an instance of a `TokenizerI` subclass. This way, you have the ability to provide your own tokenizer instance if the default tokenizer is unsuitable.

There's more...

`RegexpTokenizer` can also work by matching the gaps, as opposed to the tokens. Instead of using `re.findall()`, the `RegexpTokenizer` class will use `re.split()`. This is how the `BlanklineTokenizer` class in `nltk.tokenize` is implemented.

Simple whitespace tokenizer

The following is a simple example of using `RegexpTokenizer` to tokenize on whitespace:

```
>>> tokenizer = RegexpTokenizer('\s+', gaps=True)
>>> tokenizer.tokenize("Can't is a contraction.")
["Can't", 'is', 'a', 'contraction.']
```

Notice that punctuation still remains in the tokens. The `gaps=True` parameter means that the pattern is used to identify gaps to tokenize on. If we used `gaps=False`, then the pattern would be used to identify tokens.

See also

For simpler word tokenization, see the previous recipe.

Training a sentence tokenizer

NLTK's default sentence tokenizer is general purpose, and usually works quite well. But sometimes it is not the best choice for your text. Perhaps your text uses nonstandard punctuation, or is formatted in a unique way. In such cases, training your own sentence tokenizer can result in much more accurate sentence tokenization.

Getting ready

For this example, we'll be using the `webtext` corpus, specifically the `overheard.txt` file, so make sure you've downloaded this corpus. The text in this file is formatted as dialog that looks like this:

```
White guy: So, do you have any plans for this evening?
Asian girl: Yeah, being angry!
White guy: Oh, that sounds good.
```

As you can see, this isn't your standard paragraph of sentences formatting, which makes it a perfect case for training a sentence tokenizer.

How to do it...

NLTK provides a `PunktSentenceTokenizer` class that you can train on raw text to produce a custom sentence tokenizer. You can get raw text either by reading in a file, or from an NLTK corpus using the `raw()` method. Here's an example of training a sentence tokenizer on dialog text, using `overheard.txt` from the `webtext` corpus:

```
>>> from nltk.tokenize import PunktSentenceTokenizer
>>> from nltk.corpus import webtext
>>> text = webtext.raw('overheard.txt')
>>> sent_tokenizer = PunktSentenceTokenizer(text)
```

Let's compare the results to the default sentence tokenizer, as follows:

```
>>> sents1 = sent_tokenizer.tokenize(text)
>>> sents1[0]
'White guy: So, do you have any plans for this evening?'

>>> from nltk.tokenize import sent_tokenize
>>> sents2 = sent_tokenize(text)
>>> sents2[0]
'White guy: So, do you have any plans for this evening?'
>>> sents1[678]
'Girl: But you already have a Big Mac...'
>>> sents2[678]
'Girl: But you already have a Big Mac...\\nHobo: Oh, this is all
theatrical.'
```

While the first sentence is the same, you can see that the tokenizers disagree on how to tokenize sentence `679` (this is the first sentence where the tokenizers diverge). The default tokenizer includes the next line of dialog, while our custom tokenizer correctly thinks that the next line is a separate sentence. This difference is a good demonstration of why it can be useful to train your own sentence tokenizer, especially when your text isn't in the typical paragraph-sentence structure.

How it works...

The `PunktSentenceTokenizer` class uses an unsupervised learning algorithm to learn what constitutes a sentence break. It is unsupervised because you don't have to give it any labeled training data, just raw text. You can read more about these kinds of algorithms at `https://en.wikipedia.org/wiki/Unsupervised_learning`. The specific technique used in this case is called sentence boundary detection and it works by counting punctuation and tokens that commonly end a sentence, such as a period or newline, then using the resulting frequencies to decide what the sentence boundaries should actually look like.

This is a simplified description of the algorithm—if you'd like more details, take a look at the source code of the `nltk.tokenize.punkt.PunktTrainer` class, which can be found online at `http://www.nltk.org/_modules/nltk/tokenize/punkt.html#PunktSentenceTokenizer`.

There's more...

The `PunktSentenceTokenizer` class learns from any string, which means you can open a text file and read its content. Here is an example of reading `overheard.txt` directly instead of using the `raw()` corpus method. This assumes that the `webtext` corpus is located in the standard directory at `/usr/share/nltk_data/corpora`. We also have to pass a specific encoding to the `open()` function, as follows, because the file is not in ASCII:

```
>>> with open('/usr/share/nltk_data/corpora/webtext/overheard.txt', encoding='ISO-8859-2') as f:
...     text = f.read()
>>> sent_tokenizer = PunktSentenceTokenizer(text)
>>> sents = sent_tokenizer.tokenize(text)
>>> sents[0]
'White guy: So, do you have any plans for this evening?'
>>> sents[678]
'Girl: But you already have a Big Mac...'
```

Once you have a custom sentence tokenizer, you can use it for your own corpora. Many corpus readers accept a `sent_tokenizer` parameter, which lets you override the default sentence tokenizer object with your own sentence tokenizer. Corpus readers are covered in more detail in *Chapter 3, Creating Custom Corpora*.

See also

Most of the time, the default sentence tokenizer will be sufficient. This is covered in the first recipe, *Tokenizing text into sentences*.

Filtering stopwords in a tokenized sentence

Stopwords are common words that generally do not contribute to the meaning of a sentence, at least for the purposes of information retrieval and natural language processing. These are words such as *the* and *a*. Most search engines will filter out stopwords from search queries and documents in order to save space in their index.

Getting ready

NLTK comes with a `stopwords` corpus that contains word lists for many languages. Be sure to unzip the data file, so NLTK can find these word lists at `nltk_data/corpora/stopwords/`.

How to do it...

We're going to create a set of all English stopwords, then use it to filter stopwords from a sentence with the help of the following code:

```
>>> from nltk.corpus import stopwords
>>> english_stops = set(stopwords.words('english'))
>>> words = ["Can't", 'is', 'a', 'contraction']
>>> [word for word in words if word not in english_stops]
["Can't", 'contraction']
```

How it works...

The `stopwords` corpus is an instance of `nltk.corpus.reader.WordListCorpusReader`. As such, it has a `words()` method that can take a single argument for the file ID, which in this case is `'english'`, referring to a file containing a list of English stopwords. You could also call `stopwords.words()` with no argument to get a list of all stopwords in every language available.

There's more...

You can see the list of all English stopwords using `stopwords.words('english')` or by examining the word list file at `nltk_data/corpora/stopwords/english`. There are also stopword lists for many other languages. You can see the complete list of languages using the `fileids` method as follows:

```
>>> stopwords.fileids()
['danish', 'dutch', 'english', 'finnish', 'french', 'german',
'hungarian', 'italian', 'norwegian', 'portuguese', 'russian',
'spanish', 'swedish', 'turkish']
```

Any of these `fileids` can be used as an argument to the `words()` method to get a list of stopwords for that language. For example:

```
>>> stopwords.words('dutch')
['de', 'en', 'van', 'ik', 'te', 'dat', 'die', 'in', 'een', 'hij',
'het', 'niet', 'zijn', 'is', 'was', 'op', 'aan', 'met', 'als', 'voor',
'had', 'er', 'maar', 'om', 'hem', 'dan', 'zou', 'of', 'wat', 'mijn',
'men', 'dit', 'zo', 'door', 'over', 'ze', 'zich', 'bij', 'ook', 'tot',
'je', 'mij', 'uit', 'der', 'daar', 'haar', 'naar', 'heb', 'hoe',
'heeft', 'hebben', 'deze', 'u', 'want', 'nog', 'zal', 'me', 'zij',
'nu', 'ge', 'geen', 'omdat', 'iets', 'worden', 'toch', 'al', 'waren',
'veel', 'meer', 'doen', 'toen', 'moet', 'ben', 'zonder', 'kan',
'hun', 'dus', 'alles', 'onder', 'ja', 'eens', 'hier', 'wie', 'werd',
'altijd', 'doch', 'wordt', 'wezen', 'kunnen', 'ons', 'zelf', 'tegen',
'na', 'reeds', 'wil', 'kon', 'niets', 'uw', 'iemand', 'geweest',
'andere']
```

See also

If you'd like to create your own `stopwords` corpus, see the *Creating a wordlist corpus* recipe in *Chapter 3, Creating Custom Corpora*, to learn how to use `WordListCorpusReader`. We'll also be using stopwords in the *Discovering word collocations* recipe later in this chapter.

Looking up Synsets for a word in WordNet

WordNet is a lexical database for the English language. In other words, it's a dictionary designed specifically for natural language processing.

NLTK comes with a simple interface to look up words in WordNet. What you get is a list of **Synset** instances, which are groupings of synonymous words that express the same concept. Many words have only one Synset, but some have several. In this recipe, we'll explore a single Synset, and in the next recipe, we'll look at several in more detail.

Getting ready

Be sure you've unzipped the `wordnet` corpus at `nltk_data/corpora/wordnet`. This will allow `WordNetCorpusReader` to access it.

How to do it...

Now we're going to look up the Synset for `cookbook`, and explore some of the properties and methods of a Synset using the following code:

```
>>> from nltk.corpus import wordnet
>>> syn = wordnet.synsets('cookbook')[0]
>>> syn.name()
'cookbook.n.01'
>>> syn.definition()
'a book of recipes and cooking directions'
```

How it works...

You can look up any word in WordNet using `wordnet.synsets(word)` to get a list of Synsets. The list may be empty if the word is not found. The list may also have quite a few elements, as some words can have many possible meanings, and, therefore, many Synsets.

There's more...

Each Synset in the list has a number of methods you can use to learn more about it. The `name()` method will give you a unique name for the Synset, which you can use to get the Synset directly:

```
>>> wordnet.synset('cookbook.n.01')
Synset('cookbook.n.01')
```

The `definition()` method should be self-explanatory. Some Synsets also have an `examples()` method, which contains a list of phrases that use the word in context:

```
>>> wordnet.synsets('cooking')[0].examples()
['cooking can be a great art', 'people are needed who have experience
in cookery', 'he left the preparation of meals to his wife']
```

Working with hypernyms

Synsets are organized in a structure similar to that of an inheritance tree. More abstract terms are known as **hypernyms** and more specific terms are **hyponyms**. This tree can be traced all the way up to a root hypernym.

Hypernyms provide a way to categorize and group words based on their similarity to each other. The *Calculating WordNet Synset similarity* recipe details the functions used to calculate the similarity based on the distance between two words in the hypernym tree:

```
>>> syn.hypernyms()
[Synset('reference_book.n.01')]
>>> syn.hypernyms()[0].hyponyms()
[Synset('annual.n.02'), Synset('atlas.n.02'), Synset('cookbook.n.01'),
Synset('directory.n.01'), Synset('encyclopedia.n.01'),
Synset('handbook.n.01'), Synset('instruction_book.n.01'),
Synset('source_book.n.01'), Synset('wordbook.n.01')]
>>> syn.root_hypernyms()
[Synset('entity.n.01')]
```

As you can see, `reference_book` is a hypernym of `cookbook`, but `cookbook` is only one of the many hyponyms of `reference_book`. And all these types of books have the same root hypernym, which is `entity`, one of the most abstract terms in the English language. You can trace the entire path from entity down to `cookbook` using the `hypernym_paths()` method, as follows:

```
>>> syn.hypernym_paths()
[[Synset('entity.n.01'), Synset('physical_entity.n.01'),
Synset('object.n.01'), Synset('whole.n.02'), Synset('artifact.n.01'),
Synset('creation.n.02'), Synset('product.n.02'), Synset('work.n.02'),
Synset('publication.n.01'), Synset('book.n.01'), Synset('reference_
book.n.01'), Synset('cookbook.n.01')]]
```

The `hypernym_paths()` method returns a list of lists, where each list starts at the root hypernym and ends with the original Synset. Most of the time, you'll only get one nested list of Synsets.

Part of speech (POS)

You can also look up a simplified part-of-speech tag as follows:

```
>>> syn.pos()
'n'
```

There are four common part-of-speech tags (or POS tags) found in WordNet, as shown in the following table:

Part of speech	Tag
Noun	n
Adjective	a
Adverb	r
Verb	v

These POS tags can be used to look up specific Synsets for a word. For example, the word `'great'` can be used as a noun or an adjective. In WordNet, `'great'` has `1` noun Synset and `6` adjective Synsets, as shown in the following code:

```
>>> len(wordnet.synsets('great'))
7
>>> len(wordnet.synsets('great', pos='n'))
1
>>> len(wordnet.synsets('great', pos='a'))
6
```

These POS tags will be referenced more in the *Using WordNet for tagging* recipe in *Chapter 4, Part-of-speech Tagging*.

See also

In the next two recipes, we'll explore lemmas and how to calculate Synset similarity. And in *Chapter 2, Replacing and Correcting Words*, we'll use WordNet for lemmatization, synonym replacement, and then explore the use of antonyms.

Looking up lemmas and synonyms in WordNet

Building on the previous recipe, we can also look up lemmas in WordNet to find synonyms of a word. A **lemma** (in linguistics), is the canonical form or morphological form of a word.

How to do it...

In the following code, we'll find that there are two lemmas for the cookbook Synset using the lemmas() method:

```
>>> from nltk.corpus import wordnet
>>> syn = wordnet.synsets('cookbook')[0]
>>> lemmas = syn.lemmas()
>>> len(lemmas)
2
>>> lemmas[0].name()
'cookbook'
>>> lemmas[1].name()
'cookery_book'
>>> lemmas[0].synset() == lemmas[1].synset()
True
```

How it works...

As you can see, cookery_book and cookbook are two distinct lemmas in the same Synset. In fact, a lemma can only belong to a single Synset. In this way, a Synset represents a group of lemmas that all have the same meaning, while a lemma represents a distinct word form.

There's more...

Since all the lemmas in a Synset have the same meaning, they can be treated as synonyms. So if you wanted to get all synonyms for a Synset, you could do the following:

```
>>> [lemma.name() for lemma in syn.lemmas()]
['cookbook', 'cookery_book']
```

All possible synonyms

As mentioned earlier, many words have multiple Synsets because the word can have different meanings depending on the context. But, let's say you didn't care about the context, and wanted to get all the possible synonyms for a word:

```
>>> synonyms = []
>>> for syn in wordnet.synsets('book'):
...     for lemma in syn.lemmas():
...         synonyms.append(lemma.name())
>>> len(synonyms)
38
```

As you can see, there appears to be `38` possible synonyms for the word `'book'`. But in fact, some synonyms are verb forms, and many synonyms are just different usages of `'book'`. If, instead, we take the set of synonyms, there are fewer unique words, as shown in the following code:

```
>>> len(set(synonyms))
25
```

Antonyms

Some lemmas also have antonyms. The word `good`, for example, has 27 Synsets, five of which have lemmas with antonyms, as shown in the following code:

```
>>> gn2 = wordnet.synset('good.n.02')
>>> gn2.definition()
'moral excellence or admirableness'
>>> evil = gn2.lemmas()[0].antonyms()[0]
>>> evil.name
'evil'
>>> evil.synset().definition()
'the quality of being morally wrong in principle or practice'
>>> ga1 = wordnet.synset('good.a.01')
>>> ga1.definition()
'having desirable or positive qualities especially those suitable for
a thing specified'
>>> bad = ga1.lemmas()[0].antonyms()[0]
>>> bad.name()
'bad'
>>> bad.synset().definition()
'having undesirable or negative qualities'
```

The `antonyms()` method returns a list of lemmas. In the first case, as we can see in the previous code, the second Synset for `good` as a noun is defined as `moral excellence`, and its first antonym is `evil`, defined as `morally wrong`. In the second case, when `good` is used as an adjective to describe positive qualities, the first antonym is `bad`, which describes negative qualities.

See also

In the next recipe, we'll learn how to calculate Synset similarity. Then in *Chapter 2, Replacing and Correcting Words*, we'll revisit lemmas for lemmatization, synonym replacement, and antonym replacement.

Calculating WordNet Synset similarity

Synsets are organized in a *hypernym* tree. This tree can be used for reasoning about the similarity between the Synsets it contains. The closer the two Synsets are in the tree, the more similar they are.

How to do it...

If you were to look at all the hyponyms of `reference_book` (which is the hypernym of `cookbook`), you'd see that one of them is `instruction_book`. This seems intuitively very similar to a `cookbook`, so let's see what WordNet similarity has to say about it with the help of the following code:

```
>>> from nltk.corpus import wordnet
>>> cb = wordnet.synset('cookbook.n.01')
>>> ib = wordnet.synset('instruction_book.n.01')
>>> cb.wup_similarity(ib)
0.9166666666666666
```

So they are over 91% similar!

How it works...

The `wup_similarity` method is short for **Wu-Palmer Similarity**, which is a scoring method based on how similar the word senses are and where the Synsets occur relative to each other in the hypernym tree. One of the core metrics used to calculate similarity is the shortest path distance between the two Synsets and their common hypernym:

```
>>> ref = cb.hypernyms()[0]
>>> cb.shortest_path_distance(ref)
1
>>> ib.shortest_path_distance(ref)
1
>>> cb.shortest_path_distance(ib)
2
```

So `cookbook` and `instruction_book` must be very similar, because they are only one step away from the same `reference_book` hypernym, and, therefore, only two steps away from each other.

There's more...

Let's look at two dissimilar words to see what kind of score we get. We'll compare `dog` with `cookbook`, two seemingly very different words.

```
>>> dog = wordnet.synsets('dog')[0]
>>> dog.wup_similarity(cb)
0.38095238095238093
```

Wow, `dog` and `cookbook` are apparently 38% similar! This is because they share common hypernyms further up the tree:

```
>>> sorted(dog.common_hypernyms(cb))
[Synset('entity.n.01'), Synset('object.n.01'), Synset('physical_
entity.n.01'), Synset('whole.n.02')]
```

Comparing verbs

The previous comparisons were all between nouns, but the same can be done for verbs as well:

```
>>> cook = wordnet.synset('cook.v.01')
>>> bake = wordnet.0('bake.v.02')
>>> cook.wup_similarity(bake)
00.6666666666666666
```

The previous Synsets were obviously handpicked for demonstration, and the reason is that the hypernym tree for verbs has a lot more breadth and a lot less depth. While most nouns can be traced up to the hypernym `object`, thereby providing a basis for similarity, many verbs do not share common hypernyms, making WordNet unable to calculate the similarity. For example, if you were to use the Synset for `bake.v.01` in the previous code, instead of `bake.v.02`, the return value would be `None`. This is because the root hypernyms of both the Synsets are different, with no overlapping paths. For this reason, you also cannot calculate the similarity between words with different parts of speech.

Path and Leacock Chordorow (LCH) similarity

Two other similarity comparisons are the path similarity and the LCH similarity, as shown in the following code:

```
>>> cb.path_similarity(ib)
0.3333333333333333
>>> cb.path_similarity(dog)
0.07142857142857142
>>> cb.lch_similarity(ib)
2.538973871058276
>>> cb.lch_similarity(dog)
0.9985288301111273
```

As you can see, the number ranges are very different for these scoring methods, which is why I prefer the `wup_similarity` method.

See also

The recipe on *Looking up Synsets for a word in WordNet* has more details about hypernyms and the hypernym tree.

Discovering word collocations

Collocations are two or more words that tend to appear frequently together, such as United States. Of course, there are many other words that can come after United, such as United Kingdom and United Airlines. As with many aspects of natural language processing, context is very important. And for collocations, context is everything!

In the case of collocations, the context will be a document in the form of a list of words. Discovering collocations in this list of words means that we'll find common phrases that occur frequently throughout the text. For fun, we'll start with the script for *Monty Python and the Holy Grail*.

Getting ready

The script for *Monty Python and the Holy Grail* is found in the `webtext` corpus, so be sure that it's unzipped at `nltk_data/corpora/webtext/`.

How to do it...

We're going to create a list of all lowercased words in the text, and then produce `BigramCollocationFinder`, which we can use to find bigrams, which are pairs of words. These bigrams are found using association measurement functions in the `nltk.metrics` package, as follows:

```
>>> from nltk.corpus import webtext
>>> from nltk.collocations import BigramCollocationFinder
>>> from nltk.metrics import BigramAssocMeasures
>>> words = [w.lower() for w in webtext.words('grail.txt')]
>>> bcf = BigramCollocationFinder.from_words(words)
>>> bcf.nbest(BigramAssocMeasures.likelihood_ratio, 4)
[("'", 's'), ('arthur', ':'), ('#', '1'), ("'", 't')]
```

Well, that's not very useful! Let's refine it a bit by adding a word filter to remove punctuation and stopwords:

```
>>> from nltk.corpus import stopwords
>>> stopset = set(stopwords.words('english'))
>>> filter_stops = lambda w: len(w) < 3 or w in stopset
>>> bcf.apply_word_filter(filter_stops)
>>> bcf.nbest(BigramAssocMeasures.likelihood_ratio, 4)
[('black', 'knight'), ('clop', 'clop'), ('head', 'knight'), ('mumble',
'mumble')]
```

Much better, we can clearly see four of the most common bigrams in *Monty Python and the Holy Grail*. If you'd like to see more than four, simply increase the number to whatever you want, and the collocation finder will do its best.

How it works...

`BigramCollocationFinder` constructs two frequency distributions: one for each word, and another for bigrams. A frequency distribution, or `FreqDist` in NLTK, is basically an enhanced Python dictionary where the keys are what's being counted, and the values are the counts. Any filtering functions that are applied reduce the size of these two `FreqDists` by eliminating any words that don't pass the filter. By using a filtering function to eliminate all words that are one or two characters, and all English stopwords, we can get a much cleaner result. After filtering, the collocation finder is ready to accept a generic scoring function for finding collocations.

There's more...

In addition to `BigramCollocationFinder`, there's also `TrigramCollocationFinder`, which finds triplets instead of pairs. This time, we'll look for trigrams in Australian singles advertisements with the help of the following code:

```
>>> from nltk.collocations import TrigramCollocationFinder
>>> from nltk.metrics import TrigramAssocMeasures
>>> words = [w.lower() for w in webtext.words('singles.txt')]
>>> tcf = TrigramCollocationFinder.from_words(words)
>>> tcf.apply_word_filter(filter_stops)
>>> tcf.apply_freq_filter(3)
>>> tcf.nbest(TrigramAssocMeasures.likelihood_ratio, 4)
[('long', 'term', 'relationship')]
```

Now, we don't know whether people are looking for a long-term relationship or not, but clearly it's an important topic. In addition to the stopword filter, I also applied a frequency filter, which removed any trigrams that occurred less than three times. This is why only one result was returned when we asked for four because there was only one result that occurred more than two times.

Scoring functions

There are many more scoring functions available besides `likelihood_ratio()`. But other than `raw_freq()`, you may need a bit of a statistics background to understand how they work. Consult the NLTK API documentation for `NgramAssocMeasures` in the `nltk.metrics` package to see all the possible scoring functions.

Scoring ngrams

In addition to the `nbest()` method, there are two other ways to get ngrams (a generic term used for describing bigrams and trigrams) from a collocation finder:

- `above_score(score_fn, min_score)`: This can be used to get all ngrams with scores that are at least `min_score`. The `min_score` value that you choose will depend heavily on the `score_fn` you use.
- `score_ngrams(score_fn)`: This will return a list with tuple pairs of (ngram, score). This can be used to inform your choice for `min_score`.

See also

The `nltk.metrics` module will be used again in the *Measuring precision and recall of a classifier* and *Calculating high information words* recipes in *Chapter 7, Text Classification*.

2

Replacing and Correcting Words

In this chapter, we will cover the following recipes:

- Stemming words
- Lemmatizing words with WordNet
- Replacing words matching regular expressions
- Removing repeating characters
- Spelling correction with Enchant
- Replacing synonyms
- Replacing negations with antonyms

Introduction

In this chapter, we will go over various word replacement and correction techniques. The recipes cover the gamut of linguistic compression, spelling correction, and text normalization. All of these methods can be very useful for preprocessing text before search indexing, document classification, and text analysis.

Stemming words

Stemming is a technique to remove affixes from a word, ending up with the stem. For example, the stem of `cooking` is `cook`, and a good stemming algorithm knows that the `ing` suffix can be removed. Stemming is most commonly used by search engines for indexing words. Instead of storing all forms of a word, a search engine can store only the stems, greatly reducing the size of index while increasing retrieval accuracy.

One of the most common stemming algorithms is the **Porter stemming algorithm** by Martin Porter. It is designed to remove and replace well-known suffixes of English words, and its usage in NLTK will be covered in the next section.

> The resulting stem is not always a valid word. For example, the stem of `cookery` is `cookeri`. This is a feature, not a bug.

How to do it...

NLTK comes with an implementation of the Porter stemming algorithm, which is very easy to use. Simply instantiate the `PorterStemmer` class and call the `stem()` method with the word you want to stem:

```
>>> from nltk.stem import PorterStemmer
>>> stemmer = PorterStemmer()
>>> stemmer.stem('cooking')
'cook'
>>> stemmer.stem('cookery')
'cookeri'
```

How it works...

The `PorterStemmer` class knows a number of regular word forms and suffixes and uses this knowledge to transform your input word to a final stem through a series of steps. The resulting stem is often a shorter word, or at least a common form of the word, which has the same root meaning.

There's more...

There are other stemming algorithms out there besides the Porter stemming algorithm, such as the **Lancaster stemming algorithm**, developed at Lancaster University. NLTK includes it as the `LancasterStemmer` class. At the time of writing this book, there is no definitive research demonstrating the superiority of one algorithm over the other. However, Porter stemming algorithm is generally the default choice.

All the stemmers covered next inherit from the `StemmerI` interface, which defines the `stem()` method. The following is an inheritance diagram that explains this:

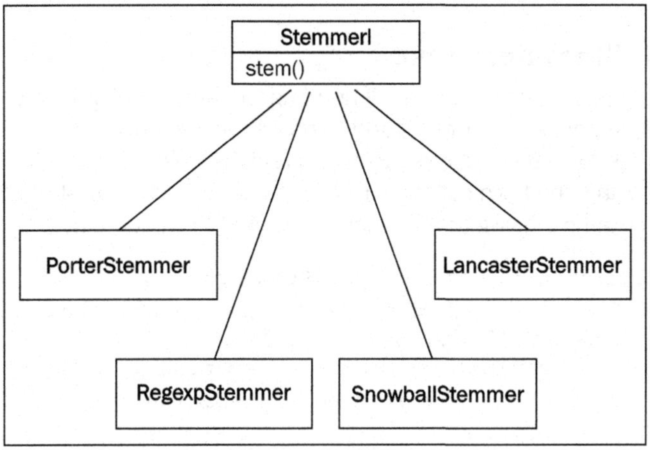

The LancasterStemmer class

The functions of the `LancasterStemmer` class are just like the functions of the `PorterStemmer` class, but can produce slightly different results. It is known to be slightly more aggressive than the `PorterStemmer` functions:

```
>>> from nltk.stem import LancasterStemmer
>>> stemmer = LancasterStemmer()
>>> stemmer.stem('cooking')
'cook'
>>> stemmer.stem('cookery')
'cookery'
```

The RegexpStemmer class

You can also construct your own stemmer using the `RegexpStemmer` class. It takes a single regular expression (either compiled or as a string) and removes any prefix or suffix that matches the expression:

```
>>> from nltk.stem import RegexpStemmer
>>> stemmer = RegexpStemmer('ing')
>>> stemmer.stem('cooking')
'cook'
>>> stemmer.stem('cookery')
'cookery'
>>> stemmer.stem('ingleside')
'leside'
```

A `RegexpStemmer` class should only be used in very specific cases that are not covered by the `PorterStemmer` or the `LancasterStemmer` class because it can only handle very specific patterns and is not a general-purpose algorithm.

The SnowballStemmer class

The `SnowballStemmer` class supports 13 non-English languages. It also provides two English stemmers: the original porter algorithm as well as the new English stemming algorithm. To use the `SnowballStemmer` class, create an instance with the name of the language you are using and then call the `stem()` method. Here is a list of all the supported languages and an example using the Spanish `SnowballStemmer` class:

```
>>> from nltk.stem import SnowballStemmer
>>> SnowballStemmer.languages('danish', 'dutch', 'english', 'finnish',
'french', 'german', 'hungarian', 'italian', 'norwegian', 'porter',
'portuguese', 'romanian', 'russian', 'spanish', 'swedish')
>>> spanish_stemmer = SnowballStemmer('spanish')
>>> spanish_stemmer.stem('hola')
u'hol'
```

See also

In the next recipe, we will cover Lemmatization, which is quite similar to stemming, but subtly different.

Lemmatizing words with WordNet

Lemmatization is very similar to stemming, but is more akin to synonym replacement. A lemma is a root word, as opposed to the root stem. So unlike stemming, you are always left with a valid word that means the same thing. However, the word you end up with can be completely different. A few examples will explain this.

Getting ready

Make sure that you have unzipped the `wordnet` corpus in `nltk_data/corpora/wordnet`. This will allow the `WordNetLemmatizer` class to access WordNet. You should also be familiar with the part-of-speech tags covered in the *Looking up Synsets for a word in WordNet* recipe of *Chapter 1, Tokenizing Text and WordNet Basics*.

How to do it...

We will use the `WordNetLemmatizer` class to find lemmas:

```
>>> from nltk.stem import WordNetLemmatizer
>>> lemmatizer = WordNetLemmatizer()
>>> lemmatizer.lemmatize('cooking')
'cooking'
>>> lemmatizer.lemmatize('cooking', pos='v')
'cook'
>>> lemmatizer.lemmatize('cookbooks')
'cookbook'
```

How it works...

The `WordNetLemmatizer` class is a thin wrapper around the `wordnet` corpus and uses the `morphy()` function of the `WordNetCorpusReader` class to find a lemma. If no lemma is found, or the word itself is a lemma, the word is returned as is. Unlike with stemming, knowing the part of speech of the word is important. As demonstrated previously, `cooking` does not return a different lemma unless you specify that the POS is a verb. This is because the default POS is a noun, and as a noun, `cooking` is its own lemma. On the other hand, `cookbooks` is a noun with its singular form, `cookbook`, as its lemma.

There's more...

Here's an example that illustrates one of the major differences between stemming and lemmatization:

```
>>> from nltk.stem import PorterStemmer
>>> stemmer = PorterStemmer()
>>> stemmer.stem('believes')
'believ'
>>> lemmatizer.lemmatize('believes')
'belief'
```

Instead of just chopping off the `es` like the `PorterStemmer` class, the `WordNetLemmatizer` class finds a valid root word. Where a stemmer only looks at the form of the word, the lemmatizer looks at the meaning of the word. By returning a lemma, you will always get a valid word.

Combining stemming with lemmatization

Stemming and lemmatization can be combined to compress words more than either process can by itself. These cases are somewhat rare, but they do exist:

```
>>> stemmer.stem('buses')
'buse'
>>> lemmatizer.lemmatize('buses')
'bus'
>>> stemmer.stem('bus')
'bu'
```

In this example, stemming saves one character, lemmatization saves two characters, and stemming the lemma saves a total of three characters out of five characters. That is nearly a 60% compression rate! This level of word compression over many thousands of words, while unlikely to always produce such high gains, can still make a huge difference.

See also

In the previous recipe, we covered the basics of stemming and WordNet was introduced in the *Looking up Synsets for a word in WordNet* and *Looking up lemmas and synonyms in WordNet* recipes of *Chapter 1, Tokenizing Text and WordNet Basics*. Looking forward, we will cover the *Using WordNet for tagging* recipe in *Chapter 4, Part-of-speech Tagging*.

Replacing words matching regular expressions

Now, we are going to get into the process of replacing words. If stemming and lemmatization are a kind of linguistic compression, then word replacement can be thought of as error correction or text normalization.

In this recipe, we will replace words based on regular expressions, with a focus on expanding contractions. Remember when we were tokenizing words in *Chapter 1, Tokenizing Text and WordNet Basics*, and it was clear that most tokenizers had trouble with contractions? This recipe aims to fix this by replacing contractions with their expanded forms, for example, by replacing "can't" with "cannot" or "would've" with "would have".

Getting ready

Understanding how this recipe works will require a basic knowledge of regular expressions and the `re` module. The key things to know are matching patterns and the `re.sub()` function.

How to do it...

First, we need to define a number of replacement patterns. This will be a list of tuple pairs, where the first element is the pattern to match with and the second element is the replacement.

Next, we will create a `RegexpReplacer` class that will compile the patterns and provide a `replace()` method to substitute all the found patterns with their replacements.

The following code can be found in the `replacers.py` module in the book's code bundle and is meant to be imported, not typed into the console:

```
import re

replacement_patterns = [
  (r'won\'t', 'will not'),
  (r'can\'t', 'cannot'),
  (r'i\'m', 'i am'),
  (r'ain\'t', 'is not'),
  (r'(\w+)\'ll', '\g<1> will'),
  (r'(\w+)n\'t', '\g<1> not'),
  (r'(\w+)\'ve', '\g<1> have'),
  (r'(\w+)\'s', '\g<1> is'),
  (r'(\w+)\'re', '\g<1> are'),
  (r'(\w+)\'d', '\g<1> would')
]

class RegexpReplacer(object):
  def __init__(self, patterns=replacement_patterns):
    self.patterns = [(re.compile(regex), repl) for (regex, repl) in
      patterns]

  def replace(self, text):
    s = text
    for (pattern, repl) in self.patterns:
      s = re.sub(pattern, repl, s)
    return s
```

How it works...

Here is a simple usage example:

```
>>> from replacers import RegexpReplacer
>>> replacer = RegexpReplacer()
>>> replacer.replace("can't is a contraction")
'cannot is a contraction'
>>> replacer.replace("I should've done that thing I didn't do")
'I should have done that thing I did not do'
```

The `RegexpReplacer.replace()` function works by replacing every instance of a replacement pattern with its corresponding substitution pattern. In replacement patterns, we have defined tuples such as `r'(\w+)\'ve'` and `'\g<1> have'`. The first element matches a group of ASCII characters followed by `'ve`. By grouping the characters before `'ve` in parenthesis, a match group is found and can be used in the substitution pattern with the `\g<1>` reference. So, we keep everything before `'ve`, then replace `'ve` with the word have. This is how `should've` can become `should have`.

There's more...

This replacement technique can work with any kind of regular expression, not just contractions. So, you can replace any occurrence of `&` with `and`, or eliminate all occurrences of `-` by replacing it with an empty string. The `RegexpReplacer` class can take any list of replacement patterns for whatever purpose.

Replacement before tokenization

Let's try using the `RegexpReplacer` class as a preliminary step before tokenization:

```
>>> from nltk.tokenize import word_tokenize
>>> from replacers import RegexpReplacer
>>> replacer = RegexpReplacer()
>>> word_tokenize("can't is a contraction")
['ca', "n't", 'is', 'a', 'contraction']
>>> word_tokenize(replacer.replace("can't is a contraction"))
['can', 'not', 'is', 'a', 'contraction']
```

Much better! By eliminating the contractions in the first place, the tokenizer will produce cleaner results. Cleaning up the text before processing is a common pattern in natural language processing.

See also

For more information on tokenization, see the first three recipes in *Chapter 1, Tokenizing Text and WordNet Basics*. For more replacement techniques, continue reading the rest of this chapter.

Removing repeating characters

In everyday language, people are often not strictly grammatical. They will write things such as `I looooooove it` in order to emphasize the word `love`. However, computers don't know that "looooooove" is a variation of "love" unless they are told. This recipe presents a method to remove these annoying repeating characters in order to end up with a *proper* English word.

Getting ready

As in the previous recipe, we will be making use of the `re` module, and more specifically, backreferences. A **backreference** is a way to refer to a previously matched group in a regular expression. This will allow us to match and remove repeating characters.

How to do it...

We will create a class that has the same form as the `RegexpReplacer` class from the previous recipe. It will have a `replace()` method that takes a single word and returns a more correct version of that word, with the dubious repeating characters removed. This code can be found in `replacers.py` in the book's code bundle and is meant to be imported:

```
import re

class RepeatReplacer(object):
  def __init__(self):
    self.repeat_regexp = re.compile(r'(\w*)(\w)\2(\w*)')
    self.repl = r'\1\2\3'

  def replace(self, word):
    repl_word = self.repeat_regexp.sub(self.repl, word)

    if repl_word != word:
      return self.replace(repl_word)
    else:
      return repl_word
```

And now some example use cases:

```
>>> from replacers import RepeatReplacer
>>> replacer = RepeatReplacer()
>>> replacer.replace('looooove')
'love'
>>> replacer.replace('oooooh')
'oh'
>>> replacer.replace('goose')
'gose'
```

How it works...

The `RepeatReplacer` class starts by compiling a regular expression to match and define a replacement string with backreferences. The `repeat_regexp` pattern matches three groups:

- `0` or more starting characters `(\w*)`
- A single character `(\w)` that is followed by another instance of that character `(\2)`
- `0` or more ending characters `(\w*)`

The replacement string is then used to keep all the matched groups, while discarding the backreference to the second group. So, the word `looooove` gets split into `(looo)(o)o(ve)` and then recombined as `loooove`, discarding the last `o`. This continues until only one `o` remains, when `repeat_regexp` no longer matches the string and no more characters are removed.

There's more...

In the preceding examples, you can see that the `RepeatReplacer` class is a bit too greedy and ends up changing `goose` into `gose`. To correct this issue, we can augment the `replace()` function with a WordNet lookup. If WordNet recognizes the word, then we can stop replacing characters. Here is the WordNet-augmented version:

```
import re
from nltk.corpus import wordnet

class RepeatReplacer(object):
  def __init__(self):
    self.repeat_regexp = re.compile(r'(\w*)(\w)\2(\w*)')
    self.repl = r'\1\2\3'
```

```
    def replace(self, word):
      if wordnet.synsets(word):
        return word
      repl_word = self.repeat_regexp.sub(self.repl, word)

      if repl_word != word:
        return self.replace(repl_word)
      else:
        return repl_word
```

Now, `goose` will be found in WordNet, and no character replacement will take place. Also, `oooooh` will become `ooh` instead of `oh` because `ooh` is actually a word in WordNet, defined as an expression of admiration or pleasure.

See also

Read the next recipe to learn how to correct misspellings. For more information on WordNet, refer to the WordNet recipes in *Chapter 1, Tokenizing Text and WordNet Basics*. We will also be using WordNet for antonym replacement later in this chapter.

Spelling correction with Enchant

Replacing repeating characters is actually an extreme form of spelling correction. In this recipe, we will take on the less extreme case of correcting minor spelling issues using **Enchant**—a spelling correction API.

Getting ready

You will need to install Enchant and a dictionary for it to use. Enchant is an offshoot of the AbiWord open source word processor, and more information on it can be found at `http://www.abisource.com/projects/enchant/`.

For dictionaries, **Aspell** is a good open source spellchecker and dictionary that can be found at `http://aspell.net/`.

Finally, you will need the **PyEnchant** library, which can be found at the following link: `http://pythonhosted.org/pyenchant/`

You should be able to install it with the `easy_install` command that comes with Python setuptools, such as by typing `sudo easy_install pyenchant` on Linux or Unix. On a Mac machine, PyEnchant may be difficult to install. If you have difficulties, consult `http://pythonhosted.org/pyenchant/download.html`.

How to do it...

We will create a new class called `SpellingReplacer` in `replacers.py`, and this time, the `replace()` method will check Enchant to see whether the word is valid. If not, we will look up the suggested alternatives and return the best match using `nltk.metrics.edit_distance()`:

```
import enchant
from nltk.metrics import edit_distance

class SpellingReplacer(object):
  def __init__(self, dict_name='en', max_dist=2):
    self.spell_dict = enchant.Dict(dict_name)
    self.max_dist = max_dist

  def replace(self, word):
    if self.spell_dict.check(word):
      return word
    suggestions = self.spell_dict.suggest(word)

    if suggestions and edit_distance(word, suggestions[0]) <=
      self.max_dist:
      return suggestions[0]
    else:
      return word
```

The preceding class can be used to correct English spellings, as follows:

```
>>> from replacers import SpellingReplacer
>>> replacer = SpellingReplacer()
>>> replacer.replace('cookbok')
'cookbook'
```

How it works...

The `SpellingReplacer` class starts by creating a reference to an Enchant dictionary. Then, in the `replace()` method, it first checks whether the given word is present in the dictionary. If it is, no spelling correction is necessary and the word is returned. If the word is not found, it looks up a list of suggestions and returns the first suggestion, as long as its edit distance is less than or equal to `max_dist`. The edit distance is the number of character changes necessary to transform the given word into the suggested word. The `max_dist` value then acts as a constraint on the Enchant `suggest` function to ensure that no unlikely replacement words are returned. Here is an example showing all the suggestions for `languege`, a misspelling of `language`:

```
>>> import enchant
>>> d = enchant.Dict('en')
>>> d.suggest('languege')
['language', 'languages', 'languor', "language's"]
```

Except for the correct suggestion, `language`, all the other words have an edit distance of three or greater. You can try this yourself with the following code:

```
>>> from nltk.metrics import edit_distance
>>> edit_distance('language', 'languege')
1
>>> edit_distance('language', 'languo')
3
```

There's more...

You can use language dictionaries other than `en`, such as `en_GB`, assuming the dictionary has already been installed. To check which other languages are available, use `enchant.list_languages()`:

```
>>> enchant.list_languages()
['en', 'en_CA', 'en_GB', 'en_US']
```

> If you try to use a dictionary that doesn't exist, you will get `enchant.DictNotFoundError`. You can first check whether the dictionary exists using `enchant.dict_exists()`, which will return `True` if the named dictionary exists, or `False` otherwise.

The en_GB dictionary

Always ensure that you use the correct dictionary for whichever language you are performing spelling correction on. The `en_US` dictionary can give you different results than `en_GB`, such as for the word `theater`. The word `theater` is the American English spelling whereas the British English spelling is `theatre`:

```
>>> import enchant
>>> dUS = enchant.Dict('en_US')
>>> dUS.check('theater')
True
>>> dGB = enchant.Dict('en_GB')
>>> dGB.check('theater')
False
```

```
>>> from replacers import SpellingReplacer
>>> us_replacer = SpellingReplacer('en_US')
>>> us_replacer.replace('theater')
'theater'
>>> gb_replacer = SpellingReplacer('en_GB')
>>> gb_replacer.replace('theater')
'theatre'
```

Personal word lists

Enchant also supports personal word lists. These can be combined with an existing dictionary, allowing you to augment the dictionary with your own words. So, let's say you had a file named `mywords.txt` that had `nltk` on one line. You could then create a dictionary augmented with your personal word list as follows:

```
>>> d = enchant.Dict('en_US')
>>> d.check('nltk')
False
>>> d = enchant.DictWithPWL('en_US', 'mywords.txt')
>>> d.check('nltk')
True
```

To use an augmented dictionary with our `SpellingReplacer` class, we can create a subclass in `replacers.py` that takes an existing spelling dictionary:

```
class CustomSpellingReplacer(SpellingReplacer):
  def __init__(self, spell_dict, max_dist=2):
    self.spell_dict = spell_dict
    self.max_dist = max_dist
```

This `CustomSpellingReplacer` class will not replace any words that you put into `mywords.txt`:

```
>>> from replacers import CustomSpellingReplacer
>>> d = enchant.DictWithPWL('en_US', 'mywords.txt')
>>> replacer = CustomSpellingReplacer(d)
>>> replacer.replace('nltk')
'nltk'
```

See also

The previous recipe covered an extreme form of spelling correction by replacing repeating characters. You can also perform spelling correction by simple word replacement as discussed in the next recipe.

Replacing synonyms

It is often useful to reduce the vocabulary of a text by replacing words with common synonyms. By compressing the vocabulary without losing meaning, you can save memory in cases such as *frequency analysis* and *text indexing*. More details about these topics are available at `https://en.wikipedia.org/wiki/Frequency_analysis` and `https://en.wikipedia.org/wiki/Full_text_search`. Vocabulary reduction can also increase the occurrence of significant collocations, which was covered in the *Discovering word collocations* recipe of *Chapter 1, Tokenizing Text and WordNet Basics*.

Getting ready

You will need a defined mapping of a word to its synonym. This is a simple controlled vocabulary. We will start by hardcoding the synonyms as a Python dictionary, and then explore other options to store synonym maps.

How to do it...

We'll first create a `WordReplacer` class in `replacers.py` that takes a word replacement mapping:

```
class WordReplacer(object):
  def __init__(self, word_map):
    self.word_map = word_map

  def replace(self, word):
    return self.word_map.get(word, word)
```

Then, we can demonstrate its usage for simple word replacement:

```
>>> from replacers import WordReplacer
>>> replacer = WordReplacer({'bday': 'birthday'})
>>> replacer.replace('bday')
'birthday'
>>> replacer.replace('happy')
'happy'
```

How it works...

The `WordReplacer` class is simply a class wrapper around a Python dictionary. The `replace()` method looks up the given word in its `word_map` dictionary and returns the replacement synonym if it exists. Otherwise, the given word is returned as is.

If you were only using the `word_map` dictionary, you wouldn't need the `WordReplacer` class and could instead call `word_map.get()` directly. However, `WordReplacer` can act as a base class for other classes that construct the `word_map` dictionary from various file formats. Read on for more information.

There's more...

Hardcoding synonyms in a Python dictionary is not a good long-term solution. Two better alternatives are to store the synonyms in a CSV file or in a YAML file. Choose whichever format is easiest for those who maintain your synonym vocabulary. Both of the classes outlined in the following section inherit the `replace()` method from `WordReplacer`.

CSV synonym replacement

The `CsvWordReplacer` class extends `WordReplacer` in `replacers.py` in order to construct the `word_map` dictionary from a CSV file:

```
import csv

class CsvWordReplacer(WordReplacer):
  def __init__(self, fname):
    word_map = {}
    for line in csv.reader(open(fname)):
      word, syn = line
      word_map[word] = syn
    super(CsvWordReplacer, self).__init__(word_map)
```

Your CSV file should consist of two columns, where the first column is the word and the second column is the synonym meant to replace it. If this file is called `synonyms.csv` and the first line is `bday, birthday`, then you can perform the following:

```
>>> from replacers import CsvWordReplacer
>>> replacer = CsvWordReplacer('synonyms.csv')
>>> replacer.replace('bday')
'birthday'
>>> replacer.replace('happy')
'happy'
```

YAML synonym replacement

If you have PyYAML installed, you can create `YamlWordReplacer` in `replacers.py` as shown in the following:

```
import yaml

class YamlWordReplacer(WordReplacer):
  def __init__(self, fname):
    word_map = yaml.load(open(fname))
    super(YamlWordReplacer, self).__init__(word_map)
```

> Download and installation instructions for PyYAML are located at `http://pyyaml.org/wiki/PyYAML`. You can also type `pip install pyyaml` on the command prompt

Your YAML file should be a simple mapping of `word: synonym`, such as `bday: birthday`. Note that the YAML syntax is very particular, and the space after the colon is required. If the file is named `synonyms.yaml`, then you can perform the following:

```
>>> from replacers import YamlWordReplacer
>>> replacer = YamlWordReplacer('synonyms.yaml')
>>> replacer.replace('bday')
'birthday'
>>> replacer.replace('happy')
'happy'
```

See also

You can use the `WordReplacer` class to perform any kind of word replacement, even spelling correction for more complicated words that can't be automatically corrected, as we did in the previous recipe. In the next recipe, we will cover antonym replacement.

Replacing negations with antonyms

The opposite of synonym replacement is **antonym replacement**. An **antonym** is a word that has the opposite meaning of another word. This time, instead of creating custom word mappings, we can use WordNet to replace words with unambiguous antonyms. Refer to the *Looking up lemmas and synonyms in WordNet* recipe in *Chapter 1, Tokenizing Text and WordNet Basics*, for more details on antonym lookups.

How to do it...

Let's say you have a sentence like `let's not uglify our code`. With antonym replacement, you can replace `not uglify` with `beautify`, resulting in the sentence `let's beautify our code`. To do this, we will create an `AntonymReplacer` class in `replacers.py` as follows:

```
from nltk.corpus import wordnet

class AntonymReplacer(object):
  def replace(self, word, pos=None):
    antonyms = set()
    for syn in wordnet.synsets(word, pos=pos):
      for lemma in syn.lemmas():
        for antonym in lemma.antonyms():
          antonyms.add(antonym.name())
    if len(antonyms) == 1:
      return antonyms.pop()
    else:
      return None

  def replace_negations(self, sent):
    i, l = 0, len(sent)
    words = []
    while i < l:
      word = sent[i]
      if word == 'not' and i+1 < l:
        ant = self.replace(sent[i+1])
        if ant:
          words.append(ant)
          i += 2
          continue
      words.append(word)
      i += 1
    return words
```

Now, we can tokenize the original sentence into `["let's", 'not', 'uglify', 'our', 'code']` and pass this to the `replace_negations()` function. Here are some examples:

```
>>> from replacers import AntonymReplacer
>>> replacer = AntonymReplacer()
>>> replacer.replace('good')
>>> replacer.replace('uglify')
'beautify'
>>> sent = ["let's", 'not', 'uglify', 'our', 'code']
>>> replacer.replace_negations(sent)
["let's", 'beautify', 'our', 'code']
```

How it works...

The `AntonymReplacer` class has two methods: `replace()` and `replace_negations()`. The `replace()` method takes a single word and an optional part-of-speech tag, then looks up the Synsets for the word in WordNet. Going through all the Synsets and every lemma of each Synset, it creates a set of all antonyms found. If only one antonym is found, then it is an unambiguous replacement. If there is more than one antonym, which can happen quite often, then we don't know for sure which antonym is correct. In the case of multiple antonyms (or no antonyms), `replace()` returns `None` as it cannot make a decision.

In `replace_negations()`, we look through a tokenized sentence for the word `not`. If `not` is found, then we try to find an antonym for the next word using `replace()`. If we find an antonym, then it is appended to the list of words, replacing `not` and the original word. All other words are appended as is, resulting in a tokenized sentence with unambiguous negations replaced by their antonyms.

There's more...

As unambiguous antonyms aren't very common in WordNet, you might want to create a custom antonym mapping in the same way we did for synonyms. This `AntonymWordReplacer` can be constructed by inheriting from both `WordReplacer` and `AntonymReplacer`:

```
class AntonymWordReplacer(WordReplacer, AntonymReplacer):
  pass
```

The order of inheritance is very important, as we want the initialization and replace function of `WordReplacer` combined with the `replace_negations` function from `AntonymReplacer`. The result is a replacer that can perform the following:

```
>>> from replacers import AntonymWordReplacer
>>> replacer = AntonymWordReplacer({'evil': 'good'})
>>> replacer.replace_negations(['good', 'is', 'not', 'evil'])
['good', 'is', 'good']
```

Of course, you can also inherit from `CsvWordReplacer` or `YamlWordReplacer` instead of `WordReplacer` if you want to load the antonym word mappings from a file.

See also

The previous recipe covers the `WordReplacer` from the perspective of synonym replacement. In *Chapter 1, Tokenizing Text and WordNet Basics*, WordNet usage is covered in detail in the *Looking up Synsets for a word in WordNet* and *Looking up lemmas and synonyms in WordNet* recipes.

3

Creating Custom Corpora

In this chapter, we will cover the following recipes:

- Setting up a custom corpus
- Creating a wordlist corpus
- Creating a part-of-speech tagged word corpus
- Creating a chunked phrase corpus
- Creating a categorized text corpus
- Creating a categorized chunk corpus reader
- Lazy corpus loading
- Creating a custom corpus view
- Creating a MongoDB-backed corpus reader
- Corpus editing with file locking

Introduction

In this chapter, we'll cover how to use corpus readers and create custom corpora. If you want to train your own model, such as a part-of-speech tagger or text classifier, you will need to create a custom corpus to train on. Model training is covered in the subsequent chapters.

Now you'll learn how to use the existing corpus data that comes with NLTK. This information is essential for future chapters when we'll need to access the corpora as training data. You've already accessed the WordNet corpus in *Chapter 1, Tokenizing Text and WordNet Basics*. This chapter will introduce you to many more corpora.

We'll also cover creating custom corpus readers, which can be used when your corpus is not in a file format that NLTK already recognizes, or if your corpus is not located in files at all, but instead is located in a database such as MongoDB. It is essential to be familiar with tokenization, which was covered in *Chapter 1, Tokenizing Text and WordNet Basics*.

Setting up a custom corpus

A **corpus** is a collection of text documents, and **corpora** is the plural of corpus. This comes from the Latin word for body; in this case, a body of text. So a **custom corpus** is really just a bunch of text files in a directory, often alongside many other directories of text files.

Getting ready

You should already have the NLTK data package installed, following the instructions at `http://www.nltk.org/data`. We'll assume that the data is installed to `C:\nltk_data` on Windows, and `/usr/share/nltk_data` on Linux, Unix, and Mac OS X.

How to do it...

NLTK defines a list of data directories, or paths, in `nltk.data.path`. Our custom corpora must be within one of these paths so it can be found by NLTK. In order to avoid conflict with the official data package, we'll create a custom `nltk_data` directory in our home directory. The following is some Python code to create this directory and verify that it is in the list of known paths specified by `nltk.data.path`:

```
>>> import os, os.path
>>> path = os.path.expanduser('~/nltk_data')
>>> if not os.path.exists(path):
...       os.mkdir(path)
>>> os.path.exists(path)
True
>>> import nltk.data
>>> path in nltk.data.path
True
```

If the last line, `path in nltk.data.path`, is `True`, then you should now have a `nltk_data` directory in your home directory. The path should be `%UserProfile%\nltk_data` on Windows, or `~/nltk_data` on Unix, Linux, and Mac OS X. For simplicity, I'll refer to the directory as `~/nltk_data`.

> If the last line does not return `True`, try creating the `nltk_data` directory manually in your home directory, then verify that the absolute path is in `nltk.data.path`. It's essential to ensure that this directory exists and is in `nltk.data.path` before continuing. You can see a list of the directories by running `python -c "import nltk.data; print(nltk.data.path)"`. Once you have your `nltk_data` directory, the convention is that corpora resides in a `corpora` subdirectory. Create this `corpora` directory within the `nltk_data` directory, so that the path is `~/nltk_data/corpora`. Finally, we'll create a subdirectory in `corpora` to hold our custom corpus. Let's call it `cookbook`, giving us the full path, which is `~/nltk_data/corpora/cookbook`. So on Unix, Linux, and Mac OS X, you could run the following to create the directory:
>
> ```
> mkdir -p ~/nltk_data/corpora/cookbook
> ```

Now, we can create a simple wordlist file and make sure it loads. In the *Spelling correction with Enchant* recipe in *Chapter 2, Replacing and Correcting Words*, we created a wordlist file called `mywords.txt`. Put this file into `~/nltk_data/corpora/cookbook/`. Now we can use `nltk.data.load()`, as shown in the following code, to load the file:

```
>>> import nltk.data
>>> nltk.data.load('corpora/cookbook/mywords.txt', format='raw')
b'nltk\n'
```

> We need to specify `format='raw'` since `nltk.data.load()` doesn't know how to interpret `.txt` files. As we'll see, it does know how to interpret a number of other file formats.

How it works...

The `nltk.data.load()` function recognizes a number of formats, such as `'raw'`, `'pickle'`, and `'yaml'`. If no format is specified, then it tries to guess the format based on the file's extension. In the previous case, we have a `.txt` file, which is not a recognized extension, so we have to specify the `'raw'` format. But, if we used a file that ended in `.yaml`, then we would not need to specify the format.

Filenames passed into `nltk.data.load()` can be *absolute* or *relative* paths. Relative paths must be relative to one of the paths specified in `nltk.data.path`. The file is found using `nltk.data.find(path)`, which searches all known paths combined with the relative path. Absolute paths do not require a search, and are used as is. When using relative paths, be sure to use choose unambiguous names for your files so as not to conflict with any existing NLTK data.

There's more...

For most corpora access, you won't actually need to use `nltk.data.load`, as that will be handled by the `CorpusReader` classes covered in the following recipes. But it's a good function to be familiar with for loading pickle files and `.yaml` files, and it also introduces the idea of putting all of your data files into a path known by NLTK.

Loading a YAML file

If you put the `synonyms.yaml` file from the *Replacing synonyms* recipe in *Chapter 2, Replacing and Correcting Words* into `~/nltk_data/corpora/cookbook` (next to `mywords.txt`), you can use `nltk.data.load()` to load it without specifying a format:

```
>>> import nltk.data
>>> nltk.data.load('corpora/cookbook/synonyms.yaml')
{'bday': 'birthday'}
```

This assumes that PyYAML is installed. If not, you can find download and installation instructions at `http://pyyaml.org/wiki/PyYAML`.

See also

In the next recipes, we'll cover various corpus readers, and then in the *Lazy corpus loading* recipe, we'll use the `LazyCorpusLoader` class, which expects corpus data to be in a `corpora` subdirectory of one of the paths specified by `nltk.data.path`.

Creating a wordlist corpus

The `WordListCorpusReader` class is one of the simplest `CorpusReader` classes. It provides access to a file containing a list of words, one word per line. In fact, you've already used it when we used the stopwords corpus in *Chapter 1, Tokenizing Text and WordNet Basics,* in the *Filtering stopwords in a tokenized sentence* and *Discovering word collocations* recipes.

Getting ready

We need to start by creating a wordlist file. This could be a single column CSV file, or just a normal text file with one word per line. Let's create a file named `wordlist` that looks like this:

```
nltk
corpus
corpora
wordnet
```

How to do it...

Now we can instantiate a `WordListCorpusReader` class that will produce a list of words from our file. It takes two arguments: the directory path containing the files, and a list of filenames. If you open the Python console in the same directory as the files, then `'.'` can be used as the directory path. Otherwise, you must use a directory path such as `nltk_data/corpora/cookbook`:

```
>>> from nltk.corpus.reader import WordListCorpusReader
>>> reader = WordListCorpusReader('.', ['wordlist'])
>>> reader.words()
['nltk', 'corpus', 'corpora', 'wordnet']
>>> reader.fileids()
['wordlist']
```

How it works...

The `WordListCorpusReader` class inherits from `CorpusReader`, which is a common base class for all corpus readers. The `CorpusReader` class does all the work of identifying which files to read, while `WordListCorpusReader` reads the files and tokenizes each line to produce a list of words. The following is an inheritance diagram:

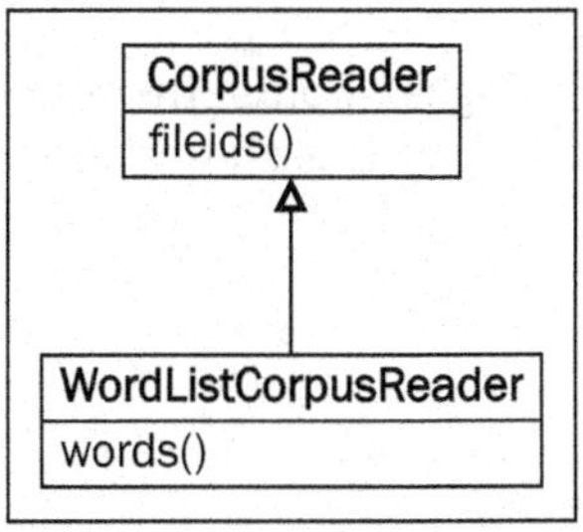

When you call the `words()` function, it calls `nltk.tokenize.line_tokenize()` on the raw file data, which you can access using the `raw()` function as follows:

```
>>> reader.raw()
'nltk\ncorpus\ncorpora\nwordnet\n'
>>> from nltk.tokenize import line_tokenize
>>> line_tokenize(reader.raw())
['nltk', 'corpus', 'corpora', 'wordnet']
```

There's more...

The `stopwords` corpus is a good example of a multifile `WordListCorpusReader`. In the *Filtering stopwords in a tokenized sentence* recipe in *Chapter 1, Tokenizing Text and WordNet Basics*, we saw that it had one wordlist file for each language, and you could access the words for that language by calling `stopwords.words(fileid)`. If you want to create your own multifile wordlist corpus, this is a great example to follow.

Names wordlist corpus

Another wordlist corpus that comes with NLTK is the `names` corpus that is shown in the following code. It contains two files: `female.txt` and `male.txt`, each containing a list of a few thousand common first names organized by gender as follows:

```
>>> from nltk.corpus import names
>>> names.fileids()
['female.txt', 'male.txt']
>>> len(names.words('female.txt'))
5001
>>> len(names.words('male.txt'))
2943
```

English words corpus

NLTK also comes with a large list of English words. There's one file with 850 basic words, and another list with over 200,000 known English words, as shown in the following code:

```
>>> from nltk.corpus import words
>>> words.fileids()
['en', 'en-basic']
>>> len(words.words('en-basic'))
850
>>> len(words.words('en'))
234936
```

See also

The *Filtering stopwords in a tokenized sentence* recipe in *Chapter 1, Tokenizing Text and WordNet Basics*, has more details on using the `stopwords` corpus. In the following recipes, we'll cover more advanced corpus file formats and corpus reader classes.

Creating a part-of-speech tagged word corpus

Part-of-speech tagging is the process of identifying the part-of-speech tag for a word. Most of the time, a tagger must first be trained on a training corpus. How to train and use a tagger is covered in detail in *Chapter 4, Part-of-speech Tagging*, but first we must know how to create and use a training corpus of part-of-speech tagged words.

Getting ready

The simplest format for a tagged corpus is of the form *word/tag*. The following is an excerpt from the `brown` corpus:

```
The/at-tl expense/nn and/cc time/nn involved/vbn are/ber
  astronomical/jj ./.
```

Each word has a tag denoting its part-of-speech. For example, `nn` refers to a noun, while a tag that starts with `vb` is a verb.

> Different corpora can use different tags to mean the same thing. For example, the `treebank` corpus uses different tags as compared to the `brown` corpus, even though both are English text. But both sets of tags can be converted into a universal tagset, described at the end of this recipe.

How to do it...

If you were to put the previous excerpt into a file called `brown.pos`, you could then create a `TaggedCorpusReader` class using the following code:

```
>>> from nltk.corpus.reader import TaggedCorpusReader
>>> reader = TaggedCorpusReader('.', r'.*\.pos')
>>> reader.words()
['The', 'expense', 'and', 'time', 'involved', 'are', ...]
>>> reader.tagged_words()
[('The', 'AT-TL'), ('expense', 'NN'), ('and', 'CC'), ...]
>>> reader.sents()
[['The', 'expense', 'and', 'time', 'involved', 'are', 'astronomical',
'.']]
>>> reader.tagged_sents()
```

```
[[('The', 'AT-TL'), ('expense', 'NN'), ('and', 'CC'), ('time', 'NN'),
('involved', 'VBN'), ('are', 'BER'), ('astronomical', 'JJ'), ('.',
'.')]]
>>> reader.paras()
[[['The', 'expense', 'and', 'time', 'involved', 'are', 'astronomical',
'.']]]
>>> reader.tagged_paras()
[[[('The', 'AT-TL'), ('expense', 'NN'), ('and', 'CC'), ('time', 'NN'),
('involved', 'VBN'), ('are', 'BER'), ('astronomical', 'JJ'), ('.',
'.')]]]
```

How it works...

This time, instead of naming the file explicitly, we use a regular expression, `r'.*\.pos'`, to match all the files whose names end with `.pos`. We could have done the same thing as we did with the `WordListCorpusReader` class, and pass `['brown.pos']` as the second argument, but this way you can see how to include multiple files in a corpus without naming each one explicitly.

The `TaggedCorpusReader` class provides a number of methods for extracting text from a corpus. First, you can get a list of all words or a list of tagged tokens. A tagged token is simply a tuple of `(word, tag)`. Next, you can get a list of every sentence and also every tagged sentence where the sentence is itself a list of words or tagged tokens. Finally, you can get a list of paragraphs, where each paragraph is a list of sentences and each sentence is a list of words or tagged tokens. The following is an inheritance diagram listing all the major methods:

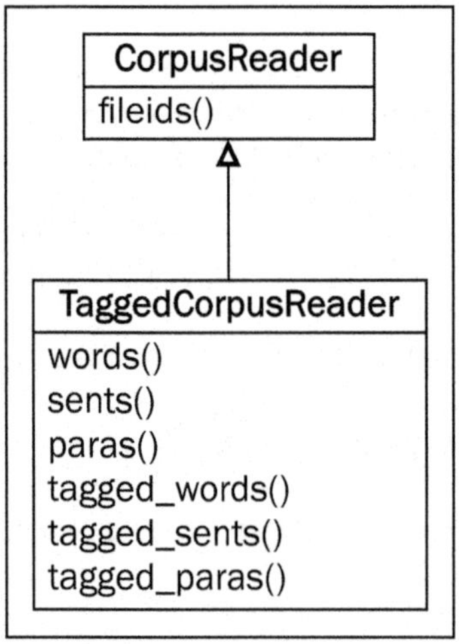

There's more...

All the functions we just demonstrated depend on tokenizers to split the text. The `TaggedCorpusReader` class tries to have good defaults, but you can customize them by passing in your own tokenizers at the time of initialization.

Customizing the word tokenizer

The default word tokenizer is an instance of `nltk.tokenize.WhitespaceTokenizer`. If you want to use a different tokenizer, you can pass that in as `word_tokenizer`, as shown in the following code:

```
>>> from nltk.tokenize import SpaceTokenizer
>>> reader = TaggedCorpusReader('.', r'.*\.pos', word_
tokenizer=SpaceTokenizer())
>>> reader.words()
['The', 'expense', 'and', 'time', 'involved', 'are', ...]
```

Customizing the sentence tokenizer

The default sentence tokenizer is an instance of `nltk.tokenize.RegexpTokenize` with `'\n'` to identify the gaps. It assumes that each sentence is on a line all by itself, and individual sentences do not have line breaks. To customize this, you can pass in your own tokenizer as `sent_tokenizer`, as shown in the following code:

```
>>> from nltk.tokenize import LineTokenizer
>>> reader = TaggedCorpusReader('.', r'.*\.pos', sent_
tokenizer=LineTokenizer())
>>> reader.sents()
[['The', 'expense', 'and', 'time', 'involved', 'are', 'astronomical',
'.']]
```

Customizing the paragraph block reader

Paragraphs are assumed to be split by blank lines. This is done with the `para_block_reader` function, which is `nltk.corpus.reader.util.read_blankline_block`. There are a number of other block reader functions in `nltk.corpus.reader.util`, whose purpose is to read blocks of text from a stream. Their usage will be covered in more detail later in the *Creating a custom corpus view* recipe, where we'll create a custom corpus reader.

Customizing the tag separator

If you don't want to use `'/'` as the word/tag separator, you can pass an alternative string to `TaggedCorpusReader` for `sep`. The default is `sep='/'`, but if you want to split words and tags with `'|'`, such as `'word|tag'`, then you should pass in `sep='|'`.

Converting tags to a universal tagset

NLTK 3.0 provides a method for converting known tagsets to a universal tagset. A **tagset** is just a list of part-of-speech tags used by one or more corpora. The **universal tagset** is a simplified and condensed tagset composed of only 12 part-of-speech tags, as shown in the following table:

Universal tag	Description
VERB	All verbs
NOUN	Common and proper nouns
PRON	Pronouns
ADJ	Adjectives
ADV	Adverbs
ADP	Prepositions and postpositions
CONJ	Conjunctions
DET	Determiners
NUM	Cardinal numbers
PRT	Participles
X	Other
.	Punctuation

Mappings from a known tagset to the universal tagset can be found at `nltk_data/taggers/universal_tagset`. For example, `treebank` tag mappings are in `nltk_data/taggers/universal_tagset/en-ptb.map`.

To map corpus tags to the universal tagset, the corpus reader must be initialized with a known tagset name. Then you pass in `tagset='universal'` to a method like `tagged_words()`, as shown in the following code:

```
>>> reader = TaggedCorpusReader('.', r'.*\.pos', tagset='en-brown')
>>> reader.tagged_words(tagset='universal')
[('The', 'DET'), ('expense', 'NOUN'), ('and', 'CONJ'), ...]
```

Most NLTK tagged corpora are initialized with a known tagset, making conversion easy. The following is an example with the `treebank` corpus:

```
>>> from nltk.corpus import treebank
>>> treebank.tagged_words()
[('Pierre', 'NNP'), ('Vinken', 'NNP'), (',', ','), ...]
>>> treebank.tagged_words(tagset='universal')
[('Pierre', 'NOUN'), ('Vinken', 'NOUN'), (',', '.'), ...]
```

If you try to map using an unknown mapping or tagset, every word will be tagged with UNK:

```
>>> treebank.tagged_words(tagset='brown')
[('Pierre', 'UNK'), ('Vinken', 'UNK'), (',', 'UNK'), ...]
```

See also

Chapter 4, Part-of-speech Tagging, will cover part-of-speech tags and tagging in much more detail. And for more on tokenizers, see the first three recipes of *Chapter 1, Tokenizing Text and WordNet Basics*.

In the next recipe, we'll create a **chunked phrase** corpus, where each phrase is also part-of-speech tagged.

Creating a chunked phrase corpus

A **chunk** is a short phrase within a sentence. If you remember sentence diagrams from grade school, they were a tree-like representation of phrases within a sentence. This is exactly what chunks are: subtrees within a sentence tree, and they will be covered in much more detail in *Chapter 5, Extracting Chunks*. The following is a sample sentence tree with three **Noun Phrase** (**NP**) chunks shown as subtrees:

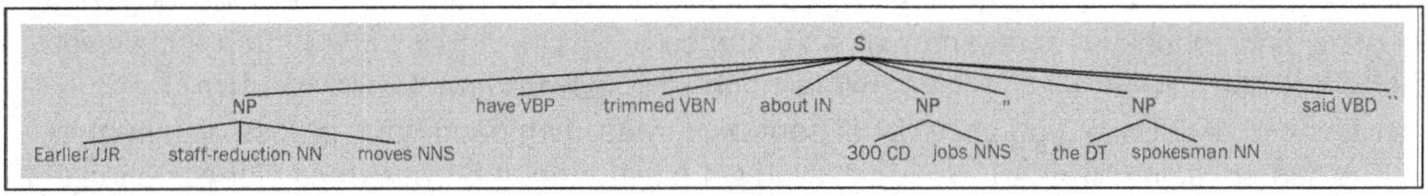

This recipe will cover how to create a corpus with sentences that contain chunks.

Getting ready

The following is an excerpt from the tagged `treebank` corpus. It has part-of-speech tags, as in the previous recipe, but it also has square brackets for denoting chunks. The text within the brackets has been highlighted to make the chunks more apparent. The following sentence is the same sentence as in the previous tree diagram, but in text form:

```
[Earlier/JJR staff-reduction/NN moves/NNS] have/VBP trimmed/VBN about/
IN [300/CD jobs/NNS] ,/, [the/DT spokesman/NN] said/VBD ./.
```

In this format, every chunk is a noun phrase. Words that are not within brackets are part of the sentence tree, but are not part of any noun phrase subtree.

How to do it...

Put the previous excerpt into a file called `treebank.chunk`, and then do the following:

```
>>> from nltk.corpus.reader import ChunkedCorpusReader
>>> reader = ChunkedCorpusReader('.', r'.*\.chunk')
>>> reader.chunked_words()
[Tree('NP', [('Earlier', 'JJR'), ('staff-reduction', 'NN'), ('moves',
'NNS')]), ('have', 'VBP'), ...]
>>> reader.chunked_sents()
[Tree('S', [Tree('NP', [('Earlier', 'JJR'), ('staff-reduction', 'NN'),
('moves', 'NNS')]), ('have', 'VBP'), ('trimmed', 'VBN'), ('about',
'IN'), Tree('NP', [('300', 'CD'), ('jobs', 'NNS')]), (',', ','),
Tree('NP', [('the', 'DT'), ('spokesman', 'NN')]), ('said', 'VBD'),
('.', '.')])]
>>> reader.chunked_paras()
[[Tree('S', [Tree('NP', [('Earlier', 'JJR'), ('staff-reduction',
'NN'), ('moves', 'NNS')]), ('have', 'VBP'), ('trimmed', 'VBN'),
('about', 'IN'), Tree('NP', [('300', 'CD'), ('jobs', 'NNS')]), (',',
','), Tree('NP', [('the', 'DT'), ('spokesman', 'NN')]), ('said',
'VBD'), ('.', '.')])]]
```

The `ChunkedCorpusReader` class provides the same methods as the `TaggedCorpusReader` for getting tagged tokens, along with three new methods for getting chunks. Each chunk is represented as an instance `of nltk.tree.Tree`. Sentence level trees look like `Tree('S', [...])` while noun phrase trees look like `Tree('NP', [...])`. In `chunked_sents()`, you get a list of sentence trees, with each noun phrase as a subtree of the sentence. In `chunked_words()`, you get a list of noun phrase trees alongside tagged tokens of words that were not in a chunk. The following is an inheritance diagram listing the major methods:

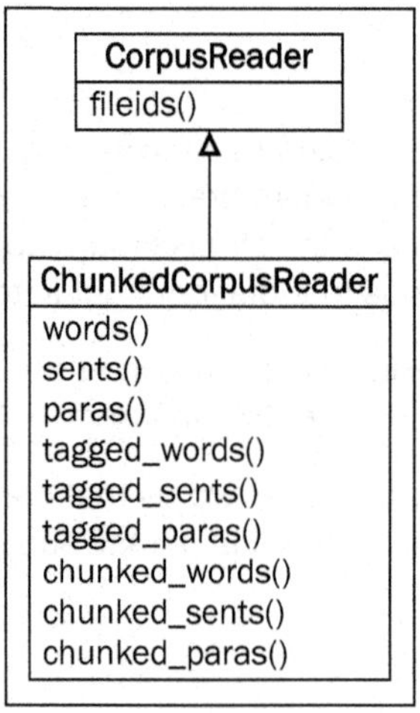

> You can draw a tree by calling the `draw()` method. Using the corpus reader defined earlier, you could do `reader.chunked_sents()[0].draw()` to get the same sentence tree diagram shown at the beginning of this recipe.

How it works...

The `ChunkedCorpusReader` class is similar to the `TaggedCorpusReader` class from the previous recipe. It has the same default `sent_tokenizer` and `para_block_reader` functions, but instead of a `word_tokenizer` function, it uses a `str2chunktree()` function. The default is `nltk.chunk.util.tagstr2tree()`, which parses a sentence string containing bracketed chunks into a sentence tree, with each chunk as a noun phrase subtree. Words are split by whitespace, and the default word/tag separator is `'/'`. If you want to customize chunk parsing, then you can pass in your own function for `str2chunktree()`.

There's more...

An alternative format for denoting chunks is called IOB tags. IOB tags are similar to part-of-speech tags, but provide a way to denote the inside, outside, and beginning of a chunk. They also have the benefit of allowing multiple different chunk phrase types, not just noun phrases. The following is an excerpt from the `conll2000` corpus. Each word is on its own line with a part-of-speech tag followed by an IOB tag:

```
Mr. NNP B-NP
Meador NNP I-NP
had VBD B-VP
been VBN I-VP
executive JJ B-NP
vice NN I-NP
president NN I-NP
of IN B-PP
Balcor NNP B-NP
. . O
```

`B-NP` denotes the beginning of a noun phrase, while `I-NP` denotes that the word is inside of the current noun phrase. `B-VP` and `I-VP` denote the beginning and inside of a verb phrase. `O` ends the sentence.

To read a corpus using the IOB format, you must use the `ConllChunkCorpusReader` class. Each sentence is separated by a blank line, but there is no separation for paragraphs. This means that the `para_*` methods are not available. If you put the previous IOB example text into a file named `conll.iob`, you can create and use a `ConllChunkCorpusReader` class with the following code. The third argument to `ConllChunkCorpusReader` should be a tuple or list specifying the types of chunks in the file, which in this case is `('NP', 'VP', 'PP')`:

```
>>> from nltk.corpus.reader import ConllChunkCorpusReader
>>> conllreader = ConllChunkCorpusReader('.', r'.*\.iob', ('NP', 'VP',
'PP'))
>>> conllreader.chunked_words()
[Tree('NP', [('Mr.', 'NNP'), ('Meador', 'NNP')]), Tree('VP', [('had',
'VBD'), ('been', 'VBN')]), ...]
>>> conllreader.chunked_sents()
[Tree('S', [Tree('NP', [('Mr.', 'NNP'), ('Meador', 'NNP')]),
Tree('VP', [('had', 'VBD'), ('been', 'VBN')]), Tree('NP',
[('executive', 'JJ'), ('vice', 'NN'), ('president', 'NN')]),
Tree('PP', [('of', 'IN')]), Tree('NP', [('Balcor', 'NNP')]), ('.',
'.')])]
>>> conllreader.iob_words()
[('Mr.', 'NNP', 'B-NP'), ('Meador', 'NNP', 'I-NP'), ...]
>>> conllreader.iob_sents()
[[('Mr.', 'NNP', 'B-NP'), ('Meador', 'NNP', 'I-NP'), ('had', 'VBD',
'B-VP'), ('been', 'VBN', 'I-VP'), ('executive', 'JJ', 'B-NP'),
('vice', 'NN', 'I-NP'), ('president', 'NN', 'I-NP'), ('of', 'IN',
'B-PP'), ('Balcor', 'NNP', 'B-NP'), ('.', '.', 'O')]]
```

The previous code also shows the `iob_words()` and `iob_sents()` methods, which return lists of three tuples of `(word, pos, iob)`. The inheritance diagram for `ConllChunkCorpusReader` looks like the following diagram, with most of the methods implemented by its superclass, `ConllCorpusReader`:

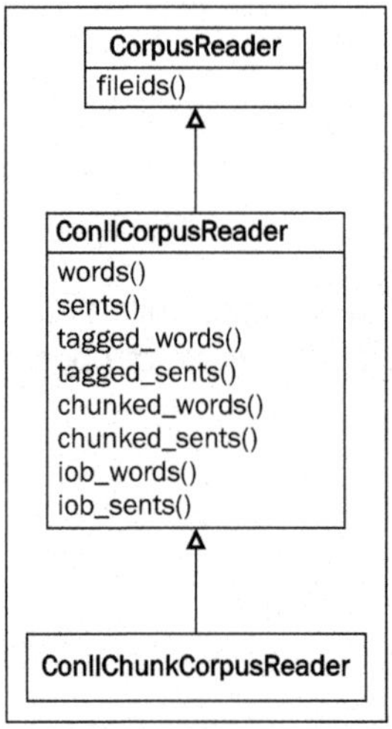

Tree leaves

When it comes to chunk trees, the leaves of a tree are the tagged tokens. So if you want to get a list of all the tagged tokens in a tree, call the `leaves()` method using the following code:

```
>>> reader.chunked_words()[0].leaves()
[('Earlier', 'JJR'), ('staff-reduction', 'NN'), ('moves', 'NNS')]
>>> reader.chunked_sents()[0].leaves()
[('Earlier', 'JJR'), ('staff-reduction', 'NN'), ('moves', 'NNS'),
('have', 'VBP'), ('trimmed', 'VBN'), ('about', 'IN'), ('300', 'CD'),
('jobs', 'NNS'), (',', ','), ('the', 'DT'), ('spokesman', 'NN'),
('said', 'VBD'), ('.', '.')]
>>> reader.chunked_paras()[0][0].leaves()
[('Earlier', 'JJR'), ('staff-reduction', 'NN'), ('moves', 'NNS'),
('have', 'VBP'), ('trimmed', 'VBN'), ('about', 'IN'), ('300', 'CD'),
('jobs', 'NNS'), (',', ','), ('the', 'DT'), ('spokesman', 'NN'),
('said', 'VBD'), ('.', '.')]
```

Treebank chunk corpus

The `nltk.corpus.treebank_chunk` corpus uses `ChunkedCorpusReader` to provide part-of-speech tagged words and noun phrase chunks of *Wall Street Journal* headlines. NLTK comes with a 5 percent sample from the Penn Treebank Project. You can find out more at `http://www.cis.upenn.edu/~treebank/home.html`.

CoNLL2000 corpus

CoNLL stands for the **Conference on Computational Natural Language Learning**. For the year 2000 conference, a shared task was undertaken to produce a corpus of chunks based on the *Wall Street Journal* corpus. In addition to **Noun Phrases** (**NP**), it also contains **Verb Phrases** (**VP**) and **Prepositional Phrases** (**PP**). This chunked corpus is available as `nltk.corpus.conll2000`, which is an instance of `ConllChunkCorpusReader`. You can read more at `http://www.cnts.ua.ac.be/conll2000/chunking/`.

See also

Chapter 5, Extracting Chunks, will cover chunk extraction in detail. Also see the previous recipe for details on getting tagged tokens from a corpus reader.

Creating a categorized text corpus

If you have a large corpus of text, you might want to categorize it into separate sections. This can be helpful for organization, or for text classification, which is covered in *Chapter 7, Text Classification*. The `brown` corpus, for example, has a number of different categories, as shown in the following code:

```
>>> from nltk.corpus import brown
>>> brown.categories()
['adventure', 'belles_lettres', 'editorial', 'fiction', 'government',
'hobbies', 'humor', 'learned', 'lore', 'mystery', 'news', 'religion',
'reviews', 'romance', 'science_fiction']
```

In this recipe, we'll learn how to create our own categorized text corpus.

Getting ready

The easiest way to categorize a corpus is to have one file for each category. The following are two excerpts from the `movie_reviews` corpus:

- movie_pos.txt:

  ```
  the thin red line is flawed but it provokes .
  ```

- movie_neg.txt:

  ```
  a big-budget and glossy production can not make up for a lack of
  spontaneity that permeates their tv show .
  ```

With these two files, we'll have two categories: `pos` and `neg`.

How to do it...

We'll use the `CategorizedPlaintextCorpusReader` class, which inherits from both `PlaintextCorpusReader` and `CategorizedCorpusReader`. These two superclasses require three arguments: the root directory, the `fileids` arguments, and a category specification:

```
>>> from nltk.corpus.reader import CategorizedPlaintextCorpusReader
>>> reader = CategorizedPlaintextCorpusReader('.', r'movie_.*\.txt',
cat_pattern=r'movie_(\w+)\.txt')
>>> reader.categories()
['neg', 'pos']
>>> reader.fileids(categories=['neg'])
['movie_neg.txt']
>>> reader.fileids(categories=['pos'])
['movie_pos.txt']
```

How it works...

The first two arguments to `CategorizedPlaintextCorpusReader` are the root directory and `fileids`, which are passed on to the `PlaintextCorpusReader` class to read in the files. The `cat_pattern` keyword argument is a regular expression for extracting the category names from the `fileids` arguments. In our case, the category is the part of the `fileid` argument after `movie_` and before `.txt`. The category must be surrounded by grouping parenthesis.

The `cat_pattern` keyword is passed to `CategorizedCorpusReader`, which overrides the common corpus reader functions such as `fileids()`, `words()`, `sents()`, and `paras()` to accept a `categories` keyword argument. This way, you could get all the `pos` sentences by calling `reader.sents(categories=['pos'])`. The `CategorizedCorpusReader` class also provides the `categories()` function, which returns a list of all the known categories in the corpus.

The `CategorizedPlaintextCorpusReader` class is an example of using multiple inheritance to join methods from multiple superclasses, as shown in the following diagram:

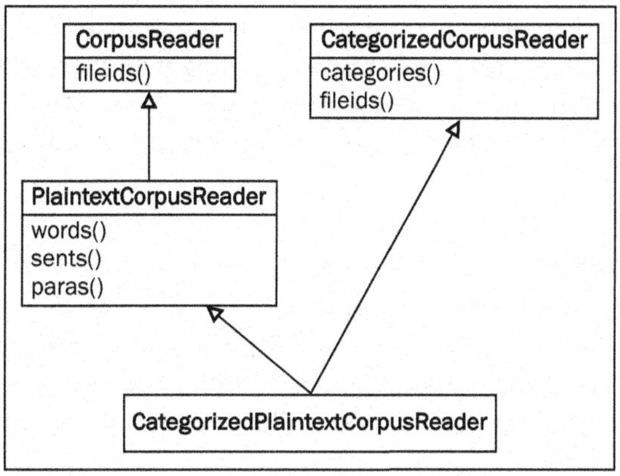

There's more...

Instead of `cat_pattern`, you could pass in a `cat_map`, which is a dictionary mapping a `fileid` argument to a list of category labels, as shown in the following code:

```
>>> reader = CategorizedPlaintextCorpusReader('.', r'movie_.*\.txt',
cat_map={'movie_pos.txt': ['pos'], 'movie_neg.txt': ['neg']})
>>> reader.categories()
['neg', 'pos']
```

Category file

A third way of specifying categories is to use the `cat_file` keyword argument to specify a filename containing a mapping of `fileid` to category. For example, the `brown` corpus has a file called `cats.txt` that looks like the following:

```
ca44 news
cb01 editorial
```

The `reuters` corpus has files in multiple categories, and its `cats.txt` looks like the following:

```
test/14840 rubber coffee lumber palm-oil veg-oil
test/14841 wheat grain
```

Categorized tagged corpus reader

The `brown` corpus reader is actually an instance of `CategorizedTaggedCorpusReader`, which inherits from `CategorizedCorpusReader` and `TaggedCorpusReader`. Just like in `CategorizedPlaintextCorpusReader`, it overrides all the methods of `TaggedCorpusReader` to allow a `categories` argument, so you can call `brown.tagged_sents(categories=['news'])` to get all the tagged sentences from the `news` category. You can use the `CategorizedTaggedCorpusReader` class just like `CategorizedPlaintextCorpusReader` for your own categorized and tagged text corpora.

Categorized corpora

The `movie_reviews` corpus reader is an instance of `CategorizedPlaintextCorpusReader`, as is the `reuters` corpus reader. But where the `movie_reviews` corpus only has two categories (`neg` and `pos`), `reuters` has 90 categories. These corpora are often used for training and evaluating classifiers, which will be covered in *Chapter 7, Text Classification*.

See also

In the next chapter, we'll create a subclass of `CategorizedCorpusReader` and `ChunkedCorpusReader` for reading a categorized chunk corpus. Also, see *Chapter 7, Text Classification* in which we use categorized text for classification.

Creating a categorized chunk corpus reader

NLTK provides a `CategorizedPlaintextCorpusReader` and `CategorizedTaggedCorpusReader` class, but there's no categorized corpus reader for chunked corpora. So in this recipe, we're going to make one.

Getting ready

Refer to the earlier recipe, *Creating a chunked phrase corpus*, for an explanation of `ChunkedCorpusReader`, and refer to the previous recipe for details on `CategorizedPlaintextCorpusReader` and `CategorizedTaggedCorpusReader`, both of which inherit from `CategorizedCorpusReader`.

How to do it...

We'll create a class called `CategorizedChunkedCorpusReader` that inherits from both `CategorizedCorpusReader` and `ChunkedCorpusReader`. It is heavily based on the `CategorizedTaggedCorpusReader` class, and also provides three additional methods for getting categorized chunks. The following code is found in `catchunked.py`:

```
from nltk.corpus.reader import CategorizedCorpusReader,
  ChunkedCorpusReader

class CategorizedChunkedCorpusReader(CategorizedCorpusReader,
  ChunkedCorpusReader):
  def __init__(self, *args, **kwargs):
    CategorizedCorpusReader.__init__(self, kwargs)
    ChunkedCorpusReader.__init__(self, *args, **kwargs)

  def _resolve(self, fileids, categories):
    if fileids is not None and categories is not None:
      raise ValueError('Specify fileids or categories, not both')
    if categories is not None:
      return self.fileids(categories)
    else:
      return fileids
```

All of the following methods call the corresponding function in `ChunkedCorpusReader` with the value returned from `_resolve()`. We'll start with the plain text methods:

```
  def raw(self, fileids=None, categories=None):
    return ChunkedCorpusReader.raw(self, self._resolve(fileids,
      categories))

  def words(self, fileids=None, categories=None):
    return ChunkedCorpusReader.words(self, self._resolve(fileids,
      categories))

  def sents(self, fileids=None, categories=None):
    return ChunkedCorpusReader.sents(self, self._resolve(fileids,
      categories))
```

```
def paras(self, fileids=None, categories=None):
  return ChunkedCorpusReader.paras(self, self._resolve(fileids,
    categories))
```

Next is the code for the tagged text methods:

```
def tagged_words(self, fileids=None, categories=None):
  return ChunkedCorpusReader.tagged_words(self,
    self._resolve(fileids, categories))

def tagged_sents(self, fileids=None, categories=None):
  return ChunkedCorpusReader.tagged_sents(self,
    self._resolve(fileids, categories))

def tagged_paras(self, fileids=None, categories=None):
  return ChunkedCorpusReader.tagged_paras(self,
    self._resolve(fileids, categories))
```

And finally, we have code for the chunked methods, which is what we've really been after:

```
def chunked_words(self, fileids=None, categories=None):
  return ChunkedCorpusReader.chunked_words(self,
    self._resolve(fileids, categories))

def chunked_sents(self, fileids=None, categories=None):
  return ChunkedCorpusReader.chunked_sents(self,
    self._resolve(fileids, categories))

def chunked_paras(self, fileids=None, categories=None):
  return ChunkedCorpusReader.chunked_paras(self,
    self._resolve(fileids, categories))
```

All these methods together give us a complete `CategorizedChunkedCorpusReader` class.

How it works...

The `CategorizedChunkedCorpusReader` class overrides all the `ChunkedCorpusReader` methods to take a `categories` argument for locating `fileids`. These `fileids` are found with the internal `_resolve()` function. This `_resolve()` function makes use of `CategorizedCorpusReader.fileids()` to return `fileids` for a given list of categories. If no categories are given, `_resolve()` just returns the given `fileids`, which could be `None`, in which case all the files are read. The initialization of both `CategorizedCorpusReader` and `ChunkedCorpusReader` is what makes all this possible. If you look at the code for `CategorizedTaggedCorpusReader`, you'll see that it's very similar.

The inheritance diagram looks like this:

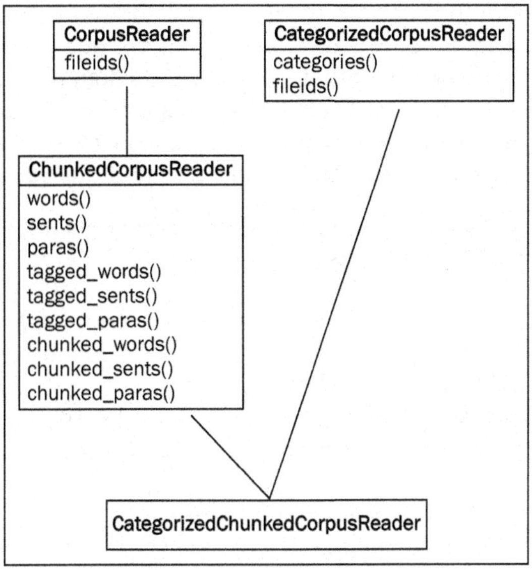

The following is example code for using the `treebank` corpus. All we're doing is making categories out of the `fileids` arguments, but the point is that you could use the same techniques to create your own categorized chunk corpus:

```
>>> import nltk.data
>>> from catchunked import CategorizedChunkedCorpusReader
>>> path = nltk.data.find('corpora/treebank/tagged')
>>> reader = CategorizedChunkedCorpusReader(path, r'wsj_.*\.pos',
cat_pattern=r'wsj_(.*)\.pos')
>>> len(reader.categories()) == len(reader.fileids())
True
>>> len(reader.chunked_sents(categories=['0001']))
16
```

We use `nltk.data.find()` to search the data directories to get a `FileSystemPathPointer` class to the `treebank` corpus. All the `treebank` tagged files start with `wsj_`, followed by a number, and end with `.pos`. The previous code turns that file number into a category.

There's more...

As covered in the *Creating a chunked phrase corpus* recipe, there's an alternative format and reader for a chunk corpus using IOB tags. To have a categorized corpus of IOB chunks, we have to make a new corpus reader.

Categorized CoNLL chunk corpus reader

The following is the code for the subclass of `CategorizedCorpusReader` and `ConllChunkReader` called `CategorizedConllChunkCorpusReader`. It overrides all methods of `ConllCorpusReader` that take a `fileids` argument, so the methods can also take a `categories` argument. The `ConllChunkCorpusReader` is just a small subclass of `ConllCorpusReader` that handles initialization; most of the work is done in `ConllCorpusReader`. This code can also be found in `catchunked.py`.

```
from nltk.corpus.reader import CategorizedCorpusReader,
ConllCorpusReader, ConllChunkCorpusReader

class CategorizedConllChunkCorpusReader(CategorizedCorpusReader,
  ConllChunkCorpusReader):
  def __init__(self, *args, **kwargs):
    CategorizedCorpusReader.__init__(self, kwargs)
    ConllChunkCorpusReader.__init__(self, *args, **kwargs)

  def _resolve(self, fileids, categories):
    if fileids is not None and categories is not None:
      raise ValueError('Specify fileids or categories, not both')
    if categories is not None:
      return self.fileids(categories)
    else:
      return fileids
```

All the following methods call the corresponding method of `ConllCorpusReader` with the value returned from `_resolve()`. We'll start with the plain text methods:

```
  def raw(self, fileids=None, categories=None):
    return ConllCorpusReader.raw(self, self._resolve(fileids,
      categories))

  def words(self, fileids=None, categories=None):
    return ConllCorpusReader.words(self, self._resolve(fileids,
      categories))

  def sents(self, fileids=None, categories=None):
    return ConllCorpusReader.sents(self, self._resolve(fileids,
      categories))
```

The `ConllCorpusReader` class does not recognize paragraphs, so there are no `*_paras()` methods. Next will be the code for the tagged and chunked methods, as follows:

```
def tagged_words(self, fileids=None, categories=None):
  return ConllCorpusReader.tagged_words(self,
    self._resolve(fileids, categories))
def tagged_sents(self, fileids=None, categories=None):
  return ConllCorpusReader.tagged_sents(self,
    self._resolve(fileids, categories))

def chunked_words(self, fileids=None, categories=None,
  chunk_types=None):
  return ConllCorpusReader.chunked_words(self,
    self._resolve(fileids, categories), chunk_types)

def chunked_sents(self, fileids=None, categories=None,
  chunk_types=None):
  return ConllCorpusReader.chunked_sents(self,
    self._resolve(fileids, categories), chunk_types)
```

For completeness, we must override the following methods of the `ConllCorpusReader` class:

```
def parsed_sents(self, fileids=None, categories=None,
  pos_in_tree=None):
  return ConllCorpusReader.parsed_sents(
    self, self._resolve(fileids, categories), pos_in_tree)

def srl_spans(self, fileids=None, categories=None):
  return ConllCorpusReader.srl_spans(self,
    self._resolve(fileids, categories))

def srl_instances(self, fileids=None, categories=None,
  pos_in_tree=None, flatten=True):
  return ConllCorpusReader.srl_instances(self,
    self._resolve(fileids, categories), pos_in_tree, flatten)

def iob_words(self, fileids=None, categories=None):
  return ConllCorpusReader.iob_words(self,
    self._resolve(fileids, categories))

def iob_sents(self, fileids=None, categories=None):
  return ConllCorpusReader.iob_sents(self,
    self._resolve(fileids, categories))
```

The inheritance diagram for this class is as follows:

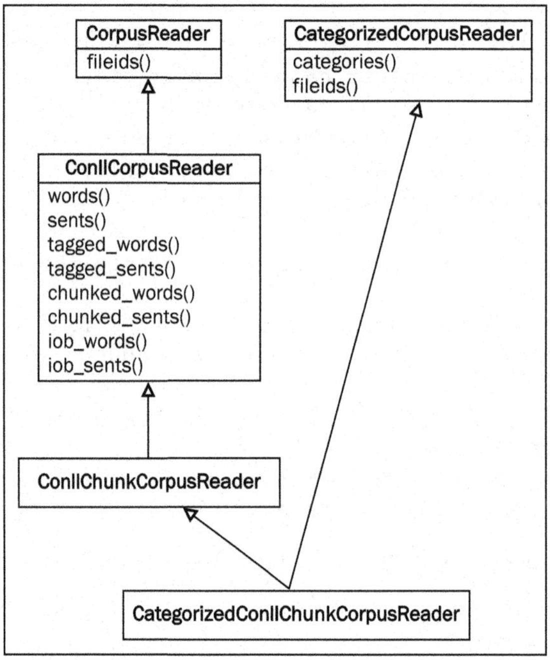

Here is example code using the `conll2000` corpus:

```
>>> import nltk.data
>>> from catchunked import CategorizedConllChunkCorpusReader
>>> path = nltk.data.find('corpora/conll2000')
>>> reader = CategorizedConllChunkCorpusReader(path, r'.*\.txt',
('NP','VP','PP'), cat_pattern=r'(.*)\.txt')
>>> reader.categories()
['test', 'train']
>>> reader.fileids()
['test.txt', 'train.txt']
>>> len(reader.chunked_sents(categories=['test']))
2012
```

Like with `treebank`, we're using the `fileids` for categories. The `ConllChunkCorpusReader` class requires a third argument to specify the chunk types. These chunk types are used to parse the IOB tags. As you learned in the *Creating a chunked phrase corpus* recipe, the `conll2000` corpus recognizes the following three chunk types:

- NP for noun phrases
- VP for verb phrases
- PP for prepositional phrases

See also

In the *Creating a chunked phrase corpus* recipe of this chapter, we covered both the `ChunkedCorpusReader` and `ConllChunkCorpusReader` classes. And in the previous recipe, we covered `CategorizedPlaintextCorpusReader` and `CategorizedTaggedCorpusReader`, which share the same superclass used by `CategorizedChunkedCorpusReader` and `CategorizedConllChunkReader`, that is, `CategorizedCorpusReader`.

Lazy corpus loading

Loading a corpus reader can be an expensive operation due to the number of files, file sizes, and various initialization tasks. And while you'll often want to specify a corpus reader in a common module, you don't always need to access it right away. To speed up module import time when a corpus reader is defined, NLTK provides a `LazyCorpusLoader` class that can transform itself into your actual corpus reader as soon as you need it. This way, you can define a corpus reader in a common module without it slowing down module loading.

How to do it...

The `LazyCorpusLoader` class requires two arguments: the name of the corpus and the corpus reader class, plus any other arguments needed to initialize the corpus reader class.

The `name` argument specifies the root directory name of the corpus, which must be within a `corpora` subdirectory of one of the paths in `nltk.data.path`. See the *Setting up a custom corpus* recipe of this chapter for more details on `nltk.data.path`.

For example, if you have a custom corpora named `cookbook` in your local `nltk_data` directory, its path would be `~/nltk_data/corpora/cookbook`. You'd then pass `'cookbook'` to `LazyCorpusLoader` as the name, and `LazyCorpusLoader` will look in `~/nltk_data/corpora` for a directory named `'cookbook'`.

The second argument to `LazyCorpusLoader` is `reader_cls`, which should be the name of a subclass of `CorpusReader`, such as `WordListCorpusReader`. You will also need to pass in any other arguments required by the `reader_cls` argument for initialization. This will be demonstrated as follows, using the same wordlist file we created in the earlier recipe, *Creating a wordlist corpus*. The third argument to `LazyCorpusLoader` is the list of filenames and `fileids` that will be passed to `WordListCorpusReader` at initialization:

```
>>> from nltk.corpus.util import LazyCorpusLoader
>>> from nltk.corpus.reader import WordListCorpusReader
>>> reader = LazyCorpusLoader('cookbook', WordListCorpusReader,
['wordlist'])
>>> isinstance(reader, LazyCorpusLoader)
True
>>> reader.fileids()
['wordlist']
>>> isinstance(reader, LazyCorpusLoader)
False
>>> isinstance(reader, WordListCorpusReader)
True
```

How it works...

The `LazyCorpusLoader` class stores all the arguments given, but otherwise does nothing until you try to access an attribute or method. This way, initialization is very fast, eliminating the overhead of loading the corpus reader immediately. As soon as you do access an attribute or method, it does the following:

1. Calls `nltk.data.find('corpora/%s' % name)` to find the corpus data root directory.
2. Instantiates the corpus reader class with the root directory and any other arguments.
3. Transforms itself into the corpus reader class.

So in the previous example code, before we call `reader.fileids()`, reader is an instance of `LazyCorpusLoader`, but after the call, reader becomes an instance of `WordListCorpusReader`.

There's more...

All of the corpora included with NLTK and defined in `nltk.corpus` are initially a `LazyCorpusLoader` class. The following is some code from `nltk.corpus` defining the `treebank` corpora:

```
treebank = LazyCorpusLoader('treebank/combined',
  BracketParseCorpusReader, r'wsj_.*\.mrg',tagset='wsj',
  encoding='ascii')
treebank_chunk = LazyCorpusLoader('treebank/tagged',
  ChunkedCorpusReader, r'wsj_.*\.pos',sent_tokenizer
  =RegexpTokenizer(r'(?<=/\.)\s*(?![^\[]*\])', gaps=True),
    para_block_reader=tagged_treebank_para_block_reader,
      encoding='ascii')
treebank_raw = LazyCorpusLoader('treebank/raw',
  PlaintextCorpusReader, r'wsj_.*', encoding='ISO-8859-2')
```

As you can see in the previous code, any number of additional arguments can be passed through by `LazyCorpusLoader` to its `reader_cls` argument.

Creating a custom corpus view

A **corpus view** is a class wrapper around a corpus file that reads in blocks of tokens as needed. Its purpose is to provide a view into a file without reading the whole file at once (since corpus files can often be quite large). If the corpus readers included by NLTK already meet all your needs, then you do not have to know anything about corpus views. But, if you have a custom file format that needs special handling, this recipe will show you how to create and use a custom corpus view. The main corpus view class is `StreamBackedCorpusView`, which opens a single file as a stream, and maintains an internal cache of blocks it has read.

Blocks of tokens are read in with a block reader function. A block can be any piece of text, such as a paragraph or a line, and tokens are parts of a block, such as individual words. In the *Creating a part-of-speech tagged word corpus* recipe, we discussed the default `para_block_reader` function of the `TaggedCorpusReader` class, which reads lines from a file until it finds a blank line, then returns those lines as a single paragraph token. The actual block reader function is `nltk.corpus.reader.util.read_blankline_block`. The `TaggedCorpusReader` class passes this block reader function into a `TaggedCorpusView` class whenever it needs to read blocks from a file. The `TaggedCorpusView` class is a subclass of `StreamBackedCorpusView` that knows to split paragraphs of word/tag into `(word, tag)` tuples.

How to do it...

We'll start with the simple case of a plain text file with a heading that should be ignored by the corpus reader. Let's make a file called `heading_text.txt` that looks like this:

```
A simple heading

Here is the actual text for the corpus.

Paragraphs are split by blanklines.

This is the 3rd paragraph.
```

Normally, we'd use the `PlaintextCorpusReader` class, but by default it will treat `A simple heading` as the first paragraph. To ignore this heading, we need to subclass the `PlaintextCorpusReader` class so we can override its `CorpusView` class variable with our own `StreamBackedCorpusView` subclass. The following is the code found in `corpus.py`:

```
from nltk.corpus.reader import PlaintextCorpusReader
from nltk.corpus.reader.util import StreamBackedCorpusView

class IgnoreHeadingCorpusView(StreamBackedCorpusView):
  def __init__(self, *args, **kwargs):
    StreamBackedCorpusView.__init__(self, *args, **kwargs)
    # open self._stream
    self._open()
    # skip the heading block
    self.read_block(self._stream)
    # reset the start position to the current position in the stream
    self._filepos = [self._stream.tell()]

class IgnoreHeadingCorpusReader(PlaintextCorpusReader):
  CorpusView = IgnoreHeadingCorpusView
```

To demonstrate that this works as expected, here is code showing that the default `PlaintextCorpusReader` class finds four paragraphs, while our `IgnoreHeadingCorpusReader` class only has three paragraphs:

```
>>> from nltk.corpus.reader import PlaintextCorpusReader
>>> plain = PlaintextCorpusReader('.', ['heading_text.txt'])
>>> len(plain.paras())
4
>>> from corpus import IgnoreHeadingCorpusReader
>>> reader = IgnoreHeadingCorpusReader('.', ['heading_text.txt'])
>>> len(reader.paras())
3
```

How it works...

The `PlaintextCorpusReader` class by design has a `CorpusView` class variable that can be overridden by subclasses. So we do just that, and make our `IgnoreHeadingCorpusView` class the `CorpusView` class variable.

> Most corpus readers do not have a `CorpusView` class variable because they require very specific corpus views.

The `IgnoreHeadingCorpusView` class is a subclass of `StreamBackedCorpusView` that does the following on initialization:

1. Opens the file using `self._open()`. This function is defined by `StreamBackedCorpusView`, and sets the internal instance variable `self._stream` to the opened file.
2. Reads one block with `read_blankline_block()`, which then reads the heading as a paragraph, and moves the stream's file position forward to the next block.
3. Resets the start file position to the current position of `self._stream`. The `self._filepos` variable is an internal index of where each block is in the file.

The following is a diagram illustrating the relationships between the classes:

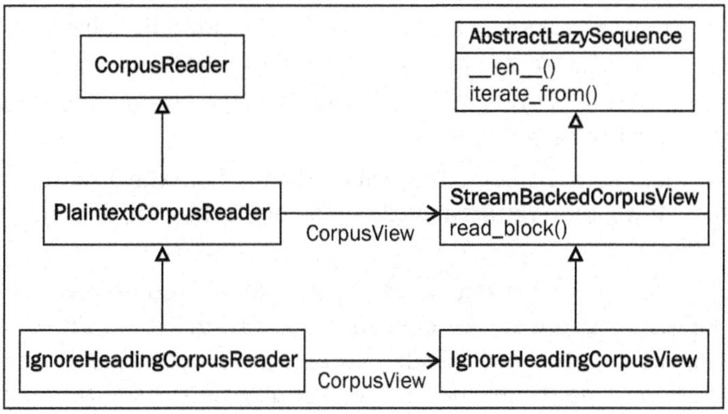

There's more...

Corpus views can get a lot fancier and more complicated, but the core concept is the same: read blocks from a stream to return a list of tokens. There are a number of block readers provided in `nltk.corpus.reader.util`, but you can always create your own. If you do want to define your own block reader function, then you have two choices on how to implement it:

1. Define it as a separate function and pass it into `StreamBackedCorpusView` as `block_reader`. This is a good option if your block reader is fairly simple, reusable, and doesn't require any outside variables or configuration.
2. Subclass `StreamBackedCorpusView` and override the `read_block()` method. This is what many custom corpus views do because the block reading is highly specialized and requires additional functions and configuration, usually provided by the corpus reader when the corpus view is initialized.

Block reader functions

The following is a survey of most of the included block readers in `nltk.corpus.reader.util`. Unless otherwise mentioned, each block reader function takes a single argument: the `stream` argument to read from:

- `read_whitespace_block()`: This will read 20 lines from the stream, splitting each line into tokens by whitespace.
- `read_wordpunct_block()`: This reads 20 lines from the stream, splitting each line using `nltk.tokenize.wordpunct_tokenize()`.
- `read_line_block()`: This reads 20 lines from the stream and returns them as a list, with each line as a token.
- `read_blankline_block()`: This will read lines from the stream until it finds a blank line. It will then return a single token of all lines found combined into a single string.
- `read_regexp_block()`: This takes two additional arguments, which must be regular expressions that can be passed to `re.match()`: `start_re` and `end_re`. The `start_re` variable matches the starting line of a block, and `end_re` matches the ending line of the block. The `end_re` variable defaults to `None`, in which case the block will end as soon as a new `start_re` match is found. The return value is a single token of all lines in the block joined into a single string.

Pickle corpus view

If you want to have a corpus of pickled objects, you can use the `PickleCorpusView`, a subclass of `StreamBackedCorpusView`, found in `nltk.corpus.reader.util`. A file consists of blocks of pickled objects, and can be created with the `PickleCorpusView.write()` class method, which takes a sequence of objects and an output file, then pickles each object using `pickle.dump()` and writes it to the file. It overrides the `read_block()` method to return a list of unpickled objects from the stream, using `pickle.load()`.

Concatenated corpus view

Also found in `nltk.corpus.reader.util` is the `ConcatenatedCorpusView` class. This class is useful if you have multiple files that you want a corpus reader to treat as a single file. A `ConcatenatedCorpusView` class is created by giving it a list of `corpus_views`, which are then iterated over as if they were a single view.

See also

The concept of block readers was introduced in the *Creating a part-of-speech tagged word corpus* recipe.

Creating a MongoDB-backed corpus reader

All the corpus readers we've dealt with so far have been file-based. That is in part due to the design of the `CorpusReader` base class, and also the assumption that most corpus data will be in text files. However, sometimes you'll have a bunch of data stored in a database that you want to access and use just like a text file corpus. In this recipe, we'll cover the case where you have documents in MongoDB, and you want to use a particular field of each document as your block of text.

Getting ready

MongoDB is a document-oriented database that has become a popular alternative to relational databases such as MySQL. The installation and setup of MongoDB is outside the scope of this book, but you can find instructions at `http://docs.mongodb.org/manual/`.

You'll also need to install PyMongo, a Python driver for MongoDB. You should be able to do this with either `easy_install` or `pip`, by typing `sudo easy_install pymongo` or `sudo pip install pymongo`.

The following code assumes that your database is on localhost port `27017`, which is the MongoDB default configuration, and that you'll be using the test database with a collection named corpus that contains documents with a text field. Explanations for these arguments are available in the PyMongo documentation at `http://api.mongodb.org/python/current/`.

How to do it...

Since the `CorpusReader` class assumes you have a file-based corpus, we can't directly subclass it. Instead, we're going to emulate both the `StreamBackedCorpusView` and `PlaintextCorpusReader` classes. The `StreamBackedCorpusView` class is a subclass of `nltk.util.AbstractLazySequence`, so we'll subclass `AbstractLazySequence` to create a MongoDB view, and then create a new class that will use the view to provide functionality similar to the `PlaintextCorpusReader` class. The following is the code, which is found in `mongoreader.py`:

```
import pymongo
from nltk.data import LazyLoader
from nltk.tokenize import TreebankWordTokenizer
from nltk.util import AbstractLazySequence, LazyMap,
  LazyConcatenation

class MongoDBLazySequence(AbstractLazySequence):
  def __init__(self, host='localhost', port=27017, db='test',
    collection='corpus', field='text'):
    self.conn = pymongo.MongoClient(host, port)
    self.collection = self.conn[db][collection]
    self.field = field

  def __len__(self):
    return self.collection.count()

  def iterate_from(self, start):
    f = lambda d: d.get(self.field, '')
    return iter(LazyMap(f, self.collection.find(fields=
      [self.field], skip=start)))

class MongoDBCorpusReader(object):
  def __init__(self, word_tokenizer=TreebankWordTokenizer(),
    sent_tokenizer=LazyLoader('tokenizers/punkt/PY3
      /english.pickle'),**kwargs):
    self._seq = MongoDBLazySequence(**kwargs)
    self._word_tokenize = word_tokenizer.tokenize
    self._sent_tokenize = sent_tokenizer.tokenize

  def text(self):
    return self._seq
```

```
def words(self):
  return LazyConcatenation(LazyMap(self._word_tokenize,
    self.text()))

def sents(self):
  return LazyConcatenation(LazyMap(self._sent_tokenize,
    self.text()))
```

How it works...

The `AbstractLazySequence` class is an abstract class that provides read-only, on-demand iteration. Subclasses must implement the `__len__()` and `iterate_from(start)` methods, while it provides the rest of the list and iterator emulation methods. By creating the `MongoDBLazySequence` subclass as our view, we can iterate over documents in the MongoDB collection on demand, without keeping all the documents in memory. The `LazyMap` class is a lazy version of Python's built-in `map()` function, and is used in `iterate_from()` to transform the document into the specific field that we're interested in. It's also a subclass of `AbstractLazySequence`.

The `MongoDBCorpusReader` class creates an internal instance of `MongoDBLazySequence` for iteration, then defines the word and sentence tokenization methods. The `text()` method simply returns the instance of `MongoDBLazySequence`, which results in a lazily evaluated list of each text field. The `words()` method uses `LazyMap` and `LazyConcatenation` to return a lazily evaluated list of all words, while the `sents()` method does the same for sentences. The `sent_tokenizer` is loaded on demand with `LazyLoader`, which is a wrapper around `nltk.data.load()`, analogous to `LazyCorpusLoader`. The `LazyConcatentation` class is a subclass of `AbstractLazySequence` too, and produces a flat list from a given list of lists (each list may also be lazy). In our case, we're concatenating the results of `LazyMap` to ensure we don't return nested lists.

There's more...

All of the parameters are configurable. For example, if you had a `db` named website, with a collection named `comments`, whose documents had a field called `comment`, you could create a `MongoDBCorpusReader` class as follows:

```
>>> reader = MongoDBCorpusReader(db='website',
  collection='comments', field='comment')
```

You can also pass in custom instances for `word_tokenizer` and `sent_tokenizer`, as long as the objects implement the `nltk.tokenize.TokenizerI` interface by providing a `tokenize(text)` method.

See also

Corpus views were covered in the previous recipe, and tokenization was covered in *Chapter 1, Tokenizing Text and WordNet Basics*.

Corpus editing with file locking

Corpus readers and views are all read-only, but there will be times when you want to add to or edit the corpus files. However, modifying a corpus file while other processes are using it, such as through a corpus reader, can lead to dangerous undefined behavior. This is where file locking comes in handy.

Getting ready

You must install the `lockfile` library using `sudo easy_install lockfile` or `sudo pip install lockfile`. This library provides cross-platform file locking, and so will work on Windows, Unix/Linux, Mac OS X, and more. You can find detailed documentation on lockfile at `http://packages.python.org/lockfile/`.

How to do it...

Here are two file editing functions: `append_line()` and `remove_line()`. Both try to acquire an exclusive lock on the file before updating it. An exclusive lock means that these functions will wait until no other process is reading from or writing to the file. Once the lock is acquired, any other process that tries to access the file will have to wait until the lock is released. This way, modifying the file will be safe and not cause any undefined behavior in other processes. These functions can be found in `corpus.py`, as follows:

```
import lockfile, tempfile, shutil

def append_line(fname, line): with lockfile.FileLock(fname):
  fp = open(fname, 'a+')
  fp.write(line)
  fp.write('\n')
  fp.close()

def remove_line(fname, line):
```

```
    with lockfile.FileLock(fname):
      tmp = tempfile.TemporaryFile()
      fp = open(fname, 'rw+')
      # write all lines from orig file, except if matches given line
      for l in fp:
        if l.strip() != line:
          tmp.write(l)

      # reset file pointers so entire files are copied
      fp.seek(0)
      tmp.seek(0)
      # copy tmp into fp, then truncate to remove trailing line(s)
      shutil.copyfileobj(tmp, fp)
      fp.truncate()
      fp.close()
      tmp.close()
```

The lock acquiring and releasing happens transparently when you do with `lockfile.FileLock(fname)`.

> Instead of using `with lockfile.FileLock(fname)`, you can also get a lock by calling `lock = lockfile.FileLock(fname)`, then call `lock.acquire()` to acquire the lock, and `lock.release()` to release the lock.

How it works...

You can use these functions as follows:

```
>>> from corpus import append_line, remove_line
>>> append_line('test.txt', 'foo')
>>> remove_line('test.txt', 'foo')
```

In `append_line()`, a lock is acquired, the file is opened in *append mode*, the text is written along with an end-of-line character, and then the file is closed, releasing the lock.

> A lock acquired by `lockfile` only protects the file from other processes that also use `lockfile`. In other words, just because your Python process has a lock with `lockfile` doesn't mean a non-Python process can't modify the file. For this reason, it's best to only use `lockfile` with files that will not be edited by an non-Python processes, or Python processes that do not use `lockfile`.

The `remove_line()` function is a bit more complicated. Because we're removing a line, and not a specific section of the file, we need to iterate over the file to find each instance of the line to remove. The easiest way to do this while writing the changes back to the file, is to use a temporary file to hold the changes, then copy that file back into the original file using `shutil.copyfileobj()`.

> The `remove_line()` function does not work on Mac OS X, but does work on Linux. For `remove_line()` to work, it must be able to open a file in both read and write modes, and Mac OS X does not allow this.

These functions are best suited for a wordlist corpus, or some other corpus type with presumably unique lines, that may be edited by multiple people at about the same time, such as through a web interface. Using these functions with a more document-oriented corpus such as `brown`, `treebank`, or `conll2000`, is probably a bad idea.

4

Part-of-speech Tagging

In this chapter, we will cover the following recipes:

- Default tagging
- Training a unigram part-of-speech tagger
- Combining taggers with backoff tagging
- Training and combining ngram taggers
- Creating a model of likely word tags
- Tagging with regular expressions
- Affix tagging
- Training a Brill tagger
- Training the TnT tagger
- Using WordNet for tagging
- Tagging proper names
- Classifier-based tagging
- Training a tagger with NLTK-Trainer

Introduction

Part-of-speech tagging is the process of converting a sentence, in the form of a list of words, into a list of tuples, where each tuple is of the form (**word, tag**). The **tag** is a part-of-speech tag, and signifies whether the word is a noun, adjective, verb, and so on.

Part-of-speech tagging is a necessary step before chunking, which is covered in *Chapter 5, Extracting Chunks*. Without the part-of-speech tags, a chunker cannot know how to extract phrases from a sentence. But with part-of-speech tags, you can tell a chunker how to identify phrases based on tag patterns.

You can also use part-of-speech tags for grammar analysis and word sense disambiguation. For example, the word *duck* could refer to a bird, or it could be a verb indicating a downward motion. Computers cannot know the difference without additional information, such as part-of-speech tags. For more on word sense disambiguation, refer to the URL `https://en.wikipedia.org/wiki/Word_sense_disambiguation`.

Most of the taggers we'll cover are trainable. They use a list of tagged sentences as their training data, such as what you get from the `tagged_sents()` method of a `TaggedCorpusReader` class (see the *Creating a part-of-speech tagged word corpus* recipe in *Chapter 3, Creating Custom Corpora,* for more details). With these training sentences, the tagger generates an internal model that will tell it how to tag a word. Other taggers use external data sources or match word patterns to choose a tag for a word.

All taggers in NLTK are in the `nltk.tag` package and inherit from the `TaggerI` base class. `TaggerI` requires all subclasses to implement a `tag()` method, which takes a list of words as input and returns a list of tagged words as output. `TaggerI` also provides an `evaluate()` method for evaluating the accuracy of the tagger (covered at the end of the *Default tagging* recipe). Many taggers can also be combined into a backoff chain, so that if one tagger cannot tag a word, the next tagger is used, and so on.

Default tagging

Default tagging provides a baseline for part-of-speech tagging. It simply assigns the same part-of-speech tag to every token. We do this using the `DefaultTagger` class. This tagger is useful as a last-resort tagger, and provides a baseline to measure accuracy improvements.

Getting ready

We're going to use the `treebank` corpus for most of this chapter because it's a common standard and is quick to load and test. But everything we do should apply equally well to `brown`, `conll2000`, and any other part-of-speech tagged corpus.

How to do it...

The `DefaultTagger` class takes a single argument, the tag you want to apply. We'll give it `NN`, which is the tag for a singular noun. `DefaultTagger` is most useful when you choose the most common part-of-speech tag. Since nouns tend to be the most common types of words, a noun tag is recommended.

```
>>> from nltk.tag import DefaultTagger
>>> tagger = DefaultTagger('NN')
>>> tagger.tag(['Hello', 'World'])
[('Hello', 'NN'), ('World', 'NN')]
```

Every tagger has a `tag()` method that takes a list of tokens, where each token is a single word. This list of tokens is usually a list of words produced by a word tokenizer (see *Chapter 1, Tokenizing Text and WordNet Basics*, for more on tokenization). As you can see, `tag()` returns a list of tagged tokens, where a tagged token is a tuple of `(word, tag)`.

How it works...

`DefaultTagger` is a subclass of `SequentialBackoffTagger`. Every subclass of `SequentialBackoffTagger` must implement the `choose_tag()` method, which takes three arguments:

- The list of tokens
- The index of the current token whose tag we want to choose
- The history, which is a list of the previous tags

`SequentialBackoffTagger` implements the `tag()` method, which calls the `choose_tag()` method of the subclass for each index in the tokens list while accumulating a history of the previously tagged tokens. This history is the reason for the *Sequential* in `SequentialBackoffTagger`. We'll get to the backoff portion of the name in the *Combining taggers with backoff tagging* recipe. Here's a diagram showing the inheritance tree:

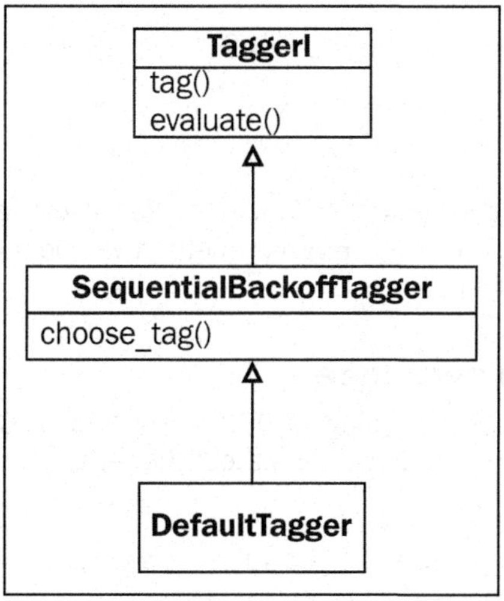

The `choose_tag()` method of `DefaultTagger` is very simple: it returns the tag we gave it at the time of initialization. It does not care about the current token or the history.

There's more...

There are a lot of different tags you could give to the `DefaultTagger` class. You can find a complete list of possible tags for the `treebank` corpus at `http://www.ling.upenn.edu/courses/Fall_2003/ling001/penn_treebank_pos.html`. These tags are also documented in *Appendix, Penn Treebank Part-of-speech Tags*.

Evaluating accuracy

To know how accurate a tagger is, you can use the `evaluate()` method, which takes a list of tagged tokens as a gold standard to evaluate the tagger. Using our default tagger created earlier, we can evaluate it against a subset of the `treebank` corpus tagged sentences.

```
>>> from nltk.corpus import treebank
>>> test_sents = treebank.tagged_sents()[3000:]
>>> tagger.evaluate(test_sents)
0.14331966328512843
```

So, by just choosing `NN` for every tag, we can achieve 14 % accuracy testing on one-fourth of the `treebank` corpus. Of course, accuracy will be different if you choose a different default tag. We'll be reusing these same `test_sents` for evaluating more taggers in the upcoming recipes.

Tagging sentences

`TaggerI` also implements a `tag_sents()` method that can be used to tag a list of sentences, instead of a single sentence. Here's an example of tagging two simple sentences:

```
>>> tagger.tag_sents([['Hello', 'world', '.'], ['How', 'are', 'you',
'?']])
[[('Hello', 'NN'), ('world', 'NN'), ('.', 'NN')], [('How', 'NN'),
('are', 'NN'), ('you', 'NN'), ('?', 'NN')]]
```

The result is a list of two tagged sentences, and of course, every tag is `NN` because we're using the `DefaultTagger` class. The `tag_sents()` method can be quiet useful if you have many sentences you wish to tag all at once.

Untagging a tagged sentence

Tagged sentences can be untagged using `nltk.tag.untag()`. Calling this function with a tagged sentence will return a list of words without the tags.

```
>>> from nltk.tag import untag
>>> untag([('Hello', 'NN'), ('World', 'NN')])
['Hello', 'World']
```

See also

For more on tokenization, see *Chapter 1, Tokenizing Text and WordNet Basics*. And to learn more about tagged sentences, see the *Creating a part-of-speech tagged word corpus* recipe in *Chapter 3, Creating Custom Corpora*. For a complete list of part-of-speech tags found in the `treebank` corpus, see *Appendix, Penn Treebank Part-of-speech Tags*.

Training a unigram part-of-speech tagger

A **unigram** generally refers to a single token. Therefore, a unigram tagger only uses a single word as its context for determining the part-of-speech tag.

`UnigramTagger` inherits from `NgramTagger`, which is a subclass of `ContextTagger`, which inherits from `SequentialBackoffTagger`. In other words, `UnigramTagger` is a context-based tagger whose context is a single word, or unigram.

How to do it...

`UnigramTagger` can be trained by giving it a list of tagged sentences at initialization.

```
>>> from nltk.tag import UnigramTagger
>>> from nltk.corpus import treebank
>>> train_sents = treebank.tagged_sents()[:3000]
>>> tagger = UnigramTagger(train_sents)
>>> treebank.sents()[0]
['Pierre', 'Vinken', ',', '61', 'years', 'old', ',', 'will', 'join',
'the', 'board', 'as', 'a', 'nonexecutive', 'director', 'Nov.', '29',
'.']
>>> tagger.tag(treebank.sents()[0])
[('Pierre', 'NNP'), ('Vinken', 'NNP'), (',', ','), ('61', 'CD'),
('years', 'NNS'), ('old', 'JJ'), (',', ','), ('will', 'MD'), ('join',
'VB'), ('the', 'DT'), ('board', 'NN'), ('as', 'IN'), ('a', 'DT'),
('nonexecutive', 'JJ'), ('director', 'NN'), ('Nov.', 'NNP'), ('29',
'CD'), ('.', '.')]
```

We use the first 3000 tagged sentences of the `treebank` corpus as the training set to initialize the `UnigramTagger` class. Then, we see the first sentence as a list of words, and can see how it is transformed by the `tag()` function into a list of tagged tokens.

How it works...

`UnigramTagger` builds a context model from the list of tagged sentences. Because `UnigramTagger` inherits from `ContextTagger`, instead of providing a `choose_tag()` method, it must implement a `context()` method, which takes the same three arguments as `choose_tag()`. The result of `context()` is, in this case, the word token. The context token is used to create the model, and also to look up the best tag once the model is created. Here's an inheritance diagram showing each class, starting at `SequentialBackoffTagger`:

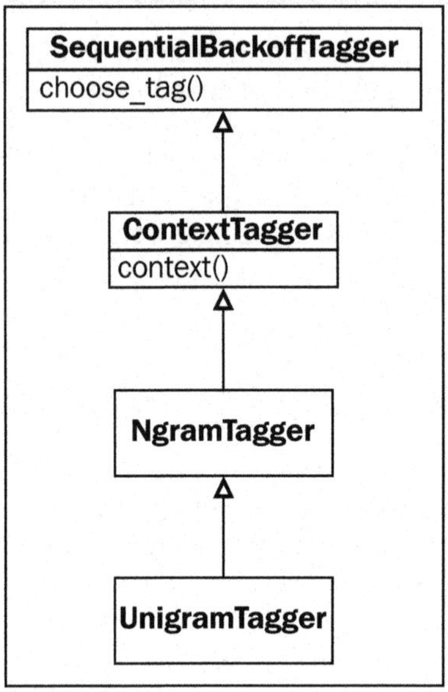

Let's see how accurate the `UnigramTagger` class is on the test sentences (see the previous recipe for how `test_sents` is created).

```
>>> tagger.evaluate(test_sents)
0.8588819339520829
```

It has almost 86 % accuracy for a tagger that only uses single word lookup to determine the part-of-speech tag. All accuracy gains from here on will be much smaller.

> Actual accuracy values may change each time you run the code. This is because the default iteration order in Python 3 is random. To get consistent accuracy values, run Python with the `PYTHONHASHSEED` environment variable set to `0` or any positive integer. For example:
>
> **`$ PYTHONHASHSEED=0 python chapter4.py`**
>
> All accuracy values in this book were calculated with `PYTHONHASHSEED=0`.

There's more...

The model building is actually implemented in `ContextTagger`. Given the list of tagged sentences, it calculates the frequency that a tag has occurred for each context. The tag with the highest frequency for a context is stored in the model.

Overriding the context model

All taggers that inherit from `ContextTagger` can take a pre-built model instead of training their own. This model is simply a Python `dict` mapping a context key to a tag. The context keys will depend on what the `ContextTagger` subclass returns from its `context()` method. For `UnigramTagger`, context keys are individual words. But for other `NgramTagger` subclasses, the context keys will be tuples.

Here's an example where we pass a very simple model to the `UnigramTagger` class instead of a training set.

```
>>> tagger = UnigramTagger(model={'Pierre': 'NN'})
>>> tagger.tag(treebank.sents()[0])
[('Pierre', 'NN'), ('Vinken', None), (',', None), ('61', None),
('years', None), ('old', None), (',', None), ('will', None), ('join',
None), ('the', None), ('board', None), ('as', None), ('a', None),
('nonexecutive', None), ('director', None), ('Nov.', None), ('29',
None), ('.', None)]
```

Since the model only contained the context key `Pierre`, only the first word got a tag. Every other word got `None` as the tag since the context word was not in the model. So, unless you know exactly what you are doing, let the tagger train its own model instead of passing in your own.

One good case for passing a self-created model to the `UnigramTagger` class is for when you have a dictionary of words and tags, and you know that every word should always map to its tag. Then, you can put this `UnigramTagger` as your first backoff tagger (covered in the next recipe) to look up tags for unambiguous words.

Minimum frequency cutoff

The `ContextTagger` class uses frequency of occurrence to decide which tag is most likely for a given context. By default, it will do this even if the context word and tag occurs only once. If you'd like to set a minimum frequency threshold, then you can pass a `cutoff` value to the `UnigramTagger` class.

```
>>> tagger = UnigramTagger(train_sents, cutoff=3)
>>> tagger.evaluate(test_sents)
0.7757392618173969
```

In this case, using `cutoff=3` has decreased accuracy, but there may be times when a cutoff is a good idea.

See also

In the next recipe, we'll cover **backoff tagging** to combine taggers, and in the *Creating a model of likely word tags* recipe, we'll learn how to statistically determine tags for very common words.

Combining taggers with backoff tagging

Backoff tagging is one of the core features of `SequentialBackoffTagger`. It allows you to chain taggers together so that if one tagger doesn't know how to tag a word, it can pass the word on to the next backoff tagger. If that one can't do it, it can pass the word on to the next backoff tagger, and so on until there are no backoff taggers left to check.

How to do it...

Every subclass of `SequentialBackoffTagger` can take a backoff keyword argument whose value is another instance of a `SequentialBackoffTagger`. So, we'll use the `DefaultTagger` class from the *Default tagging* recipe in this chapter as the backoff to the `UnigramTagger` class covered in the previous recipe, *Training a unigram part-of-speech tagger*. Refer to both the recipes for details on `train_sents` and `test_sents`.

```
>>> tagger1 = DefaultTagger('NN')
>>> tagger2 = UnigramTagger(train_sents, backoff=tagger1)
>>> tagger2.evaluate(test_sents)
0.8758471832505935
```

By using a default tag of `NN` whenever the `UnigramTagger` is unable to tag a word, we've increased the accuracy by almost 2%!

How it works...

When a `SequentialBackoffTagger` class is initialized, it creates an internal list of backoff taggers with itself as the first element. If a backoff tagger is given, then the backoff tagger's internal list of taggers is appended. Here's some code to illustrate this:

```
>>> tagger1._taggers == [tagger1]
True
>>> tagger2._taggers == [tagger2, tagger1]
True
```

The `_taggers` list is the internal list of backoff taggers that the `SequentialBackoffTagger` class uses when the `tag()` method is called. It goes through its list of taggers, calling `choose_tag()` on each one. As soon as a tag is found, it stops and returns that tag. This means that if the primary tagger can tag the word, then that's the tag that will be returned. But if it returns `None`, then the next tagger is tried, and so on until a tag is found, or else `None` is returned. Of course, `None` will never be returned if your final backoff tagger is a `DefaultTagger`.

There's more...

While most of the taggers included in NLTK are subclasses of `SequentialBackoffTagger`, not all of them are. There's a few taggers that we'll cover in the later recipes that cannot be used as part of a backoff tagging chain, such as the `BrillTagger` class. However, these taggers generally take another tagger to use as a baseline, and a `SequentialBackoffTagger` class is often a good choice for that baseline.

Saving and loading a trained tagger with pickle

Since training a tagger can take a while, and you generally only need to do the training once, pickling a trained tagger is a useful way to save it for later usage. If your trained tagger is called `tagger`, then here's how to dump and load it with `pickle`:

```
>>> import pickle
>>> f = open('tagger.pickle', 'wb')
>>> pickle.dump(tagger, f)
>>> f.close()
>>> f = open('tagger.pickle', 'rb')
>>> tagger = pickle.load(f)
```

If your tagger `pickle` file is located in an NLTK data directory, you could also use `nltk.data.load('tagger.pickle')` to load the tagger.

See also

In the next recipe, we'll combine more taggers with backoff tagging. Also, see the previous two recipes for details on the `DefaultTagger` and `UnigramTagger` classes.

Training and combining ngram taggers

In addition to UnigramTagger, there are two more NgramTagger subclasses: BigramTagger and TrigramTagger. The BigramTagger subclass uses the previous tag as part of its context, while the TrigramTagger subclass uses the previous two tags. An **ngram** is a subsequence of *n* items, so the BigramTagger subclass looks at two items (the previous tagged word and the current word), and the TrigramTagger subclass looks at three items.

These two taggers are good at handling words whose part-of-speech tag is context-dependent. Many words have a different part of speech depending on how they are used. For example, we've been talking about taggers that tag words. In this case, *tag* is used as a verb. But the result of tagging is a part-of-speech tag, so *tag* can also be a noun. The idea with the NgramTagger subclasses is that by looking at the previous words and part-of-speech tags, we can better guess the part-of-speech tag for the current word. Internally, each tagger maintains a context dictionary (implemented in the ContextTagger parent class) that is used to guess that tag based on the context. In the case of NgramTagger subclasses, the context is some number of previous tagged words.

Getting ready

Refer to the first two recipes of this chapter for details on constructing train_sents and test_sents.

How to do it...

By themselves, BigramTagger and TrigramTagger perform quite poorly. This is partly because they cannot learn context from the first word(s) in a sentence. Since a UnigramTagger class doesn't care about the previous context, it is able to have higher baseline accuracy by simply guessing the most common tag for each word.

```
>>> from nltk.tag import BigramTagger, TrigramTagger
>>> bitagger = BigramTagger(train_sents)
>>> bitagger.evaluate(test_sents)
0.11310166199007123
>>> tritagger = TrigramTagger(train_sents)
>>> tritagger.evaluate(test_sents)
0.0688107058061731
```

Where `BigramTagger` and `TrigramTagger` can make a contribution is when we combine them with backoff tagging. This time, instead of creating each tagger individually, we'll create a function that will take `train_sents`, a list of `SequentialBackoffTagger` classes, and an optional final backoff tagger, then train each tagger with the previous tagger as a backoff. Here's the code from `tag_util.py`:

```
def backoff_tagger(train_sents, tagger_classes, backoff=None):
  for cls in tagger_classes:
    backoff = cls(train_sents, backoff=backoff)

  return backoff
```

And to use it, we can do the following:

```
>>> from tag_util import backoff_tagger
>>> backoff = DefaultTagger('NN')
>>> tagger = backoff_tagger(train_sents, [UnigramTagger, BigramTagger,
TrigramTagger], backoff=backoff)
>>> tagger.evaluate(test_sents)
0.8806820634578028
```

So, we've gained almost 1% accuracy by including the `BigramTagger` and `TrigramTagger` subclasses in the backoff chain. For corpora other than `treebank`, the accuracy gain may be more or less significant, depending on the nature of the text.

How it works...

The `backoff_tagger` function creates an instance of each tagger class in the list, giving it `train_sents` and the previous tagger as a backoff. The order of the list of tagger classes is quite important: the first class in the list (`UnigramTagger`) will be trained first and given the initial backoff tagger (the `DefaultTagger`). This tagger will then become the backoff tagger for the next tagger class in the list. The final tagger returned will be an instance of the last tagger class in the list (`TrigramTagger`). Here's some code to clarify this chain:

```
>>> tagger._taggers[-1] == backoff
True
>>> isinstance(tagger._taggers[0], TrigramTagger)
True
>>> isinstance(tagger._taggers[1], BigramTagger)
True
```

So, we get a `TrigramTagger`, whose first backoff is a `BigramTagger`. Then, the next backoff will be a `UnigramTagger`, whose backoff is the `DefaultTagger`.

There's more...

The `backoff_tagger` function doesn't just work with `NgramTagger` classes, it can also be used for constructing a chain containing any subclasses of `SequentialBackoffTagger`.

`BigramTagger` and `TrigramTagger`, because they are subclasses of `NgramTagger` and `ContextTagger`, can also take a model and cutoff argument, just like the `UnigramTagger`. But unlike for `UnigramTagger`, the context keys of the model must be two tuples, where the first element is a section of the history and the second element is the current token. For the `BigramTagger`, an appropriate context key looks like `((prevtag,), word)`, and for `TrigramTagger`, it looks like `((prevtag1, prevtag2), word)`.

Quadgram tagger

The `NgramTagger` class can be used by itself to create a tagger that uses more than three ngrams for its context key.

```
>>> from nltk.tag import NgramTagger
>>> quadtagger = NgramTagger(4, train_sents)
>>> quadtagger.evaluate(test_sents)
0.058234405352903085
```

It's even worse than the `TrigramTagger`! Here's an alternative implementation of a `QuadgramTagger` class that we can include in a list to `backoff_tagger`. This code can be found in `taggers.py`.

```
from nltk.tag import NgramTagger

class QuadgramTagger(NgramTagger):
  def __init__(self, *args, **kwargs):
    NgramTagger.__init__(self, 4, *args, **kwargs)
```

This is essentially how `BigramTagger` and `TrigramTagger` are implemented: simple subclasses of `NgramTagger` that pass in the number of ngrams to look at in the `history` argument of the `context()` method.

Now, let's see how it does as part of a backoff chain.

```
>>> from taggers import QuadgramTagger
>>> quadtagger = backoff_tagger(train_sents, [UnigramTagger,
BigramTagger, TrigramTagger, QuadgramTagger], backoff=backoff)
>>> quadtagger.evaluate(test_sents)
0.8806388948845241
```

It's actually slightly worse than before, when we stopped with the `TrigramTagger`. So, the lesson is that too much context can have a negative effect on accuracy.

See also

The previous two recipes cover the `UnigramTagger` and backoff tagging.

Creating a model of likely word tags

As previously mentioned in the *Training a unigram part-of-speech tagger* recipe, using a custom model with a `UnigramTagger` class should only be done if you know exactly what you're doing. In this recipe, we're going to create a model for the most common words, most of which always have the same tag no matter what.

How to do it...

To find the most common words, we can use `nltk.probability.FreqDist` to count word frequencies in the `treebank` corpus. Then, we can create a `ConditionalFreqDist` class for tagged words, where we count the frequency of every tag for every word. Using these counts, we can construct a model of the 200 most frequent words as keys, with the most frequent tag for each word as a value. Here's the model creation function defined in `tag_util.py`.

```
from nltk.probability import FreqDist, ConditionalFreqDist

def word_tag_model(words, tagged_words, limit=200):
  fd = FreqDist(words)
  cfd = ConditionalFreqDist(tagged_words)
  most_freq = (word for word, count in fd.most_common(limit))
  return dict((word, cfd[word].max()) for word in most_freq)
```

And to use it with a `UnigramTagger` class, we can do the following:

```
>>> from tag_util import word_tag_model
>>> from nltk.corpus import treebank
>>> model = word_tag_model(treebank.words(), treebank.tagged_words())
>>> tagger = UnigramTagger(model=model)
>>> tagger.evaluate(test_sents)
0.559680552557738
```

An accuracy of almost 56% is ok, but nowhere near as good as the trained `UnigramTagger`. Let's try adding it to our backoff chain.

```
>>> default_tagger = DefaultTagger('NN')
>>> likely_tagger = UnigramTagger(model=model, backoff=default_tagger)
>>> tagger = backoff_tagger(train_sents, [UnigramTagger, BigramTagger,
TrigramTagger], backoff=likely_tagger)
>>> tagger.evaluate(test_sents)
0.8806820634578028
```

The final accuracy is exactly the same as without the `likely_tagger`. This is because the frequency calculations we did to create the model are almost exactly the same as what happens when we train a `UnigramTagger` class.

How it works...

The `word_tag_model()` function takes a list of all words, a list of all tagged words, and the maximum number of words we want to use for our model. We give the list of words to a `FreqDist` class, which counts the frequency of each word. Then, we get the top 200 words from the `FreqDist` class by calling `fd.most_common()`, which obviously returns a list of the most common words and counts. The `FreqDist` class is actually a subclass of `collections.Counter`, which provides the `most_common()` method.

Next, we give the list of tagged words to `ConditionalFreqDist`, which creates a `FreqDist` class of tags for each word, with the word as the condition. Finally, we return a `dict` of the top 200 words mapped to their most likely tag.

> In the previous edition of this book, we used the `keys()` method of the `FreqDist` class because in NLTK2, the keys were returned in sorted order, from the most frequent to the least. But in NLTK3, `FreqDist` inherits from `collections.Counter`, and the `keys()` method does not use any predictable ordering.

There's more...

It may seem useless to include this tagger as it does not change the accuracy. But the point of this recipe is to demonstrate how to construct a useful model for a `UnigramTagger` class. Custom model construction is a way to create a manual override of trained taggers that are otherwise black boxes. And by putting the `likely_tagger` at the front of the chain, we can actually improve accuracy a little bit:

```
>>> tagger = backoff_tagger(train_sents, [UnigramTagger, BigramTagger,
TrigramTagger], backoff=default_tagger)
>>> likely_tagger = UnigramTagger(model=model, backoff=tagger)
>>> likely_tagger.evaluate(test_sents)
0.8824088063889488
```

Putting custom model taggers at the front of the backoff chain gives you complete control over how specific words are tagged, while letting the trained taggers handle everything else.

See also

The *Training a unigram part-of-speech tagger* recipe has details on the `UnigramTagger` class and a simple custom model example. See the earlier *recipes Combining taggers with backoff tagging* and *Training and combining ngram taggers* for details on backoff tagging.

Tagging with regular expressions

You can use regular expression matching to tag words. For example, you can match numbers with `\d` to assign the tag **CD** (which refers to a Cardinal number). Or you could match on known word patterns, such as the suffix "ing". There's a lot of flexibility here, but be careful of over-specifying since language is naturally inexact, and there are always exceptions to the rule.

Getting ready

For this recipe to make sense, you should be familiar with the regular expression syntax and Python's `re` module.

How to do it...

The `RegexpTagger` class expects a list of two tuples, where the first element in the tuple is a regular expression and the second element is the tag. The patterns shown in the following code can be found in `tag_util.py`:

```
patterns = [
  (r'^\d+$', 'CD'),
  (r'.*ing$', 'VBG'), # gerunds, i.e. wondering
  (r'.*ment$', 'NN'), # i.e. wonderment
  (r'.*ful$', 'JJ') # i.e. wonderful
]
```

Once you've constructed this list of patterns, you can pass it into `RegexpTagger`.

```
>>> from tag_util import patterns
>>> from nltk.tag import RegexpTagger
>>> tagger = RegexpTagger(patterns)
>>> tagger.evaluate(test_sents)
0.037470321605870924
```

So, it's not too great with just a few patterns, but since `RegexpTagger` is a subclass of `SequentialBackoffTagger`, it can be a useful part of a backoff chain. For example, it could be positioned just before a `DefaultTagger` class, to tag words that the ngram tagger(s) missed.

How it works...

The `RegexpTagger` class saves the patterns given at initialization, then on each call to `choose_tag()`, it iterates over the patterns and returns the tag for the first expression that matches the current word using `re.match()`. This means that if you have two expressions that could match, the tag of the first one will always be returned, and the second expression won't even be tried.

There's more...

The `RegexpTagger` class can replace the `DefaultTagger` class if you give it a pattern such as `(r'.*', 'NN')`. This pattern should, of course, be last in the list of patterns, otherwise no other patterns will match.

See also

In the next recipe, we'll cover the `AffixTagger` class, which learns how to tag based on prefixes and suffixes of words. See the *Default tagging* recipe for details on the `DefaultTagger` class.

Affix tagging

The `AffixTagger` class is another `ContextTagger` subclass, but this time the context is either the prefix or the suffix of a word. This means the `AffixTagger` class is able to learn tags based on fixed-length substrings of the beginning or ending of a word.

How to do it...

The default arguments for an `AffixTagger` class specify three-character suffixes, and that words must be at least five characters long. If a word is less than five characters, then `None` is returned as the tag.

```
>>> from nltk.tag import AffixTagger
>>> tagger = AffixTagger(train_sents)
>>> tagger.evaluate(test_sents)
0.27558817181092166
```

So, it does ok by itself with the default arguments. Let's try it by specifying three-character prefixes.

```
>>> prefix_tagger = AffixTagger(train_sents, affix_length=3)
>>> prefix_tagger.evaluate(test_sents)
0.23587308439456076
```

To learn on two-character suffixes, the code will look like this:

```
>>> suffix_tagger = AffixTagger(train_sents, affix_length=-2)
>>> suffix_tagger.evaluate(test_sents)
0.31940427368875457
```

How it works...

A positive value for `affix_length` means that the `AffixTagger` class will learn word prefixes, essentially `word[:affix_length]`. If `affix_length` is negative, then suffixes are learned using `word[affix_length:]`.

There's more...

You can combine multiple affix taggers in a backoff chain if you want to learn on multiple character length affixes. Here's an example of four `AffixTagger` classes learning on `2` and `3` character prefixes and suffixes:

```
>>> pre3_tagger = AffixTagger(train_sents, affix_length=3)
>>> pre3_tagger.evaluate(test_sents)
0.23587308439456076
>>> pre2_tagger = AffixTagger(train_sents, affix_length=2,
backoff=pre3_tagger)
>>> pre2_tagger.evaluate(test_sents)
0.29786315562270665
>>> suf2_tagger = AffixTagger(train_sents, affix_length=-2,
backoff=pre2_tagger)
>>> suf2_tagger.evaluate(test_sents)
0.32467083962875026
>>> suf3_tagger = AffixTagger(train_sents, affix_length=-3,
backoff=suf2_tagger)
>>> suf3_tagger.evaluate(test_sents)
0.3590761925318368
```

As you can see, the accuracy goes up each time.

> The ordering in the previous block of code is not the best, nor is it the worst. I'll leave it to you to explore the possibilities and discover the best backoff chain of values for `AffixTagger` and `affix_length`.

Working with min_stem_length

The `AffixTagger` class also takes a `min_stem_length` keyword argument, with a default value of `2`. If the word length is less than `min_stem_length` plus the absolute value of `affix_length`, then `None` is returned by the `context()` method. Increasing `min_stem_length` forces the `AffixTagger` class to only learn on longer words, while decreasing `min_stem_length` will allow it to learn on shorter words. Of course, for shorter words, the `affix_length` argument could be equal to or greater than the word length, and `AffixTagger` would essentially be acting like a `UnigramTagger` class.

See also

You can manually specify prefixes and suffixes using regular expressions, as shown in the previous recipe. The *Training a unigram part-of-speech tagger* and *Training and combining ngram taggers* recipes have details on `NgramTagger` subclasses, which are also subclasses of `ContextTagger`.

Training a Brill tagger

The `BrillTagger` class is a transformation-based tagger. It is the first tagger that is not a subclass of `SequentialBackoffTagger`. Instead, the `BrillTagger` class uses a series of rules to correct the results of an initial tagger. These rules are scored based on how many errors they correct minus the number of new errors they produce.

How to do it...

Here's a function from `tag_util.py` that trains a `BrillTagger` class using `BrillTaggerTrainer`. It requires an `initial_tagger` and `train_sents`.

```
from nltk.tag import brill, brill_trainer

def train_brill_tagger(initial_tagger, train_sents, **kwargs):
  templates = [
    brill.Template(brill.Pos([-1])),
    brill.Template(brill.Pos([1])),
    brill.Template(brill.Pos([-2])),
    brill.Template(brill.Pos([2])),
    brill.Template(brill.Pos([-2, -1])),
    brill.Template(brill.Pos([1, 2])),
    brill.Template(brill.Pos([-3, -2, -1])),
    brill.Template(brill.Pos([1, 2, 3])),
    brill.Template(brill.Pos([-1]), brill.Pos([1])),
    brill.Template(brill.Word([-1])),
    brill.Template(brill.Word([1])),
```

```
        brill.Template(brill.Word([-2])),
        brill.Template(brill.Word([2])),
        brill.Template(brill.Word([-2, -1])),
        brill.Template(brill.Word([1, 2])),
        brill.Template(brill.Word([-3, -2, -1])),
        brill.Template(brill.Word([1, 2, 3])),
        brill.Template(brill.Word([-1]), brill.Word([1])),
      ]

    trainer = brill_trainer.BrillTaggerTrainer(initial_tagger,
templates, deterministic=True)
    return trainer.train(train_sents, **kwargs)
```

To use it, we can create our `initial_tagger` from a backoff chain of `NgramTagger` classes, then pass that into the `train_brill_tagger()` function to get a `BrillTagger` back.

```
>>> default_tagger = DefaultTagger('NN')
>>> initial_tagger = backoff_tagger(train_sents, [UnigramTagger,
BigramTagger, TrigramTagger], backoff=default_tagger)
>>> initial_tagger.evaluate(test_sents)
0.8806820634578028
>>> from tag_util import train_brill_tagger
>>> brill_tagger = train_brill_tagger(initial_tagger, train_sents)
>>> brill_tagger.evaluate(test_sents)
0.8827541549751781
```

So, the `BrillTagger` class has slightly increased accuracy over the `initial_tagger`.

How it works...

The `BrillTaggerTrainer` class takes an `initial_tagger` argument and a list of templates. These templates must implement the `BrillTemplateI` interface, which is found in the `nltk.tbl.template` module. The `brill.Template` class is such an implementation, and is actually imported from `nltk.tbl.template`. The `brill.Pos` and `brill.Word` classes are subclasses of `nltk.tbl.template.Feature`, and they describe what kind of features to use in the template, in this case, one or more part-of-speech tags or words.

The templates specify how to learn transformation rules. For example, `brill.Template(brill.Pos([-1]))` means that a rule can be generated using the previous part-of-speech tag. The `brill.Template(brill.Pos([1]))` statement means that you can look at the next part-of-speech tag to generate a rule. And `brill.Template(brill.Word([-2, -1]))` means you can look at the combination of the previous two words to learn a transformation rule.

The thinking behind a transformation-based tagger is this: given the correct training sentences, the output of the initial tagger, and the templates specifying features, try to generate transformation rules that correct the initial tagger's output to be more in-line with the training sentences. The job of `BrillTaggerTrainer` is to produce these rules, and to do so in a way that increases accuracy. A transformation rule that fixes one problem may cause an error in another condition; thus, every rule must be measured by how many errors it corrects versus how many new errors it introduces.

The workflow looks something like this:

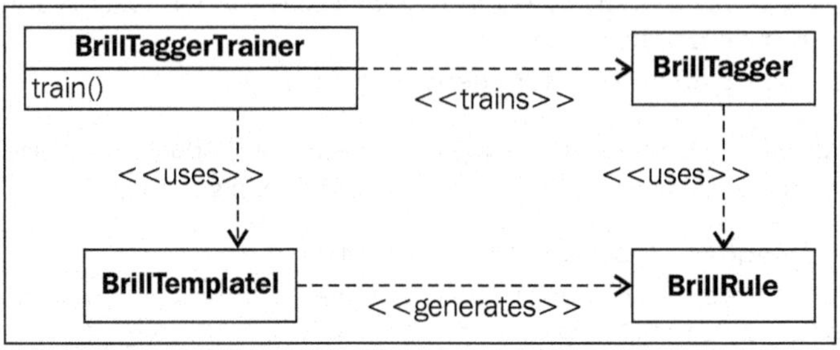

There's more...

You can control the number of rules generated using the `max_rules` keyword argument to the `BrillTaggerTrainer.train()` method. The default value is `200`. You can also control the quality of rules used with the `min_score` keyword argument. The default value is `2`, though `3` can be a good choice as well. The score is a measure of how well a rule corrects errors compared to how many new errors it introduces.

> Increasing `max_rules` or `min_score` will greatly increase training time, without necessarily increasing accuracy. Change these values with care.

Tracing

You can watch the `BrillTaggerTrainer` class do its work by passing `trace=True` into the constructor, for example, `trainer = brill.BrillTaggerTrainer(initial_tagger, templates, deterministic=True, trace=True)`. This will give you the following output:

```
TBL train (fast) (seqs: 3000; tokens: 77511; tpls: 18; min score: 2;
min acc: None)
    Finding initial useful rules...
        Found 9869 useful rules.
    Selecting rules...
```

This means it found 77511 rules with a score of at least min_score, and then it selects the best rules, keeping no more than max_rules.

The default is trace=False, which means the trainer will work silently without printing its status.

See also

The *Training and combining ngram taggers* recipe details the construction of the initial_tagger argument used earlier, and the *Default tagging* recipe explains the default_tagger argument.

Training the TnT tagger

TnT stands for **Trigrams'n'Tags**. It is a statistical tagger based on second order Markov models. The details of this are out of the scope of this book, but you can read more about the original implementation at http://www.coli.uni-saarland.de/~thorsten/tnt/.

How to do it...

The TnT tagger has a slightly different API than the previous taggers we've encountered. You must explicitly call the train() method after you've created it. Here's a basic example.

```
>>> from nltk.tag import tnt
>>> tnt_tagger = tnt.TnT()
>>> tnt_tagger.train(train_sents)
>>> tnt_tagger.evaluate(test_sents)
0.8756313403842003
```

It's quite a good tagger all by itself, only slightly less accurate than the BrillTagger class from the previous recipe. But if you do not call train() before evaluate(), you'll get an accuracy of 0%.

How it works...

The TnT tagger maintains a number of internal FreqDist and ConditionalFreqDist instances based on the training data. These frequency distributions count unigrams, bigrams, and trigrams. Then, during tagging, the frequencies are used to calculate the probabilities of possible tags for each word. So, instead of constructing a backoff chain of NgramTagger subclasses, the TnT tagger uses all the ngram models together to choose the best tag. It also tries to guess the tags for the whole sentence at once by choosing the most likely model for the entire sentence, based on the probabilities of each possible tag.

> Training is fairly quick, but tagging is significantly slower than the other taggers we've covered. This is due to all the floating point math that must be done to calculate the tag probabilities of each word.

There's more...

The `TnT` tagger accepts a few optional keyword arguments. You can pass in a tagger for unknown words as `unk`. If this tagger is already trained, then you must also pass in `Trained=True`. Otherwise, it will call `unk.train(data)` with the same data you pass into the `train()` method. Since none of the previous taggers have a public `train()` method, I recommend always passing `Trained=True` if you also pass an `unk` tagger. Here's an example using a `DefaultTagger` class, which does not require any training.

```
>>> from nltk.tag import DefaultTagger
>>> unk = DefaultTagger('NN')
>>> tnt_tagger = tnt.TnT(unk=unk, Trained=True)
>>> tnt_tagger.train(train_sents)
>>> tnt_tagger.evaluate(test_sents)
0.892467083962875
```

So, we got an almost 2% increase in accuracy! You must use a tagger that can tag a single word without having seen that word before. This is because the unknown tagger's `tag()` method is only called with a single word sentence. Other good candidates for an unknown tagger are `RegexpTagger` and `AffixTagger`. Passing in a `UnigramTagger` class that's been trained on the same data is pretty much useless, as it will have seen the exact same words and, therefore, have the same unknown word blind spots.

Controlling the beam search

Another parameter you can modify for `TnT` is `N`, which controls the number of possible solutions the tagger maintains while trying to guess the tags for a sentence. `N` defaults to `1000`. Increasing it will greatly increase the amount of memory used during tagging, without necessarily increasing the accuracy. Decreasing `N` will decrease memory usage, but could also decrease accuracy. Here's what happens when the value is changed to `N=100`.

```
>>> tnt_tagger = tnt.TnT(N=100)
>>> tnt_tagger.train(train_sents)
>>> tnt_tagger.evaluate(test_sents)
0.8756313403842003
```

So, the accuracy is exactly the same, but we use significantly less memory to achieve it. However, don't assume that accuracy will not change if you decrease `N`; experiment with your own data to be sure.

Significance of capitalization

You can pass `C=True` to the `TnT` constructor if you want capitalization of words to be significant. The default is `C=False`, which means all words are lowercase. The documentation on `C` says that treating capitalization as significant probably will not increase accuracy. In my own testing, there was a very slight (< 0.01%) increase in accuracy with `C=True`, probably because case-sensitivity can help identify proper nouns.

See also

We have covered the `DefaultTagger` class in the *Default tagging* recipe, backoff tagging in the *Combining taggers with backoff tagging* recipe, `NgramTagger` subclasses in the *Training a unigram part-of-speech tagger* and *Training and combining ngram taggers* recipes, `RegexpTagger` in the *Tagging with regular expressions recipe*, and the `AffixTagger` class in the *Affix tagging recipe*.

Using WordNet for tagging

If you remember from the *Looking up Synsets for a word in WordNet* recipe in *Chapter 1, Tokenizing Text and WordNet Basics*, WordNet Synsets specify a part-of-speech tag. It's a very restricted set of possible tags, and many words have multiple Synsets with different part-of-speech tags, but this information can be useful for tagging unknown words. WordNet is essentially a giant dictionary, and it's likely to contain many words that are not in your training data.

Getting ready

First, we need to decide how to map WordNet part-of-speech tags to the Penn Treebank part-of-speech tags we've been using. The following is a table mapping one to the other. See the *Looking up Synsets for a word in WordNet* recipe in *Chapter 1, Tokenizing Text and WordNet Basics*, for more details. The `s`, which was not shown before, is just another kind of adjective, at least for tagging purposes.

WordNet tag	Treebank tag
n	NN
a	JJ
s	JJ
r	RB
v	VB

How to do it...

Now we can create a class that will look up words in WordNet, and then choose the most common tag from the Synsets it finds. The `WordNetTagger` class defined in the following code can be found in `taggers.py`:

```
from nltk.tag import SequentialBackoffTagger
from nltk.corpus import wordnet
from nltk.probability import FreqDist

class WordNetTagger(SequentialBackoffTagger):
  '''
  >>> wt = WordNetTagger()
  >>> wt.tag(['food', 'is', 'great'])
  [('food', 'NN'), ('is', 'VB'), ('great', 'JJ')]
  '''
  def __init__(self, *args, **kwargs):
    SequentialBackoffTagger.__init__(self, *args, **kwargs)

    self.wordnet_tag_map = {
      'n': 'NN',
      's': 'JJ',
      'a': 'JJ',
      'r': 'RB',
      'v': 'VB'
    }

  def choose_tag(self, tokens, index, history):
    word = tokens[index]
    fd = FreqDist()

    for synset in wordnet.synsets(word):
      fd[synset.pos()] += 1

    return self.wordnet_tag_map.get(fd.max())
```

> Another way the FreqDist API has changed between NLTK2 and NLTK3 is that the inc() method has been removed. Instead, you must use fd[key] += 1. Since FreqDist inherits from collections.Counter, it's ok if fd[key] doesn't exist the first time you increment.

How it works...

The WordNetTagger class simply counts the number of each part-of-speech tag found in the Synsets for a word. The most common tag is then mapped to a treebank tag using internal mapping. Here's some sample usage code:

```
>>> from taggers import WordNetTagger
>>> wn_tagger = WordNetTagger()
>>> wn_tagger.evaluate(train_sents)
0.17914876598160262
```

So, it's not too accurate, but that's to be expected. We only have enough information to produce four different kinds of tags, while there are 36 possible tags in treebank. There are many words that can have different part-of-speech tags depending on their context. But if we put the WordNetTagger class at the end of an NgramTagger backoff chain, then we can improve accuracy over the DefaultTagger class.

```
>>> from tag_util import backoff_tagger
>>> from nltk.tag import UnigramTagger, BigramTagger, TrigramTagger
>>> tagger = backoff_tagger(train_sents, [UnigramTagger, BigramTagger,
TrigramTagger], backoff=wn_tagger)
>>> tagger.evaluate(test_sents)
0.8848262464925534
```

See also

The *Looking up Synsets for a word in WordNet* recipe in *Chapter 1, Tokenizing Text and WordNet Basics*, details how to use the wordnet corpus and what kinds of part-of-speech tags it knows about. And in the *Combining taggers with backoff tagging* and *Training and combining ngram taggers* recipes, we went over backoff tagging with ngram taggers.

Tagging proper names

Using the included `names` corpus, we can create a simple tagger for tagging names as proper nouns.

How to do it...

The `NamesTagger` class is a subclass of `SequentialBackoffTagger` as it's probably only useful near the end of a backoff chain. At initialization, we create a set of all names in the `names` corpus, lower-casing each name to make lookup easier. Then, we implement the `choose_tag()` method, which simply checks whether the current word is in the `names_set` list. If it is, we return the `NNP` tag (which is the tag for proper nouns). If it isn't, we return `None`, so the next tagger in the chain can tag the word. The following code can be found in `taggers.py`:

```
from nltk.tag import SequentialBackoffTagger
from nltk.corpus import names

class NamesTagger(SequentialBackoffTagger):
  def __init__(self, *args, **kwargs):
    SequentialBackoffTagger.__init__(self, *args, **kwargs)
    self.name_set = set([n.lower() for n in names.words()])

    def choose_tag(self, tokens, index, history):
      word = tokens[index]

      if word.lower() in self.name_set:
        return 'NNP'
      else:
        return None
```

How it works...

The `NamesTagger` class should be pretty self-explanatory. The usage is also simple.

```
>>> from taggers import NamesTagger
>>> nt = NamesTagger()
>>> nt.tag(['Jacob'])
[('Jacob', 'NNP')]
```

It's probably best to use the `NamesTagger` class right before a `DefaultTagger` class, so it's at the end of a backoff chain. But it could probably go anywhere in the chain since it's unlikely to mis-tag a word.

See also

The *Combining taggers with backoff tagging* recipe goes over the details of using the `SequentialBackoffTagger` subclasses.

Classifier-based tagging

The `ClassifierBasedPOSTagger` class uses classification to do part-of-speech tagging. Features are extracted from words, and then passed to an internal classifier. The classifier classifies the features and returns a label, in this case, a part-of-speech tag. Classification will be covered in detail in *Chapter 7, Text Classification*.

The `ClassifierBasedPOSTagger` class is a subclass of `ClassifierBasedTagger` that implements a feature detector that combines many of the techniques of the previous taggers into a single feature set. The feature detector finds multiple length suffixes, does some regular expression matching, and looks at the unigram, bigram, and trigram history to produce a fairly complete set of features for each word. The feature sets it produces are used to train the internal classifier, and are used for classifying words into part-of-speech tags.

How to do it...

The basic usage of the `ClassifierBasedPOSTagger` class is much like any other `SequentialBackoffTaggger`. You pass in training sentences, it trains an internal classifier, and you get a very accurate tagger.

```
>>> from nltk.tag.sequential import ClassifierBasedPOSTagger
>>> tagger = ClassifierBasedPOSTagger(train=train_sents)
>>> tagger.evaluate(test_sents)
0.9309734513274336
```

> Notice a slight modification to initialization: `train_sents` must be passed in as the `train` keyword argument.

How it works...

The `ClassifierBasedPOSTagger` class inherits from `ClassifierBasedTagger` and only implements a `feature_detector()` method. All the training and tagging is done in `ClassifierBasedTagger`. It defaults to training a `NaiveBayesClassifier` class with the given training data. Once this classifier is trained, it is used to classify word features produced by the `feature_detector()` method.

> The `ClassifierBasedTagger` class is often the most accurate tagger, but it's also one of the slowest taggers. If speed is an issue, you should stick with a `BrillTagger` class based on a backoff chain of `NgramTagger` subclasses and other simple taggers.

The `ClassifierBasedTagger` class also inherits from `FeatursetTaggerI` (which is just an empty class), creating an inheritance tree that looks like this:

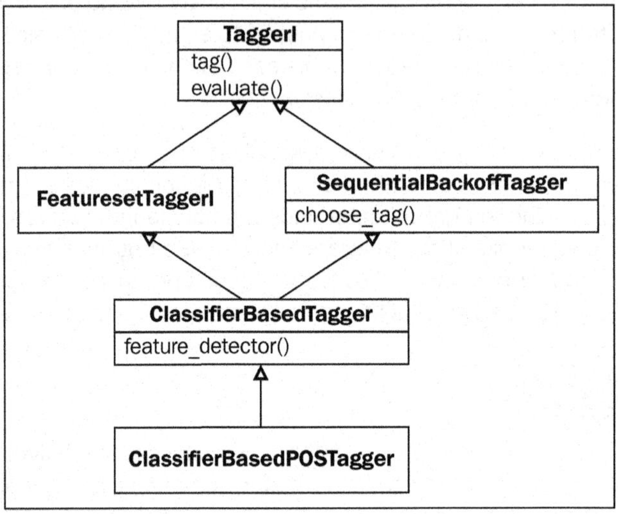

There's more...

You can use a different classifier instead of `NaiveBayesClassifier` by passing in your own `classifier_builder` function. For example, to use a `MaxentClassifier`, you'd do the following:

```
>>> from nltk.classify import MaxentClassifier
>>> me_tagger = ClassifierBasedPOSTagger(train=train_sents,
classifier_builder=MaxentClassifier.train)
>>> me_tagger.evaluate(test_sents)
0.9258363911072739
```

> The `MaxentClassifier` class takes even longer to train than `NaiveBayesClassifier`. If you have SciPy and NumPy installed, training will be faster than normal, but still slower than `NaiveBayesClassifier`.

Detecting features with a custom feature detector

If you want to do your own feature detection, there are two ways to do it:

1. Subclass `ClassifierBasedTagger` and implement a `feature_detector()` method.
2. Pass a function as the `feature_detector` keyword argument into `ClassifierBasedTagger` at initialization.

Either way, you need a feature detection method that can take the same arguments as `choose_tag(): tokens, index, history`. But instead of returning a tag, you return a `dict` of key-value features, where the key is the feature name and the value is the feature value. A very simple example would be a unigram feature detector (found in `tag_util.py`).

```
def unigram_feature_detector(tokens, index, history):
  return {'word': tokens[index]}
```

Then, using the second method, you'd pass this into `ClassifierBasedTagger` as `feature_detector`.

```
>>> from nltk.tag.sequential import ClassifierBasedTagger
>>> from tag_util import unigram_feature_detector
>>> tagger = ClassifierBasedTagger(train=train_sents, feature_
detector=unigram_feature_detector)
>>> tagger.evaluate(test_sents)
0.8733865745737104
```

Setting a cutoff probability

Because a classifier will always return the best result it can, passing in a backoff tagger is useless unless you also pass in a `cutoff_prob` argument to specify the probability threshold for classification. Then, if the probability of the chosen tag is less than `cutoff_prob`, the backoff tagger will be used. Here's an example using the `DefaultTagger` class as the backoff, and setting `cutoff_prob` to `0.3`:

```
>>> default = DefaultTagger('NN')
>>> tagger = ClassifierBasedPOSTagger(train=train_sents,
backoff=default, cutoff_prob=0.3)
>>> tagger.evaluate(test_sents)
0.9311029570472696
```

So, we get a slight increase in accuracy if the `ClassifierBasedPOSTagger` class uses the `DefaultTagger` class whenever its tag probability is less than 30%.

Using a pre-trained classifier

If you want to use a classifier that's already been trained, then you can pass that into `ClassifierBasedTagger` or `ClassifierBasedPOSTagger` as the `classifier`. In this case, the `classifier_builder` argument is ignored and no training takes place. However, you must ensure that the classifier has been trained on and can classify feature sets produced by whatever `feature_detector()` method you use.

See also

Chapter 7, Text Classification, will cover classification in depth.

Training a tagger with NLTK-Trainer

As you can tell from all the previous recipes in this chapter, there are many different ways to train taggers, and it's impossible to know which methods and parameters will work best without doing training experiments. But training experiments can be tedious, since they often involve many small code changes (and lots of cut and paste) before you converge on an optimal tagger. In an effort to simplify the process, and make my own work easier, I created a project called `NLTK-Trainer`.

NLTK-Trainer is a collection of scripts that give you the ability to run training experiments without writing a single line of code. The project is available on GitHub at `https://github.com/japerk/nltk-trainer` and has documentation at `http://nltk-trainer.readthedocs.org/`. This recipe will introduce the tagging related scripts, and will show you how to combine many of the previous recipes into a single training command. For download and installation instructions, please go to `http://nltk-trainer.readthedocs.org/`.

How to do it...

The simplest way to run `train_tagger.py` is with the name of an `NLTK` corpus. If we use the `treebank` corpus, the command and output should look something like this:

```
$ python train_tagger.py treebank
loading treebank
3914 tagged sents, training on 3914
training AffixTagger with affix -3 and backoff <DefaultTagger: tag=-None->
training <class 'nltk.tag.sequential.UnigramTagger'> tagger with backoff <AffixTagger: size=2536>
training <class 'nltk.tag.sequential.BigramTagger'> tagger with backoff <UnigramTagger: size=4933>
```

```
training <class 'nltk.tag.sequential.TrigramTagger'> tagger with backoff
<BigramTagger: size=2325>
evaluating TrigramTagger
accuracy: 0.992372
dumping TrigramTagger to /Users/jacob/nltk_data/taggers/treebank_aubt.
pickle
```

That's all it takes to train a tagger on `treebank` and have it dumped to a `pickle` file at `~/nltk_data/taggers/treebank_aubt.pickle`. "Wow, and it's over 99% accurate!" I hear you saying. But look closely at the second line of output: `3914 tagged sents, training on 3914`. This means that the tagger was trained on the entire `treebank` corpus, and then tested against those same training sentences. This is a very misleading way to evaluate any trained model. In the previous recipes, we used the first 3000 sentences for training and the remaining 914 sentences for testing, or about a 75% split. Here's how to do that with `train_tagger.py`, and also skip dumping a `pickle` file:

```
$ python train_tagger.py treebank --fraction 0.75 --no-pickle
loading treebank
3914 tagged sents, training on 2936
training AffixTagger with affix -3 and backoff <DefaultTagger: tag=-
None->
training <class 'nltk.tag.sequential.UnigramTagger'> tagger with backoff
<AffixTagger: size=2287>
training <class 'nltk.tag.sequential.BigramTagger'> tagger with backoff
<UnigramTagger: size=4176>
training <class 'nltk.tag.sequential.TrigramTagger'> tagger with backoff
<BigramTagger: size=1836>
evaluating TrigramTagger
accuracy: 0.906082
```

How it works...

The `train_tagger.py` script roughly performers the following steps:

1. Construct training and testing sentences from corpus arguments.
2. Build tagger training function from tagger arguments.
3. Train a tagger on the training sentences using the training function.
4. Evaluate and/or save the tagger.

The first argument to the script is `corpus`. This could be the name of an `NLTK` corpus that can be found in the `nltk.corpus` module, such as `treebank` or `brown`. It could also be the path to a custom corpus directory. If it's a path to a custom corpus, then you'll also need to use the `--reader` argument to specify the corpus reader class, such as `nltk.corpus.reader.tagged.TaggedCorpusReader`.

The default training algorithm is `aubt`, which is shorthand for a sequential backoff tagger composed of `AffixTagger + UnigramTagger + BigramTagger + TrigramTagger`. It's probably easiest to understand by replicating many of the previous recipes using `train_tagger.py`. Let's start with a default tagger.

```
$ python train_tagger.py treebank --no-pickle --default NN --sequential
''
loading treebank
3914 tagged sents, training on 3914
evaluating DefaultTagger
accuracy: 0.130776
```

Using `--default NN` lets us assign a default tag of `NN`, while `--sequential ''` disables the default `aubt` sequential backoff algorithm. The `--fraction` argument is omitted in this case because there's not actually any training happening.

Now let's try a unigram tagger:

```
$ python train_tagger.py treebank --no-pickle --fraction 0.75
--sequential u
loading treebank
3914 tagged sents, training on 2936
training <class 'nltk.tag.sequential.UnigramTagger'> tagger with backoff
<DefaultTagger: tag=-None->
evaluating UnigramTagger
accuracy: 0.855603
```

Specifying `--sequential u` tells `train_tagger.py` to train with a unigram tagger. As we did earlier, we can boost the accuracy a bit by using a default tagger:

```
$ python train_tagger.py treebank --no-pickle --default NN --fraction
0.75 --sequential u
loading treebank
3914 tagged sents, training on 2936
training <class 'nltk.tag.sequential.UnigramTagger'> tagger with backoff
<DefaultTagger: tag=NN>
evaluating UnigramTagger
accuracy: 0.873462
```

Now, let's try adding a bigram tagger and trigram tagger:

```
$ python train_tagger.py treebank --no-pickle --default NN --fraction
0.75 --sequential ubt
loading treebank
3914 tagged sents, training on 2936
training <class 'nltk.tag.sequential.UnigramTagger'> tagger with backoff
<DefaultTagger: tag=NN>
training <class 'nltk.tag.sequential.BigramTagger'> tagger with backoff
<UnigramTagger: size=8709>
training <class 'nltk.tag.sequential.TrigramTagger'> tagger with backoff
<BigramTagger: size=1836>
evaluating TrigramTagger
accuracy: 0.879012
```

> The `PYTHONHASHSEED` environment variable has been omitted for clarity. This means that when you run `train_tagger.py`, your output and accuracy may vary. To get consistent accuracy values, run `train_tagger.py` like this:
>
> **$ PYTHONHASHSEED=0 python train_tagger.py treebank ...**

The default training algorithm is `--sequential aubt`, and the default affix is `-3`. But you can modify this with one or more `-a` arguments. So, if we want to use an affix of `-2` as well as an affix of `-3`, you can do the following:

```
$ python train_tagger.py treebank --no-pickle --default NN --fraction
0.75 -a -3 -a -2
loading treebank
3914 tagged sents, training on 2936
training AffixTagger with affix -3 and backoff <DefaultTagger: tag=NN>
training AffixTagger with affix -2 and backoff <AffixTagger: size=2143>
training <class 'nltk.tag.sequential.UnigramTagger'> tagger with backoff
<AffixTagger: size=248>
training <class 'nltk.tag.sequential.BigramTagger'> tagger with backoff
<UnigramTagger: size=5204>
training <class 'nltk.tag.sequential.TrigramTagger'> tagger with backoff
<BigramTagger: size=1838>
evaluating TrigramTagger
accuracy: 0.908696
```

The order of multiple `-a` arguments matters, and if you switch the order, the results and accuracy will change, because the backoff order changes:

```
$ python train_tagger.py treebank --no-pickle --default NN --fraction 0.75 -a -2 -a -3
loading treebank
3914 tagged sents, training on 2936
training AffixTagger with affix -2 and backoff <DefaultTagger: tag=NN>
training AffixTagger with affix -3 and backoff <AffixTagger: size=606>
training <class 'nltk.tag.sequential.UnigramTagger'> tagger with backoff <AffixTagger: size=1313>
training <class 'nltk.tag.sequential.BigramTagger'> tagger with backoff <UnigramTagger: size=4169>
training <class 'nltk.tag.sequential.TrigramTagger'> tagger with backoff <BigramTagger: size=1829>
evaluating TrigramTagger
accuracy: 0.914367
```

You can also train a Brill tagger using the `--brill` argument. The template bounds the default to `(1, 1)` but can be customized with the `--template_bounds` argument.

```
$ python train_tagger.py treebank --no-pickle --default NN --fraction 0.75 --brill
loading treebank
3914 tagged sents, training on 2936
training AffixTagger with affix -3 and backoff <DefaultTagger: tag=NN>
training <class 'nltk.tag.sequential.UnigramTagger'> tagger with backoff <AffixTagger: size=2143>
training <class 'nltk.tag.sequential.BigramTagger'> tagger with backoff <UnigramTagger: size=4179>
training <class 'nltk.tag.sequential.TrigramTagger'> tagger with backoff <BigramTagger: size=1824>
Training Brill tagger on 2936 sentences...
Finding initial useful rules...
    Found 1304 useful rules.
Selecting rules...
evaluating BrillTagger
accuracy: 0.909138
```

Finally, you can train a classifier-based tagger with the `--classifier` argument, which specifies the name of a classifier. Be sure to also pass in `--sequential ''` because, as we learned previously, training a sequential backoff tagger in addition to a classifier-based tagger is useless. The `--default` argument is also useless, because the classifier will always guess something.

```
$ python train_tagger.py treebank --no-pickle --fraction 0.75
--sequential '' --classifier NaiveBayes
loading treebank
3914 tagged sents, training on 2936
training ['NaiveBayes'] ClassifierBasedPOSTagger
Constructing training corpus for classifier.
Training classifier (75814 instances)
training NaiveBayes classifier
evaluating ClassifierBasedPOSTagger
accuracy: 0.928646
```

There are a few other classifier algorithms available besides `NaiveBayes`, and even more if you have NumPy and SciPy installed.

> While classifier-based taggers tend to be more accurate, they are also slower to train, and much slower at tagging. If speed is important to you, I recommend sticking with sequential taggers.

There's more...

The `train_tagger.py` script supports many other arguments not shown here, all of which you can see by running the script with `--help`. A few additional arguments are presented next, followed by an introduction to two other tagging-related scripts available in `NLTK-Trainer`.

Saving a pickled tagger

Without the `--no-pickle` argument, `train_tagger.py` will save a pickled tagger at `~/nltk_data/taggers/NAME.pickle`, where `NAME` is a combination of the corpus name and training algorithm. You can specify a custom filename for your tagger using the `--filename` argument like this:

```
$ python train_tagger.py treebank --filename path/to/tagger.pickle
```

Training on a custom corpus

If you have a custom corpus that you want to use for training a tagger, you can do that by passing in the path to the corpus and the classname of a corpus reader in the `--reader` argument. The corpus path can either be absolute or relative to a `nltk_data` directory. The corpus reader class must provide a `tagged_sents()` method. Here's an example using a relative path to the `treebank` tagged corpus:

```
$ python train_tagger.py corpora/treebank/tagged --reader nltk.corpus.
reader.ChunkedCorpusReader --no-pickle --fraction 0.75
loading corpora/treebank/tagged
51002 tagged sents, training on 38252
training AffixTagger with affix -3 and backoff <DefaultTagger: tag=-
None->
training <class 'nltk.tag.sequential.UnigramTagger'> tagger with backoff
<AffixTagger: size=2092>
training <class 'nltk.tag.sequential.BigramTagger'> tagger with backoff
<UnigramTagger: size=4121>
training <class 'nltk.tag.sequential.TrigramTagger'> tagger with backoff
<BigramTagger: size=1627>
evaluating TrigramTagger
accuracy: 0.883175
```

Training with universal tags

You can train a tagger with the universal tagset using the `--tagset` argument as follows:

```
$ python train_tagger.py treebank --no-pickle --fraction 0.75 --tagset
universal
loading treebank
using universal tagset
3914 tagged sents, training on 2936
training AffixTagger with affix -3 and backoff <DefaultTagger: tag=-
None->
training <class 'nltk.tag.sequential.UnigramTagger'> tagger with backoff
<AffixTagger: size=2287>
training <class 'nltk.tag.sequential.BigramTagger'> tagger with backoff
<UnigramTagger: size=2889>
training <class 'nltk.tag.sequential.TrigramTagger'> tagger with backoff
<BigramTagger: size=1014>
evaluating TrigramTagger
accuracy: 0.934800
```

Because the universal tagset has fewer tags, these taggers tend to be more accurate; this will only work on a corpus that has universal tagset mappings. The universal tagset was covered in the *Creating a part-of-speech tagged word corpus* recipe in *Chapter 3, Creating Custom Corpora*.

Analyzing a tagger against a tagged corpus

Every previous example in this chapter has been about training and evaluating a tagger on a single corpus. But how do you know how well that tagger will perform on a different corpus? The `analyze_tagger_coverage.py` script gives you a simple way to test the performance of a tagger against another tagged corpus. Here's how to test NLTK's built-in tagger against the `treebank` corpus:

```
$ python analyze_tagger_coverage.py treebank --metrics
```

The output has been omitted for brevity, but I encourage you to run it yourself to see the results. It's especially useful for evaluating a tagger's performance on a corpus that it was not trained on, such as `conll2000` or `brown`.

If you only provide a corpus argument, this script will use NLTK's built-in tagger. To evaluate your own tagger, you can use the `--tagger` argument, which takes a path to a pickled tagger. The path can be absolute or relative to a `nltk_data` directory. For example:

```
$ python analyze_tagger_coverage.py treebank --metrics --tagger path/to/
tagger.pickle
```

You can also use a custom corpus just like we did earlier with `train_tagger.py`, but if your corpus is not tagged, then you must omit the `--metrics` argument. In that case, you will only get tag counts, with no notion of accuracy, because there are no tags to compare to.

Analyzing a tagged corpus

Finally, there is a script called `analyze_tagged_corpus.py`, which, as the name implies, will read in a tagged corpus and print out stats about the number of words and tags. You can run it as follows:

```
$ python analyze_tagged_corpus.py treebank
```

The results are available in *Appendix, Penn Treebank Part-of-speech Tags*. As with the other commands, you can pass in a custom corpus path and reader to analyze your own tagged corpus.

See also

The previous recipes in this chapter cover the details of the classes and methods that power the functionality of `train_tagger.py`. The *Training a chunker with NLTK-Trainer* recipe at the end of *Chapter 5, Extracting Chunks*, will introduce NLTK-Trainer's chunking-related scripts, and classification-related scripts will be covered in the *Training a classifier with NLTK-Trainer* recipe at the end of *Chapter 7, Text Classification*.

5
Extracting Chunks

In this chapter, we will cover the following recipes:

- Chunking and chinking with regular expressions
- Merging and splitting chunks with regular expressions
- Expanding and removing chunks with regular expressions
- Partial parsing with regular expressions
- Training a tagger-based chunker
- Classification-based chunking
- Extracting named entities
- Extracting proper noun chunks
- Extracting location chunks
- Training a named entity chunker
- Training a chunker with NLTK-Trainer

Introduction

Chunk extraction, or **partial parsing**, is the process of extracting short phrases from a part-of-speech tagged sentence. This is different from full parsing in that we're interested in standalone **chunks**, or **phrases**, instead of full parse trees (for more on parse trees, see `https://en.wikipedia.org/wiki/Parse_tree`). The idea is that meaningful phrases can be extracted from a sentence by looking for particular patterns of part-of-speech tags.

As in *Chapter 4, Part-of-speech Tagging*, we'll be using the **Penn Treebank** corpus for basic training and testing chunk extraction. We'll also be using the **CoNLL2000** corpus as it has a simpler and more flexible format that supports multiple chunk types (for more details on the `conll2000` corpus and IOB tags, see the *Creating a chunked phrase corpus* recipe in *Chapter 3, Creating Custom Corpora*).

Chunking and chinking with regular expressions

Using modified regular expressions, we can define **chunk patterns**. These are patterns of part-of-speech tags that define what kinds of words make up a chunk. We can also define patterns for what kinds of words should not be in a chunk. These unchunked words are known as **chinks**.

A `ChunkRule` class specifies what to *include* in a chunk, while a `ChinkRule` class specifies what to *exclude* from a chunk. In other words, chunking creates chunks, while chinking breaks up those chunks.

Getting ready

We first need to know how to define chunk patterns. These are modified regular expressions designed to match sequences of part-of-speech tags. An individual tag is specified by surrounding angle brackets, such as `<NN>` to match a noun tag. Multiple tags can then be combined, as in `<DT><NN>` to match a determiner followed by a noun. Regular expression syntax can be used within the angle brackets to match individual tag patterns, so you can do `<NN.*>` to match all nouns including `NN` and `NNS`. You can also use regular expression syntax outside of the angle brackets to match patterns of tags. `<DT>?<NN.*>+` will match an optional determiner followed by one or more nouns. The chunk patterns are internally converted to regular expressions using the `tag_pattern2re_pattern()` function.

```
>>> from nltk.chunk.regexp import tag_pattern2re_pattern
>>> tag_pattern2re_pattern('<DT>?<NN.*>+')
'(<(DT)>)?(<(NN[^\\{\\}<>]*)>)+'
```

You don't have to use this function to do chunking, but it might be useful or interesting to see how your chunk patterns convert to regular expressions. This function is used by the `RegexpParser` class (explained in the next section) to convert chunk patterns into regular expressions to match chunking rules.

How to do it...

The pattern for specifying a chunk is to use surrounding curly braces, such as {<DT><NN>}. To specify a chink, you flip the braces, such as }<VB>{. These rules can be combined into a **grammar** for a particular phrase type. Here's a grammar for noun phrases that combines both a chunk and a chink pattern, along with the result of parsing the sentence `the book has many chapters`:

```
>>> from nltk.chunk import RegexpParser
>>> chunker = RegexpParser(r'''
... NP:
...   {<DT><NN.*><.*>*<NN.*>}
...   }<VB.*>{
... ''')
>>> chunker.parse([('the', 'DT'), ('book', 'NN'), ('has', 'VBZ'),
('many', 'JJ'), ('chapters', 'NNS')])

Tree('S', [Tree('NP', [('the', 'DT'), ('book', 'NN')]), ('has',
'VBZ'), Tree('NP', [('many', 'JJ'), ('chapters', 'NNS')])])
```

The grammar tells the `RegexpParser` class that there are two rules for parsing `NP` chunks. The first chunk pattern says that a chunk starts with a determiner followed by any kind of noun. Then, any number of other words are allowed until a final noun is found. The second pattern says that verbs should be chinked, thus separating any large chunks that contain a verb. The result is a tree with two noun-phrase chunks: `the book` and `many chapters`.

> Tagged sentences are always parsed into a `Tree` (found in the `nltk.tree` module). The top label of the `Tree` is `S`, which stands for sentence. Any chunks found will be subtrees whose labels will refer to the chunk type. In this case, the chunk type is `NP` for noun-phrase chunks. Trees can be drawn calling the `draw()` method using `t.draw()`.

How it works...

Here's what happens, step-by-step:

1. The sentence is converted into a flat `Tree`:

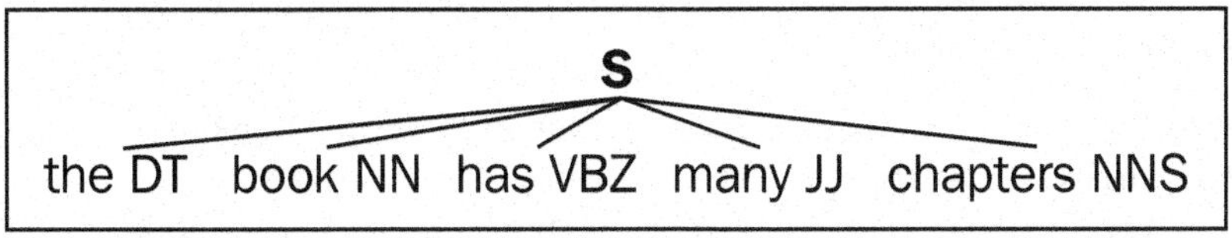

2. The `Tree` is used to create a `ChunkString`.
3. The `RegexpParser` parses the grammar to create a `NP RegexpChunkParser` with the given rules.
4. A `ChunkRule` is created and applied to the `ChunkString`, which matches the entire sentence into a chunk:

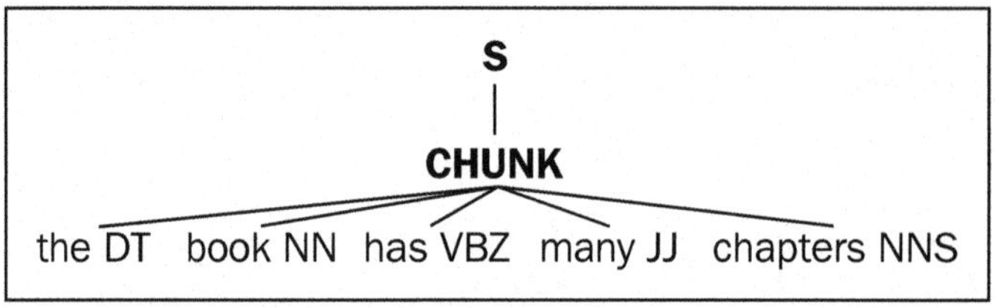

5. A `ChinkRule` is created and applied to the same `ChunkString`, which splits the big chunk into two smaller chunks with a verb between them:

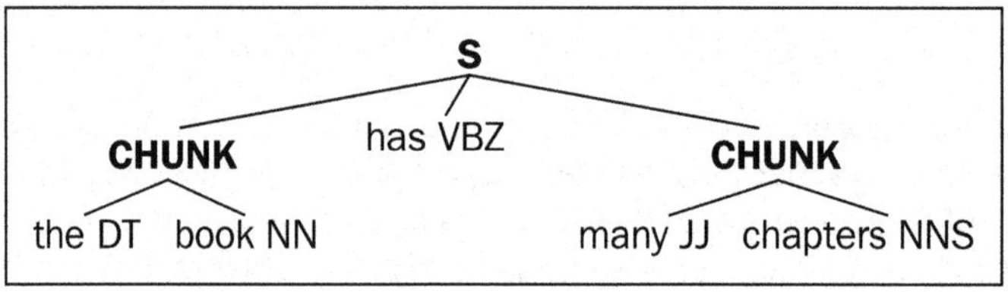

6. The `ChunkString` is converted back to a `Tree`, now with two `NP` chunk subtrees:

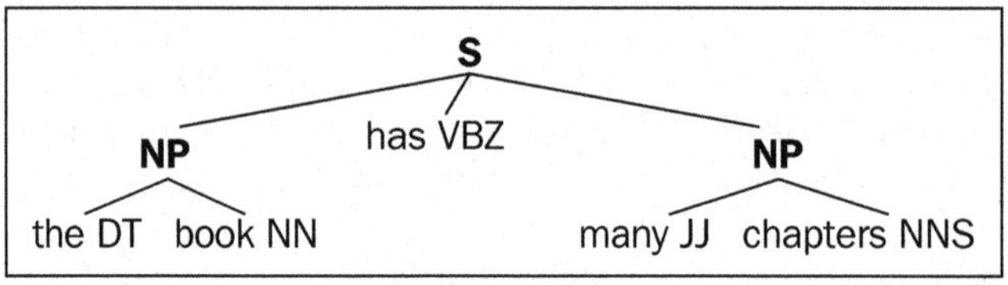

You can do this yourself using the classes in `nltk.chunk.regexp`. The `ChunkRule` and `ChinkRule` classes are both subclasses of `RegexpChunkRule`, and require two arguments: the pattern and a description of the rule. `ChunkString` is an object that starts with a flat tree, which is then modified by each rule when it is passed into the rule's `apply()` method. A `ChunkString` is converted back to a `Tree` with the `to_chunkstruct()` method. Here's some code to demonstrate this:

```
>>> from nltk.chunk.regexp import ChunkString, ChunkRule, ChinkRule
>>> from nltk.tree import Tree
>>> t = Tree('S', [('the', 'DT'), ('book', 'NN'), ('has', 'VBZ'),
```

```
'many', 'JJ'), ('chapters', 'NNS')])
>>> cs = ChunkString(t)
>>> cs
<ChunkString: '<DT><NN><VBZ><JJ><NNS>'>
>>> ur = ChunkRule('<DT><NN.*><.*>*<NN.*>', 'chunk determiners and
nouns')
>>> ur.apply(cs)
>>> cs
<ChunkString: '{<DT><NN><VBZ><JJ><NNS>}'>
>>> ir = ChinkRule('<VB.*>', 'chink verbs')
>>> ir.apply(cs)
>>> cs
<ChunkString: '{<DT><NN>}<VBZ>{<JJ><NNS>}'>
>>> cs.to_chunkstruct()
Tree('S', [Tree('CHUNK', [('the', 'DT'), ('book', 'NN')]), ('has',
'VBZ'), Tree('CHUNK', [('many', 'JJ'), ('chapters', 'NNS')])])
```

The tree diagrams shown earlier can be drawn at each step by calling `cs.to_chunkstruct().draw()`.

There's more...

You'll notice that the subtrees from the `ChunkString` class are tagged as `CHUNK` and not `NP`. That's because the rules mentioned earlier are phrase agnostic; they create chunks without needing to know what kind of chunks they are.

Internally, the `RegexpParser` class creates a `RegexpChunkParser` for each chunk phrase type. So, if you're only chunking `NP` phrases, there will only be one `RegexpChunkParser`. The `RegexpChunkParser` class gets all the rules for the specific chunk type, and handles applying the rules in order and converting the `CHUNK` trees to the specific chunk type, such as `NP`.

Here's some code to illustrate the usage of `RegexpChunkParser`. We pass both the rules mentioned earlier into the `RegexpChunkParser` class, and then parse the same sentence tree we created before. The resulting tree is just like what we got from applying both rules in order, except that `CHUNK` has been replaced with `NP` in both the subtrees. This is because `RegexpChunkParser` defaults to `chunk_label='NP'`.

```
>>> from nltk.chunk import RegexpChunkParser
>>> chunker = RegexpChunkParser([ur, ir])
>>> chunker.parse(t)
Tree('S', [Tree('NP', [('the', 'DT'), ('book', 'NN')]), ('has',
'VBZ'), Tree('NP', [('many', 'JJ'), ('chapters', 'NNS')])])
```

Parsing different chunk types

If you wanted to parse a different chunk type, then you could pass that in as `chunk_label` to `RegexpChunkParser`. Here's the same code that we saw in the previous section, but instead of `NP` subtrees, we'll call them `CP` for custom phrase:

```
>>> from nltk.chunk import RegexpChunkParser
>>> chunker = RegexpChunkParser([ur, ir], chunk_label='CP')
>>> chunker.parse(t)
Tree('S', [Tree('CP', [('the', 'DT'), ('book', 'NN')]), ('has',
'VBZ'), Tree('CP', [('many', 'JJ'), ('chapters', 'NNS')])])
```

The `RegexpParser` class does this internally when you specify multiple phrase types. This will be covered in the *Partial parsing with regular expressions* recipe.

Parsing alternative patterns

The same parsing results can be obtained using two chunk patterns in the grammar and discarding the chink pattern:

```
>>> chunker = RegexpParser(r'''
... NP:
... {<DT><NN.*>}
... {<JJ><NN.*>}
... ''')
>>> chunker.parse(t)
Tree('S', [Tree('NP', [('the', 'DT'), ('book', 'NN')]), ('has',
'VBZ'), Tree('NP', [('many', 'JJ'), ('chapters', 'NNS')])])
```

In fact, you could reduce the two chunk patterns into a single pattern.

```
>>> chunker = RegexpParser(r'''
... NP:
... {(<DT>|<JJ>)<NN.*>}
... ''')
>>> chunker.parse(t)
Tree('S', [Tree('NP', [('the', 'DT'), ('book', 'NN')]), ('has',
'VBZ'), Tree('NP', [('many', 'JJ'), ('chapters', 'NNS')])])
```

How you create and combine patterns is really up to you. Pattern creation is a process of trial and error, and entirely depends on what your data looks like and which patterns are easiest to express.

Chunk rule with context

You can also create chunk rules with a surrounding tag context. For example, if your pattern is `<DT>{<NN>}`, that will be parsed into a `ChunkRuleWithContext` class. So, context in this case is referring to the parts of the rule that are not chinks or chunks, such as `<DT>`. For example, in the phrase `the dog`, `the` would be context to the noun `dog`. Any time there's a tag on either side of the curly braces, you'll get a `ChunkRuleWithContext` class instead of a `ChunkRule` class. This can allow you to be more specific about when to parse particular kinds of chunks.

Here's an example of using `ChunkRuleWithContext` directly. It takes four arguments: the left context, the pattern to chunk, the right context, and a description:

```
>>> from nltk.chunk.regexp import ChunkRuleWithContext
>>> ctx = ChunkRuleWithContext('<DT>', '<NN.*>', '<.*>', 'chunk nouns
only after determiners')
>>> cs = ChunkString(t)
>>> cs
<ChunkString: '<DT><NN><VBZ><JJ><NNS>'>
>>> ctx.apply(cs)
>>> cs
<ChunkString: '<DT>{<NN>}<VBZ><JJ><NNS>'>
>>> cs.to_chunkstruct()
Tree('S', [('the', 'DT'), Tree('CHUNK', [('book', 'NN')]), ('has',
'VBZ'), ('many', 'JJ'), ('chapters', 'NNS')])
```

This example only chunks nouns that follow a determiner, therefore ignoring the noun that follows an adjective. Here's how it would look using the `RegexpParser` class:

```
>>> chunker = RegexpParser(r'''
... NP:
... <DT>{<NN.*>}
... ''')
>>> chunker.parse(t)
Tree('S', [('the', 'DT'), Tree('NP', [('book', 'NN')]), ('has',
'VBZ'), ('many', 'JJ'), ('chapters', 'NNS')])
```

See also

In the next recipe, we'll cover merging and splitting chunks.

Merging and splitting chunks with regular expressions

In this recipe, we'll cover two more rules for chunking. A `MergeRule` class can merge two chunks together based on the end of the first chunk and the beginning of the second chunk. A `SplitRule` class will split a chunk into two chunks based on the specified split pattern.

How to do it...

A `SplitRule` class is specified with two opposing curly braces surrounded by a pattern on either side. To split a chunk after a noun, you would do `<NN.*>}{<.*>`. A `MergeRule` class is specified by flipping the curly braces, and will join chunks where the end of the first chunk matches the left pattern and the beginning of the next chunk matches the right pattern. To merge two chunks where the first ends with a noun and the second begins with a noun, you'd use `<NN.*>{}<NN.*>`.

> Note that the order of rules is very important, and reordering can affect the results. The `RegexpParser` class applies the rules one at a time from top to bottom, so each rule will be applied to the `ChunkString` resulting from the previous rule.

An example of splitting and merging, starting with the sentence tree, is shown next:

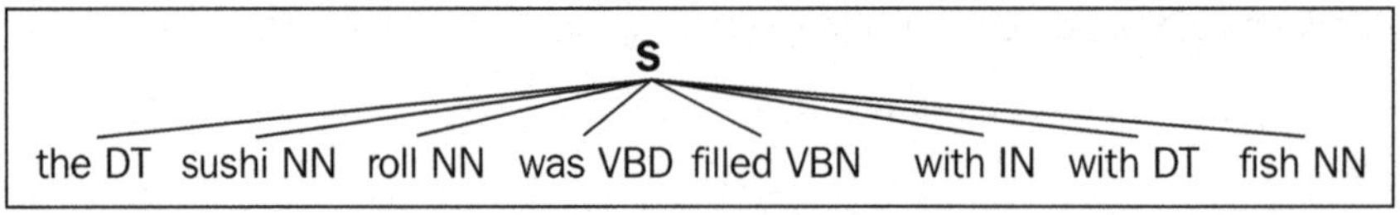

The whole sentence is chunked, as shown in the following diagram:

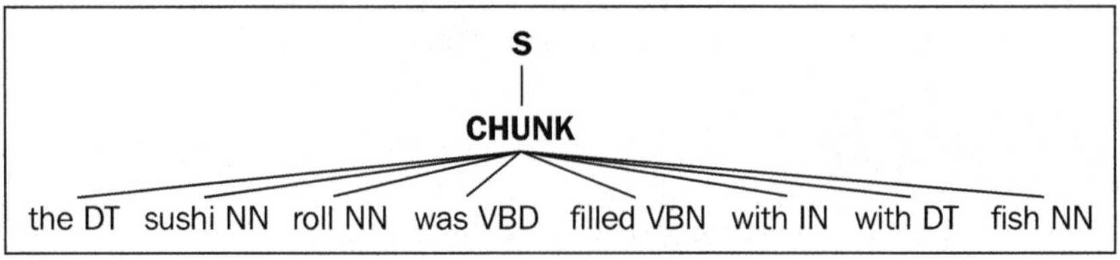

The chunk is split into multiple chunks after every noun, as shown in the following tree:

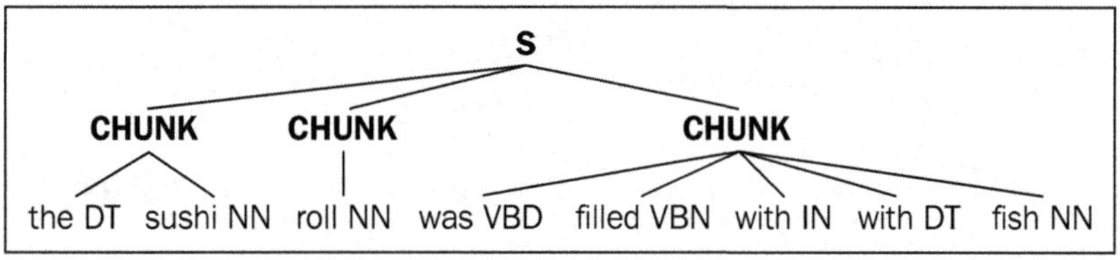

Each chunk with a determiner is split into separate chunks, creating four chunks where there were three:

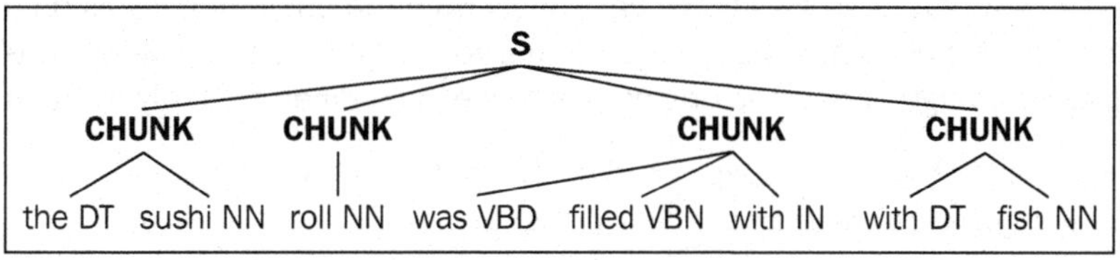

Chunks ending with a noun are merged with the next chunk if it begins with a noun, reducing the four chunks back down to three, as shown in the following diagram:

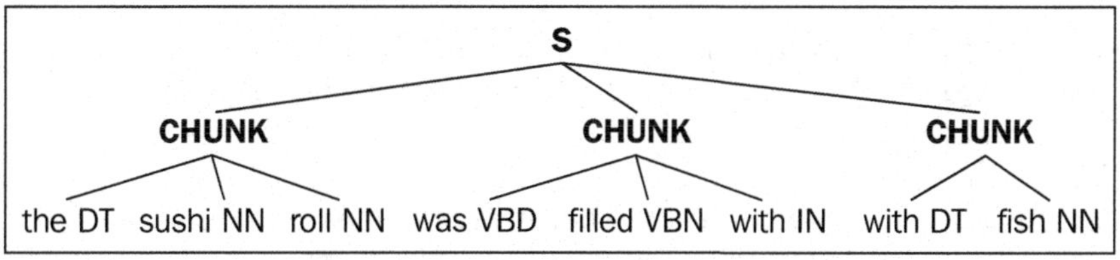

Using the `RegexpParser` class, the code looks like this:

```
>>> chunker = RegexpParser(r'''
... NP:
... {<DT><.*>*<NN.*>}
... <NN.*>}{<.*>
... <.*>}{<DT>
... <NN.*>{}<NN.*>
... ''')
>>> sent = [('the', 'DT'), ('sushi', 'NN'), ('roll', 'NN'), ('was', 'VBD'), ('filled', 'VBN'), ('with', 'IN'), ('the', 'DT'), ('fish', 'NN')]
>>> chunker.parse(sent)
Tree('S', [Tree('NP', [('the', 'DT'), ('sushi', 'NN'), ('roll', 'NN')]), Tree('NP', [('was', 'VBD'), ('filled', 'VBN'), ('with', 'IN')]), Tree('NP', [('the', 'DT'), ('fish', 'NN')])])
```

And the final tree of NP chunks is shown in the following diagram:

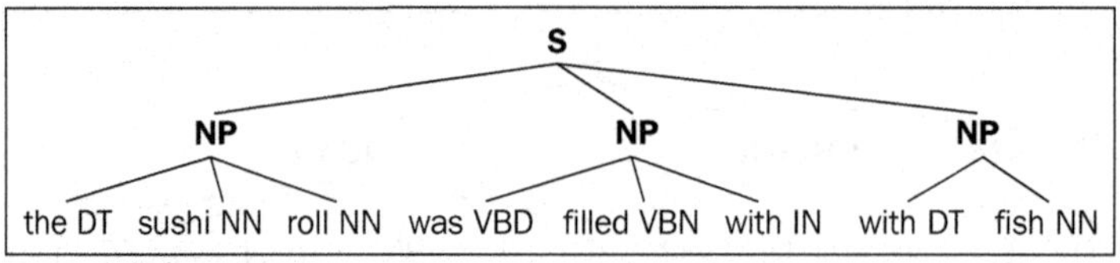

How it works...

The MergeRule and SplitRule classes take two arguments: the left pattern and the right pattern. The RegexpParser class takes care of splitting the original patterns on the curly braces to get the left and right sides, but you can also create these manually. Here's a step-by-step walkthrough of how the original sentence is modified by applying each rule:

```
>>> from nltk.chunk.regexp import MergeRule, SplitRule
>>> cs = ChunkString(Tree('S', sent))
>>> cs
<ChunkString: '<DT><NN><NN><VBD><VBN><IN><DT><NN>'>
>>> ur = ChunkRule('<DT><.*>*<NN.*>', 'chunk determiner to noun')
>>> ur.apply(cs)
>>> cs
<ChunkString: '{<DT><NN><NN><VBD><VBN><IN><DT><NN>}'>
>>> sr1 = SplitRule('<NN.*>', '<.*>', 'split after noun')
>>> sr1.apply(cs)
>>> cs
<ChunkString: '{<DT><NN>}{<NN>}{<VBD><VBN><IN><DT><NN>}'>
>>> sr2 = SplitRule('<.*>', '<DT>', 'split before determiner')
>>> sr2.apply(cs)
>>> cs
<ChunkString: '{<DT><NN>}{<NN>}{<VBD><VBN><IN>}{<DT><NN>}'>
>>> mr = MergeRule('<NN.*>', '<NN.*>', 'merge nouns')
>>> mr.apply(cs)
>>> cs
<ChunkString: '{<DT><NN><NN>}{<VBD><VBN><IN>}{<DT><NN>}'>
>>> cs.to_chunkstruct()
Tree('S', [Tree('CHUNK', [('the', 'DT'), ('sushi', 'NN'), ('roll',
'NN')]), Tree('CHUNK', [('was', 'VBD'), ('filled', 'VBN'), ('with',
'IN')]), Tree('CHUNK', [('the', 'DT'), ('fish', 'NN')])])
```

There's more...

The parsing of the rules and splitting of left and right patterns is done in the static `parse()` method of the `RegexpChunkRule` superclass. This is called by the `RegexpParser` class to get the list of rules to pass into the `RegexpChunkParser` class. Here are some examples of parsing the patterns we used earlier:

```
>>> from nltk.chunk.regexp import RegexpChunkRule
>>> RegexpChunkRule.fromstring('{<DT><.*>*<NN.*>}')
<ChunkRule: '<DT><.*>*<NN.*>'>
>>> RegexpChunkRule.fromstring('<.*>}{<DT>')
<SplitRule: '<.*>', '<DT>'>
>>> RegexpChunkRule.fromstring('<NN.*>{}<NN.*>')
<MergeRule: '<NN.*>', '<NN.*>'>
```

Specifying rule descriptions

Descriptions for each rule can be specified with a comment string after the rule (a comment string must start with `#`). If no comment string is found, the rule's description will be empty. Here's an example:

```
>>> RegexpChunkRule.fromstring('{<DT><.*>*<NN.*>} # chunk
everything').descr()
'chunk everything'
>>> RegexpChunkRule.fromstring('{<DT><.*>*<NN.*>}').descr()
''
```

Comment string descriptions can also be used within grammar strings that are passed to `RegexpParser`.

See also

The previous recipe goes over how to use `ChunkRule`, and how rules are passed into `RegexpChunkParser`.

Expanding and removing chunks with regular expressions

There are three `RegexpChunkRule` subclasses that are not supported by `RegexpChunkRule.fromstring()` or `RegexpParser`, and therefore must be created manually if you want to use them. These rules are as follows:

- `ExpandLeftRule`: Add unchunked (chink) words to the left of a chunk
- `ExpandRightRule`: Add unchunked (chink) words to the right of a chunk
- `UnChunkRule`: Unchunk any matching chunk

How to do it...

`ExpandLeftRule` and `ExpandRightRule` both take two patterns along with a description as arguments. For `ExpandLeftRule`, the first pattern is the chink we want to add to the beginning of the chunk, while the right pattern will match the beginning of the chunk we want to expand. With `ExpandRightRule`, the left pattern should match the end of the chunk we want to expand, and the right pattern matches the chink we want to add to the end of the chunk. The idea is similar to the `MergeRule` class, but in this case, we're merging chink words instead of other chunks.

`UnChunkRule` is the opposite of `ChunkRule`. Any chunk that exactly matches the `UnChunkRule` pattern will be unchunked and become a chink. Here's some code demonstrating the usage with the `RegexpChunkParser` class:

```
>>> from nltk.chunk.regexp import ChunkRule, ExpandLeftRule,
ExpandRightRule, UnChunkRule
>>> from nltk.chunk import RegexpChunkParser
>>> ur = ChunkRule('<NN>', 'single noun')
>>> el = ExpandLeftRule('<DT>', '<NN>', 'get left determiner')
>>> er = ExpandRightRule('<NN>', '<NNS>', 'get right plural noun')
>>> un = UnChunkRule('<DT><NN.*>*', 'unchunk everything')
>>> chunker = RegexpChunkParser([ur, el, er, un])
>>> sent = [('the', 'DT'), ('sushi', 'NN'), ('rolls', 'NNS')]
>>> chunker.parse(sent)
Tree('S', [('the', 'DT'), ('sushi', 'NN'), ('rolls', 'NNS')])
```

You'll notice that the end result is a flat sentence, which is exactly what we started with. That's because the final `UnChunkRule` undid the chunk created by the previous rules. Read on to see what happened step by step.

How it works...

The rules mentioned earlier were applied in the following order, starting with the sentence tree as follows:

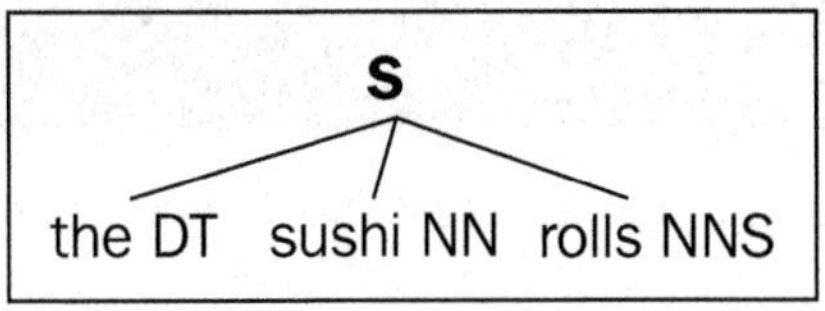

1. Make single nouns into a chunk:

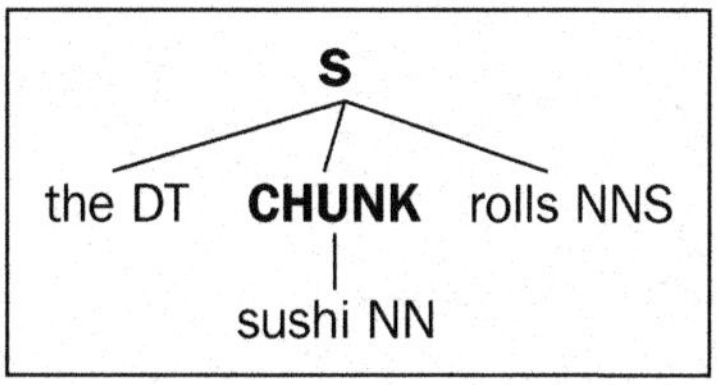

2. Expand left determiners into chunks that begin with a noun:

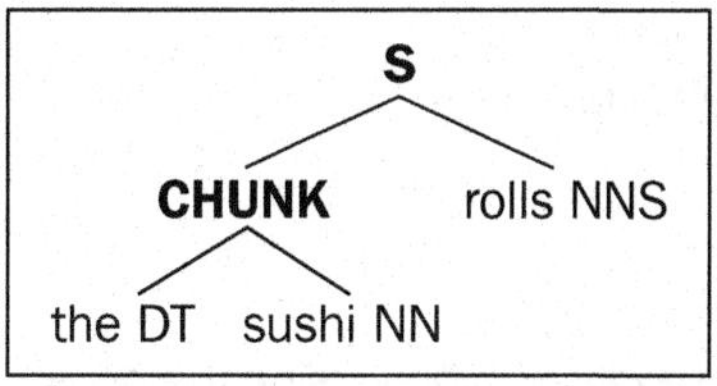

3. Expand right plural nouns into chunks that end with a noun, chunking the whole sentence as follows:

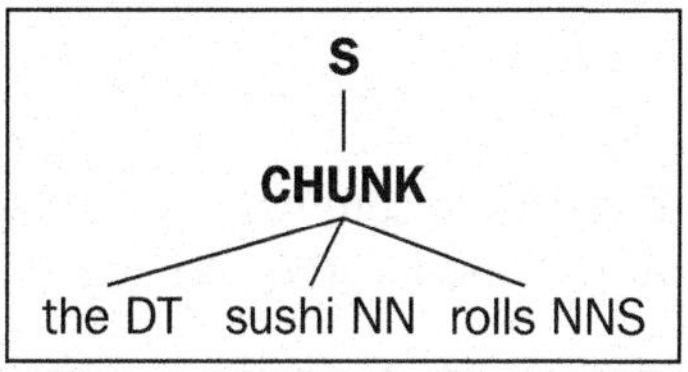

4. Unchunk every chunk that is a *determiner* + *noun* + *plural noun*, resulting in the original sentence tree:

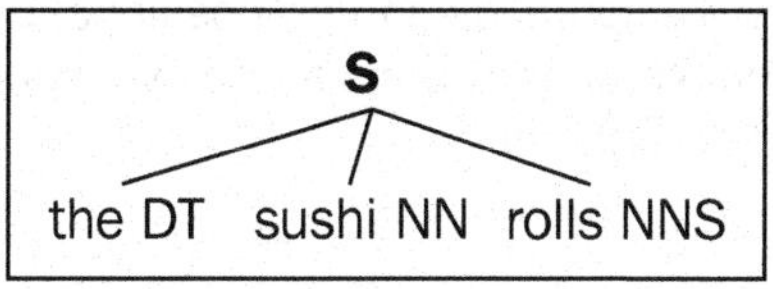

Here's the code showing each step:

```
>>> from nltk.chunk.regexp import ChunkString
>>> from nltk.tree import Tree
>>> cs = ChunkString(Tree('S', sent))
>>> cs
```

```
<ChunkString: '<DT><NN><NNS>'>
>>> ur.apply(cs)
>>> cs
<ChunkString: '<DT>{<NN>}<NNS>'>
>>> el.apply(cs)
>>> cs
<ChunkString: '{<DT><NN>}<NNS>'>
>>> er.apply(cs)
>>> cs
<ChunkString: '{<DT><NN><NNS>}'>
>>> un.apply(cs)
>>> cs
<ChunkString: '<DT><NN><NNS>'>
```

There's more...

In practice, you can probably get away with only using the previous four rules: `ChunkRule`, `ChinkRule`, `MergeRule`, and `SplitRule`. But if you do need very fine-grained control over chunk parsing and removing chunks, now you know how to do it with the expansion and unchunk rules.

See also

The previous two recipes covered the more common chunk rules that are supported by `RegexpChunkRule.fromstring()` and `RegexpParser`.

Partial parsing with regular expressions

So far, we've only been parsing noun phrases. But `RegexpParser` supports grammars with multiple phrase types, such as verb phrases and prepositional phrases. We can put the rules we've learned to use and define a grammar that can be evaluated against the `conll2000` corpus, which has `NP`, `VP`, and `PP` phrases.

How to do it...

Now, we will define a grammar to parse three phrase types. For noun phrases, we have a `ChunkRule` class that looks for an optional determiner followed by one or more nouns. We then have a `MergeRule` class for adding an adjective to the front of a noun chunk. For prepositional phrases, we simply chunk any `IN` word, such as `in` or `on`. For verb phrases, we chunk an optional modal word (such as `should`) followed by a verb.

> Each grammar rule is followed by a # comment. This comment is passed into each rule as the description. Comments are optional, but they can be helpful notes for understanding what the rule does, and will be included in trace output.

```
>>> chunker = RegexpParser(r'''
... NP:
... {<DT>?<NN.*>+}  # chunk optional determiner with nouns
... <JJ>{}<NN.*>  # merge adjective with noun chunk
... PP:
... {<IN>}       # chunk preposition
... VP:
... {<MD>?<VB.*>}  # chunk optional modal with verb
... ''')
>>> from nltk.corpus import conll2000
>>> score = chunker.evaluate(conll2000.chunked_sents())
>>> score.accuracy()
0.6148573545757688
```

When we call `evaluate()` on the `chunker` argument, we give it a list of chunked sentences and get back a `ChunkScore` object, which can give us the accuracy of the `chunker` along with a number of other metrics.

How it works...

The `RegexpParser` class parses the grammar string into sets of rules, one set of rules for each phrase type. These rules are used to create a `RegexpChunkParser` class. The rules are parsed using `RegexpChunkRule.fromstring()`, which returns one of the five subclasses: `ChunkRule`, `ChinkRule`, `MergeRule`, `SplitRule`, or `ChunkRuleWithContext`.

Now that the grammar has been translated into sets of rules, these rules are used to parse a tagged sentence into a `Tree` structure. The `RegexpParser` class inherits from `ChunkParserI`, which provides a `parse()` method to parse the tagged words. Whenever a part of the tagged tokens matches a chunk rule, a subtree is constructed so that the tagged tokens become the leaves of a `Tree` whose label is the chunk tag. The `ChunkParserI` interface also provides the `evaluate()` method, which compares the given chunked sentences to the output of the `parse()` method to construct and return a `ChunkScore` object.

There's more...

You can also evaluate this `chunker` argument on the `treebank_chunk` corpus:

```
>>> from nltk.corpus import treebank_chunk
>>> treebank_score = chunker.evaluate(treebank_chunk.chunked_sents())
>>> treebank_score.accuracy()
0.49033970276008493
```

The `treebank_chunk` corpus is a special version of the `treebank` corpus that provides a `chunked_sents()` method. The regular `treebank` corpus cannot provide that method due to its file format.

The ChunkScore metrics

The `ChunkScore` metrics provide a few other metrics besides accuracy. Of the chunks the `chunker` argument was able to guess, **precision** tells you how many were correct and **recall** tells you how well the chunker did at finding correct chunks compared to how many total chunks there were. For more about `precision` and `recall`, see `https://en.wikipedia.org/wiki/Precision_and_recall`.

```
>>> score.precision()
0.60201948127375
>>> score.recall()
0.606072502505847
```

You can also get lists of chunks that were missed by the `chunker`, chunks that were incorrectly found, correct chunks, and the total guessed chunks. These can be useful to figure out how to improve your chunk grammar:

```
>>> len(score.missed())
47161
>>> len(score.incorrect())
47967
>>> len(score.correct())
119720
>>> len(score.guessed())
120526
```

As you can see by the number of incorrect chunks, and by comparing `guessed()` and `correct()`, our chunker guessed that there were more chunks than actually existed. And it also missed a good number of correct chunks.

Looping and tracing chunk rules

If you want to apply the chunk rules in your grammar more than once, you can pass `loop=2` into `RegexpParser` at initialization. The default is `loop=1`, which will apply each rule once. Since a chunk can change after every rule application, it may sometimes make sense to re-apply the same rules multiple times.

To watch an internal trace of the chunking process, pass `trace=1` into `RegexpParser`. To get even more output, pass in `trace=2`. This will give you a printout of what the `chunker` is doing as it is doing it. Rule comments/descriptions will be included in the trace output, giving you a good idea of which rule is applied when.

See also

If coming up with regular expression chunk patterns seems like too much work, then read the next recipes, where we'll cover how to train a chunker based on a corpus of chunked sentences.

Training a tagger-based chunker

Training a chunker can be a great alternative to manually specifying regular expression chunk patterns. Instead of a pain-staking process of trial and error to get the exact right patterns, we can use existing corpus data to train chunkers much like we did for part-of-speech tagging in the previous chapter.

How to do it...

As with the part-of-speech tagging, we'll use the `treebank` corpus data for training. But this time, we'll use the `treebank_chunk` corpus, which is specifically formatted to produce chunked sentences in the form of trees. These `chunked_sents()` methods will be used by a `TagChunker` class to train a tagger-based chunker. The `TagChunker` class uses a helper function, `conll_tag_chunks()`, to extract a list of `(pos, iob)` tuples from a list of `Trees`. These `(pos, iob)` tuples are then used to train a tagger in the same way `(word, pos)` tuples were used in *Chapter 4, Part-of-speech Tagging*, to train part-of-speech taggers. But instead of learning part-of-speech tags for words, we're learning IOB tags for part-of-speech tags. Here's the code from `chunkers.py`:

```
from nltk.chunk import ChunkParserI
from nltk.chunk.util import tree2conlltags, conlltags2tree
from nltk.tag import UnigramTagger, BigramTagger
from tag_util import backoff_tagger
```

```
def conll_tag_chunks(chunk_sents):
  tagged_sents = [tree2conlltags(tree) for tree in chunk_sents]
  return [[(t, c) for (w, t, c) in sent] for sent in tagged_sents]

class TagChunker(ChunkParserI):
  def __init__(self, train_chunks, tagger_classes=[UnigramTagger,
BigramTagger]):
    train_sents = conll_tag_chunks(train_chunks)
    self.tagger = backoff_tagger(train_sents, tagger_classes)

  def parse(self, tagged_sent):
    if not tagged_sent: return None
    (words, tags) = zip(*tagged_sent)
    chunks = self.tagger.tag(tags)
    wtc = zip(words, chunks)
    return conlltags2tree([(w,t,c) for (w,(t,c)) in wtc])
```

Once we have our trained `TagChunker`, we can then evaluate the `ChunkScore` class the same way we did for the `RegexpParser` class in the previous recipes:

```
>>> from chunkers import TagChunker
>>> from nltk.corpus import treebank_chunk
>>> train_chunks = treebank_chunk.chunked_sents()[:3000]
>>> test_chunks = treebank_chunk.chunked_sents()[3000:]
>>> chunker = TagChunker(train_chunks)
>>> score = chunker.evaluate(test_chunks)
>>> score.accuracy()
0.9732039335251428
>>> score.precision()
0.9166534370535006
>>> score.recall()
0.9465573770491803
```

Pretty darn accurate! Training a chunker is clearly a great alternative to manually specified grammars and regular expressions.

How it works...

Recall from the *Creating a chunked phrase corpus* recipe in *Chapter 3, Creating Custom Corpora*, that the `conll2000` corpus defines chunks using IOB tags, which specify the type of chunk and where it begins and ends. We can train a part-of-speech tagger on these IOB tag patterns and then use that to power a `ChunkerI` subclass. But first, we need to transform a `Tree` that you'd get from the `chunked_sents()` method of a corpus into a format usable by a part-of-speech tagger. This is what `conll_tag_chunks()` does. It uses `tree2conlltags()` to convert a sentence `Tree` into a list of three tuples of the form `(word, pos, iob)`, where `pos` is the part-of-speech tag and `iob` is an IOB tag, such as `B-NP` to mark the beginning of a noun-phrase, or `I-NP` to mark that the word is inside the noun-phrase. The reverse of this method is `conlltags2tree()`. Here's some code to demonstrate these `nltk.chunk` functions:

```
>>> from nltk.chunk.util import tree2conlltags, conlltags2tree
>>> from nltk.tree import Tree
>>> t = Tree('S', [Tree('NP', [('the', 'DT'), ('book', 'NN')])])
>>> tree2conlltags(t)
[('the', 'DT', 'B-NP'), ('book', 'NN', 'I-NP')]
>>> conlltags2tree([('the', 'DT', 'B-NP'), ('book', 'NN', 'I-NP')])
Tree('S', [Tree('NP', [('the', 'DT'), ('book', 'NN')])])
```

The next step is to convert these 3-tuples into 2-tuples that the tagger can recognize. Because the `RegexpParser` class uses part-of-speech tags for chunk patterns, we'll do that here too and use part-of-speech tags as if they were words to tag. By simply dropping the word from the 3-tuples `(word, pos, iob)`, the `conll_tag_chunks()` function returns a list of 2-tuples of the form `(pos, iob)`. When we consider the previous example `Tree` in a list, the results are in a format we can feed to a tagger:

```
>>> conll_tag_chunks([t])
[[('DT', 'B-NP'), ('NN', 'I-NP')]]
```

The final step is a subclass of `ChunkParserI` called `TagChunker`. It trains on a list of chunk trees using an internal tagger. This internal tagger is composed of a `UnigramTagger` and a `BigramTagger` class in a backoff chain, using the `backoff_tagger()` method created in the *Training and combining ngram taggers* recipe in *Chapter 4, Part-of-speech Tagging*.

Finally, `ChunkerI` subclasses must implement a `parse()` method that expects a part-of-speech tagged sentence. We unzip that sentence into a list of words and part-of-speech tags. The tags are then tagged by the tagger to get IOB tags, which are then recombined with the words and part-of-speech tags to create 3-tuples we can pass to `conlltags2tree()` to return a final `Tree`.

There's more...

Since we've been talking about the conll IOB tags, let's see how the TagChunker class does on the conll2000 corpus:

```
>>> from nltk.corpus import conll2000
>>> conll_train = conll2000.chunked_sents('train.txt')
>>> conll_test = conll2000.chunked_sents('test.txt')
>>> chunker = TagChunker(conll_train)
>>> score = chunker.evaluate(conll_test)
>>> score.accuracy()
0.8950545623403762
>>> score.precision()
0.8114841974355675
>>> score.recall()
0.8644191676944863
```

Not quite as good as on treebank_chunk, but conll2000 is a much larger corpus, so it's not too surprising.

Using different taggers

If you want to use different tagger classes with the TagChunker class, you can pass them in as tagger_classes. For example, here's the TagChunker class using just a UnigramTagger class:

```
>>> from nltk.tag import UnigramTagger
>>> uni_chunker = TagChunker(train_chunks, tagger_
classes=[UnigramTagger])
>>> score = uni_chunker.evaluate(test_chunks)
>>> score.accuracy()
0.9674925924335466
```

The tagger_classes argument will be passed directly into the backoff_tagger() function, which means they must be subclasses of SequentialBackoffTagger. In testing, the default of tagger_classes=[UnigramTagger, BigramTagger] generally produces the best results, but it can vary depending on the corpus.

See also

The *Training and combing ngram taggers* recipe in *Chapter 4, Part-of-speech Tagging*, covers backoff tagging with a UnigramTagger and BigramTagger class. The ChunkScore metrics returned by the evaluate() method of a chunker are explained in the previous recipe.

Classification-based chunking

Unlike most part-of-speech taggers, the `ClassifierBasedTagger` class learns from features. That means we can create a `ClassifierChunker` class that can learn from both the words and part-of-speech tags, instead of only the part-of-speech tags as the `TagChunker` class does.

How to do it...

For the `ClassifierChunker` class, we don't want to discard the words from the training sentences as we did in the previous recipe. Instead, to remain compatible with the 2-tuple `(word, pos)` format required for training a `ClassiferBasedTagger` class, we convert the `(word, pos, iob)` 3-tuples from `tree2conlltags()` into `((word, pos), iob)` 2-tuples using the `chunk_trees2train_chunks()` function. This code can be found in `chunkers.py`:

```
from nltk.chunk import ChunkParserI
from nltk.chunk.util import tree2conlltags, conlltags2tree
from nltk.tag import ClassifierBasedTagger

def chunk_trees2train_chunks(chunk_sents):
  tag_sents = [tree2conlltags(sent) for sent in chunk_sents]
  return [[((w,t),c) for (w,t,c) in sent] for sent in tag_sents]
```

Next, we need a feature detector function to pass into `ClassifierBasedTagger`. Our default feature detector function, `prev_next_pos_iob()`, knows that the list of tokens is really a list of `(word, pos)` tuples, and can use that to return a feature set suitable for a classifier. In fact, any feature detector function used with the `ClassifierChunker` class (defined next) should recognize that tokens are a list of `(word, pos)` tuples, and have the same function signature as `prev_next_pos_iob()`. To give the classifier as much information as we can, this feature set contains the current, previous, and next word and part-of-speech tag, along with the previous IOB tag:

```
def prev_next_pos_iob(tokens, index, history):
  word, pos = tokens[index]

  if index == 0:
    prevword, prevpos, previob = ('<START>',)*3
  else:
    prevword, prevpos = tokens[index-1]
    previob = history[index-1]
```

```
    if index == len(tokens) - 1:
      nextword, nextpos = ('<END>',)*2
    else:
      nextword, nextpos = tokens[index+1]

    feats = {
      'word': word,
      'pos': pos,
      'nextword': nextword,
      'nextpos': nextpos,
      'prevword': prevword,
      'prevpos': prevpos,
      'previob': previob
    }
    return feats
```

Now, we can define the `ClassifierChunker` class, which uses an internal `ClassifierBasedTagger` with features extracted using `prev_next_pos_iob()` and training sentences from `chunk_trees2train_chunks()`. As a subclass of `ChunkerParserI`, it implements the `parse()` method, which converts the `((w, t), c)` tuples produced by the internal tagger into `Trees` using `conlltags2tree()`:

```
class ClassifierChunker(ChunkParserI):
  def __init__(self, train_sents, feature_detector=prev_next_pos_iob,
**kwargs):
    if not feature_detector:
      feature_detector = self.feature_detector

    train_chunks = chunk_trees2train_chunks(train_sents)
    self.tagger = ClassifierBasedTagger(train=train_chunks,
      feature_detector=feature_detector, **kwargs)

  def parse(self, tagged_sent):
    if not tagged_sent: return None
    chunks = self.tagger.tag(tagged_sent)
    return conlltags2tree([(w,t,c) for ((w,t),c) in chunks])
```

Using the same `train_chunks` and `test_chunks` from the `treebank_chunk` corpus in the previous recipe, we can evaluate this code from `chunkers.py`:

```
>>> from chunkers import ClassifierChunker
>>> chunker = ClassifierChunker(train_chunks)
>>> score = chunker.evaluate(test_chunks)
>>> score.accuracy()
0.9721733155838022
```

```
>>> score.precision()
0.9258838793383068
>>> score.recall()
0.9359016393442623
```

Compared to the `TagChunker` class, all the scores have gone up a bit. Let's see how it does on `conll2000`:

```
>>> chunker = ClassifierChunker(conll_train)
>>> score = chunker.evaluate(conll_test)
>>> score.accuracy()
0.9264622074002153
>>> score.precision()
0.8737924310910219
>>> score.recall()
0.9007354620620346
```

This is much improved over the `TagChunker` class.

How it works...

Like the `TagChunker` class in the previous recipe, we are training a part-of-speech tagger for IOB tagging. But in this case, we want to include the word as a feature to power a classifier. By creating nested 2-tuples of the form `((word, pos), iob)`, we can pass the word through the tagger into our feature detector function. The `chunk_trees2train_chunks()` method produces these nested 2-tuples, and `prev_next_pos_iob()` is aware of them and uses each element as a feature. The following features are extracted:

- The current word and part-of-speech tag
- The previous word, part-of-speech tag, and IOB tag
- The next word and part-of-speech tag

The arguments to `prev_next_pos_iob()` look the same as the `feature_detector()` method of the `ClassifierBasedTagger` class: `tokens`, `index`, and `history`. But this time, `tokens` will be a list of `(word, pos)` two tuples, and `history` will be a list of IOB tags. The special feature values `<START>` and `<END>` are used if there are no previous or next tokens.

The `ClassifierChunker` class uses an internal `ClassifierBasedTagger` and `prev_next_pos_iob()` as its default `feature_detector`. The results from the tagger, which are in the same nested 2-tuple form, are then reformated into 3-tuples to return a final `Tree` using `conlltags2tree()`.

There's more...

You can use your own feature detector function by passing it into the `ClassifierChunker` class as `feature_detector`. The `tokens` argument will contain a list of `(word, tag)` tuples, and `history` will be a list of the previous IOB tags found.

Using a different classifier builder

The `ClassifierBasedTagger` class defaults to using `NaiveBayesClassifier.train` as its `classifier_builder`. But you can use any classifier you want by overriding the `classifier_builder` keyword argument. Here's an example using `MaxentClassifier.train`:

```
>>> from nltk.classify import MaxentClassifier
>>> builder = lambda toks: MaxentClassifier.train(toks, trace=0, max_iter=10, min_lldelta=0.01)
>>> me_chunker = ClassifierChunker(train_chunks, classifier_builder=builder)
>>> score = me_chunker.evaluate(test_chunks)
>>> score.accuracy()
0.9743204362949285
>>> score.precision()
0.9334423548650859
>>> score.recall()
0.9357377049180328
```

Instead of using `MaxentClassifier.train` directly, I wrapped it in a `lambda` argument so that its output is quite similar to `(trace=0)` and it finishes in a reasonable amount of time. As you can see, the scores are slightly different compared to using the `NaiveBayesClassifier` class.

> The `MaxentClassifier` score values mentioned earlier were computed with the environment variable `PYTHONHASHSEED=0`. If you use a different value, or do not set this environment variable, your score values may differ.

See also

The previous recipe, *Training a tagger-based chunker*, introduced the idea of using a part-of-speech tagger for training a chunker. The *Classifier-based tagging* recipe in *Chapter 4, Part-of-speech Tagging*, describes `ClassifierBasedPOSTagger`, which is a subclass of `ClassifierBasedTagger`. And in *Chapter 7, Text Classification*, we'll cover classification in detail.

Extracting named entities

Named entity recognition is a specific kind of chunk extraction that uses entity tags instead of, or in addition to, chunk tags. Common entity tags include PERSON, ORGANIZATION, and LOCATION. Part-of-speech tagged sentences are parsed into chunk trees as with normal chunking, but the labels of the trees can be entity tags instead of chunk phrase tags.

How to do it...

NLTK comes with a pre-trained named entity chunker. This chunker has been trained on data from the ACE program, **National Institute of Standards and Technology** (**NIST**) sponsored program for **Automatic Content Extraction**, which you can read more about at http://www.itl.nist.gov/iad/894.01/tests/ace/. Unfortunately, this data is not included in the NLTK corpora, but the trained chunker is. This chunker can be used through the ne_chunk() method in the nltk.chunk module. The ne_chunk() method will chunk a single sentence into a Tree. The following is an example using ne_chunk() on the first tagged sentence of the treebank_chunk corpus:

```
>>> from nltk.chunk import ne_chunk
>>> ne_chunk(treebank_chunk.tagged_sents()[0])
Tree('S', [Tree('PERSON', [('Pierre', 'NNP')]), Tree('ORGANIZATION',
[('Vinken', 'NNP')]), (',', ','), ('61', 'CD'), ('years', 'NNS'),
('old', 'JJ'), (',', ','), ('will', 'MD'), ('join', 'VB'), ('the',
'DT'), ('board', 'NN'), ('as', 'IN'), ('a', 'DT'), ('nonexecutive',
'JJ'), ('director', 'NN'), ('Nov.', 'NNP'), ('29', 'CD'), ('.', '.')])
```

You can see that two entity tags are found: PERSON and ORGANIZATION. Each of these subtrees contains a list of the words that are recognized as a PERSON or ORGANIZATION. To extract these named entities, we can write a simple helper method that will get the leaves of all the subtrees we are interested in:

```
def sub_leaves(tree, label):
  return [t.leaves() for t in tree.subtrees(lambda s: label() ==
label)]
```

Then, we can call this method to get all the PERSON or ORGANIZATION leaves from a tree:

```
>>> tree = ne_chunk(treebank_chunk.tagged_sents()[0])
>>> from chunkers import sub_leaves
>>> sub_leaves(tree, 'PERSON')
[[('Pierre', 'NNP')]]
>>> sub_leaves(tree, 'ORGANIZATION')
[[('Vinken', 'NNP')]]
```

You will notice that the chunker has mistakenly separated Vinken into its own ORGANIZATION Tree instead of including it with the PERSON Tree containing Pierre. Such is the case with statistical natural language processing—you can't always expect perfection.

How it works...

The pre-trained named entity chunker is much like any other chunker, and in fact uses a `MaxentClassifier` powered `ClassifierBasedTagger` to determine IOB tags. But instead of `B-NP` and `I-NP` IOB tags, it uses `B-PERSON`, `I-PERSON`, `B-ORGANIZATION`, `I-ORGANIZATION`, and more. It also uses the `O` tag to mark words that are not part of a named entity (and thus are *outside* the named entity subtrees).

There's more...

To process multiple sentences at a time, you can use `chunk_ne_sents()`. Here's an example where we process the first 10 sentences from `treebank_chunk.tagged_sents()` and get `ORGANIZATION sub_leaves()`:

```
>>> from nltk.chunk import chunk_ne_sents
>>> trees = chunk_ne_sents(treebank_chunk.tagged_sents()[:10])
>>> [sub_leaves(t, 'ORGANIZATION') for t in trees]
[[[('Vinken', 'NNP')]], [[('Elsevier', 'NNP')]], [[('Consolidated', 'NNP'), ('Gold', 'NNP'), ('Fields', 'NNP')]], [], [], [[('Inc.', 'NNP')], [('Micronite', 'NN')]], [[('New', 'NNP'), ('England', 'NNP'), ('Journal', 'NNP')]], [[('Lorillard', 'NNP')]], [], []]
```

You can see that there are a couple of multiword `ORGANIZATION` chunks, such as `New England Journal`. There were also a few sentences that had no `ORGANIZATION` chunks, as indicated by the empty lists `[]`.

Binary named entity extraction

If you don't care about the particular kind of named entity to extract, you can pass `binary=True` into `ne_chunk()` or `chunk_ne_sents()`. Now, all named entities will be tagged with `NE`:

```
>>> ne_chunk(treebank_chunk.tagged_sents()[0], binary=True)
Tree('S', [Tree('NE', [('Pierre', 'NNP'), ('Vinken', 'NNP')]), (',', ','), ('61', 'CD'), ('years', 'NNS'), ('old', 'JJ'), (',', ','), ('will', 'MD'), ('join', 'VB'), ('the', 'DT'), ('board', 'NN'), ('as', 'IN'), ('a', 'DT'), ('nonexecutive', 'JJ'), ('director', 'NN'), ('Nov.', 'NNP'), ('29', 'CD'), ('.', '.')])
```

So, `binary` in this case means that an arbitrary chunk either is or is not a named entity. If we get the `sub_leaves()`, we can see that `Pierre Vinken` is correctly combined into a single named entity:

```
>>> subleaves(ne_chunk(treebank_chunk.tagged_sents()[0], binary=True), 'NE')
[[('Pierre', 'NNP'), ('Vinken', 'NNP')]]
```

See also

In the next recipe, we'll create our own simple named entity chunker.

Extracting proper noun chunks

A simple way to do named entity extraction is to chunk all proper nouns (tagged with NNP). We can tag these chunks as NAME, since the definition of a proper noun is the name of a person, place, or thing.

How to do it...

Using the RegexpParser class, we can create a very simple grammar that combines all proper nouns into a NAME chunk. Then, we can test this on the first tagged sentence of treebank_chunk to compare the results with the previous recipe:

```
>>> chunker = RegexpParser(r'''
... NAME:
...     {<NNP>+}
... ''')
>>> sub_leaves(chunker.parse(treebank_chunk.tagged_sents()[0]),
'NAME')
[[('Pierre', 'NNP'), ('Vinken', 'NNP')], [('Nov.', 'NNP')]]
```

Although we get Nov. as a NAME chunk, this isn't a wrong result, as Nov. is the name of a month.

How it works...

The NAME chunker is a simple usage of the RegexpParser class, covered in the *Chunking and chinking with regular expressions*, *Merging and splitting chunks with regular expressions*, and *Partial parsing with regular expressions* recipes. All sequences of NNP tagged words are combined into NAME chunks.

There's more...

If we wanted to be sure to only chunk the names of people, then we can build a PersonChunker class that uses the names corpus for chunking. This class can be found in chunkers.py:

```
from nltk.chunk import ChunkParserI
from nltk.chunk.util import conlltags2tree
from nltk.corpus import names
```

```
class PersonChunker(ChunkParserI):
  def __init__(self):
    self.name_set = set(names.words())

  def parse(self, tagged_sent):
    iobs = []
    in_person = False

    for word, tag in tagged_sent:
      if word in self.name_set and in_person:
        iobs.append((word, tag, 'I-PERSON'))
      elif word in self.name_set:
        iobs.append((word, tag, 'B-PERSON'))
        in_person = True
      else:
        iobs.append((word, tag, 'O'))
        in_person = False


    return conlltags2tree(iobs)
```

The `PersonChunker` class iterates over the tagged sentence, checking whether each word is in its `names_set` (constructed from the `names` corpus). If the current word is in the `names_set`, then it uses either the `B-PERSON` or `I-PERSON` IOB tags, depending on whether the previous word was also in the `names_set`. Any word that's not in the `names_set` argument gets the `O` IOB tag. When complete, the list of IOB tags is converted to a `Tree` using `conlltags2tree()`. Using it on the same tagged sentence as before, we get the following result:

```
>>> from chunkers import PersonChunker
>>> chunker = PersonChunker()
>>> sub_leaves(chunker.parse(treebank_chunk.tagged_sents()[0]),
'PERSON')
[[('Pierre', 'NNP')]]
```

We no longer get `Nov.`, but we've also lost `Vinken`, as it is not found in the `names` corpus. This recipe highlights some of the difficulties of chunk extraction and natural language processing in general:

- If you use general patterns, you'll get general results
- If you're looking for specific results, you must use specific data
- If your specific data is incomplete, your results will be incomplete too

See also

The previous recipe defines the `sub_leaves()` function used to show the found chunks. In the next recipe, we'll cover how to find `LOCATION` chunks based on the `gazetteers` corpus.

Extracting location chunks

To identify `LOCATION` chunks, we can make a different kind of `ChunkParserI` subclass that uses the `gazetteers` corpus to identify location words. The `gazetteers` corpus is a `WordListCorpusReader` class that contains the following location words:

- Country names
- U.S. states and abbreviations
- Major U.S. cities
- Canadian provinces
- Mexican states

How to do it...

The `LocationChunker` class, found in `chunkers.py`, iterates over a tagged sentence looking for words that are found in the `gazetteers` corpus. When it finds one or more location words, it creates a `LOCATION` chunk using IOB tags. The helper method `iob_locations()` is where the IOB `LOCATION` tags are produced, and the `parse()` method converts these IOB tags into a `Tree`:

```
from nltk.chunk import ChunkParserI
from nltk.chunk.util import conlltags2tree
from nltk.corpus import gazetteers

class LocationChunker(ChunkParserI):
  def __init__(self):
    self.locations = set(gazetteers.words())
    self.lookahead = 0

    for loc in self.locations:
      nwords = loc.count(' ')

      if nwords > self.lookahead:
        self.lookahead = nwords
```

```
    def iob_locations(self, tagged_sent):
      i = 0
      l = len(tagged_sent)
      inside = False

      while i < l:
        word, tag = tagged_sent[i]
        j = i + 1
        k = j + self.lookahead
        nextwords, nexttags = [], []
        loc = False

        while j < k:
          if ' '.join([word] + nextwords) in self.locations:
            if inside:
              yield word, tag, 'I-LOCATION'
            else:
              yield word, tag, 'B-LOCATION'

            for nword, ntag in zip(nextwords, nexttags):
              yield nword, ntag, 'I-LOCATION'

            loc, inside = True, True
            i = j
            break

          if j < l:
            nextword, nexttag = tagged_sent[j]
            nextwords.append(nextword)
            nexttags.append(nexttag)
            j += 1
          else:
            break

        if not loc:
          inside = False
          i += 1
          yield word, tag, 'O'

    def parse(self, tagged_sent):
      iobs = self.iob_locations(tagged_sent)
      return conlltags2tree(iobs)
```

We can use the `LocationChunker` class to parse the following sentence into two locations—`San Francisco CA is cold compared to San Jose CA`:

```
>>> from chunkers import LocationChunker
>>> t = loc.parse([('San', 'NNP'), ('Francisco', 'NNP'), ('CA', 'NNP'), ('is', 'BE'), ('cold', 'JJ'), ('compared', 'VBD'), ('to', 'TO'), ('San', 'NNP'), ('Jose', 'NNP'), ('CA', 'NNP')])
>>> sub_leaves(t, 'LOCATION')
[[('San', 'NNP'), ('Francisco', 'NNP'), ('CA', 'NNP')], [('San', 'NNP'), ('Jose', 'NNP'), ('CA', 'NNP')]]
```

And the result is that we get two `LOCATION` chunks, just as expected.

How it works...

The `LocationChunker` class starts by constructing a set of all locations in the `gazetteers` corpus. Then, it finds the maximum number of words in a single location string so it knows how many words it must look ahead when parsing a tagged sentence.

The `parse()` method calls a helper method, `iob_locations()`, which generates 3-tuples of the form `(word, pos, iob)`, where `iob` is either `O` if the word is not a location, or `B-LOCATION` or `I-LOCATION` for `LOCATION` chunks. The `iob_locations()` method finds location chunks by looking at the current word and the next words to check if the combined word is in the locations set. Multiple location words that are next to each other are then put into the same `LOCATION` chunk, such as in the previous example with `San Francisco` and `CA`.

Like in the previous recipe, it's simpler and more convenient to construct a list of `(word, pos, iob)` tuples to pass into `conlltags2tree()` to return a `Tree`. The alternative is to construct a `Tree` manually, but that requires keeping track of children, subtrees, and where you currently are in the `Tree`.

There's more...

One of the nice aspects of this `LocationChunker` class is that it doesn't care about the part-of-speech tags. As long as the location words are found in the location's set, any part-of-speech tag will do.

See also

In the next recipe, we'll cover how to train a named entity chunker using the `ieer` corpus.

Training a named entity chunker

You can train your own named entity chunker using the `ieer` corpus, which stands for **Information Extraction: Entity Recognition**. It takes a bit of extra work, though, because the `ieer` corpus has chunk trees but no part-of-speech tags for words.

How to do it...

Using the `ieertree2conlltags()` and `ieer_chunked_sents()` functions in `chunkers.py`, we can create named entity chunk trees from the `ieer` corpus to train the `ClassifierChunker` class created in the *Classification-based chunking* recipe:

```
import nltk.tag
from nltk.chunk.util import conlltags2tree
from nltk.corpus import ieer

def ieertree2conlltags(tree, tag=nltk.tag.pos_tag):
  words, ents = zip(*tree.pos())
  iobs = []
  prev = None

  for ent in ents:
    if ent == tree.label():
      iobs.append('O')
      prev = None
    elif prev == ent:
      iobs.append('I-%s' % ent)
    else:
      iobs.append('B-%s' % ent)
      prev = ent

  words, tags = zip(*tag(words))
  return zip(words, tags, iobs)

def ieer_chunked_sents(tag=nltk.tag.pos_tag):
  for doc in ieer.parsed_docs():
    tagged = ieertree2conlltags(doc.text, tag)
    yield conlltags2tree(tagged)
```

We'll use 80 out of 94 sentences for training, and the rest for testing. Then, we can see how it does on the first sentence of the `treebank_chunk` corpus:

```
>>> from chunkers import ieer_chunked_sents, ClassifierChunker
>>> from nltk.corpus import treebank_chunk
>>> ieer_chunks = list(ieer_chunked_sents())
>>> len(ieer_chunks)
94
>>> chunker = ClassifierChunker(ieer_chunks[:80])
>>> chunker.parse(treebank_chunk.tagged_sents()[0])
Tree('S', [Tree('LOCATION', [('Pierre', 'NNP'), ('Vinken', 'NNP')]),
(',', ','), Tree('DURATION', [('61', 'CD'), ('years', 'NNS')]),
Tree('MEASURE', [('old', 'JJ')]), (',', ','), ('will', 'MD'), ('join',
'VB'), ('the', 'DT'), ('board', 'NN'), ('as', 'IN'), ('a', 'DT'),
('nonexecutive', 'JJ'), ('director', 'NN'), Tree('DATE', [('Nov.',
'NNP'), ('29', 'CD')]), ('.', '.')])
```

So, it found a correct `DURATION` and `DATE`, but tagged `Pierre Vinken` as a `LOCATION`. Let's see how it scores against the rest of the `ieer` chunk trees:

```
>>> score = chunker.evaluate(ieer_chunks[80:])
>>> score.accuracy()
0.8829018388070625
>>> score.precision()
0.4088717454194793
>>> score.recall()
0.5053635280095352
```

Accuracy is pretty good, but precision and recall are very low. That means lots of false negatives and false positives.

How it works...

The truth is, we're not working with ideal training data. The `ieer` trees generated by `ieer_chunked_sents()` are not entirely accurate. First, there are no explicit sentence breaks, so each document is a single tree. Second, the words are not explicitly tagged, so we have to guess using `nltk.tag.pos_tag()`.

The `ieer` corpus provides a `parsed_docs()` method that returns a list of documents with a `text` attribute. This `text` attribute is a document `Tree` that is converted to a list of 3-tuples of the form `(word, pos, iob)`. To get these final 3-tuples, we must first flatten the `Tree` using `tree.pos()`, which returns a list of 2-tuples of the form `(word, entity)`, where `entity` is either the entity tag or the top tag of the tree. Any words whose entity is the top tag are outside the named entity chunks and get the IOB tag `O`. All words that have unique entity tags are either the beginning of or inside a named entity chunk. Once we have all the IOB tags, then we can get the part-of-speech tags of all the words and join the words, part-of-speech tags, and IOB tags into 3-tuples using `zip()`.

There's more...

Despite the non-ideal training data, the `ieer` corpus provides a good place to start for training a named entity chunker. The data comes from *New York Times* and *AP Newswire* reports. Each doc from `ieer.parsed_docs()` also contains a headline attribute that is a `Tree`:

```
>>> from nltk.corpus import ieer
>>> ieer.parsed_docs()[0].headline
Tree('DOCUMENT', ['Kenyans', 'protest', 'tax', 'hikes'])
```

See also

The *Extracting named entities* recipe covers the pre-trained named entity chunker that comes included with NLTK.

Training a chunker with NLTK-Trainer

At the end of the previous chapter, *Chapter 4*, *Part-of-speech Tagging*, we introduced NLTK-Trainer and the `train_tagger.py` script. In this recipe, we will cover the script for training chunkers: `train_chunker.py`.

> You can find NLTK-Trainer at `https://github.com/japerk/nltk-trainer` and the online documentation at `http://nltk-trainer.readthedocs.org/`.

How to do it...

As with `train_tagger.py`, the only required argument to `train_chunker.py` is the name of a corpus. In this case, we need a corpus that provides a `chunked_sents()` method, such as `treebank_chunk`. Here's an example of running `train_chunker.py` on `treebank_chunk`:

```
$ python train_chunker.py treebank_chunk
loading treebank_chunk
4009 chunks, training on 4009
training ub TagChunker
evaluating TagChunker
ChunkParse score:
    IOB Accuracy:   97.0%
    Precision:      90.8%
    Recall:         93.9%
    F-Measure:      92.3%
dumping TagChunker to /Users/jacob/nltk_data/chunkers/treebank_chunk_
ub.pickle
```

Just like with `train_tagger.py`, we can use the `--no-pickle` argument to skip saving a pickled chunker, and the `--fraction` argument to limit the training set and evaluate the chunker against a test set:

```
$ python train_chunker.py treebank_chunk --no-pickle --fraction 0.75
loading treebank_chunk
4009 chunks, training on 3007
training ub TagChunker
evaluating TagChunker
ChunkParse score:
    IOB Accuracy:   97.3%
    Precision:      91.6%
    Recall:         94.6%
    F-Measure:      93.1%
```

The score output you see is what you get when you print a `ChunkScore` object. This `ChunkScore` is the result of calling the chunker's `evaluate()` method, and has been explained in more detail earlier in this chapter in the *Partial parsing with regular expressions* recipe. Surprisingly, the chunker's scores actually increase slightly when using a smaller training set. This may indicate that the chunker training algorithm is susceptible to over-fitting, meaning that too many training examples can cause the chunker to over-value incorrect or noisy data.

> The `PYTHONHASHSEED` environment variable has been omitted for clarity. This means that when you run `train_chunker.py`, your score values may vary. To get consistent score values, run `train_chunker.py` like this:
>
> **$ PYTHONHASHSEED=0 python train_chunker.py treebank_chunk ...**

How it works...

The default training algorithm for `train_chunker.py` is to use a tagger-based chunker composed of a `BigramTagger` and `UnigramTagger` class. This is what is meant by the output line `training ub TagChunker`. The details for how to train a tag chunker have been covered earlier in this chapter in the *Training a tagger-based chunker* recipe. You can modify this algorithm using the `--sequential` argument. Here's how to train a `UnigramTagger` based chunker:

```
$ python train_chunker.py treebank_chunk --no-pickle --fraction 0.75
--sequential u
loading treebank_chunk
4009 chunks, training on 3007
training u TagChunker
evaluating TagChunker
```

```
ChunkParse score:
    IOB Accuracy:   96.7%
    Precision:      89.7%
    Recall:         93.1%
    F-Measure:      91.3%
```

And here's how to twith additional BigramTagger and TrigramTagger classes:

```
$ python train_chunker.py treebank_chunk --no-pickle --fraction 0.75
--sequential ubt
loading treebank_chunk
4009 chunks, training on 3007
training ubt TagChunker
evaluating TagChunker
ChunkParse score:
    IOB Accuracy:   97.2%
    Precision:      91.6%
    Recall:         94.4%
    F-Measure:      93.0%
```

You can also train a classifier-based chunker, which was covered in the previous recipe, *Classification-based chunking*.

```
$ python train_chunker.py treebank_chunk --no-pickle --fraction 0.75
--sequential '' --classifier NaiveBayes
loading treebank_chunk
4009 chunks, training on 3007
training ClassifierChunker with ['NaiveBayes'] classifier
Constructing training corpus for classifier.
Training classifier (71088 instances)
training NaiveBayes classifier
evaluating ClassifierChunker
ChunkParse score:
    IOB Accuracy:   97.2%
    Precision:      92.6%
    Recall:         93.6%
    F-Measure:      93.1%
```

There's more...

The `train_chunker.py` script supports many other arguments not shown here, all of which you can see by running the script with `--help`. A few additional arguments are presented next, followed by an introduction to two other chunking-related scripts available in `nltk-trainer`.

Saving a pickled chunker

Without the `--no-pickle` argument, `train_chunker.py` will save a pickled chunker at `~/nltk_data/chunkers/NAME.pickle`, where `NAME` is a combination of the corpus name and training algorithm. You can specify a custom filename for your chunker using the `--filename` argument like this:

```
$ python train_chunker.py treebank_chunker --filename path/to/
tagger.pickle
```

Training a named entity chunker

We can use `train_chunker.py` to replicate the chunker we trained on the `ieer` corpus in the *Training a named entity chunker* recipe. This is possible because the special handling required for training on `ieer` is built-in to NLTK-Trainer.

```
$ python train_chunker.py ieer --no-pickle --fraction 0.85 --sequential
'' --classifier NaiveBayes
loading ieer
converting ieer parsed docs to chunked sentences
94 chunks, training on 80
training ClassifierChunker with ['NaiveBayes'] classifier
Constructing training corpus for classifier.
Training classifier (47000 instances)
training NaiveBayes classifier
evaluating ClassifierChunker
ChunkParse score:
    IOB Accuracy:   88.3%
    Precision:      40.9%
    Recall:         50.5%
    F-Measure:      45.2%
```

Training on a custom corpus

If you have a custom corpus that you want to use for training a chunker, you can do that by passing in the path to the corpus and the classname of a corpus reader in the `--reader` argument. The corpus path can either be absolute or relative to a `nltk_data` directory. The corpus reader class must provide a `chunked_sents()` method. Here's an example using a relative path to the `treebank` chunked corpus:

```
$ python train_chunker.py corpora/treebank/tagged --reader nltk.corpus.
reader.ChunkedCorpusReader --no-pickle --fraction 0.75
loading corpora/treebank/tagged
51002 chunks, training on 38252
training ub TagChunker
evaluating TagChunker
ChunkParse score:
```

```
    IOB Accuracy:    98.4%
    Precision:       97.7%
    Recall:          98.9%
    F-Measure:       98.3%
```

Training on parse trees

The `train_chunker.py` script supports two arguments that allow it to train on full parse trees from a corpus reader's `parsed_sents()` method instead of using chunked sentences. A parse tree differs from a chunk tree in that it can be much deeper, with subphrases and even subphrases of those subphrases. But the chunking algorithms we've covered so far cannot learn from deep parse trees, so we need to flatten them somehow. The first argument is `--flatten-deep-tree`, which trains chunks from the leaf labels of a parse tree.

```
$ python train_chunker.py treebank --no-pickle --fraction 0.75 --flatten-deep-tree
loading treebank
flattening deep trees from treebank
3914 chunks, training on 2936
training ub TagChunker
evaluating TagChunker
ChunkParse score:
    IOB Accuracy:  72.4%
    Precision:     51.6%
    Recall:        52.2%
    F-Measure:     51.9%
```

We use the `treebank` corpus instead of `treebank_chunk`, because it has full parse trees accessible with the `parsed_sents()` method. The other parse tree argument is `--shallow-tree`, which trains chunks from the top-level labels of a parse tree.

```
$ python train_chunker.py treebank --no-pickle --fraction 0.75 --shallow-tree
loading treebank
creating shallow trees from treebank
3914 chunks, training on 2936
training ub TagChunker
evaluating TagChunker
ChunkParse score:
    IOB Accuracy:  73.1%
    Precision:     60.0%
    Recall:        56.2%
    F-Measure:     58.0%
```

These options are more useful for corpora that don't provide chunked sentences, such as `cess_cat` and `cess_esp`.

Analyzing a chunker against a chunked corpus

So how do you know how well a chunker will perform on a different corpus that you didn't train it on? The `analyze_chunker_coverage.py` script gives you a simple way to test the performance of a chunker against another chunked corpus. Here's how to test NLTK's built-in chunker against the `treebank_chunk` corpus:

```
$ python analyze_chunker_coverage.py treebank_chunk --score
loading tagger taggers/maxent_treebank_pos_tagger/english.pickle
loading chunker chunkers/maxent_ne_chunker/english_ace_multiclass.pickle
evaluating chunker score

ChunkParse   score:
    IOB Accuracy:  45.4%
    Precision:      0.0%
    Recall:         0.0%
    F-Measure:      0.0%

analyzing chunker coverage of treebank_chunk with NEChunkParser


IOB               Found
============  =========
FACILITY           56
GPE              1874
GSP                38
LOCATION           34
ORGANIZATION     1572
PERSON           2108
============  =========
```

As you can see, NLTK's default chunker does not do well against the `treebank_chunk` corpus. This is because the default chunker is looking for named entities, not `NP` phrases. This is shown by the coverage analysis of IOB tags that were found. These results do not necessarily mean that the default chunker is bad, just that it was not trained for finding noun phrases, and thus cannot be accurately evaluated against the `treebank_chunk` corpus.

While the `analyze_chunker_coverage.py` script defaults to using NLTK's built-in tagger and chunker, you can evaluate on your own tagger and/or chunker using the `--tagger` and/or `--chunker` arguments, both of which accept a path to a pickled tagger or chunker. Consider the following code:

```
$ python train_chunker.py treebank_chunker --tagger path/to/tagger.pickle
--chunker path/to/chunker.pickle
```

You can also use a custom corpus just like we did earlier with `train_chunker.py`; however, if your corpus is not chunked, then you must omit the `--score` argument, because you have nothing to compare the results to. In that case, you will only get IOB tag counts with no scores, because there are no chunks to compare to.

Analyzing a chunked corpus

Finally, there is a script called `analyze_chunked_corpus.py`, which as the name implies, will read in a chunked corpus and print out stats about the number of words and tags. You can run it like this:

```
$ python analyze_chunked_corpus.py treebank_chunk
```

The results are very similar to `analyze_tagged_corpus.py`, with additional columns for each IOB tag. Each IOB tag column shows the counts for each part-of-speech tag that was present in chunks for that IOB tag. For example, `NN` words (nouns) may occur 300 times in total, and for 280 of those times, the `NN` words occurred with a `NP` IOB tag, meaning that most nouns occur within noun phrases.

As with the other commands, you can pass in a custom corpus path and reader to analyze your own chunked corpus.

See also

- The *Training a tagger-based chunker*, the *Classification-based chunking*, and the *Training a named entity chunker* recipes cover many of the ideas that went into the `train_chunker.py` script
- In *Chapter 4, Part-of-speech Tagging*, we showed how to use NLTK-Trainer for training a tagger in the *Training a tagger with NLTK-Trainer* recipe

6

Transforming Chunks and Trees

In this chapter, we will cover the following recipes:

- Filtering insignificant words from a sentence
- Correcting verb forms
- Swapping verb phrases
- Swapping noun cardinals
- Swapping infinitive phrases
- Singularizing plural nouns
- Chaining chunk transformations
- Converting a chunk tree to text
- Flattening a deep tree
- Creating a shallow tree
- Converting tree labels

Introduction

Now that you know how to get chunks/phrases from a sentence, what do you do with them? This chapter will show you how to do various transforms on both chunks and trees. The **chunk transforms** are for grammatical correction and rearranging phrases without loss of meaning. The **tree transforms** give you ways to modify and flatten deep parse trees. The functions detailed in these recipes modify data, as opposed to learning from it. This means it's not safe to apply them indiscriminately. A thorough knowledge of the data you want to transform, along with a few experiments, should help you decide which functions to apply and when.

Whenever the term **chunk** is used in this chapter, it could refer to an actual chunk extracted by a chunker, or it could simply refer to a short phrase or sentence in the form of a list of tagged words. What's important in this chapter is what you can do with a chunk, not where it came from.

Filtering insignificant words from a sentence

Many of the most commonly used words are insignificant when it comes to discerning the meaning of a phrase. For example, in the phrase *the movie was terrible*, the most **significant** words are *movie* and *terrible*, while *the* and *was* are almost useless. You could get the same meaning if you took them out, that is, *movie terrible* or *terrible movie*. Either way, the sentiment is the same. In this recipe, we'll learn how to remove the insignificant words and keep the significant ones by looking at their part-of-speech tags.

Getting ready

First, we need to decide which part-of-speech tags are significant and which are not. Looking through the `treebank` corpus for stopwords yields the following table of insignificant words and tags:

Word	Tag
a	DT
all	PDT
an	DT
and	CC
or	CC
that	WDT
the	DT

Other than CC, all the tags end with DT. This means we can filter out insignificant words by looking at the tag's suffix. Refer to *Appendix*, *Penn Treebank Part-of-speech Tags*, for details on tag meanings.

How to do it...

In `transforms.py` is a function called `filter_insignificant()`. It takes a single chunk, which should be a list of tagged words, and returns a new chunk without any insignificant tagged words. It defaults to filtering out any tags that end with DT or CC:

```
def filter_insignificant(chunk, tag_suffixes=['DT', 'CC']):
  good = []
```

```
    for word, tag in chunk:
      ok = True

      for suffix in tag_suffixes:
        if tag.endswith(suffix):
          ok = False
          break

      if ok:
        good.append((word, tag))

    return good
```

And now we can use it on the part-of-speech tagged version of *the terrible movie*:

```
>>> from transforms import filter_insignificant
>>> filter_insignificant([('the', 'DT'), ('terrible', 'JJ'),
('movie', 'NN')])
[('terrible', 'JJ'), ('movie', 'NN')]
```

As you can see, the word `the` is eliminated from the chunk.

How it works...

The `filter_insignificant()` function iterates over the tagged words in the chunk. For each tag, it checks whether that tag ends with any of the `tag_suffixes`. If it does, then the tagged word is skipped. But if the tag is ok, then the tagged word is appended to a new good chunk that is returned.

There's more...

The way `filter_insignificant()` is defined, you can pass in your own tag suffixes if DT and CC are not enough, or are incorrect for your case. For example, you might decide that possessive words and pronouns such as *you*, *your*, *their*, and *theirs* are no good, but DT and CC words are ok. The tag suffixes would then be `PRP` and `PRP$`:

```
>>> filter_insignificant([('your', 'PRP$'), ('book', 'NN'), ('is',
'VBZ'), ('great', 'JJ')], tag_suffixes=['PRP', 'PRP$'])
[('book', 'NN'), ('is', 'VBZ'), ('great', 'JJ')]
```

Filtering insignificant words can be a good complement to stopword filtering for purposes such as search engine indexing and querying and text classification.

See also

This recipe is analogous to the *Filtering stopwords in a tokenized sentence* recipe in *Chapter 1, Tokenizing Text and WordNet Basics*.

Correcting verb forms

It's fairly common to find incorrect verb forms in real-world language. For example, the correct form of *is our children learning?* is *are our children learning?* The verb *is* should only be used with singular nouns, while *are* is for plural nouns, such as *children*. We can correct these mistakes by creating verb correction mappings that are used depending on whether there's a plural or singular noun in the chunk.

Getting ready

We first need to define the verb correction mappings in `transforms.py`. We'll create two mappings, one for plural to singular and another for singular to plural:

```
plural_verb_forms = {
  ('is', 'VBZ'): ('are', 'VBP'),
  ('was', 'VBD'): ('were', 'VBD')
}

singular_verb_forms = {
  ('are', 'VBP'): ('is', 'VBZ'),
  ('were', 'VBD'): ('was', 'VBD')
}
```

Each mapping has a tagged verb that maps to another tagged verb. These initial mappings cover the basics of mapping **is** to **are**, **was** to **were**, and vice versa.

How to do it...

In `transforms.py` is a function called `correct_verbs()`. Pass it a chunk with incorrect verb forms and you'll get a corrected chunk back. It uses a helper function, `first_chunk_index()`, to search the chunk for the position of the first tagged word where `pred` returns `True`. The `pred` argument should be a callable function that takes a `(word, tag)` tuple and returns `True` or `False`. Here's `first_chunk_index()`:

```
def first_chunk_index(chunk, pred, start=0, step=1):
  l = len(chunk)
  end = l if step > 0 else -1
```

```
    for i in range(start, end, step):
      if pred(chunk[i]):
        return i

    return None
```

For `first_chunk_index()` to be useful, we need to use a predicate function. In the case of `correct_verbs()`, the predicate function we need should return `True` if the tag in the `(word, tag)` argument starts with a given tag prefix, and `False` otherwise.

```
def tag_startswith(prefix):
  def f(wt):
    return wt[1].startswith(prefix)
  return f
```

The `tag_startswith()` function takes a tag prefix, such as `NN`, and returns a predicate function that will take a `(word, tag)` tuple and return `True` if the tag starts with the given prefix. A function that returns another function is called a **higher order function**. This is not as complicated as it might sound—just as you can use a function to generate and return new variables and values, some programming languages (such as Python) let you generate functions inside of other functions. In this case, we want a function that takes a single argument: `(word, tag)`. But we also want this function to have access to a prefix variable. Since we cannot add arguments to the function definition, we instead generate a higher order function that has access to the prefix variable, while preserving the single `(word, tag)` argument.

Now that we have defined `first_chunk_index()` and `tag_startswith()`, we can actually implement `correct_verbs()`. This may seem like overkill for a single function, but we will be using `first_chunk_index()` and `tag_startswith()` in subsequent recipes.

```
def correct_verbs(chunk):
  vbidx = first_chunk_index(chunk, tag_startswith('VB'))
  # if no verb found, do nothing
  if vbidx is None:
    return chunk

  verb, vbtag = chunk[vbidx]
  nnpred = tag_startswith('NN')
  # find nearest noun to the right of verb
  nnidx = first_chunk_index(chunk, nnpred, start=vbidx+1)
  # if no noun found to right, look to the left
  if nnidx is None:
    nnidx = first_chunk_index(chunk, nnpred, start=vbidx-1, step=-1)
  # if no noun found, do nothing
  if nnidx is None:
    return chunk
```

```
    noun, nntag = chunk[nnidx]
    # get correct verb form and insert into chunk
    if nntag.endswith('S'):
      chunk[vbidx] = plural_verb_forms.get((verb, vbtag), (verb, vbtag))
    else:
      chunk[vbidx] = singular_verb_forms.get((verb, vbtag), (verb,
vbtag))

    return chunk
```

When we call the preceding function on a part-of-speech tagged `is our children learning` chunk, we get back the correct form, `are our children learning`.

```
>>> from transforms import correct_verbs
>>> correct_verbs([('is', 'VBZ'), ('our', 'PRP$'), ('children',
'NNS'), ('learning', 'VBG')])
[('are', 'VBP'), ('our', 'PRP$'), ('children', 'NNS'), ('learning',
'VBG')]
```

We can also try this with a *singular noun* and an incorrect *plural verb*:

```
>>> correct_verbs([('our', 'PRP$'), ('child', 'NN'), ('were', 'VBD'),
('learning', 'VBG')])
[('our', 'PRP$'), ('child', 'NN'), ('was', 'VBD'), ('learning',
'VBG')]
```

In this case, `were` becomes `was` because `child` is a singular noun.

How it works...

The `correct_verbs()` function starts by looking for a verb in the chunk. If no verb is found, the chunk is returned with no changes. Once a verb is found, we keep the verb, its tag, and its index in the chunk. Then, we look on either side of the verb to find the nearest noun, starting on the right and looking to the left only if no noun is found on the right. If no noun is found at all, the chunk is returned as is. But if a noun is found, then we look up the correct verb form depending on whether or not the noun is plural.

Recall from *Chapter 4, Part-of-speech Tagging*, that plural nouns are tagged with `NNS`, while singular nouns are tagged with `NN`. That means we can check the plurality of a noun by looking to see whether its tag ends with `S`. Once we get the corrected verb form, it is inserted into the chunk to replace the original verb form.

See also

The next four recipes all make use of `first_chunk_index()` to perform chunk transformations.

Swapping verb phrases

Swapping the words around a verb can eliminate the passive voice from particular phrases. For example, `the book was great` can be transformed into `the great book`. This kind of normalization can also help with frequency analysis, by counting two apparently different phrases as the same phrase.

How to do it...

In `transforms.py` is a function called `swap_verb_phrase()`. It swaps the right-hand side of the chunk with the left-hand side, using the verb as the **pivot point**. It uses the `first_chunk_index()` function defined in the previous recipe to find the verb to pivot around.

```
def swap_verb_phrase(chunk):
  def vbpred(wt):
    word, tag = wt
    return tag != 'VBG' and tag.startswith('VB') and len(tag) > 2

  vbidx = first_chunk_index(chunk, vbpred)

  if vbidx is None:
    return chunk

  return chunk[vbidx+1:] + chunk[:vbidx]
```

Now we can see how it works on the part-of-speech tagged phrase `the book was great`:

```
>>> swap_verb_phrase([('the', 'DT'), ('book', 'NN'), ('was', 'VBD'),
('great', 'JJ')])
[('great', 'JJ'), ('the', 'DT'), ('book', 'NN')]
```

And the result is `great the book`. This phrase clearly isn't grammatically correct, so read on to learn how to fix it.

How it works...

Using `first_chunk_index()` from the previous recipe with the `vbpred()` function defined inline, we start by finding the first matching verb that is not a gerund (a word that ends in *ing*) tagged with VBG. Once we've found the verb, we return the chunk with the right side before the left, and remove the verb.

The reason we don't want to pivot around a gerund is that gerunds are commonly used to describe nouns, and pivoting around one would remove that description. Here's an example where you can see how not pivoting around a gerund is a good thing:

```
>>> swap_verb_phrase([('this', 'DT'), ('gripping', 'VBG'), ('book',
'NN'), ('is', 'VBZ'), ('fantastic', 'JJ')])
[('fantastic', 'JJ'), ('this', 'DT'), ('gripping', 'VBG'), ('book',
'NN')]
```

If we had pivoted around the gerund, the result would be `book is fantastic this`, and we'd lose the gerund `gripping`.

There's more...

Filtering insignificant words makes the final result more readable. By filtering either before or after `swap_verb_phrase()`, we get `fantastic gripping book` instead of `fantastic this gripping book`:

```
>>> from transforms import swap_verb_phrase, filter_insignificant
>>> swap_verb_phrase(filter_insignificant([('this', 'DT'),
('gripping', 'VBG'), ('book', 'NN'), ('is', 'VBZ'), ('fantastic',
'JJ')]))
[('fantastic', 'JJ'), ('gripping', 'VBG'), ('book', 'NN')]
>>> filter_insignificant(swap_verb_phrase([('this', 'DT'),
('gripping', 'VBG'), ('book', 'NN'), ('is', 'VBZ'), ('fantastic',
'JJ')]))
[('fantastic', 'JJ'), ('gripping', 'VBG'), ('book', 'NN')]
```

Either way, we get a shorter grammatical chunk with no loss of meaning.

See also

The previous recipe, *Correcting verb forms*, defines `first_chunk_index()`, which is used to find the verb in the chunk.

Swapping noun cardinals

In a chunk, a *cardinal* word, tagged as `CD`, refers to a number, such as *10*. These cardinals often occur before or after a noun. For normalization purposes, it can be useful to always put the cardinal before the noun.

How to do it...

The `swap_noun_cardinal()` function is defined in `transforms.py`. It swaps any cardinal that occurs immediately after a noun with the noun so that the cardinal occurs immediately before the noun. It uses a helper function, `tag_equals()`, which is similar to `tag_startswith()`, but in this case, the function it returns does an equality comparison with the given tag:

```
def tag_equals(tag):
  def f(wt):
    return wt[1] == tag
  return f
```

Now we can define `swap_noun_cardinal()`:

```
def swap_noun_cardinal(chunk):
  cdidx = first_chunk_index(chunk, tag_equals('CD'))
  # cdidx must be > 0 and there must be a noun immediately before it
  if not cdidx or not chunk[cdidx-1][1].startswith('NN'):
    return chunk

  noun, nntag = chunk[cdidx-1]
  chunk[cdidx-1] = chunk[cdidx]
  chunk[cdidx] = noun, nntag
  return chunk
```

Let's try it on a date, such as `Dec 10`, and another common phrase, `the top 10`.

```
>>> swap_noun_cardinal([('Dec.', 'NNP'), ('10', 'CD')])
[('10', 'CD'), ('Dec.', 'NNP')]
>>> swap_noun_cardinal([('the', 'DT'), ('top', 'NN'), ('10', 'CD')])
[('the', 'DT'), ('10', 'CD'), ('top', 'NN')]
```

The result is that the numbers are now in front of the noun, creating `10 Dec` and `the 10 top`.

How it works...

We start by looking for a `CD` tag in the chunk. If no `CD` is found, or if the `CD` is at the beginning of the chunk, then the chunk is returned as is. There must also be a noun immediately before the `CD`. If we do find a `CD` with a noun preceding it, then we swap the noun and cardinal.

See also

The *Correcting verb forms* recipe defines the `first_chunk_index()` function used to find tagged words in a chunk.

Swapping infinitive phrases

An infinitive phrase has the form *A of B*, such as *book of recipes*. These can often be transformed into a new form while retaining the same meaning, such as *recipes book*.

How to do it...

An infinitive phrase can be found by looking for a word tagged with `IN`. The `swap_infinitive_phrase()` function, defined in `transforms.py`, will return a chunk that swaps the portion of the phrase after the `IN` word with the portion before the `IN` word:

```
def swap_infinitive_phrase(chunk):
  def inpred(wt):
    word, tag = wt
    return tag == 'IN' and word != 'like'

  inidx = first_chunk_index(chunk, inpred)

  if inidx is None:
    return chunk

  nnidx = first_chunk_index(chunk, tag_startswith('NN'), start=inidx,
step=-1) or 0
  return chunk[:nnidx] + chunk[inidx+1:] + chunk[nnidx:inidx]
```

The function can now be used to transform `book of recipes` into `recipes book`:

```
>>> from transforms import swap_infinitive_phrase
>>> swap_infinitive_phrase([('book', 'NN'), ('of', 'IN'), ('recipes',
'NNS')])
[('recipes', 'NNS'), ('book', 'NN')]
```

How it works...

This function is similar to the `swap_verb_phrase()` function described in the *Swapping verb phrases* recipe. The `inpred` function is passed to `first_chunk_index()` to look for a word whose tag is `IN`. Next, we find the first noun that occurs before the `IN` word, so we can insert the portion of the chunk after the `IN` word between the noun and the beginning of the chunk. A more complicated example should demonstrate this:

```
>>> swap_infinitive_phrase([('delicious', 'JJ'), ('book', 'NN'),
('of', 'IN'), ('recipes', 'NNS')])
[('delicious', 'JJ'), ('recipes', 'NNS'), ('book', 'NN')]
```

We don't want the result to be `recipes delicious book`. Instead, we want to insert `recipes` before the noun `book` but after the adjective `delicious`, hence the need to find the `nnidx` occurring before the `inidx`.

There's more...

You'll notice that the `inpred` function checks to make sure the word is not `like`. That's because `like` phrases must be treated differently, as transforming them the same way will result in an ungrammatical phrase. For example, `tastes like chicken` should not be transformed into `chicken tastes`.

```
>>> swap_infinitive_phrase([('tastes', 'VBZ'), ('like', 'IN'),
('chicken', 'NN')])
[('tastes', 'VBZ'), ('like', 'IN'), ('chicken', 'NN')]
```

See also

In the next recipe, we'll learn how to transform `recipes book` into the more normal form `recipe book`.

Singularizing plural nouns

As we saw in the previous recipe, the transformation process can result in phrases such as `recipes book`. This is a `NNS` followed by a `NN`, when a more proper version of the phrase would be `recipe book`, which is a `NN` followed by another `NN`. We can do another transform to correct these improper plural nouns.

How to do it...

The `transforms.py` script defines a function called `singularize_plural_noun()` which will depluralize a plural noun (tagged with `NNS`) that is followed by another noun:

```
def singularize_plural_noun(chunk):
  nnsidx = first_chunk_index(chunk, tag_equals('NNS'))

  if nnsidx is not None and nnsidx+1 < len(chunk) and chunk[nnsidx+1]
[1][:2] == 'NN':
    noun, nnstag = chunk[nnsidx]
    chunk[nnsidx] = (noun.rstrip('s'), nnstag.rstrip('S'))

  return chunk
```

And using it on `recipes book`, we get the more correct form, `recipe book`.

```
>>> singularize_plural_noun([('recipes', 'NNS'), ('book', 'NN')])
[('recipe', 'NN'), ('book', 'NN')]
```

How it works...

We start by looking for a plural noun with the tag NNS. If found, and if the next word is a noun (determined by making sure the tag starts with NN), then we depluralize the plural noun by removing s from the right side of both the tag and the word. The tag is assumed to be capitalized, so an uppercase S is removed from the right-hand side of the tag, while a lowercase s is removed from the right-hand side of the word.

See also

The previous recipe shows how a transformation can result in a plural noun followed by a singular noun, though this could also occur naturally in real-world text.

Chaining chunk transformations

The transform functions defined in the previous recipes can be chained together to normalize chunks. The resulting chunks are often shorter with no loss of meaning.

How to do it...

In `transforms.py` is the function `transform_chunk()`. It takes a single chunk and an optional list of transform functions. It calls each transform function on the chunk, one at a time, and returns the final chunk:

```
def transform_chunk(chunk, chain=[filter_insignificant, swap_verb_
phrase, swap_infinitive_phrase, singularize_plural_noun], trace=0):
  for f in chain:
    chunk = f(chunk)

    if trace:
      print f.__name__, ':', chunk

  return chunk
```

Using it on the phrase `the book of recipes is delicious`, we get `delicious recipe book`:

```
>>> from transforms import transform_chunk
>>> transform_chunk([('the', 'DT'), ('book', 'NN'), ('of', 'IN'),
('recipes', 'NNS'), ('is', 'VBZ'), ('delicious', 'JJ')])
[('delicious', 'JJ'), ('recipe', 'NN'), ('book', 'NN')]
```

How it works...

The `transform_chunk()` function defaults to chaining the following functions in the given order:

- `filter_insignificant()`
- `swap_verb_phrase()`
- `swap_infinitive_phrase()`
- `singularize_plural_noun()`

Each function transforms the chunk that results from the previous function, starting with the original chunk.

> The order in which you apply transform functions can be significant. Experiment with your own data to determine which transforms are best, and in which order they should be applied.

There's more...

You can pass `trace=1` into `transform_chunk()` to get an output at each step:

```
>>> from transforms import transform_chunk
>>> transform_chunk([('the', 'DT'), ('book', 'NN'), ('of', 'IN'),
('recipes', 'NNS'), ('is', 'VBZ'), ('delicious', 'JJ')], trace=1)
filter_insignificant : [('book', 'NN'), ('of', 'IN'), ('recipes',
'NNS'), ('is', 'VBZ'), ('delicious', 'JJ')]
swap_verb_phrase : [('delicious', 'JJ'), ('book', 'NN'), ('of', 'IN'),
('recipes', 'NNS')]
swap_infinitive_phrase : [('delicious', 'JJ'), ('recipes', 'NNS'),
('book', 'NN')]
singularize_plural_noun : [('delicious', 'JJ'), ('recipe', 'NN'),
('book', 'NN')]
[('delicious', 'JJ'), ('recipe', 'NN'), ('book', 'NN')]
```

This shows you the result of each transform function, which is then passed in to the next transform until a final chunk is returned.

See also

The transform functions used were defined in the previous recipes of this chapter.

Converting a chunk tree to text

At some point, you may want to convert a `Tree` or subtree back to a sentence or chunk string. This is mostly straightforward, except when it comes to properly outputting punctuation.

How to do it...

We'll use the first tree of the `treebank_chunk` corpus as our example. The obvious first step is to join all the words in the tree with a space:

```
>>> from nltk.corpus import treebank_chunk
>>> tree = treebank_chunk.chunked_sents()[0]
>>> ' '.join([w for w, t in tree.leaves()])
'Pierre Vinken , 61 years old , will join the board as a nonexecutive
director Nov. 29 .'
```

But as you can see, the punctuation isn't quite right. The commas and period are treated as individual words, and so get the surrounding spaces as well. But we can fix this using regular expression substitution. This is implemented in the `chunk_tree_to_sent()` function found in `transforms.py`:

```
import re
punct_re = re.compile(r'\s([,\.;\?])')

def chunk_tree_to_sent(tree, concat=' '):
  s = concat.join([w for w, t in tree.leaves()])
  return re.sub(punct_re, r'\g<1>', s)
```

Using `chunk_tree_to_sent()` results in a cleaner sentence, with no space before each punctuation mark:

```
>>> from transforms import chunk_tree_to_sent
>>> chunk_tree_to_sent(tree)
'Pierre Vinken, 61 years old, will join the board as a nonexecutive
director Nov. 29.'
```

How it works...

To correct the extra spaces in front of the punctuation, we create a regular expression, `punct_re`, that will match a space followed by any of the known punctuation characters. We have to escape both `'.'` and `'?'` with a `'\'` since they are special characters. The punctuation is surrounded by parentheses so we can use the matched group for substitution.

Once we have our regular expression, we define `chunk_tree_to_sent()`, whose first step is to join the words by a concatenation character that defaults to a space. Then, we can call `re.sub()` to replace all the punctuation matches with just the punctuation group. This eliminates the space in front of the punctuation characters, resulting in a more correct string.

There's more...

We can simplify this function a little using `nltk.tag.untag()` to get words from the tree's leaves, instead of using our own list comprehension:

```
import nltk.tag, re
punct_re = re.compile(r'\s([,\.;\?])')

def chunk_tree_to_sent(tree, concat=' '):
  s = concat.join(nltk.tag.untag(tree.leaves()))
  return re.sub(punct_re, r'\g<1>', s)
```

See also

The `nltk.tag.untag()` function is covered at the end of the *Default tagging* recipe in *Chapter 4, Part-of-speech Tagging.*

Flattening a deep tree

Some of the included corpora contain parsed sentences, which are often deep trees of nested phrases. Unfortunately, these trees are too deep to use for training a chunker, since IOB tag parsing is not designed for nested chunks. To make these trees usable for chunker training, we must flatten them.

Getting ready

We're going to use the first parsed sentence of the `treebank` corpus as our example. Here's a diagram showing how deeply nested this tree is:

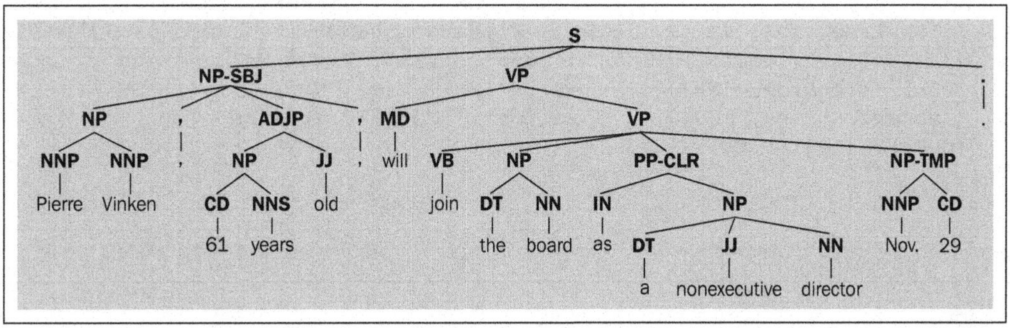

You may notice that the part-of-speech tags are part of the tree structure instead of being included with the word. This will be handled later using the `Tree.pos()` method, which was designed specifically for combining words with preterminal `Tree` labels such as part-of-speech tags.

How to do it...

In `transforms.py` is a function named `flatten_deeptree()`. It takes a single `Tree` and will return a new `Tree` that keeps only the lowest-level trees. It uses a helper function, `flatten_childtrees()`, to do most of the work:

```
from nltk.tree import Tree

def flatten_childtrees(trees):
  children = []

  for t in trees:
    if t.height() < 3:
      children.extend(t.pos())
    elif t.height() == 3:
      children.append(Tree(t.label(), t.pos()))
    else:
      children.extend(flatten_childtrees([c for c in t]))

  return children

def flatten_deeptree(tree):
  return Tree(tree.label(), flatten_childtrees([c for c in tree]))
```

We can use it on the first parsed sentence of the `treebank` corpus to get a flatter tree:

```
>>> from nltk.corpus import treebank
>>> from transforms import flatten_deeptree
>>> flatten_deeptree(treebank.parsed_sents()[0])
Tree('S', [Tree('NP', [('Pierre', 'NNP'), ('Vinken', 'NNP')]), (',',
','), Tree('NP', [('61', 'CD'), ('years', 'NNS')]), ('old', 'JJ'),
(',', ','), ('will', 'MD'), ('join', 'VB'), Tree('NP', [('the',
'DT'), ('board', 'NN')]), ('as', 'IN'), Tree('NP', [('a', 'DT'),
('nonexecutive', 'JJ'), ('director', 'NN')]), Tree('NP-TMP', [('Nov.',
'NNP'), ('29', 'CD')]), ('.', '.')])
```

The result is a much flatter `Tree` that only includes `NP` phrases. Words that are not part of an `NP` phrase are separated. This flatter tree is shown in the following diagram:

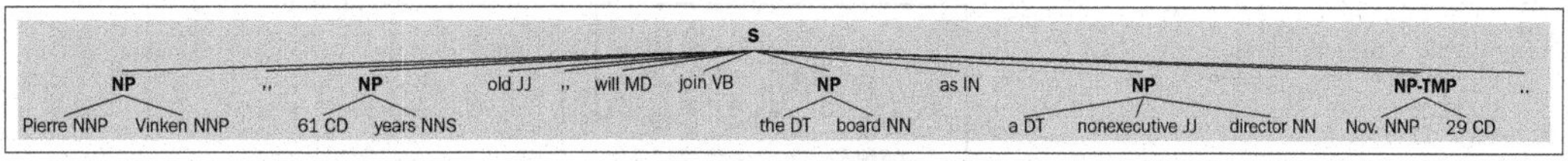

This `Tree` is quite similar to the first chunk `Tree` from the `treebank_chunk` corpus. The main difference is that the rightmost `NP Tree` is separated into two subtrees above, one of them named `NP-TMP`.

The first tree from `treebank_chunk` is shown in the following diagram for comparison. The main difference is the right side of the tree, which has only one `NP` subtree instead of two subtrees:

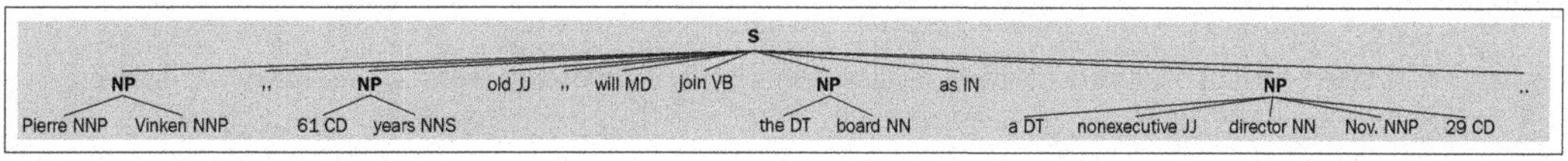

How it works...

The solution is composed of two functions: `flatten_deeptree()` returns a new `Tree` from the given tree by calling `flatten_childtrees()` on each of the given tree's children.

The `flatten_childtrees()` function is a recursive function that drills down into the `Tree` until it finds child trees whose `height()` is equal to or less than `3`. A `Tree` whose `height()` is less than `3` looks like this:

```
>>> from nltk.tree import Tree
>>> Tree('NNP', ['Pierre']).height()
2
```

These short trees are converted into lists of tuples using the `pos()` function.

```
>>> Tree('NNP', ['Pierre']).pos()
[('Pierre', 'NNP')]
```

Trees whose `height()` is equal to `3` are the lowest level trees that we're interested in keeping. These trees look like this:

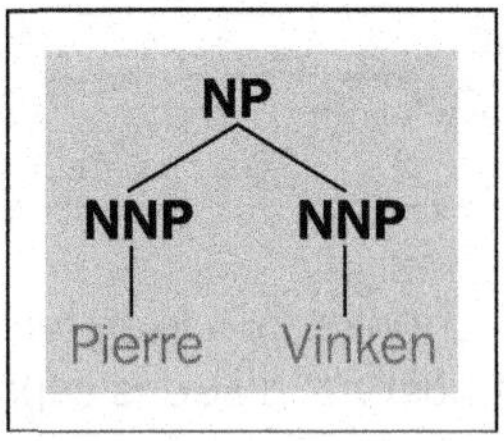


```
>>> Tree('NP', [Tree('NNP', ['Pierre']), Tree('NNP', ['Vinken'])]).
height()
3
```

And when we call `pos()` on that tree, we get:

```
>>> Tree('NP', [Tree('NNP', ['Pierre']), Tree('NNP', ['Vinken'])]).
pos()
[('Pierre', 'NNP'), ('Vinken', 'NNP')]
```

The recursive nature of `flatten_childtrees()` eliminates all trees whose height is greater than `3`.

There's more...

Flattening a deep `Tree` allows us to call `nltk.chunk.util.tree2conlltags()` on the flattened `Tree`, a necessary step to train a chunker. If you try to call this function before flattening the `Tree`, you get a `ValueError` exception:

```
>>> from nltk.chunk.util import tree2conlltags
>>> tree2conlltags(treebank.parsed_sents()[0])
Traceback (most recent call last):
  File "<stdin>", line 1, in <module>
  File "/usr/local/lib/python2.6/dist-packages/nltk/chunk/util.py",
line 417, in tree2conlltags
    raise ValueError, "Tree is too deeply nested to be printed in
CoNLL format"
ValueError: Tree is too deeply nested to be printed in CoNLL format
```

But after flattening, there's no problem:

```
>>> tree2conlltags(flatten_deeptree(treebank.parsed_sents()[0]))
[('Pierre', 'NNP', 'B-NP'), ('Vinken', 'NNP', 'I-NP'), (',', ',',
'O'), ('61', 'CD', 'B-NP'), ('years', 'NNS', 'I-NP'), ('old', 'JJ',
'O'), (',', ',', 'O'), ('will', 'MD', 'O'), ('join', 'VB', 'O'),
('the', 'DT', 'B-NP'), ('board', 'NN', 'I-NP'), ('as', 'IN', 'O'),
('a', 'DT', 'B-NP'), ('nonexecutive', 'JJ', 'I-NP'), ('director',
'NN', 'I-NP'), ('Nov.', 'NNP', 'B-NP-TMP'), ('29', 'CD', 'I-NP-TMP'),
('.', '.', 'O')]
```

Being able to flatten trees opens up the possibility of training a chunker on corpora consisting of deep parse trees.

The cess_esp and cess_cat treebank

The `cess_esp` and `cess_cat` corpora are Spanish and Catalan corpora that have parsed sentences but no chunked sentences. In other words, they have deep trees that must be flattened in order to train a chunker. In fact, the trees are so deep that a diagram would be overwhelming, but the flattening can be demonstrated by showing the `height()` of the tree before and after flattening:

```
>>> from nltk.corpus import cess_esp
>>> cess_esp.parsed_sents()[0].height()
22
>>> flatten_deeptree(cess_esp.parsed_sents()[0]).height()
3
```

See also

The *Training a tagger-based chunker* recipe in *Chapter 5, Extracting Chunks*, covers training a chunker using IOB tags.

Creating a shallow tree

In the previous recipe, we flattened a deep `Tree` by only keeping the lowest level subtrees. In this recipe, we'll keep only the highest level subtrees instead.

How to do it...

We'll be using the first parsed sentence from the `treebank` corpus as our example. Recall from the previous recipe that the sentence `Tree` looks like this:

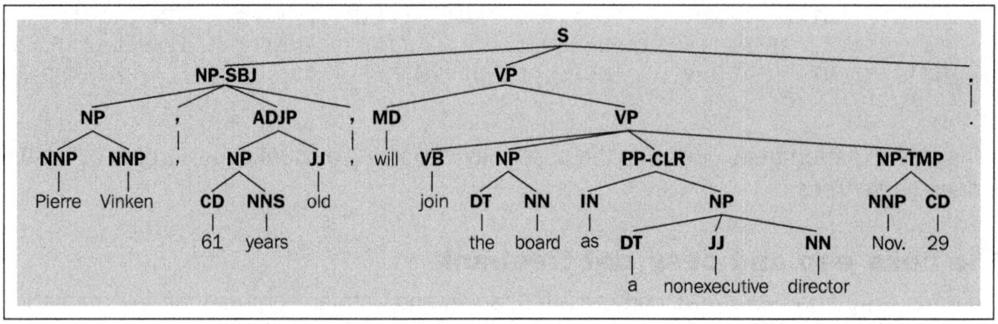

The `shallow_tree()` function defined in `transforms.py` eliminates all the nested subtrees, keeping only the top subtree labels:

```
from nltk.tree import Tree

def shallow_tree(tree):
  children = []

  for t in tree:
    if t.height() < 3:
      children.extend(t.pos())
    else:
      children.append(Tree(t.label(), t.pos()))

  return Tree(tree.label(), children)
```

Using it on the first parsed sentence in `treebank` results in a `Tree` with only two subtrees:

```
>>> from transforms import shallow_tree
>>> shallow_tree(treebank.parsed_sents()[0])
Tree('S', [Tree('NP-SBJ', [('Pierre', 'NNP'), ('Vinken', 'NNP'), (',',
','), ('61', 'CD'), ('years', 'NNS'), ('old', 'JJ'), (',', ',')]),
Tree('VP', [('will', 'MD'), ('join', 'VB'), ('the', 'DT'), ('board',
'NN'), ('as', 'IN'), ('a', 'DT'), ('nonexecutive', 'JJ'), ('director',
'NN'), ('Nov.', 'NNP'), ('29', 'CD')]), ('.', '.')])
```

We can visually and programmatically see the difference in the following diagram:

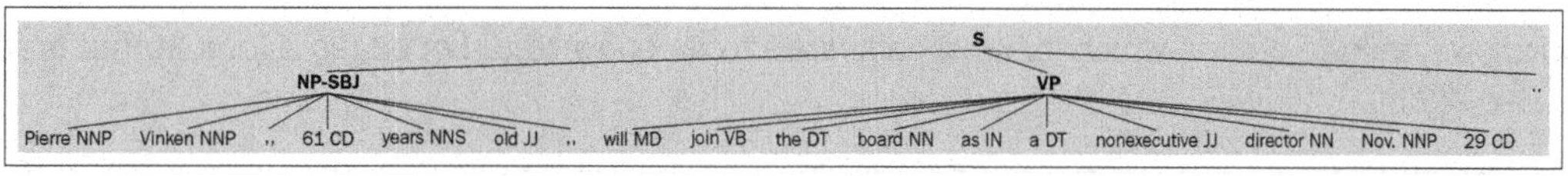


```
>>> treebank.parsed_sents()[0].height()
7
>>> shallow_tree(treebank.parsed_sents()[0]).height()
3
```

As in the previous recipe, the height of the new tree is `3` so it can be used for training a chunker.

How it works...

The `shallow_tree()` function iterates over each of the top-level subtrees in order to create new child trees. If the `height()` of a subtree is less than `3`, then that subtree is replaced by a list of its part-of-speech tagged children. All other subtrees are replaced by a new `Tree` whose children are the part-of-speech tagged leaves. This eliminates all nested subtrees while retaining the top-level subtrees.

This function is an alternative to `flatten_deeptree()` from the previous recipe, for when you want to keep the higher-level tree labels and ignore the lower-level labels.

See also

The previous recipe covers how to flatten a `Tree` and keep the lowest-level subtrees, as opposed to keeping the highest-level subtrees.

Converting tree labels

As you've seen in previous recipes, parse trees often have a variety of `Tree` label types that are not present in chunk trees. If you want to use parse trees to train a chunker, then you'll probably want to reduce this variety by converting some of these tree labels to more common label types.

Getting ready

First, we have to decide which `Tree` labels need to be converted. Let's take a look at that first `Tree` again:

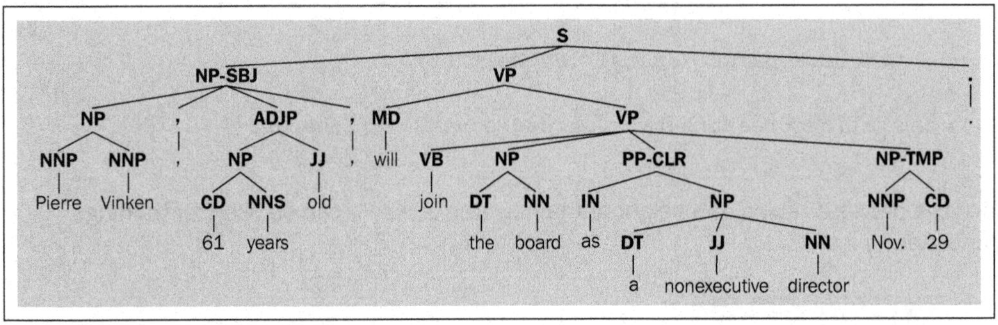

Immediately, you can see that there are two alternative `NP` subtrees: `NP-SBJ` and `NP-TMP`. Let's convert both of those to `NP`. The mapping will be as follows:

Original Label	New Label
NP-SBJ	NP
NP-TMP	NP

How to do it...

In `transforms.py` is the function `convert_tree_labels()`. It takes two arguments: the `Tree` to convert and a label conversion mapping. It returns a new `Tree` with all matching labels replaced based on the values in the mapping:

```
from nltk.tree import Tree

def convert_tree_labels(tree, mapping):
  children = []

  for t in tree:
    if isinstance(t, Tree):
      children.append(convert_tree_labels(t, mapping))
    else:
      children.append(t)

  label = mapping.get(tree.label(), tree.label())
  return Tree(label, children)
```

Using the mapping table we saw earlier, we can pass it in as a `dict` to `convert_tree_labels()` and convert the first parsed sentence from `treebank`:

```
>>> from transforms import convert_tree_labels
>>> mapping = {'NP-SBJ': 'NP', 'NP-TMP': 'NP'}
>>> convert_tree_labels(treebank.parsed_sents()[0], mapping)
Tree('S', [Tree('NP', [Tree('NP', [Tree('NNP', ['Pierre']),
Tree('NNP', ['Vinken'])]), Tree(',', [',']), Tree('ADJP', [Tree('NP',
[Tree('CD', ['61']), Tree('NNS', ['years'])]), Tree('JJ', ['old'])]),
Tree(',', [','])]), Tree('VP', [Tree('MD', ['will']), Tree('VP',
[Tree('VB', ['join']), Tree('NP', [Tree('DT', ['the']), Tree('NN',
['board'])]), Tree('PP-CLR', [Tree('IN', ['as']), Tree('NP',
[Tree('DT', ['a']), Tree('JJ', ['nonexecutive']), Tree('NN',
['director'])])]), Tree('NP', [Tree('NNP', ['Nov.']), Tree('CD',
['29'])])])]), Tree('.', ['.'])])
```

As you can see in the following diagram, the `NP-*` subtrees have been replaced with `NP` subtrees:

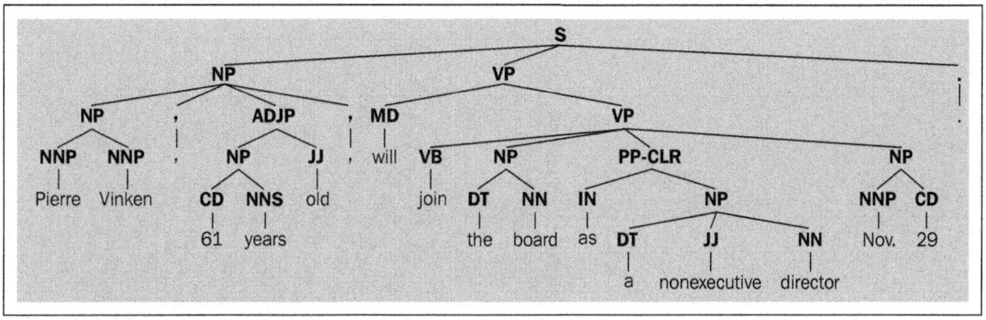

How it works...

The `convert_tree_labels()` function recursively converts every child subtree using the mapping. The `Tree` is then rebuilt with the converted labels and children until the entire `Tree` has been converted.

The result is a brand new `Tree` instance with new subtrees whose labels have been converted.

See also

The previous two recipes cover different methods of flattening a parse `Tree`, both of which can produce subtrees that may require mapping before using them to train a chunker. Chunker training is covered in the *Training a tagger-based chunker* recipe in *Chapter 5, Extracting Chunks*.

7
Text Classification

In this chapter, we will cover the following recipes:

- Bag of words feature extraction
- Training a Naive Bayes classifier
- Training a decision tree classifier
- Training a maximum entropy classifier
- Training scikit-learn classifiers
- Measuring precision and recall of a classifier
- Calculating high information words
- Combining classifiers with voting
- Classifying with multiple binary classifiers
- Training a classifier with NLTK-Trainer

Introduction

Text classification is a way to categorize documents or pieces of text. By examining the word usage in a piece of text, classifiers can decide what class label to assign to it. A **binary classifier** decides between two labels, such as positive or negative. The text can either be one label or another, but not both, whereas a **multi-label classifier** can assign one or more labels to a piece of text.

Classification works by learning from **labeled feature sets**, or training data, to later classify an **unlabeled feature set**. A labeled feature set is simply a tuple that looks like `(feat, label)`, while an unlabeled feature set is a `feat` by itself. A **feature set** is basically a key-value mapping of feature names to feature values. In the case of text classification, the feature names are usually words, and the values are all `True`. As the documents may have unknown words, and the number of possible words may be very large, words that don't occur in the text are omitted, instead of including them in a feature set with the value `False`.

An **instance** is another term for a feature set. It represents a single occurrence of a combination of features. I will use instance and feature set interchangeably. A **labeled feature set** is an instance with a known class label that we can use for training or evaluation. To summarize, `(feat, label)` is a labeled feature set, or labeled instance. `feat` is a feature set, normally represented as a key-value dictionary. When `feat` does not have an associated label, it is also called an **unlabeled feature set**, or instance.

Bag of words feature extraction

Text feature extraction is the process of transforming what is essentially a list of words into a feature set that is usable by a classifier. The NLTK classifiers expect `dict` style feature sets, so we must therefore transform our text into a `dict`. The **bag of words** model is the simplest method; it constructs a word presence feature set from all the words of an instance. This method doesn't care about the order of the words, or how many times a word occurs, all that matters is whether the word is present in a list of words.

How to do it...

The idea is to convert a list of words into a `dict`, where each word becomes a key with the value `True`. The `bag_of_words()` function in `featx.py` looks like this:

```
def bag_of_words(words):
  return dict([(word, True) for word in words])
```

We can use it with a list of words; in this case, the tokenized sentence `the quick brown fox`:

```
>>> from featx import bag_of_words
>>> bag_of_words(['the', 'quick', 'brown', 'fox'])
{'quick': True, 'brown': True, 'the': True, 'fox': True}
```

The resulting `dict` is known as a **bag of words** because the words are not in order, and it doesn't matter where in the list of words they occurred, or how many times they occurred. All that matters is that the word is found at least once.

> You can use different values than `True`, but it is important to keep in mind that the NLTK classifiers learn from the unique combination of `(key, value)`. That means that `('fox', 1)` is treated as a different feature than `('fox', 2)`.

How it works...

The `bag_of_words()` function is a very simple list comprehension that constructs a `dict` from the given words, where every word gets the value `True`.

Since we have to assign a value to each word in order to create a `dict`, `True` is a logical choice for the value to indicate word presence. If we knew the universe of all possible words, we could assign the value `False` to all the words that are not in the given list of words. But most of the time, we don't know all the possible words beforehand. Plus, the `dict` that would result from assigning `False` to every possible word would be very large (assuming all words in the English language are possible). So instead, to keep feature extraction simple and use less memory, we stick to assigning the value `True` to all words that occur at least once. We don't assign the value `False` to any word since we don't know what the set of possible words are; we only know about the words we are given.

There's more...

In the default bag of words model, all words are treated equally. But that's not always a good idea. As we already know, some words are so common that they are practically meaningless. If you have a set of words that you want to exclude, you can use the `bag_of_words_not_in_set()` function in `featx.py`:

```
def bag_of_words_not_in_set(words, badwords):
  return bag_of_words(set(words) - set(badwords))
```

This function can be used, among other things, to filter stopwords. Here's an example where we filter the word `the` from `the quick brown fox`:

```
>>> from featx import bag_of_words_not_in_set
>>> bag_of_words_not_in_set(['the', 'quick', 'brown', 'fox'], ['the'])
{'quick': True, 'brown': True, 'fox': True}
```

As expected, the resulting `dict` has `quick`, `brown`, and `fox`, but not `the`.

Filtering stopwords

Stopwords are words that are often useless in NLP, in that they don't convey much meaning, such as the word `the`. Here's an example of using the `bag_of_words_not_in_set()` function to filter all English stopwords:

```
from nltk.corpus import stopwords

def bag_of_non_stopwords(words, stopfile='english'):
  badwords = stopwords.words(stopfile)
  return bag_of_words_not_in_set(words, badwords)
```

You can pass a different language filename as the `stopfile` keyword argument if you are using a language other than English. Using this function produces the same result as the previous example:

```
>>> from featx import bag_of_non_stopwords
>>> bag_of_non_stopwords(['the', 'quick', 'brown', 'fox'])
{'quick': True, 'brown': True, 'fox': True}
```

Here, `the` is a stopword, so it is not present in the returned `dict`.

Including significant bigrams

In addition to single words, it often helps to include significant bigrams. As significant bigrams are less common than most individual words, including them in the bag of words model can help the classifier make better decisions. We can use the `BigramCollocationFinder` class covered in the *Discovering word collocations* recipe of *Chapter 1, Tokenizing Text and WordNet Basics*, to find significant bigrams. The `bag_of_bigrams_words()` function found in `featx.py` will return a `dict` of all words along with the 200 most significant bigrams:

```
from nltk.collocations import BigramCollocationFinder
from nltk.metrics import BigramAssocMeasures

def bag_of_bigrams_words(words, score_fn=BigramAssocMeasures.chi_sq,
n=200):
  bigram_finder = BigramCollocationFinder.from_words(words)
  bigrams = bigram_finder.nbest(score_fn, n)
  return bag_of_words(words + bigrams)
```

The bigrams will be present in the returned `dict` as `(word1, word2)` and will have the value as `True`. Using the same example words as we did earlier, we get all words plus every bigram:

```
>>> from featx import bag_of_bigrams_words
>>> bag_of_bigrams_words(['the', 'quick', 'brown', 'fox'])
{'brown': True, ('brown', 'fox'): True, ('the', 'quick'):
True, 'fox': True, ('quick', 'brown'): True, 'quick': True, 'the':
True}
```

You can change the maximum number of bigrams found by altering the keyword argument *n*.

See also

The *Discovering word collocations* recipe of *Chapter 1, Tokenizing Text and WordNet Basics*, covers the `BigramCollocationFinder` class in more detail. In the next recipe, we will train a `NaiveBayesClassifier` class using feature sets created with the bag of words model.

Training a Naive Bayes classifier

Now that we can extract features from text, we can train a classifier. The easiest classifier to get started with is the `NaiveBayesClassifier` class. It uses the **Bayes theorem** to predict the probability that a given feature set belongs to a particular label. The formula is:

```
P(label | features) = P(label) * P(features | label) / P(features)
```

The following list describes the various parameters from the previous formula:

- `P(label)`: This is the prior probability of the label occurring, which is the likelihood that a random feature set will have the label. This is based on the number of training instances with the label compared to the total number of training instances. For example, if 60/100 training instances have the label, the prior probability of the label is 60%.
- `P(features | label)`: This is the prior probability of a given feature set being classified as that label. This is based on which features have occurred with each label in the training data.
- `P(features)`: This is the prior probability of a given feature set occurring. This is the likelihood of a random feature set being the same as the given feature set, and is based on the observed feature sets in the training data. For example, if the given feature set occurs twice in 100 training instances, the prior probability is 2%.
- `P(label | features)`: This tells us the probability that the given features should have that label. If this value is high, then we can be reasonably confident that the label is correct for the given features.

Getting ready

We are going to be using the `movie_reviews` corpus for our initial classification examples. This corpus contains two categories of text: `pos` and `neg`. These categories are exclusive, which makes a classifier trained on them a **binary classifier**. Binary classifiers have only two classification labels, and will always choose one or the other.

Each file in the `movie_reviews` corpus is composed of either positive or negative movie reviews. We will be using each file as a single instance for both training and testing the classifier. Because of the nature of the text and its categories, the classification we will be doing is a form of sentiment analysis. If the classifier returns `pos`, then the text expresses a positive sentiment, whereas if we get `neg`, then the text expresses a negative sentiment.

How to do it...

For training, we need to first create a list of labeled feature sets. This list should be of the form `[(featureset, label)]`, where the `featureset` variable is a `dict` and `label` is the known class label for the `featureset`. The `label_feats_from_corpus()` function in `featx.py` takes a corpus, such as `movie_reviews`, and a `feature_detector` function, which defaults to `bag_of_words`. It then constructs and returns a mapping of the form `{label: [featureset]}`. We can use this mapping to create a list of labeled training instances and testing instances. The reason to do it this way is to get a fair sample from each label. It is important to get a fair sample, because parts of the corpus may be (unintentionally) biased towards one label or the other. Getting a fair sample should eliminate this possible bias:

```
import collections

def label_feats_from_corpus(corp, feature_detector=bag_of_words):
  label_feats = collections.defaultdict(list)
  for label in corp.categories():
    for fileid in corp.fileids(categories=[label]):
      feats = feature_detector(corp.words(fileids=[fileid]))
      label_feats[label].append(feats)
  return label_feats
```

Once we can get a mapping of `label | feature sets`, we want to construct a list of labeled training instances and testing instances. The `split_label_feats()` function in `featx.py` takes a mapping returned from `label_feats_from_corpus()` and splits each list of feature sets into labeled training and testing instances:

```
def split_label_feats(lfeats, split=0.75):
  train_feats = []
  test_feats = []
  for label, feats in lfeats.items():
    cutoff = int(len(feats) * split)
    train_feats.extend([(feat, label) for feat in feats[:cutoff]])
    test_feats.extend([(feat, label) for feat in feats[cutoff:]])
  return train_feats, test_feats
```

Using these functions with the `movie_reviews` corpus gives us the lists of labeled feature sets we need to train and test a classifier:

```
>>> from nltk.corpus import movie_reviews
>>> from featx import label_feats_from_corpus, split_label_feats
>>> movie_reviews.categories()
['neg', 'pos']
>>> lfeats = label_feats_from_corpus(movie_reviews)
>>> lfeats.keys()
```

```
dict_keys(['neg', 'pos'])
>>> train_feats, test_feats = split_label_feats(lfeats, split=0.75)
>>> len(train_feats)
1500
>>> len(test_feats)
500
```

So there are 1000 `pos` files, 1000 `neg` files, and we end up with 1500 labeled training instances and 500 labeled testing instances, each composed of equal parts of `pos` and `neg`. If we were using a different dataset, where the classes were not balanced, our training and testing data would have the same imbalance.

Now we can train a `NaiveBayesClassifier` class using its `train()` class method:

```
>>> from nltk.classify import NaiveBayesClassifier
>>> nb_classifier = NaiveBayesClassifier.train(train_feats)
>>> nb_classifier.labels()
['neg', 'pos']
```

Let's test the classifier on a couple of made up reviews. The `classify()` method takes a single argument, which should be a feature set. We can use the same `bag_of_words()` feature detector on a list of words to get our feature set:

```
>>> from featx import bag_of_words
>>> negfeat = bag_of_words(['the', 'plot', 'was', 'ludicrous'])
>>> nb_classifier.classify(negfeat)
'neg'
>>> posfeat = bag_of_words(['kate', 'winslet', 'is', 'accessible'])
>>> nb_classifier.classify(posfeat)
'pos'
```

How it works...

The `label_feats_from_corpus()` function assumes that the corpus is categorized, and that a single file represents a single instance for feature extraction. It iterates over each category label, and extracts features from each file in that category using the `feature_detector()` function, which defaults to `bag_of_words()`. It returns a `dict` whose keys are the category labels, and the values are lists of instances for that category.

If we had `label_feats_from_corpus()` return a list of labeled feature sets instead of a `dict`, it would be much harder to get balanced training data. The list would be ordered by label, and if you took a slice of it, you would almost certainly be getting far more of one label than another. By returning a `dict`, you can take slices from the feature sets of each label, in the same proportion that exists in the data.

Now we need to split the labeled feature sets into training and testing instances using `split_label_feats()`. This function allows us to take a fair sample of labeled feature sets from each label, using the `split` keyword argument to determine the size of the sample. The `split` argument defaults to `0.75`, which means the first 75% of the labeled feature sets for each label will be used for training, and the remaining 25% will be used for testing.

Once we have gotten our training and testing feats split up, we train a classifier using the `NaiveBayesClassifier.train()` method. This class method builds two probability distributions for calculating prior probabilities. These are passed into the `NaiveBayesClassifier` constructor. The `label_probdist` constructor contains the prior probability for each label, or `P(label)`. The `feature_probdist` constructor contains `P(feature name = feature value | label)`. In our case, it will store `P(word=True | label)`. Both are calculated based on the frequency of occurrence of each label and each feature name and value in the training data.

The `NaiveBayesClassifier` class inherits from `ClassifierI`, which requires subclasses to provide a `labels()` method, and at least one of the `classify()` or `prob_classify()` methods. The following diagram shows other methods, which will be covered shortly:

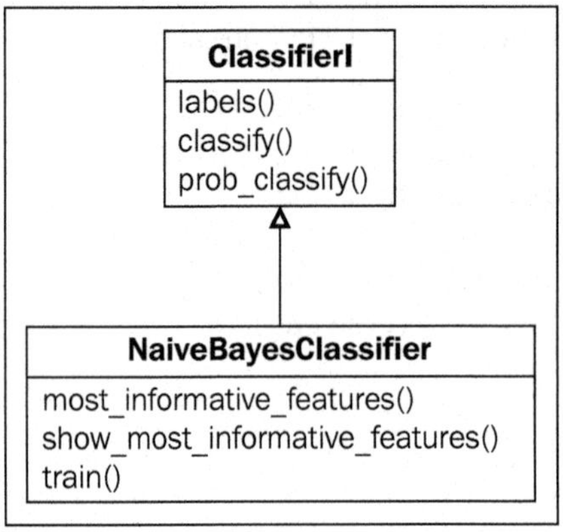

There's more...

We can test the accuracy of the classifier using `nltk.classify.util.accuracy()` and the `test_feats` variable created previously:

```
>>> from nltk.classify.util import accuracy
>>> accuracy(nb_classifier, test_feats)
0.728
```

This tells us that the classifier correctly guessed the label of nearly 73% of the test feature sets.

> The code in this chapter is run with the `PYTHONHASHSEED=0` environment variable so that accuracy calculations are consistent. If you run the code with a different value for `PYTHONHASHSEED`, or without setting this environment variable, your accuracy values may differ.

Classification probability

While the `classify()` method returns only a single label, you can use the `prob_classify()` method to get the classification probability of each label. This can be useful if you want to use probability thresholds for classification:

```
>>> probs = nb_classifier.prob_classify(test_feats[0][0])
>>> probs.samples()
dict_keys(['neg', 'pos'])
>>> probs.max()
'pos'
>>> probs.prob('pos')
0.9999999646430913
>>> probs.prob('neg')
3.535688969240647e-08
```

In this case, the classifier says that the first test instance is nearly 100% likely to be `pos`. Other instances may have more mixed probabilities. For example, if the classifier says an instance is 60% `pos` and 40% `neg`, that means the classifier is 60% sure the instance is `pos`, but there is a 40% chance that it is `neg`. It can be useful to know this for situations where you only want to use strongly classified instances, with a threshold of 80% or greater.

Most informative features

The `NaiveBayesClassifier` class has two methods that are quite useful for learning about your data. Both methods take a keyword argument `n` to control how many results to show. The `most_informative_features()` method returns a list of the form `[(feature name, feature value)]` ordered by most informative to least informative. In our case, the feature value will always be `True`:

```
>>> nb_classifier.most_informative_features(n=5)
[('magnificent', True), ('outstanding', True), ('insulting', True),
('vulnerable', True), ('ludicrous', True)]
```

The `show_most_informative_features()` method will print out the results from `most_informative_features()` and will also include the probability of a feature pair belonging to each label:

```
>>> nb_classifier.show_most_informative_features(n=5)
Most Informative Features

    magnificent = True      pos : neg = 15.0 : 1.0
    outstanding = True      pos : neg = 13.6 : 1.0
    insulting = True        neg : pos = 13.0 : 1.0
    vulnerable = True       pos : neg = 12.3 : 1.0
    ludicrous = True        neg : pos = 11.8 : 1.0
```

The informativeness, or information gain, of each feature pair is based on the prior probability of the feature pair occurring for each label. More informative features are those that occur primarily in one label and not on the other. The less informative features are those that occur frequently with both labels. Another way to state this is that the entropy of the classifier decreases more when using a more informative feature. See `https://en.wikipedia.org/wiki/Information_gain_in_decision_trees` for more on information gain and entropy (while it specifically mentions decision trees, the same concepts are applicable to all classifiers).

Training estimator

During training, the `NaiveBayesClassifier` class constructs probability distributions for each feature using an `estimator` parameter, which defaults to `nltk.probability.ELEProbDist`. The estimator is used to calculate the probability of a `label` parameter given a specific feature. In `ELEProbDist`, **ELE** stands for **Expected Likelihood Estimate**, and the formula for calculating the label probabilities for a given feature is *(c+0.5)/(N+B/2)*. Here, *c* is the count of times a single feature occurs, *N*

is the total number of feature outcomes observed, and *B* is the number of bins or unique features in the feature set. In cases where the feature values are all `True`, *N == B*. In other cases, where the number of times a feature occurs is recorded, then *N >= B*.

You can use any `estimator` parameter you want, and there are quite a few to choose from. The only constraints are that it must inherit from `nltk.probability.ProbDistI` and its constructor must take a `bins` keyword argument. Here's an example using the `LaplaceProdDist` class, which uses the formula *(c+1)/(N+B)*:

```
>>> from nltk.probability import LaplaceProbDist
>>> nb_classifier = NaiveBayesClassifier.train(train_feats,
estimator=LaplaceProbDist)
>>> accuracy(nb_classifier, test_feats)
0.716
```

As you can see, accuracy is slightly lower, so choose your `estimator` parameter carefully.

You cannot use `nltk.probability.MLEProbDist` as the estimator, or any `ProbDistI` subclass that does not take the `bins` keyword argument. Training will fail with `TypeError: __init__() got an unexpected keyword argument 'bins'`.

Manual training

You don't have to use the `train()` class method to construct a `NaiveBayesClassifier`. You can instead create the `label_probdist` and `feature_probdist` variables manually. The `label_probdist` variable should be an instance of `ProbDistI`, and should contain the prior probabilities for each label. The `feature_probdist` variable should be a `dict` whose keys are tuples of the form `(label, feature name)` and whose values are instances of `ProbDistI` that have the probabilities for each feature value. In our case, each `ProbDistI` should have only one value, `True=1`. Here's a very simple example using a manually constructed `DictionaryProbDist` class:

```
>>> from nltk.probability import DictionaryProbDist
>>> label_probdist = DictionaryProbDist({'pos': 0.5, 'neg': 0.5})
>>> true_probdist = DictionaryProbDist({True: 1})
>>> feature_probdist = {('pos', 'yes'): true_probdist, ('neg', 'no'): 
true_probdist}
>>> classifier = NaiveBayesClassifier(label_probdist, feature_
probdist)
>>> classifier.classify({'yes': True})
'pos'
>>> classifier.classify({'no': True})
'neg'
```

See also

In the next recipes, we will train two more classifiers, `DecisionTreeClassifier` and `MaxentClassifier`. In the *Measuring precision and recall of a classifier* recipe in this chapter, we will use precision and recall instead of accuracy to evaluate the classifiers. And then in the *Calculating high information words* recipe, we will see how using only the most informative features can improve classifier performance.

The `movie_reviews` corpus is an instance of `CategorizedPlaintextCorpusReader`, which is covered in the *Creating a categorized text corpus* recipe in *Chapter 3, Creating Custom Corpora*.

Training a decision tree classifier

The `DecisionTreeClassifier` class works by creating a tree structure, where each node corresponds to a feature name and the branches correspond to the feature values. Tracing down the branches, you get to the leaves of the tree, which are the classification labels.

How to do it...

Using the same `train_feats` and `test_feats` variables we created from the `movie_reviews` corpus in the previous recipe, we can call the `DecisionTreeClassifier.train()` class method to get a trained classifier. We pass `binary=True` because all of our features are binary: either the word is present or it's not. For other classification use cases where you have multivalued features, you will want to stick to the default `binary=False`.

> In this context, `binary` refers to *feature values*, and is not to be confused with a *binary classifier*. Our word features are binary because the value is either `True` or the word is not present. If our features could take more than two values, we would have to use `binary=False`. A **binary classifier**, on the other hand, is a classifier that only chooses between two labels. In our case, we are training a binary `DecisionTreeClassifier` on binary features. But it's also possible to have a binary classifier with non-binary features, or a non-binary classifier with binary features.

The following is the code for training and evaluating the accuracy of a `DecisionTreeClassifier` class:

```
>>> from nltk.classify import DecisionTreeClassifier
>>> dt_classifier = DecisionTreeClassifier.train(train_feats,
binary=True, entropy_cutoff=0.8, depth_cutoff=5, support_cutoff=30)
>>> accuracy(dt_classifier, test_feats)
0.688
```

The `DecisionTreeClassifier` class can take much longer to train than the `NaiveBayesClassifier` class. For that reason, I have overridden the default parameters so it trains faster. These parameters will be explained later.

How it works...

The `DecisionTreeClassifier` class, like the `NaiveBayesClassifier` class, is also an instance of `ClassifierI`, as shown in the following diagram:

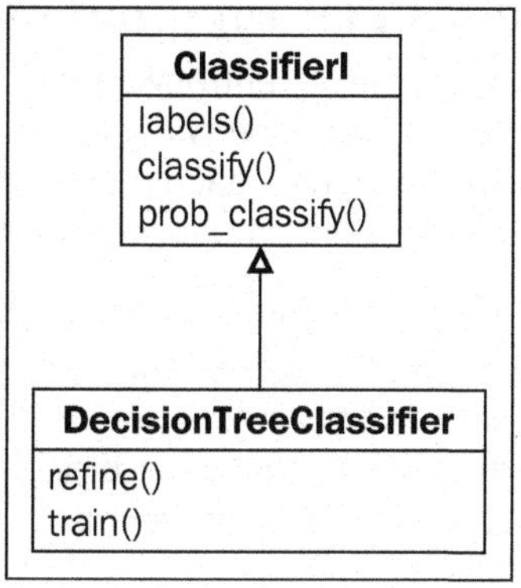

During training, the `DecisionTreeClassifier` class creates a tree where the child nodes are also instances of `DecisionTreeClassifier`. The leaf nodes contain only a single label, while the intermediate child nodes contain decision mappings for each feature. These decisions map each feature value to another `DecisionTreeClassifier`, which itself may contain decisions for another feature, or it may be a final leaf node with a classification label. The `train()` class method builds this tree from the ground up, starting with the leaf nodes. It then refines itself to minimize the number of decisions needed to get to a label by putting the most informative features at the top.

To classify, the `DecisionTreeClassifier` class looks at the given feature set and traces down the tree, using known feature names and values to make decisions. Because we are creating a binary tree, each `DecisionTreeClassifier` instance also has a default decision tree, which it uses when a known feature is not present in the feature set being classified. This is a common occurrence in text-based feature sets, and indicates that a known word was not in the text being classified. This also contributes information towards a classification decision.

There's more...

The parameters passed into `DecisionTreeClassifier.train()` can be tweaked to improve accuracy or decrease training time. Generally, if you want to improve accuracy, you must accept a longer training time and if you want to decrease the training time, the accuracy will most likely decrease as well. But be careful not to optimize for accuracy too much. A really high accuracy may indicate overfitting, which means the classifier will be excellent at classifying the training data, but not so good on data it has never seen. See `https://en.wikipedia.org/wiki/Over_fitting` for more on this concept.

Controlling uncertainty with entropy_cutoff

Entropy is the uncertainty of the outcome. As entropy approaches 1.0, uncertainty increases. Conversely, as entropy approaches 0.0, uncertainty decreases. In other words, when you have similar probabilities, the entropy will be high as each probability has a similar likelihood (or uncertainty of occurrence). But the more the probabilities differ, the lower the entropy will be.

The `entropy_cutoff` value is used during the tree refinement process. The tree refinement process is how the decision tree decides to create new branches. If the entropy of the probability distribution of label choices in the tree is greater than the `entropy_cutoff` value, then the tree is refined further by creating more branches. But if the entropy is lower than the `entropy_cutoff` value, then tree refinement is halted.

Entropy is calculated by giving `nltk.probability.entropy()` a `MLEProbDist` value created from a `FreqDist` of label counts. Here's an example showing the entropy of various `FreqDist` values. The value of `'pos'` is kept at `30`, while the value of `'neg'` is manipulated to show that when `'neg'` is close to `'pos'`, entropy increases, but when it is closer to `1`, entropy decreases:

```
>>> from nltk.probability import FreqDist, MLEProbDist, entropy
>>> fd = FreqDist({'pos': 30, 'neg': 10})
>>> entropy(MLEProbDist(fd))
0.8112781244591328
>>> fd['neg'] = 25
>>> entropy(MLEProbDist(fd))
0.9940302114769565
>>> fd['neg'] = 30
>>> entropy(MLEProbDist(fd))
1.0
>>> fd['neg'] = 1
>>> entropy(MLEProbDist(fd))
0.20559250818508304
```

What this all means is that if the label occurrence is very skewed one way or the other, the tree doesn't need to be refined because entropy/uncertainty is low. But when the entropy is greater than `entropy_cutoff`, then the tree must be refined with further decisions to reduce the uncertainty. Higher values of `entropy_cutoff` will decrease both accuracy and training time.

Controlling tree depth with depth_cutoff

The `depth_cutoff` value is also used during refinement to control the depth of the tree. The final decision tree will never be deeper than the `depth_cutoff` value. The default value is `100`, which means that classification may require up to 100 decisions before reaching a leaf node. Decreasing the `depth_cutoff` value will decrease the training time and most likely decrease the accuracy as well.

Controlling decisions with support_cutoff

The `support_cutoff` value controls how many labeled feature sets are required to refine the tree. As the `DecisionTreeClassifier` class refines itself, labeled feature sets are eliminated once they no longer provide value to the training process. When the number of labeled feature sets is less than or equal to `support_cutoff`, refinement stops, at least for that section of the tree.

Another way to look at it is that `support_cutoff` specifies the minimum number of instances that are required to make a decision about a feature. If `support_cutoff` is `20`, and you have less than 20 labeled feature sets with a given feature, then you don't have enough instances to make a good decision, and refinement around that feature must come to a stop.

See also

The previous recipe covered the creation of training and test feature sets from the `movie_reviews` corpus. In the next recipe, we will cover training a `MaxentClassifier` class, and in the *Measuring precision and recall of a classifier* recipe in this chapter, we will use precision and recall to evaluate all the classifiers.

Training a maximum entropy classifier

The third classifier we will cover is the `MaxentClassifier` class, also known as a **conditional exponential classifier** or **logistic regression classifier**. The **maximum entropy classifier** converts labeled feature sets to vectors using encoding. This encoded vector is then used to calculate weights for each feature that can then be combined to determine the most likely label for a feature set. For more details on the math behind this, see `https://en.wikipedia.org/wiki/Maximum_entropy_classifier`.

Getting ready

The `MaxentClassifier` class requires the `NumPy` package. This is because the feature encodings use `NumPy` arrays. You can find installation details at the following link:

`http://www.scipy.org/Installing_SciPy`

> The `MaxentClassifier` class algorithms can be quite memory hungry, so you may want to quit all your other programs while training a `MaxentClassifier` class, just to be safe.

How to do it...

We will use the same `train_feats` and `test_feats` variables from the `movie_reviews` corpus that we constructed before, and call the `MaxentClassifier.train()` class method. Like the `DecisionTreeClassifier` class, `MaxentClassifier.train()` has its own specific parameters that I have tweaked to speed up training. These parameters will be explained in more detail later:

```
>>> from nltk.classify import MaxentClassifier
>>> me_classifier = MaxentClassifier.train(train_feats, trace=0, max_
iter=1, min_lldelta=0.5)
>>> accuracy(me_classifier, test_feats)
0.5
```

The reason this classifier has such a low accuracy is because I set the parameters such that it is unable to learn a more accurate model. This is due to the time required to train a suitable model using the default `iis` algorithm. A better algorithm is `gis`, which can be trained like this:

```
>>> me_classifier = MaxentClassifier.train(train_feats,
algorithm='gis', trace=0, max_iter=10, min_lldelta=0.5)
>>> accuracy(me_classifier, test_feats)
0.722
```

The `gis` algorithm is a bit faster and generally more accurate than the default `iis` algorithm, and can be allowed to run for up to 10 iterations in a reasonable amount of time. Both `iis` and `gis` will be explained in more detail in the next section.

> If training is taking a long time, you can usually cut it off manually by hitting *Ctrl* + *C*. This should stop the current iteration and still return a classifier based on whatever state the model is in.

How it works...

Like the previous classifiers, `MaxentClassifier` inherits from `ClassifierI`, as shown in the following diagram:

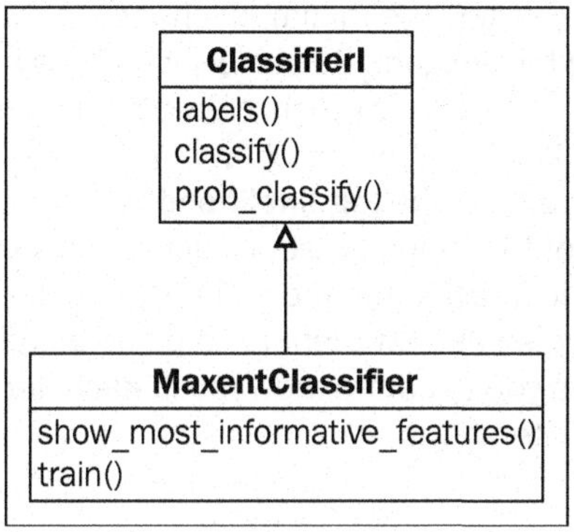

Depending on the algorithm, `MaxentClassifier.train()` calls one of the training functions in the `nltk.classify.maxent` module. The default algorithm is `iis`, and the function used is `train_maxent_classifier_with_iis()`. The other algorithm that's included is `gis`, which uses the `train_maxent_classifier_with_gis()` function. **GIS** stands for **General Iterative Scaling**, while **IIS** stands for **Improved Iterative Scaling**. The only difference between these two algorithms that really matters is that `gis` is much faster than `iis`.

If `megam` is installed and you specify the `megam` algorithm, then `train_maxent_classifier_with_megam()` is used (`megam` is covered in more detail in the next section).

> Previous versions of NLTK provided additional algorithms if SciPy was installed. These algorithms have been removed, but many other algorithms can be used in conjunction with `scikit-learn`, which we will cover in the next recipe, *Training scikit-learn classifiers*.

The basic idea behind the maximum entropy model is to build some probability distributions that fit the observed data and then choose whichever probability distribution has the highest entropy. The `gis` and `iis` algorithms do so by iteratively improving the weights used to classify features. This is where the `max_iter` and `min_lldelta` parameters come into play.

The `max_iter` variable specifies the maximum number of iterations to go through and update the weights. More iterations will generally improve accuracy, but only up to a point. Eventually, the changes from one iteration to the next will hit a plateau and further iterations are useless.

The `min_lldelta` variable specifies the minimum change in the log likelihood required to continue iteratively improving the weights. Before beginning training iterations, an instance of `nltk.classify.util.CutoffChecker` is created. When its `check()` method is called, it uses functions such as `nltk.classify.util.log_likelihood()` to decide whether the cutoff limits have been reached. The **log likelihood** is the log (using `math.log()`) of the average label probability of the training data (which is the log of the average likelihood of a label). As the log likelihood increases, the model improves. But it too will reach a plateau where further increases are so small that there is no point in continuing. Specifying the `min_lldelta` variable allows you to control how much each iteration must increase the log likelihood before stopping the iterations.

There's more...

Like the `NaiveBayesClassifier` class, you can see the most informative features by calling the `show_most_informative_features()` method:

```
>>> me_classifier.show_most_informative_features(n=4)
-0.740 worst==True and label is 'pos'

0.740 worst==True and label is 'neg'

0.715 bad==True and label is 'neg'

-0.715 bad==True and label is 'pos'
```

The numbers shown are the weights for each feature. This tells us that the word `worst` is negatively weighted towards the `pos` label, and positively weighted towards the `neg` label. In other words, if the word `worst` is found in the feature set, then there's a strong possibility that the text should be classified `neg`.

Megam algorithm

If you have installed the `megam` package, then you can use the `megam` algorithm. It's faster than the included algorithms and much more accurate, but it can also be difficult to install. Installation instructions and information can be found at the following link:

`http://www.umiacs.umd.edu/~hal/megam/`

The `nltk.classify.megam.config_megam()` function can be used to specify where the `megam` executable is found. Or, if `megam` can be found in the standard executable paths, NLTK will configure it automatically:

```
>>> me_classifier = MaxentClassifier.train(train_feats,
algorithm='megam', trace=0, max_iter=10)
[Found megam: /usr/local/bin/megam]
>>> accuracy(me_classifier, test_feats)
0.8679999999999999
```

See also

The *Bag of words feature extraction* and the *Training a Naive Bayes classifier* recipes in this chapter show how to construct the training and testing features from the `movie_reviews` corpus. The next recipe shows how to train even more accurate classifiers with `scikit-learn`. After that, we will cover how and why to evaluate a classifier using precision and recall instead of accuracy, in the *Measuring precision and recall of a classifier* recipe.

Training scikit-learn classifiers

Scikit-learn is one of the best machine learning libraries available in any programming language. It contains all sorts of machine learning algorithms for many different purposes, but they all follow the same fit/predict design pattern:

- Fit the model to the data
- Use the model to make predictions

We won't be accessing the `scikit-learn` models directly in this recipe. Instead, we'll be using NLTK's `SklearnClassifier` class, which is a wrapper class around a `scikit-learn` model to make it conform to NLTK's `ClassifierI` interface. This means that the `SklearnClassifier` class can be trained and used much like the classifiers we've used in the previous recipes in this chapter.

> I may use the terms `scikit-learn` and `sklearn` interchangeably in this recipe.

Getting ready

To use the `SklearnClassifier` class, you must have `scikit-learn` installed. Instructions are available online at `http://scikit-learn.org/stable/install.html`. If you have all the dependencies installed, such as `NumPy` and `SciPy`, you should be able to install `scikit-learn` with `pip`:

```
$ pip install scikit-learn
```

To test if everything is installed correctly, try to import the `SklearnClassifier` class:

```
>>> from nltk.classify import scikitlearn
```

If the import fails, then you are still missing `scikit-learn` and its dependencies.

How to do it...

Training an `SklearnClassifier` class has a slightly different series of steps than classifiers covered in the previous recipes of this chapter:

1. Create training features (covered in the previous recipes).
2. Choose and import an `sklearn` algorithm.
3. Construct an `SklearnClassifier` class with the chosen algorithm.
4. Train the `SklearnClassifier` class with your training features.

The main difference with NLTK classifiers is that steps 3 and 4 are usually combined. Let's put this into practice using the `MultinomialNB` classifier from `sklearn`. Refer to the earlier recipe, *Training a Naive Bayes classifier*, for details on constructing `train_feats` and `test_feats`:

```
>>> from nltk.classify.scikitlearn import SklearnClassifier
>>> from sklearn.naive_bayes import MultinomialNB
>>> sk_classifier = SklearnClassifier(MultinomialNB())
>>> sk_classifier.train(train_feats)
<SklearnClassifier(MultinomialNB(alpha=1.0, class_prior=None,
fit_prior=True))>
```

Now that we have a trained classifier, we can evaluate the accuracy:

```
>>> accuracy(sk_classifier, test_feats)
0.83
```

How it works...

The `SklearnClassifier` class is a small wrapper class whose main job is to convert NLTK feature dictionaries into `sklearn` compatible feature vectors. Here's the complete class code, minus all comments, docstrings, and most imports:

```
from sklearn.feature_extraction import DictVectorizer
from sklearn.preprocessing import LabelEncoder

class SklearnClassifier(ClassifierI):
    def __init__(self, estimator, dtype=float, sparse=True):
        self._clf = estimator
        self._encoder = LabelEncoder()
        self._vectorizer = DictVectorizer(dtype=dtype, sparse=sparse)
```

```
    def batch_classify(self, featuresets):
        X = self._vectorizer.transform(featuresets)
        classes = self._encoder.classes_
        return [classes[i] for i in self._clf.predict(X)]

    def batch_prob_classify(self, featuresets):
        X = self._vectorizer.transform(featuresets)
        y_proba_list = self._clf.predict_proba(X)
        return [self._make_probdist(y_proba) for y_proba in y_proba_
list]

    def labels(self):
        return list(self._encoder.classes_)

    def train(self, labeled_featuresets):
        X, y = list(compat.izip(*labeled_featuresets))
        X = self._vectorizer.fit_transform(X)
        y = self._encoder.fit_transform(y)
        self._clf.fit(X, y)
        return self

    def _make_probdist(self, y_proba):
        classes = self._encoder.classes_
        return DictionaryProbDist(dict((classes[i], p) for i, p in
enumerate(y_proba)))
```

The class is initialized with an estimator, which is the algorithm we pass in, such as `MultinomialNB`. It then creates a `LabelEncoder` and `DictVectorizer` object. The `LabelEncoder` object transforms label strings to numbers. For example, the `pos` class may be encoded as `1`, and the `neg` class may be encoded as `0`. The `DictVectorizer` object is for transforming the NLTK feature dictionaries into `sklearn` compatible feature vectors.

In the `train()` method, the labeled feature sets are first encoded and transformed using the `LabelEncoder` and `DictVectorizer` objects. Then, the model we gave as an estimator, such as `MultinomialNB`, is fit to the data. Because the `sk_classifier` class is created before it is trained, you might forget to train it before you try to do any classification. Luckily, this will produce an exception with the message `'DictVectorizer' object has no attribute 'vocabulary_'`. Since Python dictionaries are unordered (unlike vectors), the `DictVectorizer` object must maintain a vocabulary in order to know where in the vector a feature value belongs. This ensures that new feature dictionaries are vectorized in a manner consistent with the training features.

To classify a feature set, it is transformed to a vector and then passed to the trained model's `predict()` method. This is done in the `batch_classify()` method.

There's more...

The scikit-learn model contains many different algorithms for classification, and this recipe covers only a few. But not all the classification algorithms are compatible with the SklearnClassifier class, because it uses sparse vectors. Sparse vectors are more efficient because they only store the data they need, using a kind of data compression. However, some algorithms, such as sklearn's DecisionTreeClassifier, require dense vectors, which store every entry in the vector, even if it has no value. If you try a different algorithm with the SklearnClassifier class and get an exception, this is probably why.

Comparing Naive Bayes algorithms

As you saw earlier, the MultinomialNB algorithm got an accuracy of 83%. This is much higher than the 72.8% accuracy we got from NLTK's NaiveBayesClassifier class. The big difference between these two algorithms is that MultinomialNB can work with discrete feature values, such as word frequencies, whereas NaiveBayesClassifier class assumes a small set of feature values, such as strings or Booleans. There is another sklearn Naive Bayes algorithm, BernoulliNB, which can also work with discrete values by binarizing those values, so that the final values are 1 or 0. Our features are actually already binarized, because the feature values are True or False:

```
>>> from sklearn.naive_bayes import BernoulliNB
>>> sk_classifier = SklearnClassifier(BernoulliNB())
>>> sk_classifier.train(train_feats)
<SklearnClassifier(BernoulliNB(alpha=1.0, binarize=0.0, class_
prior=None, fit_prior=True))>
>>> accuracy(sk_classifier, test_feats)
0.812
```

Clearly, the sklearn algorithm performs better than NLTK's Naive Bayes implementation. The sklearn classifiers also have a much smaller memory footprint, and will produce much smaller pickle files on disk. Their classification speed is often slightly slower than the NaiveBayesClassifier class, but I think the accuracy and memory gains are quite worth it.

Training with logistic regression

Earlier in this chapter, we covered the maximum entropy classifier. This algorithm is also known as **logistic regression**, and scikit-learn provides a corresponding implementation.

```
>>> from sklearn.linear_model import LogisticRegression
>>> sk_classifier = SklearnClassifier(LogisticRegression())
<SklearnClassifier(LogisticRegression(C=1.0, class_weight=None,
dual=False, fit_intercept=True,
              intercept_scaling=1, penalty='l2', random_state=None,
tol=0.0001))>
>>> sk_classifier.train(train_feats)
>>> accuracy(sk_classifier, test_feats)
0.892
```

Again, we see that the sklearn algorithm has better performance than NLTK's `MaxentClassifier`, which only had 72.2% accuracy. The logistic regression algorithm also has a much faster training time than the IIS or GIS algorithms, even when those algorithms have a limited number of iterations. This can be explained by sklearn's focus on optimized numeric processing using NumPy.

Training with LinearSVC

A third family of algorithms that NLTK does not support directly is **Support Vector Machines**, or **SVM**. These algorithms have been shown to be effective at learning on high-dimensional data, such as text classification, where every word feature counts as a dimension. You can learn more about support vector machines at `https://en.wikipedia.org/wiki/Support_vector_machine`. Here are some examples of using the `sklearn` implementations:

```
>>> from sklearn.svm import SVC
>>> sk_classifier = SklearnClassifier(svm.SVC())
>>> sk_classifier.train(train_feats)
<SklearnClassifier(SVC(C=1.0, cache_size=200, class_weight=None,
coef0=0.0, degree=3, gamma=0.0,
  kernel='rbf', max_iter=-1, probability=False, random_state=None,
  shrinking=True, tol=0.001, verbose=False))>
>>> accuracy(sk_classifier, test_feats)
0.69

>>> from sklearn.svm import LinearSVC
>>> sk_classifier = SklearnClassifier(LinearSVC())
>>> sk_classifier.train(train_feats)
<SklearnClassifier(LinearSVC(C=1.0, class_weight=None, dual=True, fit_
intercept=True,
         intercept_scaling=1, loss='l2', multi_class='ovr',
penalty='l2',
         random_state=None, tol=0.0001, verbose=0))>
>>> accuracy(sk_classifier, test_feats)
0.864

>>> from sklearn.svm import NuSVC
>>> sk_classifier = SklearnClassifier(svm.NuSVC())
>>> sk_classifier.train(train_feats)
/Users/jacob/py3env/lib/python3.3/site-packages/scipy/sparse/
compressed.py:119: UserWarning: indptr array has non-integer dtype
(float64)
  % self.indptr.dtype.name)
<SklearnClassifier(NuSVC(cache_size=200, coef0=0.0, degree=3,
gamma=0.0, kernel='rbf',
   max_iter=-1, nu=0.5, probability=False, random_state=None,
   shrinking=True, tol=0.001, verbose=False))>
>>> accuracy(sk_classifier, test_feats)
0.882
```

You can see that in this case, `NuSVC` is the most accurate SVM classifier, just above `LinearSVC`, while `SVC` is much less accurate than either. These accuracy differences are a result of the different algorithm implementations and the default parameters. You can learn more about these specific implementations at the following link:

http://scikit-learn.org/stable/modules/svm.html

See also

If you are interested in exploring more aspects of machine learning with Python, the `scikit-learn` documentation is a great place to start:

http://scikit-learn.org/stable/documentation.html

Earlier in this chapter, we covered the *Training a Naive Bayes classifier* and *Training a maximum entropy classifier* recipes. We will use the `LinearSVC` and `NuSVC` classifiers again in the following recipes.

Measuring precision and recall of a classifier

In addition to accuracy, there are a number of other metrics used to evaluate classifiers. Two of the most common are **precision** and **recall**. To understand these two metrics, we must first understand **false positives** and **false negatives**. False positives happen when a classifier classifies a feature set with a label it shouldn't have gotten. False negatives happen when a classifier doesn't assign a label to a feature set that should have it. In a binary classifier, these errors happen at the same time.

Here's an example: the classifier classifies a movie review as `pos` when it should have been `neg`. This counts as a false positive for the `pos` label, and a false negative for the `neg` label. If the classifier had correctly guessed `neg`, then it would count as a **true positive** for the `neg` label, and a **true negative** for the `pos` label.

How does this apply to precision and recall? Precision is the *lack of false positives*, and recall is the *lack of false negatives*. As you will see, these two metrics are often in competition: the more precise a classifier is, the lower the recall, and vice versa.

How to do it...

Let's calculate the precision and recall of the `NaiveBayesClassifier` class we trained in the *Training a Naive Bayes classifier* recipe. The `precision_recall()` function in `classification.py` looks like this:

```
import collections
from nltk import metrics
```

```
def precision_recall(classifier, testfeats):
  refsets = collections.defaultdict(set)
  testsets = collections.defaultdict(set)

  for i, (feats, label) in enumerate(testfeats):
    refsets[label].add(i)
    observed = classifier.classify(feats)
    testsets[observed].add(i)

  precisions = {}
  recalls = {}

  for label in classifier.labels():
    precisions[label] = metrics.precision(refsets[label],
testsets[label])
    recalls[label] = metrics.recall(refsets[label], testsets[label])

  return precisions, recalls
```

This function takes two arguments:

- The trained classifier
- Labeled test features, also known as a gold standard

These are the same arguments you pass to `accuracy()`. The `precision_recall()` function returns two dictionaries; the first holds the precision for each label, and the second holds the recall for each label. Here's an example usage with `nb_classifier` and `test_feats` we created in the *Training a Naive Bayes classifier* recipe earlier:

```
>>> from classification import precision_recall
>>> nb_precisions, nb_recalls = precision_recall(nb_classifier,
test_feats)
>>> nb_precisions['pos']
0.6413612565445026
>>> nb_precisions['neg']
0.9576271186440678
>>> nb_recalls['pos']
0.98
>>> nb_recalls['neg']
0.452
```

This tells us that while the `NaiveBayesClassifier` class can correctly identify most of the `pos` feature sets (high recall), it also classifies many of the `neg` feature sets as `pos` (low precision). This behavior contributes to high precision but low recall for the `neg` label—as the `neg` label isn't given often (low recall), when it is, it's very likely to be correct (high precision). The conclusion could be that there are certain common words that are biased towards the `pos` label, but occur frequently enough in the `neg` feature sets to cause mis-classifications. To correct this behavior, we will use only the most informative words in the next recipe, *Calculating high information words*.

How it works...

To calculate precision and recall, we must build two sets for each label. The first set is known as the **reference set**, and contains all the correct values. The second set is called the **test set**, and contains the values guessed by the classifier. These two sets are compared to calculate the precision or recall for each label.

Precision is defined as the size of the intersection of both sets divided by the size of the test set. In other words, the percentage of the test set that was guessed correctly. In Python, the code is `float(len(reference.intersection(test))) / len(test)`.

Recall is the size of the intersection of both sets divided by the size of the reference set, or the percentage of the reference set that was guessed correctly. The Python code is `float(len(reference.intersection(test))) / len(reference)`.

The `precision_recall()` function in `classification.py` iterates over the labeled test features and classifies each one. We store the numeric index of the feature set (starting with `0`) in the reference set for the known training label, and also store the index in the test set for the guessed label. If the classifier guesses `pos` but the training label is `neg`, then the index is stored in the reference set for `neg` and the test set for `pos`.

> We use the numeric index because the feature sets aren't hashable, and we need a unique value for each feature set.

The `nltk.metrics` package contains functions for calculating both precision and recall, so all we really have to do is build the sets and then call the appropriate function.

There's more...

Let's try it with the `MaxentClassifier` class of GIS, which we trained in the *Training a maximum entropy classifier* recipe:

```
>>> me_precisions, me_recalls = precision_recall(me_classifier,
test_feats)
>>> me_precisions['pos']
0.6456692913385826
>>> me_precisions['neg']
0.9663865546218487
>>> me_recalls['pos']
0.984
>>> me_recalls['neg']
0.46
```

This classifier is just as biased as the `NaiveBayesClassifier` class. Chances are it would be less biased if allowed to train for more iterations and/or approach a smaller log likelihood change. Now, let's try the `SklearnClassifier` class of `NuSVC` from the previous recipe, *Training scikit-learn classifiers*:

```
>>> sk_precisions, sk_recalls = precision_recall(sk_classifier,
test_feats)
>>> sk_precisions['pos']
0.9063829787234042
>>> sk_precisions['neg']
0.8603773584905661
>>> sk_recalls['pos']
0.852
>>> sk_recalls['neg']
0.912
```

In this case, the label bias is much less significant, and the reason is that the `SklearnClassifier` class of `NuSVC` weighs its features according to its own internal model. This is also true for logistic regression and many of the other `scikit-learn` algorithms. Words that are more significant are those that occur primarily in a single label, and will get higher weights in the model. Words that are common to both labels will get lower weights, as they are less significant.

F-measure

The **F-measure** is defined as the weighted harmonic mean of precision and recall. If *p* is the precision, and *r* is the recall, the formula is:

1/(alpha/p + (1-alpha)/r)

Here, *alpha* is a weighing constant that defaults to `0.5`. You can use `nltk.metrics.f_measure()` to get the F-measure. It takes the same arguments as for the `precision()` and `recall()` functions: a reference set and a test set. It's often used instead of accuracy to measure a classifier, because if either precision or recall are very low, it will be reflected in the F-measure, but not necessarily in the accuracy. However, I find precision and recall to be much more useful metrics by themselves, as the F-measure can obscure the kinds of imbalances we saw with the `NaiveBayesClassifier` class.

See also

In the *Training a Naive Bayes classifier* recipe, we collected training and testing feature sets and trained the `NaiveBayesClassifier` class. The `MaxentClassifier` class was trained in the *Training a maximum entropy classifier* recipe, and the `SklearnClassifier` class was trained in the *Training scikit-learn classifiers* recipe. In the next recipe, we will explore eliminating the less significant words, and use only the high information words to create our feature sets.

Calculating high information words

A **high information** word is a word that is strongly biased towards a single classification label. These are the kinds of words we saw when we called the `show_most_informative_features()` method on both the `NaiveBayesClassifier` class and the `MaxentClassifier` class. Somewhat surprisingly, the top words are different for both classifiers. This discrepancy is due to how each classifier calculates the significance of each feature, and it's actually beneficial to have these different methods as they can be combined to improve accuracy, as we will see in the next recipe, *Combining classifiers with voting*.

The **low information** words are words that are common to all labels. It may be counter-intuitive, but eliminating these words from the training data can actually improve accuracy, precision, and recall. The reason this works is that using only high information words reduces the noise and confusion of a classifier's internal model. If all the words/features are highly biased one way or the other, it's much easier for the classifier to make a correct guess.

How to do it...

First, we need to calculate the high information words in the `movie_review` corpus. We can do this using the `high_information_words()` function in `featx.py`:

```
from nltk.metrics import BigramAssocMeasures
from nltk.probability import FreqDist, ConditionalFreqDist

def high_information_words(labelled_words, score_
fn=BigramAssocMeasures.chi_sq, min_score=5):
  word_fd = FreqDist()
  label_word_fd = ConditionalFreqDist()

  for label, words in labelled_words:
    for word in words:
      word_fd[word] += 1
      label_word_fd[label][word] += 1

  n_xx = label_word_fd.N()
  high_info_words = set()

  for label in label_word_fd.conditions():
    n_xi = label_word_fd[label].N()
    word_scores = collections.defaultdict(int)
```

```
    for word, n_ii in label_word_fd[label].items():
      n_ix = word_fd[word]
      score = score_fn(n_ii, (n_ix, n_xi), n_xx)
      word_scores[word] = score

    bestwords = [word for word, score in word_scores.items() if score
>= min_score]
    high_info_words |= set(bestwords)
return high_info_words
```

It takes one argument from a list of two tuples of the form `[(label, words)]` where `label` is the classification label, and `words` is a list of words that occur under that label. It returns a set of the high information words.

Once we have the high information words, we use the feature detector function `bag_of_words_in_set()`, also found in `featx.py`, which will let us filter out all low information words.

```
def bag_of_words_in_set(words, goodwords):
  return bag_of_words(set(words) & set(goodwords))
```

With this new feature detector, we can call `label_feats_from_corpus()` and get a new `train_feats` and `test_feats` function using `split_label_feats()`. These two functions were covered in the *Training a Naive Bayes classifier* recipe earlier in this chapter.

```
>>> from featx import high_information_words, bag_of_words_in_set
>>> labels = movie_reviews.categories()
>>> labeled_words = [(l, movie_reviews.words(categories=[l])) for l
in labels]
>>> high_info_words = set(high_information_words(labeled_words))
>>> feat_det = lambda words: bag_of_words_in_set(words, high_info_
words)
>>> lfeats = label_feats_from_corpus(movie_reviews, feature_
detector=feat_det)
>>> train_feats, test_feats = split_label_feats(lfeats)
```

Now that we have new training and testing feature sets, let's train and evaluate a `NaiveBayesClassifier` class:

```
>>> nb_classifier = NaiveBayesClassifier.train(train_feats)
>>> accuracy(nb_classifier, test_feats)
0.91
>>> nb_precisions, nb_recalls = precision_recall(nb_classifier,
test_feats)
>>> nb_precisions['pos']
0.8988326848249028
```

```
>>> nb_precisions['neg']
0.9218106995884774
>>> nb_recalls['pos']
0.924
>>> nb_recalls['neg']
0.896
```

While the `neg` precision and `pos` recall have both decreased somewhat, `neg` recall and `pos` precision have increased drastically. Accuracy is now a little higher than the `MaxentClassifier` class.

How it works...

The `high_information_words()` function starts by counting the frequency of every word, as well as the conditional frequency for each word within each label. This is why we need the words to be labeled, so we know how often each word occurs for each label.

Once we have the `FreqDist` and `ConditionalFreqDist` variables, we can score each word on a per-label basis.

The default `score_fn` is `nltk.metrics.BigramAssocMeasures.chi_sq()`, which calculates the chi-square score for each word using the following parameters:

- `n_ii`: This is the frequency of the word for the label
- `n_ix`: This is the total frequency of the word across all labels
- `n_xi`: This is the total frequency of all words that occurred for the label
- `n_xx`: This is the total frequency for all words in all labels

The formula is `n_xx * nltk.metrics.BigramAssocMeasures.phi_sq`. The `phi_sq()` function is the squared Pearson correlation coefficient, which you can read more about at `https://en.wikipedia.org/wiki/Pearson_product-moment_correlation_coefficient`.

The simplest way to think about these numbers is that the closer `n_ii` is to `n_ix`, the higher the score. Or, the more often a word occurs in a label, relative to its overall occurrence, the higher the score.

Once we have the scores for each word in each label, we can filter out all words whose score is below the `min_score` threshold. We keep the words that meet or exceed the threshold and return all high scoring words in each label.

> It is recommended to experiment with different values of `min_score` to see what happens. In some cases, less words may improve the metrics even more, while in other cases more words is better.

There's more...

There are a number of other scoring functions available in the `BigramAssocMeasures` class, such as `phi_sq()` for phi-square, `pmi()` for pointwise mutual information, and `jaccard()` for using the Jaccard index. They all take the same arguments, and so can be used interchangeably with `chi_sq()`. These functions are all documented in `http://www.nltk.org/_modules/nltk/metrics/association.html` with links to the source code of the formulas.

The MaxentClassifier class with high information words

Let's evaluate the `MaxentClassifier` class using the high information words feature sets:

```
>>> me_classifier = MaxentClassifier.train(train_feats,
algorithm='gis', trace=0, max_iter=10, min_lldelta=0.5)
>>> accuracy(me_classifier, test_feats)
0.912
>>> me_precisions, me_recalls = precision_recall(me_classifier,
test_feats)
>>> me_precisions['pos']
0.8992248062015504
>>> me_precisions['neg']
0.9256198347107438
>>> me_recalls['pos']
0.928
>>> me_recalls['neg']
0.896
```

This also led to significant improvements for `MaxentClassifier`. But as we'll see, not all algorithms will benefit from high information word filtering, and in some cases, accuracy will decrease.

The DecisionTreeClassifier class with high information words

Now, let's evaluate the `DecisionTreeClassifier` class:

```
>>> dt_classifier = DecisionTreeClassifier.train(train_feats,
binary=True, depth_cutoff=20, support_cutoff=20, entropy_cutoff=0.01)
>>> accuracy(dt_classifier, test_feats)
0.68600000000000005
>>> dt_precisions, dt_recalls = precision_recall(dt_classifier, test_
feats)
>>> dt_precisions['pos']
0.6741573033707865
>>> dt_precisions['neg']
```

```
0.69957081545064381
>>> dt_recalls['pos']
0.71999999999999997
>>> dt_recalls['neg']
0.65200000000000002
```

The accuracy is about the same, even with a larger `depth_cutoff`, and smaller `support_cutoff` and `entropy_cutoff`. These results lead me to believe that the `DecisionTreeClassifier` class was already putting the high information features at the top of the tree, and it will only improve if we increase the depth significantly. But that could make training time prohibitively long and risk over-fitting the tree.

The SklearnClassifier class with high information words

Let's evaluate the `LinearSVC SklearnClassifier` with the same `train_feats` function:

```
>>> sk_classifier = SklearnClassifier(LinearSVC()).train(train_feats)
>>> accuracy(sk_classifier, test_feats)
0.86
>>> sk_precisions, sk_recalls = precision_recall(sk_classifier,
test_feats)
>>> sk_precisions['pos']
0.871900826446281
>>> sk_precisions['neg']
0.8488372093023255
>>> sk_recalls['pos']
0.844
>>> sk_recalls['neg']
0.876
```

Its accuracy before was 86.4%, so we actually got a very slight decrease. In general, support vector machine and logistic regression-based algorithms will benefit less, or perhaps even be harmed, by pre-filtering the training features. This is because these algorithms are able to learn feature weights that correspond to the significance of each feature, whereas Naive Bayes algorithms do not.

See also

We started this chapter with the *Bag of words feature extraction* recipe. The `NaiveBayesClassifier` class was originally trained in the *Training a Naive Bayes classifier* recipe, and the `MaxentClassifier` class was trained in the *Training a maximum entropy classifier* recipe. Details on precision and recall can be found in the *Measuring precision and recall of a classifier* recipe. We will be using only high information words in the next two recipes, where we combine classifiers.

Combining classifiers with voting

One way to improve classification performance is to combine classifiers. The simplest way to combine multiple classifiers is to use voting, and choose whichever label gets the most votes. For this style of voting, it's best to have an odd number of classifiers so that there are no ties. This means combining at least three classifiers together. The individual classifiers should also use different algorithms; the idea is that multiple algorithms are better than one, and the combination of many can compensate for individual bias. However, combining a poorly performing classifier with better performing classifiers is generally not a good idea, because the poor performance of one classifier can bring the total accuracy down.

Getting ready

As we need to have at least three trained classifiers to combine, we are going to use a `NaiveBayesClassifier` class, a `DecisionTreeClassifier` class, and a `MaxentClassifier` class, all trained on the highest information words of the `movie_reviews` corpus. These were all trained in the previous recipe, so we will combine these three classifiers with voting.

How to do it...

In the `classification.py` module, there is a `MaxVoteClassifier` class:

```
import itertools
from nltk.classify import ClassifierI
from nltk.probability import FreqDist

class MaxVoteClassifier(ClassifierI):
  def __init__(self, *classifiers):
    self._classifiers = classifiers
    self._labels = sorted(set(itertools.chain(*[c.labels() for c
in classifiers])))

  def labels(self):
    return self._labels

  def classify(self, feats):
    counts = FreqDist()

    for classifier in self._classifiers:
      counts[classifier.classify(feats)] += 1

    return counts.max()
```

To create it, you pass in a list of classifiers that you want to combine. Once created, it works just like any other classifier. Though it may take about three times longer to classify, it should generally be at least as accurate as any individual classifier.

```
>>> from classification import MaxVoteClassifier
>>> mv_classifier = MaxVoteClassifier(nb_classifier, dt_classifier, me_classifier, sk_classifier)
>>> mv_classifier.labels()
['neg', 'pos']
>>> accuracy(mv_classifier, test_feats)
0.894
>>> mv_precisions, mv_recalls = precision_recall(mv_classifier, test_feats)
>>> mv_precisions['pos']
0.9156118143459916
>>> mv_precisions['neg']
0.8745247148288974
>>> mv_recalls['pos']
0.868
>>> mv_recalls['neg']
0.92
```

These metrics are about on-par with the best sklearn classifiers, as well as the `MaxentClassifier` and `NaiveBayesClassifier` classes with high information features. Some numbers are slightly better, some worse. It's likely that a significant improvement to the `DecisionTreeClassifier` class could produce better numbers.

How it works...

The `MaxVoteClassifier` class extends the `nltk.classify.ClassifierI` interface, which requires the implementation of at least two methods:

- The `labels()` method must return a list of possible labels. This will be the union of the `labels()` method of each classifier passed in at initialization.
- The `classify()` method takes a single feature set and returns a label. The `MaxVoteClassifier` class iterates over its classifiers and calls `classify()` on each of them, recording their label as a vote in a `FreqDist` variable. The label with the most votes is returned using `FreqDist.max()`.

The following is the inheritance diagram:

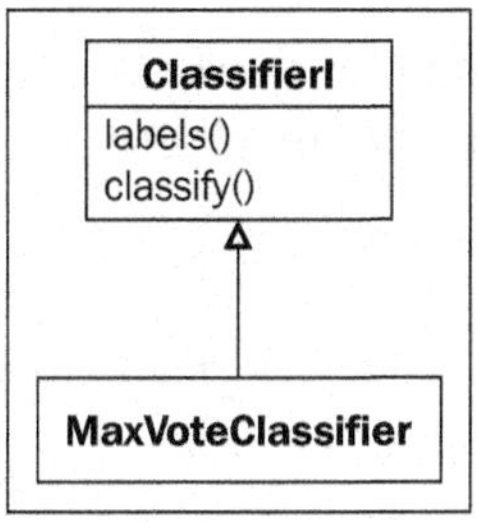

While it doesn't check for this, the `MaxVoteClassifier` class assumes that all the classifiers passed in at initialization use the same labels. Breaking this assumption may lead to odd behavior.

See also

In the previous recipe, we trained a `NaiveBayesClassifier` class, a `MaxentClassifier` class, and a `DecisionTreeClassifier` class using only the highest information words. In the next recipe, we will use the `reuters` corpus and combine many binary classifiers in order to create a multi-label classifier.

Classifying with multiple binary classifiers

So far we have focused on **binary classifiers**, which classify with one of two possible labels. The same techniques for training a binary classifier can also be used to create a multi-class classifier, which is a classifier that can classify with one of the many possible labels. But there are also cases where you need to be able to classify with multiple labels. A classifier that can return more than one label is a **multi-label classifier**.

A common technique for creating a multi-label classifier is to combine many binary classifiers, one for each label. You train each binary classifier so that it either returns a known label or returns something else to signal that the label does not apply. Then, you can run all the binary classifiers on your feature set to collect all the applicable labels.

Getting ready

The `reuters` corpus contains multi-labeled text that we can use for training and evaluation:

```
>>> from nltk.corpus import reuters
>>> len(reuters.categories())
90
```

We will train one binary classifier per label, which means we will end up with 90 binary classifiers.

How to do it...

First, we should calculate the high information words in the `reuters` corpus. This is done with the `reuters_high_info_words()` function in `featx.py`:

```
from nltk.corpus import reuters

def reuters_high_info_words(score_fn=BigramAssocMeasures.chi_sq):
  labeled_words = []

  for label in reuters.categories():
    labeled_words.append((label, reuters.words(categories=[label])))

  return high_information_words(labeled_words, score_fn=score_fn)
```

Then, we need to get training and test feature sets based on those high information words. This is done with the `reuters_train_test_feats()` function, also found in `featx.py`. It defaults to using `bag_of_words()` as its `feature_detector`, but we will be overriding this using `bag_of_words_in_set()` to use only the high information words:

```
def reuters_train_test_feats(feature_detector=bag_of_words):
  train_feats = []
  test_feats = []
  for fileid in reuters.fileids():
    if fileid.startswith('training'):
      featlist = train_feats
    else: # fileid.startswith('test')
      featlist = test_feats
    feats = feature_detector(reuters.words(fileid))
    labels = reuters.categories(fileid)
    featlist.append((feats, labels))
  return train_feats, test_feats
```

We can use these two functions to get a list of multi-labeled training and testing feature sets.

```
>>> from featx import reuters_high_info_words, reuters_train_test_
feats
>>> rwords = reuters_high_info_words()
>>> featdet = lambda words: bag_of_words_in_set(words, rwords)
>>> multi_train_feats, multi_test_feats = reuters_train_test_
feats(featdet)
```

The `multi_train_feats` and `multi_test_feats` functions are multi-labeled feature sets. That means they have a list of labels instead of a single label, and they look like `[(featureset, [label])]`, as each feature set can have one or more labels. With this training data, we can train multiple binary classifiers. The `train_binary_classifiers()` function in `classification.py` takes a training function, a list of multi-label feature sets, and a set of possible labels to return a `dict` of `label : binary classifier`:

```
def train_binary_classifiers(trainf, labelled_feats, labelset):
  pos_feats = collections.defaultdict(list)
  neg_feats = collections.defaultdict(list)
  classifiers = {}

  for feat, labels in labelled_feats:
    for label in labels:
      pos_feats[label].append(feat)

    for label in labelset - set(labels):
      neg_feats[label].append(feat)

  for label in labelset:
    postrain = [(feat, label) for feat in pos_feats[label]]
    negtrain = [(feat, '!%s' % label) for feat in neg_feats[label]]
    classifiers[label] = trainf(postrain + negtrain)

  return classifiers
```

To use this function, we need to provide a training function that takes a single argument, which is the training data. This will be a simple lambda wrapper around a sklearn logistic regression `SklearnClassifier` class.

```
>>> from classification import train_binary_classifiers
>>> trainf = lambda train_feats: SklearnClassifier(LogisticRegressi
on()).train(train_feats)
>>> labelset = set(reuters.categories())
>>> classifiers = train_binary_classifiers(trainf, multi_train_feats,
labelset)
>>> len(classifiers)
90
```

Also in `classification.py`, we can define a `MultiBinaryClassifier` class, which takes a list of labeled classifiers of the form `[(label, classifier)]`, where the `classifier` is assumed to be a binary classifier that either returns the `label` or something else if the `label` doesn't apply.

```
from nltk.classify import MultiClassifierI

class MultiBinaryClassifier(MultiClassifierI):
  def __init__(self, *label_classifiers):
    self._label_classifiers = dict(label_classifiers)
    self._labels = sorted(self._label_classifiers.keys())

  def labels(self):
    return self._labels

  def classify(self, feats):
    lbls = set()

    for label, classifier in self._label_classifiers.items():
      if classifier.classify(feats) == label:
        lbls.add(label)

    return lbls
```

Now we can construct this class using the binary classifiers we just created:

```
>>> from classification import MultiBinaryClassifier
>>> multi_classifier = MultiBinaryClassifier(*classifiers.items())
```

To evaluate this classifier, we can use precision and recall, but not accuracy. That's because the accuracy function assumes single values, and doesn't take into account partial matches. For example, if the `multi_classifier` returns three labels for a feature set, and two of them are correct but the third is not, then the `accuracy()` function would mark that as incorrect. So, instead of using accuracy, we will use **masi distance**, which measures the partial overlap between two sets using the formula from this paper:

`http://citeseerx.ist.psu.edu/viewdoc/summary?doi=10.1.1.113.3752`

If the masi distance is close to `0`, the better the match. But if the masi distance is close to `1`, there is little or no overlap. A lower average masi distance, therefore, means more accurate partial matches. The `multi_metrics()` function in `classification.py` calculates the precision and recall of each label, along with the average masi distance.

```
import collections
from nltk import metrics

def multi_metrics(multi_classifier, test_feats):
  mds = []
```

```
    refsets = collections.defaultdict(set)
    testsets = collections.defaultdict(set)

    for i, (feat, labels) in enumerate(test_feats):
      for label in labels:
        refsets[label].add(i)

      guessed = multi_classifier.classify(feat)

      for label in guessed:
        testsets[label].add(i)

      mds.append(metrics.masi_distance(set(labels), guessed))

    avg_md = sum(mds) / float(len(mds))
    precisions = {}
    recalls = {}

    for label in multi_classifier.labels():
      precisions[label] = metrics.precision(refsets[label],
  testsets[label])
      recalls[label] = metrics.recall(refsets[label], testsets[label])

    return precisions, recalls, avg_md
```

Using this with the `multi_classifier` function we just created gives us the following results:

```
>>> from classification import multi_metrics
>>> multi_precisions, multi_recalls, avg_md = multi_metrics
(multi_classifier, multi_test_feats)
>>> avg_md
0.23310715863026216
```

So our average masi distance isn't too bad. Lower is better, which means our multi-label classifier is only partially accurate. Let's take a look at a few precisions and recalls:

```
>>> multi_precisions['soybean']
0.7857142857142857
>>> multi_recalls['soybean']
0.3333333333333333
>>> len(reuters.fileids(categories=['soybean']))
111
```

```
>>> multi_precisions['sunseed']
1.0
>>> multi_recalls['sunseed']
2.0
>>> len(reuters.fileids(categories=['crude']))
16
```

In general, the labels that have more feature sets will have higher precision and recall, and those with less feature sets will have lower performance. Many of the categories have 0 values, because when there are not a lot of feature sets for a classifier to learn from, you can't expect it to perform well.

How it works...

The `reuters_high_info_words()` function is fairly simple; it constructs a list of `[(label, words)]` for each category of the `reuters` corpus, then passes it into the `high_information_words()` function to return a list of the most informative words in the `reuters` corpus.

With the resulting set of words, we create a feature detector function using the `bag_of_words_in_set()` function. This is then passed into the `reuters_train_test_feats()` function, which returns two lists, the first containing `[(feats, labels)]` for all the training files, and the second list has the same for all the test files.

Next, we train a binary classifier for each label using the `train_binary_classifiers()` function. This function constructs two lists for each label, one containing positive training feature sets and the other containing negative training feature sets. The **positive feature sets** are those feature sets that classify for the label. The **negative feature sets** for a label comes from the positive feature sets for all other labels. For example, a feature set that is positive for `zinc` and `sunseed` is a negative example for all the other 88 labels. Once we have positive and negative feature sets for each label, we can train a binary classifier for each label using the given training function.

With the resulting dictionary of binary classifiers, we create an instance of the `MultiBinaryClassifier` class. This class extends the `nltk.classify.MultiClassifierI` interface, which requires at least two functions:

- The `labels()` function must return a list of possible labels.
- The `classify()` function takes a single feature set and returns a set of labels. To create this set, we iterate over the binary classifiers, and any time a call to the `classify()` function returns its label, we add it to the set. If it returns something else, we continue.

The following is the inheritance diagram:

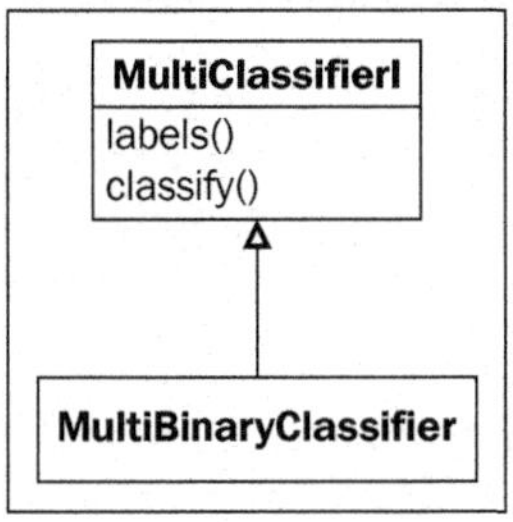

Finally, we evaluate the multi-label classifier using the `multi_metrics()` function. It is similar to the `precision_recall()` function from the *Measuring precision and recall of a classifier* recipe, but in this case, we know that the classifier is an instance of the `MultiClassifierI` interface and it can therefore return multiple labels. It also keeps track of the masi distance for each set of classification labels using the `nltk.metrics.masi_distance()` function. The `multi_metrics()` function returns three values:

- A dictionary of precisions for each label
- A dictionary of recalls for each label
- The average masi distance for each feature set

There's more...

The nature of the `reuters` corpus introduces the **class-imbalance problem**. This problem occurs when some labels have very few feature sets, and other labels have many. The binary classifiers that have few positive instances to train on, end up with far more negative instances, and are therefore strongly biased towards the negative label. There's nothing inherently wrong about this, as the bias reflects the data, but the negative instances can overwhelm the classifier to the point where it's nearly impossible to get a positive result. There are a number of advanced techniques for overcoming this problem, but they are out of the scope of this book. The paper available at `http://www.ijetae.com/files/Volume2Issue4/IJETAE_0412_07.pdf` provides a good starting reference of techniques to overcome this problem.

See also

The `SklearnClassifier` class is covered in the *Training scikit-learn classifiers* recipe in this chapter. The *Measuring precision and recall of a classifier* recipe shows how to evaluate a classifier, while the *Calculating high information words* recipe describes how to use only the best features.

Training a classifier with NLTK-Trainer

In this recipe, we'll cover the `train_classifier.py` script from NLTK-Trainer, which lets you train NLTK classifiers from the command line. NLTK-Trainer was previously introduced at the end of *Chapter 4, Part-of-speech Tagging*, and again at the end of *Chapter 5, Extracting Chunks*.

> You can find NLTK-Trainer at `https://github.com/japerk/nltk-trainer` and the online documentation at `http://nltk-trainer.readthedocs.org/`.

How to do it...

Like `train_tagger.py` and `train_chunker.py`, the only required argument for `train_classifier.py` is the name of a corpus. The corpus must have a `categories()` method, because text classification is all about learning to classify categories. Here's an example of running `train_classifier.py` on the `movie_reviews` corpus:

```
$ python train_classifier.py movie_reviews
loading movie_reviews
2 labels: ['neg', 'pos']
using bag of words feature extraction
2000 training feats, 2000 testing feats
training NaiveBayes classifier
accuracy: 0.967000
neg precision: 1.000000
neg recall: 0.934000
neg f-measure: 0.965874
pos precision: 0.938086
pos recall: 1.000000
pos f-measure: 0.968054
dumping NaiveBayesClassifier to ~/nltk_data/classifiers/movie_
reviews_NaiveBayes.pickle
```

We can use the `--no-pickle` argument to skip saving the classifier and the `--fraction` argument to limit the training set and evaluate the classifier against a test set. This example replicates what we did earlier in the *Training a Naive Bayes classifier recipe*.

```
$ python train_classifier.py movie_reviews --no-pickle --fraction 0.75
loading movie_reviews
2 labels: ['neg', 'pos']
using bag of words feature extraction
1500 training feats, 500 testing feats
training NaiveBayes classifier
accuracy: 0.726000
neg precision: 0.952000
neg recall: 0.476000
neg f-measure: 0.634667
pos precision: 0.650667
pos recall: 0.976000
pos f-measure: 0.780800
```

You can see that not only do we get accuracy, we also get the precision and recall of each class, like we covered earlier in the recipe, *Measuring precision and recall of a classifier*.

> The `PYTHONHASHSEED` environment variable has been omitted for clarity. This means that when you run `train_classifier.py`, your accuracy, precision, and recall values may vary. To get consistent values, run `train_classifier.py` like this:
>
> **`$ PYTHONHASHSEED=0 python train_classifier.py movie_reviews`**

How it works...

The `train_classifier.py` script goes through a series of steps to train a classifier:

1. Loads the categorized corpus.
2. Extracts features.
3. Trains the classifier.

Depending on the arguments used, there may be further steps, such as evaluating the classifier and/or saving the classifier.

The default feature extraction is a bag of words, which we covered in the first recipe of this chapter, *Bag of words feature extraction*. And the default classifier is the `NaiveBayesClassifier` class, which we covered earlier in the *Training a Naive Bayes classifier* recipe. You can choose a different classifier using the `--classifier` argument. Here's an example with `DecisionTreeClassifier`, replicating the same arguments we used in the *Training a decision tree classifier* recipe:

```
$ python train_classifier.py movie_reviews --no-pickle --fraction 0.75
--classifier DecisionTree --trace 0 --entropy_cutoff 0.8 --depth_cutoff 5
--support_cutoff 30 --binary
accuracy: 0.672000
neg precision: 0.683761
neg recall: 0.640000
neg f-measure: 0.661157
pos precision: 0.661654
pos recall: 0.704000
pos f-measure: 0.682171
```

There's more...

The `train_classifier.py` script supports many other arguments not shown here, all of which you can see by running the script with `--help`. Some additional arguments are presented next along with examples for other classification algorithms, followed by an introduction to another classification-related script available in `nltk-trainer`.

Saving a pickled classifier

Without the `--no-pickle` argument, `train_classifier.py` will save a pickled classifier at `~/nltk_data/classifiers/NAME.pickle`, where `NAME` is a combination of the corpus name and training algorithm. You can specify a custom filename for your classifier using the `--filename` argument like this:

```
$ python train_classifier.py movie_reviews --filename path/to/classifier.
pickle
```

Using different training instances

By default, `train_classifier.py` uses individual files as training instances. That means a single categorized file will be used as one instance. But you can instead use paragraphs or sentences as training instances. Here's an example using sentences from the `movie_reviews` corpus:

```
$ python train_classifier.py movie_reviews --no-pickle --fraction 0.75
--instances sents
loading movie_reviews
2 labels: ['neg', 'pos']
using bag of words feature extraction
50820 training feats, 16938 testing feats
training NaiveBayes classifier
accuracy: 0.638623
```

```
neg precision: 0.694942
neg recall: 0.470786
neg f-measure: 0.561313
pos precision: 0.610546
pos recall: 0.800580
pos f-measure: 0.692767
```

To use paragraphs instead of files or sentences, you can do `--instances paras`.

The most informative features

In the earlier recipe, *Training a Naive Bayes classifier*, we covered how to see the most informative features. This can also be done as an argument in `train_classifier.py`:

```
$ python train_classifier.py movie_reviews --no-pickle --fraction 0.75
--show-most-informative 5
loading movie_reviews
2 labels: ['neg', 'pos']
using bag of words feature extraction
1500 training feats, 500 testing feats
training NaiveBayes classifier
accuracy: 0.726000
neg precision: 0.952000
neg recall: 0.476000
neg f-measure: 0.634667
pos precision: 0.650667
pos recall: 0.976000
pos f-measure: 0.780800
5 most informative features

Most Informative Features
             finest = True              pos : neg    =     13.4 : 1.0
         astounding = True              pos : neg    =     11.0 : 1.0
             avoids = True              pos : neg    =     11.0 : 1.0
             inject = True              neg : pos    =     10.3 : 1.0
          strongest = True              pos : neg    =     10.3 : 1.0
```

The Maxent and LogisticRegression classifiers

In the *Training a maximum entropy classifier* recipe, we covered the `MaxentClassifier` class with the GIS algorithm. Here's how to use `train_classifier.py` to do this:

```
$ python train_classifier.py movie_reviews --no-pickle --fraction 0.75
--classifier GIS --max_iter 10 --min_lldelta 0.5
loading movie_reviews
2 labels: ['neg', 'pos']
using bag of words feature extraction
1500 training feats, 500 testing feats
training GIS classifier
  ==> Training (10 iterations)
accuracy: 0.712000
neg precision: 0.964912
neg recall: 0.440000
neg f-measure: 0.604396
pos precision: 0.637306
pos recall: 0.984000
pos f-measure: 0.773585
```

If you have `scikit-learn` installed, then you can use many different sklearn algorithms for classification. In the *Training scikit-learn classifiers* recipe, we covered the `LogisticRegression` classifier, so here's how to do it with `train_classifier.py`:

```
$ python train_classifier.py movie_reviews --no-pickle --fraction 0.75
--classifier sklearn.LogisticRegression
loading movie_reviews
2 labels: ['neg', 'pos']
using bag of words feature extraction
1500 training feats, 500 testing feats
training sklearn.LogisticRegression with {'penalty': 'l2', 'C': 1.0}
using dtype bool
training sklearn.LogisticRegression classifier
accuracy: 0.856000
neg precision: 0.847656
neg recall: 0.868000
neg f-measure: 0.857708
pos precision: 0.864754
pos recall: 0.844000
pos f-measure: 0.854251
```

SVMs

SVM classifiers were introduced in the *Training scikit-learn classifiers* recipe, and can also be used with `train_classifier.py`. Here's the parameters for `LinearSVC`:

```
$ python train_classifier.py movie_reviews --no-pickle --fraction 0.75
--classifier sklearn.LinearSVC
loading movie_reviews
2 labels: ['neg', 'pos']
using bag of words feature extraction
1500 training feats, 500 testing feats
training sklearn.LinearSVC with {'penalty': 'l2', 'loss': 'l2', 'C': 1.0}
using dtype bool
training sklearn.LinearSVC classifier
accuracy: 0.860000
neg precision: 0.851562
neg recall: 0.872000
neg f-measure: 0.861660
pos precision: 0.868852
pos recall: 0.848000
pos f-measure: 0.858300
```

And here's the parameters for `NuSVC`:

```
$ python train_classifier.py movie_reviews --no-pickle --fraction 0.75
--classifier sklearn.NuSVC
loading movie_reviews
2 labels: ['neg', 'pos']
using bag of words feature extraction
1500 training feats, 500 testing feats
training sklearn.NuSVC with {'kernel': 'rbf', 'nu': 0.5}
using dtype bool
training sklearn.NuSVC classifier
accuracy: 0.850000
neg precision: 0.827715
neg recall: 0.884000
neg f-measure: 0.854932
pos precision: 0.875536
pos recall: 0.816000
pos f-measure: 0.844720
```

Combining classifiers

In the *Combining classifiers with voting* recipe, we covered how to combine multiple classifiers into a single classifier using a max vote method. The `train_classifier.py` script can also combine classifiers, but it uses a slightly different algorithm. Instead of counting votes, it sums probabilities together to produce a final probability distribution, which is then used to classify each instance. Here's an example with three sklearn classifiers:

```
$ python train_classifier.py movie_reviews --no-pickle --fraction 0.75
--classifier sklearn.LogisticRegression sklearn.MultinomialNB sklearn.
NuSVC
loading movie_reviews
2 labels: ['neg', 'pos']
using bag of words feature extraction
1500 training feats, 500 testing feats
training sklearn.LogisticRegression with {'penalty': 'l2', 'C': 1.0}
using dtype bool
training sklearn.MultinomialNB with {'alpha': 1.0}
using dtype bool
training sklearn.NuSVC with {'kernel': 'rbf', 'nu': 0.5}
using dtype bool
training sklearn.LogisticRegression classifier
training sklearn.MultinomialNB classifier
training sklearn.NuSVC classifier
accuracy: 0.856000
neg precision: 0.839695
neg recall: 0.880000
neg f-measure: 0.859375
pos precision: 0.873950
pos recall: 0.832000
pos f-measure: 0.852459
```

High information words and bigrams

In the *Calculating high information words* recipe, we calculated the information gain of words, and then used only words with high information gain as features. The `train_classifier.py` script can do this too:

```
$ python train_classifier.py movie_reviews --no-pickle --fraction 0.75
--classifier NaiveBayes --min_score 5 --ngrams 1 2
```

```
loading movie_reviews
2 labels: ['neg', 'pos']
calculating word scores
using bag of words from known set feature extraction
9989 words meet min_score and/or max_feats
1500 training feats, 500 testing feats
training NaiveBayes classifier
accuracy: 0.860000
neg precision: 0.901786
neg recall: 0.808000
neg f-measure: 0.852321
pos precision: 0.826087
pos recall: 0.912000
pos f-measure: 0.866920
```

Cross-fold validation

Cross-fold validation is a method for evaluating a classification algorithm. The typical way to do it is using 10 folds, leaving one fold out for testing. What this means is that the training corpus is first split into 10 parts (or folds). Then, it is trained on nine of the folds and tested against the remaining fold. This is repeated nine more times, choosing a different fold to leave out for testing each time. By using a different set of training and testing examples each time, you can avoid any bias that might be present in the training set. Here's how to do this with `train_classifier.py`:

```
$ python train_classifier.py movie_reviews --classifier sklearn.
LogisticRegression --cross-fold 10
...
mean and variance across folds
------------------------------
accuracy mean: 0.870000
accuracy variance: 0.000365
neg precision mean: 0.866884
neg precision variance: 0.000795
pos precision mean: 0.873236
pos precision variance: 0.001157
neg recall mean: 0.875482
neg recall variance: 0.000706
pos recall mean: 0.864537
```

```
pos recall variance: 0.001091
neg f_measure mean: 0.870630
neg f_measure variance: 0.000290
pos f_measure mean: 0.868246
pos f_measure variance: 0.000610
```

Most of the output has been omitted for clarity. What really matters is the final evaluation, which is the mean and variance of the results across all folds.

Analyzing a classifier

Also included in NLTK-Trainer is a script called `analyze_classifier_coverage.py`. As the name implies, you can use it to see how a classifier categorizes a given corpus. It expects the name of a corpus and a path to a pickled classifier to run on the corpus. If the corpus is categorized, you can also use the `--metrics` argument to get the accuracy, precision, and recall. The script supports many of the same corpus-related arguments as `train_classifier.py`, and also has an optional `--speed` argument, so you can see how fast the classifier is. Here's an example of analyzing a pickled `NaiveBayesClassifier` class against the `movie_reviews` corpus:

```
$ python analyze_classifier_coverage.py movie_reviews --classifier
classifiers/movie_reviews_NaiveBayes.pickle --metrics --speed
loading time: 0secs
accuracy: 0.967
neg precision: 1.000000
neg recall: 0.934000
neg f-measure: 0.965874
pos precision: 0.938086
pos recall: 1.000000
pos f-measure: 0.968054
neg 934
pos 1066
average time per classify: 3secs / 2000 feats = 1.905661 ms/feat
```

See also

NLTK-Trainer was introduced at the end of *Chapter 4, Part-of-speech Tagging*, in the *Training a tagger with NLTK-Trainer* recipe. It was also covered at the end of *Chapter 5, Extracting Chunks*, in the *Training a chunker with NLTK-Trainer* recipe. All the previous recipes in the chapter explain various aspects of how the `train_classifier.py` script works.

8

Distributed Processing and Handling Large Datasets

In this chapter, we will cover the following recipes:

- Distributed tagging with execnet
- Distributed chunking with execnet
- Parallel list processing with execnet
- Storing a frequency distribution in Redis
- Storing a conditional frequency distribution in Redis
- Storing an ordered dictionary in Redis
- Distributed word scoring with Redis and execnet

Introduction

NLTK is great for in-memory, single-processor natural language processing. However, there are times when you have a lot of data to process and want to take advantage of multiple CPUs, multicore CPUs, and even multiple computers. Or, you might want to store frequencies and probabilities in a persistent, shared database so multiple processes can access it simultaneously. For the first case, we'll be using **execnet** to do parallel and distributed processing with NLTK. For the second case, you'll learn how to use the Redis data structure server/database to store frequency distributions and more.

Distributed tagging with execnet

Execnet is a distributed execution library for Python. It allows you to create gateways and channels for remote code execution. A **gateway** is a connection from the calling process to a remote environment. The remote environment can be a local subprocess or an SSH connection to a remote node. A **channel** is created from a gateway and handles communication between the channel creator and the remote code. In this way, execnet is a kind of **Message Passing Interface** (**MPI**), where the gateway creates the connection and the channel is used to send messages back and forth.

Since many NLTK processes take 100% CPU during computation, execnet is an ideal way to distribute that computation for maximum resource usage. You can create one gateway per CPU core, and it doesn't matter whether the cores are in your local computer or spread across remote machines. In many situations, you only need to have the trained objects and data on a single machine and can send the objects and data to the remote nodes as needed.

Getting ready

You'll need to install `execnet` for this to work. It should be as simple as `sudo pip install execnet` or `sudo easy_install execnet`. The current version of `execnet`, as of this writing, is 1.2. The `execnet` home page, which has API documentation and examples, is at `http://codespeak.net/execnet/`.

How to do it...

We start by importing the required modules, as well as an additional module, `remote_tag.py`, that will be explained in the *How it works...* section. We also need to import `pickle` so we can serialize (transmit) the tagger. Execnet does not natively know how to deal with complex objects such as a part-of-speech tagger, so we must dump the tagger to a string using `pickle.dumps()`. We'll use the default tagger that's used by the `nltk.tag.pos_tag()` function, but you could use any pre-trained part-of-speech tagger as long as it implements the `TaggerI` interface.

Once we have a serialized tagger, we start execnet by making a gateway with `execnet.makegateway()`. The default gateway creates a Python subprocess, and we can call the `remote_exec()` function of the `remote_tag` module to create a channel. With an open channel, we send over the serialized tagger, followed by the first tokenized sentence of the `treebank` corpus.

> You don't have to do any special serialization of simple types such as lists and tuples, since `execnet` already knows how to handle serializing the built-in types.

Now, if we call `channel.receive()`, we get back a tagged sentence that is equivalent to the first tagged sentence in the `treebank` corpus, so we know the tagging worked. We end by exiting the gateway, which closes the channel and kills the subprocess.

```
>>> import execnet, remote_tag, nltk.tag, nltk.data
>>> from nltk.corpus import treebank
>>> import pickle
>>> pickled_tagger = pickle.dumps(nltk.data.load(nltk.tag._POS_
TAGGER))
>>> gw = execnet.makegateway()
>>> channel = gw.remote_exec(remote_tag)

>>> channel.send(pickled_tagger)
>>> channel.send(treebank.sents()[0])

>>> tagged_sentence = channel.receive()
>>> tagged_sentence == treebank.tagged_sents()[0]
True
>>> gw.exit()
```

Visually, the communication process looks like this:

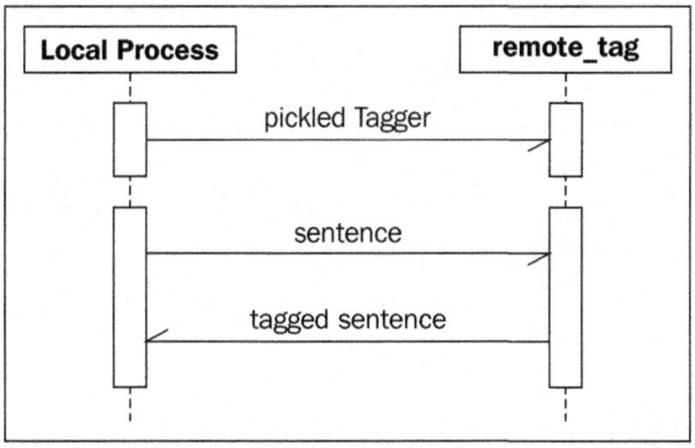

How it works...

The gateway's `remote_exec()` method takes a single argument that can be one of the following three types:

- A string of code to execute remotely
- The name of a **pure function** that will be serialized and executed remotely
- The name of a **pure module** whose source will be executed remotely

We use option three with the `remote_tag.py` module, which is defined as follows:

```
import pickle

if __name__ == '__channelexec__':
  tagger = pickle.loads(channel.receive())

  for sentence in channel:
    channel.send(tagger.tag(sentence))
```

A **pure module** is a module that is self-contained: it can only access Python modules that are available where it executes, and does not have access to any variables or states that exist wherever the gateway is initially created. Similarly, a **pure function** is a self-contained function, with no external dependencies. To detect that the module is being executed by `execnet`, you can look at the `__name__` variable. If it's equal to `'__channelexec__'`, then it is being used to create a remote channel. This is similar to doing if `__name__ == '__main__'` to check if a module is being executed on the command line.

The first thing we do is call `channel.receive()` to get the serialized tagger, which we load using `pickle.loads()`. You may notice that `channel` is not imported anywhere—that's because it is included in the global namespace of the module. Any module that `execnet` executes remotely has access to the `channel` variable in order to communicate with the `channel` creator.

Once we have the `tagger`, we iteratively `tag()` each tokenized sentence that we receive from the channel. This allows us to tag as many sentences as the sender wants to send, as iteration will not stop until the channel is closed. What we've essentially created is a compute node for part-of-speech tagging that dedicates 100% of its resources to tagging whatever sentences it receives. As long as the channel remains open, the node is available for processing.

There's more...

This is a simple example that opens a single gateway and channel. But `execnet` can do a lot more, such as opening multiple channels to increase parallel processing, as well as opening gateways to remote hosts over SSH to do distributed processing.

Creating multiple channels

We can create multiple channels, one per gateway, to make the processing more parallel. Each gateway creates a new subprocess (or remote interpreter if using an SSH gateway), and we use one channel per gateway for communication. Once we've created two channels, we can combine them using the `MultiChannel` class, which allows us to iterate over the channels and make a receive queue to receive messages from each channel.

After creating each channel and sending the tagger, we cycle through the channels to send an even number of sentences to each channel for tagging. Then, we collect all the responses from the `queue`. A call to `queue.get()` will return a 2-tuple of `(channel, message)` in case you need to know which channel the message came from.

> If you don't want to wait forever, you can also pass a `timeout` keyword argument with the maximum number of seconds you want to wait, as in `queue.get(timeout=4)`. This can be a good way to handle network errors.

Once all the tagged sentences have been collected, we can exit the gateways. Here's the code:

```
>>> import itertools
>>> gw1 = execnet.makegateway()
>>> gw2 = execnet.makegateway()
>>> ch1 = gw1.remote_exec(remote_tag)
>>> ch1.send(pickled_tagger)
>>> ch2 = gw2.remote_exec(remote_tag)
>>> ch2.send(pickled_tagger)
>>> mch = execnet.MultiChannel([ch1, ch2])
>>> queue = mch.make_receive_queue()
>>> channels = itertools.cycle(mch)
>>> for sentence in treebank.sents()[:4]:
...     channel = next(channels)
...     channel.send(sentence)
>>> tagged_sentences = []
>>> for i in range(4):
...     channel, tagged_sentence = queue.get()
...     tagged_sentences.append(tagged_sentence)
>>> len(tagged_sentences)
4
>>> gw1.exit()
>>> gw2.exit()
```

In the example code, we're only sending four sentences, but in real-life, you'd want to send thousands. A single computer can tag four sentences very quickly, but when thousands, or hundreds of thousands of sentences need to be tagged, sending sentences to multiple computers can be much faster than waiting for a single computer to do it all.

Local versus remote gateways

The default gateway spec is popen, which creates a Python subprocess on the local machine. This means `execnet.makegateway()` is equivalent to `execnet.makegateway('popen')`. If you have password-less SSH access to a remote machine, then you can create a remote gateway using `execnet.makegateway('ssh=remotehost')`, where remotehost should be the hostname of the machine. An SSH gateway spawns a new Python interpreter for executing the code remotely. As long as the code you're using for remote execution is **pure**, you only need a Python interpreter on the remote machine.

Channels work exactly the same no matter what kind of gateway is used; the only difference will be communication time. This means you can mix and match local subprocesses with remote interpreters to distribute your computations across many machines in a network. There are many more details on gateways in the API documentation at http://codespeak.net/execnet/basics.html.

See also

Part-of-speech tagging and taggers are covered in detail in *Chapter 4*, *Part-of-speech Tagging*. In the next recipe, we'll use execnet to do distributed chunk extraction.

Distributed chunking with execnet

In this recipe, we'll do chunking and tagging over an execnet gateway. This will be very similar to the tagging in the previous recipe, but we'll be sending two objects instead of one, and we will be receiving a Tree instead of a list, which requires pickling and unpickling for serialization.

Getting ready

As in the previous recipe, you must have execnet installed.

How to do it...

The setup code is very similar to the last recipe, and we'll use the same pickled tagger as well. First, we'll pickle the default chunker used by `nltk.chunk.ne_chunk()`, though any chunker would do. Next, we make a gateway for the remote_chunk module, get a channel, and send the pickled tagger and chunker over. Then, we receive a pickled Tree, which we can unpickle and inspect to see the result. Finally, we exit the gateway:

```
>>> import execnet, remote_chunk
>>> import nltk.data, nltk.tag, nltk.chunk
>>> import pickle
>>> from nltk.corpus import treebank_chunk
```

```
>>> tagger = pickle.dumps(nltk.data.load(nltk.tag._POS_TAGGER))
>>> chunker = pickle.dumps(nltk.data.load(nltk.chunk._MULTICLASS_NE_
CHUNKER))
>>> gw = execnet.makegateway()
>>> channel = gw.remote_exec(remote_chunk)
>>> channel.send(tagger)
>>> channel.send(chunker)
>>> channel.send(treebank_chunk.sents()[0])
>>> chunk_tree = pickle.loads(channel.receive())
>>> chunk_tree
Tree('S', [Tree('PERSON', [('Pierre', 'NNP')]), Tree('ORGANIZATION',
[('Vinken', 'NNP')]), (',', ','), ('61', 'CD'), ('years', 'NNS'),
('old', 'JJ'), (',', ','), ('will', 'MD'), ('join', 'VB'), ('the',
'DT'), ('board', 'NN'), ('as', 'IN'), ('a', 'DT'), ('nonexecutive',
'JJ'), ('director', 'NN'), ('Nov.', 'NNP'), ('29', 'CD'), ('.', '.')])
>>> gw.exit()
```

The communication this time is slightly different, as shown in the following diagram:

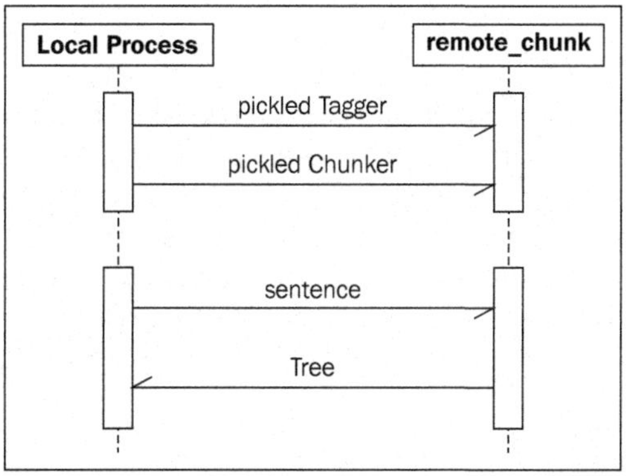

How it works...

The `remote_chunk.py` module is just a little bit more complicated than the `remote_tag.py` module from the previous recipe. In addition to receiving a pickled `tagger`, it also expects to receive a pickled `chunker` that implements the `ChunkerI` interface. Once it has both a `tagger` and a `chunker`, it expects to receive any number of tokenized sentences, which it tags and parses into a `Tree`. This `Tree` is then pickled and sent back over the channel:

```
import pickle

if __name__ == '__channelexec__':
  tagger = pickle.loads(channel.receive())
  chunker = pickle.loads(channel.receive())
```

```
for sentence in channel:
  chunk_tree = chunker.parse(tagger.tag(sent))
  channel.send(pickle.dumps(chunk_tree))
```

> The `Tree` must be pickled because it is not a simple built-in type.

There's more...

Note that the `remote_chunk` module is pure. Its only external dependency is the `pickle` module, which is part of the Python standard library. It doesn't need to import any NLTK modules in order to use the `tagger` or `chunker`, because all the necessary data is pickled and sent over the `channel`. As long as you structure your remote code like this, with no external dependencies, you only need NLTK to be installed on a single machine—the one that starts the gateway and sends the objects over the channel.

Python subprocesses

If you look at your task/system monitor (or `top` on *nix) while running the `execnet` code, you may notice a few extra Python processes. Every gateway spawns a new, self-contained, shared-nothing Python interpreter process, which is killed when you call the `exit()` method. Unlike with threads, there is no shared memory to worry about, and no global interpreter lock to slow things down. All you have are separate communicating processes. This is true whether the processes are local or remote. Instead of locking and synchronization, all you have to worry about is the order in which the messages are sent and received.

See also

The previous recipe explains `execnet` gateways and channels in detail. In the next recipe, we'll use `execnet` to process a list in parallel.

Parallel list processing with execnet

This recipe presents a pattern for using `execnet` to process a list in parallel. It's a function pattern for mapping each element in the list to a new value, using `execnet` to do the mapping in parallel.

How to do it...

First, we need to decide exactly what we want to do. In this example, we'll just double integers, but we could do any pure computation. Following is the `remote_double.py` module, which will be executed by `execnet`. It receives a 2-tuple of `(i, arg)`, assumes `arg` is a number, and sends back `(i, arg*2)`. The need for `i` will be explained in the next section.

```
if __name__ == '__channelexec__':
  for (i, arg) in channel:
    channel.send((i, arg * 2))
```

To use this module to double every element in a list, we import the `plists` module (explained in the *How it works...* section) and call `plists.map()` with the `remote_double` module, and a list of integers to double.

```
>>> import plists, remote_double
>>> plists.map(remote_double, range(10))
[0, 2, 4, 6, 8, 10, 12, 14, 16, 18]
```

Communication between channels is very simple, as shown in the following diagram:

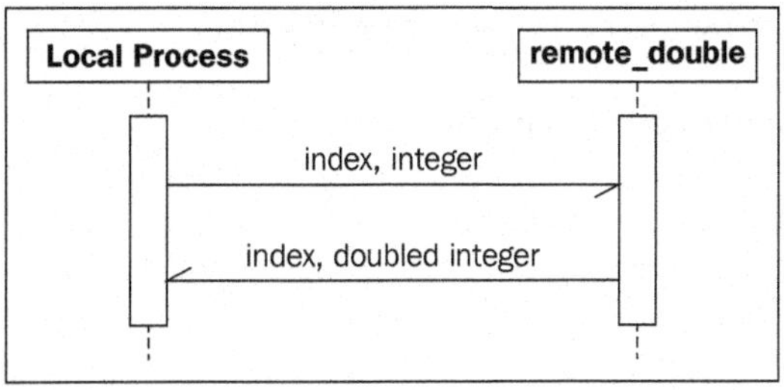

How it works...

The `map()` function is defined in `plists.py`. It takes a pure module, a list of arguments, and an optional list of 2-tuples consisting of `(spec, count)`. The default specs are `[('popen', 2)]`, which means we'll open two local gateways and channels. Once these channels are opened, we put them into an `itertools` cycle, which creates an infinite iterator that cycles back to the beginning once it hits the end.

Now we can send each argument in `args` to a `channel` for processing, and since the channels are cycled, each channel gets an almost even distribution of arguments. This is where `i` comes in—we don't know in what order we'll get the results back, so `i`, as the index of each `arg` in the list, is passed to the channel and back so we can combine the results in the original order. We then wait for the results with a `MultiChannel` receive queue and insert them into a prefilled list that's the same length as the original `args`. Once we have all the expected results, we can exit the gateways and return the results:

```
import itertools, execnet

def map(mod, args, specs=[('popen', 2)]):

  gateways = []
  channels = []


  for spec, count in specs:
    for i in range(count):
      gw = execnet.makegateway(spec)
      gateways.append(gw)
      channels.append(gw.remote_exec(mod))

  cyc = itertools.cycle(channels)

  for i, arg in enumerate(args):
    channel = next(cyc)
    channel.send((i, arg))

  mch = execnet.MultiChannel(channels)
  queue = mch.make_receive_queue()
  l = len(args)
  results = [None] * l # creates a list of length l, where every
element is None

  for i in range(l):
    channel, (i, result) = queue.get()
    results[i] = result

  for gw in gateways:
    gw.exit()

  return results
```

There's more...

You can increase the parallelization by modifying the specs, as follows:

```
>>> plists.map(remote_double, range(10), [('popen', 4)])
[0, 2, 4, 6, 8, 10, 12, 14, 16, 18]
```

However, more parallelization does not necessarily mean faster processing. It depends on the available resources, and the more gateways and channels you have open, the more overhead is required. Ideally, there should be one gateway and channel per CPU core to get maximum resource utilization.

You can use `plists.map()` with any pure module as long as it receives and sends back 2-tuples where `i` is the first element. This pattern is most useful when you have a bunch of numbers to crunch and want to process them as quickly as possible.

See also

The previous two recipes cover `execnet` features in greater detail.

Storing a frequency distribution in Redis

The `nltk.probability.FreqDist` class is used in many classes throughout NLTK for storing and managing frequency distributions. It's quite useful, but it's all in-memory, and doesn't provide a way to persist the data. A single `FreqDist` is also not accessible to multiple processes. We can change all that by building a `FreqDist` on top of Redis.

Redis is a **data structure server** that is one of the more popular *NoSQL* databases. Among other things, it provides a network-accessible database for storing dictionaries (also known as **hash maps**). Building a `FreqDist` interface to a Redis hash map will allow us to create a persistent `FreqDist` that is accessible to multiple local and remote processes at the same time.

> Most Redis operations are **atomic**, so it's even possible to have multiple processes write to the `FreqDist` concurrently.

Getting ready

For this and the subsequent recipes, we need to install both `Redis` and `redis-py`. The Redis website is at `http://redis.io/` and includes many documentation resources. To use hash maps, you should install the latest version, which at the time of this writing is 2.8.9.

The Redis Python driver, `redis-py`, can be installed using `pip install redis` or `easy_install redis`. The latest version at this time is 2.9.1. The `redis-py` home page is at `http://github.com/andymccurdy/redis-py/`.

Once both are installed and a `redis-server` process is running, you're ready to go. Let's assume `redis-server` is running on localhost on port `6379` (the default host and port).

How to do it...

The `FreqDist` class extends the standard library `collections.Counter` class, which makes a `FreqDist` a small wrapper with a few extra methods, such as `N()`. The `N()` method returns the number of sample outcomes, which is the sum of all the values in the frequency distribution.

We can create an API-compatible class on top of Redis by extending a `RedisHashMap` (which will be explained in the next section) and then implementing the `N()` method. Since the `FreqDist` only stores integers, we also override a few other methods to ensure values are always integers. This `RedisHashFreqDist` (defined in `redisprob.py`) sums all the values in the hash map for the `N()` method:

```
from rediscollections import RedisHashMap

class RedisHashFreqDist(RedisHashMap):
  def N(self):
    return int(sum(self.values()))

  def __missing__(self, key):
    return 0

  def __getitem__(self, key):
    return int(RedisHashMap.__getitem__(self, key) or 0)

  def values(self):
    return [int(v) for v in RedisHashMap.values(self)]

  def items(self):
    return [(k, int(v)) for (k, v) in RedisHashMap.items(self)]
```

We can use this class just like a `FreqDist`. To instantiate it, we must pass a `Redis` connection and the name of our hash map. The name should be a unique reference to this particular `FreqDist` so that it doesn't clash with any other keys in `Redis`.

```
>>> from redis import Redis
>>> from redisprob import RedisHashFreqDist
>>> r = Redis()
>>> rhfd = RedisHashFreqDist(r, 'test')
```

```
>>> len(rhfd)
0
>>> rhfd['foo'] += 1
>>> rhfd['foo']
1
>>> rhfd.items()
>>> len(rhfd)
1
```

> The name of the hash map and the sample keys will be encoded to replace whitespace and `&` characters with _. This is because the `Redis` protocol uses these characters for communication. It's best if the name and keys don't include whitespace to begin with.

How it works...

Most of the work is done in the `RedisHashMap` class, found in `rediscollections.py`, which extends `collections.MutableMapping` and then overrides all methods that require Redis-specific commands. Here's an outline of each method that uses a specific Redis command:

- `__len__()`: This uses the `hlen` command to get the number of elements in the hash map
- `__contains__()`: This uses the `hexists` command to check if an element exists in the hash map
- `__getitem__()`: This uses the `hget` command to get a value from the hash map
- `__setitem__()`: This uses the `hset` command to set a value in the hash map
- `__delitem__()`: This uses the `hdel` command to remove a value from the hash map
- `keys()`: This uses the `hkeys` command to get all the keys in the hash map
- `values()`: This uses the `hvals` command to get all the values in the hash map
- `items()`: This uses the `hgetall` command to get a dictionary containing all the keys and values in the hash map
- `clear()`: This uses the `delete` command to remove the entire hash map from Redis

> Extending `collections.MutableMapping` provides a number of other `dict` compatible methods based on the previous methods, such as `update()` and `setdefault()`, so we don't have to implement them ourselves.

The initialization used for `RedisHashFreqDist` is actually implemented here, and requires a `Redis` connection and a name for the hash map. The connection and name are both stored internally to use with all the subsequent commands. As mentioned earlier, whitespace is replaced by an underscore in the name and all keys for compatibility with the Redis network protocol.

```
import collections, re

white = re.compile('[\s&]+')

def encode_key(key):
  return white.sub('_', key.strip())

class RedisHashMap(collections.MutableMapping):
  def __init__(self, r, name):
    self._r = r
    self._name = encode_key(name)

  def __iter__(self):
    return self.items()

  def __len__(self):
    return self._r.hlen(self._name)

  def __contains__(self, key):
    return self._r.hexists(self._name, encode_key(key))

  def __getitem__(self, key):
    return self._r.hget(self._name, encode_key(key))

  def __setitem__(self, key, val):
    self._r.hset(self._name, encode_key(key), val)

  def __delitem__(self, key):
    self._r.hdel(self._name, encode_key(key))

  def keys(self):
    return self._r.hkeys(self._name)

  def values(self):
    return self._r.hvals(self._name)

  def items(self):
    return self._r.hgetall(self._name).items()

  def get(self, key, default=0):
    return self[key] or default

  def clear(self):
    self._r.delete(self._name)
```

There's more...

The `RedisHashMap` can be used by itself as a persistent key-value dictionary. However, while the hash map can support a large number of keys and arbitrary string values, its storage structure is more optimal for integer values and smaller numbers of keys. However, don't let that stop you from taking full advantage of Redis. It's very fast (for a network server) and does its best to efficiently encode whatever data you throw at it.

> While Redis is quite fast for a network database, it will be significantly slower than the in-memory `FreqDist`. There's no way around this, but while you sacrifice speed, you gain persistence and the ability to do concurrent processing.

See also

In the next recipe, we'll create a conditional frequency distribution based on the `Redis` frequency distribution created here.

Storing a conditional frequency distribution in Redis

The `nltk.probability.ConditionalFreqDist` class is a container for `FreqDist` instances, with one `FreqDist` per condition. It is used to count frequencies that are dependent on another condition, such as another word or a class label. We used this class in the *Calculating high information words* recipe in *Chapter 7, Text Classification*. Here, we'll create an API-compatible class on top of Redis using the `RedisHashFreqDist` from the previous recipe.

Getting ready

As in the previous recipe, you'll need to have `Redis` and `redis-py` installed with an instance of `redis-server` running.

How to do it...

We define a `RedisConditionalHashFreqDist` class in `redisprob.py` that extends `nltk.probability.ConditionalFreqDist` and overrides the `__getitem__()` method. We override `__getitem__()` so we can create an instance of `RedisHashFreqDist` instead of a `FreqDist`:

```
from nltk.probability import ConditionalFreqDist
from rediscollections import encode_key
```

```
class RedisConditionalHashFreqDist(ConditionalFreqDist):
  def __init__(self, r, name, cond_samples=None):
    self._r = r
    self._name = name
    ConditionalFreqDist.__init__(self, cond_samples)

    for key in self._r.keys(encode_key('%s:*' % name)):
      condition = key.split(':')[1]
      self[condition] # calls self.__getitem__(condition)

  def __getitem__(self, condition):
    if condition not in self._fdists:
      key = '%s:%s' % (self._name, condition)
      val = RedisHashFreqDist(self._r, key)
      super(RedisConditionalHashFreqDist, self).__setitem__(condition,
val)

    return super(RedisConditionalHashFreqDist, self).__getitem__
(condition)

  def clear(self):
    for fdist in self.values():
      fdist.clear()
```

An instance of this class can be created by passing in a `Redis` connection and a **base name**. After that, it works just like a `ConditionalFreqDist`:

```
>>> from redis import Redis
>>> from redisprob import RedisConditionalHashFreqDist
>>> r = Redis()
>>> rchfd = RedisConditionalHashFreqDist(r, 'condhash')
>>> rchfd.N()
0
>>> rchfd.conditions()
[]

>>> rchfd['cond1']['foo'] += 1
>>> rchfd.N()
1
>>> rchfd['cond1']['foo']
1
>>> rchfd.conditions()
['cond1']
>>> rchfd.clear()
```

How it works...

The RedisConditionalHashFreqDist uses name prefixes to reference RedisHashFreqDist instances. The name passed into the RedisConditionalHashFreqDist is a base name that is combined with each condition to create a unique name for each RedisHashFreqDist. For example, if the base name of the RedisConditionalHashFreqDist is 'condhash', and the condition is 'cond1', then the final name for the RedisHashFreqDist is 'condhash:cond1'. This naming pattern is used at initialization to find all the existing hash maps using the keys command. By searching for all keys matching 'condhash:*', we can identify all the existing conditions and create an instance of RedisHashFreqDist for each.

Combining strings with colons is a common naming convention for Redis keys as a way to define namespaces. In our case, each RedisConditionalHashFreqDist instance defines a single namespace of hash maps.

There's more...

RedisConditionalHashFreqDist also defines a clear() method. This is a helper method that calls clear() on all the internal RedisHashFreqDist instances. The clear() method is not defined in ConditionalFreqDist.

See also

The previous recipe covers RedisHashFreqDist in detail. Also, see the *Calculating high information words* recipe in *Chapter 7, Text Classification*, for example usage of ConditionalFreqDist.

Storing an ordered dictionary in Redis

An ordered dictionary is like a normal dict, but the keys are ordered by an ordering function. In the case of Redis, it supports ordered dictionaries whose keys are strings and whose values are floating point scores. This structure can come in handy in cases where we need to calculate the information gain (covered in the *Calculating high information words* recipe in *Chapter 7, Text Classification*), and when you want to store all the words and scores for later use.

Getting ready

Again, you'll need Redis and redis-py installed with an instance of redis-server running, as explained in the earlier recipe, *Storing a frequency distribution in Redis*.

How to do it...

The `RedisOrderedDict` class in `rediscollections.py` extends `collections.MutableMapping` to get a number of `dict` compatible methods for free. Then, it implements all the key methods that require `Redis` ordered set (also known as **Zset**) commands:

```
class RedisOrderedDict(collections.MutableMapping):
  def __init__(self, r, name):
    self._r = r
    self._name = encode_key(name)

  def __iter__(self):
    return iter(self.items())

  def __len__(self):
    return self._r.zcard(self._name)

  def __getitem__(self, key):
    return self._r.zscore(self._name, encode_key(key))

  def __setitem__(self, key, score):
    self._r.zadd(self._name, encode_key(key), score)

  def __delitem__(self, key):
    self._r.zrem(self._name, encode_key(key))

  def keys(self, start=0, end=-1):
    # we use zrevrange to get keys sorted by high value instead of by
lowest
    return self._r.zrevrange(self._name, start, end)

  def values(self, start=0, end=-1):
    return [v for (k, v) in self.items(start=start, end=end)]

  def items(self, start=0, end=-1):
    return self._r.zrevrange(self._name, start, end, withscores=True)

  def get(self, key, default=0):
    return self[key] or default

  def iteritems(self):
    return iter(self)

  def clear(self):
    self._r.delete(self._name)
```

You can create an instance of `RedisOrderedDict` by passing in a `Redis` connection and a unique name:

```
>>> from redis import Redis
>>> from rediscollections import RedisOrderedDict
>>> r = Redis()
>>> rod = RedisOrderedDict(r, 'test')
>>> rod.get('bar')
>>> len(rod)
0
>>> rod['bar'] = 5.2
>>> rod['bar']
5.2000000000000002
>>> len(rod)
1
>>> rod.items()
[(b'bar', 5.2)]
>>> rod.clear()
```

> By default, keys are returned as binary strings. If you want a plain string, you can convert the keys using `key.decode()`. You can always look up values with normal strings.

How it works...

Much of the code may look similar to the `RedisHashMap`, which is to be expected since they both extend `collections.MutableMapping`. The main difference here is that `RedisOrderedSet` orders keys by floating point values, and so it is not suited for arbitrary key-value storage like the `RedisHashMap`. Here's an outline explaining each key method and how they work with Redis:

- `__len__()`: This uses the `zcard` command to get the number of elements in the ordered set.
- `__getitem__()`: This uses the `zscore` command to get the score of a key, and returns 0 if the key does not exist.
- `__setitem__()`: This uses the `zadd` command to add a key to the ordered set with the given score, or updates the score if the key already exists.
- `__delitem__()`: This uses the `zrem` command to remove a key from the ordered set.
- `keys()`: This uses the `zrevrange` command to get all the keys in the ordered set, sorted by the highest score. It takes two optional keyword arguments, `start` and `end`, to more efficiently get a slice of the ordered keys.

- `values()`: This extracts all the scores from the `items()` method.
- `items()`: This uses the `zrevrange` command to get the scores of each key in order to return a list of 2-tuples ordered by the highest score. Like `keys()`, it takes `start` and `end` keyword arguments to efficiently get a slice.
- `clear()`: This uses the `delete` command to remove the entire ordered set from `Redis`.

> The default ordering of items in a `Redis` ordered set is low-to-high, so that the key with the lowest score comes first. This is the same as Python's default list ordering when you call `sort()` or `sorted()`, but this is not what we want when it comes to scoring. For storing scores, we expect items to be sorted from high-to-low, which is why `keys()` and `items()` use `zrevrange` instead of `zrange`.

All the Redis commands are documented at `http://redis.io/commands`.

There's more...

As mentioned previously, the `keys()` and `items()` methods take optional `start` and `end` keyword arguments to get a slice of the results. This makes `RedisOrderedDict` optimal for storing scores and getting the top *N* keys.

> The `start` and `end` keyword arguments are inclusive, so if you use `start=0` and `end=2`, you will get up to three elements.

Here's a simple example where we assign three word scores and get the top two:

```
>>> from redis import Redis
>>> from rediscollections import RedisOrderedDict
>>> r = Redis()
>>> rod = RedisOrderedDict(r, 'scores')
>>> rod['best'] = 10
>>> rod['worst'] = 0.1
>>> rod['middle'] = 5
>>> rod.keys()
[b'best', b'middle', b'worst']
>>> rod.keys(start=0, end=1)
[b'best', b'middle']
>>> rod.clear()
```

See also

The *Calculating high information words* recipe in *Chapter 7, Text Classification*, describes how to calculate information gain, which is a good case for storing word scores in a `RedisOrderedDict`. The *Storing a frequency distribution in Redis* recipe introduces `Redis` and the `RedisHashMap`.

Distributed word scoring with Redis and execnet

We can use `Redis` and `execnet` together to do distributed word scoring. In the *Calculating high information words* recipe in *Chapter 7, Text Classification*, we calculated the information gain of each word in the `movie_reviews` corpus using a `FreqDist` and `ConditionalFreqDist`. Now that we have `Redis`, we can do the same thing using a `RedisHashFreqDist` and a `RedisConditionalHashFreqDist`, and then store the scores in a `RedisOrderedDict`. We can use `execnet` to distribute the counting in order to get a better performance out of `Redis`.

Getting ready

`Redis`, `redis-py`, and `execnet` must be installed, and an instance of `redis-server` must be running on localhost.

How to do it...

We start by getting a list of `(label, words)` tuples for each label in the `movie_reviews` corpus (which only has `pos` and `neg` labels). Then, we get the `word_scores` using `score_words()` from the `dist_featx` module. The `word_scores` function is an instance of `RedisOrderedDict`, and we can see that the total number of words is 39,764. Using the `keys()` method, we can then get the top 1,000 words and inspect the top five, just to see what they are. Once we've gotten all we want from `word_scores`, we can delete the keys in `Redis`, as we no longer need the data.

```
>>> from dist_featx import score_words
>>> from nltk.corpus import movie_reviews
>>> labels = movie_reviews.categories()
>>> labelled_words = [(l, movie_reviews.words(categories=[l])) for l
in labels]
>>> word_scores = score_words(labelled_words)
>>> len(word_scores)
39767
>>> topn_words = word_scores.keys(end=1000)
```

```
>>> topn_words[0:5]
[b'bad', b',', b'and', b'?', b'movie']
>>> from redis import Redis
>>> r = Redis()
>>> [r.delete(key) for key in ['word_fd', 'label_word_fd:neg',
'label_word_fd:pos', 'word_scores']]
[1, 1, 1, 1]
```

The `score_words()` function from `dist_featx` can take a while to complete, so expect to wait a couple of minutes. The overhead of using `execnet` and `Redis` means it will take significantly longer than a nondistributed, in-memory version of the function.

How it works...

The `dist_featx.py` module contains the `score_words()` function, which does the following:

- Opens gateways and channels, sending initialization data to each channel
- Sends each `(label, words)` tuple over a channel for counting
- Sends a `done` message to each channel, waits for a `done` reply back, then closes the channels and gateways
- Calculates the score of each word based on the counts and stores in a `RedisOrderedDict`

In our case of counting words in the `movie_reviews` corpus, calling `score_words()` opens two gateways and channels, one for counting the `pos` words and the other for counting the `neg` words. The communication looks like the following diagram:

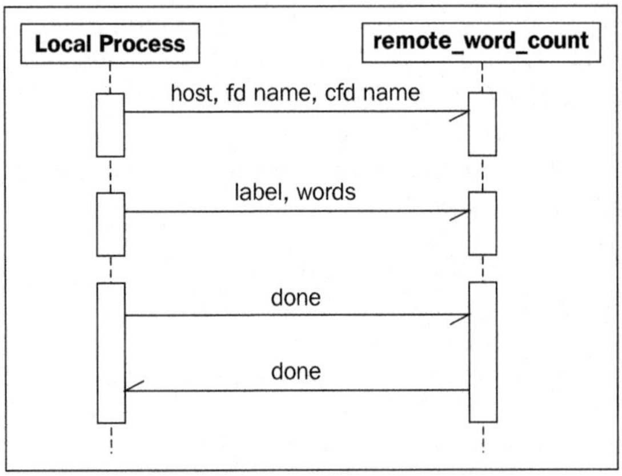

Once the counting is finished, we can score all the words and store the results. The code itself is as follows:

```
import itertools, execnet, remote_word_count
from nltk.metrics import BigramAssocMeasures
from redis import Redis
from redisprob import RedisHashFreqDist, RedisConditionalHashFreqDist
from rediscollections import RedisOrderedDict

def score_words(labelled_words, score_fn=BigramAssocMeasures.chi_sq,
host='localhost', specs=[('popen', 2)]):
  gateways = []
  channels = []

  for spec, count in specs:
    for i in range(count):
      gw = execnet.makegateway(spec)
      gateways.append(gw)
      channel = gw.remote_exec(remote_word_count)
      channel.send((host, 'word_fd', 'label_word_fd'))
      channels.append(channel)

  cyc = itertools.cycle(channels)

  for label, words in labelled_words:
    channel = next(cyc)
    channel.send((label, list(words)))

  for channel in channels:
    channel.send('done')
    assert 'done' == channel.receive()
    channel.waitclose(5)

  for gateway in gateways:
    gateway.exit()

  r = Redis(host)
  fd = RedisHashFreqDist(r, 'word_fd')
  cfd = RedisConditionalHashFreqDist(r, 'label_word_fd')
  word_scores = RedisOrderedDict(r, 'word_scores')
  n_xx = cfd.N()

  for label in cfd.conditions():
    n_xi = cfd[label].N()
```

```
    for word, n_ii in cfd[label].iteritems():
      word = word.decode()
      n_ix = fd[word]

      if n_ii and n_ix and n_xi and n_xx:
        score = score_fn(n_ii, (n_ix, n_xi), n_xx)
        word_scores[word] = score

  return word_scores
```

> Note that this scoring method will only be accurate for comparing two labels. If there are more than two labels, a different scoring method should be used, and its requirements will dictate how you store word scores.

The `remote_word_count.py` module looks like the following code:

```
from redis import Redis
from redisprob import RedisHashFreqDist, RedisConditionalHashFreqDist

if __name__ == '__channelexec__':
  host, fd_name, cfd_name = channel.receive()
  r = Redis(host)
  fd = RedisHashFreqDist(r, fd_name)
  cfd = RedisConditionalHashFreqDist(r, cfd_name)

  for data in channel:
    if data == 'done':
      channel.send('done')
      break

    label, words = data

    for word in words:
      fd[word] += 1
      cfd[label][word] += 1
```

You'll notice that this is not a pure module, as it requires being able to import both `redis` and `redisprob`. The reason is that instances of `RedisHashFreqDist` and `RedisConditionalHashFreqDist` cannot be pickled and sent over the `channel`. Instead, we send the hostname and key names over the channel so we can create the instances in the remote module. Once we have the instances, there are two kinds of data we can receive over the `channel`:

- A `done` message, which signals that there is no more data coming in over the channel. We reply back with another `done` message, then exit the loop to close the channel.
- A 2-tuple of `(label, words)`, which we then iterate over to increment counts in both the `RedisHashFreqDist` and `RedisConditionalHashFreqDist`.

There's more...

In this particular case, it would be faster to compute the scores without using `Redis` or `execnet`. However, by using `Redis`, we can store the scores persistently for later examination and usage. Being able to inspect all the word counts and scores manually is a great way to learn about your data. We can also tweak feature extraction without having to re-compute the scores. For example, you could use `featx.bag_of_words_in_set()` (found in *Chapter 7, Text Classification*) with the top `N` words from the `RedisOrderedDict`, where `N` could be 1,000, 2,000, or whatever number you want. If our data size is much greater, the benefits of `execnet` will be much more apparent. Horizontal scalability using `execnet` or some other method to distribute computations across many nodes becomes more valuable as the size of the data you need to process increases. This method of word scoring is much slower than if we weren't using `Redis`, but the benefit is that the numbers are stored persistently.

See also

The *Calculating high information words* recipe in *Chapter 7, Text Classification*, introduces information gain scoring of words for feature extraction and classification. The first three recipes of this chapter show how to use `execnet`, while the next three recipes describe `RedisHashFreqDist`, `RedisConditionalHashFreqDist`, and `RedisOrderedDict`, respectively.

9
Parsing Specific Data Types

In this chapter, we will cover the following recipes:

- Parsing dates and times with dateutil
- Timezone lookup and conversion
- Extracting URLs from HTML with lxml
- Cleaning and stripping HTML
- Converting HTML entities with BeautifulSoup
- Detecting and converting character encodings

Introduction

This chapter covers parsing specific kinds of data, focusing primarily on dates, times, and HTML. Luckily, there are a number of useful libraries to accomplish this, so we don't have to delve into tricky and overly complicated regular expressions. These libraries can be great complements to NLTK:

- `dateutil` provides datetime parsing and timezone conversion
- `lxml` and `BeautifulSoup` can parse, clean, and convert HTML
- `charade` and `UnicodeDammit` can detect and convert text character encoding

These libraries can be useful for preprocessing text before passing it to an NLTK object, or postprocessing text that has been processed and extracted using NLTK. Coming up is an example that ties many of these tools together.

Let's say you need to parse a blog article about a restaurant. You can use `lxml` or `BeautifulSoup` to extract the article text, outbound links, and the date and time when the article was written. The date and time can then be parsed to a Python `datetime` object with `dateutil`. Once you have the article text, you can use `charade` to ensure it's `utf-8` before cleaning out the HTML and running it through NLTK-based part-of-speech tagging, chunk extraction, and/or text classification to create additional metadata about the article. Real-world text processing often requires more than just NLTK-based natural language processing, and the functionality covered in this chapter can help with those additional requirements.

Parsing dates and times with dateutil

If you need to parse dates and times in Python, there is no better library than `dateutil`. The `parser` module can parse `datetime` strings in many more formats than can be shown here, while the `tz` module provides everything you need for looking up timezones. When combined, these modules make it quite easy to parse strings into timezone-aware `datetime` objects.

Getting ready

You can install `dateutil` using `pip` or `easy_install`, that is, `sudo pip install dateutil==2.0` or `sudo easy_install dateutil==2.0`. You need the 2.0 version for Python 3 compatibility. The complete documentation can be found at `http://labix.org/python-dateutil`.

How to do it...

Let's dive into a few parsing examples:

```
>>> from dateutil import parser
>>> parser.parse('Thu Sep 25 10:36:28 2010')
datetime.datetime(2010, 9, 25, 10, 36, 28)
>>> parser.parse('Thursday, 25. September 2010 10:36AM')
datetime.datetime(2010, 9, 25, 10, 36)
>>> parser.parse('9/25/2010 10:36:28')
datetime.datetime(2010, 9, 25, 10, 36, 28)
>>> parser.parse('9/25/2010')
datetime.datetime(2010, 9, 25, 0, 0)
>>> parser.parse('2010-09-25T10:36:28Z')
datetime.datetime(2010, 9, 25, 10, 36, 28, tzinfo=tzutc())
```

As you can see, all it takes is importing the parser module and calling the `parse()` function with a datetime string. The parser will do its best to return a sensible `datetime` object, but if it cannot parse the string, it will raise a `ValueError`.

How it works...

The parser does not use regular expressions. Instead, it looks for recognizable tokens and does its best to guess what those tokens refer to. The order of these tokens matters; for example, some cultures use a date format that looks like *Month/Day/Year* (the default order), while others use a *Day/Month/Year* format. To deal with this, the `parse()` function takes an optional keyword argument, `dayfirst`, which defaults to `False`. If you set it to `True`, it can correctly parse dates in the latter format.

```
>>> parser.parse('25/9/2010', dayfirst=True)
datetime.datetime(2010, 9, 25, 0, 0)
```

Another ordering issue can occur with two-digit years. For example, `'10-9-25'` is ambiguous. Since `dateutil` defaults to the *Month-Day-Year* format, `'10-9-25'` is parsed to the year 2025. But if you pass `yearfirst=True` into `parse()`, it will be parsed to the year 2010:

```
>>> parser.parse('10-9-25')
datetime.datetime(2025, 10, 9, 0, 0)
>>> parser.parse('10-9-25', yearfirst=True)
datetime.datetime(2010, 9, 25, 0, 0)
```

There's more...

The `dateutil` parser can also do fuzzy parsing, which allows it to ignore extraneous characters in a datetime string. With the default value of `False`, `parse()` will raise a `ValueError` when it encounters unknown tokens. But if `fuzzy=True`, then a `datetime` object can usually be returned:

```
>>> try:
...     parser.parse('9/25/2010 at about 10:36AM')
... except ValueError:
...     'cannot parse'
'cannot parse'
>>> parser.parse('9/25/2010 at about 10:36AM', fuzzy=True)
datetime.datetime(2010, 9, 25, 10, 36)
```

See also

In the next recipe, we'll use the `tz` module of `dateutil` to do timezone lookup and conversion.

Timezone lookup and conversion

Most datetime objects returned from the dateutil parser are naïve, meaning they don't have an explicit tzinfo, which specifies the timezone and UTC offset. In the previous recipe, only one of the examples had a tzinfo, and that's because it's in the standard ISO format for UTC datetime strings. UTC is the coordinated universal time, and is basically the same as GMT. **ISO** is the **International Standards Organization**, which among other things, specifies standard datetime formatting.

Python datetime objects can either be naïve or aware. If a datetime object has a tzinfo, then it is aware. Otherwise, the datetime is naïve. To make a naïve datetime object timezone aware, you must give it an explicit tzinfo. However, the Python datetime library only defines an abstract baseclass for tzinfo, and leaves it up to others to actually implement tzinfo creation. This is where the tz module of dateutil comes in—it provides everything you need to look up timezones from your OS timezone data.

Getting ready

dateutil should be installed using pip or easy_install. You should also make sure your operating system has timezone data. On Linux, this is usually found in /usr/share/zoneinfo, and the Ubuntu package is called tzdata. If you have a number of files and directories in /usr/share/zoneinfo, such as America/ and Europe/, then you should be ready to proceed. The upcoming examples show directory paths for Ubuntu Linux.

How to do it...

Let's start by getting a UTC tzinfo object. This can be done by calling tz.tzutc(), and you can check that the offset is 0 by calling the utcoffset() method with a UTC datetime object:

```
>>> from dateutil import tz
>>> tz.tzutc()
tzutc()
>>> import datetime
>>> tz.tzutc().utcoffset(datetime.datetime.utcnow())
datetime.timedelta(0)
```

To get `tzinfo` objects for other timezones, you can pass in a timezone file path to the `gettz()` function:

```
>>> tz.gettz('US/Pacific')
tzfile('/usr/share/zoneinfo/US/Pacific')
>>> tz.gettz('US/Pacific').utcoffset(datetime.datetime.utcnow())
datetime.timedelta(-1, 61200)
>>> tz.gettz('Europe/Paris')
tzfile('/usr/share/zoneinfo/Europe/Paris')
>>> tz.gettz('Europe/Paris').utcoffset(datetime.datetime.utcnow())
datetime.timedelta(0, 7200)
```

You can see that the UTC offsets are `timedelta` objects, where the first number is days and the second number is seconds.

> If you're storing datetimes in a database, it's a good idea to store them all in UTC to eliminate any timezone ambiguity. Even if the database can recognize timezones, it's still good practice.

To convert a non-UTC `datetime` object to UTC, it must be made timezone aware. If you try to convert a naïve `datetime` to UTC, you'll get a `ValueError` exception. To make a naïve `datetime` timezone aware, you simply call the `replace()` method with the correct `tzinfo`. Once a `datetime` object has a `tzinfo`, then UTC conversion can be performed by calling the `astimezone()` method with `tz.tzutc()`.

```
>>> pst = tz.gettz('US/Pacific')
Y
>>> dt = datetime.datetime(2010, 9, 25, 10, 36)
>>> dt.tzinfo
>>> dt.astimezone(tz.tzutc())
Traceback (most recent call last):
  File "/usr/lib/python2.6/doctest.py", line 1248, in __run
  compileflags, 1) in test.globs
  File "<doctest __main__[22]>", line 1, in <module>
  dt.astimezone(tz.tzutc())
ValueError: astimezone() cannot be applied to a naive datetime
>>> dt.replace(tzinfo=pst)
datetime.datetime(2010, 9, 25, 10, 36, tzinfo=tzfile('/usr/share/
zoneinfo/US/Pacific'))
>>> dt.replace(tzinfo=pst).astimezone(tz.tzutc())
datetime.datetime(2010, 9, 25, 17, 36, tzinfo=tzutc())
```

> The `tzfile` paths vary across operating systems, so your `tzfile` paths may differ from the examples. There is no cause for concern, unless you are getting different `datetime` values.

How it works...

The `tzutc` and `tzfile` objects are both subclasses of `tzinfo`. As such, they know the correct UTC offset for timezone conversion (which is `0` for `tzutc`). A `tzfile` object knows how to read your operating system's `zoneinfo` files to get the necessary offset data. The `replace()` method of a `datetime` object does what the name implies—it replaces attributes. Once a `datetime` has a `tzinfo`, the `astimezone()` method will be able to convert the time using the UTC offsets, and then replace the current `tzinfo` with the new `tzinfo`.

> Note that both `replace()` and `astimezone()` return new `datetime` objects. They do not modify the current object.

There's more...

You can pass a `tzinfos` keyword argument into the `dateutil` parser to detect the otherwise unrecognized timezones:

```
>>> parser.parse('Wednesday, Aug 4, 2010 at 6:30 p.m. (CDT)',
fuzzy=True)
datetime.datetime(2010, 8, 4, 18, 30)
>>> tzinfos = {'CDT': tz.gettz('US/Central')}
>>> parser.parse('Wednesday, Aug 4, 2010 at 6:30 p.m. (CDT)',
fuzzy=True, tzinfos=tzinfos)
datetime.datetime(2010, 8, 4, 18, 30, tzinfo=tzfile('/usr/share/
zoneinfo/US/Central'))
```

In the first instance, we get a naïve `datetime` since the timezone is not recognized. But when we pass in the `tzinfos` mapping, we get a timezone-aware `datetime`.

Local timezone

If you want to look up your local timezone, you can call `tz.tzlocal()`, which will use whatever your operating system thinks is the local timezone. In Ubuntu Linux, this is usually specified in the `/etc/timezone` file.

Custom offsets

You can create your own `tzinfo` object with a custom UTC offset using the `tzoffset` object. A custom offset of 1 hour could be created as follows:

```
>>> tz.tzoffset('custom', 3600)
tzoffset('custom', 3600)
```

You must provide a name as the first argument and the offset time in seconds as the second argument.

See also

The previous recipe, *Parsing dates and times with dateutil*, covers parsing `datetime` strings with `dateutil.parser`.

Extracting URLs from HTML with lxml

A common task when parsing HTML is extracting links. This is one of the core functions of every general web crawler. There are a number of Python libraries for parsing HTML, and `lxml` is one of the best. As you'll see, it comes with some great helper functions geared specifically towards link extraction.

Getting ready

`lxml` is a Python binding for the C libraries `libxml2` and `libxslt`. This makes it a very fast XML and HTML parsing library, while still being Pythonic. But that also means you need to install the C libraries for it to work. Installation instructions are available at `http://lxml.de/installation.html`. But if you're running Ubuntu Linux, installation is as easy as `sudo apt-get install python-lxml`. You can also try doing `pip install lxml`. The latest version as of this writing is 3.3.5.

How to do it...

`lxml` comes with an `html` module designed specifically for parsing HTML. Using the `fromstring()` function, we can parse an HTML string and get a list of all the links. The `iterlinks()` method generates 4-tuples of the form `(element, attr, link, pos)`:

- `element`: This is the parsed node of the anchor tag from which the `link` is extracted. If you're just interested in the `link`, you can ignore this.
- `attr`: This is the attribute the `link` came from, which is usually `'href'`.
- `link`: This is the actual URL extracted from the anchor tag.
- `pos`: This is the numeric index of the anchor tag in the document. The first tag has a `pos` of `0`, the second has a `pos` of `1`, and so on.

Here's some code to demonstrate:

```
>>> from lxml import html
>>> doc = html.fromstring('Hello <a href="/world">world</a>')
>>> links = list(doc.iterlinks())
>>> len(links)
1
```

```
>>> (el, attr, link, pos) = links[0]
>>> attr
'href'
>>> link
'/world'
>>> pos
0
```

How it works...

`lxml` parses the HTML into an `ElementTree`. This is a tree structure of parent nodes and child nodes, where each node represents an HTML tag and contains all the corresponding attributes of that tag. Once the tree is created, it can be iterated on to find elements, such as the **a** or **anchor** tag. The core tree handling code is in the `lxml.etree` module, while the `lxml.html` module contains only HTML-specific functions for creating and iterating a tree. For complete documentation, see the `lxml` tutorial at `http://lxml.de/tutorial.html`.

There's more...

You'll notice that the link mentioned earlier is **relative**, meaning it's not an absolute URL. We can make it **absolute** by calling the `make_links_absolute()` method with a base URL before extracting the links:

```
>>> doc.make_links_absolute('http://hello')
>>> abslinks = list(doc.iterlinks())
>>> (el, attr, link, pos) = abslinks[0]
>>> link
'http://hello/world'
```

Extracting links directly

If you don't want to do anything other than extract links, you can call the `iterlinks()` function with an HTML string:

```
>>> links = list(html.iterlinks('Hello <a href="/world">world</a>'))
>>> links[0][2]
'/world'
```

Parsing HTML from URLs or files

Instead of parsing an HTML string using the `fromstring()` function, you can call the `parse()` function with a URL or filename; for example, `html.parse('http://my/url')` or `html.parse('/path/to/file')`. The result will be the same as if you loaded the URL or file into a string yourself and then called `fromstring()`.

Extracting links with XPaths

Instead of using the `iterlinks()` method, you can also get links using the `xpath()` method, which is a general way to extract whatever you want from HTML or XML parse trees:

```
>>> doc.xpath('//a/@href')[0]
'http://hello/world'
```

For more on XPath syntax, see `http://www.w3schools.com/XPath/xpath_syntax.asp`.

See also

In the next recipe, we'll cover cleaning and stripping HTML.

Cleaning and stripping HTML

Cleaning up text is one of the unfortunate but entirely necessary aspects of text processing. When it comes to parsing HTML, you probably don't want to deal with any embedded JavaScript or CSS, and are only interested in the tags and text.

Getting ready

You'll need to install `lxml`. See the previous recipe or `http://lxml.de/installation.html` for installation instructions.

How to do it...

We can use the `clean_html()` function in the `lxml.html.clean` module to remove unnecessary HTML tags and embedded JavaScript from an HTML string:

```
>>> import lxml.html.clean
>>> lxml.html.clean.clean_html('<html><head></head><body
onload=loadfunc()>my text</body></html>')
'<div><body>my text</body></div>'
```

The result is much cleaner and easier to deal with.

How it works...

The lxml.html.clean_html() function parses the HTML string into a tree and then iterates over and removes all nodes that should be removed. It also cleans nodes of unnecessary attributes (such as embedded JavaScript) using regular expression matching and substitution.

There's more...

The lxml.html.clean module defines a default Cleaner class that's used when you call clean_html(). You can customize the behavior of this class by creating your own instance and calling its clean_html() method. For more details on this class, see http://lxml.de/lxmlhtml.html#cleaning-up-html.

See also

The lxml.html module was introduced in the previous recipe for parsing HTML and extracting links. In the next recipe, we'll cover unescaping HTML entities.

Converting HTML entities with BeautifulSoup

HTML entities are strings such as "&" or "<". These are encodings of normal ASCII characters that have special uses in HTML. For example, "<" is the entity for "<", but you can't just have "<" within HTML tags because it is the beginning character for an HTML tag, hence the need to escape it and define the "<" entity. "&" is the entity code for "&", which as we've just seen is the beginning character for an entity code. If you need to process the text within an HTML document, then you'll want to convert these entities back to their normal characters so you can recognize them and handle them appropriately.

Getting ready

You'll need to install BeautifulSoup, which you should be able to do with sudo pip install beautifulsoup4 or sudo easy_install beautifulsoup4. You can read more about BeautifulSoup at http://www.crummy.com/software/BeautifulSoup/.

How to do it...

`BeautifulSoup` is an HTML parser library that can also be used for entity conversion. It's quite simple: create an instance of `BeautifulSoup` given a string containing HTML entities, then get the `string` attribute:

```
>>> from bs4 import BeautifulSoup
>>> BeautifulSoup('&lt;').string
'<'
>>> BeautifulSoup('&amp;').string
'&'
```

However, the reverse is not true. If you try to do `BeautifulSoup('<')`, you will get a `None` result because that is not valid in HTML.

How it works...

To convert the HTML entities, `BeautifulSoup` looks for tokens that look like an entity and replaces them with their corresponding value in the `htmlentitydefs.name2codepoint` dictionary from the Python standard library. It can do this if the entity token is within an HTML tag, or when it's in a normal string.

There's more...

`BeautifulSoup` is an excellent HTML and XML parser in its own right, and can be a great alternative to `lxml`. It's particularly good at handling malformed HTML. You can read more about how to use it at `http://www.crummy.com/software/BeautifulSoup/bs4/doc/`.

Extracting URLs with BeautifulSoup

Here's an example of using `BeautifulSoup` to extract URLs, like we did in the *Extracting URLs from HTML with lxml* recipe. You first create the `soup` with an HTML string, call the `findAll()` method with `'a'` to get all anchor tags, and pull out the `'href'` attribute to get the URLs:

```
>>> from bs4 import BeautifulSoup
>>> soup = BeautifulSoup('Hello <a href="/world">world</a>')
>>> [a['href'] for a in soup.findAll('a')]
['/world']
```

See also

In the *Extracting URLs from HTML with lxml* recipe, we covered how to use `lxml` to extract URLs from an HTML string, and we also covered the *Cleaning and stripping HTML* recipe after that.

Detecting and converting character encodings

A common occurrence with text processing is finding text that has nonstandard character encoding. Ideally, all text would be ASCII or utf-8, but that's just not the reality. In cases when you have non-ASCII or non-utf-8 text and you don't know what the character encoding is, you'll need to detect it and convert the text to a standard encoding before doing further processing.

Getting ready

You'll need to install the `charade` module using `sudo pip install charade` or `sudo easy_install charade`. You can learn more about `charade` at `https://pypi.python.org/pypi/charade`.

How to do it...

Encoding detection and conversion functions are provided in `encoding.py`. These are simple wrapper functions around the `charade` module. To detect the encoding of a string, call `encoding.detect(string)`. You'll get back a `dict` containing two attributes: `confidence` and `encoding`. The `confidence` attribute is a probability of how confident `charade` is that the value for `encoding` is correct.

```
# -*- coding: utf-8 -*-
import charade

def detect(s):
  try:
    if isinstance(s, str):
      return charade.detect(s.encode())
    else:
      return charade.detect(s)
  except UnicodeDecodeError:
    return charade.detect(s.encode('utf-8'))

def convert(s):
  if isinstance(s, str):
    s = s.encode()

  encoding = detect(s)['encoding']

  if encoding == 'utf-8':
    return s.decode()
  else:
    return s.decode(encoding)
```

And here's some example code using `detect()` to determine character encoding:

```
>>> import encoding
>>> encoding.detect('ascii')
{'confidence': 1.0, 'encoding': 'ascii'}
>>> encoding.detect('abcdé')
{'confidence': 0.505, 'encoding': 'utf-8'}
>>> encoding.detect(bytes('\222\222\223\225', 'latin-1'))
{'confidence': 0.5, 'encoding': 'windows-1252'}
```

To convert a string to a standard `unicode` encoding, call `encoding.convert()`. This will decode the string from its original encoding and then re-encode it as utf-8.

```
>>> encoding.convert('ascii')
'ascii'
>>> encoding.convert('abcdé')
'abcdé'
>>> encoding.convert((bytes('\222\222\223\225', 'latin-1'))
'\u2019\u2019\u201c\u2022'
```

How it works...

The `detect()` function is a wrapper around `charade.detect()` that can encode strings and handle `UnicodeDecodeError` exceptions. The `charade.detect()` method expects a `bytes` object, not a string, so in these cases, the string is encoded before trying to detect the encoding.

The `convert()` function first calls `detect()` to get the encoding and, then returns a decoded string.

There's more...

The comment at the top of the module, `# -*- coding: utf-8 -*-`, is a hint to the Python interpreter that tells which encoding to use for the strings in the code. This is helpful for when you have non-ASCII strings in your source code, and is documented in detail at `http://www.python.org/dev/peps/pep-0263/`.

Converting to ASCII

If you want pure ASCII text, with non-ASCII characters converted to ASCII equivalents or dropped if there is no equivalent character, then you can use the `unicodedata.normalize()` function:

```
>>> import unicodedata
>>> unicodedata.normalize('NFKD', 'abcd\xe9').encode('ascii',
'ignore')
b'abcde'
```

Specifying `'NFKD'` as the first argument ensures that the non-ASCII characters are replaced with their equivalent ASCII versions, and the final call to `encode()` with `'ignore'` as the second argument will remove any extraneous unicode characters. This returns a `bytes` object, which you can call `decode()` on to get a string.

UnicodeDammit conversion

The `BeautifulSoup` library contains a helper class called `UnicodeDammit`, which can do automatic conversion to unicode. Its usage is very simple:

```
>>> from bs4 import UnicodeDammit
>>> UnicodeDammit('abcd\xe9').unicode_markup
'abcdé'
```

Installing `BeautifulSoup` is covered in the previous recipe, *Converting HTML entities with BeautifulSoup*.

See also

Encoding detection and conversion is a recommended first step before doing HTML processing with `lxml` or `BeautifulSoup`, covered in the *Extracting URLs from HTML with lxml* and *Converting HTML entities with BeautifulSoup* recipes.

10
Penn Treebank Part-of-speech Tags

The following is a table of all the part-of-speech tags that occur in the treebank corpus distributed with NLTK. The tags and counts shown here were acquired using the following code:

```
>>> from nltk.probability import FreqDist
>>> from nltk.corpus import treebank
>>> fd = FreqDist()
>>> for word, tag in treebank.tagged_words():
...     fd[tag] += 1
>>> fd.items()
```

The FreqDist fd contains all the counts shown here for every tag in the treebank corpus. You can inspect each tag count individually, by doing fd[tag], for example, fd['DT']. Punctuation tags are also shown, along with special tags such as -NONE-, which signifies that the part-of-speech tag is unknown. Descriptions of most of the tags can be found at the following link:
http://www.ling.upenn.edu/courses/Fall_2003/ling001/penn_treebank_pos.html

Part-of-speech tag	**Frequency of occurrence**
#	16
$	724
''	694
,	4886
-LRB-	120
-NONE-	6592
-RRB-	126
.	384

Part-of-speech tag	Frequency of occurrence
:	563
''	712
CC	2265
CD	3546
DT	8165
EX	88
FW	4
IN	9857
JJ	5834
JJR	381
JJS	182
LS	13
MD	927
NN	13166
NNP	9410
NNPS	244
NNS	6047
PDT	27
POS	824
PRP	1716
PRP$	766
RB	2822
RBR	136
RBS	35
RP	216
SYM	1
TO	2179
UH	3
VB	2554
VBD	3043
VBG	1460
VBN	2134
VBP	1321
VBZ	2125
WDT	445
WP	241
WP$	14
WRB	178

Module 3

Mastering Natural Language Processing with Python

Maximize your NLP capabilities while creating amazing NLp projects in Python

1
Working with Strings

Natural Language Processing (**NLP**) is concerned with the interaction between natural language and the computer. It is one of the major components of **Artificial Intelligence** (**AI**) and computational linguistics. It provides a seamless interaction between computers and human beings and gives computers the ability to understand human speech with the help of machine learning. The fundamental data type used to represent the contents of a file or a document in programming languages (for example, C, C++, JAVA, Python, and so on) is known as string. In this chapter, we will explore various operations that can be performed on strings that will be useful to accomplish various NLP tasks.

This chapter will include the following topics:

- Tokenization of text
- Normalization of text
- Substituting and correcting tokens
- Applying Zipf's law to text
- Applying similarity measures using the Edit Distance Algorithm
- Applying similarity measures using Jaccard's Coefficient
- Applying similarity measures using Smith Waterman

Tokenization

Tokenization may be defined as the process of splitting the text into smaller parts called tokens, and is considered a crucial step in NLP.

When NLTK is installed and Python IDLE is running, we can perform the tokenization of text or paragraphs into individual sentences. To perform tokenization, we can import the sentence tokenization function. The argument of this function will be text that needs to be tokenized. The `sent_tokenize` function uses an instance of NLTK known as `PunktSentenceTokenizer`. This instance of NLTK has already been trained to perform tokenization on different European languages on the basis of letters or punctuation that mark the beginning and end of sentences.

Tokenization of text into sentences

Now, let's see how a given text is tokenized into individual sentences:

```
>>> import nltk
>>> text=" Welcome readers. I hope you find it interesting. Please do
reply."
>>> from nltk.tokenize import sent_tokenize
>>> sent_tokenize(text)
[' Welcome readers.', 'I hope you find it interesting.', 'Please do
reply.']
```

So, a given text is split into individual sentences. Further, we can perform processing on the individual sentences.

To tokenize a large number of sentences, we can load `PunktSentenceTokenizer` and use the `tokenize()` function to perform tokenization. This can be seen in the following code:

```
>>> import nltk
>>> tokenizer=nltk.data.load('tokenizers/punkt/english.pickle')
>>> text=" Hello everyone. Hope all are fine and doing well. Hope you
find the book interesting"
>>> tokenizer.tokenize(text)
[' Hello everyone.', 'Hope all are fine and doing well.', 'Hope you
find the book interesting']
```

Tokenization of text in other languages

For performing tokenization in languages other than English, we can load the respective language pickle file found in `tokenizers/punkt` and then tokenize the text in another language, which is an argument of the `tokenize()` function. For the tokenization of French text, we will use the `french.pickle` file as follows:

```
>> import nltk
>>> french_tokenizer=nltk.data.load('tokenizers/punkt/french.pickle')
```

```
>>> french_tokenizer.tokenize('Deux agressions en quelques jours,
voilà ce qui a motivé hier matin le débrayage  collège franco-
britanniquedeLevallois-Perret. Deux agressions en quelques jours,
voilà ce qui a motivé hier matin le débrayage  Levallois. L'équipe
pédagogique de ce collège de 750 élèves avait déjà été choquée
par l'agression, janvier , d'un professeur d'histoire. L'équipe
pédagogique de ce collège de 750 élèves avait déjà été choquée par
l'agression, mercredi , d'un professeur d'histoire')
['Deux agressions en quelques jours, voilà ce qui a motivé hier
matin le débrayage  collège franco-britanniquedeLevallois-Perret.',
'Deux agressions en quelques jours, voilà ce qui a motivé hier matin
le débrayage  Levallois.', 'L'équipe pédagogique de ce collège de
750 élèves avait déjà été choquée par l'agression, janvier , d'un
professeur d'histoire.', 'L'équipe pédagogique de ce collège de
750 élèves avait déjà été choquée par l'agression, mercredi , d'un
professeur d'histoire']
```

Tokenization of sentences into words

Now, we'll perform processing on individual sentences. Individual sentences are tokenized into words. Word tokenization is performed using a `word_tokenize()` function. The `word_tokenize` function uses an instance of NLTK known as `TreebankWordTokenizer` to perform word tokenization.

The tokenization of English text using `word_tokenize` is shown here:

```
>>> import nltk
>>> text=nltk.word_tokenize("PierreVinken , 59 years old , will join
as a nonexecutive director on Nov. 29 .»)
>>> print(text)
[' PierreVinken', ',', '59', ' years', ' old', ',', 'will', 'join',
'as', 'a', 'nonexecutive', 'director' , 'on', 'Nov.', '29', '.']
```

Tokenization of words can also be done by loading `TreebankWordTokenizer` and then calling the `tokenize()` function, whose argument is a sentence that needs to be tokenized into words. This instance of NLTK has already been trained to perform the tokenization of sentence into words on the basis of spaces and punctuation.

The following code will help us obtain user input, tokenize it, and evaluate its length:

```
>>> import nltk
>>> from nltk import word_tokenize
>>> r=input("Please write a text")
Please write a textToday is a pleasant day
>>> print("The length of text is",len(word_tokenize(r)),"words")
The length of text is 5 words
```

Tokenization using TreebankWordTokenizer

Let's have a look at the code that performs tokenization using `TreebankWordTokenizer`:

```
>>> import nltk
>>> from nltk.tokenize import TreebankWordTokenizer
>>> tokenizer = TreebankWordTokenizer()
>>> tokenizer.tokenize("Have a nice day. I hope you find the book
interesting")
['Have', 'a', 'nice', 'day.', 'I', 'hope', 'you', 'find', 'the',
'book', 'interesting']
```

`TreebankWordTokenizer` uses conventions according to Penn Treebank Corpus. It works by separating contractions. This is shown here:

```
>>> import nltk
>>> text=nltk.word_tokenize(" Don't hesitate to ask questions")
>>> print(text)
['Do', "n't", 'hesitate', 'to', 'ask', 'questions']
```

Another word tokenizer is `PunktWordTokenizer`. It works by splitting punctuation; each word is kept instead of creating an entirely new token. Another word tokenizer is `WordPunctTokenizer`. It provides splitting by making punctuation an entirely new token. This type of splitting is usually desirable:

```
>>> from nltk.tokenize import WordPunctTokenizer
>>> tokenizer=WordPunctTokenizer()
>>> tokenizer.tokenize(" Don't hesitate to ask questions")
['Don', "'", 't', 'hesitate', 'to', 'ask', 'questions']
```

The inheritance tree for tokenizers is given here:

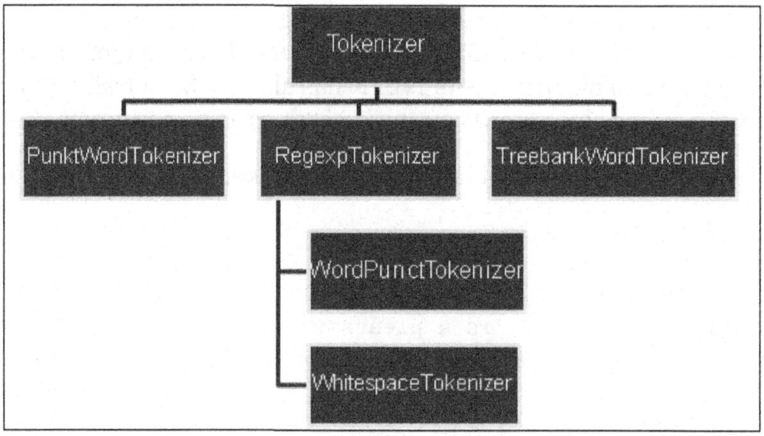

Tokenization using regular expressions

The tokenization of words can be performed by constructing **regular expressions** in these two ways:

- By matching with words
- By matching spaces or gaps

We can import `RegexpTokenizer` from NLTK. We can create a Regular Expression that can match the tokens present in the text:

```
>>> import nltk
>>> from nltk.tokenize import RegexpTokenizer
>>> tokenizer=RegexpTokenizer([\w]+")
>>> tokenizer.tokenize("Don't hesitate to ask questions")
["Don't", 'hesitate', 'to', 'ask', 'questions']
```

Instead of instantiating class, an alternative way of tokenization would be to use this function:

```
>>> import nltk
>>> from nltk.tokenize import regexp_tokenize
>>> sent="Don't hesitate to ask questions"
>>> print(regexp_tokenize(sent, pattern='\w+|\$[\d\.]+|\S+'))
['Don', "'t", 'hesitate', 'to', 'ask', 'questions']
```

`RegularexpTokenizer` uses the `re.findall()` function to perform tokenization by matching tokens. It uses the `re.split()` function to perform tokenization by matching gaps or spaces.

Let's have a look at an example of how to tokenize using whitespaces:

```
>>> import nltk
>>> from nltk.tokenize import RegexpTokenizer
>>> tokenizer=RegexpTokenizer('\s+',gaps=True)
>>> tokenizer.tokenize("Don't hesitate to ask questions")
["Don't", 'hesitate', 'to', 'ask', 'questions']
```

To select the words starting with a capital letter, the following code is used:

```
>>> import nltk
>>> from nltk.tokenize import RegexpTokenizer
>>> sent=" She secured 90.56 % in class X . She is a meritorious
student"
>>> capt = RegexpTokenizer('[A-Z]\w+')
>>> capt.tokenize(sent)
['She', 'She']
```

The following code shows how a predefined Regular Expression is used by a subclass of `RegexpTokenizer`:

```
>>> import nltk
>>> sent=" She secured 90.56 % in class X . She is a meritorious
student"
>>> from nltk.tokenize import BlanklineTokenizer
>>> BlanklineTokenizer().tokenize(sent)
[' She secured 90.56 % in class X \n. She is a meritorious student\n']
```

The tokenization of strings can be done using whitespace—tab, space, or newline:

```
>>> import nltk
>>> sent=" She secured 90.56 % in class X . She is a meritorious
student"
>>> from nltk.tokenize import WhitespaceTokenizer
>>> WhitespaceTokenizer().tokenize(sent)
['She', 'secured', '90.56', '%', 'in', 'class', 'X', '.', 'She', 'is',
'a', 'meritorious', 'student']
```

`WordPunctTokenizer` makes use of the regular expression `\w+|[^\w\s]+` to perform the tokenization of text into alphabetic and non-alphabetic characters.

Tokenization using the `split()` method is depicted in the following code:

```
>>>import nltk
>>>sent= She secured 90.56 % in class X. She is a meritorious student"
>>> sent.split()
['She', 'secured', '90.56', '%', 'in', 'class', 'X', '.', 'She', 'is',
'a', 'meritorious', 'student']
>>> sent.split('')
['', 'She', 'secured', '90.56', '%', 'in', 'class', 'X', '.', 'She',
'is', 'a', 'meritorious', 'student']
>>> sent=" She secured 90.56 % in class X \n. She is a meritorious
student\n"
>>> sent.split('\n')
[' She secured 90.56 % in class X ', '. She is a meritorious student',
'']
```

Similar to `sent.split('\n')`, `LineTokenizer` works by tokenizing text into lines:

```
>>> import nltk
>>> from nltk.tokenize import BlanklineTokenizer
>>> sent=" She secured 90.56 % in class X \n. She is a meritorious
student\n"
>>> BlanklineTokenizer().tokenize(sent)
[' She secured 90.56 % in class X \n. She is a meritorious student\n']
```

```
>>> from nltk.tokenize import LineTokenizer
>>> LineTokenizer(blanklines='keep').tokenize(sent)
[' She secured 90.56 % in class X ', '. She is a meritorious student']
>>> LineTokenizer(blanklines='discard').tokenize(sent)
[' She secured 90.56 % in class X ', '. She is a meritorious student']
```

`SpaceTokenizer` works similar to `sent.split('')`:

```
>>> import nltk
>>> sent=" She secured 90.56 % in class X \n. She is a meritorious
student\n"
>>> from nltk.tokenize import SpaceTokenizer
>>> SpaceTokenizer().tokenize(sent)
['', 'She', 'secured', '90.56', '%', 'in', 'class', 'X', '\n.', 'She',
'is', 'a', 'meritorious', 'student\n']
```

`nltk.tokenize.util` module works by returning the sequence of tuples that are offsets of the tokens in a sentence:

```
>>> import nltk
>>> from nltk.tokenize import WhitespaceTokenizer
>>> sent=" She secured 90.56 % in class X \n. She is a meritorious
student\n"
>>> list(WhitespaceTokenizer().span_tokenize(sent))
[(1, 4), (5, 12), (13, 18), (19, 20), (21, 23), (24, 29), (30, 31),
(33, 34), (35, 38), (39, 41), (42, 43), (44, 55), (56, 63)]
```

Given a sequence of spans, the sequence of relative spans can be returned:

```
>>> import nltk
>>> from nltk.tokenize import WhitespaceTokenizer
>>> from nltk.tokenize.util import spans_to_relative
>>> sent=" She secured 90.56 % in class X \n. She is a meritorious
student\n"
>>>list(spans_to_relative(WhitespaceTokenizer().span_tokenize(sent)))
[(1, 3), (1, 7), (1, 5), (1, 1), (1, 2), (1, 5), (1, 1), (2, 1), (1,
3), (1, 2), (1, 1), (1, 11), (1, 7)]
```

`nltk.tokenize.util.string_span_tokenize(sent,separator)` will return the offsets of tokens in sent by splitting at each incidence of the separator:

```
>>> import nltk
>>> from nltk.tokenize.util import string_span_tokenize
>>> sent=" She secured 90.56 % in class X \n. She is a meritorious
student\n"
>>> list(string_span_tokenize(sent, ""))
[(1, 4), (5, 12), (13, 18), (19, 20), (21, 23), (24, 29), (30, 31),
(32, 34), (35, 38), (39, 41), (42, 43), (44, 55), (56, 64)]
```

Normalization

In order to carry out processing on natural language text, we need to perform normalization that mainly involves eliminating punctuation, converting the entire text into lowercase or uppercase, converting numbers into words, expanding abbreviations, canonicalization of text, and so on.

Eliminating punctuation

Sometimes, while tokenizing, it is desirable to remove punctuation. Removal of punctuation is considered one of the primary tasks while doing normalization in NLTK.

Consider the following example:

```
>>> text=[" It is a pleasant evening.","Guests, who came from US
arrived at the venue","Food was tasty."]
>>> from nltk.tokenize import word_tokenize
>>> tokenized_docs=[word_tokenize(doc) for doc in text]
>>> print(tokenized_docs)
[['It', 'is', 'a', 'pleasant', 'evening', '.'], ['Guests', ',', 'who',
'came', 'from', 'US', 'arrived', 'at', 'the', 'venue'], ['Food',
'was', 'tasty', '.']]
```

The preceding code obtains the tokenized text. The following code will remove punctuation from tokenized text:

```
>>> import re
>>> import string
>>> text=[" It is a pleasant evening.","Guests, who came from US
arrived at the venue","Food was tasty."]
>>> from nltk.tokenize import word_tokenize
>>> tokenized_docs=[word_tokenize(doc) for doc in text]
>>> x=re.compile('[%s]' % re.escape(string.punctuation))
>>> tokenized_docs_no_punctuation = []
>>> for review in tokenized_docs:
    new_review = []
    for token in review:
    new_token = x.sub(u'', token)
    if not new_token == u'':
            new_review.append(new_token)
    tokenized_docs_no_punctuation.append(new_review)
>>> print(tokenized_docs_no_punctuation)
[['It', 'is', 'a', 'pleasant', 'evening'], ['Guests', 'who', 'came',
'from', 'US', 'arrived', 'at', 'the', 'venue'], ['Food', 'was',
'tasty']]
```

Conversion into lowercase and uppercase

A given text can be converted into lowercase or uppercase text entirely using the functions `lower()` and `upper()`. The task of converting text into uppercase or lowercase falls under the category of normalization.

Consider the following example of case conversion:

```
>>> text='HARdWork IS KEy to SUCCESS'
>>> print(text.lower())
hardwork is key to success
>>> print(text.upper())
HARDWORK IS KEY TO SUCCESS
```

Dealing with stop words

Stop words are words that need to be filtered out during the task of information retrieval or other natural language tasks, as these words do not contribute much to the overall meaning of the sentence. There are many search engines that work by deleting stop words so as to reduce the search space. Elimination of `stopwords` is considered one of the normalization tasks that is crucial in NLP.

NLTK has a list of stop words for many languages. We need to unzip `datafile` so that the list of stop words can be accessed from `nltk_data/corpora/stopwords/`:

```
>>> import nltk
>>> from nltk.corpus import stopwords
>>> stops=set(stopwords.words('english'))
>>> words=["Don't", 'hesitate','to','ask','questions']
>>> [word for word in words if word not in stops]
["Don't", 'hesitate', 'ask', 'questions']
```

The instance of `nltk.corpus.reader.WordListCorpusReader` is a `stopwords` corpus. It has the `words()` function, whose argument is `fileid`. Here, it is English; this refers to all the stop words present in the English file. If the `words()` function has no argument, then it will refer to all the stop words of all the languages.

Other languages in which stop word removal can be done, or the number of languages whose file of stop words is present in NLTK can be found using the `fileids()` function:

```
>>> stopwords.fileids()
['danish', 'dutch', 'english', 'finnish', 'french', 'german',
'hungarian', 'italian', 'norwegian', 'portuguese', 'russian',
'spanish', 'swedish', 'turkish']
```

Any of these previously listed languages can be used as an argument to the `words()` function so as to get the stop words in that language.

Calculate stopwords in English

Let's see an example of how to calculate `stopwords`:

```
>>> import nltk
>>> from nltk.corpus import stopwords
>>> stopwords.words('english')
['i', 'me', 'my', 'myself', 'we', 'our', 'ours', 'ourselves', 'you',
'your', 'yours', 'yourself', 'yourselves', 'he', 'him', 'his',
'himself', 'she', 'her', 'hers', 'herself', 'it', 'its', 'itself',
'they', 'them', 'their', 'theirs', 'themselves', 'what', 'which',
'who', 'whom', 'this', 'that', 'these', 'those', 'am', 'is', 'are',
'was', 'were', 'be', 'been', 'being', 'have', 'has', 'had', 'having',
'do', 'does', 'did', 'doing', 'a', 'an', 'the', 'and', 'but', 'if',
'or', 'because', 'as', 'until', 'while', 'of', 'at', 'by', 'for',
'with', 'about', 'against', 'between', 'into', 'through', 'during',
'before', 'after', 'above', 'below', 'to', 'from', 'up', 'down', 'in',
'out', 'on', 'off', 'over', 'under', 'again', 'further', 'then',
'once', 'here', 'there', 'when', 'where', 'why', 'how', 'all', 'any',
'both', 'each', 'few', 'more', 'most', 'other', 'some', 'such', 'no',
'nor', 'not', 'only', 'own', 'same', 'so', 'than', 'too', 'very', 's',
't', 'can', 'will', 'just', 'don', 'should', 'now']
>>> def para_fraction(text):
stopwords = nltk.corpus.stopwords.words('english')
para = [w for w in text if w.lower() not in stopwords]
return len(para) / len(text)

>>> para_fraction(nltk.corpus.reuters.words())
0.7364374824583169

>>> para_fraction(nltk.corpus.inaugural.words())
0.5229560503653893
```

Normalization may also involve converting numbers into words (for example, `1` can be replaced by `one`) and expanding abbreviations (for instance, `can't` can be replaced by `cannot`). This can be achieved by representing them in replacement patterns. This is discussed in the next section.

Substituting and correcting tokens

In this section, we will discuss the replacement of tokens with other tokens. We will also about how we can correct the spelling of tokens by replacing incorrectly spelled tokens with correctly spelled tokens.

Replacing words using regular expressions

In order to remove errors or perform text normalization, word replacement is done. One way by which text replacement is done is by using regular expressions. Previously, we faced problems while performing tokenization for contractions. Using text replacement, we can replace contractions with their expanded versions. For example, `doesn't` can be replaced by `does not`.

We will begin by writing the following code, naming this program `replacers.py`, and saving it in the `nltkdata` folder:

```
import re
replacement_patterns = [
(r'won\'t', 'will not'),
(r'can\'t', 'cannot'),
(r'i\'m', 'i am'),
(r'ain\'t', 'is not'),
(r'(\w+)\'ll', '\g<1> will'),
(r'(\w+)n\'t', '\g<1> not'),
(r'(\w+)\'ve', '\g<1> have'),
(r'(\w+)\'s', '\g<1> is'),
(r'(\w+)\'re', '\g<1> are'),
(r'(\w+)\'d', '\g<1> would')
]
class RegexpReplacer(object):
    def __init__(self, patterns=replacement_patterns):
        self.patterns = [(re.compile(regex), repl) for (regex, repl)
in
        patterns]
    def replace(self, text):
        s = text
        for (pattern, repl) in self.patterns:
            (s, count) = re.subn(pattern, repl, s)
        return s
```

Here, replacement patterns are defined in which the first term denotes the pattern to be matched and the second term is its corresponding replacement pattern. The `RegexpReplacer` class has been defined to perform the task of compiling pattern pairs and it provides a method called `replace()`, whose function is to perform the replacement of a pattern with another pattern.

Example of the replacement of a text with another text

Let's see an example of how we can substitute a text with another text:

```
>>> import nltk
>>> from replacers import RegexpReplacer
>>> replacer= RegexpReplacer()
>>> replacer.replace("Don't hesitate to ask questions")
'Do not hesitate to ask questions'
>>> replacer.replace("She must've gone to the market but she didn't
go")
'She must have gone to the market but she did not go'
```

The function of `RegexpReplacer.replace()` is substituting every instance of a replacement pattern with its corresponding substitution pattern. Here, `must've` is replaced by `must have` and `didn't` is replaced by `did not`, since the replacement pattern in `replacers.py` has already been defined by tuple pairs, that is, `(r'(\w+)\'ve', '\g<1> have')` and `(r'(\w+)n\'t', '\g<1> not')`.

We can not only perform the replacement of contractions; we can also substitute a token with any other token.

Performing substitution before tokenization

Tokens substitution can be performed prior to tokenization so as to avoid the problem that occurs during tokenization for contractions:

```
>>> import nltk
>>> from nltk.tokenize import word_tokenize
>>> from replacers import RegexpReplacer
>>> replacer=RegexpReplacer()
>>> word_tokenize("Don't hesitate to ask questions")
['Do', "n't", 'hesitate', 'to', 'ask', 'questions']
>>> word_tokenize(replacer.replace("Don't hesitate to ask questions"))
['Do', 'not', 'hesitate', 'to', 'ask', 'questions']
```

Dealing with repeating characters

Sometimes, people write words involving repeating characters that cause grammatical errors. For instance consider a sentence, `I like it lotttttt`. Here, `lotttttt` refers to `lot`. So now, we'll eliminate these repeating characters using the backreference approach, in which a character refers to the previous characters in a group in a regular expression. This is also considered one of the normalization tasks.

Firstly, append the following code to the previously created `replacers.py`:

```
class RepeatReplacer(object):
    def __init__(self):
        self.repeat_regexp = re.compile(r'(\w*)(\w)\2(\w*)')
        self.repl = r'\1\2\3'
    def replace(self, word):
        repl_word = self.repeat_regexp.sub(self.repl, word)
        if repl_word != word:
            return self.replace(repl_word)
        else:
            return repl_word
```

Example of deleting repeating characters

Let's see an example of how we can delete repeating characters from a token:

```
>>> import nltk
>>> from replacers import RepeatReplacer
>>> replacer=RepeatReplacer()
>>> replacer.replace('lotttt')
'lot'
>>> replacer.replace('ohhhhh')
'oh'
>>> replacer.replace('ooohhhhh')
'oh'
```

The `RepeatReplacer` class works by compiling regular expressions and replacement strings and is defined using `backreference.Repeat_regexp`, which is present in `replacers.py`. It matches the starting characters that can be zero or many `(\w*)`, ending characters that can be zero or many `(\w*)`, or a character `(\w)` that is followed by same character.

For example, `lotttt` is split into `(lo)(t)t(tt)`. Here, one `t` is reduced and the string becomes lottt. The process of splitting continues, and finally, the resultant string obtained is lot.

The problem with `RepeatReplacer` is that it will convert `happy` to `hapy`, which is inappropriate. To avoid this problem, we can embed `wordnet` along with it.

In the `replacers.py` program created previously, add the following lines to include `wordnet`:

```
import re
from nltk.corpus import wordnet
```

```
class RepeatReplacer(object):
    def __init__(self):
        self.repeat_regexp = re.compile(r'(\w*)(\w)\2(\w*)')
        self.repl = r'\1\2\3'
    def replace(self, word):
        if wordnet.synsets(word):
            return word
        repl_word = self.repeat_regexp.sub(self.repl, word)
        if repl_word != word:
            return self.replace(repl_word)
        else:
            return repl_word
```

Now, let's take a look at how the previously mentioned problem can be overcome:

```
>>> import nltk
>>> from replacers import RepeatReplacer
>>> replacer=RepeatReplacer()
>>> replacer.replace('happy')
'happy'
```

Replacing a word with its synonym

Now we will see how we can substitute a given word by its synonym. To the already existing `replacers.py`, we can add a class called `WordReplacer` that provides mapping between a word and its synonym:

```
class WordReplacer(object):
    def __init__(self, word_map):
        self.word_map = word_map
    def replace(self, word):
        return self.word_map.get(word, word)
```

Example of substituting word a with its synonym

Let's have a look at an example of substituting a word with its synonym:

```
>>> import nltk
>>> from replacers import WordReplacer
>>> replacer=WordReplacer({'congrats':'congratulations'})
>>> replacer.replace('congrats')
'congratulations'
>>> replacer.replace('maths')
'maths'
```

In this code, the `replace()` function looks for the corresponding synonym for a word in `word_map`. If the synonym is present for a given word, then the word will be replaced by its synonym. If the synonym for a given word is not present, then no replacement will be performed; the same word will be returned.

Applying Zipf's law to text

Zipf's law states that the frequency of a token in a text is directly proportional to its rank or position in the sorted list. This law describes how tokens are distributed in languages: some tokens occur very frequently, some occur with intermediate frequency, and some tokens rarely occur.

Let's see the code for obtaining the log-log plot in NLTK that is based on Zipf's law:

```
>>> import nltk
>>> from nltk.corpus import gutenberg
>>> from nltk.probability import FreqDist
>>> import matplotlib
>>> import matplotlib.pyplot as plt
>>> matplotlib.use('TkAgg')
>>> fd = FreqDist()
>>> for text in gutenberg.fileids():
. . . for word in gutenberg.words(text):
. . . fd.inc(word)
>>> ranks = []
>>> freqs = []
>>> for rank, word in enumerate(fd):
. . . ranks.append(rank+1)
. . . freqs.append(fd[word])
. . .
>>> plt.loglog(ranks, freqs)
>>> plt.xlabel('frequency(f)', fontsize=14, fontweight='bold')
>>> plt.ylabel('rank(r)', fontsize=14, fontweight='bold')
>>> plt.grid(True)
>>> plt.show()
```

The preceding code will obtain a plot of rank versus the frequency of words in a document. So, we can check whether Zipf's law holds for all the documents or not by seeing the proportionality relationship between rank and the frequency of words.

Similarity measures

There are many similarity measures that can be used for performing NLP tasks. The `nltk.metrics` package in NLTK is used to provide various evaluation or similarity measures, which is conducive to perform various NLP tasks.

In order to test the performance of taggers, chunkers, and so on, in NLP, the standard scores retrieved from information retrieval can be used.

Let's have a look at how the output of named entity recognizer can be analyzed using the standard scores obtained from a training file:

```
>>> from __future__ import print_function
>>> from nltk.metrics import *
>>> training='PERSON OTHER PERSON OTHER OTHER ORGANIZATION'.split()
>>> testing='PERSON OTHER OTHER OTHER OTHER OTHER'.split()
>>> print(accuracy(training,testing))
0.6666666666666666
>>> trainset=set(training)
>>> testset=set(testing)
>>> precision(trainset,testset)
1.0
>>> print(recall(trainset,testset))
0.6666666666666666
>>> print(f_measure(trainset,testset))
0.8
```

Applying similarity measures using Ethe edit distance algorithm

Edit distance or the Levenshtein edit distance between two strings is used to compute the number of characters that can be inserted, substituted, or deleted in order to make two strings equal.

The operations performed in Edit Distance include the following:

- Copying letters from the first string to the second string (cost 0) and substituting a letter with another (cost 1):

  D(i-1,j-1) + d(si,tj)(Substitution / copy)

- Deleting a letter in the first string (cost 1)

  D(i,j-1)+1 (deletion)

- Inserting a letter in the second string (cost 1):

  D(i,j) = min D(i-1,j)+1 (insertion)

The Python code for Edit Distance that is included in the `nltk.metrics` package is as follows:

```
from __future__ import print_function
def _edit_dist_init(len1, len2):
    lev = []
    for i in range(len1):
        lev.append([0] * len2)  # initialize 2D array to zero
    for i in range(len1):
        lev[i][0] = i           # column 0: 0,1,2,3,4,...
    for j in range(len2):
        lev[0][j] = j           # row 0: 0,1,2,3,4,...
    return lev

def_edit_dist_step(lev,i,j,s1,s2,transpositions=False):
c1 =s1[i-1]
c2 =s2[j-1]

# skipping a character in s1
a =lev[i-1][j] +1
# skipping a character in s2
b =lev[i][j -1]+1
# substitution
c =lev[i-1][j-1]+(c1!=c2)
# transposition
d =c+1 # never picked by default
if transpositions and i>1 and j>1:
if s1[i -2]==c2 and s2[j -2]==c1:
d =lev[i-2][j-2]+1
# pick the cheapest
lev[i][j] =min(a,b,c,d)

def edit_distance(s1, s2, transpositions=False):
    # set up a 2-D array
    len1 = len(s1)
    len2 = len(s2)
    lev = _edit_dist_init(len1 + 1, len2 + 1)

    # iterate over the array
    for i in range(len1):
```

```
        for j in range(len2):
            _edit_dist_step(lev, i + 1, j + 1, s1, s2,
transpositions=transpositions)
    return lev[len1][len2]
```

Let's have a look at the Edit Distance calculated in NLTK using the `nltk.metrics` package:

```
>>> import nltk
>>> from nltk.metrics import *
>>> edit_distance("relate","relation")
3
>>> edit_distance("suggestion","calculation")
7
```

Here, when we calculate the edit distance between `relate` and `relation`, three operations (one substitution and two insertions) are performed. While calculating the edit distance between `suggestion` and `calculation`, seven operations (six substitutions and one insertion) are performed.

Applying similarity measures using Jaccard's Coefficient

Jaccard's coefficient, or Tanimoto coefficient, may be defined as a measure of the overlap of two sets, X and Y.

It may be defined as follows:

- $Jaccard(X,Y)=|X\cap Y|/|X\cup Y|$
- $Jaccard(X,X)=1$
- $Jaccard(X,Y)=0 \text{ if } X\cap Y=0$

The code for Jaccard's similarity may be given as follows:

```
def jacc_similarity(query, document):
first=set(query).intersection(set(document))
second=set(query).union(set(document))
return len(first)/len(second)
```

Let's have a look at the implementation of Jaccard's similarity coefficient using NLTK:

```
>>> import nltk
>>> from nltk.metrics import *
```

```
>>> X=set([10,20,30,40])
>>> Y=set([20,30,60])
>>> print(jaccard_distance(X,Y))
0.6
```

Applying similarity measures using the Smith Waterman distance

The Smith Waterman distance is similar to edit distance. This similarity metric was developed in order to detect the optical alignments between related protein sequences and DNA. It consists of costs to be assigned to and functions for alphabet mapping to cost values (substitution); cost is also assigned to gap G (insertion or deletion):

1. *0* //start over
2. *D(i-1,j-1) -d(si,tj)* //subst/copy
3. *D(i,j) = max D(i-1,j)-G* //insert
1. *D(i,j-1)-G* //delete

> Distance is maximum over all *i,j* in table of *D(i,j)*

4. *G = 1* //example value for gap
5. *d(c,c) = -2* //context dependent substitution cost
6. *d(c,d) = +1* //context dependent substitution cost

Similar to Edit distance, the Python code for Smith Waterman can be embedded with the `nltk.metrics` package to perform string similarity using Smith Waterman in NLTK.

Other string similarity metrics

Binary distance is a string similarity metric. It returns the value `0.0` if two labels are identical; otherwise, it returns the value `1.0`.

The Python code for Binary distance metrics is:

```
def binary_distance(label1, label2):
 return 0.0 if label1 == label2 else 1.0
```

Let's see how Binary distance metrics is implemented in NLTK:

```
>>> import nltk
>>> from nltk.metrics import *
>>> X = set([10,20,30,40])
>>> Y= set([30,50,70])
>>> binary_distance(X, Y)
1.0
```

Masi distance is based on partial agreement when multiple labels are present.

The Python code included in `nltk.metrics` for `masi` distance is as follows:

```
def masi_distance(label1, label2):
    len_intersection = len(label1.intersection(label2))
    len_union = len(label1.union(label2))
    len_label1 = len(label1)
    len_label2 = len(label2)
    if len_label1 == len_label2 and len_label1 == len_intersection:
        m = 1
    elif len_intersection == min(len_label1, len_label2):
        m = 0.67
    elif len_intersection > 0:
        m = 0.33
    else:
        m = 0

    return 1 - (len_intersection / float(len_union)) * m
```

Let's see the implementation of `masi` distance in NLTK:

```
>>> import nltk
>>> from __future__ import print_function
>>> from nltk.metrics import *
>>> X = set([10,20,30,40])
>>> Y= set([30,50,70])
>>> print(masi_distance(X,Y))
0.945
```

Summary

In this chapter, you have learned various operations that can be performed on a text that is a collection of strings. You have understood the concept of tokenization, substitution, and normalization, and applied various similarity measures to strings using NLTK. We have also discussed Zipf's law, which may be applicable to some of the existing documents.

In the next chapter, we'll discuss various language modeling techniques and different NLP tasks.

2

Statistical Language Modeling

Computational linguistics is an emerging field that is widely used in analytics, software applications, and contexts where people communicate with machines. Computational linguistics may be defined as a subfield of artificial intelligence. Applications of computational linguistics include machine translation, speech recognition, intelligent Web searching, information retrieval, and intelligent spelling checkers. It is important to understand the preprocessing tasks or the computations that can be performed on natural language text. In the following chapter, we will discuss ways to calculate word frequencies, the **Maximum Likelihood Estimation** (**MLE**) model, interpolation on data, and so on. But first, let's go through the various topics that we will cover in this chapter. They are as follows:

- Calculating word frequencies (1-gram, 2-gram, 3-gram)
- Developing MLE for a given text
- Applying smoothing on the MLE model
- Developing a back-off mechanism for MLE
- Applying interpolation on data to get a mix and match
- Evaluating a language model through perplexity
- Applying Metropolis-Hastings in modeling languages
- Applying Gibbs sampling in language processing

Understanding word frequency

Collocations may be defined as the collection of two or more tokens that tend to exist together. For example, the United States, the United Kingdom, Union of Soviet Socialist Republics, and so on.

Unigram represents a single token. The following code will be used for generate `unigrams` for Alpino Corpus:

```
>>> import nltk
>>> from nltk.util import ngrams
>>> from nltk.corpus import alpino
>>> alpino.words()
['De', 'verzekeringsmaatschappijen', 'verhelen', ...]>>>
unigrams=ngrams(alpino.words(),1)
>>> for i in unigrams:
print(i)
```

Consider another example for generating `quadgrams` or `fourgrams` from `alpinocorpus`:

```
>>> import nltk
>>> from nltk.util import ngrams
>>> from nltk.corpus import alpino
>>> alpino.words()
['De', 'verzekeringsmaatschappijen', 'verhelen', ...]
>>> quadgrams=ngrams(alpino.words(),4)
>>> for i in quadgrams:
print(i)
```

`bigram` refers to a pair of tokens. To find bigrams in the text, firstly, lowercased words are searched, a list of lowercased words in the text is created, and `BigramCollocationFinder` is produced. The `BigramAssocMeasures` found in the `nltk.metrics` package can be used to find bigrams in the text:

```
>>> import nltk
>>> from nltk.collocations import BigramCollocationFinder
>>> from nltk.corpus import webtext
>>> from nltk.metrics import BigramAssocMeasures
>>> tokens=[t.lower() for t in webtext.words('grail.txt')]
>>> words=BigramCollocationFinder.from_words(tokens)
>>> words.nbest(BigramAssocMeasures.likelihood_ratio, 10)
[("'", 's'), ('arthur', ':'), ('#', '1'), ("'", 't'), ('villager',
'#'), ('#', '2'), (']', '['), ('1', ':'), ('oh', ','), ('black',
'knight')]
```

In the preceding code, we can add a word filter that can be used to eliminate `stopwords` and punctuation:

```
>>> from nltk.corpus import stopwords
>>> from nltk.corpus import webtext
>>> from nltk.collocations import BigramCollocationFinder
>>> from nltk.metrics import BigramAssocMeasures
```

```
>>> set = set(stopwords.words('english'))
>>> stops_filter = lambda w: len(w) < 3 or w in set
>>> tokens=[t.lower() for t in webtext.words('grail.txt')]
>>> words=BigramCollocationFinder.from_words(tokens)
>>> words.apply_word_filter(stops_filter)
>>> words.nbest(BigramAssocMeasures.likelihood_ratio, 10)
[('black', 'knight'), ('clop', 'clop'), ('head', 'knight'), ('mumble',
'mumble'), ('squeak', 'squeak'), ('saw', 'saw'), ('holy', 'grail'),
('run', 'away'), ('french', 'guard'), ('cartoon', 'character')]
```

Here, we can change the frequency of bigrams from 10 to any other number.

Another way of generating bigrams from a text is using collocation finders. This is given in the following code:

```
>>> import nltk
>>> from nltk.collocation import *
>>> text1="Hardwork is the key to success. Never give up!"
>>> word = nltk.wordpunct_tokenize(text1)
>>> finder = BigramCollocationFinder.from_words(word)
>>> bigram_measures = nltk.collocations.BigramAssocMeasures()
>>> value = finder.score_ngrams(bigram_measures.raw_freq)
>>> sorted(bigram for bigram, score in value)
[('.', 'Never'), ('Hardwork', 'is'), ('Never', 'give'), ('give',
'up'), ('is', 'the'), ('key', 'to'), ('success', '.'), ('the', 'key'),
('to', 'success'), ('up', '!')]
```

We will now see another code for generating bigrams from `alpino corpus`:

```
>>> import nltk
>>> from nltk.util import ngrams
>>> from nltk.corpus import alpino
>>> alpino.words()
['De', 'verzekeringsmaatschappijen', 'verhelen', ...]
>>> bigrams_tokens=ngrams(alpino.words(),2)
>>> for i in bigrams_tokens:
print(i)
```

This code will generate bigrams from `alpino corpus`.

We will now see the code for generating `trigrams`:

```
>>> import nltk
>>> from nltk.util import ngrams
>>> from nltk.corpus import alpino
>>> alpino.words()
```

```
['De', 'verzekeringsmaatschappijen', 'verhelen', ...]>>> trigrams_
tokens=ngrams(alpino.words(),3)
>>> for i in trigrams_tokens:
print(i)
```

For generating `fourgrams` and generating the frequency of `fourgrams`, the following code is used:

```
>>> import nltk
>>> import nltk
>>> from nltk.collocations import *
>>> text="Hello how are you doing ? I hope you find the book
interesting"
>>> tokens=nltk.wordpunct_tokenize(text)
>>> fourgrams=nltk.collocations.QuadgramCollocationFinder.from_
words(tokens)
>>> for fourgram, freq in fourgrams.ngram_fd.items():
print(fourgram,freq)

('hope', 'you', 'find', 'the') 1
('Hello', 'how', 'are', 'you') 1
('you', 'doing', '?', 'I') 1
('are', 'you', 'doing', '?') 1
('how', 'are', 'you', 'doing') 1
('?', 'I', 'hope', 'you') 1
('doing', '?', 'I', 'hope') 1
('find', 'the', 'book', 'interesting') 1
('you', 'find', 'the', 'book') 1
('I', 'hope', 'you', 'find') 1
```

We will now see the code for generating `ngrams` for a given sentence:

```
>>> import nltk
>>> sent=" Hello , please read the book thoroughly . If you have any
queries , then don't hesitate to ask . There is no shortcut to success
."
>>> n=5
>>> fivegrams=ngrams(sent.split(),n)
>>> for grams in fivegrams:
    print(grams)


('Hello', ',', 'please', 'read', 'the')
(',', 'please', 'read', 'the', 'book')
('please', 'read', 'the', 'book', 'thoroughly')
('read', 'the', 'book', 'thoroughly', '.')
```

```
('the', 'book', 'thoroughly', '.', 'If')
('book', 'thoroughly', '.', 'If', 'you')
('thoroughly', '.', 'If', 'you', 'have')
('.', 'If', 'you', 'have', 'any')
('If', 'you', 'have', 'any', 'queries')
('you', 'have', 'any', 'queries', ',')
('have', 'any', 'queries', ',', 'then')
('any', 'queries', ',', 'then', "don't")
('queries', ',', 'then', "don't", 'hesitate')
(',', 'then', "don't", 'hesitate', 'to')
('then', "don't", 'hesitate', 'to', 'ask')
("don't", 'hesitate', 'to', 'ask', '.')
('hesitate', 'to', 'ask', '.', 'There')
('to', 'ask', '.', 'There', 'is')
('ask', '.', 'There', 'is', 'no')
('.', 'There', 'is', 'no', 'shortcut')
('There', 'is', 'no', 'shortcut', 'to')
('is', 'no', 'shortcut', 'to', 'success')
('no', 'shortcut', 'to', 'success', '.')
```

Develop MLE for a given text

MLE, also referred to as multinomial logistic regression or a conditional exponential classifier, is an essential task in the field of NLP. It was first introduced in 1996 by Berger and Della Pietra. Maximum Entropy is defined in NLTK in the `nltk.classify.maxent` module. In this module, all the probability distributions are considered that are in accordance with the training data. This model is used to refer to two features, namely input-feature and joint feature. An input feature may be called the feature of unlabeled words. A joined feature may be called the feature of labeled words. MLE is used to generate `freqdist` that contains the probability distribution for a given occurrence in a text. `param freqdist` consists of frequency distribution on which probability distribution is based.

We'll now see the code for the Maximum Entropy Model in NLTK:

```
from__future__import print_function,unicode_literals
__docformat__='epytext en'

try:
import numpy
except ImportError:
    pass
```

```
import tempfile
import os
from collections import defaultdict
from nltk import compat
from nltk.data import gzip_open_unicode
from nltk.util import OrderedDict
from nltk.probability import DictionaryProbDist
from nltk.classify.api import ClassifierI
from nltk.classify.util import CutoffChecker,accuracy,log_likelihood
from nltk.classify.megam import (call_megam,
write_megam_file,parse_megam_weights)
from nltk.classify.tadm import call_tadm,write_tadm_file,parse_tadm_
weights
```

In the preceding code, `nltk.probability` consists of the `FreqDist` class that can be used to determine the frequency of the occurrence of individual tokens in a text.

The `ProbDistI` is used to determine the probability distribution of individual occurrences in a text. There are basically two kinds of probability distributions: Derived Probability Distribution and Analytic Probability Distribution. Distributed Probability Distributions are obtained from frequency distribution. Analytic Probability Distributions are obtained from parameters, such as variance.

In order to obtain the frequency distribution, the maximum likelihood estimate is used. It computes the probability of every occurrence on the basis of its frequency in the frequency distribution:

```
class MLEProbDist(ProbDistI):

    def __init__(self, freqdist, bins=None):
        self._freqdist = freqdist

    def freqdist(self):
"""
```

It will find the frequency distribution on the basis of probability distribution:

```
"""
    return self._freqdist

    def prob(self, sample):
        return self._freqdist.freq(sample)

    def max(self):
        return self._freqdist.max()
```

```
    def samples(self):
        return self._freqdist.keys()

    def __repr__(self):
"""
        It will return string representation of ProbDist
"""
        return '<MLEProbDist based on %d samples>' % self._
freqdist.N()


class LidstoneProbDist(ProbDistI):
"""
```

It is used to obtain frequency distribution. It is represented by a real number, Gamma, whose range lies between `0` and `1`. The `LidstoneProbDist` calculates the probability of a given observation with count `c`, outcomes `N`, and bins `B` as follows: *(c+Gamma)/(N+B*Gamma)*.

It also means that Gamma is added to the count of each bin and MLE is computed from the given frequency distribution:

```
"""
SUM_TO_ONE = False
    def __init__(self, freqdist, gamma, bins=None):
"""
```

Lidstone is used to compute the probability distribution in order to obtain `freqdist`.

`paramfreqdist` may be defined as the frequency distribution on which probability estimates are based.

`param` bins may be defined as sample values that can be obtained from the probability distribution. The sum of probabilities is equal to one:

```
"""
        if (bins == 0) or (bins is None and freqdist.N() == 0):
            name = self.__class__.__name__[:-8]
            raise ValueError('A %s probability distribution ' % name +
'must have at least one bin.')
        if (bins is not None) and (bins < freqdist.B()):
            name = self.__class__.__name__[:-8]
            raise ValueError('\nThe number of bins in a %s
distribution ' % name +
```

```
'(%d) must be greater than or equal to\n' % bins +
'the number of bins in the FreqDist used ' +
'to create it (%d).' % freqdist.B())

        self._freqdist = freqdist
        self._gamma = float(gamma)
        self._N = self._freqdist.N()

        if bins is None:
            bins = freqdist.B()
        self._bins = bins

        self._divisor = self._N + bins * gamma
        if self._divisor == 0.0:
            # In extreme cases we force the probability to be 0,
            # which it will be, since the count will be 0:
            self._gamma = 0
            self._divisor = 1

def freqdist(self):
"""
```

It obtains frequency distribution, which is based upon the probability distribution:

```
    """
        return self._freqdist

def prob(self, sample):
c = self._freqdist[sample]
        return (c + self._gamma) / self._divisor

   def max(self):
 # To obtain most probable sample, choose the one
# that occurs very frequently.
        return self._freqdist.max()

def samples(self):
        return self._freqdist.keys()

def discount(self):
    gb = self._gamma * self._bins
        return gb / (self._N + gb)

    def __repr__(self):
"""
```

```
        String representation of ProbDist is obtained.


"""
        return '<LidstoneProbDist based on %d samples>' % self._
freqdist.N()


class LaplaceProbDist(LidstoneProbDist):
"""
```

It is used to obtain frequency distribution. It calculates the probability of a sample with count c, outcomes `N`, and bins `B` as follows:

(c+1)/(N+B)

It also means that 1 is added to the count of every bin, and the maximum likelihood is estimated for the resultant frequency distribution:

```
"""
    def __init__(self, freqdist, bins=None):
"""
```

`LaplaceProbDist` is used to obtain the probability distribution for generating `freqdist`.

`param freqdist` is used to obtain the frequency distribution, which is based on probability estimates.

`Param` bins may be defined as the frequency of sample values that can be generated. The sum of probabilities must be `1`:

```
"""
        LidstoneProbDist.__init__(self, freqdist, 1, bins)

    def __repr__(self):
"""
        String representation of ProbDist is obtained.
"""
        return '<LaplaceProbDist based on %d samples>' % self._
freqdist.N()

class ELEProbDist(LidstoneProbDist):
"""
```

It is used to obtain frequency distribution. It calculates the probability of a sample with count c, outcomes N, and bins B as follows:

(c+0.5)/(N+B/2)

It also means that `0.5` is added to the count of every bin and the maximum likelihood is estimated for the resultant frequency distribution:

```
"""
        def __init__(self, freqdist, bins=None):
"""
```

The expected likelihood estimation is used to obtain the probability distribution for generating `freqdist.param.freqdist` is used to obtain the frequency distribution, which is based on probability estimates.

`param` bins may be defined as the frequency of sample values that can be generated. The sum of probabilities must be 1:

```
"""
LidstoneProbDist.__init__(self, freqdist, 0.5, bins)

        def __repr__(self):
"""
                String representation of ProbDist is obtained.
        """
                return '<ELEProbDist based on %d samples>' % self._
freqdist.N()



class WittenBellProbDist(ProbDistI):
"""
```

The `WittenBellProbDist` is used to obtain the probability distribution. It is used to obtain the uniform probability mass on the basis of the frequency of the sample seen before. The probability mass for the sample is given as follows:

T / (N + T)

Here, *T* is the number of samples observed and *N* is total number of events observed. It is equal to the maximum likelihood estimate of a new sample that is occurring. The sum of all the probabilities is equal to 1:

```
        Here,
                p = T / Z (N + T), if count = 0
                p = c / (N + T), otherwise
```

```
"""

    def __init__(self, freqdist, bins=None):
"""
```

It obtains the probability distribution. This probability is used to provide the uniform probability mass to an unseen sample. The probability mass for the sample is given as follows:

T / (N + T)

Here, *T* is the number of samples observed and *N* is the total number of events observed. It is equal to the maximum likelihood estimate of a new sample that is occurring. The sum of all the probabilities is equal to *1*:

```
    Here,
          p = T / Z (N + T), if count = 0
          p = c / (N + T), otherwise
```

Z is the normalizing factor that is calculated using these values and a bin value.

`Param freqdist` is used to estimate the frequency counts from which the probability distribution is obtained.

`Param` bins may be defined as the number of possible types of samples:

```
"""
        assert bins is None or bins >= freqdist.B(),\
'bins parameter must not be less than %d=freqdist.B()' % freqdist.B()
        if bins is None:
            bins = freqdist.B()
        self._freqdist = freqdist
        self._T = self._freqdist.B()
        self._Z = bins - self._freqdist.B()
        self._N = self._freqdist.N()
        # self._P0 is P(0), precalculated for efficiency:
        if self._N==0:
            # if freqdist is empty, we approximate P(0) by a
UniformProbDist:
            self._P0 = 1.0 / self._Z
        else:
            self._P0 = self._T / float(self._Z * (self._N + self._T))

    def prob(self, sample):
        # inherit docs from ProbDistI
        c = self._freqdist[sample]
```

```
        return (c / float(self._N + self._T) if c != 0 else self._P0)

    def max(self):
        return self._freqdist.max()

    def samples(self):
        return self._freqdist.keys()

    def freqdist(self):
        return self._freqdist

    def discount(self):
        raise NotImplementedError()

    def __repr__(self):
"""
        String representation of ProbDist is obtained.


"""
        return '<WittenBellProbDist based on %d samples>' % self._
freqdist.N()
```

We can perform testing using maximum likelihood estimation. Let's consider the following code for MLE in NLTK:

```
>>> import nltk
>>> from nltk.probability import *
>>> train_and_test(mle)
28.76%
>>> train_and_test(LaplaceProbDist)
69.16%
>>> train_and_test(ELEProbDist)
76.38%
>>> def lidstone(gamma):
    return lambda fd, bins: LidstoneProbDist(fd, gamma, bins)

>>> train_and_test(lidstone(0.1))
86.17%
>>> train_and_test(lidstone(0.5))
76.38%
>>> train_and_test(lidstone(1.0))
69.16%
```

Hidden Markov Model estimation

Hidden Markov Model (**HMM**) comprises of observed states and the latent states that help in determining them. Consider the diagrammatic description of HMM. Here, x represents the latent state and y represents the observed state.

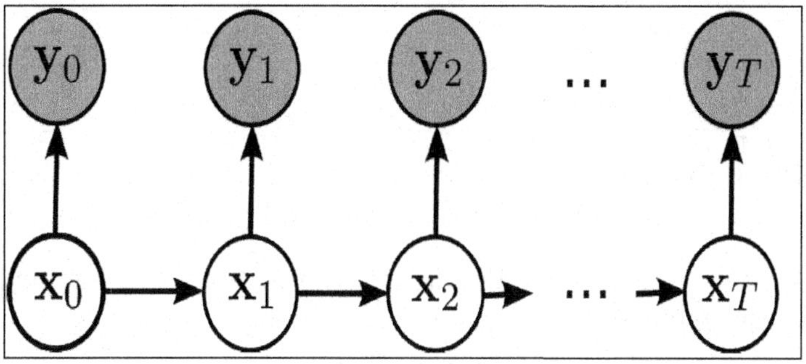

We can perform testing using HMM estimation. Let's consider the `Brown` Corpus and the code given here:

```
>>> import nltk
>>> corpus = nltk.corpus.brown.tagged_sents(categories='adventure')
[:700]
>>> print(len(corpus))
700
>>> from nltk.util import unique_list
>>> tag_set = unique_list(tag for sent in corpus for (word,tag) in
sent)
>>> print(len(tag_set))
104
>>> symbols = unique_list(word for sent in corpus for (word,tag) in
sent)
>>> print(len(symbols))
1908
>>> print(len(tag_set))
104
>>> symbols = unique_list(word for sent in corpus for (word,tag) in
sent)
>>> print(len(symbols))
1908
>>> trainer = nltk.tag.HiddenMarkovModelTrainer(tag_set, symbols)
>>> train_corpus = []
>>> test_corpus = []
>>> for i in range(len(corpus)):
if i % 10:
```

```
train_corpus += [corpus[i]]
else:
test_corpus += [corpus[i]]


>>> print(len(train_corpus))
630
>>> print(len(test_corpus))
70
>>> def train_and_test(est):
hmm = trainer.train_supervised(train_corpus, estimator=est)
print('%.2f%%' % (100 * hmm.evaluate(test_corpus)))
```

In the preceding code, we have created a 90% training and 10% testing file and we have tested the estimator.

Applying smoothing on the MLE model

Smoothing is used to handle the words that have not occurred previously. So, the probability of unknown words is 0. To solve this problem, smoothing is used.

Add-one smoothing

In the 18th century, Laplace invented add-one smoothing. In add-one smoothing, 1 is added to the count of each word. Instead of 1, any other value can also be added to the count of unknown words so that unknown words can be handled and their probability is non-zero. Pseudo count is the value (that is, either 1 or nonzero) that is added to the counts of unknown words to make their probability nonzero.

Let's consider the following code for add-one smoothing in NLTK:

```
>>> import nltk
>>> corpus=u"<s> hello how are you doing ? Hope you find the book
interesting. </s>".split()
>>> sentence=u"<s>how are you doing</s>".split()
>>> vocabulary=set(corpus)
>>> len(vocabulary)
13
>>> cfd = nltk.ConditionalFreqDist(nltk.bigrams(corpus))
>>> # The corpus counts of each bigram in the sentence:
>>> [cfd[a][b] for (a,b) in nltk.bigrams(sentence)]
[0, 1, 0]
>>> # The counts for each word in the sentence:
>>> [cfd[a].N() for (a,b) in nltk.bigrams(sentence)]
```

```
[0, 1, 2]
>>> # There is already a FreqDist method for MLE probability:
>>> [cfd[a].freq(b) for (a,b) in nltk.bigrams(sentence)]
[0, 1.0, 0.0]
>>> # Laplace smoothing of each bigram count:
>>> [1 + cfd[a][b] for (a,b) in nltk.bigrams(sentence)]
[1, 2, 1]
>>> # We need to normalise the counts for each word:
>>> [len(vocabulary) + cfd[a].N() for (a,b) in nltk.bigrams(sentence)]
[13, 14, 15]
>>> # The smoothed Laplace probability for each bigram:
>>> [1.0 * (1+cfd[a][b]) / (len(vocabulary)+cfd[a].N()) for (a,b) in
nltk.bigrams(sentence)]
[0.07692307692307693, 0.14285714285714285, 0.06666666666666667]
```

Consider another way of performing Add-one smoothing or generating a Laplace probability distribution:

```
>>> # MLEProbDist is the unsmoothed probability distribution:
>>> cpd_mle = nltk.ConditionalProbDist(cfd, nltk.MLEProbDist,
bins=len(vocabulary))
>>> # Now we can get the MLE probabilities by using the .prob method:
>>> [cpd_mle[a].prob(b) for (a,b) in nltk.bigrams(sentence)]
[0, 1.0, 0.0]
>>> # LaplaceProbDist is the add-one smoothed ProbDist:
>>> cpd_laplace = nltk.ConditionalProbDist(cfd, nltk.LaplaceProbDist,
bins=len(vocabulary))
>>> # Getting the Laplace probabilities is the same as for MLE:
>>> [cpd_laplace[a].prob(b) for (a,b) in nltk.bigrams(sentence)]
[0.07692307692307693, 0.14285714285714285, 0.06666666666666667]
```

Good Turing

Good Turing was introduced by Alan Turing along with his statistical assistant I.J. Good. It is an efficient smoothing method that increases the performance of statistical techniques performed for linguistic tasks, such as word sense disambiguation (WSD), named entity recognition (NER), spelling correction, machine translation, and so on. This method helps to predict the probability of unseen objects. In this method, binomial distribution is exhibited by our objects of interest. This method is used to compute the mass probability for zero or low count samples on the basis of higher count samples . Simple Good Turing performs approximation from frequency to frequency by linear regression into a linear line in log space. If $c\backslash$ is the adjusted count, it will compute the following:

$c\backslash = (c + 1)\, N(c + 1) / N(c)$ *for* $c >= 1$

The samples with zero frequency in training = *N(1)* for *c* == *0*.

Here, *c* is the original count and *N(i)* is the number of event types observed with count `i`.

Bill Gale and Geoffrey Sampson have presented Simple Good Turing:

```
class SimpleGoodTuringProbDist(ProbDistI):
"""


    Given a pair (pi, qi),  where pi refers to the frequency and
    qi refers to the frequency of frequency, our aim is to minimize
the
    square variation. E(p) and E(q) is the mean of pi and qi.

    - slope,  b = sigma ((pi-E(p)(qi-E(q))) / sigma ((pi-E(p))(pi-
E(p)))
    - intercept: a = E(q) - b.E(p)
"""
    SUM_TO_ONE = False
    def __init__(self, freqdist, bins=None):
"""
        param freqdist refers to the count of frequency from which
probability
        distribution is estimated.
        Param bins is used to estimate the possible number of samples.
"""
        assert bins is None or bins > freqdist.B(),\
'bins parameter must not be less than %d=freqdist.B()+1' %
(freqdist.B()+1)
        if bins is None:
            bins = freqdist.B() + 1
        self._freqdist = freqdist
        self._bins = bins
        r, nr = self._r_Nr()
        self.find_best_fit(r, nr)
        self._switch(r, nr)
        self._renormalize(r, nr)

    def _r_Nr_non_zero(self):
        r_Nr = self._freqdist.r_Nr()
        del r_Nr[0]
        return r_Nr
```

```
    def _r_Nr(self):
"""
Split the frequency distribution in two list (r, Nr), where Nr(r) > 0
"""
        nonzero = self._r_Nr_non_zero()

        if not nonzero:
            return [], []
        return zip(*sorted(nonzero.items()))

    def find_best_fit(self, r, nr):
"""
        Use simple linear regression to tune parameters self._slope
and
        self._intercept in the log-log space based on count and
Nr(count)
        (Work in log space to avoid floating point underflow.)
"""
        # For higher sample frequencies the data points becomes
horizontal
        # along line Nr=1. To create a more evident linear model in
log-log
        # space, we average positive Nr values with the surrounding
zero
        # values. (Church and Gale, 1991)

        if not r or not nr:
            # Empty r or nr?
            return

        zr = []
        for j in range(len(r)):
            i = (r[j-1] if j > 0 else 0)
            k = (2 * r[j] - i if j == len(r) - 1 else r[j+1])
            zr_ = 2.0 * nr[j] / (k - i)
            zr.append(zr_)

        log_r = [math.log(i) for i in r]
        log_zr = [math.log(i) for i in zr]

        xy_cov = x_var = 0.0
        x_mean = 1.0 * sum(log_r) / len(log_r)
        y_mean = 1.0 * sum(log_zr) / len(log_zr)
        for (x, y) in zip(log_r, log_zr):
```

```
            xy_cov += (x - x_mean) * (y - y_mean)
            x_var += (x - x_mean)**2
        self._slope = (xy_cov / x_var if x_var != 0 else 0.0)
        if self._slope >= -1:
            warnings.warn('SimpleGoodTuring did not find a proper best
fit '
'line for smoothing probabilities of occurrences. '
'The probability estimates are likely to be '
'unreliable.')
        self._intercept = y_mean - self._slope * x_mean

    def _switch(self, r, nr):
"""
        Calculate the r frontier where we must switch from Nr to Sr
        when estimating E[Nr].
"""
        for i, r_ in enumerate(r):
            if len(r) == i + 1 or r[i+1] != r_ + 1:
                # We are at the end of r, or there is a gap in r
                self._switch_at = r_
                break

            Sr = self.smoothedNr
            smooth_r_star = (r_ + 1) * Sr(r_+1) / Sr(r_)
            unsmooth_r_star = 1.0 * (r_ + 1) * nr[i+1] / nr[i]

            std = math.sqrt(self._variance(r_, nr[i], nr[i+1]))
            if abs(unsmooth_r_star-smooth_r_star) <= 1.96 * std:
                self._switch_at = r_
                break

    def _variance(self, r, nr, nr_1):
        r = float(r)
        nr = float(nr)
        nr_1 = float(nr_1)
        return (r + 1.0)**2 * (nr_1 / nr**2) * (1.0 + nr_1 / nr)

    def _renormalize(self, r, nr):
"""
```

Renormalization is very crucial to ensure that the proper distribution of probability is obtained. It can be obtained by making the probability estimate of an unseen sample *N(1)/N* and then, renormalizing all the previously seen sample probabilities:

```
"""
        prob_cov = 0.0
        for r_, nr_ in zip(r, nr):
            prob_cov  += nr_ * self._prob_measure(r_)
        if prob_cov:
            self._renormal = (1 - self._prob_measure(0)) / prob_cov

    def smoothedNr(self, r):
"""
        Return the number of samples with count r.


"""

        # Nr = a*r^b (with b < -1 to give the appropriate hyperbolic
        # relationship)
        # Estimate a and b by simple linear regression technique on
        # the logarithmic form of the equation: log Nr = a + b*log(r)

        return math.exp(self._intercept + self._slope * math.log(r))

    def prob(self, sample):
"""
        Return the sample's probability.

"""
        count = self._freqdist[sample]
        p = self._prob_measure(count)
        if count == 0:
            if self._bins == self._freqdist.B():
                p = 0.0
            else:
                p = p / (1.0 * self._bins - self._freqdist.B())
        else:
            p = p * self._renormal
        return p

    def _prob_measure(self, count):
        if count == 0 and self._freqdist.N() == 0 :
            return 1.0
        elif count == 0 and self._freqdist.N() != 0:
            return 1.0 * self._freqdist.Nr(1) / self._freqdist.N()
```

```
        if self._switch_at > count:
            Er_1 = 1.0 * self._freqdist.Nr(count+1)
            Er = 1.0 * self._freqdist.Nr(count)
        else:
            Er_1 = self.smoothedNr(count+1)
            Er = self.smoothedNr(count)

        r_star = (count + 1) * Er_1 / Er
        return r_star / self._freqdist.N()

    def check(self):
        prob_sum = 0.0
        for i in  range(0, len(self._Nr)):
            prob_sum += self._Nr[i] * self._prob_measure(i) / self._
renormal
        print("Probability Sum:", prob_sum)
        #assert prob_sum != 1.0, "probability sum should be one!"

    def discount(self):
"""
        It is used to provide the total probability transfers from the
        seen events to the unseen events.
"""
        return  1.0 * self.smoothedNr(1) / self._freqdist.N()

    def max(self):
        return self._freqdist.max()

    def samples(self):
        return self._freqdist.keys()

    def freqdist(self):
        return self._freqdist

    def __repr__(self):
"""
        It obtains the string representation of ProbDist.
"""
        return '<SimpleGoodTuringProbDist based on %d samples>'\
                % self._freqdist.N()
```

Let's see the code for Simple Good Turing in NLTK:

```
>>> gt = lambda fd, bins: SimpleGoodTuringProbDist(fd, bins=1e5)
>>> train_and_test(gt)
5.17%
```

Kneser Ney estimation

Kneser Ney is used with trigrams. Let's see the following code in NLTK for the Kneser Ney estimation:

```
>>> import nltk
>>> corpus = [[((x[0],y[0],z[0]),(x[1],y[1],z[1]))
    for x, y, z in nltk.trigrams(sent)]
  for sent in corpus[:100]]
>>> tag_set = unique_list(tag for sent in corpus for (word,tag) in
sent)
>>> len(tag_set)
906
>>> symbols = unique_list(word for sent in corpus for (word,tag) in
sent)
>>> len(symbols)
1341
>>> trainer = nltk.tag.HiddenMarkovModelTrainer(tag_set, symbols)
>>> train_corpus = []
>>> test_corpus = []
>>> for i in range(len(corpus)):
if i % 10:
train_corpus += [corpus[i]]
else:
test_corpus += [corpus[i]]

>>> len(train_corpus)
90
>>> len(test_corpus)
10
>>> kn = lambda fd, bins: KneserNeyProbDist(fd)
>>> train_and_test(kn)
0.86%
```

Witten Bell estimation

Witten Bell is the smoothing algorithm that was designed to deal with unknown words having zero probability. Let's consider the following code for Witten Bell estimation in NLTK:

```
>>> train_and_test(WittenBellProbDist)
6.90%
```

Develop a back-off mechanism for MLE

Katz back-off may be defined as a generative n gram language model that computes the conditional probability of a given token given its previous information in n gram. According to this model, in training, if n gram is seen more than n times, then the conditional probability of a token, given its previous information, is proportional to the MLE of that n gram. Else, the conditional probability is equivalent to the back-off conditional probability of (n-1) gram.

The following is the code for Katz's back-off model in NLTK:

```
def prob(self, word, context):
"""
Evaluate the probability of this word in this context using Katz
Backoff.
: param word: the word to get the probability of
: type word: str
:param context: the context the word is in
:type context: list(str)
"""
context = tuple(context)
if(context+(word,) in self._ngrams) or (self._n == 1):
return self[context].prob(word)
else:
return self._alpha(context) * self._backoff.prob(word,context[1:])
```

Applying interpolation on data to get mix and match

The limitation of using an additive smoothed bigram is that we back off to a state of ignorance when we deal with rare text. For example, the word captivating occurs five times in a training data: thrice followed by *by* and twice followed by *the*. With additive smoothing, the occurrence of *a* and *new* before captivating is the same. Both the occurrences are plausible, but the former is more probable as compared to latter. This problem can be rectified using unigram probabilities. We can develop an interpolation model in which both the unigram and bigram probabilities can be combined.

In SRILM, we perform interpolation by first training a unigram model with `-order 1` and `-order 2` used for the bigram model:

```
ngram - count - text / home / linux / ieng6 / ln165w / public / data
/ engand hintrain . txt \ - vocab / home / linux / ieng6 / ln165w /
public / data / engandhinlexicon . txt \ - order 1 - addsmooth 0.0001
- lm wsj1 . lm
```

Evaluate a language model through perplexity

The `nltk.model.ngram` module in NLTK has a submodule, `perplexity(text)`. This submodule evaluates the perplexity of a given text. Perplexity is defined as 2**Cross Entropy for the text. Perplexity defines how a probability model or probability distribution can be useful to predict a text.

The code for evaluating the perplexity of text as present in the `nltk.model.ngram` module is as follows:

```
def perplexity(self, text):
"""
        Calculates the perplexity of the given text.
        This is simply 2 ** cross-entropy for the text.

        :param text: words to calculate perplexity of
        :type text: list(str)
"""

        return pow(2.0, self.entropy(text))
```

Applying metropolis hastings in modeling languages

There are various ways to perform processing on posterior distribution in **Markov Chain Monte Carlo** (**MCMC**). One way is using the Metropolis-Hastings sampler. In order to implement the Metropolis-Hastings algorithm, we require standard uniform distribution, proposal distribution, and target distribution that is proportional to posterior probability. An example of Metropolis-Hastings is discussed in the following topic.

Applying Gibbs sampling in language processing

With the help of Gibbs sampling, Markov chain is built by sampling from the conditional probability. When the iteration over all the parameters is completed, then one cycle of the Gibbs sampler is completed. When it is not possible to sample from conditional distribution, then Metropolis-Hastings can be used. This is referred to as Metropolis within Gibbs. Gibbs sampling may be defined as Metropolis-hastings with special proposal distribution. On each iteration, we draw a proposal for a new value of a specific parameter.

Consider an example of throwing two coins that is characterized by the number of heads and the number of tosses of a coin:

```
def bern(theta,z,N):
"""Bernoulli likelihood with N trials and z successes."""
return np.clip(theta**z*(1-theta)**(N-z),0,1)
def bern2(theta1,theta2,z1,z2,N1,N2):
"""Bernoulli likelihood with N trials and z successes."""
return bern(theta1,z1,N1)*bern(theta2,z2,N2)
def make_thetas(xmin,xmax,n):
xs=np.linspace(xmin,xmax,n)
widths=(xs[1:]-xs[:-1])/2.0
thetas=xs[:-1]+widths
returnt hetas
def make_plots(X,Y,prior,likelihood,posterior,projection=None):
fig,ax=plt.subplots(1,3,subplot_kw=dict(projection=projection,aspect='
equal'),figsize=(12,3))
ifprojection=='3d':
ax[0].plot_surface(X,Y,prior,alpha=0.3,cmap=plt.cm.jet)
ax[1].plot_surface(X,Y,likelihood,alpha=0.3,cmap=plt.cm.jet)
ax[2].plot_surface(X,Y,posterior,alpha=0.3,cmap=plt.cm.jet)
else:
ax[0].contour(X,Y,prior)
ax[1].contour(X,Y,likelihood)
ax[2].contour(X,Y,posterior)
ax[0].set_title('Prior')
ax[1].set_title('Likelihood')
ax[2].set_title('Posteior')
plt.tight_layout()
thetas1=make_thetas(0,1,101)
thetas2=make_thetas(0,1,101)
X,Y=np.meshgrid(thetas1,thetas2)
```

For Metropolis, the following values are considered:

```
a=2
b=3

z1=11
N1=14
z2=7
N2=14

prior=lambdatheta1,theta2:stats.beta(a,b).pdf(theta1)*stats.beta(a,b).
pdf(theta2)
```

```
lik=partial(bern2,z1=z1,z2=z2,N1=N1,N2=N2)
target=lambdatheta1,theta2:prior(theta1,theta2)*lik(theta1,theta2)

theta=np.array([0.5,0.5])
niters=10000
burnin=500
sigma=np.diag([0.2,0.2])

thetas=np.zeros((niters-burnin,2),np.float)
foriinrange(niters):
new_theta=stats.multivariate_normal(theta,sigma).rvs()
p=min(target(*new_theta)/target(*theta),1)
ifnp.random.rand()<p:
theta=new_theta
ifi>=burnin:
thetas[i-burnin]=theta
kde=stats.gaussian_kde(thetas.T)
XY=np.vstack([X.ravel(),Y.ravel()])
posterior_metroplis=kde(XY).reshape(X.shape)
make_plots(X,Y,prior(X,Y),lik(X,Y),posterior_metroplis)
make_plots(X,Y,prior(X,Y),lik(X,Y),posterior_
metroplis,projection='3d')
```

For Gibbs, the following values are considered:

```
a=2
b=3

z1=11
N1=14
z2=7
N2=14

prior=lambda theta1,theta2:stats.beta(a,b).pdf(theta1)*stats.
beta(a,b).pdf(theta2)
lik=partial(bern2,z1=z1,z2=z2,N1=N1,N2=N2)
target=lambdatheta1,theta2:prior(theta1,theta2)*lik(theta1,theta2)

theta=np.array([0.5,0.5])
niters=10000
burnin=500
sigma=np.diag([0.2,0.2])

thetas=np.zeros((niters-burnin,2),np.float)
foriinrange(niters):
```

```
theta=[stats.beta(a+z1,b+N1-z1).rvs(),theta[1]]
theta=[theta[0],stats.beta(a+z2,b+N2-z2).rvs()]

ifi>=burnin:
thetas[i-burnin]=theta
kde=stats.gaussian_kde(thetas.T)
XY=np.vstack([X.ravel(),Y.ravel()])
posterior_gibbs=kde(XY).reshape(X.shape)
make_plots(X,Y,prior(X,Y),lik(X,Y),posterior_gibbs)
make_plots(X,Y,prior(X,Y),lik(X,Y),posterior_gibbs,projection='3d')
```

In the preceding codes of Metropolis and Gibbs, 2D and 3D plots of prior, likelihood, and posterior would be obtained.

Summary

In this chapter, we have discussed about word frequencies (unigram, bigram, and trigram). You have studied Maximum Likelihood Estimation and its implementation in NLTK. We have discussed about the interpolation method, the backoff method, Gibbs sampling, and Metropolis-hastings. We have also discussed how we can perform language modeling through perplexity.

In the next chapter, we will discuss about Stemmer and Lemmatizer, and creating the Morphological generator using machine learning tools.

3
Morphology – Getting Our Feet Wet

Morphology may be defined as the study of the composition of words using morphemes. A morpheme is the smallest unit of language that has meaning. In this chapter, we will discuss stemming and lemmatizing, stemmer and lemmatizer for non-English languages, developing a morphological analyzer and morphological generator using machine learning tools, search engines, and many such concepts.

In brief, this chapter will include the following topics:

- Introducing morphology
- Understanding stemmer
- Understanding lemmatization
- Developing a stemmer for non-English languages
- Morphological analyzer
- Morphological generator
- Search engine

Introducing morphology

Morphology may be defined as the study of the production of tokens with the help of **morphemes**. A morpheme is the basic unit of language carrying meaning. There are two types of morpheme: stems and affixes (suffixes, prefixes, infixes, and circumfixes).

Stems are also referred to as free morphemes, since they can even exist without adding affixes. Affixes are referred to as bound morphemes, since they cannot exist in a free form and they always exist along with free morphemes. Consider the word `unbelievable`. Here, `believe` is a stem or a free morpheme. It can exist on its own. The morphemes `un` and `able` are affixes or bound morphemes. They cannot exist in a free form, but they exist together with stem. There are three kinds of language, namely **isolating languages**, **agglutinative languages**, and **inflecting languages**. Morphology has a different meaning in all these languages. Isolating languages are those languages in which words are merely free morphemes and they do not carry any tense (past, present, and future) and number (singular or plural) information. Mandarin Chinese is an example of an isolating language. Agglutinative languages are those in which small words combine together to convey compound information. Turkish is an example of an agglutinative language. Inflecting languages are those in which words are broken down into simpler units, but all these simpler units exhibit different meanings. Latin is an example of an inflecting language. Morphological processes are of the following types: inflection, derivation, semiaffixes and combining forms, and cliticization. Inflection means transforming the word into a form so that it represents person, number, tense, gender, case, aspect, and mood. Here, the syntactic category of a token remains the same. In derivation, the syntactic category of a word is also changed. Semiaffixes are bound morphemes that exhibit words, such as quality, for example, noteworthy, antisocial, anticlockwise, and so on.

Understanding stemmer

Stemming may be defined as the process of obtaining a stem from a word by eliminating the affixes from a word. For example, in the case of the word `raining`, stemmer would return the root word or stem word `rain` by removing the affix from raining. In order to increase the accuracy of information retrieval, search engines mostly use stemming to get the stems and store them as indexed words. Search engines call words with the same meaning synonyms, which may be a kind of query expansion known as conflation. *Martin Porter* has designed a well-known stemming algorithm known as the *Porter stemming algorithm*. This algorithm is basically designed to replace and eliminate some well-known suffices present in English words. To perform stemming in NLTK, we can simply do an instantiation of the `PorterStemmer` class and then perform stemming by calling the `stem` method.

Let's see the code for stemming using the `PorterStemmer` class in NLTK:

```
>>> import nltk
>>> from nltk.stem import PorterStemmer
>>> stemmerporter = PorterStemmer()
>>> stemmerporter.stem('working')
```

```
'work'
>>> stemmerporter.stem('happiness')
'happi'
```

The `PorterStemmer` class has been trained and has knowledge of the many stems and word forms of English. The process of stemming takes place in a series of steps and transforms the word into a shorter word or a word that has a similar meaning to the root word. The **Stemmer I** interface defines the `stem()` method, and all the stemmers are inherited from the **Stemmer I** interface. The inheritance diagram is depicted here:

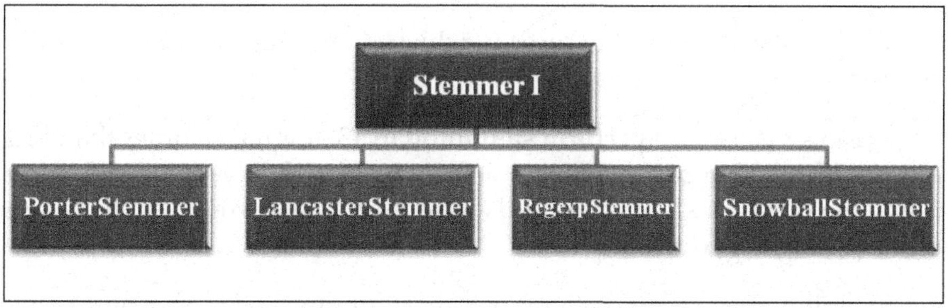

Another stemming algorithm known as the *Lancaster stemming algorithm* was introduced at Lancaster University. Similar to the `PorterStemmer` class, the `LancasterStemmer` class is used in NLTK to implement Lancaster stemming. However, one of the major differences between the two algorithms is that Lancaster stemming involves the use of more words of different sentiments as compared to Porter Stemming.

Let's consider the following code that depicts Lancaster stemming in NLTK:

```
>>> import nltk
>>> from nltk.stem import LancasterStemmer
>>> stemmerlan=LancasterStemmer()
>>> stemmerlan.stem('working')
'work'
>>> stemmerlan.stem('happiness')
'happy'
```

We can also build our own stemmer in NLTK using `RegexpStemmer`. It works by accepting a string and eliminating the string from the prefix or suffix of a word when a match is found.

Let's consider an example of stemming using `RegexpStemmer` in NLTK:

```
>>> import nltk
>>> from nltk.stem import RegexpStemmer
>>> stemmerregexp=RegexpStemmer('ing')
>>> stemmerregexp.stem('working')
'work'
>>> stemmerregexp.stem('happiness')
'happiness'
>>> stemmerregexp.stem('pairing')
'pair'
```

We can use `RegexpStemmer` in the cases in which stemming cannot be performed using `PorterStemmer` and `LancasterStemmer`.

`SnowballStemmer` is used to perform stemming in 13 languages other than English. In order to perform stemming using `SnowballStemmer`, firstly, an instance is created in the language in which stemming needs to be performed. Then, using the `stem()` method, stemming is performed.

Consider the following example of performing stemming in Spanish and French in NLTK using `SnowballStemmer`:

```
>>> import nltk
>>> from nltk.stem import SnowballStemmer
>>> SnowballStemmer.languages
('danish', 'dutch', 'english', 'finnish', 'french', 'german',
'hungarian', 'italian', 'norwegian', 'porter', 'portuguese',
'romanian', 'russian', 'spanish', 'swedish')
>>> spanishstemmer=SnowballStemmer('spanish')
>>> spanishstemmer.stem('comiendo')
'com'
>>> frenchstemmer=SnowballStemmer('french')
>>> frenchstemmer.stem('manger')
'mang'
```

`Nltk.stem.api` consists of the `Stemmer I` class in which the `stem` function is performed.

Consider the following code present in NLTK that enables us to perform stemming:

```
Class StemmerI(object):
"""
It is an interface that helps to eliminate morphological affixes from
the tokens and the process is known as stemming.
"""
```

```
def stem(self, token):
"""
Eliminate affixes from token and stem is returned.
"""
raise NotImplementedError()
```

Let's see the code used to perform stemming using multiple stemmers:

```
>>> import nltk
>>> from nltk.stem.porter import PorterStemmer
>>> from nltk.stem.lancaster import LancasterStemmer
>>> from nltk.stem import SnowballStemmer
>>> def obtain_tokens():
With open('/home/p/NLTK/sample1.txt') as stem: tok = nltk.word_
tokenize(stem.read())
return tokens
>>> def  stemming(filtered):
stem=[]
for x in filtered:
stem.append(PorterStemmer().stem(x))
return stem
>>>  if_name_=="_main_":
tok= obtain_tokens()
>>>print("tokens is %s")%(tok)
>>>stem_tokens= stemming(tok)
>>>print("After stemming is %s")%stem_tokens
>>>res=dict(zip(tok,stem_tokens))
>>>print("{tok:stemmed}=%s")%(result)
```

Understanding lemmatization

Lemmatization is the process in which we transform the word into a form with a different word category. The word formed after lemmatization is entirely different. The built-in `morphy()` function is used for lemmatization in `WordNetLemmatizer`. The inputted word is left unchanged if it is not found in WordNet. In the argument, `pos` refers to the part of speech category of the inputted word.

Consider an example of lemmatization in NLTK:

```
>>> import nltk
>>> from nltk.stem import WordNetLemmatizer
>>> lemmatizer_output=WordNetLemmatizer()
>>> lemmatizer_output.lemmatize('working')
'working'
```

```
>>> lemmatizer_output.lemmatize('working',pos='v')
'work'
>>> lemmatizer_output.lemmatize('works')
'work'
```

The `WordNetLemmatizer` library may be defined as a wrapper around the so-called WordNet corpus, and it makes use of the `morphy()` function present in `WordNetCorpusReader` to extract a lemma. If no lemma is extracted, then the word is only returned in its original form. For example, for `works`, the lemma returned is the singular form, `work`.

Let's consider the following code that illustrates the difference between stemming and lemmatization :

```
>>> import nltk
>>> from nltk.stem import PorterStemmer
>>> stemmer_output=PorterStemmer()
>>> stemmer_output.stem('happiness')
'happi'
>>> from nltk.stem import WordNetLemmatizer
>>> lemmatizer_output=WordNetLemmatizer()
>>> lemmatizer_output.lemmatize('happiness')
'happiness'
```

In the preceding code, `happiness` is converted to `happi` by stemming. Lemmatization doesn't find the root word for `happiness`, so it returns the word `happiness`.

Developing a stemmer for non-English language

Polyglot is a software that is used to provide models called morfessor models that are used to obtain morphemes from tokens. The Morpho project's goal is to create unsupervised data-driven processes. The main aim of the Morpho project is to focus on the creation of morphemes, which is the smallest unit of syntax. Morphemes play an important role in natural language processing. Morphemes are useful in automatic recognition and the creation of language. With the help of the vocabulary dictionaries of Polyglot, morfessor models on the 50,000 tokens of different languages were used.

Let's see the code for obtaining the language table using `polyglot`:

```
from polyglot.downloader import downloader
print(downloader.supported_languages_table("morph2"))
```

The output obtained from preceding code is the languages listed here:

1. Piedmontese language	2. Lombard language	3. Gan Chinese
4. Sicilian	5. Scots	6. Kirghiz, Kyrgyz
7. Pashto, Pushto	8. Kurdish	9. Portuguese
10. Kannada	11. Korean	12. Khmer
13. Kazakh	14. Ilokano	15. Polish
16. Panjabi, Punjabi	17. Georgian	18. Chuvash
19. Alemannic	20. Czech	21. Welsh
22. Chechen	23. Catalan; Valencian	24. Northern Sami
25. Sanskrit (Sa?sk?ta)	26. Slovene	27. Javanese
28. Slovak	29. Bosnian-Croatian-Serbian	30. Bavarian
31. Swedish	32. Swahili	33. Sundanese
34. Serbian	35. Albanian	36. Japanese
37. Western Frisian	38. French	39. Finnish
40. Upper Sorbian	41. Faroese	42. Persian
43. Sinhala, Sinhalese	44. Italian	45. Amharic
46. Aragonese	47. Volapük	48. Icelandic
49. Sakha	50. Afrikaans	51. Indonesian
52. Interlingua	53. Azerbaijani	54. Ido
55. Arabic	56. Assamese	57. Yoruba
58. Yiddish	59. Waray-Waray	60. Croatian
61. Hungarian	62. Haitian; Haitian Creole	63. Quechua
64. Armenian	65. Hebrew (modern)	66. Silesian
67. Hindi	68. Divehi; Dhivehi; Mald...	69. German
70. Danish	71. Occitan	72. Tagalog
73. Turkmen	74. Thai	75. Tajik
76. Greek, Modern	77. Telugu	78. Tamil
79. Oriya	80. Ossetian, Ossetic	81. Tatar
82. Turkish	83. Kapampangan	84. Venetian
85. Manx	86. Gujarati	87. Galician
88. Irish	89. Scottish Gaelic; Gaelic	90. Nepali
91. Cebuano	92. Zazaki	93. Walloon
94. Dutch	95. Norwegian	96. Norwegian Nynorsk
97. West Flemish	98. Chinese	99. Bosnian
100. Breton	101. Belarusian	102. Bulgarian
103. Bashkir	104. Egyptian Arabic	105. Tibetan Standard, Tib...
106. Bengali	107. Burmese	108. Romansh
109. Marathi (Mara?hi)	110. Malay	111. Maltese
112. Russian	113. Macedonian	114. Malayalam
115. Mongolian	116. Malagasy	117. Vietnamese
118. Spanish; Castilian	119. Estonian	120. Basque
121. Bishnupriya Manipuri	122. Asturian	123. English
124. Esperanto	125. Luxembourgish, Letzeb...	126. Latin
127. Uighur, Uyghur	128. Ukrainian	129. Limburgish, Limburgan...
130. Latvian	131. Urdu	132. Lithuanian
133. Fiji Hindi	134. Uzbek	135. Romanian, Moldavian, ...

The necessary models can be downloaded using the following code:

```
%%bash
polyglot download morph2.en morph2.ar

[polyglot_data] Downloading package morph2.en to
[polyglot_data]     /home/rmyeid/polyglot_data...
[polyglot_data]   Package morph2.en is already up-to-date!
[polyglot_data] Downloading package morph2.ar to
[polyglot_data]     /home/rmyeid/polyglot_data...
[polyglot_data]   Package morph2.ar is already up-to-date!
```

Consider an example that is used to obtain an output from `polyglot`:

```
from polyglot.text import Text, Word
tokens =["unconditional" ,"precooked", "impossible", "painful",
"entered"]
for s in tokens:
s=Word(s, language="en")
print("{:<20}{}".format(s,s.morphemes))

unconditional['un','conditional']
precooked['pre','cook','ed']
impossible['im','possible']
painful['pain','ful']
entered['enter','ed']
```

If tokenization is not performed properly, then we can perform morphological analysis for the process of splitting the text into the original constituents:

```
sent="Ihopeyoufindthebookinteresting"
para=Text(sent)
para.language="en"
para.morphemes
WordList(['I','hope','you','find','the','book','interesting'])
```

Morphological analyzer

Morphological analysis may be defined as the process of obtaining grammatical information from tokens, given their suffix information. Morphological analysis can be performed in three ways: morpheme-based morphology (or anitem and arrangement approach), lexeme-based morphology (or an item and process approach), and word-based morphology (or a word and paradigm approach). A morphological analyzer may be defined as a program that is responsible for the analysis of the morphology of a given input token. It analyzes a given token and generates morphological information, such as gender, number, class, and so on, as an output.

In order to perform morphological analysis on a given non-whitespace token, the `pyEnchant` dictionary is used.

Let's consider the following code that performs morphological analysis:

```
>>> import enchant
>>> s = enchant.Dict("en_US")
>>> tok=[]
>>> def tokenize(st1):
if not st1:return
for j in xrange(len(st1),-1,-1):
if s.check(st1[0:j]):
tok.append(st1[0:i])
st1=st[j:]
tokenize(st1)
break
>>> tokenize("itismyfavouritebook")
>>> tok
['it', 'is', 'my','favourite','book']
>>> tok=[ ]
>>> tokenize("ihopeyoufindthebookinteresting")
>>> tok
['i','hope','you','find','the','book','interesting']
```

We can determine the category of the word with the help of the following points:

- **Morphological hints**: The suffix's information helps us detect the category of a word. For example, the -ness and -ment suffixes exist with nouns.
- **Syntactic hints**: Contextual information is conducive to determine the category of a word. For example, if we have found the word that has the noun category, then syntactic hints will be useful for determining whether an adjective would appear before the noun or after the noun category.
- **Semantic hints**: A semantic hint is also useful for determining the word's category. For example, if we already know that a word represents the name of a location, then it will fall under the noun category.
- **Open class**: This is class of words that are not fixed, and their number keeps on increasing every day, whenever a new word is added to their list. Words in the open class are usually nouns. Prepositions are mostly in a closed class. For example, there can be an unlimited number of words in the of Persons list. So, it is an open class.
- **Morphology captured by the Part of Speech tagset**: The Part of Speech tagset captures information that helps us perform morphology. For example, the word `plays` would appear with the third person and a singular noun.

- **Omorfi:Omorfi** (**Open morphology of Finnish**) is a package that has been licensed by GNU GPL version 3. It is used for performing numerous tasks, such as language modeling, morphological analysis, rule-based machine translation, information retrieval, statistical machine translation, morphological segmentation, ontologies, and spell checking and correction.

Morphological generator

A morphological generator is a program that performs the task of morphological generation. Morphological generation may be considered an opposite task of morphological analysis. Here, given the description of a word in terms of number, category, stem, and so on, the original word is retrieved. For example, if *root* = *go*, *part of speech* = *verb*, *tense*= *present*, and if it occurs along with a third person and singular subject, then a morphological generator would generate its surface form, goes.

There is a lot of Python-based software that performs morphological analysis and generation. Some of them are as follows:

- **ParaMorfo**: It is used to perform morphological generation and analysis of Spanish and Guarani nouns, adjectives, and verbs.
- **HornMorpho**: It is used for the morphological generation and analysis of Oromo and Amharic nouns and verbs, as well as Tigrinya verbs.
- **AntiMorfo**: It is used for the morphological generation and analysis of Quechua adjectives, verbs, and nouns, as well as Spanish verbs.
- **MorfoMelayu**: It is used for the morphological analysis of Malay words.

Other examples of software that is used to perform morphological analysis and generation are as follows:

- Morph is a morphological generator and analyzer for English for the RASP system
- Morphy is a morphological generator, analyzer, and POS tagger for German
- Morphisto is a morphological generator and analyzer for German
- Morfette performs supervised learning (inflectional morphology) for Spanish and French

Search engine

PyStemmer 1.0.1 consists of Snowball stemming algorithms that are used for performing information retrieval tasks and for constructing a search engine. It consists of the Porter stemming algorithm and many other stemming algorithms that are useful for performing stemming and information retrieval tasks in many languages, including many European languages.

We can construct a vector space search engine by converting the texts into vectors.

The following are the steps involved in constructing a vector space search engine:

1. Consider the following code for the removal of stopwords and tokenization:

   A stemmer is a program that accepts words and converts them into stems. Tokens that have the same stem have nearly the same meanings. Stopwords are also eliminated from a text.

   ```
   def eliminatestopwords(self,list):
   """
   Eliminate words which occur often and have not much significance
   from context point of view.
   """
   return[ word for word in list if word not in self.stopwords ]

   def tokenize(self,string):
   """
   Perform the task of splitting text into stop words and tokens
   """
   Str=self.clean(str)
   Words=str.split("")
   return [self.stemmer.stem(word,0,len(word)-1) for word in words]
   ```

2. Consider the following code for mapping keywords into vector dimensions:

   ```
   def obtainvectorkeywordindex(self, documentList):
   """
   In the document vectors,  generate the keyword for the given
   position of element
   """


   #Perform mapping of text into strings
   vocabstring = "".join(documentList)

   vocablist = self.parser.tokenise(vocabstring)
   ```

```
#Eliminate common words that have no search significance
vocablist = self.parser.eliminatestopwords(vocablist)
uniqueVocablist = util.removeDuplicates(vocablist)

vectorIndex={}
 offset=0
#Attach a position to keywords that performs mapping with
dimension that is used to depict this token
 for word in uniqueVocablist:
vectorIndex[word]=offset
offset+=1
 return vectorIndex  #(keyword:position)
```

3. Here, a simple term count model is used. Consider the following code for the conversion of text strings into vectors:

```
def constructVector(self, wordString):

        # Initialise the vector with 0's
        Vector_val = [0] * len(self.vectorKeywordIndex)
        tokList = self.parser.tokenize(tokString)
        tokList = self.parser.eliminatestopwords(tokList)
        for word in toklist:
                vector[self.vectorKeywordIndex[word]] += 1;
# simple Term Count Model is used
        return vector
```

4. Searching similar documents by finding the cosine of an angle between the vectors of a document, we can prove whether two given documents are similar or not. If the cosine value is 1, then the angle's value is 0 degrees and the vectors are said to be parallel (this means that the documents are said to be related). If the cosine value is 0 and value of the angle is 90 degrees, then the vectors are said to be perpendicular (this means that the documents are not said to be related). Let's see the code for computing the cosine between the text vectors using SciPy:

```
def cosine(vec1, vec2):
"""
                cosine  = ( X * Y ) / ||X|| x ||Y||
"""
return float(dot(vec1,vec2) / (norm(vec1) * norm(vec2)))
```

5. We perform the mapping of keywords to vector space. We construct a temporary text that represents the items to be searched and then compare it with document vectors with the help of cosine measurement. Let's see the following code for searching the vector space:

```
def searching(self,searchinglist):
""" search for text that are  matched on the  basis oflist of
items """
        askVector = self.buildQueryVector(searchinglist)

ratings = [util.cosine(askVector, textVector) for textVector in
self.documentVectors]
        ratings.sort(reverse=True)
        return ratings
```

6. We will now consider the following code that can be used for detecting languages from the source text:

```
>>>  import nltk
>>>  import sys
>>> try:
from nltk import wordpunct_tokenize
from nltk.corpus import stopwords
except ImportError:
print( 'Error has occured')



#-----------------------------------------------------------------
-----
>>> def _calculate_languages_ratios(text):
"""
Compute probability of given document that can be written in
different languages and give a dictionary that appears like
{'german': 2, 'french': 4, 'english': 1}
"""
 languages_ratios = {}
'''
nltk.wordpunct_tokenize() splits all punctuations into separate
tokens
 wordpunct_tokenize("I hope you like the book interesting .")
[' I',' hope ','you ','like ','the ','book' ,'interesting ','.']
'''

tok = wordpunct_tokenize(text)
wor = [word.lower() for word in tok]

  # Compute occurence of unique stopwords in a text
for language in stopwords.fileids():
stopwords_set = set(stopwords.words(language))
```

```
words_set = set(words)
common_elements = words_set.intersection(stopwords_set)
languages_ratios[language] = len(common_elements)
# language "score"
return languages_ratios

#---------------------------------------------------------------

>>> def detect_language(text):
"""
Compute the probability of given text that is written in different
languages and obtain the one that is highest scored. It makes
use of stopwords calculation approach, finds out unique stopwords
present in a analyzed text.
"""
ratios = _calculate_languages_ratios(text)
most_rated_language = max(ratios, key=ratios.get)
return most_rated_language



if __name__=='__main__':

 text = '''
All over this cosmos, most of the people believe that there is
an invisible supreme power that is the creator and the runner of
this world. Human being is supposed to be the most intelligent and
loved creation by that power and that is being searched by human
beings in different ways into different things. As a result people
reveal His assumed form as per their own perceptions and beliefs.
It has given birth to different religions and people are divided
on the name of religion viz. Hindu, Muslim, Sikhs, Christian etc.
People do not stop at this. They debate the superiority of one
over the other and fight to establish their views. Shrewd people
like politicians oppose and support them at their own convenience
to divide them and control them. It has intensified to the extent
that even parents of a
new born baby teach it about religious differences and recommend
their own religion superior to that of others and let the child
learn to hate other people just because of religion. Jonathan
Swift, an eighteenth century novelist, observes that we have just
enough religion to make us hate, but not enough to make us love
one another.
The word 'religion' does not have a derogatory meaning - A literal
meaning of religion is 'A
personal or institutionalized system grounded in belief in a God
or Gods and the activities connected
```

```
with this'. At its basic level, 'religion is just a set of
teachings that tells people how to lead a good
life'. It has never been the purpose of religion to divide people
into groups of isolated followers that
cannot live in harmony together. No religion claims to teach
intolerance or even instructs its believers to segregate a
certain religious group or even take the fundamental rights of
an individual solely based on their religious choices. It is also
said that 'Majhab nhi sikhata aaps mai bair krna'.But this very
majhab or religion takes a very heinous form when it is misused
by the shrewd politicians and the fanatics e.g. in Ayodhya on 6th
December, 1992 some right wing political parties
and communal organizations incited the Hindus to demolish the 16th
century Babri Masjid in the
name of religion to polarize Hindus votes. Muslim fanatics in
Bangladesh retaliated and destroyed a
number of temples, assassinated innocent Hindus and raped Hindu
girls who had nothing to do with
the demolition of Babri Masjid. This very inhuman act has been
presented by Taslima Nasrin, a Bangladeshi Doctor-cum-Writer
in her controversial novel 'Lajja' (1993) in which, she seems
to utilizes fiction's mass emotional appeal, rather than its
potential for nuance and universality.
'''

>>> language = detect_language(text)

>>> print(language)
```

The preceding code will search for stopwords and detect the language of the text, that is, English.

Summary

The field of computational linguistics has numerous applications. We need to perform preprocessing on our original text in order to implement or build an application. In this chapter, we have discussed stemming, lemmatization, and morphological analysis and generation, and their implementation in NLTK. We have also discussed search engines and their implementation.

In the next chapter, we will discuss parts of speech, tagging, and chunking.

4

Parts-of-Speech Tagging – Identifying Words

Parts-of-speech (**POS**) tagging is one of the many tasks in NLP. It is defined as the process of assigning a particular parts-of-speech tag to individual words in a sentence. The parts-of-speech tag identifies whether a word is a noun, verb, adjective, and so on. There are numerous applications of parts-of-speech tagging, such as information retrieval, machine translation, NER, language analysis, and so on.

This chapter will include the following topics:

- Creating POS tagged corpora
- Selecting a machine learning algorithm
- Statistical modeling involving the n-gram approach
- Developing a chunker using POS tagged data

Introducing parts-of-speech tagging

Parts-of-speech tagging is the process of assigning a category (for example, noun, verb, adjective, and so on) tag to individual tokens in a sentence. In NLTK, taggers are present in the `nltk.tag` package and it is inherited by the `TaggerIbase` class.

Consider an example to implement POS tagging for a given sentence in NLTK:

```
>>> import nltk
>>> text1=nltk.word_tokenize("It is a pleasant day today")
>>> nltk.pos_tag(text1)
[('It', 'PRP'), ('is', 'VBZ'), ('a', 'DT'), ('pleasant', 'JJ'),
('day', 'NN'), ('today', 'NN')]
```

We can implement the `tag()` method in all the subclasses of `TaggerI`. In order to evaluate tagger, `TaggerI` has provided the `evaluate()` method. A combination of taggers can be used to form a back-off chain so that the next tagger can be used for tagging if one tagger is not tagging.

Let's see the list of available tags provided by **Penn Treebank** (`https://www.ling.upenn.edu/courses/Fall_2003/ling001/penn_treebank_pos.html`):

```
CC - Coordinating conjunction
CD - Cardinal number
DT - Determiner
EX - Existential there
FW - Foreign word
IN - Preposition or subordinating conjunction
JJ - Adjective
JJR - Adjective, comparative
JJS - Adjective, superlative
LS - List item marker
MD - Modal
NN - Noun, singular or mass
NNS - Noun, plural
NNP - Proper noun, singular
NNPS - Proper noun, plural
PDT - Predeterminer
POS - Possessive ending
PRP - Personal pronoun
PRP$ - Possessive pronoun (prolog version PRP-S)
RB - Adverb
RBR - Adverb, comparative
RBS - Adverb, superlative
RP - Particle
SYM - Symbol
TO - to
UH - Interjection
VB - Verb, base form
VBD - Verb, past tense
VBG - Verb, gerund or present participle
VBN - Verb, past participle
VBP - Verb, non-3rd person singular present
VBZ - Verb, 3rd person singular present
WDT - Wh-determiner
WP - Wh-pronoun
WP$ - Possessive wh-pronoun (prolog version WP-S)
WRB - Wh-adverb
```

NLTK may provide the information of tags. Consider the following code, which provides information about the `NNS` tag:

```
>>> nltk.help.upenn_tagset('NNS')
NNS: noun, common, plural
    undergraduates scotches bric-a-brac products bodyguards facets
coasts
    divestitures storehouses designs clubs fragrances averages
    subjectivists apprehensions muses factory-jobs ...
```

Let's see another example in which a regular expression may also be queried:

```
>>> nltk.help.upenn_tagset('VB.*')
VB: verb, base form
    ask assemble assess assign assume atone attention avoid bake
balkanize
    bank begin behold believe bend benefit bevel beware bless boil
bomb
    boost brace break bring broil brush build ...
VBD: verb, past tense
    dipped pleaded swiped regummed soaked tidied convened halted
registered
    cushioned exacted snubbed strode aimed adopted belied figgered
    speculated wore appreciated contemplated ...
VBG: verb, present participle or gerund
    telegraphing stirring focusing angering judging stalling lactating
    hankerin' alleging veering capping approaching traveling besieging
    encrypting interrupting erasing wincing ...
VBN: verb, past participle
    multihulled dilapidated aerosolized chaired languished panelized
used
 experimented flourished imitated reunifed factored condensed sheared
    unsettled primed dubbed desired ...
VBP: verb, present tense, not 3rd person singular
    predominate wrap resort sue twist spill cure lengthen brush
terminate
    appear tend stray glisten obtain comprise detest tease attract
    emphasize mold postpone sever return wag ...
VBZ: verb, present tense, 3rd person singular
    bases reconstructs marks mixes displeases seals carps weaves
snatches
    slumps stretches authorizes smolders pictures emerges stockpiles
    seduces fizzes uses bolsters slaps speaks pleads ...R
```

The preceding code gives information regarding all the tags of verb phrases.

Let's look at an example that depicts words' sense disambiguation achieved through POS tagging:

```
>>> import nltk
>>> text=nltk.word_tokenize("I cannot bear the pain of bear")
>>> nltk.pos_tag(text)
[('I', 'PRP'), ('can', 'MD'), ('not', 'RB'), ('bear', 'VB'), ('the',
'DT'), ('pain', 'NN'), ('of', 'IN'), ('bear', 'NN')]
```

Here, in the previous sentence, `bear` is a verb, which means to tolerate, and it also is an animal, which means that it is a noun.

In NLTK, a tagged token is represented as a tuple consisting of a token and its tag. We can create this tuple in NLTK using the `str2tuple()` function:

```
>>> import nltk
>>> taggedword=nltk.tag.str2tuple('bear/NN')
>>> taggedword
('bear', 'NN')
>>> taggedword[0]
'bear'
>>> taggedword[1]
'NN'
```

Let's consider an example in which sequences of tuples can be generated from the given text:

```
>>> import nltk
>>> sentence='''The/DT sacred/VBN Ganga/NNP flows/VBZ in/IN this/DT
region/NN ./. This/DT is/VBZ a/DT pilgrimage/NN ./. People/NNP from/IN
all/DT over/IN the/DT country/NN visit/NN this/DT place/NN ./. '''
>>> [nltk.tag.str2tuple(t) for t in sentence.split()]
[('The', 'DT'), ('sacred', 'VBN'), ('Ganga', 'NNP'), ('flows', 'VBZ'),
('in', 'IN'), ('this', 'DT'), ('region', 'NN'), ('.', '.'), ('This',
'DT'), ('is', 'VBZ'), ('a', 'DT'), ('pilgrimage', 'NN'), ('.', '.'),
('People', 'NNP'), ('from', 'IN'), ('all', 'DT'), ('over', 'IN'),
('the', 'DT'), ('country', 'NN'), ('visit', 'NN'), ('this', 'DT'),
('place', 'NN'), ('.', '.')]
```

Now, consider the following code that converts the tuple (`word` and `pos` tag) into a word and a tag:

```
>>> import nltk
>>> taggedtok = ('bear', 'NN')
>>> from nltk.tag.util import tuple2str
>>> tuple2str(taggedtok)
'bear/NN'
```

Let's see the occurrence of some common tags in the Treebank corpus:

```
>>> import nltk
>>> from nltk.corpus import treebank
>>> treebank_tagged = treebank.tagged_words(tagset='universal')
>>> tag = nltk.FreqDist(tag for (word, tag) in treebank_tagged)
>>> tag.most_common()
[('NOUN', 28867), ('VERB', 13564), ('.', 11715), ('ADP', 9857),
('DET', 8725), ('X', 6613), ('ADJ', 6397), ('NUM', 3546), ('PRT',
3219), ('ADV', 3171), ('PRON', 2737), ('CONJ', 2265)]
```

Consider the following code, which calculates the number of tags occurring before a noun tag:

```
>>> import nltk
>>> from nltk.corpus import treebank
>>> treebank_tagged = treebank.tagged_words(tagset='universal')
>>> tagpairs = nltk.bigrams(treebank_tagged)
>>> preceders_noun = [x[1] for (x, y) in tagpairs if y[1] == 'NOUN']
>>> freqdist = nltk.FreqDist(preceders_noun)
>>> [tag for (tag, _) in freqdist.most_common()]
['NOUN', 'DET', 'ADJ', 'ADP', '.', 'VERB', 'NUM', 'PRT', 'CONJ',
'PRON', 'X', 'ADV']
```

We can also provide POS tags to tokens using dictionaries in Python. Let's see the following code that illustrates the creation of a tuple (`word:pos` tag) using dictionaries in Python:

```
>>> import nltk
>>> tag={}
>>> tag
{}
>>> tag['beautiful']='ADJ'
>>> tag
{'beautiful': 'ADJ'}
>>> tag['boy']='N'
>>> tag['read']='V'
>>> tag['generously']='ADV'
>>> tag
{'boy': 'N', 'beautiful': 'ADJ', 'generously': 'ADV', 'read': 'V'}
```

Default tagging

Default tagging is a kind of tagging that assigns identical parts-of-speech tags to all the tokens. The subclass of `SequentialBackoffTagger` is `DefaultTagger`. The `choose_tag()` method must be implemented by `SequentialBackoffTagger`. This method includes the following arguments:

- A collection of tokens
- The index of the token that should be tagged
- The previous tags list

The hierarchy of tagger is depicted as follows:

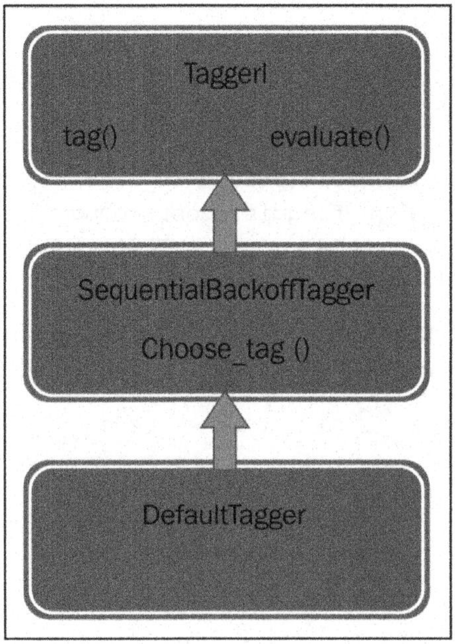

Let's now see the following code, which depicts the working of `DefaultTagger`:

```
>>> import nltk
>>> from nltk.tag import DefaultTagger
>>> tag = DefaultTagger('NN')
>>> tag.tag(['Beautiful', 'morning'])
[('Beautiful', 'NN'), ('morning', 'NN')]
```

We can convert a tagged sentence into an untagged sentence with the help of `nltk.tag.untag()`. After calling this function, the tags on individual tokens will be eliminated.

Let's see the code for untagging a sentence:

```
>>> from nltk.tag import untag
>>> untag([('beautiful', 'NN'), ('morning', 'NN')])
['beautiful', 'morning']
```

Creating POS-tagged corpora

A **corpus** may be known as a collection of documents. A **corpora** is the collection of multiple corpus.

Let's see the following code, which will generate a `data` directory inside the `home` directory:

```
>>> import nltk
>>> import os,os.path
>>> create = os.path.expanduser('~/nltkdoc')
>>> if not os.path.exists(create):
  os.mkdir(create)


>>> os.path.exists(create)
True
>>> import nltk.data
>>> create in nltk.data.path
True
```

This code will create a data directory named `~/nltkdoc` inside the `home` directory. The last line of this code will return `True` and will ensure that the `data` directory has been created. If the last line of the code returns `False`, then it means that the `data` directory has not been created and we need to create it manually. After creating the `data` directory manually, we can test the last line and it will then return `True`. Within this directory, we can create another directory named `nltkcorpora` that will hold the whole corpus. The path will be `~/nltkdoc/nltkcorpora`. Also, we can create a subdirectory named `important` that will hold all the necessary files.

The path will be `~/nltkdoc/nltkcorpora/important`.

Let's see the following code to load a text file into the subdirectory:

```
>>> import nltk.data
>>> nltk.data.load('nltkcorpora/important/firstdoc.txt',format='raw')
'nltk\n'
```

Here, in the previous code, we have mentioned `format='raw'`, since `nltk.data.load()` cannot interpret `.txt` files.

There is a word list corpus in NLTK known as the `Names` corpus. It consists of two files, namely, `male.txt` and `female.txt`.

Let's see the code to generate the length of `male.txt` and `female.txt`:

```
>>> import nltk
>>> from nltk.corpus import names
>>> names.fileids()
['female.txt', 'male.txt']
>>> len(names.words('male.txt'))
2943
>>> len(names.words('female.txt'))
5001
```

NLTK also consists of a large collection of English words. Let's see the code that describes the number of words present in the English word file:

```
>>> import nltk
>>> from nltk.corpus import words
>>> words.fileids()
['en', 'en-basic']
>>> len(words.words('en'))
235886
>>> len(words.words('en-basic'))
850
```

Consider the following code used in NLTK for defining the **Maxent Treebank** POS tagger:

```
def pos_tag(tok):
    """
```

We can use POS tagger given by NLTK to tag a list of tokens:

```
>>> from nltk.tag import pos_tag
>>> from nltk.tokenize import word_tokenize
>>> pos_tag(word_tokenize("Papa's favourite hobby is reading."))
        [('Papa', 'NNP'), ("'s", 'POS'), ('favourite', 'JJ'),
('hobby', 'NN'), ('is',
        'VBZ'), ('reading', 'VB'),  ('.', '.')]

    :param tokens: list of tokens that need to be tagged
    :type tok: list(str)
    :return: The tagged tokens
```

```
        :rtype: list(tuple(str, str))
        """
        tagger = load(_POS_TAGGER)
        return tagger.tag(tok)

    def batch_pos_tag(sent):
        """
        We can use part of speech tagger given by NLTK to perform tagging
    of list of tokens.
        """
        tagger = load(_POS_TAGGER)
        return tagger.batch_tag(sent)
```

Selecting a machine learning algorithm

POS tagging is also referred to as word category disambiguation or grammatical tagging. POS tagging may be of two types: rule-based or stochastic/probabilistic. E. Brill's tagger is based on the rule-based tagging algorithm.

A POS classifier takes a document as input and obtains word features. It trains itself with the help of these word features combined with the already available training labels. This type of classifier is referred to as a second order classifier, and it makes use of the bootstrap classifier in order to generate the tags for words.

A `backoff` classifier is one in which backoff procedure is performed. The output is obtained in such a manner that the trigram POS tagger relies on the bigram POS tagger, which in turn relies on the unigram POS tagger.

While training a POS classifier, a feature set is generated. This feature set may comprise the following:

- Information about the current word
- Information about the previous word or prefix
- Information about the next word or successor

In NLTK, `FastBrillTagger` is based on unigram. It makes use of a dictionary of words that are already known and the pos tag information.

Let's see the code for `FastBrillTagger` used in NLTK:

```
from nltk.tag import UnigramTagger
from nltk.tag import FastBrillTaggerTrainer

from nltk.tag.brill import SymmetricProximateTokensTemplate
```

```
from nltk.tag.brill import ProximateTokensTemplate
from nltk.tag.brill import ProximateTagsRule
from nltk.tag.brill import ProximateWordsRule

ctx = [ # Context = surrounding words and tags.
    SymmetricProximateTokensTemplate(ProximateTagsRule, (1, 1)),
    SymmetricProximateTokensTemplate(ProximateTagsRule, (1, 2)),
    SymmetricProximateTokensTemplate(ProximateTagsRule, (1, 3)),
    SymmetricProximateTokensTemplate(ProximateTagsRule, (2, 2)),
    SymmetricProximateTokensTemplate(ProximateWordsRule, (0, 0)),
    SymmetricProximateTokensTemplate(ProximateWordsRule, (1, 1)),
    SymmetricProximateTokensTemplate(ProximateWordsRule, (1, 2)),
    ProximateTokensTemplate(ProximateTagsRule, (-1, -1), (1, 1)),
]

tagger = UnigramTagger(sentences)
tagger = FastBrillTaggerTrainer(tagger, ctx, trace=0)
tagger = tagger.train(sentences, max_rules=100)
```

Classification may be defined as the process of deciding a POS tag for a given input.

In **supervised classification**, a training corpus is used that comprises a word and its correct tag. In **unsupervised classification**, any pair of words and a correct tag list does not exist:

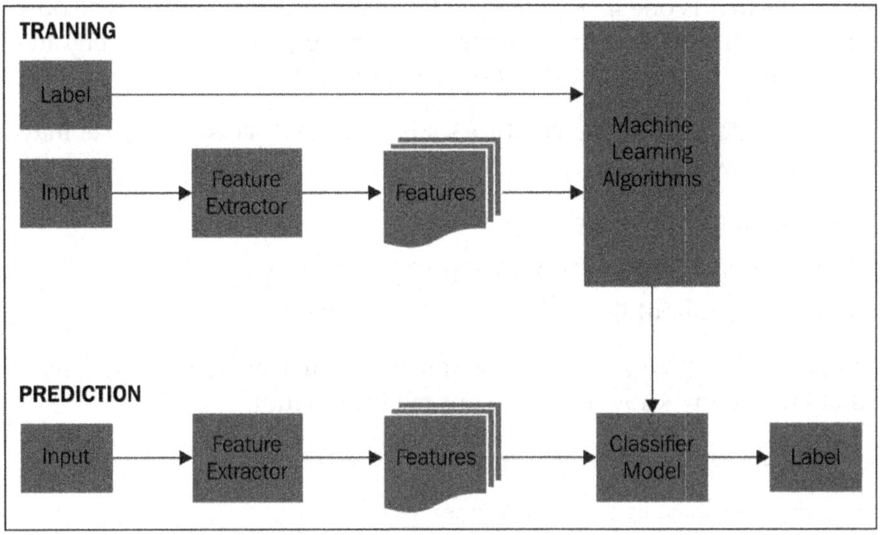

In supervised classification, during training, a feature extractor accepts the input and labels and generates a set of features. These features set along with the label act as input to machine learning algorithms. During the testing or prediction phase, a feature extractor is used that generates features from unknown inputs, and the output is sent to a classifier model that generates an output in the form of label or pos tag information with the help of machine learning algorithms.

The **maximum entropy** classifier is one in that searches the parameter set in order to maximize the total likelihood of the corpus used for training.

It may be defined as follows:

```
P(features_word) = Σx |in| corpus P(label_word(x)|features_word(x))
P(label_word|features_word) = P(label_word, features_word)
/ Σlabel_word P(label_word, features_word)
```

Statistical modeling involving the n-gram approach

Unigram means a single word. In a unigram tagger, a single token is used to find the particular parts-of-speech tag.

Training of `UnigramTagger` can be performed by providing it with a list of sentences at the time of initialization.

Let's see the following code in NLTK, which performs `UnigramTagger` training:

```
>>> import nltk
>>> from nltk.tag import UnigramTagger
>>> from nltk.corpus import treebank
>>> training= treebank.tagged_sents()[:7000]
>>> unitagger=UnigramTagger(training)
>>> treebank.sents()[0]
['Pierre', 'Vinken', ',', '61', 'years', 'old', ',', 'will', 'join',
'the', 'board', 'as', 'a', 'nonexecutive', 'director', 'Nov.', '29',
'.']
>>> unitagger.tag(treebank.sents()[0])
[('Pierre', 'NNP'), ('Vinken', 'NNP'), (',', ','), ('61', 'CD'),
('years', 'NNS'), ('old', 'JJ'), (',', ','), ('will', 'MD'), ('join',
'VB'), ('the', 'DT'), ('board', 'NN'), ('as', 'IN'), ('a', 'DT'),
('nonexecutive', 'JJ'), ('director', 'NN'), ('Nov.', 'NNP'), ('29',
'CD'), ('.', '.')]
```

In the preceding code, we have performed training using the first 7000 sentences of the Treebank corpus.

The hierarchy followed by `UnigramTagger` is depicted in the following inheritance diagram:

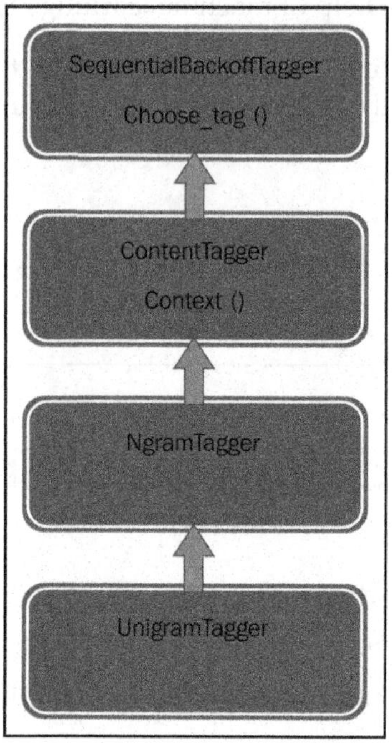

To evaluate `UnigramTagger`, let's see the following code, which calculates the accuracy:

```
>>> import nltk
>>> from nltk.corpus import treebank
>>> from nltk.tag import UnigramTagger
>>> training= treebank.tagged_sents()[:7000]
>>> unitagger=UnigramTagger(training)
>>> testing = treebank.tagged_sents()[2000:]
>>> unitagger.evaluate(testing)
0.963400866227395
```

So, it is 96% accurate in correctly performing pos tagging.

Since `UnigramTagger` inherits from `ContextTagger`, we can map the context key with a specific tag.

Consider the following example of tagging using `UnigramTagger`:

```
>>> import nltk
>>> from nltk.corpus import treebank
>>> from nltk.tag import UnigramTagger
>>> unitag = UnigramTagger(model={'Vinken': 'NN'})
>>> unitag.tag(treebank.sents()[0])
[('Pierre', None), ('Vinken', 'NN'), (',', None), ('61', None),
('years', None), ('old', None), (',', None), ('will', None), ('join',
None), ('the', None), ('board', None), ('as', None), ('a', None),
('nonexecutive', None), ('director', None), ('Nov.', None), ('29',
None), ('.', None)]
```

Here, in the preceding code, `UnigramTagger` only tags `'Vinken'` with the `'NN'` tag and the rest are tagged with the `'None'` tag since we have provided the tag for the word `'Vinken'` in the context model and no other words are included in the context model.

In a given context, `ContextTagger` uses the frequency of a given tag to decide the occurrence of the most probable tag. In order to use minimum threshold frequency, we can pass a specific value to the cutoff value. Let's see the code that evaluates `UnigramTagger`:

```
>>> unitagger = UnigramTagger(training, cutoff=5)
>>> unitagger.evaluate(testing)
0.7974218445306567
```

Backoff tagging may be defined as a feature of `SequentialBackoffTagger`. All the taggers are chained together so that if one of the taggers is unable to tag a token, then the token may be passed to the next tagger.

Let's see the following code, which uses back-off tagging. Here, `DefaultTagger` and `UnigramTagger` are used to tag a token. If any tagger of them is unable to tag a word, then the next tagger may be used to tag it:

```
>>> import nltk
>>> from nltk.tag import UnigramTagger
>>> from nltk.tag import DefaultTagger
>>> from nltk.corpus import treebank
>>> testing = treebank.tagged_sents()[2000:]
>>> training= treebank.tagged_sents()[:7000]
>>> tag1=DefaultTagger('NN')
>>> tag2=UnigramTagger(training,backoff=tag1)
>>> tag2.evaluate(testing)
0.963400866227395
```

The subclasses of `NgramTagger` are`UnigramTagger`, `BigramTagger`, and `TrigramTagger`. `BigramTagger` makes use of the previous tag as contextual information. `TrigramTagger` uses the previous two tags as contextual information.

Consider the following code, which illustrates the implementation of `BigramTagger`:

```
>>> import nltk
>>> from nltk.tag import BigramTagger
>>> from nltk.corpus import treebank
>>> training_1= treebank.tagged_sents()[:7000]
>>> bigramtagger=BigramTagger(training_1)
>>> treebank.sents()[0]
['Pierre', 'Vinken', ',', '61', 'years', 'old', ',', 'will', 'join',
'the', 'board', 'as', 'a', 'nonexecutive', 'director', 'Nov.', '29',
'.']
>>> bigramtagger.tag(treebank.sents()[0])
[('Pierre', 'NNP'), ('Vinken', 'NNP'), (',', ','), ('61', 'CD'),
('years', 'NNS'), ('old', 'JJ'), (',', ','), ('will', 'MD'), ('join',
'VB'), ('the', 'DT'), ('board', 'NN'), ('as', 'IN'), ('a', 'DT'),
('nonexecutive', 'JJ'), ('director', 'NN'), ('Nov.', 'NNP'), ('29',
'CD'), ('.', '.')]
>>> testing_1 = treebank.tagged_sents()[2000:]
>>> bigramtagger.evaluate(testing_1)
0.922942709936983
```

Let's see another code for `BigramTagger` and `TrigramTagger`:

```
>>> import nltk
>>> from nltk.tag import BigramTagger, TrigramTagger
>>> from nltk.corpus import treebank
>>> testing = treebank.tagged_sents()[2000:]
>>> training= treebank.tagged_sents()[:7000]
>>> bigramtag = BigramTagger(training)
>>> bigramtag.evaluate(testing)
0.9190426339881356
>>> trigramtag = TrigramTagger(training)
>>> trigramtag.evaluate(testing)
0.9101956195989079
```

`NgramTagger` can be used to generate a tagger for *n* greater than three as well. Let's see the following code in NLTK, which develops `QuadgramTagger`:

```
>>> import nltk
>>> from nltk.corpus import treebank
>>> from nltk import NgramTagger
>>> testing = treebank.tagged_sents()[2000:]
```

```
>>> training= treebank.tagged_sents()[:7000]
>>> quadgramtag = NgramTagger(4, training)
>>> quadgramtag.evaluate(testing)
0.9429767842847466
```

The `AffixTagger` is also a `ContextTagger` in that makes use of a prefix or suffix as the contextual information.

Let's see the following code, which uses `AffixTagger`:

```
>>> import nltk
>>> from nltk.corpus import treebank
>>> from nltk.tag import AffixTagger
>>> testing = treebank.tagged_sents()[2000:]
>>> training= treebank.tagged_sents()[:7000]
>>> affixtag = AffixTagger(training)
>>> affixtag.evaluate(testing)
0.29043249789601167
```

Let's see the following code, which learns the use of four character prefixes:

```
>>> import nltk
>>> from nltk.tag import AffixTagger
>>> from nltk.corpus import treebank
>>> testing = treebank.tagged_sents()[2000:]
>>> training= treebank.tagged_sents()[:7000]
>>> prefixtag = AffixTagger(training, affix_length=4)
>>> prefixtag.evaluate(testing)
0.21103516226368618
```

Consider the following code, which learns the use of three character suffixes:

```
>>> import nltk
>>> from nltk.tag import AffixTagger
>>> from nltk.corpus import treebank
>>> testing = treebank.tagged_sents()[2000:]
>>> training= treebank.tagged_sents()[:7000]
>>> suffixtag = AffixTagger(training, affix_length=-3)
>>> suffixtag.evaluate(testing)
0.29043249789601167
```

Consider the following code in NLTK, which that combines many affix taggers in the back-off chain:

```
>>> import nltk
>>> from nltk.tag import AffixTagger
>>> from nltk.corpus import treebank
```

```
>>> testing = treebank.tagged_sents()[2000:]
>>> training= treebank.tagged_sents()[:7000]
>>> prefixtagger=AffixTagger(training,affix_length=4)
>>> prefixtagger.evaluate(testing)
0.21103516226368618
>>> prefixtagger3=AffixTagger(training,affix_
length=3,backoff=prefixtagger)
>>> prefixtagger3.evaluate(testing)
0.25906767658107027
>>> suffixtagger3=AffixTagger(training,affix_length=-
3,backoff=prefixtagger3)
>>> suffixtagger3.evaluate(testing)
0.2939630929654946
>>> suffixtagger4=AffixTagger(training,affix_length=-
4,backoff=suffixtagger3)
>>> suffixtagger4.evaluate(testing)
0.3316090892296324
```

The **TnT** is **Trigrams n Tags**. `TnT` is a statistical-based tagger that is based on the second order Markov models.

Let's see the code in NLTK for `TnT`:

```
>>> import nltk
>>> from nltk.tag import tnt
>>> from nltk.corpus import treebank
>>> testing = treebank.tagged_sents()[2000:]
>>> training= treebank.tagged_sents()[:7000]
>>> tnt_tagger=tnt.TnT()
>>> tnt_tagger.train(training)
>>> tnt_tagger.evaluate(testing)
0.9882176652913768
```

`TnT` computes `ConditionalFreqDist` and `internalFreqDist` from the training text. These instances are used to compute unigrams, bigrams, and trigrams. In order to choose the best tag, TnT uses the ngram model.

Consider the following code of a `DefaultTagger` in which, if the value of the unknown tagger is provided explicitly, then `TRAINED` will be set to `TRUE`:

```
>>> import nltk
>>> from nltk.tag import DefaultTagger
>>> from nltk.tag import tnt
>>> from nltk.corpus import treebank
>>> testing = treebank.tagged_sents()[2000:]
>>> training= treebank.tagged_sents()[:7000]
```

```
>>> tnt_tagger=tnt.TnT()
>>> unknown=DefaultTagger('NN')
>>> tagger_tnt=tnt.TnT(unk=unknown,Trained=True)
>>> tnt_tagger.train(training)
>>> tnt_tagger.evaluate(testing)
0.988238192006897
```

Developing a chunker using pos-tagged corpora

Chunking is the process used to perform entity detection. It is used for the segmentation and labeling of multiple sequences of tokens in a sentence.

To design a chunker, a chunk grammar should be defined. A chunk grammar holds the rules of how chunking should be done.

Let's consider the example that performs *Noun Phrase Chunking* by forming the chunk rules:

```
>>> import nltk
>>> sent=[("A","DT"),("wise", "JJ"), ("small", "JJ"),("girl", "NN"),
("of", "IN"), ("village", "N"),  ("became", "VBD"), ("leader", "NN")]
>>> sent=[("A","DT"),("wise", "JJ"), ("small", "JJ"),("girl", "NN"),
("of", "IN"), ("village", "NN"),  ("became", "VBD"), ("leader", "NN")]
>>> grammar = "NP: {<DT>?<JJ>*<NN><IN>?<NN>*}"
>>> find = nltk.RegexpParser(grammar)
>>> res = find.parse(sent)
>>> print(res)
(S
  (NP A/DT wise/JJ small/JJ girl/NN of/IN village/NN)
  became/VBD
  (NP leader/NN))
>>> res.draw()
```

The following parse tree is generated:

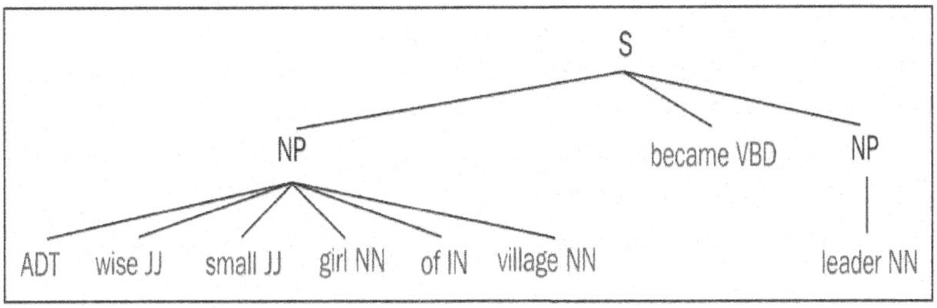

Here, the chunk rule for **Noun Phrase** is defined by keeping **DT** as optional, any number of **JJ**, followed by **NN**, optional **IN**, and any number of **NN**.

Consider another example in which the **Noun Phrase** chunk rule is created with any number of nouns:

```
>>> import nltk
>>> noun1=[("financial","NN"),("year","NN"),("account","NN"),("summar
y","NN")]
>>> gram="NP:{<NN>+}"
>>> find = nltk.RegexpParser(gram)
>>> print(find.parse(noun1))
(S (NP financial/NN year/NN account/NN summary/NN))
>>> x=find.parse(noun1)
>>> x.draw()
```

The output in the form of the parse tree is given here:

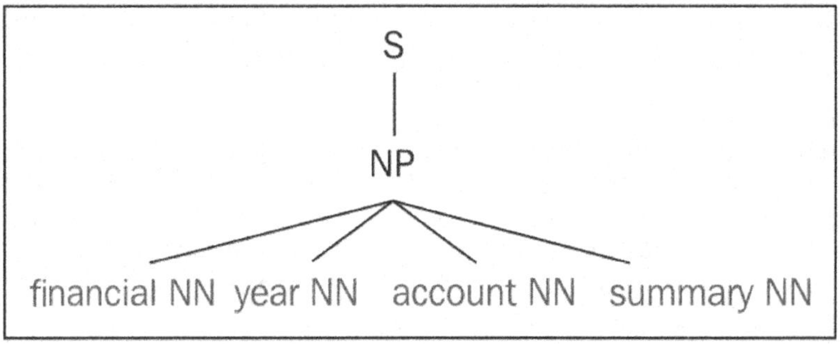

Chunking is the process in which some of the parts of a chunk are eliminated. Either an entire chunk may be used, a part of the chunk may be used from the middle and the remaining parts are eliminated, or a part of chunk may be used either from the beginning of the chunk or from the end of the chunk and the remaining part of the chunk is removed.

Consider the code for `UnigramChunker` in NLTK, which has been developed to perform chunking and parsing:

```
class UnigramChunker(nltk.ChunkParserI):
  def _init_(self,training):
    training_data=[[(x,y) for p,x,y in nltk.chunk.treeconlltags(sent)]
        for sent in training]
    self.tagger=nltk.UnigramTagger(training_data)
```

```
    def parsing(self,sent):
      postags=[pos1 for (word1,pos1) in sent]
      tagged_postags=self.tagger.tag(postags)
      chunk_tags=[chunking for (pos1,chunktag) in tagged_postags]
      conll_tags=[(word,pos1,chunktag) for ((word,pos1),chunktag)
          in zip(sent, chunk_tags)]
      return nltk.chunk.conlltaags2tree(conlltags)
```

Consider the following code, which can be used to estimate the accuracy of the chunker after it is trained:

```
import nltk.corpus, nltk.tag

def ubt_conll_chunk_accuracy(train_sents, test_sents):
    chunks_train =conll_tag_chunks(training)
    chunks_test =conll_tag_chunks(testing)

    chunker1 =nltk.tag.UnigramTagger(chunks_train)
    print 'u:', nltk.tag.accuracy(chunker1, chunks_test)

    chunker2 =nltk.tag.BigramTagger(chunks_train, backoff=chunker1)
    print 'ub:', nltk.tag.accuracy(chunker2, chunks_test)

    chunker3 =nltk.tag.TrigramTagger(chunks_train, backoff=chunker2)
    print 'ubt:', nltk.tag.accuracy(chunker3, chunks_test)

    chunker4 =nltk.tag.TrigramTagger(chunks_train, backoff=chunker1)
    print 'ut:', nltk.tag.accuracy(chunker4, chunks_test)

    chunker5 =nltk.tag.BigramTagger(chunks_train, backoff=chunker4)
    print 'utb:', nltk.tag.accuracy(chunker5, chunks_test)

# accuracy test for conll chunking
conll_train =nltk.corpus.conll2000.chunked_sents('train.txt')
conll_test =nltk.corpus.conll2000.chunked_sents('test.txt')
ubt_conll_chunk_accuracy(conll_train, conll_test)

# accuracy test for treebank chunking
treebank_sents =nltk.corpus.treebank_chunk.chunked_sents()
ubt_conll_chunk_accuracy(treebank_sents[:2000], treebank_sents[2000:])
```

Summary

In this chapter, we have discussed POS tagging, different POS taggers, and the approaches used for POS tagging. You have also learned about statistical modeling involving the n-gram approach, and have developed a chunker using POS tags information.

In the following chapter, we will discuss Treebank construction, CFG construction, different parsing algorithms, and so on.

5
Parsing – Analyzing Training Data

Parsing, also referred to as syntactic analysis, is one of the tasks in NLP. It is defined as the process of finding whether a character sequence, written in natural language, is in accordance with the rules defined in formal grammar. It is the process of breaking the sentences into words or phrase sequences and providing them a particular component category (noun, verb, preposition, and so on).

This chapter will include the following topics:

- Treebank construction
- Extracting **Context-free Grammar** (CFG) rules from Treebank
- Creating a probabilistic Context-free Grammar from CFG
- CYK chart parsing algorithm
- Earley chart parsing algorithm

Introducing parsing

Parsing is one of the steps involved in NLP. It is defined as the process of determining the part-of-speech category for an individual component in a sentence and analyzing whether a given sentence is in accordance with grammar rules or not. The term parsing has been derived from the Latin word *pars* (oration is) which means part-of-speech.

Consider an example—*Ram bought a book*. This sentence is grammatically correct. But, instead of this sentence, if we have a sentence Book bought a Ram, then by adding the semantic information to the parse tree so constructed, we can conclude that although the sentence is grammatically correct, it is not semantically correct. So, the generation of a parse tree is followed by adding meaning to it as well. A parser is a software that accepts an input text and constructs a parse tree or a syntax tree. Parsing may be divided into two categories Top-down Parsing and Bottom-up Parsing. In Top-down Parsing, we begin from the start symbol and continue till we reach individual components. Some of the Top-down Parsers include the Recursive Descent Parser, LL Parser, and Earley Parser. In Bottom-up Parsing, we start from individual components and continue till we reach the start symbol. Some Bottom-up Parsers include the Operator-precedence parser, Simple precedence parser, Simple LR Parser, LALR Parser, Canonical LR (*LR(1)*) Parser, GLR Parser, CYK or (alternatively CKY) Parser, Recursive ascent parser, and Shift-reduce parser.

The `nltk.parse.api.ParserI` class is defined in NLTK. This class is used to obtain parses or syntactic structures for a given sentence. Parsers can be used to obtain syntactic structures, discourse structures, and morphological trees.

Chart parsing follows the dynamic programming approach. In this, once some results are obtained, these may be treated as the intermediate results and may be reused to obtain future results. Unlike in Top-down parsing, the same task is not performed again and again.

Treebank construction

The `nltk.corpus.package` consists of a number of `corpus reader`classes that can be used to obtain the contents of various corpora.

Treebank corpus can also be accessed from `nltk.corpus`. Identifiers for files can be obtained using `fileids()`:

```
>>> import nltk
>>> import nltk.corpus
>>> print(str(nltk.corpus.treebank).replace('\\\\','/'))
<BracketParseCorpusReader in 'C:/nltk_data/corpora/treebank/combined'>
>>> nltk.corpus.treebank.fileids()
['wsj_0001.mrg', 'wsj_0002.mrg', 'wsj_0003.mrg', 'wsj_0004.
mrg', 'wsj_0005.mrg', 'wsj_0006.mrg', 'wsj_0007.mrg', 'wsj_0008.
mrg', 'wsj_0009.mrg', 'wsj_0010.mrg', 'wsj_0011.mrg', 'wsj_0012.
mrg', 'wsj_0013.mrg', 'wsj_0014.mrg', 'wsj_0015.mrg', 'wsj_0016.
mrg', 'wsj_0017.mrg', 'wsj_0018.mrg', 'wsj_0019.mrg', 'wsj_0020.
mrg', 'wsj_0021.mrg', 'wsj_0022.mrg', 'wsj_0023.mrg', 'wsj_0024.
mrg', 'wsj_0025.mrg', 'wsj_0026.mrg', 'wsj_0027.mrg', 'wsj_0028.mrg',
'wsj_0029.mrg', 'wsj_0030.mrg', 'wsj_0031.mrg', 'wsj_0032.
```

```
mrg', 'wsj_0033.mrg', 'wsj_0034.mrg', 'wsj_0035.mrg', 'wsj_0036.
mrg', 'wsj_0037.mrg', 'wsj_0038.mrg', 'wsj_0039.mrg', 'wsj_0040.
mrg', 'wsj_0041.mrg', 'wsj_0042.mrg', 'wsj_0043.mrg', 'wsj_0044.
mrg', 'wsj_0045.mrg', 'wsj_0046.mrg', 'wsj_0047.mrg', 'wsj_0048.
mrg', 'wsj_0049.mrg', 'wsj_0050.mrg', 'wsj_0051.mrg', 'wsj_0052.
mrg', 'wsj_0053.mrg', 'wsj_0054.mrg', 'wsj_0055.mrg', 'wsj_0056.
mrg', 'wsj_0057.mrg', 'wsj_0058.mrg', 'wsj_0059.mrg', 'wsj_0060.
mrg', 'wsj_0061.mrg', 'wsj_0062.mrg', 'wsj_0063.mrg', 'wsj_0064.
mrg', 'wsj_0065.mrg', 'wsj_0066.mrg', 'wsj_0067.mrg', 'wsj_0068.
mrg', 'wsj_0069.mrg', 'wsj_0070.mrg', 'wsj_0071.mrg', 'wsj_0072.
mrg', 'wsj_0073.mrg', 'wsj_0074.mrg', 'wsj_0075.mrg', 'wsj_0076.
mrg', 'wsj_0077.mrg', 'wsj_0078.mrg', 'wsj_0079.mrg', 'wsj_0080.
mrg', 'wsj_0081.mrg', 'wsj_0082.mrg', 'wsj_0083.mrg', 'wsj_0084.
mrg', 'wsj_0085.mrg', 'wsj_0086.mrg', 'wsj_0087.mrg', 'wsj_0088.
mrg', 'wsj_0089.mrg', 'wsj_0090.mrg', 'wsj_0091.mrg', 'wsj_0092.
mrg', 'wsj_0093.mrg', 'wsj_0094.mrg', 'wsj_0095.mrg', 'wsj_0096.
mrg', 'wsj_0097.mrg', 'wsj_0098.mrg', 'wsj_0099.mrg', 'wsj_0100.
mrg', 'wsj_0101.mrg', 'wsj_0102.mrg', 'wsj_0103.mrg', 'wsj_0104.
mrg', 'wsj_0105.mrg', 'wsj_0106.mrg', 'wsj_0107.mrg', 'wsj_0108.
mrg', 'wsj_0109.mrg', 'wsj_0110.mrg', 'wsj_0111.mrg', 'wsj_0112.
mrg', 'wsj_0113.mrg', 'wsj_0114.mrg', 'wsj_0115.mrg', 'wsj_0116.
mrg', 'wsj_0117.mrg', 'wsj_0118.mrg', 'wsj_0119.mrg', 'wsj_0120.
mrg', 'wsj_0121.mrg', 'wsj_0122.mrg', 'wsj_0123.mrg', 'wsj_0124.
mrg', 'wsj_0125.mrg', 'wsj_0126.mrg', 'wsj_0127.mrg', 'wsj_0128.
mrg', 'wsj_0129.mrg', 'wsj_0130.mrg', 'wsj_0131.mrg', 'wsj_0132.
mrg', 'wsj_0133.mrg', 'wsj_0134.mrg', 'wsj_0135.mrg', 'wsj_0136.
mrg', 'wsj_0137.mrg', 'wsj_0138.mrg', 'wsj_0139.mrg', 'wsj_0140.
mrg', 'wsj_0141.mrg', 'wsj_0142.mrg', 'wsj_0143.mrg', 'wsj_0144.
mrg', 'wsj_0145.mrg', 'wsj_0146.mrg', 'wsj_0147.mrg', 'wsj_0148.
mrg', 'wsj_0149.mrg', 'wsj_0150.mrg', 'wsj_0151.mrg', 'wsj_0152.
mrg', 'wsj_0153.mrg', 'wsj_0154.mrg', 'wsj_0155.mrg', 'wsj_0156.
mrg', 'wsj_0157.mrg', 'wsj_0158.mrg', 'wsj_0159.mrg', 'wsj_0160.
mrg', 'wsj_0161.mrg', 'wsj_0162.mrg', 'wsj_0163.mrg', 'wsj_0164.
mrg', 'wsj_0165.mrg', 'wsj_0166.mrg', 'wsj_0167.mrg', 'wsj_0168.
mrg', 'wsj_0169.mrg', 'wsj_0170.mrg', 'wsj_0171.mrg', 'wsj_0172.
mrg', 'wsj_0173.mrg', 'wsj_0174.mrg', 'wsj_0175.mrg', 'wsj_0176.
mrg', 'wsj_0177.mrg', 'wsj_0178.mrg', 'wsj_0179.mrg', 'wsj_0180.
mrg', 'wsj_0181.mrg', 'wsj_0182.mrg', 'wsj_0183.mrg', 'wsj_0184.
mrg', 'wsj_0185.mrg', 'wsj_0186.mrg', 'wsj_0187.mrg', 'wsj_0188.
mrg', 'wsj_0189.mrg', 'wsj_0190.mrg', 'wsj_0191.mrg', 'wsj_0192.
mrg', 'wsj_0193.mrg', 'wsj_0194.mrg', 'wsj_0195.mrg', 'wsj_0196.mrg',
'wsj_0197.mrg', 'wsj_0198.mrg', 'wsj_0199.mrg']
>>> from nltk.corpus import treebank
>>> print(treebank.words('wsj_0007.mrg'))
['McDermott', 'International', 'Inc.', 'said', '0', ...]
>>> print(treebank.tagged_words('wsj_0007.mrg'))
[('McDermott', 'NNP'), ('International', 'NNP'), ...]
```

Let's see the code in NLTK for accessing the Penn Treebank Corpus, which uses the Treebank Corpus Reader contained in the corpus module:

```
>>> import nltk
>>> from nltk.corpus import treebank
>>> print(treebank.parsed_sents('wsj_0007.mrg')[2])
(S
  (NP-SBJ
    (NP (NNP Bailey) (NNP Controls))
    (, ,)
    (VP
      (VBN based)
      (NP (-NONE- *))
      (PP-LOC-CLR
        (IN in)
        (NP (NP (NNP Wickliffe)) (, ,) (NP (NNP Ohio)))))
    (, ,))
  (VP
    (VBZ makes)
    (NP
      (JJ computerized)
      (JJ industrial)
      (NNS controls)
      (NNS systems)))
  (. .))

>>> import nltk
>>> from nltk.corpus import treebank_chunk
>>> treebank_chunk.chunked_sents()[1]
Tree('S', [Tree('NP', [('Mr.', 'NNP'), ('Vinken', 'NNP')]), ('is',
'VBZ'), Tree('NP', [('chairman', 'NN')]), ('of', 'IN'), Tree('NP',
[('Elsevier', 'NNP'), ('N.V.', 'NNP')]), (',', ','), Tree('NP',
[('the', 'DT'), ('Dutch', 'NNP'), ('publishing', 'VBG'), ('group',
'NN')]), ('.', '.')])
>>> treebank_chunk.chunked_sents()[1].draw()
```

The preceding code obtains the following parse tree:

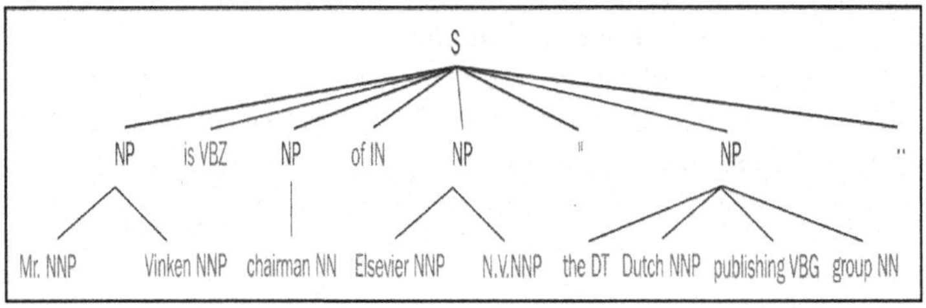

```
>>> import nltk
>>> from nltk.corpus import treebank_chunk
>>> treebank_chunk.chunked_sents()[1].leaves()
[('Mr.', 'NNP'), ('Vinken', 'NNP'), ('is', 'VBZ'), ('chairman',
'NN'), ('of', 'IN'), ('Elsevier', 'NNP'), ('N.V.', 'NNP'), (',', ','),
('the', 'DT'), ('Dutch', 'NNP'), ('publishing', 'VBG'), ('group',
'NN'), ('.', '.')]
>>> treebank_chunk.chunked_sents()[1].pos()
[(('Mr.', 'NNP'), 'NP'), (('Vinken', 'NNP'), 'NP'), (('is', 'VBZ'),
'S'), (('chairman', 'NN'), 'NP'), (('of', 'IN'), 'S'), (('Elsevier',
'NNP'), 'NP'), (('N.V.', 'NNP'), 'NP'), ((',', ','), 'S'), (('the',
'DT'), 'NP'), (('Dutch', 'NNP'), 'NP'), (('publishing', 'VBG'), 'NP'),
(('group', 'NN'), 'NP'), (('.', '.'), 'S')]
>>> treebank_chunk.chunked_sents()[1].productions()
[S -> NP ('is', 'VBZ') NP ('of', 'IN') NP (',', ',') NP ('.', '.'),
NP -> ('Mr.', 'NNP') ('Vinken', 'NNP'), NP -> ('chairman', 'NN'), NP
-> ('Elsevier', 'NNP') ('N.V.', 'NNP'), NP -> ('the', 'DT') ('Dutch',
'NNP') ('publishing', 'VBG') ('group', 'NN')]
```

Part of speech annotations are included in the `tagged_words()` method:

```
>>> nltk.corpus.treebank.tagged_words()
[('Pierre', 'NNP'), ('Vinken', 'NNP'), (',', ','), ...]
```

The type of tags and the count of these tags used in the Penn Treebank Corpus are shown here:

#	16
$	724
''	
,	4,886
-LRB-	120
-NONE-	6,592
-RRB-	126
.	384
:	563
``	712
CC	2,265
CD	3,546
DT	8,165
EX	88
FW	4

IN	9,857
JJ	5,834
JJR	381
JJS	182
LS	13
MD	927
NN	13,166
NNP	9,410
NNPS	244
NNS	6,047
PDT	27
POS	824
PRP	1,716
PRP$	766
RB	2,822
RBR	136
RBS	35
RP	216
SYM	1
TO	2,179
UH	3
VB	2,554
VBD	3,043
VBG	1,460
VBN	2,134
VBP	1,321
VBZ	2,125
WDT	445
WP	241
WP$	14

The tags and frequency can be obtained from the following code:

```
>>> import nltk
>>> from nltk.probability import FreqDist
>>> from nltk.corpus import treebank
>>> fd = FreqDist()
```

```
>>> fd.items()
dict_items([])
```

The preceding code obtains a list of tags and the frequency of each tag in the Treebank corpus.

Let's see the code in NLTK for accessing the Sinica Treebank Corpus:

```
>>> import nltk
>>> from nltk.corpus import sinica_treebank
>>> print(sinica_treebank.sents())
[['一'], ['友情'], ['嘉珍', '和', '我', '住在', '同一條', '巷子'], ...]
>>> sinica_treebank.parsed_sents()[27]
Tree('S', [Tree('NP', [Tree('NP', [Tree('N·的', [Tree('Nhaa', ['我']),
Tree('DE', ['的'])]), Tree('Ncb', ['腦海'])]), Tree('Ncda', ['中'])]),
Tree('Dd', ['頓時']), Tree('DM', ['一片']), Tree('VH11', ['空白'])])
```

Extracting Context Free Grammar (CFG) rules from Treebank

CFG was defined for natural languages in 1957 by Noam Chomsky. A CFG consists of the following components:

- A set of non terminal nodes (*N*)
- A set of terminal nodes (*T*)
- Start symbol (*S*)
- A set of production rules (*P*) of the form:

  $A \rightarrow a$

CFG rules are of two types—Phrase structure rules and Sentence structure rules.

A Phrase Structure Rule can be defined as follows—$A \rightarrow a$, where *A* *Î N* and *a* consists of Terminals and Non terminals.

In Sentence level Construction of CFG, there are four structures:

- **Declarative structure**: Deals with declarative sentences (the subject is followed by a predicate).
- **Imperative structure**: Deals with imperative sentences, commands, or suggestions (sentences begin with a verb phrase and do not include a subject).

- **Yes-No structure**: Deals with question-answering sentences. The answers to these questions are either *yes* or *no*.
- **Wh-question structure**: Deals with question-answering sentences. Questions that begin following *Wh* words (Who, What, How, When, Where, Why, and Which).

General CFG rules are summarized here:

- *S→NP VP*
- *S→VP*
- *S→Aux NP VP*
- *S→Wh-NP VP*
- *S→Wh-NP Aux NP VP*
- *NP→(Det) (AP) Nom (PP)*
- *VP→Verb (NP) (NP) (PP)**
- *VP→Verb S*
- *PP→Prep (NP)*
- *AP→(Adv) Adj (PP)*

Consider an example that depicts the use of Context-free Grammar rules in NLTK:

```
>>> import nltk
>>> from nltk import Nonterminal, nonterminals, Production, CFG
>>> nonterminal1 = Nonterminal('NP')
>>> nonterminal2 = Nonterminal('VP')
>>> nonterminal3 = Nonterminal('PP')
>>> nonterminal1.symbol()
'NP'
>>> nonterminal2.symbol()
'VP'
>>> nonterminal3.symbol()
'PP'
>>> nonterminal1==nonterminal2
False
>>> nonterminal2==nonterminal3
False
>>> nonterminal1==nonterminal3
False
>>> S, NP, VP, PP = nonterminals('S, NP, VP, PP')
>>> N, V, P, DT = nonterminals('N, V, P, DT')
>>> production1 = Production(S, [NP, VP])
```

```
>>> production2 = Production(NP, [DT, NP])
>>> production3 = Production(VP, [V, NP,NP,PP])
>>> production1.lhs()
S
>>> production1.rhs()
(NP, VP)
>>> production3.lhs()
VP
>>> production3.rhs()
(V, NP, NP, PP)
>>> production3 == Production(VP, [V,NP,NP,PP])
True
>>> production2 == production3
False
```

An example for accessing ATIS grammar in NLTK is as follows:

```
>>> import nltk
>>> gram1 = nltk.data.load('grammars/large_grammars/atis.cfg')
>>> gram1
<Grammar with 5517 productions>
```

Extract the testing sentences from ATIS as follows:

```
>>> import nltk
>>> sent = nltk.data.load('grammars/large_grammars/atis_sentences.
txt')
>>> sent = nltk.parse.util.extract_test_sentences(sent)
>>> len(sent)
98
>>> testingsent=sent[25]
>>> testingsent[1]
11
>>> testingsent[0]
['list', 'those', 'flights', 'that', 'stop', 'over', 'in', 'salt',
'lake', 'city', '.']
>>> sent=testingsent[0]
```

Bottom-up parsing:

```
>>> import nltk
>>> gram1 = nltk.data.load('grammars/large_grammars/atis.cfg')
>>> sent = nltk.data.load('grammars/large_grammars/atis_sentences.
txt')
>>> sent = nltk.parse.util.extract_test_sentences(sent)
>>> testingsent=sent[25]
```

```
>>> sent=testingsent[0]
>>> parser1 = nltk.parse.BottomUpChartParser(gram1)
>>> chart1 = parser1.chart_parse(sent)
>>> print((chart1.num_edges()))
13454
>>> print((len(list(chart1.parses(gram1.start())))))
11
```

Bottom-up, Left Corner parsing:

```
>>> import nltk
>>> gram1 = nltk.data.load('grammars/large_grammars/atis.cfg')
>>> sent = nltk.data.load('grammars/large_grammars/atis_sentences.
txt')
>>> sent = nltk.parse.util.extract_test_sentences(sent)
>>> testingsent=sent[25]
>>> sent=testingsent[0]
>>> parser2 = nltk.parse.BottomUpLeftCornerChartParser(gram1)
>>> chart2 = parser2.chart_parse(sent)
>>> print((chart2.num_edges()))
8781
>>> print((len(list(chart2.parses(gram1.start())))))
11
```

Left Corner parsing with a Bottom-up filter:

```
>>> import nltk
>>> gram1 = nltk.data.load('grammars/large_grammars/atis.cfg')
>>> sent = nltk.data.load('grammars/large_grammars/atis_sentences.
txt')
>>> sent = nltk.parse.util.extract_test_sentences(sent)
>>> testingsent=sent[25]
>>> sent=testingsent[0]
>>> parser3 = nltk.parse.LeftCornerChartParser(gram1)
>>> chart3 = parser3.chart_parse(sent)
>>> print((chart3.num_edges()))
1280
>>> print((len(list(chart3.parses(gram1.start())))))
11
```

Top-down parsing:

```
>>> import nltk
>>> gram1 = nltk.data.load('grammars/large_grammars/atis.cfg')
>>> sent = nltk.data.load('grammars/large_grammars/atis_sentences.
txt')
```

```
>>> sent = nltk.parse.util.extract_test_sentences(sent)
>>> testingsent=sent[25]
>>> sent=testingsent[0]
>>>parser4 = nltk.parse.TopDownChartParser(gram1)
>>> chart4 = parser4.chart_parse(sent)
>>> print((chart4.num_edges()))
37763
>>> print((len(list(chart4.parses(gram1.start())))))
11
```

Incremental Bottom-up parsing:

```
>>> import nltk
>>> gram1 = nltk.data.load('grammars/large_grammars/atis.cfg')
>>> sent = nltk.data.load('grammars/large_grammars/atis_sentences.
txt')
>>> sent = nltk.parse.util.extract_test_sentences(sent)
>>> testingsent=sent[25]
>>> sent=testingsent[0]
>>> parser5 = nltk.parse.IncrementalBottomUpChartParser(gram1)
>>> chart5 = parser5.chart_parse(sent)
>>> print((chart5.num_edges()))
13454
>>> print((len(list(chart5.parses(gram1.start())))))
11
```

Incremental Bottom-up, Left Corner parsing:

```
>>> import nltk
>>> gram1 = nltk.data.load('grammars/large_grammars/atis.cfg')
>>> sent = nltk.data.load('grammars/large_grammars/atis_sentences.
txt')
>>> sent = nltk.parse.util.extract_test_sentences(sent)
>>> testingsent=sent[25]
>>> sent=testingsent[0]
>>> parser6 = nltk.parse.IncrementalBottomUpLeftCornerChartParser(gr
am1)
>>> chart6 = parser6.chart_parse(sent)
>>> print((chart6.num_edges()))
8781
>>> print((len(list(chart6.parses(gram1.start())))))
11
```

Incremental Left Corner parsing with a Bottom-up filter:

```
>>> import nltk
>>> gram1 = nltk.data.load('grammars/large_grammars/atis.cfg')
>>> sent = nltk.data.load('grammars/large_grammars/atis_sentences.
txt')
>>> sent = nltk.parse.util.extract_test_sentences(sent)
>>> testingsent=sent[25]
>>> sent=testingsent[0]
>>> parser7 = nltk.parse.IncrementalLeftCornerChartParser(gram1)
>>> chart7 = parser7.chart_parse(sent)
>>> print((chart7.num_edges()))
1280
>>> print((len(list(chart7.parses(gram1.start())))))
11
```

Incremental Top-down parsing:

```
>>> import nltk
>>> gram1 = nltk.data.load('grammars/large_grammars/atis.cfg')
>>> sent = nltk.data.load('grammars/large_grammars/atis_sentences.
txt')
>>> sent = nltk.parse.util.extract_test_sentences(sent)
>>> testingsent=sent[25]
>>> sent=testingsent[0]
>>> parser8 = nltk.parse.IncrementalTopDownChartParser(gram1)
>>> chart8 = parser8.chart_parse(sent)
>>> print((chart8.num_edges()))
37763
>>> print((len(list(chart8.parses(gram1.start())))))
11
```

Earley parsing:

```
>>> import nltk
>>> gram1 = nltk.data.load('grammars/large_grammars/atis.cfg')
>>> sent = nltk.data.load('grammars/large_grammars/atis_sentences.
txt')
>>> sent = nltk.parse.util.extract_test_sentences(sent)
>>> testingsent=sent[25]
>>> sent=testingsent[0]
>>> parser9 = nltk.parse.EarleyChartParser(gram1)
>>> chart9 = parser9.chart_parse(sent)
>>> print((chart9.num_edges()))
37763
>>> print((len(list(chart9.parses(gram1.start())))))
11
```

Creating a probabilistic Context Free Grammar from CFG

In **Probabilistic Context-free Grammar** (PCFG), probabilities are attached to all the production rules present in CFG. The sum of these probabilities is 1. It generates the same parse structures as CFG, but it also assigns a probability to each parse tree. The probability of a parsed tree is obtained by taking the product of probabilities of all the production rules used in building the tree.

Let's see the following code in NLTK, that illustrates the formation of rules in PCFG:

```
>>> import nltk
>>> from nltk.corpus import treebank
>>> from itertools import islice
>>> from nltk.grammar import PCFG, induce_pcfg, toy_pcfg1, toy_pcfg2
>>> gram2 = PCFG.from string("""
A -> B B [.3] | C B C [.7]
B -> B D [.5] | C [.5]
C -> 'a' [.1] | 'b' [0.9]
D -> 'b' [1.0]
""")
>>> prod1 = gram2.productions()[0]
>>> prod1
A -> B B [0.3]
>>> prod2 = gram2.productions()[1]
>>> prod2
A -> C B C [0.7]
>>> prod2.lhs()
A
>>> prod2.rhs()
(C, B, C)
>>> print((prod2.prob()))
0.7
>>> gram2.start()
A
>>> gram2.productions()
[A -> B B [0.3], A -> C B C [0.7], B -> B D [0.5], B -> C [0.5], C ->
'a' [0.1], C -> 'b' [0.9], D -> 'b' [1.0]]
```

Let's see the code in NLTK that illustrates Probabilistic Chart Parsing:

```
>>> import nltk
>>> from nltk.corpus import treebank
>>> from itertools import islice
>>> from nltk.grammar import PCFG, induce_pcfg, toy_pcfg1, toy_pcfg2
>>> tokens = "Jack told Bob to bring my cookie".split()
>>> grammar = toy_pcfg2
>>> print(grammar)
Grammar with 23 productions (start state = S)
    S -> NP VP [1.0]
    VP -> V NP [0.59]
    VP -> V [0.4]
    VP -> VP PP [0.01]
    NP -> Det N [0.41]
    NP -> Name [0.28]
    NP -> NP PP [0.31]
    PP -> P NP [1.0]
    V -> 'saw' [0.21]
    V -> 'ate' [0.51]
    V -> 'ran' [0.28]
    N -> 'boy' [0.11]
    N -> 'cookie' [0.12]
    N -> 'table' [0.13]
    N -> 'telescope' [0.14]
    N -> 'hill' [0.5]
    Name -> 'Jack' [0.52]
    Name -> 'Bob' [0.48]
    P -> 'with' [0.61]
    P -> 'under' [0.39]
    Det -> 'the' [0.41]
    Det -> 'a' [0.31]
    Det -> 'my' [0.28]
```

CYK chart parsing algorithm

The drawback of Recursive Descent Parsing is that it causes the Left Recursion Problem and is very complex. So, CYK chart parsing was introduced. It uses the Dynamic Programming approach. CYK is one of the simplest chart parsing algorithms. The CYK algorithm is capable of constructing a chart in *O(n3)* time. Both CYK and Earley are Bottom-up chart parsing algorithms. But, the Earley algorithm also makes use of Top-down predictions when invalid parses are constructed.

Consider the following example of CYK parsing:

```
tok = ["the", "kids", "opened", "the", "box", "on", "the", "floor"]
gram = nltk.parse_cfg("""
S -> NP VP
NP -> Det N | NP PP
VP -> V NP | VP PP
PP -> P NP
Det -> 'the'
N -> 'kids' | 'box' | 'floor'
V -> 'opened' P -> 'on'
 """)
```

Consider the following code to construct the initializing table:

```
def init_nfst(tok, gram):
numtokens1 = len(tok)
 # fill w/ dots
nfst = [["." for i in range(numtokens1+1)] !!!!!!! for j in
range(numtokens1+1)]
# fill in diagonal
for i in range(numtokens1):
prod= gram.productions(rhs=tok[i])
nfst[i][i+1] = prod[0].lhs()
return nfst
```

Consider the following code to fill in the table:

```
def complete_nfst(nfst, tok, trace=False):
index1 = {} for prod in gram.productions():
#make lookup reverse
index1[prod.rhs()] = prod.lhs()
numtokens1 = len(tok) for span in range(2, numtokens1+1):
for start in range(numtokens1+1-span):
#go down towards diagonal
end1 = start1 + span for mid in range(start1+1, end1):
nt1, nt2 = nfst[start1][mid1], nfst[mid1][end1]
if (nt1,nt2) in index1:
if trace:
print "[%s] %3s [%s] %3s [%s] ==> [%s] %3s [%s]" % \ (start, nt1,
mid1, nt2, end1, start1, index[(nt1,nt2)], end) nfst[start1][end1] =
index[(nt1,nt2)]
return nfst
```

Following is the code in Python for constructing the display table:

```
def display(wfst, tok):
print '\nWFST ' + ' '.join([("%-4d" % i) for i in range(1,
len(wfst))])
for i in range(len(wfst)-1):
print "%d " % i,
for j in range(1, len(wfst)):
print "%-4s" % wfst[i][j],
print
```

The result can be obtained from the following code:

```
tok = ["the", "kids", "opened", "the", "box", "on", "the", "floor"]
res1 = init_wfst(tok, gram)
display(res1, tok)
res2 = complete_wfst(res1,tok)
display(res2, tok)
```

Earley chart parsing algorithm

Earley algorithm was given by Earley in 1970. This algorithm is similar to Top-down parsing. It can handle left-recursion, and it doesn't need CNF. It fills in a chart in the left to right manner.

Consider an example that illustrates parsing using the Earley chart parser:

```
>>> import nltk
>>> nltk.parse.earleychart.demo(print_times=False, trace=1,sent='I saw
a dog', numparses=2)
* Sentence:
I saw a dog
['I', 'saw', 'a', 'dog']

|.    I    .   saw   .    a    .   dog   .|
|[---------]         .         .         .| [0:1] 'I'
|.         [---------]         .         .| [1:2] 'saw'
|.         .         [---------]         .| [2:3] 'a'
|.         .         .         [---------]| [3:4] 'dog'
|>         .         .         .         .| [0:0] S  -> * NP VP
|>         .         .         .         .| [0:0] NP -> * NP PP
|>         .         .         .         .| [0:0] NP -> * Det Noun
|>         .         .         .         .| [0:0] NP -> * 'I'
|[---------]         .         .         .| [0:1] NP -> 'I' *
|[--------->         .         .         .| [0:1] S  -> NP * VP
```

```
|[--------->         .         .         .| [0:1] NP -> NP * PP
|.         >         .         .         .| [1:1] VP -> * VP PP
|.         >         .         .         .| [1:1] VP -> * Verb NP
|.         >         .         .         .| [1:1] VP -> * Verb
|.         >         .         .         .| [1:1] Verb -> * 'saw'
|.         [---------]         .         .| [1:2] Verb -> 'saw' *
|.         [--------->         .         .| [1:2] VP -> Verb * NP
|.         [---------]         .         .| [1:2] VP -> Verb *
|[-------------------]         .         .| [0:2] S  -> NP VP *
|.         [--------->         .         .| [1:2] VP -> VP * PP
|.         .         >         .         .| [2:2] NP -> * NP PP
|.         .         >         .         .| [2:2] NP -> * Det Noun
|.         .         >         .         .| [2:2] Det -> * 'a'
|.         .         [---------]         .| [2:3] Det -> 'a' *
|.         .         [--------->         .| [2:3] NP -> Det * Noun
|.         .         .         >         .| [3:3] Noun -> * 'dog'
|.         .         .         [---------]| [3:4] Noun -> 'dog' *
|.         .         [-------------------]| [2:4] NP -> Det Noun *
|.         [-----------------------------]| [1:4] VP -> Verb NP *
|.         .         [------------------->| [2:4] NP -> NP * PP
|[=======================================]| [0:4] S  -> NP VP *
|.         [----------------------------->| [1:4] VP -> VP * PP
```

Consider an example that illustrates parsing using the Chart parser in NLTK:

```
>>> import nltk
>>> nltk.parse.chart.demo(2, print_times=False, trace=1,sent='John saw
a dog', numparses=1)
* Sentence:
John saw a dog
['John', 'saw', 'a', 'dog']

* Strategy: Bottom-up

|.   John  .   saw   .    a    .   dog   .|
|[---------]         .         .         .| [0:1] 'John'
|.         [---------]         .         .| [1:2] 'saw'
|.         .         [---------]         .| [2:3] 'a'
|.         .         .         [---------]| [3:4] 'dog'
|>         .         .         .         .| [0:0] NP -> * 'John'
|[---------]         .         .         .| [0:1] NP -> 'John' *
|>         .         .         .         .| [0:0] S  -> * NP VP
|>         .         .         .         .| [0:0] NP -> * NP PP
|[--------->         .         .         .| [0:1] S  -> NP * VP
```

```
|[--------->         .         .         .| [0:1] NP -> NP * PP
|.         >         .         .         .| [1:1] Verb -> * 'saw'
|.         [---------]         .         .| [1:2] Verb -> 'saw' *
|.         >         .         .         .| [1:1] VP -> * Verb NP
|.         >         .         .         .| [1:1] VP -> * Verb
|.         [--------->         .         .| [1:2] VP -> Verb * NP
|.         [---------]         .         .| [1:2] VP -> Verb *
|.         >         .         .         .| [1:1] VP -> * VP PP
|[-------------------]         .         .| [0:2] S  -> NP VP *
|.         [--------->         .         .| [1:2] VP -> VP * PP
|.         .         >         .         .| [2:2] Det -> * 'a'
|.         .         [---------]         .| [2:3] Det -> 'a' *
|.         .         >         .         .| [2:2] NP -> * Det Noun
|.         .         [--------->         .| [2:3] NP -> Det * Noun
|.         .         .         >         .| [3:3] Noun -> * 'dog'
|.         .         .         [---------]| [3:4] Noun -> 'dog' *
|.         .         [-------------------]| [2:4] NP -> Det Noun *
|.         .         >         .         .| [2:2] S  -> * NP VP
|.         .         >         .         .| [2:2] NP -> * NP PP
|.         [-----------------------------]| [1:4] VP -> Verb NP *
|.         .         [------------------->| [2:4] S  -> NP * VP
|.         .         [------------------->| [2:4] NP -> NP * PP
|[=======================================]| [0:4] S  -> NP VP *
|.         [---------------------------->| [1:4] VP -> VP * PP
Nr edges in chart: 33
(S (NP John) (VP (Verb saw) (NP (Det a) (Noun dog))))
```

Consider an example that illustrates parsing using the Stepping Chart parser in NLTK:

```
>>> import nltk
>>> nltk.parse.chart.demo(5, print_times=False, trace=1,sent='John saw
a dog', numparses=2)
* Sentence:
John saw a dog
['John', 'saw', 'a', 'dog']

* Strategy: Stepping (top-down vs bottom-up)

*** SWITCH TO TOP DOWN
|[---------]         .         .         .| [0:1] 'John'
|.         [---------]         .         .| [1:2] 'saw'
|.         .         [---------]         .| [2:3] 'a'
|.         .         .         [---------]| [3:4] 'dog'
|>         .         .         .         .| [0:0] S  -> * NP VP
```

```
|>         .         .         .         .| [0:0] NP -> * NP PP
|>         .         .         .         .| [0:0] NP -> * Det Noun
|>         .         .         .         .| [0:0] NP -> * 'John'
|[---------]         .         .         .| [0:1] NP -> 'John' *
|[--------->         .         .         .| [0:1] S  -> NP * VP
|[--------->         .         .         .| [0:1] NP -> NP * PP
|.         >         .         .         .| [1:1] VP -> * VP PP
|.         >         .         .         .| [1:1] VP -> * Verb NP
|.         >         .         .         .| [1:1] VP -> * Verb
|.         >         .         .         .| [1:1] Verb -> * 'saw'
|.         [---------]         .         .| [1:2] Verb -> 'saw' *
|.         [--------->         .         .| [1:2] VP -> Verb * NP
|.         [---------]         .         .| [1:2] VP -> Verb *
|[-------------------]         .         .| [0:2] S  -> NP VP *
|.         [--------->         .         .| [1:2] VP -> VP * PP
|.         .         >         .         .| [2:2] NP -> * NP PP
|.         .         >         .         .| [2:2] NP -> * Det Noun
*** SWITCH TO BOTTOM UP
|.         .         >         .         .| [2:2] Det -> * 'a'
|.         .         .         >         .| [3:3] Noun -> * 'dog'
|.         .         [---------]         .| [2:3] Det -> 'a' *
|.         .         .         [---------]| [3:4] Noun -> 'dog' *
|.         .         [--------->         .| [2:3] NP -> Det * Noun
|.         .         [-------------------]| [2:4] NP -> Det Noun *
|.         [-----------------------------]| [1:4] VP -> Verb NP *
|.         .         [------------------->| [2:4] NP -> NP * PP
|[=======================================]| [0:4] S  -> NP VP *
|.         [----------------------------->| [1:4] VP -> VP * PP
|.         .         >         .         .| [2:2] S  -> * NP VP
|.         .         [------------------->| [2:4] S  -> NP * VP
*** SWITCH TO TOP DOWN
|.         .         .         .         >| [4:4] VP -> * VP PP
|.         .         .         .         >| [4:4] VP -> * Verb NP
|.         .         .         .         >| [4:4] VP -> * Verb
*** SWITCH TO BOTTOM UP
*** SWITCH TO TOP DOWN
*** SWITCH TO BOTTOM UP
*** SWITCH TO TOP DOWN
*** SWITCH TO BOTTOM UP
*** SWITCH TO TOP DOWN
*** SWITCH TO BOTTOM UP
Nr edges in chart: 37
```

Let's see the code for Feature chart parsing in NLTK:

```
>>> import nltk
>>>nltk.parse.featurechart.demo(print_times=False,print_
grammar=True,parser=nltk.parse.featurechart.FeatureChartParser,sent='I
saw a dog')

Grammar with 18 productions (start state = S[])
    S[] -> NP[] VP[]
    PP[] -> Prep[] NP[]
    NP[] -> NP[] PP[]
    VP[] -> VP[] PP[]
    VP[] -> Verb[] NP[]
    VP[] -> Verb[]
    NP[] -> Det[pl=?x] Noun[pl=?x]
    NP[] -> 'John'
    NP[] -> 'I'
    Det[] -> 'the'
    Det[] -> 'my'
    Det[-pl] -> 'a'
    Noun[-pl] -> 'dog'
    Noun[-pl] -> 'cookie'
    Verb[] -> 'ate'
    Verb[] -> 'saw'
    Prep[] -> 'with'
    Prep[] -> 'under'

* FeatureChartParser
Sentence: I saw a dog
|. I .saw. a .dog.|
|[---]   .   .   .| [0:1] 'I'
|.   [---]   .   .| [1:2] 'saw'
|.   .   [---]   .| [2:3] 'a'
|.   .   .   [---]| [3:4] 'dog'
|[---]   .   .   .| [0:1] NP[] -> 'I' *
|[--->   .   .   .| [0:1] S[] -> NP[] * VP[] {}
|[--->   .   .   .| [0:1] NP[] -> NP[] * PP[] {}
|.   [---]   .   .| [1:2] Verb[] -> 'saw' *
|.   [--->   .   .| [1:2] VP[] -> Verb[] * NP[] {}
|.   [---]   .   .| [1:2] VP[] -> Verb[] *
|.   [--->   .   .| [1:2] VP[] -> VP[] * PP[] {}
|[-------]   .   .| [0:2] S[] -> NP[] VP[] *
|.   .   [---]   .| [2:3] Det[-pl] -> 'a' *
|.   .   [--->   .| [2:3] NP[] -> Det[pl=?x] * Noun[pl=?x] {?x: False}
```

```
|.    .    .    [---]|  [3:4] Noun[-pl] -> 'dog' *
|.    .    [-------]|  [2:4] NP[] -> Det[-pl] Noun[-pl] *
|.    .    [------->|  [2:4] S[] -> NP[] * VP[] {}
|.    .    [------->|  [2:4] NP[] -> NP[] * PP[] {}
|.    [-----------]|  [1:4] VP[] -> Verb[] NP[] *
|.    [----------->|  [1:4] VP[] -> VP[] * PP[] {}
|[===============]|  [0:4] S[] -> NP[] VP[] *
(S[]
  (NP[] I)
  (VP[] (Verb[] saw) (NP[] (Det[-pl] a) (Noun[-pl] dog))))
```

The following code is found in NLTK for the implementation of the Earley algorithm:

```
def demo(print_times=True, print_grammar=False,
         print_trees=True, trace=2,
         sent='I saw John with a dog with my cookie', numparses=5):
    """
    A demonstration of the Earley parsers.
    """
    import sys, time
    from nltk.parse.chart import demo_grammar

    # The grammar for ChartParser and SteppingChartParser:
    grammar = demo_grammar()
    if print_grammar:
        print("* Grammar")
        print(grammar)

    # Tokenize the sample sentence.
    print("* Sentence:")
    print(sent)
    tokens = sent.split()
    print(tokens)
    print()

    # Do the parsing.
    earley = EarleyChartParser(grammar, trace=trace)
    t = time.clock()
    chart = earley.chart_parse(tokens)
    parses = list(chart.parses(grammar.start()))
    t = time.clock()-t

    # Print results.
    if numparses:
        assert len(parses)==numparses, 'Not all parses found'
    if print_trees:
```

```
            for tree in parses: print(tree)
        else:
            print("Nr trees:", len(parses))
        if print_times:
            print("Time:", t)

    if __name__ == '__main__': demo()
```

Summary

In this chapter, we discussed Parsing, accessing the Treebank Corpus, and the implementation of Context-free Grammar, Probabilistic Context-free Grammar, the CYK algorithm, and the Earley algorithm. Hence, in this chapter, we discussed about the syntactic analysis phase of NLP.

In the next chapter, we will discuss about semantic analysis, which is another phase of NLP. We will discuss about NER using different approaches and obtain ways for performing disambiguation tasks.

6

Semantic Analysis – Meaning Matters

Semantic analysis, or meaning generation is one of the tasks in NLP. It is defined as the process of determining the meaning of character sequences or word sequences. It may be used for performing the task of disambiguation.

This chapter will include the following topics:

- NER
- NER system using the HMM
- Training NER using machine learning toolkits
- NER using POS tagging
- Generation of the synset id from Wordnet
- Disambiguating senses using Wordnet

Introducing semantic analysis

NLP means performing computations on natural language. One of the steps performed while processing a natural language is semantic analysis. While analyzing an input sentence, if the syntactic structure of a sentence is built, then the semantic analysis of a sentence will be done. Semantic interpretation means mapping a meaning to a sentence. Contextual interpretation is mapping the logical form to the knowledge representation. The primitive or the basic unit of semantic analysis is referred to as meaning or sense. One of the tools dealing with senses is ELIZA. ELIZA was developed in the sixties by Joseph Weizenbaum. It made use of substitution and pattern matching techniques to analyze the sentence and provide an output to the given input. MARGIE was developed by Robert Schank in the seventies. It could represent all the English verbs using 11 primitives. MARGIE could interpret the sense of a sentence and represent it with the help of primitives. It further gave way to the concept of scripts. From MARGIE, **Script Applier Mechanism (SAM)** was developed. It could translate a sentence from different languages, such as English, Chinese, Russian, Dutch, and Spanish. In order to perform processing on textual data, a Python library or TextBlob is used. TextBlob provides APIs for performing NLP tasks, such as Part-of-Speech tagging, extraction of Noun Phrases, classification, machine translation, sentiment analysis.

Semantic analysis can be used to query a database and retrieve information. Another Python library, Gensim, can be used to perform document indexing, topic modeling, and similarity retrieval. Polyglot is an NLP tool that supports various multilingual applications. It provides NER for 40 different languages, tokenization for 165 different languages, language detection for 196 different languages, sentiment analysis for 136 different languages, POS tagging for 16 different languages, Morphological Analysis for 135 different languages, word embedding for 137 different languages, and transliteration for 69 different languages. MontyLingua is an NLP tool that is used to perform the semantic interpretation of English text. From English sentences, it extracts semantic information, such as verbs, nouns, adjectives, dates, phrases, and so on.

Sentences can be formally represented using logics. The basic expressions or sentences in propositional logic are represented using propositional symbols, such as P,Q, R, and so on. Complex expressions in propositional logic can be represented using Boolean operators. For example, to represent the sentence *If it is raining, I'll wear a raincoat* using propositional logic:

- **P**: It is raining.
- **Q**: I'll wear raincoat.
- **P→Q**: If it is raining, I'll wear a raincoat.

Consider the following code to represent operators used in NLTK:

```
>>> import nltk
>>> nltk.boolean_ops()
negation  -
conjunction       &
disjunction       |
implication       ->
equivalence       <->
```

Well-formed Formulas (WFF) are formed using propositional symbols or using a combination of propositional symbols and Boolean operators.

Let's see the following code in NLTK, that categorizes logical expressions into different subclasses:

```
>>> import nltk
>>> input_expr = nltk.sem.Expression.from string
>>> input_expr('X | (Y -> Z)')
<OrExpression (X | (Y -> Z))>
>>> input_expr('-(X & Y)')
<NegatedExpression -(X & Y)>
>>> input_expr('X & Y')
<AndExpression (X & Y)>
>>> input_expr('X <-> -- X')
<IffExpression (X <-> --X)>
```

For mapping `True` or `False` values to logical expressions, the `Valuation` function is used in NLTK:

```
>>> import nltk
>>> value = nltk.Valuation([('X', True), ('Y', False), ('Z', True)])
>>> value['Z']
True
>>> domain = set()
>>> v = nltk.Assignment(domain)
>>> u = nltk.Model(domain, value)
>>> print(u.evaluate('(X & Y)', v))
False
>>> print(u.evaluate('-(X & Y)', v))
True
>>> print(u.evaluate('(X & Z)', v))
True
>>> print(u.evaluate('(X | Y)', v))
True
```

First order predicate logic involving constants and predicates in NLTK are depicted in the following code:

```
>>> import nltk
>>> input_expr = nltk.sem.Expression.from string
>>> expression = input_expr('run(marcus)', type_check=True)
>>> expression.argument
<ConstantExpressionmarcus>
>>> expression.argument.type
e
>>> expression.function
<ConstantExpression run>
>>> expression.function.type
<e,?>
>>> sign = {'run': '<e, t>'}
>>> expression = input_expr('run(marcus)', signature=sign)
>>> expression.function.type
e
```

The `signature` is used in NLTK to map associated types and non-logical constants. Consider the following code in NLTK that helps to generate a query and retrieve data from the database:

```
>>> import nltk
>>> nltk.data.show_cfg('grammars/book_grammars/sql1.fcfg')
% start S
S[SEM=(?np + WHERE + ?vp)] -> NP[SEM=?np] VP[SEM=?vp]
VP[SEM=(?v + ?pp)] -> IV[SEM=?v] PP[SEM=?pp]
VP[SEM=(?v + ?ap)] -> IV[SEM=?v] AP[SEM=?ap]
VP[SEM=(?v + ?np)] -> TV[SEM=?v] NP[SEM=?np]
VP[SEM=(?vp1 + ?c + ?vp2)] -> VP[SEM=?vp1] Conj[SEM=?c] VP[SEM=?vp2]
NP[SEM=(?det + ?n)] ->Det[SEM=?det] N[SEM=?n]
NP[SEM=(?n + ?pp)]  -> N[SEM=?n] PP[SEM=?pp]
NP[SEM=?n]  -> N[SEM=?n]  | CardN[SEM=?n]
CardN[SEM='1000'] -> '1,000,000'
PP[SEM=(?p + ?np)] -> P[SEM=?p] NP[SEM=?np]
AP[SEM=?pp] -> A[SEM=?a] PP[SEM=?pp]
NP[SEM='Country="greece"'] -> 'Greece'
NP[SEM='Country="china"'] -> 'China'
Det[SEM='SELECT'] -> 'Which' | 'What'
Conj[SEM='AND'] -> 'and'
N[SEM='City FROM city_table'] -> 'cities'
N[SEM='Population'] -> 'populations'
IV[SEM=''] -> 'are'
```

```
TV[SEM=''] -> 'have'
A -> 'located'
P[SEM=''] -> 'in'
P[SEM='>'] -> 'above'
>>> from nltk import load_parser
>>> test = load_parser('grammars/book_grammars/sql1.fcfg')
>>> q=" What cities are in Greece"
>>> t = list(test.parse(q.split()))
>>> ans = t[0].label()['SEM']
>>> ans = [s for s in ans if s]
>>> q = ' '.join(ans)
>>> print(q)
SELECT City FROM city_table WHERE Country="greece"
>>> from nltk.sem import chat80
>>> r = chat80.sql_query('corpora/city_database/city.db', q)
>>> for p in r:
print(p[0], end=" ")

athens
```

Introducing NER

Named entity recognition (NER) is the process in which proper nouns or named entities are located in a document. Then, these Named Entities are classified into different categories, such as Name of Person, Location, Organization, and so on.

There are 12 NER tagsets defined by IIIT-Hyderabad IJCNLP 2008. These are described here:

SNO.	Named entity tag	Meaning
1	NEP	Name of Person
2	NED	Name of Designation
3	NEO	Name of Organization
4	NEA	Name of Abbreviation
5	NEB	Name of Brand
6	NETP	Title of Person
7	NETO	Title of Object
8	NEL	Name of Location

SNO.	Named entity tag	Meaning
9	NETI	Time
10	NEN	Number
11	NEM	Measure
12	NETE	Terms

One of the applications of NER is information extraction. In NLTK, we can perform the task of information extraction by storing the tuple (entity, relation, entity), and then, the entity value can be retrieved.

Consider an example in NLTK that shows how information extraction is performed:

```
>>> import nltk
>>> locations=[('Jaipur', 'IN', 'Rajasthan'),('Ajmer', 'IN',
'Rajasthan'),('Udaipur', 'IN', 'Rajasthan'),('Mumbai', 'IN',
'Maharashtra'),('Ahmedabad', 'IN', 'Gujrat')]
>>> q = [x1 for (x1, relation, x2) in locations if x2=='Rajasthan']
>>> print(q)
['Jaipur', 'Ajmer', 'Udaipur']
```

The `nltk.tag.stanford` module is used that makes use of stanford taggers to perform NER. We can download tagger models from `http://nlp.stanford.edu/software`.

Let's see the following example in NLTK that can be used to perform NER using the `Stanford` tagger:

```
>>> from nltk.tag import StanfordNERTagger
>>> sentence = StanfordNERTagger('english.all.3class.distsim.crf.ser.
gz')
>>> sentence.tag('John goes to NY'.split())
[('John', 'PERSON'), ('goes', 'O'), ('to', 'O'),('NY', 'LOCATION')]
```

A classifier has been trained in NLTK to detect Named Entities. Using the function `nltk.ne.chunk()`, named entities can be identified from a text. If the parameter binary is set to `true`, then the named entities are detected and tagged with the `NE` tag; otherwise the named entities are tagged with tags such as PERSON, GPE, and ORGANIZATION.

Let's see the following code, that detects Named Entities, if they exist, and tags them with the `NE` tag:

```
>>> import nltk
>>> sentences1 = nltk.corpus.treebank.tagged_sents()[17]
>>> print(nltk.ne_chunk(sentences1, binary=True))
(S
  The/DT
total/NN
of/IN
  18/CD
deaths/NNS
from/IN
malignant/JJ
mesothelioma/NN
  ,/,
lung/NN
cancer/NN
and/CC
asbestosis/NN
was/VBD
far/RB
higher/JJR
than/IN
  */-NONE-
expected/VBN
  *?*/-NONE-
  ,/,
the/DT
researchers/NNS
said/VBD
  0/-NONE-
  *T*-1/-NONE-
  ./.)
>>> sentences2 = nltk.corpus.treebank.tagged_sents()[7]
>>> print(nltk.ne_chunk(sentences2, binary=True))
(S
  A/DT
  (NE Lorillard/NNP)
spokewoman/NN
said/VBD
  ,/,
  ``/``
  This/DT
```

```
is/VBZ
an/DT
old/JJ
story/NN
  ./.)
>>> print(nltk.ne_chunk(sentences2))
(S
  A/DT
  (ORGANIZATION Lorillard/NNP)
spokewoman/NN
said/VBD
  ,/,
  ``/``
  This/DT
is/VBZ
an/DT
old/JJ
story/NN
  ./.)
```

Consider another example in NLTK that can be used to detect named entities:

```
>>> import nltk
>>> from nltk.corpus import conll2002
>>> for documents in conll2002.chunked_sents('ned.train')[25]:
print(documents)


(PER Vandenbussche/Adj)
('zelf', 'Pron')
('besloot', 'V')
('dat', 'Conj')
('het', 'Art')
('hof', 'N')
('"', 'Punc')
('de', 'Art')
('politieke', 'Adj')
('zeden', 'N')
('uit', 'Prep')
('het', 'Art')
('verleden', 'N')
('"', 'Punc')
('heeft', 'V')
('willen', 'V')
('veroordelen', 'V')
('.', 'Punc')
```

A `chunker` is a program that is used to partition plain text into a sequence of semantically related words. To perform NER in NLTK, default chunkers are used. Default chunkers are chunkers based on classifiers that have been trained on the ACE corpus. Other chunkers have been trained on parsed or chunked NLTK corpora. The languages covered by these NLTK chunkers are as follows:

- Dutch
- Spanish
- Portuguese
- English

Consider another example in NLTK that identifies named entities and categorizes into different named entity classes:

```
>>> import nltk
>>> sentence = "I went to Greece to meet John";
>>> tok=nltk.word_tokenize(sentence)
>>> pos_tag=nltk.pos_tag(tok)
>>> print(nltk.ne_chunk(pos_tag))
(S
  I/PRP
went/VBD
to/TO
  (GPE Greece/NNP)
to/TO
meet/VB
  (PERSON John/NNP))
```

A NER system using Hidden Markov Model

HMM is one of the popular statistical approaches of NER. An HMM is defined as a **Stochastic Finite State Automaton (SFSA)** consisting of a finite set of states that are associated with the definite probability distribution. States are unobserved or hidden. HMM generates optimal state sequences as an output. HMM is based on the Markov Chain property. According to the Markov Chain property, the probability of the occurrence of the next state is dependent on the previous tag. It is the simplest approach to implement. The drawback of HMM is that it requires a large amount of training and it cannot be used for large dependencies. HMM consists of the following:

- Set of states, *S*, where $|S|=N$. Here, *N* is the total number of states.
- Start state, *S0*.

- Output alphabet, *O*; | *O* | =*k*. *k* is the total number of output alphabets.
- Transition probability, *A*.
- Emission probability, *B*.
- Initial state probabilities, π.

HMM is represented by the following tuple—$\lambda= (A, B, \pi)$.

Start probability or initial state probability may be defined as the probability that a particular tag occurs first in a sentence.

Transition probability (*A=aij*) may be defined as the probability of the occurrence of the next tag *j* in a sentence given the occurrence of the particular tag *i* at present.

A=aij= the number of transitions from state *si* to *sj* /the number of transitions from state *si*

Emission probability (*B=bj(O)*) may be defined as the probability of the occurrence of an output sequence given a state *j*.

B=bj(k)= the number of times in state *j* and observing the symbol *k* /the expected number of times in state *j*.

The Baum Welch algorithm is used to find the maximum likelihood and the posterior mode estimates for HMM parameters. The forward-backward algorithm is used to find the posterior marginals of all the hidden state variables given a sequence of emissions or observations.

There are three steps involved in performing NER using HMM—Annotation, HMM train, and HMM test. The Annotation module converts raw text into annotated or trainable data. During HMM train, we compute HMM parameters—start probability, transition probability, and emission probability. During HMM test, the Viterbi algorithm is used. that finds out the optimal tag sequence.

Consider an example of chunking using the HMM in NLTK. Using chunking, the NP and VP chunks can be obtained. NP chunks can further be processed to obtain proper nouns or named entities:

```
>>> import nltk
>>> nltk.tag.hmm.demo_pos()

HMM POS tagging demo

Training HMM...
Testing...
```

```
Test: the/AT fulton/NP county/NN grand/JJ jury/NN said/VBD friday/
NR an/AT investigation/NN of/IN atlanta's/NP$ recent/JJ primary/NN
election/NN produced/VBD ``/`` no/AT evidence/NN ''/'' that/CS any/DTI
irregularities/NNS took/VBD place/NN ./.

Untagged: the fulton county grand jury said friday an investigation of
atlanta's recent primary election produced `` no evidence '' that any
irregularities took place .

HMM-tagged: the/AT fulton/NP county/NN grand/JJ jury/NN said/
VBD friday/NR an/AT investigation/NN of/IN atlanta's/NP$ recent/
JJ primary/NN election/NN produced/VBD ``/`` no/AT evidence/NN ''/''
that/CS any/DTI irregularities/NNS took/VBD place/NN ./.

Entropy: 18.7331739705

------------------------------------------------------------

Test: the/AT jury/NN further/RBR said/VBD in/IN term-end/NN
presentments/NNS that/CS the/AT city/NN executive/JJ committee/NN ,/,
which/WDT had/HVD over-all/JJ charge/NN of/IN the/AT election/NN ,/,
``/`` deserves/VBZ the/AT praise/NN and/CC thanks/NNS of/IN the/AT
city/NN of/IN atlanta/NP ''/'' for/IN the/AT manner/NN in/IN which/WDT
the/AT election/NN was/BEDZ conducted/VBN ./.

Untagged: the jury further said in term-end presentments that the
city executive committee , which had over-all charge of the election
, `` deserves the praise and thanks of the city of atlanta '' for the
manner in which the election was conducted .

HMM-tagged: the/AT jury/NN further/RBR said/VBD in/IN term-end/AT
presentments/NN that/CS the/AT city/NN executive/NN committee/NN ,/,
which/WDT had/HVD over-all/VBN charge/NN of/IN the/AT election/NN ,/,
``/`` deserves/VBZ the/AT praise/NN and/CC thanks/NNS of/IN the/AT
city/NN of/IN atlanta/NP ''/'' for/IN the/AT manner/NN in/IN which/WDT
the/AT election/NN was/BEDZ conducted/VBN ./.

Entropy: 27.0708725519

------------------------------------------------------------

Test: the/AT september-october/NP term/NN jury/NN had/HVD been/BEN
charged/VBN by/IN fulton/NP superior/JJ court/NN judge/NN durwood/
NP pye/NP to/TO investigate/VB reports/NNS of/IN possible/JJ ``/``
irregularities/NNS ''/'' in/IN the/AT hard-fought/JJ primary/NN which/
WDT was/BEDZ won/VBN by/IN mayor-nominate/NN ivan/NP allen/NP jr./NP
./.
```

```
Untagged: the september-october term jury had been charged by fulton
superior court judge durwoodpye to investigate reports of possible ``
irregularities '' in the hard-fought primary which was won by mayor-
nominate ivanallenjr. .

HMM-tagged: the/AT september-october/JJ term/NN jury/NN had/HVD been/
BEN charged/VBN by/IN fulton/NP superior/JJ court/NN judge/NN durwood/
TO pye/VB to/TO investigate/VB reports/NNS of/IN possible/JJ ``/``
irregularities/NNS ''/'' in/IN the/AT hard-fought/JJ primary/NN which/
WDT was/BEDZ won/VBN by/IN mayor-nominate/NP ivan/NP allen/NP jr./NP
./.

Entropy: 33.8281874237

------------------------------------------------------------

Test: ``/`` only/RB a/AT relative/JJ handful/NN of/IN such/JJ reports/
NNS was/BEDZ received/VBN ''/'' ,/, the/AT jury/NN said/VBD ,/, ``/``
considering/IN the/AT widespread/JJ interest/NN in/IN the/AT election/
NN ,/, the/AT number/NN of/IN voters/NNS and/CC the/AT size/NN of/IN
this/DT city/NN ''/'' ./.

Untagged: `` only a relative handful of such reports was received '' ,
the jury said , `` considering the widespread interest in the election
, the number of voters and the size of this city '' .

HMM-tagged: ``/`` only/RB a/AT relative/JJ handful/NN of/IN such/JJ
reports/NNS was/BEDZ received/VBN ''/'' ,/, the/AT jury/NN said/VBD
,/, ``/`` considering/IN the/AT widespread/JJ interest/NN in/IN the/AT
election/NN ,/, the/AT number/NN of/IN voters/NNS and/CC the/AT size/
NN of/IN this/DT city/NN ''/'' ./.

Entropy: 11.4378198596

------------------------------------------------------------

Test: the/AT jury/NN said/VBD it/PPS did/DOD find/VB that/CS many/AP
of/IN georgia's/NP$ registration/NN and/CC election/NN laws/NNS ``/``
are/BER outmoded/JJ or/CC inadequate/JJ and/CC often/RB ambiguous/JJ
''/'' ./.

Untagged: the jury said it did find that many of georgia's
registration and election laws `` are outmoded or inadequate and often
ambiguous '' .

HMM-tagged: the/AT jury/NN said/VBD it/PPS did/DOD find/VB that/CS
many/AP of/IN georgia's/NP$ registration/NN and/CC election/NN laws/
NNS ``/`` are/BER outmoded/VBG or/CC inadequate/JJ and/CC often/RB
ambiguous/VB ''/'' ./.
```

```
Entropy: 20.8163623192

------------------------------------------------------------

Test: it/PPS recommended/VBD that/CS fulton/NP legislators/NNS act/VB
``/`` to/TO have/HV these/DTS laws/NNS studied/VBN and/CC revised/VBN
to/IN the/AT end/NN of/IN modernizing/VBG and/CC improving/VBG them/
PPO ''/'' ./.

Untagged: it recommended that fulton legislators act `` to have these
laws studied and revised to the end of modernizing and improving them
'' .

HMM-tagged: it/PPS recommended/VBD that/CS fulton/NP legislators/
NNS act/VB ``/`` to/TO have/HV these/DTS laws/NNS studied/VBD and/CC
revised/VBD to/IN the/AT end/NN of/IN modernizing/NP and/CC improving/
VBG them/PPO ''/'' ./.

Entropy: 20.3244921203

------------------------------------------------------------

Test: the/AT grand/JJ jury/NN commented/VBD on/IN a/AT number/NN of/
IN other/AP topics/NNS ,/, among/IN them/PPO the/AT atlanta/NP and/
CC fulton/NP county/NN purchasing/VBG departments/NNS which/WDT it/
PPS said/VBD ``/`` are/BER well/QL operated/VBN and/CC follow/VB
generally/RB accepted/VBN practices/NNS which/WDT inure/VB to/IN the/
AT best/JJT interest/NN of/IN both/ABX governments/NNS ''/'' ./.

Untagged: the grand jury commented on a number of other topics ,
among them the atlanta and fulton county purchasing departments which
it said `` are well operated and follow generally accepted practices
which inure to the best interest of both governments '' .

HMM-tagged: the/AT grand/JJ jury/NN commented/VBD on/IN a/AT number/
NN of/IN other/AP topics/NNS ,/, among/IN them/PPO the/AT atlanta/
NP and/CC fulton/NP county/NN purchasing/NN departments/NNS which/WDT
it/PPS said/VBD ``/`` are/BER well/RB operated/VBN and/CC follow/VB
generally/RB accepted/VBN practices/NNS which/WDT inure/VBZ to/IN the/
AT best/JJT interest/NN of/IN both/ABX governments/NNS ''/'' ./.

Entropy: 31.3834231469

------------------------------------------------------------

Test: merger/NN proposed/VBN

Untagged: merger proposed
```

```
HMM-tagged: merger/PPS proposed/VBD

Entropy: 5.6718203946

------------------------------------------------------------

Test: however/WRB ,/, the/AT jury/NN said/VBD it/PPS believes/VBZ
``/`` these/DTS two/CD offices/NNS should/MD be/BE combined/VBN to/TO
achieve/VB greater/JJR efficiency/NN and/CC reduce/VB the/AT cost/NN
of/IN administration/NN ''/'' ./.

Untagged: however , the jury said it believes `` these two offices
should be combined to achieve greater efficiency and reduce the cost
of administration '' .

HMM-tagged: however/WRB ,/, the/AT jury/NN said/VBD it/PPS believes/
VBZ ``/`` these/DTS two/CD offices/NNS should/MD be/BE combined/VBN
to/TO achieve/VB greater/JJR efficiency/NN and/CC reduce/VB the/AT
cost/NN of/IN administration/NN ''/'' ./.

Entropy: 8.27545943909

------------------------------------------------------------

Test: the/AT city/NN purchasing/VBG department/NN ,/, the/AT jury/NN
said/VBD ,/, ``/`` is/BEZ lacking/VBG in/IN experienced/VBN clerical/
JJ personnel/NNS as/CS a/AT result/NN of/IN city/NN personnel/NNS
policies/NNS ''/'' ./.

Untagged: the city purchasing department , the jury said , `` is
lacking in experienced clerical personnel as a result of city
personnel policies '' .

HMM-tagged: the/AT city/NN purchasing/NN department/NN ,/, the/
AT jury/NN said/VBD ,/, ``/`` is/BEZ lacking/VBG in/IN experienced/
AT clerical/JJ personnel/NNS as/CS a/AT result/NN of/IN city/NN
personnel/NNS policies/NNS ''/'' ./.

Entropy: 16.7622537278

------------------------------------------------------------

accuracy over 284 tokens: 92.96
```

The outcome of an NER tagger may be defined as a *response* and an interpretation of human beings as *answer key*. So, we provide the following definitions:

- **Correct**: If the response is exactly the same as answer key
- **Incorrect**: If the response is not same as answer key
- **Missing**: If answer key is found tagged, but response is not tagged
- **Spurious**: If response is found tagged, but answer key is not tagged

Performance of an NER-based system can be judged by using the following parameters:

- **Precision (P)**: It is defined as follows:

  P=Correct/ (Correct+Incorrect+Missing)

- **Recall (R)**: It is defined as follows:

  R=Correct/ (Correct+Incorrect+Spurious)

- **F-Measure**: It is defined as follows:

  *F-Measure = (2*PREC*REC)/(PRE+REC)*

Training NER using Machine Learning Toolkits

NER can be performed using the following approaches:

- Rule-based or Handcrafted approach:
  - List Lookup approach
  - Linguistic approach
- Machine Learning-based approach or Automated approach:
  - Hidden Markov Model
  - Maximum Entropy Markov Model
  - Conditional Random Fields
  - Support Vector Machine
  - Decision Trees

It has been proved experimentally that Machine learning-based approaches outperform Rule-based approaches. Also, if a combination of Rule-based approaches and Machine Learning-based approaches is used, then the performance of NER will increase.

NER using POS tagging

Using POS tagging, NER can be performed. The POS tags that can be used are as follows (they are available at `https://www.ling.upenn.edu/courses/Fall_2003/ling001/penn_treebank_pos.html`):

Tag	Description
CC	Coordinating conjunction
CD	Cardinal number
DT	Determiner
EX	Existential there
FW	Foreign word
IN	Preposition or subordinating conjunction
JJ	Adjective
JJR	Adjective, comparative
JJS	Adjective, superlative
LS	List item marker
MD	Modal
NN	Noun, singular or mass
NNS	Noun, plural
NNP	Proper noun, singular
NNPS	Proper noun, plural
PDT	Predeterminer
POS	Possessive ending
PRP	Personal pronoun
PRP$	Possessive pronoun
RB	Adverb
RBR	Adverb, comparative
RBS	Adverb, superlative
RP	Particle
SYM	Symbol
TO	To
UH	Interjection
VB	Verb, base form
VBD	Verb, past tense
VBG	Verb, gerund or present participle
VBN	Verb, past participle

Tag	Description
VBP	Verb, non-3rd person singular present
VBZ	Verb, 3rd person singular present
WDT	Wh-determiner
WP	Wh-pronoun
WP$	Possessive wh-pronoun
WRB	Wh-adverb

If POS tagging is performed, then using POS information, named entities can be identified. The tokens tagged with the `NNP` tag are Named Entities.

Consider the following example in NLTK in which POS tagging is used to perform NER:

```
>>> import nltk
>>> from nltk import pos_tag, word_tokenize
>>> pos_tag(word_tokenize("John and Smith are going to NY and
Germany"))
[('John', 'NNP'), ('and', 'CC'), ('Smith', 'NNP'), ('are', 'VBP'),
('going', 'VBG'), ('to', 'TO'), ('NY', 'NNP'), ('and', 'CC'),
('Germany', 'NNP')]
```

Here, the named entities are—`John`, `Smith`, `NY`, and `Germany` since they are tagged with the NNP tag.

Let's see another example in which POS tagging is performed in NLTK and the POS tag information is used to detect Named Entities:

```
>>> import nltk
>>> from nltk.corpus import brown
>>> from nltk.tag import UnigramTagger
>>> tagger = UnigramTagger(brown.tagged_sents(categories='news')
[:700])
>>> sentence = ['John','and','Smith','went','to','NY','and','Germany']
>>> for word, tag in tagger.tag(sentence):
print(word,'->',tag)


John -> NP
and -> CC
Smith -> None
went -> VBD
to -> TO
```

```
NY -> None
and -> CC
Germany -> None
```

Here, John has been tagged with the `NP` tag, so it is identified as a named entity. Some of the tokens here are tagged with the `None` tag because these tokens have not been trained.

Generation of the synset id from Wordnet

Wordnet may be defined as an English lexical database. The conceptual dependency between words, such as hypernym, synonym, antonym, and hyponym, can be found using synsets.

Consider the following code in NLTK for the generation of synsets:

```
def all_synsets(self, pos=None):
        """Iterate over all synsets with a given part of speech tag.
        If no pos is specified, all synsets for all parts of speech
        will be loaded.
        """
        if pos is None:
            pos_tags = self._FILEMAP.keys()
        else:
            pos_tags = [pos]

        cache = self._synset_offset_cache
        from_pos_and_line = self._synset_from_pos_and_line

        # generate all synsets for each part of speech
        for pos_tag in pos_tags:
            # Open the file for reading.  Note that we can not re-use
            # the file poitners from self._data_file_map here, because
            # we're defining an iterator, and those file pointers
might
            # be moved while we're not looking.
            if pos_tag == ADJ_SAT:
                pos_tag = ADJ
            fileid = 'data.%s' % self._FILEMAP[pos_tag]
            data_file = self.open(fileid)

            try:
                # generate synsets for each line in the POS file
                offset = data_file.tell()
```

```
                line = data_file.readline()
                while line:
                    if not line[0].isspace():
                        if offset in cache[pos_tag]:
                            # See if the synset is cached
                            synset = cache[pos_tag][offset]
                        else:
                            # Otherwise, parse the line
                            synset = from_pos_and_line(pos_tag, line)
                            cache[pos_tag][offset] = synset

                        # adjective satellites are in the same file as
                        # adjectives so only yield the synset if it's
actually
                        # a satellite
                        if synset._pos == ADJ_SAT:
                            yield synset

                        # for all other POS tags, yield all synsets
(this means
                        # that adjectives also include adjective
satellites)
                        else:
                            yield synset
                    offset = data_file.tell()
                    line = data_file.readline()

            # close the extra file handle we opened
            except:
                data_file.close()
                raise
            else:
                data_file.close()
```

Let's see the following code in NLTK, that is used to look up a word using synsets:

```
>>> import nltk
>>> from nltk.corpus import wordnet
>>> from nltk.corpus import wordnet as wn
>>> wn.synsets('cat')
[Synset('cat.n.01'), Synset('guy.n.01'), Synset('cat.n.03'),
Synset('kat.n.01'), Synset('cat-o'-nine-tails.n.01'),
Synset('caterpillar.n.02'), Synset('big_cat.n.01'),
Synset('computerized_tomography.n.01'), Synset('cat.v.01'),
Synset('vomit.v.01')]
```

```
>>> wn.synsets('cat', pos=wn.VERB)
[Synset('cat.v.01'), Synset('vomit.v.01')]
>>> wn.synset('cat.n.01')
Synset('cat.n.01')
```

Here, `cat.n.01` means that `cat` is of the noun category and only one meaning of `cat` exists:

```
>>> print(wn.synset('cat.n.01').definition())
feline mammal usually having thick soft fur and no ability to roar:
domestic cats; wildcats
>>> len(wn.synset('cat.n.01').examples())
0
>>> wn.synset('cat.n.01').lemmas()
[Lemma('cat.n.01.cat'), Lemma('cat.n.01.true_cat')]
>>> [str(lemma.name()) for lemma in wn.synset('cat.n.01').lemmas()]
['cat', 'true_cat']
>>> wn.lemma('cat.n.01.cat').synset()
Synset('cat.n.01')
```

Let's see the following example in NLTK, that depicts the use of Synsets and Open Multilingual Wordnet using ISO 639 language codes:

```
>>> import nltk
>>> from nltk.corpus import wordnet
>>> from nltk.corpus import wordnet as wn
>>> sorted(wn.langs())
['als', 'arb', 'cat', 'cmn', 'dan', 'eng', 'eus', 'fas', 'fin', 'fra',
'fre', 'glg', 'heb', 'ind', 'ita', 'jpn', 'nno', 'nob', 'pol', 'por',
'spa', 'tha', 'zsm']
>>> wn.synset('cat.n.01').lemma_names('ita')
['gatto']
>>> sorted(wn.synset('cat.n.01').lemmas('dan'))
[Lemma('cat.n.01.kat'), Lemma('cat.n.01.mis'), Lemma('cat.n.01.
missekat')]
>>> sorted(wn.synset('cat.n.01').lemmas('por'))
[Lemma('cat.n.01.Gato-doméstico'), Lemma('cat.n.01.Gato_doméstico'),
Lemma('cat.n.01.gato'), Lemma('cat.n.01.gato')]
>>> len(wordnet.all_lemma_names(pos='n', lang='jpn'))
66027
>>> cat = wn.synset('cat.n.01')
>>> cat.hypernyms()
[Synset('feline.n.01')]
>>> cat.hyponyms()
[Synset('domestic_cat.n.01'), Synset('wildcat.n.03')]
```

```
>>> cat.member_holonyms()
[]
>>> cat.root_hypernyms()
[Synset('entity.n.01')]
>>> wn.synset('cat.n.01').lowest_common_hypernyms(wn.
synset('dog.n.01'))
[Synset('carnivore.n.01')]
```

Disambiguating senses using Wordnet

Disambiguation is the task of distinguishing two or more of the same spellings or the same sounding words on the basis of their sense or meaning.

Following are the implementations of disambiguation or the WSD task using Python technologies:

- Lesk algorithms:
  - Original Lesk
  - Cosine Lesk (use cosines to calculate overlaps instead of using raw counts)
  - Simple Lesk (with definitions, example(s), and hyper+hyponyms)
  - Adapted/extended Lesk
  - Enhanced Lesk
- Maximizing similarity:
  - Information content
  - Path similarity
- Supervised WSD:
  - **It Makes Sense (IMS)**
  - SVM WSD
- Vector Space models:
  - Topic Models, LDA
  - LSI/LSA
  - NMF
- Graph-based models:
  - Babelfly
  - UKB

- Baselines:
    - Random sense
    - Highest lemma counts
    - First NLTK sense

Wordnet sense similarity in NLTK involves the following algorithms:

- **Resnik Score**: On comparing two tokens, a score (Least Common Subsumer) is returned that decides the similarity of two tokens
- **Wu-Palmer Similarity**: Defines the similarity between two tokens on the basis of the depth of two senses and Least Common Subsumer
- **Path Distance Similarity**: The similarity of two tokens is determined on the basis of the shortest distance that is computed in the is-a taxonomy
- **Leacock Chodorow Similarity**: A similarity score is returned on the basis of the shortest path and the depth (maximum) in which the senses exist in the taxonomy
- **Lin Similarity**: A similarity score is returned on the basis of the information content of the Least Common Subsumer and two input Synsets
- **Jiang-Conrath Similarity**: A similarity score is returned on the basis of the content information of Least Common Subsumer and two input Synsets

Consider the following example in NLTK, which depicts path similarity:

```
>>> import nltk
>>> from nltk.corpus import wordnet
>>> from nltk.corpus import wordnet as wn
>>> lion = wn.synset('lion.n.01')
>>> cat = wn.synset('cat.n.01')
>>> lion.path_similarity(cat)
0.25
```

Consider the following example in NLTK that depicts Leacock Chodorow Similarity:

```
>>> import nltk
>>> from nltk.corpus import wordnet
>>> from nltk.corpus import wordnet as wn
>>> lion = wn.synset('lion.n.01')
>>> cat = wn.synset('cat.n.01')
>>> lion.lch_similarity(cat)
2.2512917986064953
```

Consider the following example in NLTK that depicts Wu-Palmer Similarity:

```
>>> import nltk
>>> from nltk.corpus import wordnet
>>> from nltk.corpus import wordnet as wn
>>> lion = wn.synset('lion.n.01')
>>> cat = wn.synset('cat.n.01')
>>> lion.wup_similarity(cat)
0.896551724137931
```

Consider the following example in NLTK that depicts Resnik Similarity, Lin Similarity, and Jiang-Conrath Similarity:

```
>>> import nltk
>>> from nltk.corpus import wordnet
>>> from nltk.corpus import wordnet as wn
>>> from nltk.corpus import wordnet_ic
>>> brown_ic = wordnet_ic.ic('ic-brown.dat')
>>> semcor_ic = wordnet_ic.ic('ic-semcor.dat')
>>> from nltk.corpus import genesis
>>> genesis_ic = wn.ic(genesis, False, 0.0)
>>> lion = wn.synset('lion.n.01')
>>> cat = wn.synset('cat.n.01')
>>> lion.res_similarity(cat, brown_ic)
8.663481537685325
>>> lion.res_similarity(cat, genesis_ic)
7.339696591781995
>>> lion.jcn_similarity(cat, brown_ic)
0.36425897775957294
>>> lion.jcn_similarity(cat, genesis_ic)
0.3057800856788946
>>> lion.lin_similarity(cat, semcor_ic)
0.8560734335071154
```

Let's see the following code in NLTK based on Wu-Palmer Similarity and Path Distance Similarity:

```
from nltk.corpus import wordnet as wn
def getSenseSimilarity(worda,wordb):

"""

find similarity betwwn word senses of two words

"""
```

```
wordasynsets = wn.synsets(worda)

wordbsynsets = wn.synsets(wordb)

synsetnamea = [wn.synset(str(syns.name)) for syns in wordasynsets]

   synsetnameb = [wn.synset(str(syns.name)) for syns in wordbsynsets]


for sseta, ssetb in [(sseta,ssetb) for sseta in synsetnamea\

for ssetb in synsetnameb]:

pathsim = sseta.path_similarity(ssetb)

wupsim = sseta.wup_similarity(ssetb)

if pathsim != None:

print "Path Sim Score: ",pathsim," WUP Sim Score: ",wupsim,\

"\t",sseta.definition, "\t", ssetb.definition


if __name__ == "__main__":

#getSenseSimilarity('walk','dog')

getSenseSimilarity('cricket','ball')
```

Consider the following code of a Lesk algorithm in NLTK , which is used to perform the disambiguation task:

```
from nltk.corpus import wordnet


def lesk(context_sentence, ambiguous_word, pos=None, synsets=None):
    """Return a synset for an ambiguous word in a context.

    :param iter context_sentence: The context sentence where the
ambiguous word
    occurs, passed as an iterable of words.
    :param str ambiguous_word: The ambiguous word that requires WSD.
    :param str pos: A specified Part-of-Speech (POS).
```

```
    :param iter synsets: Possible synsets of the ambiguous word.
    :return: ``lesk_sense`` The Synset() object with the highest
signature overlaps.

//    This function is an implementation of the original Lesk
algorithm (1986) [1].

    Usage example::

>>> lesk(['I', 'went', 'to', 'the', 'bank', 'to', 'deposit', 'money',
'.'], 'bank', 'n')
        Synset('savings_bank.n.02')


    context = set(context_sentence)
    if synsets is None:
        synsets = wordnet.synsets(ambiguous_word)

    if pos:
        synsets = [ss for ss in synsets if str(ss.pos()) == pos]

    if not synsets:
        return None

    _, sense = max(
        (len(context.intersection(ss.definition().split())), ss) for
ss in synsets
    )

    return sense
```

Summary

In this chapter, we have discussed Semantic Analysis, which is also one of the phase of Natural Language Processing. We have discussed NER, NER using HMM, NER using Machine Learning Toolkits, Performance Metrics of NER, NER using POS tagging, and WSD using Wordnet and the Generation of Synsets.

In the next chapter, we will discuss sentiment analysis using NER and machine learning approaches. We will also discuss the evaluation of the NER system.

7

Sentiment Analysis – I Am Happy

Sentiment analysis or sentiment generation is one of the tasks in NLP. It is defined as the process of determining the sentiments behind a character sequence. It may be used to determine whether the speaker or the person expressing the textual thoughts is in a happy or sad mood, or it represents a neutral expression.

This chapter will include the following topics:

- Introducing sentiment analysis
- Sentiment analysis using NER
- Sentiment analysis using machine learning
- Evaluation of the NER system

Introducing sentiment analysis

Sentiment analysis may be defined as a task performed on natural languages. Here, computations are performed on the sentences or words expressed in natural language to determine whether they express a positive, negative, or a neutral sentiment. Sentiment analysis is a subjective task, since it provides the information about the text being expressed. Sentiment analysis may be defined as a classification problem in which classification may be of two types—binary categorization (positive or negative) and multi-class categorization (positive, negative, or neutral). Sentiment analysis is also referred to as **text sentiment analysis**. It is a text mining approach in which we determine the sentiments or the emotions behind the text. When we combine sentiment analysis with topic mining, then it is referred to as **topic-sentiment analysis**. Sentiment analysis can be performed using a lexicon. The lexicon could be domain-specific or of a general purpose nature. Lexicon may contain a list of positive expressions, negative expressions, neutral expressions, and stop words. When a testing sentence appears, then a simple look up operation can be performed through this lexicon.

One example of the word list is—**Affective Norms for English Words (ANEW)**. It is an English word list found at the University of Florida. It consists of 1034 words for dominance, valence, and arousal. It was formed by Bradley and Lang. This word list was constructed for academic purposes and not for research purposes. Other variants are **DANEW** (Dutch ANEW) and **SPANEW** (Spanish ANEW).

AFINN consists of 2477 words (earlier 1468 words). This word list was formed by Finn Arup Nielson. The main purpose for creating this word list was to perform sentiment analysis for Twitter texts. A valence value ranging from *-5* to *+5* is allotted to each word.

The **Balance Affective** word list consists of 277 English words. The valence code ranges from 1 to 4. 1 means positive, 2 means negative, 3 means anxious, and 4 means neutral.

Berlin Affective Word List (BAWL) consists of 2,200 words in German. Another version of BAWL is **Berlin Affective Word List Reloaded (BAWL-R)** that comprises of additional arousal for words.

Bilingual Finnish Affective Norms comprises 210 British English as well as Finnish nouns. It also comprises taboo words.

Compass DeRose Guide to Emotion Words consists of emotional words in English. This was formed by Steve J. DeRose. Words were classified, but there was no valence and arousal.

Dictionary of Affect in Language (DAL) comprises emotional words that can be used for sentiment analysis. It was formed by Cynthia M. Whissell. So, it is also referred to as **Whissell's Dictionary of Affect in Language (WDAL)**.

General Inquirer consists of many dictionaries. In this, the positive list comprises 1915 words and the negative list comprises 2291 words.

Hu-Liu opinion Lexicon (HL) comprises a list of 6800 words (positive and negative).

Leipzig Affective Norms for German (LANG) is a list that consists of 1000 nouns in German, and the rating has been done based on valence, concreteness, and arousal.

Loughran and McDonald Financial Sentiment Dictionaries were created by Tim Loughran and Bill McDonald. These dictionaries consist of words for financial documents, which are positive, negative, or modal words.

Moors consist of a list of words in Dutch related to dominance, arousal, and valence.

NRC Emotion Lexicon comprises of a list of words developed through Amazon Mechanical Turk by Saif M. Mohammad.

OpinionFinder's **Subjectivity Lexicon** comprises a list of 8221 words (positive or negative).

SentiSense comprises 2,190 synsets and 5,496 words based on 14 emotional categories.

Warringer comprises 13,915 words in English collected from Amazon Mechanical Turk that are related to dominance, arousal, and valence.

labMT is a word list consisting of 10,000 words.

Let's consider the following example in NLTK, which performs sentiment analysis for movie reviews:

```
import nltk
import random
from nltk.corpus import movie_reviews
docs = [(list(movie_reviews.words(fid)), cat)
        for cat in movie_reviews.categories()
        for fid in movie_reviews.fileids(cat)]
random.shuffle(docs)

all_tokens = nltk.FreqDist(x.lower() for x in movie_reviews.words())
token_features = all_tokens.keys()[:2000]
print token_features[:100]
```

```
    [',', 'the', '.', 'a', 'and', 'of', 'to', "'", 'is', 'in', 's',
'"', 'it', 'that', '-', ')', '(', 'as', 'with', 'for', 'his', 'this',
'film', 'i', 'he', 'but', 'on', 'are', 't', 'by', 'be', 'one',
'movie', 'an', 'who', 'not', 'you', 'from', 'at', 'was', 'have',
'they', 'has', 'her', 'all', '?', 'there', 'like', 'so', 'out',
'about', 'up', 'more', 'what', 'when', 'which', 'or', 'she', 'their',
':', 'some', 'just', 'can', 'if', 'we', 'him', 'into', 'even', 'only',
'than', 'no', 'good', 'time', 'most', 'its', 'will', 'story', 'would',
'been', 'much', 'character', 'also', 'get', 'other', 'do', 'two',
'well', 'them', 'very', 'characters', ';', 'first', '--', 'after',
'see', '!', 'way', 'because', 'make', 'life']

def doc_features(doc):
    doc_words = set(doc)
    features = {}
    for word in token_features:
        features['contains(%s)' % word] = (word in doc_words)
    return features

print doc_features(movie_reviews.words('pos/cv957_8737.txt
feature_sets = [(doc_features(d), c) for (d,c) in doc]
train_sets, test_sets = feature_sets[100:], feature_sets[:100]
classifiers = nltk.NaiveBayesClassifier.train(train_sets)
print nltk.classify.accuracy(classifiers, test_sets)

    0.86

classifier.show_most_informative_features(5)

     Most Informative Features
contains(damon) = True              pos : neg    =    11.2 : 1.0
contains(outstanding) = True        pos : neg    =    10.6 : 1.0
contains(mulan) = True              pos : neg    =     8.8 : 1.0
contains(seagal) = True             neg : pos    =     8.4 : 1.0
contains(wonderfully) = True        pos : neg    =     7.4 : 1.0
```

Here, it is checked whether the informative features are present in the document or not.

Consider another example of semantic analysis. First, the preprocessing of text is performed. In this, individual sentences are identified in a given text. Then, tokens are identified in the sentences. Each token further comprises three entities, namely, word, lemma, and tag.

Let's see the following code in NLTK for the preprocessing of text:

```
importnltk

class Splitter(object):
def __init__(self):
self.nltk_splitter = nltk.data.load('tokenizers/punkt/english.pickle')
self.nltk_tokenizer = nltk.tokenize.TreebankWordTokenizer()

def split(self, text):
sentences = self.nltk_splitter.tokenize(text)
tokenized_sentences = [self.nltk_tokenizer.tokenize(sent) for sent in
sentences]
return tokenized_sentences
classPOSTagger(object):
def __init__(self):
pass

def pos_tag(self, sentences):

pos = [nltk.pos_tag(sentence) for sentence in sentences]
pos = [[(word, word, [postag]) for (word, postag) in sentence] for
sentence in pos]
returnpos
```

The lemmas generated will be same as the word forms. Tags are the POS tags. Consider the following code, which generates three tuples for each token, that is, word, lemma, and the POS tag:

```
text = """Why are you looking disappointed. We will go to restaurant
for dinner."""
splitter = Splitter()
postagger = POSTagger()
splitted_sentences = splitter.split(text)
print splitted_sentences
[['Why','are','you','looking','disappointed','.'], ['We','will','go','
to','restaurant','for','dinner','.']]

pos_tagged_sentences = postagger.pos_tag(splitted_sentences)

print pos_tagged_sentences
[[('Why','Why',['WP']),('are','are',['VBZ']),('you','you',['PRP']
),('looking','looking',['VB']),('disappointed','disappointed',['
VB']),('.','.',['.'])],[('We','We',['PRP']),('will','will',['VBZ']),('
go','go',['VB']),('to','to',['TO']),('restaurant','restaurant',['NN'])
,('for','for',['IN']),('dinner','dinner',['NN']),('.','.',['.'])]]
```

We can construct two kinds of dictionary consisting of positive and negative expressions. We can then perform tagging on our processed text using dictionaries.

Let's consider the following NLTK code for tagging using dictionaries:

```
classDictionaryTagger(object):
def __init__(self, dictionary_paths):
files = [open(path, 'r') for path in dictionary_paths]
dictionaries = [yaml.load(dict_file) for dict_file in files]
map(lambda x: x.close(), files)
self.dictionary = {}
self.max_key_size = 0
forcurr_dict in dictionaries:
for key in curr_dict:
if key in self.dictionary:
self.dictionary[key].extend(curr_dict[key])
else:
self.dictionary[key] = curr_dict[key]
self.max_key_size = max(self.max_key_size, len(key))

def tag(self, postagged_sentences):
return [self.tag_sentence(sentence) for sentence in postagged_
sentences]

def tag_sentence(self, sentence, tag_with_lemmas=False):
tag_sentence = []
        N = len(sentence)
ifself.max_key_size == 0:
self.max_key_size = N
i = 0
while (i< N):
j = min(i + self.max_key_size, N) #avoid overflow
tagged = False
while (j >i):
expression_form = ' '.join([word[0] for word in sentence[i:j]]).
lower()
expression_lemma = ' '.join([word[1] for word in sentence[i:j]]).
lower()
iftag_with_lemmas:
literal = expression_lemma
else:
literal = expression_form
if literal in self.dictionary:
    is_single_token = j - i == 1
original_position = i
i = j
taggings = [tag for tag in self.dictionary[literal]]
```

```
tagged_expression = (expression_form, expression_lemma, taggings)
ifis_single_token: #if the tagged literal is a single token, conserve
its previous taggings:
original_token_tagging = sentence[original_position][2]
tagged_expression[2].extend(original_token_tagging)
tag_sentence.append(tagged_expression)
tagged = True
else:
                    j = j - 1
if not tagged:
tag_sentence.append(sentence[i])
i += 1
return tag_sentence
```

Here, words in the preprocessed text are tagged as positive or negative with the help of dictionaries.

Let's see the following code in NLTK, which can be used to compute the number of positive expressions and negative expressions:

```
def value_of(sentiment):
if sentiment == 'positive': return 1
if sentiment == 'negative': return -1
return 0
def sentiment_score(review):
return sum ([value_of(tag) for sentence in dict_tagged_sentences for
token in sentence for tag in token[2]])
```

The `nltk.sentiment.util` module is used in NLTK to perform sentiment analysis using Hu-Liu lexicon. This module counts the number of positive, negative, and neutral expressions, with the help of the lexicon, and then decides on the basis of majority counts whether the text consist of a positive, negative, or neutral sentiment. The words which are not available in the lexicon are considered neutral.

Sentiment analysis using NER

NER is the process of finding named entities and then categorizing named entities into different named entity classes. NER can be performed using different techniques, such as the Rule-based approach, List look up approach, and Statistical approaches (Hidden Markov Model, Maximum Entropy Markov Model, Support Vector Machine, Conditional Random Fields, and Decision Trees).

If named entities are identified in the list, then they may be removed or filtered out from the sentences. Similarly, stop words may also be removed. Now, sentiment analysis may be performed on the remaining words, since named entities are words that do not contribute to sentiment analysis.

Sentiment analysis using machine learning

The `nltk.sentiment.sentiment_analyzer` module in NLTK is used to perform sentiment analysis. It is based on machine learning techniques.

Let's see the following code of the `nltk.sentiment.sentiment_analyzer` module in NLTK:

```
from __future__ import print_function
from collections import defaultdict

from nltk.classify.util import apply_features, accuracy as eval_
accuracy
from nltk.collocations import BigramCollocationFinder
from nltk.metrics import (BigramAssocMeasures, precision as eval_
precision,
    recall as eval_recall, f_measure as eval_f_measure)

from nltk.probability import FreqDist

from nltk.sentiment.util import save_file, timer
class SentimentAnalyzer(object):
    """
    A tool for Sentiment Analysis which is based on machine learning
techniques.
    """
    def __init__(self, classifier=None):
        self.feat_extractors = defaultdict(list)
        self.classifier = classifier
```

Consider the following code, which will return all the words (duplicates) from a text:

```
     def all_words(self, documents, labeled=None):
        all_words = []
        if labeled is None:
            labeled = documents and isinstance(documents[0], tuple)
        if labeled == True:
            for words, sentiment in documents:
                all_words.extend(words)
        elif labeled == False:
```

```
            for words in documents:
                all_words.extend(words)
        return all_words
```

Consider the following code, which will apply the feature extraction function to the text:

```
    def apply_features(self, documents, labeled=None):

        return apply_features(self.extract_features, documents,
labeled)
```

Consider the following code, which will return the word's features:

```
    def unigram_word_feats(self, words, top_n=None, min_freq=0):
        unigram_feats_freqs = FreqDist(word for word in words)
        return [w for w, f in unigram_feats_freqs.most_common(top_n)
                if unigram_feats_freqs[w] > min_freq]
```

The following code returns the bigram features:

```
    def bigram_collocation_feats(self, documents, top_n=None, min_freq=3,
                                 assoc_measure=BigramAssocMeasures.
pmi):
        finder = BigramCollocationFinder.from_documents(documents)
        finder.apply_freq_filter(min_freq)
        return finder.nbest(assoc_measure, top_n)
```

Let's see the following code, which can be used to classify a given instance using the available feature set:

```
    def classify(self, instance):
        instance_feats = self.apply_features([instance],
labeled=False)
        return self.classifier.classify(instance_feats[0])
```

Let's see the following code, which can be used for the extraction of features from the text:

```
    def add_feat_extractor(self, function, **kwargs):
        self.feat_extractors[function].append(kwargs)

    def extract_features(self, document):
        all_features = {}
        for extractor in self.feat_extractors:
            for param_set in self.feat_extractors[extractor]:
                feats = extractor(document, **param_set)
            all_features.update(feats)
        return all_features
```

Let's see the following code that can be used to perform training on the training file. `Save_classifier` is used to save the output in a file:

```
def train(self, trainer, training_set, save_classifier=None,
**kwargs):
        print("Training classifier")
        self.classifier = trainer(training_set, **kwargs)
        if save_classifier:
            save_file(self.classifier, save_classifier)

        return self.classifier
```

Let's see the following code that can be used to perform testing and performance evaluation of our classifier using test data:

```
def evaluate(self, test_set, classifier=None, accuracy=True, f_
measure=True,
                precision=True, recall=True, verbose=False):
        if classifier is None:
            classifier = self.classifier
        print("Evaluating {0} results...".format(type(classifier).__
name__))
        metrics_results = {}
        if accuracy == True:
            accuracy_score = eval_accuracy(classifier, test_set)
            metrics_results['Accuracy'] = accuracy_score

        gold_results = defaultdict(set)
        test_results = defaultdict(set)
        labels = set()
        for i, (feats, label) in enumerate(test_set):
            labels.add(label)
            gold_results[label].add(i)
            observed = classifier.classify(feats)
            test_results[observed].add(i)

        for label in labels:
            if precision == True:
                precision_score = eval_precision(gold_results[label],
                    test_results[label])
                metrics_results['Precision [{0}]'.format(label)] =
precision_score
            if recall == True:
                recall_score = eval_recall(gold_results[label],
                    test_results[label])
```

```
                metrics_results['Recall [{0}]'.format(label)] =
recall_score
            if f_measure == True:
                f_measure_score = eval_f_measure(gold_results[label],
                    test_results[label])
                metrics_results['F-measure [{0}]'.format(label)] = f_
measure_score

        if verbose == True:
            for result in sorted(metrics_results):
                print('{0}: {1}'.format(result, metrics_
results[result]))

        return metrics_results
```

Twitter can be considered as one of the most popular blogging services that is used to create messages referred to as *tweets*. These tweets comprise words that are either related to positive, negative, or neutral sentiments.

For performing sentiment analysis, we can use machine learning classifiers, statistical classifiers, or automated classifiers, such as the Naive Bayes Classifier, Maximum Entropy Classifier, Support Vector Machine Classifier, and so on.

These machine learning classifiers or automated classifiers are used to perform supervised classification, since they require training data for classification.

Let's see the following code in NLTK for feature extraction:

```
stopWords = []

#If there is occurrence of two or more same character, then replace it
with the character itself.
def replaceTwoOrMore(s):
    pattern = re.compile(r"(.)\1{1,}", re.DOTALL)
    return pattern.sub(r"\1\1", s)
def getStopWordList(stopWordListFileName):
    # This function will read the stopwords from a file and builds a
list.
    stopWords = []
    stopWords.append('AT_USER')
    stopWords.append('URL')

    fp = open(stopWordListFileName, 'r')
    line = fp.readline()
    while line:
```

```
            word = line.strip()
            stopWords.append(word)
            line = fp.readline()
        fp.close()
        return stopWords

    def getFeatureVector(tweet):
        featureVector = []
        #Tweets are  firstly split into words
        words = tweet.split()
        for w in words:
            #replace two or more with two occurrences
            w = replaceTwoOrMore(w)
            #strip punctuation
            w = w.strip('\'"?,.')
            #Words begin with alphabet is checked.
            val = re.search(r"^[a-zA-Z][a-zA-Z0-9]*$", w)
            #If there is a stop word, then it is ignored.
            if(w in stopWords or val is None):
                continue
            else:
                featureVector.append(w.lower())
        return featureVector
    #end

    #Tweets are read one by one and then processed.
    fp = open('data/sampleTweets.txt', 'r')
    line = fp.readline()

    st = open('data/feature_list/stopwords.txt', 'r')
    stopWords = getStopWordList('data/feature_list/stopwords.txt')

    while line:
        processedTweet = processTweet(line)
        featureVector = getFeatureVector(processedTweet)
        print featureVector
        line = fp.readline()
    #end loop
    fp.close()

    #Tweets are read one by one and then processed.
    inpTweets = csv.reader(open('data/sampleTweets.csv', 'rb'),
    delimiter=',', quotechar='|')
    tweets = []
```

```
for row in inpTweets:
    sentiment = row[0]
    tweet = row[1]
    processedTweet = processTweet(tweet)
    featureVector = getFeatureVector(processedTweet, stopWords)
    tweets.append((featureVector, sentiment));

#Features Extraction takes place using following method
def extract_features(tweet):
    tweet_words = set(tweet)
    features = {}
    for word in featureList:
        features['contains(%s)' % word] = (word in tweet_words)
    return features
```

During the training of a classifier, the input to the machine learning algorithm is a label and features. Features are obtained from the feature extractor when the input is given to the feature extractor. During prediction, a label is provided as an output of a classifier model and the input of the classifier model is the features that are obtained using the feature extractor. Let's have a look at a diagram explaining the same process:

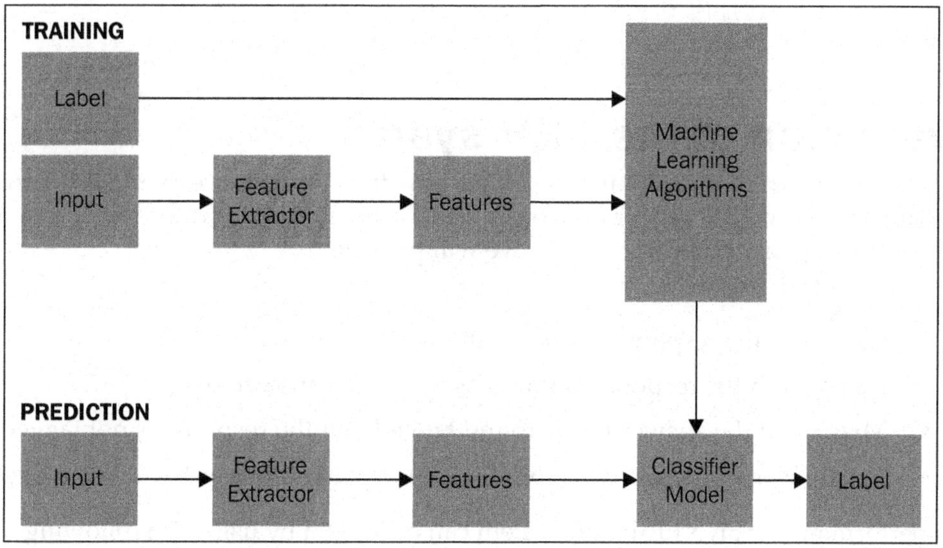

Now, let's see the following code that can be used to perform sentiment analysis using the Naive Bayes Classifier:

```
NaiveBClassifier = nltk.NaiveBayesClassifier.train(training_set)
# Testing the classifiertestTweet = 'I liked this book on Sentiment
Analysis a lot.'
processedTestTweet = processTweet(testTweet)
print NaiveBClassifier.classify(extract_features(getFeatureVector(proc
essedTestTweet)))
testTweet = 'I am so badly hurt'
processedTestTweet = processTweet(testTweet)
print NBClassifier.classify(extract_features(getFeatureVector(process
edTestTweet)))
```

Let's see the following code on sentiment analysis using maximum entropy:

```
MaxEntClassifier = nltk.classify.maxent.MaxentClassifier.
train(training_set, 'GIS', trace=3, \
                    encoding=None, labels=None, sparse=True, gaussian_
prior_sigma=0, max_iter = 10)
testTweet = 'I liked the book on sentiment analysis a lot'
processedTestTweet = processTweet(testTweet)
print MaxEntClassifier.classify(extract_features(getFeatureVector(proc
essedTestTweet)))
print MaxEntClassifier.show_most_informative_features(10)
```

Evaluation of the NER system

Performance metrics or evaluation helps to show the performance of an NER system. The outcome of an NER tagger may be defined as the *response* and the interpretation of human beings as the *answer key*. So, we will provide
the following definitions:

- **Correct**: If the response is exactly the same as the answer key
- **Incorrect**: If the response is not the same as the answer key
- **Missing**: If the answer key is found tagged, but the response is not tagged
- **Spurious**: If the response is found tagged, but the answer key is not tagged

The performance of an NER-based system can be judged by using the following parameters:

- **Precision (P)**: *P=Correct/(Correct+Incorrect+Missing)*
- **Recall (R)**: *R=Correct/(Correct+Incorrect+Spurious)*
- **F-Measure**: *F-Measure = (2*P*R)/(P+R)*

Let's see the code for NER using the HMM:

```
#*******   Function to find all tags in corpus   **********

def find_tag_set(tra_lines):
global tag_set

tag_set = [ ]

for line in tra_lines:
tok = line.split()
for t in tok:
wd = t.split("/")
if not wd[1] in tag_set:
tag_set.append(wd[1])

return

#*******   Function to find frequency of each tag in tagged corpus
**********

defcnt_tag(tr_ln):
global start_li
global li
global tag_set
global c
global line_cnt
global lines

lines = tr_ln

start_li = [ ]    # list of starting tags

find_tag_set(tr_ln)


line_cnt  = 0
for line in lines:
tok = line.split()
x = tok[0].split("/")
if  not x[1] in start_li:
start_li.append(x[1])
line_cnt = line_cnt + 1
```

```
find_freq_tag()

find_freq_srttag()

return

def find_freq_tag():
global tag_cnt
global tag_set
tag_cnt={}
i = 0
for w in tag_set:
cal_freq_tag(tag_set[i])
i = i + 1
tag_cnt.update({w:freq_tg})
return


defcal_freq_tag(tg):
global freq_tg
global lines
freq_tg = 0

for line in lines:
freq_tg = freq_tg + line.count(tg)

return

#*******   Function to find frequency of each starting tag in tagged
corpus  **********


def find_freq_srttag():
global lst
lst = {}        # start probability

i  = 0
for w in start_li:
        cc = freq_srt_tag(start_li[i])
prob = cc / line_cnt

lst.update({start_li[i]:prob})
i = i + 1
return
```

```
def freq_srt_tag(stg):
global lines
freq_srt_tg = 0

for line in lines:
tok = line.split()
ifstg in tok[0]:
freq_srt_tg = freq_srt_tg + 1

return(freq_srt_tg)

import tkinter as tk
import vit
import random
import cal_start_p
import calle_prob
import trans_mat
import time
import trans
import dict5
from tkinter import *
from tkinter import ttk
from tkinter.filedialog import askopenfilename
from tkinter.messagebox import showerror
import languagedetect1
import languagedetect3
e_dict = dict()
t_dict = dict()

def calculate1(*args):
import listbox1
def calculate2(*args):
import listbox2
def calculate3(*args):
import listbox3


def dispdlg():
global file_name
root = tk.Tk()
root.withdraw()
file_name = askopenfilename()
return
```

```
def tranhmm():
ttk.Style().configure("TButton", padding=6, relief="flat",background="
Pink",foreground="Red")
ttk.Button(mainframe, text="BROWSE", command=find_train_corpus).
grid(column=7, row=5, sticky=W)

# The following code will be used to display or accept the testing
corpus from the user.
def testhmm():
ttk.Button(mainframe, text="Develop a new testing Corpus",
command=calculate3).grid(column=9, row=5, sticky=E)

ttk.Button(mainframe, text="BROWSE", command=find_obs).grid(column=9,
row=7, sticky=E)


#In HMM, We require parameters such as Start Probability, Transition
Probability and Emission Probability. The following code is used to
calculate emission probability matrix

def cal_emit_mat():
global emission_probability
global corpus
global tlines

calle_prob.m_prg(e_dict,corpus,tlines)

emission_probability = e_dict

return

# to calculate states


def cal_states():
global states
global tlines

cal_start_p.cnt_tag(tlines)

states = cal_start_p.tag_set

return
```

```
# to take observations


def find_obs():
global observations
global test_lines
global tra
global w4
global co
global tra
global wo1
global wo2
global test1
global wo3
global te
global definitionText
global definitionScroll
global dt2
global ds2
global dt11
global ds11

wo3=[ ]
woo=[ ]
wo1=[ ]
wo2=[ ]
    co=0
w4=[ ]
if(flag2!=0):
definitionText11.pack_forget()
definitionScroll11.pack_forget()
dt1.pack_forget()
ds1.pack_forget()
dispdlg()
f = open(file_name,"r+",encoding = 'utf-8')
test_lines = f.readlines()
f.close()
fname="C:/Python32/file_name1"




for x in states:
if not x in start_probability:
```

```
start_probability.update({x:0.0})
for line in test_lines:
ob = line.split()
observations = ( ob )




fe=open("C:\Python32\output3_file","w+",encoding = 'utf-8')
fe.write("")
fe.close()
ff=open("C:\Python32\output4_file","w+",encoding = 'utf-8')


ff.write("")
ff.close()
ff7=open("C:\Python32\output5_file","w+",encoding = 'utf-8')
ff7.write("")
ff7.close()
ff8=open("C:\Python32\output6_file","w+",encoding = 'utf-8')
ff8.write("")
ff8.close()
ff81=open("C:\Python32\output7_file","w+",encoding = 'utf-8')
ff81.write("")
ff81.close()
dict5.search_obs_train_corpus(file1,fname,tlines,test_
lines,observations, states, start_probability, transition_probability,
emission_probability)

f20 = open("C:\Python32\output5_file","r+",encoding = 'utf-8')
te = f20.readlines()
tee=f20.read()
f = open(fname,"r+",encoding = 'utf-8')
train_llines = f.readlines()



ds11 = Scrollbar(root)
dt11 = Text(root, width=10, height=20,fg='black',bg='pink',yscrollcom
mand=ds11.set)
ds11.config(command=dt11.yview)
dt11.insert("1.0",train_llines)
dt11.insert("1.0","\n")
dt11.insert("1.0","\n")
```

```
dt11.insert("1.0","******TRAINING SENTENCES******")


    # an example of how to add new text to the text area
dt11.pack(padx=10,pady=150)
ds11.pack(padx=10,pady=150)

ds11.pack(side=LEFT, fill=BOTH)
dt11.pack(side=LEFT, fill=BOTH, expand=True)

ds2 = Scrollbar(root)
dt2 = Text(root, width=10, height=10,fg='black',bg='pink',yscrollcomm
and=ds2.set)
ds2.config(command=dt2.yview)
dt2.insert("1.0",test_lines)
dt2.insert("1.0","\n")
dt2.insert("1.0","\n")
dt2.insert("1.0","*********TESTING SENTENCES*********")



    # an example of how to add new text to the text area
dt2.pack(padx=10,pady=150)
ds2.pack(padx=10,pady=150)

ds2.pack(side=LEFT, fill=BOTH)
dt2.pack(side=LEFT, fill=BOTH, expand=True)


definitionScroll = Scrollbar(root)
definitionText = Text(root, width=10, height=10,fg='black',bg='pink',y
scrollcommand=definitionScroll.set)
definitionScroll.config(command=definitionText.yview)
definitionText.insert("1.0",te)
definitionText.insert("1.0","\n")
definitionText.insert("1.0","\n")
definitionText.insert("1.0","*********OUTPUT*********")



    # an example of how to add new text to the text area
definitionText.pack(padx=10,pady=150)
definitionScroll.pack(padx=10,pady=150)
```

```
definitionScroll.pack(side=LEFT, fill=BOTH)
definitionText.pack(side=LEFT, fill=BOTH, expand=True)

l = tk.Label(root, text="NOTE:*****The Entities which are not tagged
in Output are not Named Entities*****" , fg='black', bg='pink')
l.place(x = 500, y = 650, width=500, height=25)



    #ttk.Button(mainframe, text="View Parameters", command=parame).
grid(column=11, row=10, sticky=E)
    #definitionText.place(x= 19, y = 200,height=25)

f20.close()

f14 = open("C:\Python32\output2_file","r+",encoding = 'utf-8')
testl = f14.readlines()
for lines in testl:
toke = lines.split()
for t in toke:
w4.append(t)
f14.close()
f12 = open("C:\Python32\output_file","w+",encoding = 'utf-8')
f12.write("")
f12.close()


ttk.Button(mainframe, text="SAVE OUTPUT", command=save_output).
grid(column=11, row=7, sticky=E)
ttk.Button(mainframe, text="NER EVALUATION", command=evaluate).
grid(column=13, row=7, sticky=E)
ttk.Button(mainframe, text="REFRESH", command=ref).grid(column=15,
row=7, sticky=E)

return
def ref():
root.destroy()
import new1
return
```

Let's see the following code in Python, which will be used to evaluate the output produced by NER using HMM:

```
def evaluate():
global wDict
```

```
global woe
global woe1
global woe2
woe1=[ ]
woe=[ ]
woe2=[ ]
ws=[ ]
wDict = {}
i=0
    j=0
    k=0
sp=0
f141 = open("C:\Python32\output1_file","r+",encoding = 'utf-8')
tesl = f141.readlines()
for lines in tesl:
toke = lines.split()
for t in toke:
ws.append(t)
if t in wDict: wDict[t] += 1
else: wDict[t] = 1
for line in tlines:
tok = line.split()

for t in tok:
wd = t.split("/")
if(wd[1]!='OTHER'):
if t in wDict: wDict[t] += 1
else: wDict[t] = 1
print ("words  in train corpus ",wDict)
for key  in wDict:
i=i+1
print("total words in Dictionary are:",i)
for line in train_lines:
toe=line.split()
for t1 in toe:
if '/' not in t1:
sp=sp+1
woe2.append(t1)
print("Spurious words are")
for w in woe2:
print(w)
print("Total spurious words are:",sp)
for l in te:
to=l.split()
```

```
for t1 in to:
if '/' in t1:
                  #print(t1)
if t1 in ws or t1 in wDict:
woe.append(t1)
                       j=j+1
if t1 not in wDict:
wdd=t1.split("/")
ifwdd[0] not in woe2:
woe1.append(t1)
                            k=k+1
print("Word found in Dict are:")
for w in woe:
print(w)
print("Word not found in Dict are:")
for w in woe1:
print(w)
print("Total correctly tagged words are:",j)
print("Total incorrectly tagged words are:",k)
pr=(j)/(j+k)
re=(j)/(j+k+sp)
f141.close()
root=Tk()
root.title("NER EVALUATION")
root.geometry("1000x1000")

ds21 = Scrollbar(root)
dt21 = Text(root, width=10, height=10,fg='black',bg='pink',yscrollcom
mand=ds21.set)
ds21.config(command=dt21.yview)
dt21.insert("1.0",(2*pr*re)/(pr+re))
dt21.insert("1.0","\n")
dt21.insert("1.0","F-MEASURE=")
dt21.insert("1.0","\n")
dt21.insert("1.0","F-MEASURE=(2*PRECISION*RECALL)/(PRECISION+RECALL)")
dt21.insert("1.0","\n")
dt21.insert("1.0","\n")
dt21.insert("1.0",re)
dt21.insert("1.0","RECALL=")
dt21.insert("1.0","\n")
dt21.insert("1.0","RECALL= CORRECT/(CORRECT +INCORRECT +SPURIOUS)")
dt21.insert("1.0","\n")
dt21.insert("1.0","\n")
dt21.insert("1.0",pr)
```

```
dt21.insert("1.0","PRECISION=")
dt21.insert("1.0","\n")
dt21.insert("1.0","PRECISION= CORRECT/(CORRECT +INCORRECT +MISSING)")
dt21.insert("1.0","\n")
dt21.insert("1.0","\n")
dt21.insert("1.0","Total No. of Missing words are: 0")
dt21.insert("1.0","\n")
dt21.insert("1.0","\n")
dt21.insert("1.0",sp)
dt21.insert("1.0","Total No. of Spurious Words are:")
dt21.insert("1.0","\n")
for w in woe2:
dt21.insert("1.0",w)
dt21.insert("1.0"," ")
dt21.insert("1.0","Total Spurious Words are:")
dt21.insert("1.0","\n")
dt21.insert("1.0","\n")
dt21.insert("1.0",k)
dt21.insert("1.0","Total No. of Incorrectly tagged words are:")
dt21.insert("1.0","\n")
for w in woe1:
dt21.insert("1.0",w)
dt21.insert("1.0"," ")
dt21.insert("1.0","Total Incorrectly tagged words are:")
dt21.insert("1.0","\n")
dt21.insert("1.0","\n")
dt21.insert("1.0",j)
dt21.insert("1.0","Total No. of Correctly tagged words are:")
dt21.insert("1.0","\n")
for w in woe:
dt21.insert("1.0",w)
dt21.insert("1.0"," ")
dt21.insert("1.0","Total Correctly tagged words are:")
dt21.insert("1.0","\n")
dt21.insert("1.0","\n")
dt21.insert("1.0","***************PERFORMANCE EVALUATION OF
NERHMM***************")


    # an example of how to add new text to the text area
dt21.pack(padx=5,pady=5)
ds21.pack(padx=5,pady=5)
```

```
ds21.pack(side=LEFT, fill=BOTH)
dt21.pack(side=LEFT, fill=BOTH, expand=True)
root.mainloop()
return
def save_output():
    #dispdlg()
f = open("C:\Python32\save","w+",encoding = 'utf-8')
f20 = open("C:\Python32\output5_file","r+",encoding = 'utf-8')
te = f20.readlines()
for t in te:
f.write(t)
f.close()
f20.close()

# to calculate start probability matrix

def cal_srt_prob():
global start_probability

start_probability = cal_start_p.lst

return

# to print vitarbi parameter if required

def pr_param():
l1 = tk.Label(root, text="HMM Training is going on.....Don't Click any
Button!!",fg='black',bg='pink')
l1.place(x = 300, y = 150,height=25)

print("states")
print(states)
print(" ")
print(" ")
print("start probability")
print(start_probability)
print(" ")
print(" ")
print("transition probability")
print(transition_probability)
print(" ")
print(" ")
print("emission probability")
print(emission_probability)
```

```
l1 = tk.Label(root, text="
")
l1.place(x = 300, y = 150,height=25)
global flag1
    flag1=0
global flag2
    flag2=0
ttk.Button(mainframe, text="View Parameters", command=parame).
grid(column=7, row=5, sticky=W)
return

def parame():
global flag2
    flag2=flag1+1
global definitionText11
global definitionScroll11
definitionScroll11 = Scrollbar(root)
definitionText11 = Text(root, width=10, height=10,fg='black',bg='pink'
,yscrollcommand=definitionScroll11.set)

    #definitionText.place(x= 19, y = 200,height=25)
definitionScroll11.config(command=definitionText11.yview)

definitionText11.delete("1.0", END)    # an example of how to delete
all current text
definitionText11.insert("1.0",emission_probability )
definitionText11.insert("1.0","\n")
definitionText11.insert("1.0","Emission Probability")
definitionText11.insert("1.0","\n")
definitionText11.insert("1.0",transition_probability)
definitionText11.insert("1.0","Transition Probability")
definitionText11.insert("1.0","\n")
definitionText11.insert("1.0",start_probability)
definitionText11.insert("1.0","Start Probability")


     # an example of how to add new text to the text area
definitionText11.pack(padx=10,pady=175)
definitionScroll11.pack(padx=10,pady=175)

definitionScroll11.pack(side=LEFT, fill=BOTH)
definitionText11.pack(side=LEFT, fill=BOTH, expand=True)

return
```

```
# to calculate transition probability matrix


def cat_trans_prob():
global transition_probability
global corpus
global tlines

trans_mat.main_prg(t_dict,corpus,tlines)

transition_probability = t_dict
return

def find_train_corpus():
global train_lines
global tlines
global c
global corpus
global words1
global w1
global train1
global fname
global file1
global ds1
global dt1
global w21
words1=[ ]
    c=0
w1=[ ]
w21=[ ]
f11 = open("C:\Python32\output1_file","w+",encoding='utf-8')
f11.write("")
f11.close()
fr = open("C:\Python32\output_file","w+",encoding='utf-8')
fr.write("")
fr.close()
fgl=open("C:\Python32\ladetect1","w+",encoding = 'utf-8')
fgl.write("")
fgl.close()

fgl=open("C:\Python32\ladetect","w+",encoding = 'utf-8')
fgl.write("")
fgl.close()
dispdlg()
```

```
f = open(file_name,"r+",encoding = 'utf-8')
train_lines = f.readlines()

ds1 = Scrollbar(root)
dt1 = Text(root, width=10, height=10,fg='black',bg='pink',yscrollcomm
and=ds1.set)
ds1.config(command=dt1.yview)
dt1.insert("1.0",train_lines)
dt1.insert("1.0","\n")
dt1.insert("1.0","\n")
dt1.insert("1.0","*********TRAINING SENTENCES*********")


    # an example of how to add new text to the text area
dt1.pack(padx=10,pady=175)
ds1.pack(padx=10,pady=175)

ds1.pack(side=LEFT, fill=BOTH)
dt1.pack(side=LEFT, fill=BOTH, expand=True)
fname="C:/Python32/file_name1"
f = open(file_name,"r+",encoding = 'utf-8')
    file1=file_name
p = open(fname,"w+",encoding = 'utf-8')

corpus = f.read()
for line in train_lines:
tok = line.split()
for t in tok:
n=t.split()

le=len(t)
i=0
            j=0
for n1 in n:
while(j<le):

if(n1[j]!='/'):
i=i+1
                        j=j+1
else:
                        j=j+1
if(i==le):
p.write(t)
p.write("/OTHER ")          #Handling Spurious words
```

```
else:
p.write(t)
p.write(" ")

p.write("\n")




p.close()
fname="C:/Python32/file_name1"
f00 = open(fname,"r+",encoding = 'utf-8')
tlines = f00.readlines()
for line in tlines:
tok = line.split()
for t in tok:
wd = t.split("/")
if(wd[1]!='OTHER'):
if not wd[0] in words1:
words1.append(wd[0])
w1.append(wd[1])
f00.close()

f157 = open("C:\Python32\input_file","w+",encoding='utf-8')
f157.write("")
f157.close()
f1 = open("C:\Python32\input_file","w+",encoding='utf-8')   #input_
file has list of Named Entities of training file
for w in words1:
f1.write(w)
f1.write("\n")
f1.close()
fr=open("C:\Python32\detect","w+",encoding = 'utf-8')
fr.write("")
fr.close()


f.close()
f.close()


cal_states()
cal_emit_mat()
cal_srt_prob()
cat_trans_prob()
```

```
pr_param()


return

root=Tk()
root.title("NAMED ENTITY RECOGNITION IN NATURAL LANGUAGES USING HIDDEN
MARKOV MODEL")
root.geometry("1000x1000")

mainframe = ttk.Frame(root, padding="20 20 12 12")
mainframe.grid(column=0, row=0, sticky=(N, W, E, S))

b=StringVar()
a=StringVar()

ttk.Style().configure("TButton", padding=6, relief="flat",background="
Pink", foreground="Red")
ttk.Button(mainframe, text="ANNOTATION", command=calculate1).
grid(column=5, row=3, sticky=W)

ttk.Button(mainframe, text="TRAIN HMM", command=tranhmm).
grid(column=7, row=3, sticky=E)

ttk.Button(mainframe, text="TEST HMM", command=testhmm).grid(column=9,
row=3, sticky=E)

ttk.Button(mainframe, text="HELP", command=hmmhelp).grid(column=11,
row=3, sticky=E)


# To call viterbi for particular observations find in find_obs

def call_vitar():
global test_lines
global train_lines
global corpus
global observations
global states
global start_probability
global transition_probability
global emission_probability

find_train_corpus()
```

```
cal_states()
find_obs()
cal_emit_mat()
cal_srt_prob()
cat_trans_prob()

    # print("Vitarbi Parameters are for selected corpus")
    # pr_param()

     # -----------------To add all states not in start probability ---
-------------

for x in states:
if not x in start_probability:
start_probability.update({x:0.0})


for line in test_lines:

ob = line.split()
observations = ( ob )
print(" ")
print(" ")
print(line)
print("*************************")
print(vit.viterbi(observations, states, start_probability, transition_
probability, emission_probability),bg='Pink',fg='Red')
return



root.mainloop()
```

The preceding code in Python shows how NER is performed using the HMM, and how an NER system is evaluated using performance metrics (Precision, Recall and F-Measure).

Summary

In this chapter, we have discussed sentiment analysis using NER and machine learning techniques. We have also discussed the evaluation of an NER-based system..

In the next chapter, we'll discuss information retrieval, text summarization, stop word removal, question-answering system, and more.

8

Information Retrieval – Accessing Information

Information retrieval is one of the many applications of natural language processing. Information retrieval may be defined as the process of retrieving information (for example, the number of times the word *Ganga* has appeared in the document) corresponding to a query that has been made by the user.

This chapter will include the following topics:

- Introducing information retrieval
- Stop word removal
- Information retrieval using a vector space model
- Vector space scoring and query operator interactions
- Developing an IR system using latent semantic indexing
- Text summarization
- Question-answering system

Introducing information retrieval

Information retrieval may be defined as the process of retrieving the most suitable information as a response to the query being made by the user. In information retrieval, the search is performed based on metadata or context-based indexing. One example of information retrieval is Google Search in which, corresponding to each user query, a response is provided on the basis of the information retrieval algorithm being used. An indexing mechanism is used by the information retrieval algorithm. The indexing mechanism used is known as an inverted index. An IR system builds an index postlist to perform the information retrieval task.

Boolean retrieval is an information retrieval task in which a Boolean operation is applied to the postlist in order to retrieve relevant information.

The accuracy of an information retrieval task is measured in terms of precision and recall.

Suppose that a given IR system returns X documents when a query is fired. But the actual or gold set of documents that needs to be returned is Y.

Recall may be defined as the fraction of gold documents that a system finds. It may be defined as the ratio of true positives to the combination of true positives and false negatives.

$Recall\ (R) = (X \cap Y)/Y$

Precision may be defined as the fraction of documents that an IR system detects and are correct.

$Precision\ (P) = (X \cap Y)/X$

F-Measure may be defined as the harmonic mean of precision and recall.

$F\text{-}Measure = 2 * (X \cap Y)/(X + Y)$

Stop word removal

While performing information retrieval , it is important to detect the stop words in a document and eliminate them.

Let's see the following code that can be used to provide the collection of stop words that can be detected in the English text in NLTK:

```
>>> import nltk
>>> fromnltk.corpus import stopwords
>>> stopwords.words('english')
['i', 'me', 'my', 'myself', 'we', 'our', 'ours', 'ourselves', 'you',
'your', 'yours', 'yourself', 'yourselves', 'he', 'him', 'his',
'himself', 'she', 'her', 'hers', 'herself', 'it', 'its', 'itself',
'they', 'them', 'their', 'theirs', 'themselves', 'what', 'which',
'who', 'whom', 'this', 'that', 'these', 'those', 'am', 'is', 'are',
'was', 'were', 'be', 'been', 'being', 'have', 'has', 'had', 'having',
'do', 'does', 'did', 'doing', 'a', 'an', 'the', 'and', 'but', 'if',
'or', 'because', 'as', 'until', 'while', 'of', 'at', 'by', 'for',
'with', 'about', 'against', 'between', 'into', 'through', 'during',
'before', 'after', 'above', 'below', 'to', 'from', 'up', 'down', 'in',
'out', 'on', 'off', 'over', 'under', 'again', 'further', 'then',
'once', 'here', 'there', 'when', 'where', 'why', 'how', 'all', 'any',
```

```
'both', 'each', 'few', 'more', 'most', 'other', 'some', 'such', 'no',
'nor', 'not', 'only', 'own', 'same', 'so', 'than', 'too', 'very', 's',
't', 'can', 'will', 'just', 'don', 'should', 'now']
```

NLTK consists of stop word corpus that comprises of 2,400 stop words from 11 different languages.

Let's see the following code in NLTK that can be used to find the fraction of words in a text that are not stop words:

```
>>> def not_stopwords(text):
    stopwords = nltk.corpus.stopwords.words('english')
    content = [w for w in text if w.lower() not in stopwords]
    return len(content) / len(text)

>>> not_stopwords(nltk.corpus.reuters.words())
0.7364374824583169
```

Let's see the following code in NLTK that can be used to remove the stop words from a given text. Here, the `lower()` function is used prior to the elimination of stop words so that the stop words in capital letters, such as A, are first converted into lower case letters and then eliminated:

```
import nltk
from collections import Counter
import string
fromnltk.corpus import stopwords

def get_tokens():
    with open('/home/d/TRY/NLTK/STOP.txt') as stopl:
        tokens = nltk.word_tokenize(stopl.read().lower().
translate(None, string.punctuation))
    return tokens

if __name__ == "__main__":

    tokens = get_tokens()
    print("tokens[:20]=%s") %(tokens[:20])

    count1 = Counter(tokens)
    print("before: len(count1) = %s") %(len(count1))

    filtered1 = [w for w in tokens if not w in stopwords.
words('english')]
```

```
print("filtered1 tokens[:20]=%s") %(filtered1[:20])

count1 = Counter(filtered1)
print("after: len(count1) = %s") %(len(count1))

print("most_common = %s") %(count.most_common(10))

tagged1 = nltk.pos_tag(filtered1)
print("tagged1[:20]=%s") %(tagged1[:20])
```

Information retrieval using a vector space model

In a vector space model, documents are represented as vectors. One of the methods of representing documents as vectors is using **TF-IDF (Term Frequency-Inverse Document Frequency)**.

Term frequency may be defined as the total number of times a given token exists in a document divided by the total number of tokens. It may also be defined as the frequency of the occurrence of certain terms in a given document.

The formula for term frequency (TF) is given as follows:

$TF(t,d) = 0.5 + (0.5 * f(t,d)) / max \{f(w,d) : w \in d\}$

IDF may be defined as the inverse of document frequency. It is also defined as the document count that lies in the corpus in which a given term coexists.

IDF can be computed by finding the logarithm of the total number of documents present in a given corpus divided by the number of documents in which a particular token exists.

The formula for *IDF(t,d)* may be stated as follows:

$IDF(t,D)= log(N/\{d \in D : t \in d\})$

The TF-IDF score can be obtained by multiplying both scores. This is written as follows:

$TF\text{-}IDF(t, d, D) = TF(t,d) * IDF(t,D)$

TF-IDF provides the estimate of the frequency of a term as present in the given document and how much it is being spread across the corpus.

In order to compute TF-IDF for a given document, the following steps are required:

- Tokenization of documents
- Computation of vector space model
- Computation of TF-IDF for each document

The process of tokenization involves tokenizing the text into sentences first. The individual sentences are then tokenized into words. The words, which are of no significance during information retrieval, also known as stop words, can then be removed.

Let's see the following code that can be used for performing tokenization on each document in a corpus:

```
authen = OAuthHandler(CLIENT_ID, CLIENT_SECRET, CALLBACK)
authen.set_access_token(ACCESS_TOKEN)
ap = API(authen)


venue = ap.venues(id='4bd47eeb5631c9b69672a230')
stopwords = nltk.corpus.stopwords.words('english')
tokenizer = RegexpTokenizer("[\w']+", flags=re.UNICODE)


def freq(word, tokens):
return tokens.count(word)


#Compute the frequency for each term.
vocabulary = []
docs = {}
all_tips = []
for tip in (venue.tips()):
tokens = tokenizer.tokenize(tip.text)

bitokens = bigrams(tokens)
tritokens = trigrams(tokens)
tokens = [token.lower() for token in tokens if len(token) > 2]
tokens = [token for token in tokens if token not in stopwords]

bitokens = [' '.join(token).lower() for token in bitokens]
bitokens = [token for token in bitokens if token not in stopwords]

tritokens = [' '.join(token).lower() for token in tritokens]
```

```
tritokens = [token for token in tritokens if token not in stopwords]

ftokens = []
ftokens.extend(tokens)
ftokens.extend(bitokens)
ftokens.extend(tritokens)
docs[tip.text] = {'freq': {}}

for token in ftokens:
docs[tip.text]['freq'][token] = freq(token, ftokens)

print docs
```

The next step performed after tokenization is the normalization of the `tf` vector. Let's see the following code that performs the normalization of the `tf` vector:

```
authen = OAuthHandler(CLIENT_ID, CLIENT_SECRET, CALLBACK)
authen.set_access_token(ACCESS_TOKEN)
ap = API(auth)


venue = ap.venues(id='4bd47eeb5631c9b69672a230')
stopwords = nltk.corpus.stopwords.words('english')
tokenizer = RegexpTokenizer("[\w']+", flags=re.UNICODE)


def freq(word, tokens):
return tokens.count(word)


def word_count(tokens):
return len(tokens)


def tf(word, tokens):
return (freq(word, tokens) / float(word_count(tokens)))

#Compute the frequency for each term.
vocabulary = []
docs = {}
all_tips = []
for tip in (venue.tips()):
tokens = tokenizer.tokenize(tip.text)

bitokens = bigrams(tokens)
```

```
tritokens = trigrams(tokens)
tokens = [token.lower() for token in tokens if len(token) > 2]
tokens = [token for token in tokens if token not in stopwords]

bitokens = [' '.join(token).lower() for token in bitokens]
bitokens = [token for token in bitokens if token not in stopwords]

tritokens = [' '.join(token).lower() for token in tritokens]
tritokens = [token for token in tritokens if token not in stopwords]

ftokens = []
ftokens.extend(tokens)
ftokens.extend(bitokens)
ftokens.extend(tritokens)
docs[tip.text] = {'freq': {}, 'tf': {}}

for token in ftokens:
        #The Computed  Frequency
docs[tip.text]['freq'][token] = freq(token, ftokens)
        # Normalized Frequency
docs[tip.text]['tf'][token] = tf(token, ftokens)


print docs
```

Let's see the following code for computing the TF-IDF:

```
authen = OAuthHandler(CLIENT_ID, CLIENT_SECRET, CALLBACK)
authen.set_access_token(ACCESS_TOKEN)
ap = API(authen)


venue = ap.venues(id='4bd47eeb5631c9b69672a230')
stopwords = nltk.corpus.stopwords.words('english')
tokenizer = RegexpTokenizer("[\w']+", flags=re.UNICODE)


def freq(word, doc):
return doc.count(word)


def word_count(doc):
return len(doc)


def tf(word, doc):
```

```
return (freq(word, doc) / float(word_count(doc)))


def num_docs_containing(word, list_of_docs):
count = 0
for document in list_of_docs:
if freq(word, document) > 0:
count += 1
return 1 + count


def idf(word, list_of_docs):
return math.log(len(list_of_docs) /
float(num_docs_containing(word, list_of_docs)))


#Compute the frequency for each term.
vocabulary = []
docs = {}
all_tips = []
for tip in (venue.tips()):
tokens = tokenizer.tokenize(tip.text)

bitokens = bigrams(tokens)
tritokens = trigrams(tokens)
tokens = [token.lower() for token in tokens if len(token) > 2]
tokens = [token for token in tokens if token not in stopwords]

bitokens = [' '.join(token).lower() for token in bitokens]
bitokens = [token for token in bitokens if token not in stopwords]

tritokens = [' '.join(token).lower() for token in tritokens]
tritokens = [token for token in tritokens if token not in stopwords]

ftokens = []
ftokens.extend(tokens)
ftokens.extend(bitokens)
ftokens.extend(tritokens)
docs[tip.text] = {'freq': {}, 'tf': {}, 'idf': {}}

for token in ftokens:
        #The frequency computed for each tip
docs[tip.text]['freq'][token] = freq(token, ftokens)
        #The term-frequency (Normalized Frequency)
```

```
docs[tip.text]['tf'][token] = tf(token, ftokens)

vocabulary.append(ftokens)

for doc in docs:
for token in docs[doc]['tf']:
        #The Inverse-Document-Frequency
docs[doc]['idf'][token] = idf(token, vocabulary)

print docs
```

TF-IDF is computed by finding the product of TF and IDF. The large value of TF-IDF is computed when there is an occurrence of high term frequency and low document frequency.

Let's see the following code for computing the TF-IDF for each term in a document:

```
authen = OAuthHandler(CLIENT_ID, CLIENT_SECRET, CALLBACK)
authen.set_access_token(ACCESS_TOKEN)
ap = API(authen)


venue = ap.venues(id='4bd47eeb5631c9b69672a230')
stopwords = nltk.corpus.stopwords.words('english')
tokenizer = RegexpTokenizer("[\w']+", flags=re.UNICODE)


def freq(word, doc):
return doc.count(word)


def word_count(doc):
return len(doc)


def tf(word, doc):
return (freq(word, doc) / float(word_count(doc)))


def num_docs_containing(word, list_of_docs):
count = 0
for document in list_of_docs:
if freq(word, document) > 0:
count += 1
```

```
return 1 + count


def idf(word, list_of_docs):
return math.log(len(list_of_docs) /
float(num_docs_containing(word, list_of_docs)))


def tf_idf(word, doc, list_of_docs):
return (tf(word, doc) * idf(word, list_of_docs))

#Compute the frequency for each term.
vocabulary = []
docs = {}
all_tips = []
for tip in (venue.tips()):
tokens = tokenizer.tokenize(tip.text)

bitokens = bigrams(tokens)
tritokens = trigrams(tokens)
tokens = [token.lower() for token in tokens if len(token) > 2]
tokens = [token for token in tokens if token not in stopwords]

bitokens = [' '.join(token).lower() for token in bitokens]
bitokens = [token for token in bitokens if token not in stopwords]

tritokens = [' '.join(token).lower() for token in tritokens]
tritokens = [token for token in tritokens if token not in stopwords]

ftokens = []
ftokens.extend(tokens)
ftokens.extend(bitokens)
ftokens.extend(tritokens)
docs[tip.text] = {'freq': {}, 'tf': {}, 'idf': {},
                        'tf-idf': {}, 'tokens': []}

for token in ftokens:
        #The frequency computed for each tip
docs[tip.text]['freq'][token] = freq(token, ftokens)
        #The term-frequency (Normalized Frequency)
docs[tip.text]['tf'][token] = tf(token, ftokens)
docs[tip.text]['tokens'] = ftokens
```

```
vocabulary.append(ftokens)

for doc in docs:
for token in docs[doc]['tf']:
        #The Inverse-Document-Frequency
docs[doc]['idf'][token] = idf(token, vocabulary)
        #The tf-idf
docs[doc]['tf-idf'][token] = tf_idf(token, docs[doc]['tokens'],
vocabulary)

#Now let's find out the most relevant words by tf-idf.
words = {}
for doc in docs:
for token in docs[doc]['tf-idf']:
if token not in words:
words[token] = docs[doc]['tf-idf'][token]
else:
if docs[doc]['tf-idf'][token] > words[token]:
words[token] = docs[doc]['tf-idf'][token]

for item in sorted(words.items(), key=lambda x: x[1], reverse=True):
print "%f <= %s" % (item[1], item[0])
```

Let's see the following code for mapping keywords to the vector's dimension:

```
>>> def getVectkeyIndex(self,documentList):
    vocabString=" ".join(documentList)
    vocabList=self.parser.tokenise(vocabString)
    vocabList=self.parser.removeStopWords(vocabList)
    uniquevocabList=util.removeDuplicates(vocabList)
    vectorIndex={}
    offset=0


for word in uniquevocabList:
        vectorIndex[word]=offset
        offset+=1
return vectorIndex
```

Let's see the following code for mapping document strings to vectors:

```
>>> def makeVect(self,wordString):
    vector=[0]*len(self.vectorkeywordIndex)
    wordList=self.parser.tokenise(wordString)
    wordList=self.parser.removeStopWords(wordList)
    for word in wordList:
        vector[self.vectorkeywordIndex[word]]+=1;
    return vector
```

Vector space scoring and query operator interaction

Vector space model is used for the representation of meanings in the form of vectors of lexical items. A vector space model can easily be modeled using linear algebra. So the similarity between vectors can be computed easily.

Vector size is used to represent the size of the vector being used that represents a particular context. The window-based method and dependency-based method are used for the modeling context. In the window-based method, the context is determined using the occurrence of words within the window of a particular size. In a dependency-based method, the context is determined when there is an occurrence of a word in a particular syntactic relation with the corresponding target word. Features or contextual words are stemmed and lemmatized. Similarity metrics can be used to compute the similarity between the two vectors.

Let's see the following list of similarity metrics:

Measure	Definition
Euclidean	$\frac{1}{1+\sqrt{\sum_{i=1}^{n}(u_i - v_i)^2}}$
Cityblock	$\frac{1}{1+\sum_{i=1}^{n}\lvert u_i - v_i\rvert}$
Chebyshev	$\frac{1}{1+\max_i \lvert u_i - v_i\rvert}$
Cosine	$\frac{u.v}{\lvert u\rvert\lvert v\rvert}$
Correlation	$\frac{(u-\mu_u).(v-\mu_v)}{\lvert u\rvert\lvert v\rvert}$
Dice	$\frac{2\sum_{i=0}^{n} min(u_i, v_i)}{\sum_{i=0}^{n} u_i + v_i}$
Jaccard	$\frac{u.v}{\sum_{i=0}^{n} u_i + v_i}$
Jaccard2	$\frac{\sum_{i=0}^{n} min(u_i, v_i)}{\sum_{i=0}^{n} max(u_i, v_i)}$
Lin	$\frac{\sum_{i=0}^{n} u_i + v_i}{\lvert u\rvert + \lvert v\rvert}$

Tanimoto	$\frac{u.v}{\lvert u\rvert+\lvert v\rvert-u.v}$
Jensen-Shannon Div	$1-\frac{\frac{1}{2}\left(D\left(u\middle\|\frac{u+v}{2}\right)+D\left(v\middle\|\frac{u+v}{2}\right)\right)}{\sqrt{2\log 2}}$
α **-skew**	$1-\frac{D\left(u\|\alpha v+(1-\alpha)u\right)}{\sqrt{2\log 2}}$

Weighting scheme is another term that is very important as it provides information that the given context is more related to the target word.

Let's see the list of weighting schemes that can be considered:

Scheme	Definition
None	$w_{ij}=f_{ij}$
TF-IDF	$w_{ij}=\log\left(f_{ij}\right)\times\log\left(\frac{N}{n_j}\right)$
TF-ICF	$w_{ij}=\log\left(f_{ij}\right)\times\log\left(\frac{N}{f_j}\right)$
Okapi BM25	$w_{ij}=\frac{f_{ij}}{0.5+1.5\times\frac{f_j}{\frac{f_j}{j}}+f_{ij}}\log\frac{N-n_j+0.5}{f_{ij}+0.5}$
ATC	$w_{ij}=\frac{\left(0.5+0.5\times\frac{f_{ij}}{\max_f}\right)\log\left(\frac{N}{n_j}\right)}{\sqrt{\Sigma_{i=1}^{N}\left[\left(0.5+0.5\times\frac{f_{ij}}{\max_f}\right)\log\left(\frac{N}{n_j}\right)\right]^2}}$
LTU	$w_{ij}=\frac{\left(\log\left(f_{ij}\right)+1.0\right)\log\left(\frac{N}{n_j}\right)}{0.8+0.2\times f_j\times\frac{j}{f_j}}$
MI	$w_{ij}=\log\frac{P\left(t_{ij}\mid c_j\right)}{P\left(t_{ij}\right)P\left(c_j\right)}$

PosMI	$\max(0, MI)$
T-Test	$w_{ij} = \frac{p(t_{ij} \mid c_j) - P(t_{ij})P(c_j)}{\sqrt{P(t_{ij})P(c_j)}}$
χ^2	$see(Curran, 2004, p.83)$
Lin98a	$w_{ij} = \frac{f_{ij} \times f}{f_i \times f_j}$
Lin98b	$w_{ij} = -1 \times \log \frac{n_j}{N}$
Gref94	$w_{ij} = \frac{\log f_{ij} + 1}{\log n_i + 1}$

Developing an IR system using latent semantic indexing

Latent semantic indexing can be used for performing categorization with the help of minimum training.

Latent semantic indexing is a technique that can be used for processing text. It can perform the following:

- Automatic categorization of text
- Conceptual information retrieval
- Cross-lingual information retrieval

Latent semantic method may be defined as an information retrieval and indexing method. It makes use of a mathematical technique known as **Singular Value Decomposition** (**SVD**). SVD is used for the detection of patterns having a certain relation with the concepts contained in a given unstructured text.

Some of the applications of latent semantic indexing include the following:

- Information discovery
- Automated document classification text summarization[20] (eDiscovery, Publishing)
- Relationship discovery
- Automatic generation of the link charts of individuals and organizations

- Matching technical papers and grants with reviewers
- Online customer support
- Determining document authorship
- Automatic keyword annotation of images
- Understanding software source code
- Filtering spam
- Information visualization
- Essay scoring
- Literature-based discovery

Text summarization

Text summarization is the process of generating summaries from a given long text. Based on the Luhn work, *The Automatic Creation of Literature Abstracts* (1958), a naïve summarization approach known as NaiveSumm is developed. It makes use of a word's frequencies for the computation and extraction of sentences that consist of the most frequent words. Using this approach, text summarization can be performed by extracting a few specific sentences.

Let's see the following code in NLTK that can be used for performing text summarization:

```
from nltk.tokenize import sent_tokenize,word_tokenize
from nltk.corpus import stopwords
from collections import defaultdict
from string import punctuation
from heapq import nlargest

class Summarize_Frequency:
  def __init__(self, cut_min=0.2, cut_max=0.8):
    """
     Initilize the text summarizer.
     Words that have a frequency term lower than cut_min
     or higer than cut_max will be ignored.
    """
    self._cut_min = cut_min
    self._cut_max = cut_max
    self._stopwords = set(stopwords.words('english') +
list(punctuation))

  def _compute_frequencies(self, word_sent):
```

```
        """
          Compute the frequency of each of word.
          Input:
           word_sent, a list of sentences already tokenized.
          Output:
           freq, a dictionary where freq[w] is the frequency of w.
        """
        freq = defaultdict(int)
        for s in word_sent:
          for word in s:
            if word not in self._stopwords:
              freq[word] += 1
        # frequencies normalization and fitering
        m = float(max(freq.values()))
        for w in freq.keys():
          freq[w] = freq[w]/m
          if freq[w] >= self._cut_max or freq[w] <= self._cut_min:
            del freq[w]
        return freq

      def summarize(self, text, n):
        """
    list of (n) sentences are returned.
    summary of text is returned.
        """
        sents = sent_tokenize(text)
        assert n <= len(sents)
        word_sent = [word_tokenize(s.lower()) for s in sents]
        self._freq = self._compute_frequencies(word_sent)
        ranking = defaultdict(int)
        for i,sent in enumerate(word_sent):
          for w in sent:
            if w in self._freq:
              ranking[i] += self._freq[w]
        sents_idx = self._rank(ranking, n)
        return [sents[j] for j in sents_idx]

      def _rank(self, ranking, n):
        """ return the first n sentences with highest ranking """
        return nlargest(n, ranking, key=ranking.get)
```

The preceding code computes the term frequency for each word and then the most frequent words, such as determiners, may be eliminated as they are not of much use while performing information retrieval tasks.

Question-answering system

Question-answering systems are referred to as intelligent systems that can be used to provide responses for the questions being asked by the user based on certain facts or rules stored in the knowledge base. So the accuracy of a question-answering system to provide a correct response depends on the rules or facts stored in the knowledge base.

One of the many issues involved in a question-answering system is how the responses and questions would be represented in the system. Responses may be retrieved and then represented using text summarization or parsing. Another issue involved in the question-answering system is how the questions and the corresponding answers are represented in a knowledge base.

To build a question-answering system, various approaches, such as the named entity recognition, information retrieval, information extraction, and so on, can be applied.

A question-answering system involves three phases:

- Extraction of facts
- Understanding of questions
- Generation of answers

Extraction of facts is performed in order to understand domain-specific data and generate a response for a given query.

Extraction of facts can be performed in two ways using: extraction of entity and extraction of relation. The process of extraction of entity or extraction of proper nouns is referred to as NER. The process of extraction of relation is based on the extraction of semantic information from the text.

Understanding of questions involves the generation of a parse tree from a given text.

The generation of answers involves obtaining the most likely response for a given query that can be understood by the user.

Let's see the following code in NLTK that can be used to accept a query from a user user. This query can be processed by removing stop words from it so that information retrieval can be performed post processing:

```
import nltk
from nltk import *
import string
print "Enter your question"
ques=raw input()
```

```
ques=ques.lower()
stopwords=nltk.corpus.stopwords.words('english')
cont=nltk.word_tokenize(question)
analysis_keywords=list( set(cont) -set(stopwords) )
```

Summary

In this chapter, we have discussed information retrieval. We have mainly learned about stop words removal. Stop words are eliminated so that information retrieval and text summarization tasks become faster. We have also discussed the implementation of text summarization, question-answering systems, and vector space models.

In the next chapter, we'll study the concepts of discourse analysis and anaphora resolution.

9

Discourse Analysis – Knowing Is Believing

Discourse analysis is another one of the applications of Natural Language Processing. Discourse analysis may be defined as the process of determining contextual information that is useful for performing other tasks, such as **anaphora resolution (AR)** (we will cover this section later in this chapter), NER, and so on.

This chapter will include the following topics:

- Introducing discourse analysis
- Discourse analysis using Centering Theory
- Anaphora resolution

Introducing discourse analysis

The word *discourse* in linguistic terms means language in use. Discourse analysis may be defined as the process of performing text or language analysis, which involves text interpretation and knowing the social interactions. Discourse analysis may involve dealing with morphemes, n-grams, tenses, verbal aspects, page layouts, and so on. Discourse may be defined as the sequential set of sentences.

In most cases, we can interpret the meaning of the sentence on the basis of the preceding sentences.

Consider a discourse *John went to the club on Saturday. He met Sam.*" Here, *He* refers to John.

Discourse Representation Theory (**DRT**) has been developed to provide a means for performing AR. A **Discourse Representation Structure** (**DRS**) has been developed that provides the meaning of discourse with the help of discourse referents and conditions. Discourse referents refer to variables used in first-order logic and things under consideration in a discourse. A discourse representation structure's conditions refer to the atomic formulas used in first-order predicate logic.

First Order Predicate Logic (**FOPL**) was developed to extend the idea of propositional logic. FOPL involves the use of functions, arguments, and quantifiers. Two types of quantifiers are used to represent the general sentences, namely, universal quantifiers and existential quantifiers. In FOPL, connectives, constants, and variables are also used. For instance, `Robin is a bird` can be represented in FOPL as `bird (robin)`.

Let's see an example of the discourse representation structure:

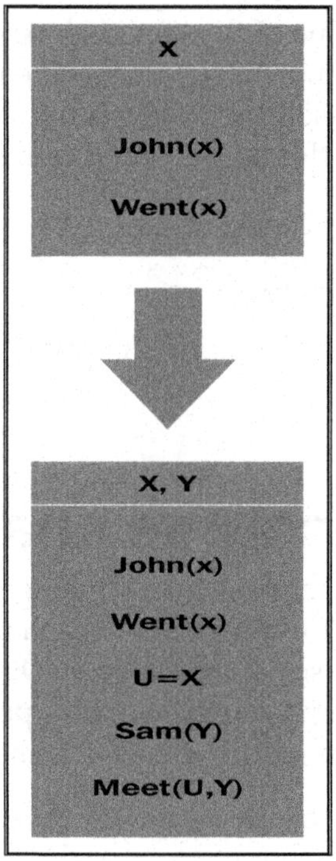

The preceding diagram is a representation of the following sentences:

1. John went to a club
2. John went to a club. He met Sam.

Here, the discourse consists of two sentences. Discourse Structure Representation may represent the entire text. For computationally processing DRS, it needs to be converted into a linear format.

The NLTK module that can be used to provide first order predicate logic implementation is `nltk.sem.logic`. Its UML diagram is shown here:

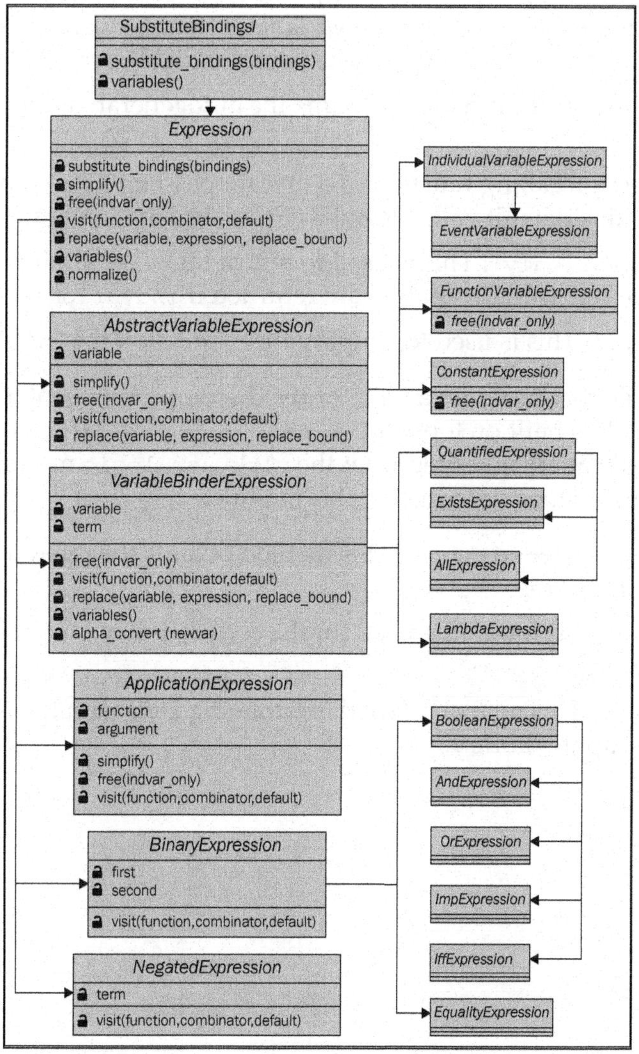

The `nltk.sem.logic` module is used to define the expressions of first order predicate logic. Its UML diagram is comprised of various classes that are required for the representation of objects in first order predicate logic as well as their methods. The methods that are included are as follows:

- `substitute_bindings(bindings)`: Here, binding represents variable-to-expression mapping. It replaces variables present in the expression with a specific value.
- `Variables()`: This comprises a set of all the variables that need to be replaced. It consists of constants as well as free variables.
- `replace(variable, expression, replace_bound)`: This is used for substituting the expression for a variable instance; `replace_bound` is used to specify whether we need to replace bound variables or not.
- `Normalize()`: This is used to rename the autogenerated unique variables.
- `Visit(self,function,combinatory,default)`: This is used to visit subexpression calling functions; results are passed to the combinator that begins with a default value. Results of the combination are returned.
- `free(indvar_only)`: This is used to return the set of all the free variables of the object. Individual variables are returned if `indvar_only` is set to `True`.
- `Simplify()`: This is used to simplify the expression that represents an object.

The NLTK module that provides a base for the discourse representation theory is `nltk.sem.drt`. It is built on top of `nltk.sem.logic`. Its UML class diagram comprises classes that are inherited from the `nltk.sem.logic` module. The following are the methods described in this module:

- The `get_refs(recursive)`: This method obtains the referents for the current discourse.
- The `fol()`: This method is used for the conversion of DRS into first order predicate logic.
- The `draw()`: This method is used for drawing DRS with the help of the Tkinter graphics library.

Let's see the UML class diagram of the `nltk.sem.drt` module:

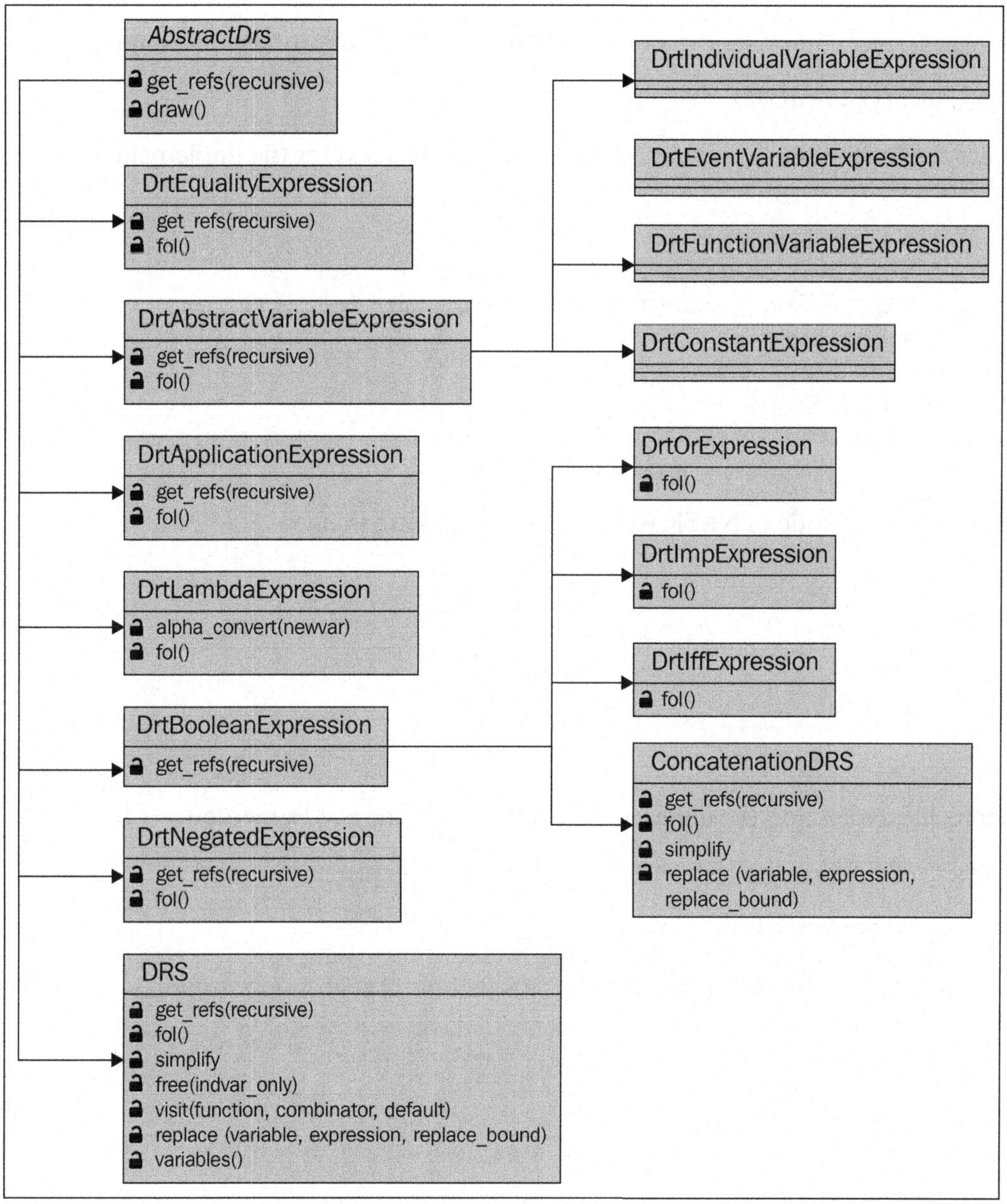

The NLTK module that provides access to WordNet 3.0 is `nltk.corpus.reader.wordnet`.

Linear format comprises discourse referents and DRS conditions, for example:

([x], [John(x), Went(x)])

Let's see the following code in NLTK, which can be used for the implementation of DRS:

```
>>> import nltk
>>> expr_read = nltk.sem.DrtExpression.from string
>>> expr1 = expr_read('([x], [John(x), Went(x)])')
>>> print(expr1)
([x],[John(x), Went(x)])
>>> expr1.draw()
>>> print(expr1.fol())
exists x.(John(x) & Went(x))
```

The preceding code of NLTK will draw the following image:

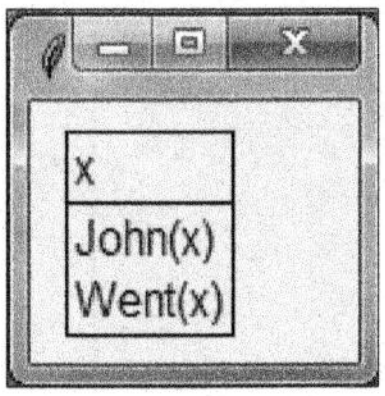

Here, the expression is converted into FOPL using the `fol()` method.

Let's see the following code in NLTK for the other expression:

```
>>> import nltk
>>> expr_read = nltk.sem.DrtExpression.from string
>>> expr2 = expr_read('([x,y], [John(x), Went(x),Sam(y),Meet(x,y)])')
>>> print(expr2)
([x,y],[John(x), Went(x), Sam(y), Meet(x,y)])
>>> expr2.draw()
>>> print(expr2.fol())
exists x y.(John(x) & Went(x) & Sam(y) & Meet(x,y))
```

The `fol()` function is used to obtain the first order predicate logic equivalent of the expression. The preceding code displays the following image:

We can perform the concatenation of two DRS using the DRS concatenation operator (+). Let's see the following code in NLTK that can be used to perform the concatenation of two DRS:

```
>>> import nltk
>>> expr_read = nltk.sem.DrtExpression.from string
>>> expr3 = expr_read('([x], [John(x), eats(x)])+
([y],[Sam(y),eats(y)])')
>>> print(expr3)
(([x],[John(x), eats(x)]) + ([y],[Sam(y), eats(y)]))
>>> print(expr3.simplify())
([x,y],[John(x), eats(x), Sam(y), eats(y)])
>>> expr3.draw()
```

The preceding code draws the following image:

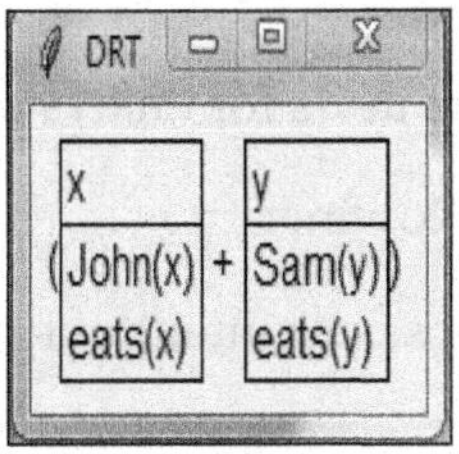

Here, `simplify()` is used to simplify the expression.

Let's see the following code in NLTK, which can be used to embed one DRS into another:

```
>>> import nltk
>>> expr_read = nltk.sem.DrtExpression.from string
>>> expr4 = expr_read('([],[(([x],[student(x)])-
>([y],[book(y),read(x,y)]))])')
>>> print(expr4.fol())
all x.(student(x) -> exists y.(book(y) & read(x,y)))
```

Let's see another example that can be used to combine two sentences. Here, PRO has been used and `resolve_anaphora()` is used to perform AR:

```
>>> import nltk
>>> expr_read = nltk.sem.DrtExpression.from string
>>> expr5 = expr_read('([x,y],[ram(x),food(y),eats(x,y)])')
>>> expr6 = expr_read('([u,z],[PRO(u),coffee(z),drinks(u,z)])')
>>> expr7=expr5+expr6
>>> print(expr7.simplify())
([u,x,y,z],[ram(x), food(y), eats(x,y), PRO(u), coffee(z),
drinks(u,z)])
>>> print(expr7.simplify().resolve_anaphora())
([u,x,y,z],[ram(x), food(y), eats(x,y), (u = [x,y,z]), coffee(z),
drinks(u,z)])
```

Discourse analysis using Centering Theory

Discourse analysis using Centering Theory is the first step toward corpus annotation. It also involves the task of AR. In Centering Theory, we perform the task of segmenting discourse into various units for analysis.

Centering Theory involves the following:

- Interaction between purposes or intentions of discourse participants and discourse
- Attention of participants
- Discourse structure

Centering is related to participants attention and how the local as well as global structures affect expressions and the coherence of discourse.

Anaphora resolution

AR may be defined as the process by which a pronoun or a noun phrase used in the sentence is resolved and refers to a specific entity on the basis of discourse knowledge.

For example:

```
John helped Sara. He was kind.
```

Here, `He` refers to `John`.

AR is of three types, namely:

- **Pronominal**: Here, the referent is referred to by a pronoun. For example, `Sam` found the love of his life. Here, 'his' refers to 'Sam'.
- **Definite noun phrase**: Here, the antecedent may be referred to by the phrase of the form, `<the><noun phrase>`. For example, `The relationship could not last long`. Here, `The relationship` refers to `the love` in the previous sentence.
- **Quantifier/ordinal**: The quantifier, such as one, and the ordinal, such as first, are also examples of AR. For example, `He began a new one`. Here, `one` refers to `the relationship`.

In cataphora, the referent precedes the antecedent. For example, `After his class, Sam will go home`. Here, `his` refers to `Sam`.

For integrating some extensions in a NLTK architecture, a new module is developed on top of the existing modules, `nltk.sem.logic` and `nltk.sem.drt`. The new module acts like a replacement for the `nltk.sem.drt` module. There is a replacement of all the classes with the enhanced classes.

A method called `resolve()` can be called indirectly and directly from a class called `AbstractDRS()`. It then provides a list consisting of resolved copies of a particular object. An object that needs to be resolved must override the `readings()` method. The `resolve()` method is used to generate readings using the `traverse()` function. The `traverse()` function is used to perform sorting on the list of operations. A priority order list includes the following:

- Binding operations
- Local accommodation operations
- Intermediate accommodation operations
- Global accommodation operations

Let's see the flow diagram of the `traverse()` function:

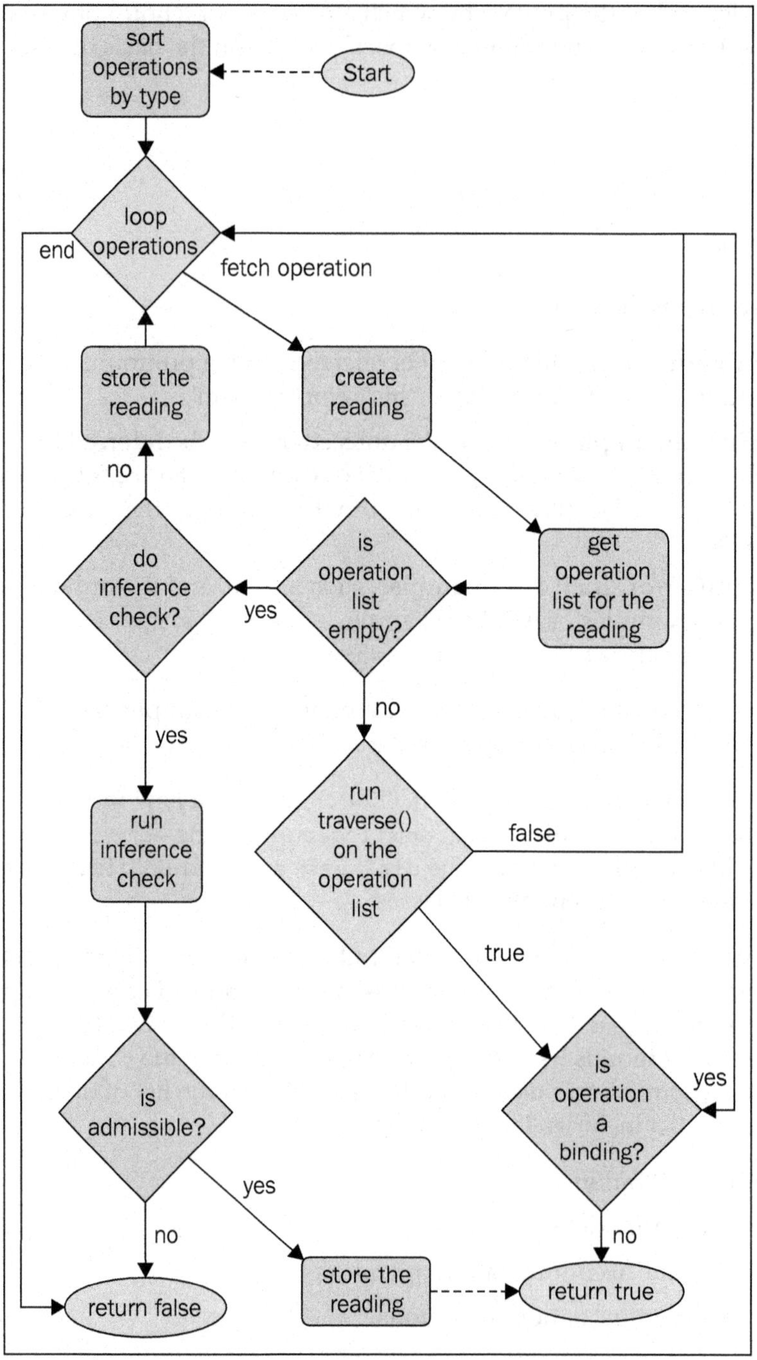

After the priority order of operations is generated, the following takes place:

- Readings are generated from the operation with the help of the `deepcopy()` method. The current operation is taken as an argument.
- When the `readings()` method runs, a list of operations are performed.
- Till the list of operations is not empty, run is performed on those operations.
- If there are no operations left to be performed, admissibility check will be run on the final reading; if the check is successful, it will be stored.

In `AbstractDRS()`, the `resolve()` method is defined. It is defined as follows:

def resolve(self, verbose=False)

The `PresuppositionDRS` class includes the following methods:

- `find_bindings(drs_list, collect_event_data)`: Bindings are found from the list of DRS instances using the `is_possible_binding` method. Collection of participation information is done if `collect_event_data` is set to `True`.
- `is_possible_binding(cond)`: This finds out whether the condition is a binding candidate and makes sure that it is an unary predicate with the features that match the trigger conditions.
- `is_presupposition.cond(cond)`: This is used to identify a trigger condition among all the conditions.
- `presupposition_readings(trail)`: This is like readings in the subclasses of `PresuppositionDRS`.

Let's see the classes that are inherited from `AbstractDRS`:

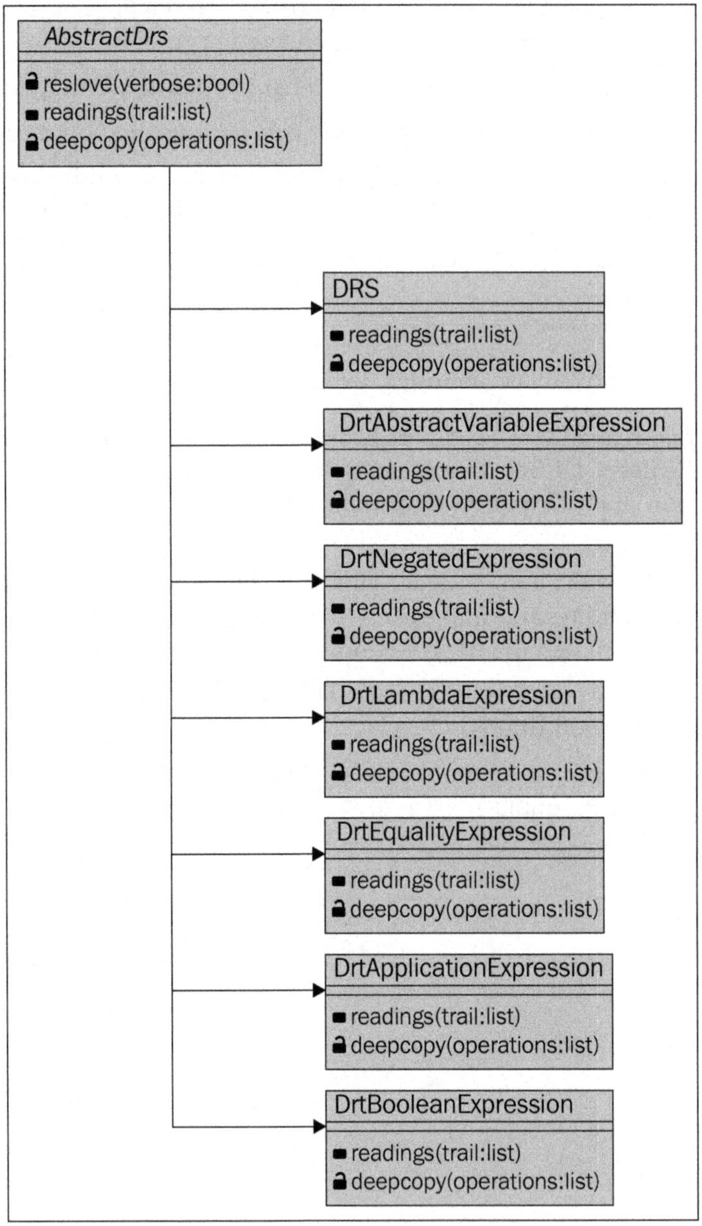

Let's see the classes that are inherited in `DRTAbstractVariableExpression`:

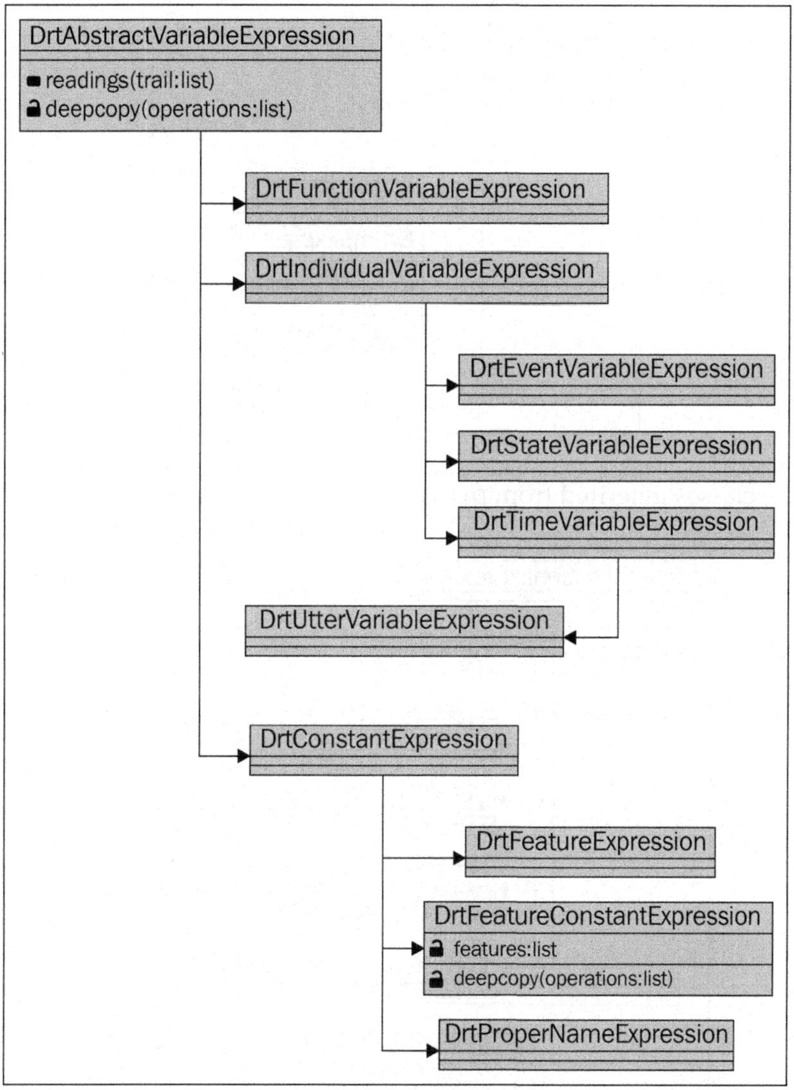

Let's see the classes inherited from `DrtBooleanExpression`:

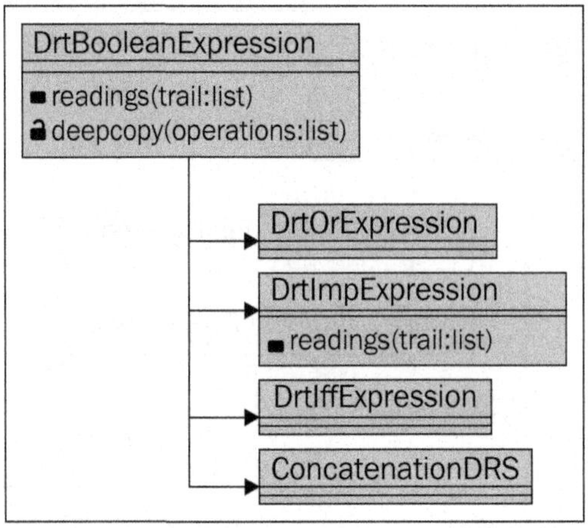

Let's see the classes inherited from `DrtApplicationExpression`:

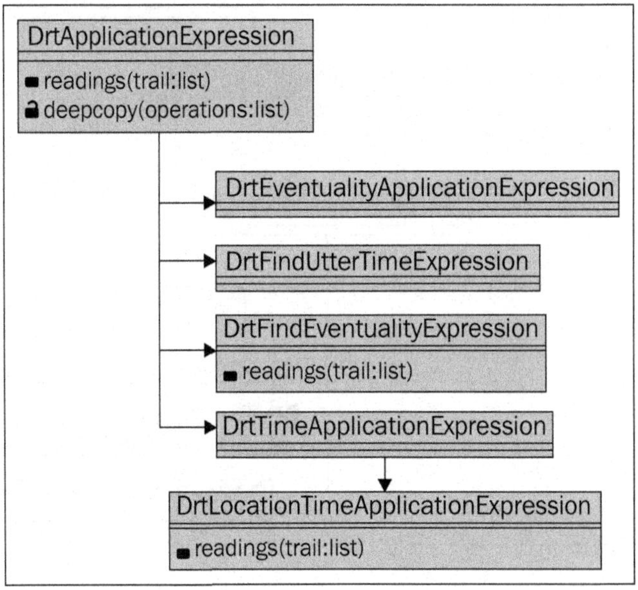

Let's see the classes inherited from DRS:

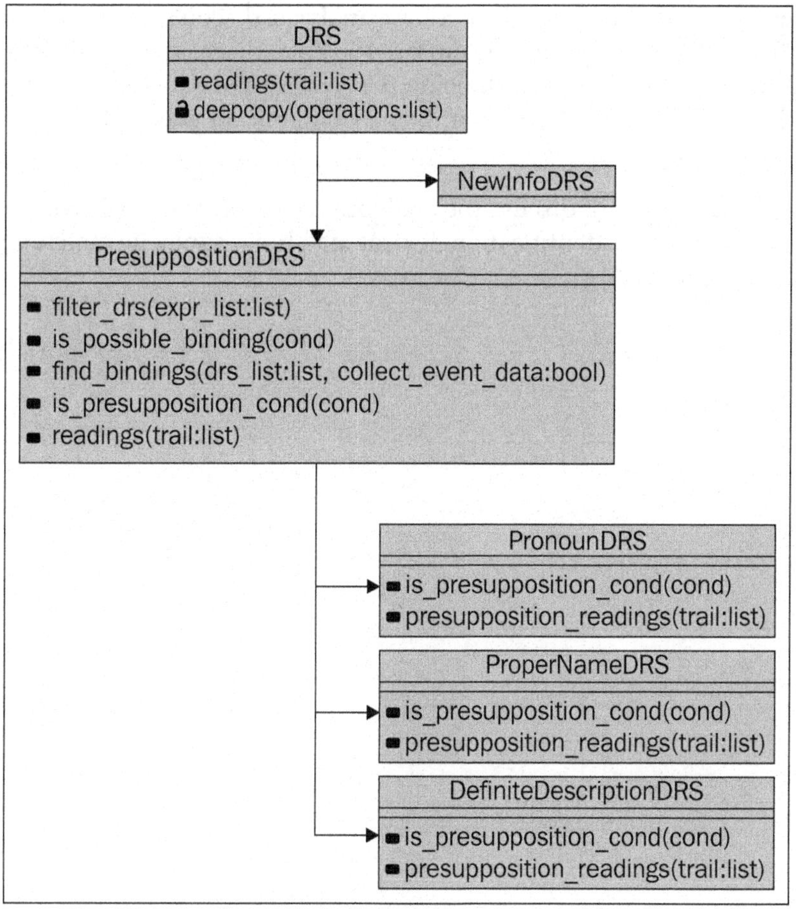

Summary

In this chapter, we have discussed discourse analysis, discourse analysis using Centering Theory, and anaphora resolution. We have discussed the discourse representation structure that is built using first order predicate logic. We have also discussed how NLTK can be used to implement first order predicate logic using UML diagrams.

In the next chapter, we will discuss the evaluation of NLP Tools. We will also discuss various metrics for error identification, lexical matching, syntactic matching, and shallow semantic matching.

10

Evaluation of NLP Systems – Analyzing Performance

The evaluation of NLP systems is performed so that we can analyze whether a given NLP system produces the desired result or not and the desired performance is achieved or not. Evaluation may be performed automatically using predefined metrics, or it may be performed manually by comparing human output with the output obtained by an NLP system.

This chapter will include the following topics:

- The need for the evaluation of NLP systems
- Evaluation of NLP tools (POS Taggers, Stemmers, and Morphological Analyzers)
- Parser evaluation using gold data
- The evaluation of an IR system
- Metrics for error identification
- Metrics based on lexical matching
- Metrics based on syntactic matching
- Metrics using shallow semantic matching

The need for evaluation of NLP systems

Evaluation of NLP systems is done so as to analyze whether the output given by the NLP systems is similar to the one expected from the human output. If errors in the module are identified at an early stage, then the cost of correcting the NLP system is reduced to quite an extent.

Suppose we want to evaluate a tagger. We can do this by comparing the output of the tagger with the human output. Many a times, we do not have access to an impartial or expert human. So we can construct a gold standard test data to perform the evaluation of our tagger. This is a corpus, which has been tagged manually and is considered as a standard corpus that can be used for the evaluation of our tagger. The tagger is considered as correct if the output in the form of a tag given by the tagger is the same as that provided by the gold standard test data.

Creation of a gold standard annotated corpus is a major task and is also very expensive. It is performed by manually tagging a given test data. The tags chosen in this manner are taken as standard tags that can be used to represent a wide range of information.

Evaluation of NLP tools (POS taggers, stemmers, and morphological analyzers)

We can perform the evaluation of NLP systems, such as POS taggers, stemmers, morphological analyzers, NER-based systems, machine translators, and so on. Consider the following code in NLTK that can be used to train a unigram tagger. Sentence tagging is performed and then an evaluation is done to check whether the output given by the tagger is the same as the gold standard test data:

```
>>> import nltk
>>>from nltk.corpus import brown
>>> sentences=brown.tagged_sents(categories='news')
>>> sent=brown.sents(categories='news')
>>> unigram_sent=nltk.UnigramTagger(sentences)
>>> unigram_sent.tag(sent[2008])
[('Others', 'NNS'), (',', ','), ('which', 'WDT'), ('are', 'BER'),
('reached', 'VBN'), ('by', 'IN'), ('walking', 'VBG'), ('up', 'RP'),
('a', 'AT'), ('single', 'AP'), ('flight', 'NN'), ('of', 'IN'),
('stairs', 'NNS'), (',', ','), ('have', 'HV'), ('balconies', 'NNS'),
('.', '.')]
>>> unigram_sent.evaluate(sentences)
0.9349006503968017
```

Consider the following code in NLTK in which the training and testing of Unigram tagger is performed on separate data. A given data is split into 80% training data and 20% testing data:

```
>>> import nltk
>>> from nltk.corpus import brown
>>> sentences=brown.tagged_sents(categories='news')
>>> sz=int(len(sentences)*0.8)
```

```
>>> sz
3698
>>> training_sents = sentences[:sz]
>>> testing_sents=sentences[sz:]
>>> unigram_tagger=nltk.UnigramTagger(training_sents)
>>> unigram_tagger.evaluate(testing_sents)
0.8028325063827737
```

Consider the following code in NLTK that demonstrates the use of N-Gram tagger. Here, Training corpus consists of tagged data. Also, in the following example, we have used a special case of n-gram tagger, that is, bigram tagger:

```
>>> import nltk
>>> from nltk.corpus import brown
>>> sentences=brown.tagged_sents(categories='news')
>>> sz=int(len(sentences)*0.8)
>>> training_sents = sentences[:sz]
>>> testing_sents=sentences[sz:]
>>> bigram_tagger=nltk.UnigramTagger(training_sents)
>>> bigram_tagger=nltk.BigramTagger(training_sents)
>>> bigram_tagger.tag(sentences[2008])
[(('Others', 'NNS'), None), ((',', ','), None), (('which', 'WDT'),
None), (('are', 'BER'), None), (('reached', 'VBN'), None), (('by',
'IN'), None), (('walking', 'VBG'), None), (('up', 'IN'), None), (('a',
'AT'), None), (('single', 'AP'), None), (('flight', 'NN'), None),
(('of', 'IN'), None), (('stairs', 'NNS'), None), ((',', ','), None),
(('have', 'HV'), None), (('balconies', 'NNS'), None), (('.', '.'),
None)]
>>> un_sent=sentences[4203]
>>> bigram_tagger.tag(un_sent)
[(('The', 'AT'), None), (('population', 'NN'), None), (('of', 'IN'),
None), (('the', 'AT'), None), (('Congo', 'NP'), None), (('is', 'BEZ'),
None), (('13.5', 'CD'), None), (('million', 'CD'), None), ((',',
','), None), (('divided', 'VBN'), None), (('into', 'IN'), None),
(('at', 'IN'), None), (('least', 'AP'), None), (('seven', 'CD'),
None), (('major', 'JJ'), None), (('``', '``'), None), (('culture',
'NN'), None), (('clusters', 'NNS'), None), (("''", "''"), None),
(('and', 'CC'), None), (('innumerable', 'JJ'), None), (('tribes',
'NNS'), None), (('speaking', 'VBG'), None), (('400', 'CD'), None),
(('separate', 'JJ'), None), (('dialects', 'NNS'), None), (('.', '.'),
None)]
>>> bigram_tagger.evaluate(testing_sents)
0.09181559805385615
```

Another way of tagging can be performed by means of bootstrapping different methods. In this approach, tagging can be performed using a bigram `Tagger`. If the tag is not found using the bigram `Tagger`, then a back-off method involving a unigram `Tagger` can be used. Also, if a tag is not found using a unigram `Tagger`, then a back-off method involving a default tagger can be used.

Let's see the following code in NLTK that implements combined `Tagger`:

```
>>> import nltk
>>> from nltk.corpus import brown
>>> sentences=brown.tagged_sents(categories='news')
>>> sz=int(len(sentences)*0.8)
>>> training_sents = sentences[:sz]
>>> testing_sents=sentences[sz:]
>>> s0=nltk.DefaultTagger('NNP')
>>> s1=nltk.UnigramTagger(training_sents,backoff=s0)
>>> s2=nltk.BigramTagger(training_sents,backoff=s1)
>>> s2.evaluate(testing_sents)
0.8122260224480948
```

The linguists use the following clues to determine the category of a word:

- Morphological clues
- Syntactic clues
- Semantic clues

Morphological clues are those in which prefix, suffix, infix, and affix information are used to determine the category of a word. For example, *ment* is a suffix that combines with a verb to form a noun, such as *establish* + *ment* = *establishment* and *achieve* + *ment* = *achievement*.

Syntactic clues can be useful in determining the category of a word. For example, let's assume that nouns are already known. Now, adjectives can be determined. Adjectives can occur either after a noun or after a word, such as very, in a sentence.

Semantic information can also be used to determine the category of a word. If the meaning of a word is known, then its category can easily be known.

Let's see the following code in NLTK that can be used for the evaluation of a chunk parser:

```
>>> import nltk
>>> chunkparser = nltk.RegexpParser("")
>>> print(nltk.chunk.accuracy(chunkparser, nltk.corpus.conll2000.
chunked_sents('train.txt', chunk_types=('NP',))))
0.44084599507856814
```

Let's see another code in NLTK that is based on the evaluation of a naïve chunk parser that looks for tags, such as CD, JJ, and so on:

```
>>> import nltk
>>> grammar = r"NP: {<[CDJNP].*>+}"
>>> cp = nltk.RegexpParser(grammar)
>>> print(nltk.chunk.accuracy(cp, nltk.corpus.conll2000.chunked_
sents('train.txt', chunk_types=('NP',))))
0.8744798726662164
```

The following code in NLTK is used to compute the conditional frequency distribution for chunked data:

```
def chunk_tags(train):
    """Generate a following tags list that appears inside chunks"""
    cfreqdist = nltk.ConditionalFreqDist()
    for t in train:
        for word, tag, chunktag in nltk.chunk.tree2conlltags(t):
            if chtag == "O":
                cfreqdist[tag].inc(False)
            else:
                cfreqdist[tag].inc(True)
    return [tag for tag in cfreqdist.conditions() if cfreqdist[tag].
max() == True]
>>> training_sents = nltk.corpus.conll2000.chunked_sents('train.txt',
chunk_types=('NP',))
>>> print chunked_tags(train_sents)
['PRP$', 'WDT', 'JJ', 'WP', 'DT', '#', '$', 'NN', 'FW', 'POS',
'PRP', 'NNS', 'NNP', 'PDT', 'RBS', 'EX', 'WP$', 'CD', 'NNPS', 'JJS',
'JJR']
```

Let's see the following code for performing the evaluation of `chunker` in NLTK. Here, two entities, namely `guessed` and `correct`, are used. Guessed entities are those that are returned by a chunk parser. Correct entities are those set of chunks that are defined in the test corpus:

```
>>> import nltk
>>> correct = nltk.chunk.tagstr2tree(
"[ the/DT little/JJ cat/NN ] sat/VBD on/IN [ the/DT mat/NN ]")
>>> print(correct.flatten())
(S the/DT little/JJ cat/NN sat/VBD on/IN the/DT mat/NN)
>>> grammar = r"NP: {<[CDJNP].*>+}"
>>> cp = nltk.RegexpParser(grammar)
>>> grammar = r"NP: {<PRP|DT|POS|JJ|CD|N.*>+}"
```

```
>>> chunk_parser = nltk.RegexpParser(grammar)
>>> tagged_tok = [("the", "DT"), ("little", "JJ"), ("cat",
"NN"),("sat", "VBD"), ("on", "IN"), ("the", "DT"), ("mat", "NN")]
>>> chunkscore = nltk.chunk.ChunkScore()
>>> guessed = cp.parse(correct.flatten())
>>> chunkscore.score(correct, guessed)
>>> print(chunkscore)
ChunkParse score:
    IOB Accuracy: 100.0%
    Precision:    100.0%
    Recall:       100.0%
    F-Measure:    100.0%
```

Let's see the following code in NLTK that can be used for the evaluation of unigram `chunker` and bigram `chunker`:

```
>>>chunker_data = [[(t,c) for w,t,c in nltk.chunk.
tree2conlltags(chtree)]
>>>              for chtree in nltk.corpus.conll2000.chunked_
sents('train.txt')]
>>> unigram_chunk = nltk.UnigramTagger(chunker_data)
>>> print nltk.tag.accuracy(unigram_chunk, chunker_data)
0.781378851068
>>> bigram_chunk = nltk.BigramTagger(chunker_data, backoff=unigram_
chunker)
>>> print nltk.tag.accuracy(bigram_chunk, chunker_data)
0.893220987404
```

Consider the following code in which the suffix of a word is used to determine the part of a speech tag. A classifier is trained to provide a list of informative suffixes. A feature extractor function has been used that checks the suffixes that are present in a given word:

```
>>> from nltk.corpus import brown
>>> suffix_freqdist = nltk.FreqDist()
>>> for wrd in brown.words():
...     wrd = wrd.lower()
...     suffix_freqdist[wrd[-1:]] += 1
...     suffix_fdist[wrd[-2:]] += 1
...     suffix_fdist[wrd[-3:]] += 1
>>> common_suffixes = [suffix for (suffix, count) in suffix_freqdist.
most_common(100)]
>>> print(common_suffixes)
['e', ',', '.', 's', 'd', 't', 'he', 'n', 'a', 'of', 'the',
 'y', 'r', 'to', 'in', 'f', 'o', 'ed', 'nd', 'is', 'on', 'l',
```

```
'g', 'and', 'ng', 'er', 'as', 'ing', 'h', 'at', 'es', 'or',
're', 'it', '``', 'an', "''", 'm', ';', 'i', 'ly', 'ion', ...]
```

```
>>> def pos_feature(wrd):
...     feature = {}
...     for suffix in common_suffixes:
...         feature['endswith({})'.format(suffix)] = wrd.lower().
endswith(suffix)
...     return feature
>>> tagged_wrds = brown.tagged_wrds(categories='news')
>>> featureset = [(pos_feature(n), g) for (n,g) in tagged_wrds]
>>> size = int(len(featureset) * 0.1)
>>> train_set, test_set = featureset[size:], featureset[:size]
>>> classifier1 = nltk.DecisionTreeClassifier.train(train_set)
>>> nltk.classify.accuracy(classifier1, test_set)
0.62705121829935351
```

```
>>> classifier.classify(pos_features('cats'))
'NNS'

>>> print(classifier.pseudocode(depth=4))
if endswith(,) == True: return ','
if endswith(,) == False:
  if endswith(the) == True: return 'AT'
  if endswith(the) == False:
    if endswith(s) == True:
      if endswith(is) == True: return 'BEZ'
      if endswith(is) == False: return 'VBZ'
    if endswith(s) == False:
      if endswith(.) == True: return '.'
      if endswith(.) == False: return 'NN'
```

Consider the following code in NLTK for building a regular expression tagger. Here, tags are assigned on the basis of matching patterns:

```
>>> import nltk
>>> from nltk.corpus import brown
>>> sentences = brown.tagged_sents(categories='news')
>>> sent = brown.sents(categories='news')
>>> pattern = [
(r'.*ing$', 'VBG'),                # for gerunds
(r'.*ed$', 'VBD'),                 # for simple past
```

```
(r'.*es$', 'VBZ'),                    # for 3rd singular present
(r'.*ould$', 'MD'),                   # for modals
(r'.*\'s$', 'NN$'),                   # for possessive nouns
(r'.*s$', 'NNS'),                     # for plural nouns
(r'^-?[0-9]+(.[0-9]+)?$', 'CD'),  #  for cardinal numbers
 (r'.*', 'NN')                         # for nouns (default)
]
>>> regexpr_tagger = nltk.RegexpTagger(pattern)
>>> regexpr_tagger.tag(sent[3])
 [('``', 'NN'), ('Only', 'NN'), ('a', 'NN'), ('relative', 'NN'),
('handful', 'NN'), ('of', 'NN'), ('such', 'NN'), ('reports', 'NNS'),
('was', 'NNS'), ('received', 'VBD'), ("''", 'NN'), (',', 'NN'),
('the', 'NN'), ('jury', 'NN'), ('said', 'NN'), (',', 'NN'), ('``',
'NN'), ('considering', 'VBG'), ('the', 'NN'), ('widespread', 'NN'),
('interest', 'NN'), ('in', 'NN'), ('the', 'NN'), ('election', 'NN'),
(',', 'NN'), ('the', 'NN'), ('number', 'NN'), ('of', 'NN'), ('voters',
'NNS'), ('and', 'NN'), ('the', 'NN'), ('size', 'NN'), ('of', 'NN'),
('this', 'NNS'), ('city', 'NN'), ("''", 'NN'), ('.', 'NN')]
>>> regexp_tagger.evaluate(sentences)
0.20326391789486245
```

Consider the following code to build a lookup tagger. In building up a lookup tagger, a list of frequently used words is maintained along with their tag information. Some of the words have been assigned the `None` tag because they do not exist among the list of the most frequently occurring words:

```
>>> import nltk
>>> from nltk.corpus import brown
>>> freqd = nltk.FreqDist(brown.words(categories='news'))
>>> cfreqd = nltk.ConditionalFreqDist(brown.tagged_
words(categories='news'))
>>> mostfreq_words = freqd.most_common(100)
>>> likelytags = dict((word, cfreqd[word].max()) for (word, _) in
mostfreq_words)
>>> baselinetagger = nltk.UnigramTagger(model=likelytags)
>>> baselinetagger.evaluate(brown_tagged_sents)
0.45578495136941344
>>> sent = brown.sents(categories='news')[3]
>>> baselinetagger.tag(sent)
[('``', '``'), ('Only', None), ('a', 'AT'), ('relative', None),
('handful', None), ('of', 'IN'), ('such', None), ('reports', None),
('was', 'BEDZ'), ('received', None), ("''", "''"), (',', ','),
('the', 'AT'), ('jury', None), ('said', 'VBD'), (',', ','),
```

```
('``', '``'), ('considering', None), ('the', 'AT'), ('widespread',
None),
('interest', None), ('in', 'IN'), ('the', 'AT'), ('election', None),
(',', ','), ('the', 'AT'), ('number', None), ('of', 'IN'),
('voters', None), ('and', 'CC'), ('the', 'AT'), ('size', None),
('of', 'IN'), ('this', 'DT'), ('city', None), ("''", "''"), ('.',
'.')]
>>> baselinetagger = nltk.UnigramTagger(model=likely_tags,
...                                     backoff=nltk.
DefaultTagger('NN'))
def performance(cfreqd, wordlist):
    lt = dict((word, cfreqd[word].max()) for word in wordlist)
    baseline_tagger = nltk.UnigramTagger(model=lt, backoff=nltk.
DefaultTagger('NN'))
    return baseline_tagger.evaluate(brown.tagged_
sents(categories='news'))

def display():
    import pylab
    word_freqs = nltk.FreqDist(brown.words(categories='news')).most_
common()
    words_by_freq = [w for (w, _) in word_freqs]
    cfd = nltk.ConditionalFreqDist(brown.tagged_
words(categories='news'))
    sizes = 2 ** pylab.arange(15)
    perfs = [performance(cfd, words_by_freq[:size]) for size in sizes]
    pylab.plot(sizes, perfs, '-bo')
    pylab.title('Lookup Tagger Performance with Varying Model Size')
    pylab.xlabel('Model Size')
    pylab.ylabel('Performance')
    pylab.show()
display()
```

Let's see the following stemming code in NLTK using `lancasterstemmer`. The evaluation of such a `stemmer` can be done using gold test data:

```
>>> import nltk
>>> from nltk.stem.lancaster import LancasterStemmer
>>> stri=LancasterStemmer()
>>> stri.stem('achievement')
'achiev'
```

Consider the following code in NLTK that can be used for designing a classifier-based chunker. It makes use of the Maximum Entropy classifier:

```
class ConseNPChunkTagger(nltk.TaggerI):

    def __init__(self, train_sents):
        train_set = []
        for tagsent in train_sents:
            untagsent = nltk.tag.untag(tagsent)
            history = []
            for i, (word, tag) in enumerate(tagsent):
                featureset = npchunk_features(untagsent, i, history)
                train_set.append( (featureset, tag) )
                history.append(tag)
        self.classifier = nltk.MaxentClassifier.train(
            train_set, algorithm='megam', trace=0)

    def tag(self, sentence):
        history = []
        for i, word in enumerate(sentence):
            featureset = npchunk_features(sentence, i, history)
            tag = self.classifier.classify(featureset)
            history.append(tag)
        return zip(sentence, history)

class ConseNPChunker(nltk.ChunkParserI): [4]
    def __init__(self, train_sents):
        tagsent = [[((w,t),c) for (w,t,c) in
                        nltk.chunk.tree2conlltags(sent)]
                      for sent in train_sents]
      self.tagger = ConseNPChunkTagger(tagsent)

    def parse(self, sentence):
        tagsent = self.tagger.tag(sentence)
        conlltags = [(w,t,c) for ((w,t),c) in tagsent]
        return nltk.chunk.conlltags2tree(conlltags)
```

In the following code, the evaluation of chunker is performed with the use of a feature extractor. The resultant chunker is similar to the unigram chunker:

```
>>> def npchunk_features(sentence, i, history):
...     word, pos = sentence[i]
...     return {"pos": pos}
>>> chunker = ConseNPChunker(train_sents)
```

```
>>> print(chunker.evaluate(test_sents))
ChunkParse score:
    IOB Accuracy:  92.9%
    Precision:     79.9%
    Recall:        86.7%
    F-Measure:     83.2%
```

In the following code, the features of the previous part of the speech tag are also added. This involves the interaction between tags. So the resultant `chunker` is similar to the bigram `chunker`:

```
>>> def npchunk_features(sentence, i, history):
...     word, pos = sentence[i]
...     if i == 0:
...         previword, previpos = "<START>", "<START>"
...     else:
...         previword, previpos = sentence[i-1]
...     return {"pos": pos, "previpos": previpos}
>>> chunker = ConseNPChunker(train_sents)
>>> print(chunker.evaluate(test_sents))
ChunkParse score:
    IOB Accuracy:  93.6%
    Precision:     81.9%
    Recall:        87.2%
    F-Measure:     84.5%
```

Consider the following code for `chunker` in which features for the current word are added to improve the performance of a `chunker`:

```
>>> def npchunk_features(sentence, i, history):
...     word, pos = sentence[i]
...     if i == 0:
...         previword, previpos = "<START>", "<START>"
...     else:
...         previword, previpos = sentence[i-1]
...     return {"pos": pos, "word": word, "previpos": previpos}
>>> chunker = ConseNPChunker(train_sents)
>>> print(chunker.evaluate(test_sents))
ChunkParse score:
    IOB Accuracy:  94.5%
    Precision:     84.2%
    Recall:        89.4%
    F-Measure:     86.7%
```

Let's consider the code in NLTK in which the collection of features, such as paired features, lookahead features, complex contextual features, and so on, are added to enhance the performance of a `chunker`:

```
>>> def npchunk_features(sentence, i, history):
...     word, pos = sentence[i]
...     if i == 0:
...         previword, previpos = "<START>", "<START>"
...     else:
...         previword, previpos = sentence[i-1]
...     if i == len(sentence)-1:
...         nextword, nextpos = "<END>", "<END>"
...     else:
...         nextword, nextpos = sentence[i+1]
...     return {"pos": pos,
...             "word": word,
...             "previpos": previpos,
...             "nextpos": nextpos,
...             "previpos+pos": "%s+%s" % (previpos, pos),
...             "pos+nextpos": "%s+%s" % (pos, nextpos),
...             "tags-since-dt": tags_since_dt(sentence, i)}
>>> def tags_since_dt(sentence, i):
...     tags = set()
...     for word, pos in sentence[:i]:
...         if pos == 'DT':
...             tags = set()
...         else:
...             tags.add(pos)
...     return '+'.join(sorted(tags))


>>> chunker = ConsecutiveNPChunker(train_sents)
>>> print(chunker.evaluate(test_sents))
ChunkParse score:
    IOB Accuracy:  96.0%
    Precision:     88.6%
    Recall:        91.0%
    F-Measure:     89.8%
```

The evaluation of Morphological Analyzer can also be performed using gold data. The human expected output is already stored to form a gold set and then the output of the morphological analyzer is compared with the gold data.

Parser evaluation using gold data

Parser evaluation can be done using the gold data or the standard data against which the output of the parser is matched.

Firstly, training of parser model is performed on the training data. Then parsing is done on the unseen data or testing data.

The following two measures can be used to evaluate the performance of a parser:

- **Labelled Attachment Score** (LAS)
- **Labelled Exact Match** (LEM)

In both cases, parser's output is compared with testing data. A good parsing algorithm is one that gives the highest LAS and LEM scores. The training and testing data that we use for parsing may consist of parts of speech tags that are gold standard tags, since they have been assigned manually. Parser evaluation can be done using metrics, such as Recall, Precision, and F-Measure.

Here, precision may be defined as the number of correct entities produced by parser divided by the total number of entities produced by parser.

Recall may be defined as the number of correct entities produced by parser divided by the total number of entities in the gold standard parse trees.

F-Score may be defined as the harmonic mean of recall and precision.

Evaluation of IR system

IR is also one of the applications of Natural Language Processing.

Following are the aspects that can be considered while performing the evaluation of the IR system:

- Resources required
- Presentation of documents
- Market evaluation or appealing to the user
- Retrieval speed
- Assistance in constituting queries
- Ability to find required documents

Evaluation is usually done by comparing one system with another.

IR systems can be compared on the basis of a set of documents, set of queries, techniques used, and so on. Metrics used for performance evaluation are Precision, Recall, and F-Measure. Let's learn a bit more about them:

- **Precision**: It is defined as the proportion of a retrieved set that is relevant.

  Precision = | relevant ∩ retrieved | ÷ | retrieved | = P(relevant | retrieved)

- **Recall**: It is defined as the proportion of all the relevant documents in the collection included in the retrieved set.

  Recall = | relevant ∩ retrieved | ÷ | relevant | = P(retrieved | relevant)

- **F-Measure**: It can be obtained using Precision and Recall as follows:

  *F-Measure = (2*Precision*Recall) / (Precision + Recall)*

Metrics for error identification

Error identification is a very important aspect that affects the performance of an NLP system. Searching tasks may involve the following terminologies:

- **True Positive (TP)**: This may be defined as the set of relevant documents that is correctly identified as the relevant document.
- **True Negative (TN)**: This may be defined as the set of irrelevant documents that is correctly identified as the irrelevant document.
- **False Positive (FP)**: This is also referred to as Type I error and is the set of irrelevant documents that is incorrectly identified as the relevant document.
- **False Negative (FN)**: This is also referred to as Type II error and is the set of relevant documents that is incorrectly identified as the irrelevant document.

On the basis of the previously mentioned terminologies, we have the following metrics:

- *Precision (P) - TP/(TP+FP)*
- *Recall (R) - TP/(TP+FN)*
- *F-Measure – 2*P*R/(P+R)*

Metrics based on lexical matching

We can also perform the analysis of performance at word level or lexical level.

Consider the following code in NLTK in which movie reviews have been taken and marked as either positive or negative. A feature extractor is constructed that checks whether a given word is present in a document or not:

```
>>> from nltk.corpus import movie_reviews
>>> docs = [(list(movie_reviews.words(fileid)), category)
...              for category in movie_reviews.categories()
...              for fileid in movie_reviews.fileids(category)]
>>> random.shuffle(docs)
all_wrds = nltk.FreqDist(w.lower() for w in movie_reviews.words())
word_features = list(all_wrds)[:2000]

def doc_features(doc):
    doc_words = set(doc)
    features = {}
    for word in word_features:
        features['contains({})'.format(word)] = (word in doc_words)
    return features
>>> print(doc_features(movie_reviews.words('pos/cv957_8737.txt')))
{'contains(waste)': False, 'contains(lot)': False, ...}
featuresets = [(doc_features(d), c) for (d,c) in docs]
train_set, test_set = featuresets[100:], featuresets[:100]
classifier = nltk.NaiveBayesClassifier.train(train_set)
>>> print(nltk.classify.accuracy(classifier, test_set))
0.81
>>> classifier.show_most_informative_features(5)
Most Informative Features
   contains(outstanding) = True              pos : neg    =     11.1 :
1.0
        contains(seagal) = True              neg : pos    =      7.7 :
1.0
   contains(wonderfully) = True              pos : neg    =      6.8 :
1.0
         contains(damon) = True              pos : neg    =      5.9 :
1.0
        contains(wasted) = True              neg : pos    =      5.8 :
1.0
```

Consider the following code in NLTK that describes `nltk.metrics.distance`, which provides metrics to determine whether a given output is the same as the expected output:

```
from __future__ import print_function
from __future__ import division
def _edit_dist_init(len1, len2):
    lev = []
    for i in range(len1):
        lev.append([0] * len2)  # initialization of 2D array to zero
    for i in range(len1):
        lev[i][0] = i           # column 0: 0,1,2,3,4,...
    for j in range(len2):
        lev[0][j] = j           # row 0: 0,1,2,3,4,...
    return lev

def _edit_dist_step(lev, i, j, s1, s2, transpositions=False):
    c1 = s1[i - 1]
    c2 = s2[j - 1]

    # skipping a character in s1
    a = lev[i - 1][j] + 1
    # skipping a character in s2
    b = lev[i][j - 1] + 1
    # substitution
    c = lev[i - 1][j - 1] + (c1 != c2)

    # transposition
    d = c + 1  # never picked by default
    if transpositions and i > 1 and j > 1:
        if s1[i - 2] == c2 and s2[j - 2] == c1:
            d = lev[i - 2][j - 2] + 1

    # pick the cheapest
    lev[i][j] = min(a, b, c, d)


def edit_distance(s1, s2, transpositions=False):

    # set up a 2-D array
    len1 = len(s1)
    len2 = len(s2)
    lev = _edit_dist_init(len1 + 1, len2 + 1)
```

```
    # iterate over the array
    for i in range(len1):
        for j in range(len2):
            _edit_dist_step(lev, i + 1, j + 1, s1, s2,
transpositions=transpositions)
    return lev[len1][len2]


def binary_distance(label1, label2):
    """Simple equality test.

    0.0 if the labels are identical, 1.0 if they are different.

>>> from nltk.metrics import binary_distance
>>> binary_distance(1,1)
    0.0

>>> binary_distance(1,3)
    1.0
    """

    return 0.0 if label1 == label2 else 1.0


def jaccard_distance(label1, label2):
    """Distance metric comparing set-similarity.
    """
    return (len(label1.union(label2)) - len(label1.
intersection(label2)))/len(label1.union(label2))

def masi_distance(label1, label2)

    len_intersection = len(label1.intersection(label2))
    len_union = len(label1.union(label2))
    len_label1 = len(label1)
    len_label2 = len(label2)
    if len_label1 == len_label2 and len_label1 == len_intersection:
        m = 1
    elif len_intersection == min(len_label1, len_label2):
        m = 0.67
    elif len_intersection > 0:
        m = 0.33
    else:
        m = 0
```

```
    return 1 - (len_intersection / len_union) * m


def interval_distance(label1,label2):

    try:
        return pow(label1 - label2, 2)
#        return pow(list(label1)[0]-list(label2)[0],2)
    except:
        print("non-numeric labels not supported with interval
distance")


def presence(label):

    return lambda x, y: 1.0 * ((label in x) == (label in y))


def fractional_presence(label):
    return lambda x, y:\
        abs(((1.0 / len(x)) - (1.0 / len(y)))) * (label in x and label
in y) \
        or 0.0 * (label not in x and label not in y) \
        or abs((1.0 / len(x))) * (label in x and label not in y) \
        or ((1.0 / len(y))) * (label not in x and label in y)


def custom_distance(file):
    data = {}
    with open(file, 'r') as infile:
        for l in infile:
            labelA, labelB, dist = l.strip().split("\t")
            labelA = frozenset([labelA])
            labelB = frozenset([labelB])
            data[frozenset([labelA,labelB])] = float(dist)
    return lambda x,y:data[frozenset([x,y])]


def demo():
    edit_distance_examples = [
        ("rain", "shine"), ("abcdef", "acbdef"), ("language",
"lnaguaeg"),
        ("language", "lnaugage"), ("language", "lngauage")]
    for s1, s2 in edit_distance_examples:
```

```
        print("Edit distance between '%s' and '%s':" % (s1, s2), edit_
distance(s1, s2))
    for s1, s2 in edit_distance_examples:
        print("Edit distance with transpositions between '%s' and
'%s':" % (s1, s2), edit_distance(s1, s2, transpositions=True))

    s1 = set([1, 2, 3, 4])
    s2 = set([3, 4, 5])
    print("s1:", s1)
    print("s2:", s2)
    print("Binary distance:", binary_distance(s1, s2))
    print("Jaccard distance:", jaccard_distance(s1, s2))
    print("MASI distance:", masi_distance(s1, s2))

if __name__ == '__main__':
    demo()
```

Metrics based on syntactic matching

Syntactic matching can be done by performing the task of chunking. In NLTK, a module called `nltk.chunk.api` is provided that helps to identify chunks and returns a parse tree for a given chunk sequence.

The module called `nltk.chunk.named_entity` is used to identify a list of named entities and also to generate a parse structure. Consider the following code in NLTK based on syntactic matching:

```
>>> import nltk
>>> from nltk.tree import Tree
>>> print(Tree(1,[2,Tree(3,[4]),5]))
(1 2 (3 4) 5)
>>> ct=Tree('VP',[Tree('V',['gave']),Tree('NP',['her'])])
>>> sent=Tree('S',[Tree('NP',['I']),ct])
>>> print(sent)
(S (NP I) (VP (V gave) (NP her)))
>>> print(sent[1])
(VP (V gave) (NP her))
>>> print(sent[1,1])
(NP her)
>>> t1=Tree.from string("(S(NP I) (VP (V gave) (NP her)))")
>>> sent==t1
True
>>> t1[1][1].set_label('X')
>>> t1[1][1].label()
```

```
'X'
>>> print(t1)
(S (NP I) (VP (V gave) (X her)))
>>> t1[0],t1[1,1]=t1[1,1],t1[0]
>>> print(t1)
(S (X her) (VP (V gave) (NP I)))
>>> len(t1)
2
```

Metrics using shallow semantic matching

WordNet Similarity is used to perform semantic matching. In this, a similarity of a given text is computed against the hypothesis. The Natural Language Toolkit can be used to compute: path distance, Leacock-Chodorow Similarity, Wu-Palmer Similarity, Resnik Similarity, Jiang-Conrath Similarity, and Lin Similarity between words present in the text and the hypothesis. In these metrics, we compare the similarity between word senses rather than words.

During Shallow Semantic analysis, NER and coreference resolution are also performed.

Consider the following code in NLTK that computes `wordnet` similarity:

```
>>> wordnet.N['dog'][0].path_similarity(wordnet.N['cat'][0])
0.20000000000000001
>>> wordnet.V['run'][0].path_similarity(wordnet.V['walk'][0])
0.25
```

Summary

In this chapter, we discussed the evaluation of NLP systems (POS tagger, stemmer, and morphological analyzer). You learned about various metrics used for performing the evaluation of NLP systems based on error identification, lexical matching, syntactic matching, and shallow semantic matching. We also discussed parser evaluation performed using gold data. Evaluation can be done using three metrics, namely Precision, Recall, and F-Measure. You also learned about the evaluation of IR system.

Bibliography

This course is a blend of text and quizzes, all packaged up keeping your journey in mind. It includes content from the following Packt products:

- *NLTK Essentials, Nitin Hardeniya*
- *Python 3 Text Processing with NLTK 3 Cookbook, Jacob Perkins*
- *Mastering Natural Language Processing with Python, Deepti Chopra, Nisheeth Joshi, Iti Mathur*

Index

Symbols

A

B

C

D

E

F

G

H

I

J

K

L

M

O

P

Q

R

S

T

U

V

W

X

Y

Z

CPSIA information can be obtained
at www.ICGtesting.com
Printed in the USA
LVOW04s0025260917
549923LV00033B/902/P